Quick Reference Guide to Protocol Descriptions

Lock Manager Portocol Procedures, Versions 1, 2, and 3

Name	Description	
NULL	Do nothing	
TEST	Test for a lock	296
LOCK	Create a lock	299
CANCEL	Cancel a lock	302
UNLOCK	Remove a lock	304
GRANTED	Lock granted	305
TEST_MSG	Test lock message	296
LOCK_MSG	Create a lock message	299
CANCEL_MSG	Cancel a lock message	302
UNLOCK_MSG	Unlock message	304
GRANTED_MSG	Lock granted message	305
TEST_RES	Test lock result	296
LOCK_RES	Create a lock result	299
CANCEL_RES	Cancel a lock result	302
UNLOCK_RES	Unlock result	304
GRANTED_RES	Lock granted result	305
SHARE	Share a file	308
UNSHARE	Unshare a file	310
NM_LOCK	Nonmonitored lock	311
FREE_ALL	Free all locks	311

PCNFSD Protocol Procedures, Versions 1 and 2

Name	Description	Version 1 Page	Version 2 Page
NULL	Null procedure		
INFO	Determine supported services		391
PR_INIT	Prepare for remote printing	389	393
PR_START	Submit job for printing	390	394
PR_LIST	List printers on server		395
PR_QUEUE	List printer jobs queued		396
PR_STATUS	Determine printer status		398
PR_CANCEL	Cancel print job		399
PR_ADMIN	Printer administration		400
PR_REQUEUE	Change print job queue position		401
PR_HOLD	Hold print job in queue		403
PR_RELEASE	Release hold on print job		404
MAPID	Translate between username and ID		405
AUTH	Perform user authentication	388	407
ALERT	Send message to server administrator		408

NFS ILLUSTRATED

NFS ILLUSTRATED

Brent Callaghan

ADDISON–WESLEY

An Imprint of Addison Wesley Longman, Inc.

Reading, Massachusetts • Harlow, England • Menlo Park, California
Berkeley, California • Don Mills, Ontario • Sydney
Bonn • Amsterdam • Tokyo • Mexico City

Many of the designations used by manufacturers and sellers to distinguish their products are claimed as trademarks. Where those designations appear in this book and Addison-Wesley was aware of a trademark claim, the designations have been printed in initial caps or all caps.

The author and publisher have taken care in the preparation of this book but make no expressed or implied warranty of any kind and assume no responsibility for errors or omissions. No liability is assumed for incidental or consequential damages in connection with or arising out of the use of the information or programs contained herein.

The publisher offers discounts on this book when ordered in quantity for special sales. For more information, please contact:

Corporate, Government, and Special Sales
Addison Wesley Longman, Inc.
One Jacob Way
Reading, Massachusetts 01867

Library of Congress Cataloging-in-Publication Data

Callaghan, Brent
    NFS illustrated / Brent Callaghan
        p.   cm. — (Addison-Wesley professional computing series)
    Includes bibliographical references and index.
    ISBN 0-201-32570-5
        1. Network File System (Computer network protocol)   I. Title.   II. Series

    TK5105.574 .C35 2000
    004.6'2--dc21   99-056696

ISBN 0-201-32570-5

Text printed on recycled and acid-free paper.

1 2 3 4 5 6 7 8 9 10–CRW–03 02 01 00 99
First Printing, December 1999

To Barbara, Luke, and Eli

Contents

Preface   *xvii*

1   Introduction   **1**
1.1 File Access and File Transfer   2
1.2 Early File Access Protocols   4
1.3 ONC RPC   6
1.4 Organization of This Book   6

2   XDR—External Data Representation   **9**
2.1   Protocols and Transportable Data   9
2.2   A Canonical Standard   11
2.3   XDR Unit   12
2.4   Primitive XDR Data Types   13
    2.4.1   Integer   13
    2.4.2   Unsigned Integer   14
    2.4.3   Boolean   14
    2.4.4   Hyper Integer and Unsigned Hyper Integer   15
    2.4.5   Fixed-Length Opaque Data   15
    2.4.6   Variable-Length Opaque Data   15
    2.4.7   String   15
2.5   Structured XDR Data Types   16
    2.5.1   Fixed-Length Array   16
    2.5.2   Variable-Length Array   16
    2.5.3   Discriminated Union   17
    2.5.4   Linked Lists   17
2.6   XDR Language   17
    2.6.1   Notational Conventions   18
    2.6.2   Lexical Notes   18
    2.6.3   Syntax Information   19
    2.6.4   Syntax Notes   20

	2.6.5	Example of an XDR Data Description	20
	2.6.6	XDR Language Variant in This Book	21
2.7	Summary		23

3   ONC RPC   25

3.1	Remote Procedure Call Model		25
3.2	RPC Transport Independence and Semantics		27
3.3	Program Numbers and Versioning		29
3.4	Requirements of the RPC Protocol		30
3.5	RPC Call Message		31
3.6	RPC Reply Message		33
3.7	Record-Marking Standard		36
3.8	Portmapper and Rpcbind		38
	3.8.1	Portmap Protocol	39
	3.8.2	Rpcbind Protocol	40
3.9	Summary		41

4   RPC Authentication   43

4.1	RPC Credential and Verifier		43
4.2	Authentication Flavors		44
4.3	Null Authentication		44
4.4	System Authentication		45
4.5	Diffie-Hellman Authentication		48
	4.5.1	Naming	49
	4.5.2	DH Authentication Verifiers	49
	4.5.3	Nicknames and Clock Synchronization	50
	4.5.4	DH Authentication Protocol	51
	4.5.5	DH Full Network Name Credential and Verifier	51
	4.5.6	DH Nickname Credential and Verifier	53
	4.5.7	Server Verifier	54
	4.5.8	Diffie-Hellman Encryption	56
	4.5.9	Weaknesses of DH Authentication	57
4.6	Kerberos Version 4 Authentication		58
	4.6.1	Kerberos Naming	59
	4.6.2	Kerberos-Based Authentication Protocol Specification	59
	4.6.3	Kerberos Full Network Name Credential and Verifier	59
	4.6.4	Kerberos Nickname Credential and Verifier	61
	4.6.5	Server Verifier	62
	4.6.6	Kerberos-Specific Authentication Status Values	62
	4.6.7	Weaknesses of Kerberos Authentication	63
4.7	RPCSEC_GSS Authentication		64
	4.7.1	RPCSEC_GSS Security Protocol	65
	4.7.2	RPCSEC_GSS Credential	66
	4.7.3	Context Creation	66
	4.7.4	Successful Creation Response	68

	4.7.5	Unsuccessful Context Creation	70
	4.7.6	RPC Data Exchange	70
	4.7.7	Data Integrity Protection	71
	4.7.8	Data Privacy	73
	4.7.9	Server Processing of RPC Data Requests	74
	4.7.10	Server's Reply	75
	4.7.11	RPCSEC_GSS Errors	75
	4.7.12	Performance of RPCSEC_GSS	76
	4.7.13	Snoop Trace of Session	76
4.8	Connection-Based Security		78
4.9	Summary		80

5 NFS Filesystem Model   **81**

5.1	Filesystem and Filesystem Objects		81
5.2	Filehandles		83
5.3	Pathnames		85
	5.3.1	Filename Component Handling	85
	5.3.2	Pathname Evaluation	86
5.4	Stateless Server		87
	5.4.1	Server Recovery	88
	5.4.2	Idempotent Operations	88
	5.4.3	Statelessness and High Availability	89
5.5	Summary		90

6 NFS Version 2   **91**

6.1	Common Data Types		92
6.2	Server Procedures		98
	6.2.1	Procedure 0: NULL—Do Nothing	99
	6.2.2	Procedure 1: GETATTR—Get File Attributes	100
	6.2.3	Procedure 2: SETATTR—Set File Attributes	102
	6.2.4	Procedure 4: LOOKUP—Look Up File Name	104
	6.2.5	Procedure 5: READLINK—Read from Symbolic Link	106
	6.2.6	Procedure 6: READ—Read from File	107
	6.2.7	Procedure 8: WRITE—Write to File	109
	6.2.8	Procedure 9: CREATE—Create File	112
	6.2.9	Procedure 10: REMOVE—Remove File	115
	6.2.10	Procedure 11: RENAME—Rename File	116
	6.2.11	Procedure 12: LINK—Create Link to File	119
	6.2.12	Procedure 13: SYMLINK—Create Symbolic Link	120
	6.2.13	Procedure 14: MKDIR—Create Directory	122
	6.2.14	Procedure 15: RMDIR—Remove Directory	124
	6.2.15	Procedure 16: READDIR—Read from Directory	126
	6.2.16	Procedure 17: STATFS—Get Filesystem Attributes	128

7 NFS Version 3   **131**

7.1	Changes from the NFS Version 2 Protocol		132
	7.1.1	Deleted Procedures	132
	7.1.2	Modified Procedures	132
	7.1.3	New Procedures	133

	7.1.4	Filehandle Size	134
	7.1.5	Maximum Data Sizes	134
	7.1.6	Error Return	134
	7.1.7	File Type	135
	7.1.8	File Attributes	135
	7.1.9	Set File Attributes	135
	7.1.10	32-Bit Clients/Servers and 64-Bit Clients/Servers	135
7.2	Basic Data Types		136
	7.2.1	Sizes	136
	7.2.2	Basic Data Types	137
7.3	Server Procedures		147
	7.3.1	Procedure 0: NULL—Do Nothing	149
	7.3.2	Procedure 1: GETATTR—Get File Attributes	149
	7.3.3	Procedure 2: SETATTR—Set File Attributes	151
	7.3.4	Procedure 3: LOOKUP—Look Up Filename	155
	7.3.5	Procedure 4: ACCESS—Check Access Permission	158
	7.3.6	Procedure 5: READLINK—Read from Symbolic Link	162
	7.3.7	Procedure 6: READ—Read from File	164
	7.3.8	Procedure 7: WRITE—Write to File	168
	7.3.9	Procedure 8: CREATE—Create a File	174
	7.3.10	Procedure 9: MKDIR—Create a Directory	179
	7.3.11	Procedure 10: SYMLINK—Create a Symbolic Link	182
	7.3.12	Procedure 11: MKNOD—Create a Special Device	186
	7.3.13	Procedure 12: REMOVE—Remove a File	190
	7.3.14	Procedure 13: RMDIR—Remove Directory	192
	7.3.15	Procedure 14: RENAME—Rename File or Directory	195
	7.3.16	Procedure 15: LINK—Create Link to an Object	199
	7.3.17	Procedure 16: READDIR—Read from Directory	202
	7.3.18	Procedure 17: READDIRPLUS—Extended Read from Directory	205
	7.3.19	Procedure 18: FSSTAT—Get Dynamic Filesystem Information	212
	7.3.20	Procedure 19: FSINFO—Get Static Filesystem Information	214
	7.3.21	Procedure 20: PATHCONF—Retrieve POSIX Information	218
	7.3.22	Procedure 21: COMMIT—Commit Cached Data on a Server to Stable Storage	221
8	**NFS Implementation**		**225**
8.1	File Attributes		225
8.2	Unsupported Procedures		225
8.3	Multiple Version Support		226
8.4	Last Close Problem		227
8.5	Crossing of Server Mountpoints		228
8.6	Problems with Hierarchical Mounts		230
8.7	Permission Issues		230
	8.7.1	Identifying Users	231
	8.7.2	Access to Open Files	231
	8.7.3	UID/GID Mapping	232

	8.7.4	Checking File Access	232
	8.7.5	Executable Files	233
8.8	Concurrent RPC Calls		234
8.9	Duplicate Request Cache		234
8.10	Synchronous Operations and Stable Storage		236
8.11	Adaptive Retransmission for UDP		239
8.12	Read-ahead and Write-behind		241
8.13	Write Gathering		243
8.14	Caching Policies		244
	8.14.1	Cached Objects	245
	8.14.2	Cache Consistency	246
	8.14.3	Close-to-Open Consistency	248
	8.14.4	Read and Write Caching	248
	8.14.5	Disk Caching	249
	8.14.6	Disconnection and Reconnection	250
8.15	Connectathon		252
8.16	Summary		253

9	**NFS MOUNT Protocol**		**255**
9.1	Protocol Revisions		256
9.2	Transport		257
9.3	Authentication		257
9.4	Access Lists		258
9.5	Server Procedures		259
	9.5.1	Procedure 0: NULL—Do Nothing	259
	9.5.2	Procedure 1: MOUNTPROC_MNT—Add MOUNT Entry	260
	9.5.3	Procedure 2: MOUNTPROC_DUMP—Return MOUNT Entries	263
	9.5.4	Procedure 3: MOUNTPROC_UMNT—Remove MOUNT Entry	264
	9.5.5	Procedure 4: MOUNTPROC_UMNTALL— Remove All MOUNT Entries	265
	9.5.6	Procedure 5: MOUNTPROC_EXPORT—Return Export List	265
	9.5.7	Procedure 6: MOUNTPROC_EXPORTALL— Return Export List	267
	9.5.8	Procedure 7: MOUNTPROC_PATHCONF— POSIX Pathconf Information	267
9.6	MOUNT Table		270
9.7	Submounts		271
9.8	Export Limitations		273
9.9	Summary		275

10   NFS Lock Manager Protocol   277

     10.1   Monitored Locking   278

     10.2   Advisory vs. Mandatory Locks   281

     10.3   Exclusive and Nonexclusive Locks   281

     10.4   Asynchronous Procedures and Callback   282

     10.5   DOS/Windows File Sharing Procedures   283

     10.6   Server Crash Recovery   284

     10.7   Lockd and Statd Implementation   287

     10.8   Client Crash Recovery   288

     10.9   Deadlock Detection   289

     10.10 Locking Cached or Mapped Files   290

     10.11 Transport and Authentication   291

     10.12 Basic Data Types   292

     10.13 Errors   294

     10.14 Lock Manager Procedures   294
            10.14.1   Procedure 0: NULL—Do Nothing   295
            10.14.2   Procedure 1: NLM_TEST—Test for a Lock   296
            10.14.3   Procedure 2: NLM_LOCK—Create a Lock   299
            10.14.4   Procedure 3: NLM_CANCEL—Cancel a Lock   302
            10.14.5   Procedure 4: NLM_UNLOCK—Remove a Lock   304
            10.14.6   Procedure 5: NLM_GRANTED—Lock Is Granted   305
            10.14.7   Procedure 20: NLM_SHARE—Share a File   308
            10.14.8   Procedure 21: NLM_UNSHARE—Unshare a File   310
            10.14.9   Procedure 22: NLM_NM_LOCK—Establish
                      a Nonmonitored Lock   311
            10.14.10 Procedure 23: NLM_FREE_ALL—Free All Locks   311

     10.15 Network Status Monitor Protocol   312
            10.15.1   Procedure 0: SM_NULL—Do Nothing   313
            10.15.2   Procedure 1: SM_STAT—Check Status   313
            10.15.3   Procedure 2: SM_MON—Monitor a Host   314
            10.15.4   Procedure 3: SM_UNMON—Unmonitor a Host   316
            10.15.5   Procedure 4: SM_UNMON_ALL—Unmonitor
                      All Hosts   317
            10.15.6   Procedure 5: SM_SIMU_CRASH—Simulate a Crash   317
            10.15.7   Procedure 6: SM_NOTIFY—Notify a Host   318

     10.16 Summary   318

11   Automounting   321

     11.1   Automounter as NFS Server   322

     11.2   Problems with Symbolic Links   324

     11.3   Automounting with Autofs   327

     11.4   Automounter Maps   329
            11.4.1   Master Map   329
            11.4.2   Direct Map   329

	11.4.3	Indirect Map	330
	11.4.4	Executable Map	331
11.5	Offset Mounts	332
11.6	Multiple Mounts	333
11.7	Replica Servers	334
11.8	Map Variables and Key Substitution	337
11.9	MOUNT Options	339
11.10	Amd Automounter	339
	11.10.1 Nonblocking Operation	339
	11.10.2 Server Keepalives	340
	11.10.3 Map Syntax	340
11.11	Summary	341

12   NFS Variants   **343**

12.1	Spritely NFS	343
	12.1.1 Stateful Server	344
	12.1.2 Callback	344
	12.1.3 Write-behind	345
	12.1.4 Recovery	347
	12.1.5 Performance	348
	12.1.6 Summary	349
12.2	NQNFS	349
	12.2.1 Leases	350
	12.2.2 Recovery	351
	12.2.3 Other Features	352
	12.2.4 Summary	352
12.3	Trusted NFS	352
	12.3.1 AUTH_MLS Credential	353
	12.3.2 Extended Attributes	354
	12.3.3 Filename Attributes	355
	12.3.4 TNFS Interoperability	356
	12.3.5 Summary	356
12.4	NASD NFS	356
	12.4.1 NASD Storage	357
	12.4.2 Locating the Data	358
	12.4.3 Data Security	358
	12.4.4 Summary	359

13   Other Distributed Filesystems   **361**

13.1	Remote File Sharing	361
	13.1.1 Remote System Calls	361
	13.1.2 RFS Naming	362
	13.1.3 Security and UID/GID Mapping	363
	13.1.4 Summary	363
13.2	Andrew File System	364
	13.2.1 File Caching	364
	13.2.2 Shared Namespace	366
	13.2.3 Volume Movement	367

	13.2.4	Read-only Replication	368
	13.2.5	Security	368
	13.2.6	Summary	368
13.3	DCE/DFS		369
	13.3.1	Cache Consistency with Tokens	369
	13.3.2	DFS Namespace	370
	13.3.3	Episode File System	371
	13.3.4	Summary	371
13.4	SMB File Access		372
	13.4.1	Namespace	372
	13.4.2	Session Setup	373
	13.4.3	PC File Semantics	373
	13.4.4	Batched Requests	374
	13.4.5	File Locking	374
	13.4.6	Opportunistic Locks	374
	13.4.7	The Samba Server	376
	13.4.8	Summary	376

14 PC NFS   **379**

14.1	File Naming	379
14.2	File Attributes	381
14.3	Text Files	382
14.4	Symbolic Links	382
14.5	PCNFSD Protocol	384
	14.5.1 Printing	385
	14.5.2 Comment Strings	387
	14.5.3 Transport and Authentication	387
14.6	PCNFSD Version 1	387
	14.6.1 Procedure 1: PCNFSD_AUTH—Perform User Authentication	388
	14.6.2 Procedure 2: PCNFSD_PR_INIT—Prepare for Remote Printing	389
	14.6.3 Procedure 3: PCNFSD_PR_START—Submit Print Job	390
14.7	PCNFSD Version 2	391
	14.7.1 Procedure 1: PCNFSD2_INFO—Determine Supported Services	391
	14.7.2 Procedure 2: PCNFSD2_PR_INIT—Prepare for Remote Printing	393
	14.7.3 Procedure 3: PCNFSD2_PR_START—Submit Job for Printing	394
	14.7.4 Procedure 4: PCNFSD2_PR_LIST—List Printers on Server	395
	14.7.5 Procedure 5: PCNFSD2_PR_QUEUE—List Printer Jobs Queued	396
	14.7.6 Procedure 6: PCNFSD2_PR_STATUS—Determine Printer Status	398
	14.7.7 Procedure 7: PCNFSD2_PR_CANCEL—Cancel a Print Job	399

14.7.8   Procedure 8: PCNFSD2_PR_ADMIN—Printer
         Administration   400
14.7.9   Procedure 9: PCNFSD2_PR_REQUEUE—Change
         Print Job Queue Position   401
14.7.10 Procedure 10: PCNFSD2_PR_HOLD—Hold a Print
         Job in the Queue   403
14.7.11 Procedure 11: PCNFSD2_PR_RELEASE—Release
         Hold on a Print Job   404
14.7.12 Procedure 12: PCNFSD2_MAPID—Translate
         Between Username and ID   405
14.7.13 Procedure 13: PCNFSD2_AUTH—Perform User
         Authentication   407
14.7.14 Procedure 14: PCNFSD2_ALERT—Send Message
         to Server Administrator   408

14.8   BWNFSD/HCLNFSD Protocol   409

14.9   Summary   410

15 NFS Benchmarks   413

15.1   Factors Affecting Performance   414
       15.1.1   Memory   414
       15.1.2   CPU   414
       15.1.3   Network   415
       15.1.4   Network Interfaces   416
       15.1.5   Server Data Bus   417
       15.1.6   NVRAM   417
       15.1.7   Disk Controllers   417
       15.1.8   Disk Spindles   417

15.2   Workload   418
       15.2.1   Operation Mix   418
       15.2.2   Working Set   419
       15.2.3   File and Directory Size   419

15.3   Nfsstone   419

15.4   Nhfsstone   421

15.5   SFS 1.0 and 1.1   422
       15.5.1   Running the SFS Benchmark   423
       15.5.2   Workload   424
       15.5.3   Server Configuration   426
       15.5.4   Cluster Challenge   426

15.6   SFS 2.0   428

15.7   Summary   430

16 WebNFS   431

16.1   Internet and NFS over TCP   431

16.2   Internet and NFS Version 3   432

16.3   Firewalls   433

16.4   Public Filehandle   433

16.5   Multicomponent LOOKUP   434

16.5.1 Pathname Evaluation and Latency   434
16.5.2 Initialization Overhead   435
16.5.3 Pathname Evaluation   435
16.5.4 Server Evaluation of Pathname   436
16.5.5 Symbolic Links   436

16.6 NFS URL   438
16.6.1 URL Structure   438
16.6.2 Absolute vs. Relative Paths   438

16.7 WebNFS Client Characteristics   439
16.7.1 Mountpoint Crossing   441
16.7.2 Fetching a File   441
16.7.3 Fetching a Directory   442
16.7.4 Fetching a Symbolic Link   442
16.7.5 Document Types   442

16.8 WebNFS Server Requirements   442
16.8.1 Evaluating a Multicomponent LOOKUP   442
16.8.2 Canonical vs. Native Path   444
16.8.3 Client and Server Port   444

16.9 WebNFS Security Negotiation   445

16.10 Summary   447

17 NFS Version 4   449

17.1 An IETF Protocol   450

17.2 NFS Version 4 Working Group Charter   451

17.3 Improved Access and Good Performance
       on the Internet   452
17.3.1 Protocol Integration   452
17.3.2 Latency   453
17.3.3 Bandwidth   455
17.3.4 Efficient Caching   456
17.3.5 Proxy Caching   456
17.3.6 Scalability   457
17.3.7 Availability   458

17.4 Strong Security with Negotiation Built into the
       Protocol   459
17.4.1 Connection-Based Security   459
17.4.2 RPC-Based Security   459

17.5 Better Cross-Platform Interoperability   460
17.5.1 File Attributes   460
17.5.2 Representing User and Group IDs   461
17.5.3 Access Control Lists   462
17.5.4 File Locking   462
17.5.5 Internationalization   463

17.6 Designed for Protocol Extensions   465

17.7 Summary   466

References   467

Index   475

Preface

I have been working with the NFS protocol since I joined Sun Microsystems in 1986. At that time the NFS market was expanding rapidly and I was excited to be working with the group, led by Bob Lyon, that developed the protocol and its first implementation in SunOS. In the NFS group, the protocol was a powerful but raw technology that needed to be exploited. We wanted it to run on as many platforms as possible, so an NFS porting group was assigned the task of helping other companies implement NFS on their computers.

Our NFS evangelism was a little ahead of its time. Before the phrase "open systems" had yet become hackneyed, we'd made the source code for Sun RPC available for free download via FTP server[1] and organized the first Connectathon event. At Connectathon our enthusiasm for NFS was shared with engineers from other companies who brought along their machines, source code, and junk food and spent a few days connected to a network, testing their NFS client and server implementations against each other.

Implementations of the NFS protocol have been successful in bringing remote file access to programs through existing interfaces. There is no need to change the software for remote file access or to name files differently. NFS has been almost *too* successful at making remote files indistinguishable from local files. For instance, a program that backs up files on a local disk to tape needs to avoid stumbling into NFS filesystems. For everyone but system administrators, NFS is invisible—if you ignore the rare "NFS server not responding" message.

It's easy to forget NFS is there. NFS has no programming interface of its own. Even software engineers have no need to deal with NFS directly. There are no conference tutorials called "Programming with NFS," there are no magazine screen shots of NFS-enabled applications, and there are no demonstrations of NFS at trade shows. Except for server administrators, NFS seems not to exist.

---

1. It is still available today via the Connectathon Web site (*www.connectathon.org*).

There are many server implementations of the NFS protocol, each with its own features. Each of these server implementations has its own documentation, each slightly different. Perhaps this explains why there are so few NFS books available. NFS is never more than a chapter in a book about the operating system in which it is embedded.

Although NFS implementations vary, there is an underlying invariant: the protocol itself. NFS is not a single protocol. Not only are there two versions of the protocol in use now, but there is a third version in development as well. The NFS protocol is layered on XDR and RPC protocols, and no implementation is complete without the MOUNT and Lock Manager protocols. I wanted to bring all the NFS protocols together into a single volume along with other topics unique to NFS, such as Connectathon and the SPEC SFS benchmarks.

I wanted this book to describe the protocol in detail in a more interesting way than a dry, text-only specification. I was inspired by Richard Stevens's book *TCP/IP Illustrated, Volume 1.* This book is an excellent example of network protocols animated through the use of diagrams and real protocol traces that show the protocol in action. I have used that book as a model for my own description of the NFS protocols. I hope you will appreciate it as a useful reference.

Acknowledgments

Many people have helped me write this book. I attribute the idea for the book to Carol Long, my first editor at Addison Wesley Longman. Thanks to Richard Stevens and John Ousterhout for the advice and encouragement I needed to begin this venture. I'm grateful to my editor, Mary O'Brien, for her generous support and encouragement over the two years it took to write the book and to Elizabeth Spainhour for prompt handling of my drafts and reviews.

I'm very grateful to fellow NFS engineer Mike Eisler, who gave me prompt and insightful feedback on several drafts. Agnes Jacob did me a great favor in filling a draft with lots of yellow sticky notes with suggestions that helped improve the readability of some of my more obscure text. I'm thankful that Mike Kupfer and Salit Gazit were able to guide me through the mysteries of the Network Lock Manager—their experience with this protocol was invaluable. David Robinson and Spencer Shepler, who both spent several years developing the SPEC SFS benchmarks, corrected my description of SFS benchmarking and offered useful background material.

Thanks to Alex Chiu for the corrections he provided to my account of the WebNFS security negotiation protocol. Carl Beame and Fred Whiteside were invaluable in their review of the PC-NFS chapter. In particular, they provided me with useful material on their BWNFSD daemon implementation. Thanks to Jeff Mogul for his thorough review of my short description of his work on Spritely NFS and to Rick Macklem for checking my description of his NQNFS variant of NFS version 2. I'm grateful to Gary Winiger for the corrections and additional material he offered for the section on Trusted NFS (TNFS).

Special thanks to my technical reviewers for tolerating my lengthy (and sometimes incomplete) manuscripts. To be a useful reference, a technical book depends heavily on the accumulated experience of its reviewers. Thanks to Ran Atkinson, Richard Basch, Bob Gilligan, Clemens Huebner, Ron Hutchins, Kirk McKusick, Tom McNeal, Vernon Schryver, Hal Stern, Dana Treadwell, and Andy Watson.

I'm grateful to my employer, Sun Microsystems, Inc., for giving me the time and resources to write this book. A special thanks to my managers for their unwavering support: Cindy Vinores, David Brittle, and Bev Crair. Thanks to Professional Computing Series editors Brian Kernighan and Craig Partridge for their detailed and helpful reviews.

Finally, I'm grateful for the patience and understanding of my family: my wife, Barbara, and sons, Luke and Eli. Not only did they cheerfully put up with my frequent absences to work on "The Book," they also provided needed encouragement.

Chapter 1

Introduction

The NFS™ protocol (hereafter simply called "NFS") is a network protocol that makes files stored on a file server accessible to any computer on a network. In this book I describe not only the NFS protocol and its implementation, but other protocols that NFS depends on. The book is intended for people who are interested in a better understanding of the NFS protocol: developers interested in creating new NFS implementations or system administrators and users curious about how NFS works. For such a popular protocol, it is unusual that there are no books that describe it in detail. NFS is accorded a mention in many books that describe TCP/IP-based protocols, but there is no reference that provides a complete description of NFS that extends to the companion protocols such as MOUNT, Network Lock Manager, and PCNFSD. I hope this book provides a valuable reference.

This book assumes that you are already familiar, at some basic level, with the concepts of TCP/IP networking and have a reasonable working knowledge of computer filesystems, programming languages, and operating systems principles. If you wish to brush up on some of this knowledge, I recommend Richard Stevens's book *TCP/IP Illustrated, Volume 1* [Stevens94] as an excellent introduction to TCP/IP networking. It not only describes the protocols on which NFS and ONC RPC are built, but also includes a chapter on version 2 of the NFS protocol. For a more complete introduction to distributed systems and network protocols, I recommend *Distributed Systems, Concepts and Design,* by George Coulouris, Jean Dollimore, and Tim Kindberg [Coulouris+96]. It also includes a chapter that discusses NFS along with other distributed filesystem protocols.

You will notice that the book emphasizes *protocol* over *implementation*. In most chapters, NFS and the protocols it depends on are discussed at the level of a protocol specification: What are the bits that move across the wire and what do they mean? There are many implementations of NFS, each with its own features and administration requirements. A description of the details of these implementations is best left for other books or technical manuals. However, if there were no mention of implementation, this book would be just a very dry protocol specification. Chapter 8 is dedicated to a discussion of issues common to all implementations of NFS, and the protocol descriptions themselves have an Implementation section for every protocol procedure.

1.1   File Access and File Transfer

File transfer was one of the first "killer apps" for computer networks beginning with the FTP[1] protocol designed for use on the ARPANET in 1971. The objective of file *transfer* is to move an entire file across a network from one computer to another, which is more convenient than transporting the file on a floppy disk or magnetic tape. FTP supports a number of different file types, displays directory listings, and allows some directory manipulation on the server. With FTP, files can be created, removed, and renamed. However, FTP does not allow file content to be manipulated directly by applications. You need to transfer a file in its entirety to a local disk before you can view or change it. The need for file transfer makes accessing remote data less attractive. You need to remember which files are "remote" and which are "local." A remote file that needs file transfer cannot be opened directly by a program. It must be transferred to a local disk before it can be viewed and transferred back if it has been modified. The management of transferred files can cause problems: you need to find a location on disk with enough space and assign a name to a transferred file. Your local disk may also become cluttered with transferred files that you have forgotten about.

File *access* protocols like NFS are designed to remove the need to transfer the file (Figure 1.1). The file stays where it is, on the server, and is manipulated in place. In-place manipulation has obvious benefits if the changes are minor. For instance, it's easy to append a new record to a large file just by sending the data in the new record. The file transfer alternative requires the file to be transferred in its entirety in both directions. File access protocols have significant advantages over file transfer protocols:

- *You get just what you need.* If the client application wants only a small piece of the file, then only that piece needs to be transferred. For instance, a multipage document may consist of an initial table of contents that describes the location of data within the file. The client may obtain the table of contents, then obtain the data of interest from a location within the file.

- *Remote files appear to be local.* A remote file access protocol makes a remote server's files appear as if they were on a local disk. The user of an application no longer has to consciously transfer a file before accessing it.

---

1. See RFC 959.

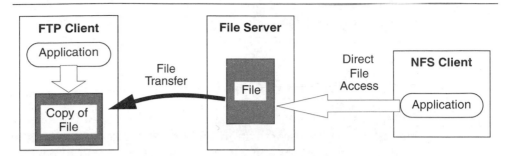

FIGURE 1.1 A file transfer protocol like FTP must move the file in its entirety to the client's disk before an application can access it. A file access protocol like NFS allows the application to access the file directly on the server.

- *No stale data.* Since file access protocols access the server's file directly, the file data are always up to date (assuming that there is no inconsistency caused by caching).

- *Diskless clients.* If the client has no disk or less than enough disk space left to hold a large file, then the file cannot be transferred. A file access protocol has no local storage requirements.

- *No waiting.* File transfer generally requires that the entire file be transferred before the data can be accessed by an application. A file access protocol can provide data to an application as soon as it arrives from the file server.

- *File locking.* Using a file access protocol, a client application can lock a file on the server to prevent other clients from obtaining or changing the data. Locking avoids problems caused by clients overwriting each other's changes to a file.

With all these clear advantages, what are the disadvantages? Why do file transfer protocols like FTP continue to be so popular? To make a remote file-system appear to be local, the client and file server need a network connection that is approximately as fast as the local disk drive connection; otherwise, the illusion of a "local" disk cannot be maintained. The File Transfer Protocol was written for the ARPANET, which at the time could transmit data at a speed of 56K bits/sec; however, the speed of a local SCSI disk connection was approximately 12M bits/sec—that's about 200 times faster! It took Ethernet and Token Ring networks that could move data at 1M bytes/sec to bring the speed of network access close enough to that of local SCSI connections for remote access to become practical. On high speed, local area networks' file access protocols are most popular, but for modem users, where bandwidth is still a precious commodity, file transfer is easier to use.

NFS versions 2 and 3 are designed for these high-speed, local area networks. In the final chapter of the book I discuss the challenges facing NFS version 4, designed to be competitive with the FTP protocol on the Internet.

1.2 Early File Access Protocols

The high-speed networking that became available in the early 1980s created interest in many researchers in building file access protocols. At about this time, interest was growing in protocols based on Remote Procedure Calls (RPC). NFS was not the first, nor did it support many of the features offered by some of its predecessors. Perhaps the feature that most distinguished NFS from the others was its publication as a *protocol* from which many different implementations could be built. The other distributed filesystems of the time were described as *implementations.* This feature, a distributed filesystem as a protocol, continues to distinguish NFS today.

AT&T's RFS filesystem (described in chapter 13) was a contemporary of NFS but a commercial failure due to its complexity and poor performance. The Apollo DOMAIN operating system supported remote file access, though it was so tightly integrated with the operating system and Apollo hardware that it was impractical to implement it on other operating systems. The LOCUS distributed operating system [Popek+83], developed at UCLA in the early 1980s, provided many advanced remote file access features, such as consistent, high-performance caching, location independence, file migration and replication, and crash recovery. However, like RFS and DOMAIN, its distributed filesystem was inextricably integrated with the LOCUS operating system. Its fate was tied to a complex implementation with limited portability.

The Newcastle Connection [Brownbridge+82] was another remote file access implementation that preceded NFS by several years, and it succeeded in building expectations of a distributed filesystem that could be ported to other UNIX-like operating systems (Figure 1.2). The Newcastle Connection achieved its portability by implementing a distributed filesystem outside the

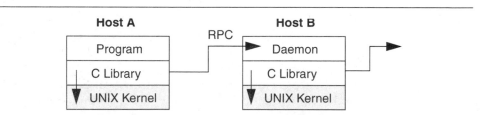

FIGURE 1.2 Newcastle Connection implementation. A modified C library intercepted UNIX I/O system calls, redirecting them locally or remotely. Remote calls were handled by an RPC protocol.

UNIX kernel through a modified C library on the clients and a user-level daemon process on the server. The C library interposed functions to intercept UNIX system calls for file I/O. System calls that related to local files were simply forwarded to the kernel, but calls destined for files on other computers were packaged into an RPC call and sent via the network (originally a Cambridge Token Ring) to a daemon on the remote computer. Its use of a remote system call model was similar to that of RFS. A simple naming convention was used to distinguish remote files from local files. A superroot directory above the local root directory was assumed to contain the hostnames of other computers. Above this superroot the hierarchy could extend further to include named departments or organizations.

Once a file was opened, the Newcastle Connection client code would use a table of file descriptors to distinguish remote files from local files (Figure 1.3). On the server, a daemon process would accept remote system calls from clients and apply them locally. Since servers could also run the Newcastle Connection client code, the calls made by the daemon process could be forwarded to other servers. To create a user context for the remote calls, the daemon process would fork a new process to handle the remote calls for a specific process on the client. If the client process forked a new child process, then the server process would also fork a new child. To control access to the server's filesystems, a system administrator could maintain a list of users to which access was authorized.

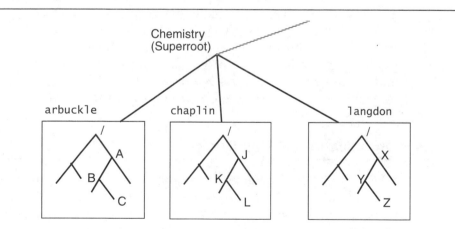

FIGURE 1.3 Newcastle Connection naming. Using the notion of a superroot directory that has hostnames for entries, a process on "arbuckle" could open the file Z on "langdon" with path /../langdon/X/Y/Z. Going higher, a file on a computer in another university department might be named with the hostname /../../physics/fermi/M/N/O.

The Newcastle Connection was popular in the early 1980s because it provided UNIX users with the advantages of a distributed filesystem. These users' previous experience with remote file access was through file transfer via ftp or uucp[2] commands. While the Newcastle Connection was convenient for casual access to remote files, performance was not as good as a local disk, since the code did no caching of data or file attributes. An additional problem was the requirement for programs to be relinked with a new C library that would interpose system calls. It was common to encounter programs that were linked with a C library that did not include the magic interposition functions and hence could not make use of the Newcastle Connection namespace. These limitations of the Newcastle Connection may have influenced the NFS design team in choosing a kernel-based client that would be more transparent to applications—no need to relink or recompile. Also, a kernel-based implementation would be able to cache file attributes and data that could be shared across multiple processes.

1.3   ONC RPC

The NFS protocol marks the genesis of the ONC RPC protocol (Figure 1.4). The Remote Procedure Call programming paradigm was based on work at Xerox PARC in the early 1980s that led to the Xerox Courier RPC system. Bob Lyon, one of the Sun designers of the NFS protocol, decided to create NFS as an RPC protocol. Protocol simplicity and high performance were cornerstones of NFS design and are reflected in the clean design of ONC RPC and its use of XDR encoding. With the NFS protocol as its initial motivation, the ONC RPC protocol led to further protocols such as portmapper, NIS, and eventually a public specification of the protocol, along with a C/C++ API, source code, and documentation. Several hundred ONC RPC-based protocols have been implemented, each registered with a unique program number.

1.4   Organization of This Book

The NFS protocol is built on the foundations of the XDR and ONC RPC protocols, so they are introduced in chapters 2 and 3. Since NFS security is implemented within the RPC protocol, it is appropriate to describe that next, in chapter 4. The protocol descriptions in all chapters use a variant of the RPC language described in [RFC 1832]. The RPC language syntax is described in sections 2.6.3 and 2.6.4.

---

2. UNIX to UNIX CoPy. A variation of the UNIX cp command that copied files from one UNIX system to another over a serial line or modem connection.

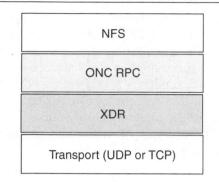

FIGURE 1.4 NFS protocol layering. The NFS protocol is built on ONC RPC, which uses XDR to encode data for transmission over a network transport.

Chapter 5 introduces the filesystem model that the NFS protocol assumes. The common filesystem model is a strength of the NFS protocol. NFS clients are much easier to implement because the peculiarities of different server filesystems are mapped into a common model. Chapters 6 and 7 describe versions 2 and 3 of the protocol, procedure by procedure. I illustrate these protocols in use with examples of real protocol calls and replies through *snoop* traces. Snoop is a packet-sniffing program that captures protocol packets from the network and displays their contents. Snoop is bundled with the Solaris and Irix operating systems. Another packet-sniffing program, *tcpdump*, is more widely available than snoop, but it does not provide as much detail as snoop for the NFS, MOUNT, and Network Lock Manager protocols. Chapter 8 covers implementation issues that are encountered by anyone attempting to build an NFS client or server.

The NFS protocol cannot implement a complete distributed filesystem without two important companion protocols; chapters 9 and 10 describe the MOUNT and Network Lock Manager protocols that enable the mounting of NFS filesystems and file locking functions.

Chapter 11 describes the automounter. The automounter is an example of the NFS approach to protocol layering. The NFS protocol itself does not implement a global namespace. It depends on the automounter to implement a namespace above it. The scope of the book broadens still further with chapter 12, NFS Variants. These variant protocols explore extensions to the NFS protocol. Some of these extensions were later incorporated into NFS version 3. Chapter 13 expands this survey to other distributed filesystem implementations that are not derived from NFS. Chapter 14 focuses on the challenges involved in implementing NFS on PC operating systems. Included in this chapter is a description of the PCNFSD protocol that is used by PC clients.

Server implementations of the NFS protocol owe much of their good performance to the SPEC SFS benchmarks, also known as LADDIS. Chapter 15 gives a history of these benchmarks, beginning with *nfsstone*. Chapter 16 is dedicated to WebNFS, a recent addition to the NFS protocol. WebNFS simplifies the connection to NFS servers, making it possible to connect to servers through firewalls. The WebNFS chapter is a good introduction to the final chapter, which speculates on the features of NFS version 4. At the time of writing, the NFS version 4 specification is still under development, yet the requirements for this new protocol are clear: to run well over the Internet and to further extend the interoperability and security of the protocol. Hopefully, a future revision of this book will add a complete description of this protocol when it becomes an Internet standard.

Chapter 2

XDR—External Data Representation

The NFS protocol data in RPC messages must be represented in a format that can be understood by both the sender and the recipient computer. This chapter explains the need for the common data representation provided by XDR, then examines the representation of primitive values such as integers and strings, followed by structured types such as arrays, linked lists, and discriminated unions. The chapter closes with a description of the XDR language: a notation for describing XDR encoded data. This chapter is not intended to be a complete description of all XDR types. For instance, there is no mention of *enum* and *void* types, nor of the XDR floating point data types such as *float*, *double,* and *quadruple*. It describes only the data types used by the NFS protocol and related protocols presented in this book. For a more complete description see [Bloomer92], [RFC 1832], or [X/OpenNFS96] in the References section near the end of the book.

2.1 Protocols and Transportable Data

Network protocols must use a common encoding scheme to represent the data that flies across the wires. Just as people represent their thoughts and ideas in different languages and character sets, computers also use a variety of data encoding schemes to represent their data internally. Back in the 1950s and 1960s, computer manufacturers found it advantageous to represent text using a common encoding scheme so that the letter "A" on one computer could be written to a tape or transmitted on a wire and read as the letter "A" by another computer of a different model or even a different manufacturer. These character encoding schemes have names like ASCII and UTF-8.

As well as having their own representations for characters, computers also differ in their representations for other data, like integers, floating point numbers, boolean values, and collections of values such as variable-length lists and tree structures. Some network protocols, like HTTP for Web pages and SMTP for mail, convert the protocol elements to readable ASCII text, which is then "parsed" by the recipient. For instance, the date field used in the HTTP 1.1 protocol is defined by RFC 1123 as an ASCII string that looks like this: "Date: Sun, 06 Nov 1999 08:49:37 GMT." The word "Date" labels the field and the colon is a delimiter for the value. The value is represented as day of week, day, month, year, and time in hours, minutes, and seconds. Representation of protocol elements as text fields has some good features:

- Network engineers can read the raw protocol traffic without the need for protocol interpreter software, which makes these text-based protocols easier to debug.
- Client and server implementations can be built using simple data formatting functions, like the *printf* function in the C language, to create and parse network messages.
- The protocol elements themselves are inherently variable length.

Text representation also has several disadvantages:

- It takes more space to encode data this way (the value part of the date field shown above requires 29 bytes, whereas a binary representation, such as a UNIX time, can represent dates in as little as 8 bytes).
- Parsing of variable-length fields and text to binary data conversion is expensive in CPU cycles.
- Data in text fields must be carefully inspected in case they contain characters that might be confused with protocol delimiters. Such "special" characters must be escaped in some way.

XDR is a standard for encoding binary data in a common, interoperable format. RPC-based protocols like NFS use XDR to encode data in network call and reply messages. As Figure 2.1 explains, without a standard data representation machines cannot accurately exchange binary data. Not only might the byte order be different, but the machines might have different data alignment requirements or different representations for floating point numbers and more elaborate structured items like linked lists, which contain pointers that are meaningless outside the address space in which they were created.

XDR provides a similar function to that of the ISO Abstract Syntax Notation.[1] While XDR uses *implicit* typing, ASN uses *explicit* typing, labeling each data item with a type code. XDR uses no data typing. There is an implicit assumption that the application parsing an XDR stream knows what type of data to expect. Use of implicit typing provides a more compact data representation, since type codes do not need to be included with the data and there is

---

1. ISO ASN.1 X.209

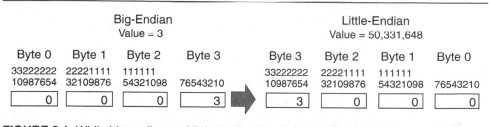

FIGURE 2.1 While big-endian and little-endian machines may both represent an integer as a two's-complement, 32-bit integer, they store these values with different byte orders in memory. If the big-endian machine transmits the integer as a byte stream, the little-endian machine will receive the bytes in reverse order and interpret the 32-bit integer incorrectly.

no overhead in interpreting the type codes. Additionally, most client-server protocols already define a well-known sequence of data fields, which makes the inclusion of data type tags redundant. XDR can be used selectively to label variable data types through the use of a discriminant tag. ASN.1 also includes an explicit length with each data item.

The length field allows a parser to skip or postpone the evaluation of unknown data fields. It also allows some flexibility in the representation of data. For instance, an XDR protocol that encodes an integer will represent it in 4 bytes even if the value is small and can be represented in a smaller number of bytes. An ASN.1 protocol allows the length to vary according to the amount of storage required. The saving in space provided by the flexible data lengths of ASN.1 is usually negated by the additional space required to store the length field itself.

2.2 A Canonical Standard

The XDR standard assumes that 8-bit bytes, or *octets,* are portable and defines each data type as a sequence of bytes. XDR uses a *canonical* data representation; that is, every data type has just one XDR encoding: a single byte order for integers (big-endian), a single floating point representation (IEEE standard), and so on. Any program that needs to transmit data to another machine (either on a network or via a medium such as tape or floppy disk) can convert its local representation of the data to the XDR encoding. A program that receives this XDR encoded data simply converts the data back to its own local representation.

An alternative coding is used by an alternative remote procedure call system, DCE/RPC, which evolved from the NCS RPC that was developed by Apollo Computer. Rather than use a canonical encoding, DCE/RPC allows alternative encodings, sometimes called "receiver makes it right" because the sender typically uses its native encoding style and the receiver is responsible for converting the encoded data to its own representation. For instance, an Intel-based sender uses a native little-endian format. If received by another Intel machine, then no data manipulation is required since the data are already in native format. A big-endian receiver detects the little-endian data and performs the appropriate conversion. DCE/RPC supports multiple formats for floating point representations as well.

XDR's use of a canonical standard is sometimes criticized for being wasteful. For example, if a program on a little-endian machine transmits an array of integers to a program on another little-endian machine, then the programs each incur the unnecessary overhead of a conversion between little-endian and big-endian representations. In practice, this overhead is not significant except perhaps in the rare case where the programs are exchanging large arrays of integers.

Some have suggested that the XDR use of big-endian representation for integer values favors Sun Microsystems' computers since they used Motorola 680x CPUs followed by SPARC CPUs—both big-endian. VAX and Intel 808x CPUs are little-endian. The big-endian representation for XDR was based on big-endian *network byte order* used in the headers of Internet protocols like UDP and TCP. In practice, the additional byte swapping required of little-endian architectures in marshaling XDR data is not significant for most protocols. Typically, the amount of integer data is small and the processing overhead is dwarfed by other data movement and protocol processing.

2.3   XDR Unit

XDR data items are encoded as a sequence of XDR data units, each containing four 8-bit bytes, or 32 bits. Any encoded data item that is not a multiple of 4 bytes in length must be padded with zero bytes (Figure 2.2).

The minimum data unit requirement achieves suitable alignment on most computer architectures, and the zero padding allows fields to be efficiently compared or checksummed. Although XDR is commonly perceived as just a standard for the representation of data, its alignment and padding requirements are important for the portability of groups of data.

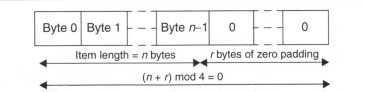

FIGURE 2.2 An XDR field always contains an integral number of 4-byte XDR units.

Alignment	Data Alignment in Memory (bytes)											
	0	1	2	3	4	5	6	7	8	9	10	11
8-bit	tag				flags	link						
16-bit	tag					flags	link					
32-bit	tag							flags			link	

FIGURE 2.3 Data alignment in memory.

For instance, the C structure

```
struct mydata {
    int     tag;
    char    flags;
    short   link;
```

might be represented in a computer's memory in several different ways depending on the padding and alignment requirements of the C compiler and the computer architecture. In each case in Figure 2.3 the structure fields are a 32-bit, an 8-bit, and a 16-bit quantity, but the padding requirements increase with the alignment unit. Although 8-bit alignment is the most efficient because it requires no padding, it increases marshaling overhead for modern computer architectures with stricter alignments.

2.4 Primitive XDR Data Types

Each of the following sections describes a data type within the XDR standard.

2.4.1 Integer

An XDR integer is a 32-bit field that represents an integer in two's complement form in the range [−2,147,483,648, 2,147,483,647]. The byte order is big-endian (i.e., the most significant byte is 0 and the least significant is 3).

MSB			LSB
Byte 0	Byte 1	Byte 2	Byte 3

32 bits

Two's complement form is commonly used on computers to represent signed binary numbers. In straight binary representation, each digit represents a power of two with increasing weights from right to left; for example, in an 8-bit field the value 12 would be represented as

```
00001100 = 0 x 2⁷ + 0 x 2⁶ + 0 x 2⁵ + 1 x 2⁴ + 1 x 2³ + 1 x 2² +
           0 x 2¹ + 0 x 2⁰
         = 8 + 4 + 0 + 0
         = 12
```

The leftmost digit of a number represented in two's complement form has a negative weight, so negative 12 is represented as

```
11110100 = -1 x 2⁷ + 1 x 2⁶ + 1 x 2⁵ + 1 x 2⁴ + 0 x 2³ + 1 x 2² +
           0 x 2¹ + 0 x 2⁰
         = -128 + 64 + 32 + 16 + 0 + 4 + 0 + 0
         = -12
```

A nice feature of two's complement form is that the normal rules for binary addition work correctly. It's also easy to negate a number (make it negative): simply complement each bit and add one to the result.

2.4.2   Unsigned Integer

An XDR unsigned integer is a bit field that represents a nonnegative integer in the range [0, 4294967295]. Like the signed integer, the byte order is big-endian; that is, the most significant byte is 0 and the least significant is 3. Unlike a signed integer, the most significant bit has a positive weight.

MSB			LSB
Byte 0	Byte 1	Byte 2	Byte 3

32 bits

2.4.3   Boolean

A boolean value is represented as a signed integer with assigned values: 0 = false and 1 = true.

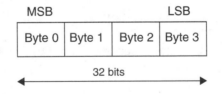

MSB			LSB
Byte 0	Byte 1	Byte 2	Byte 3
= 0	= 0	= 0	= 0 or 1

32 bits

2.4.4   Hyper Integer and Unsigned Hyper Integer

Hyper integers are extensions of the 32-bit integer encodings to 64 bits.

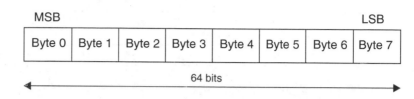

2.4.5   Fixed-Length Opaque Data

XDR allows an uninterpreted sequence of bytes (numbered 0 through $n-1$) to be conveyed from one machine to another. Byte m of the sequence always precedes byte $m+1$ of the sequence. Other than preserving the original byte order, the data format is not interpreted. Where the opaque data is fixed length it is assumed that the recipient has knowledge of the number of bytes in the sequence. As with any XDR field, it must contain an integral number of 4-byte XDR units so up to 3 pad bytes may be appended to the end of the sequence.

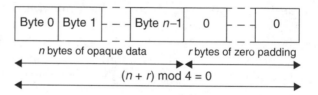

2.4.6   Variable-Length Opaque Data

Where the number of bytes is not known to the recipient, XDR allows opaque data to have a prepended integer containing the byte count The byte count does not include any pad bytes.

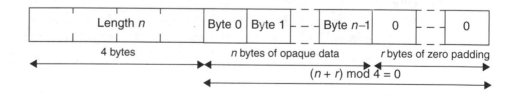

2.4.7   String

A string of ASCII characters can be encoded as variable-length opaque data. Although the standard describes these as "ASCII" bytes, they can be regarded as simple 8-bit bytes with no particular character encoding assumed. The string length does not include any pad bytes. Although it is a convention of C programs to terminate strings with a null byte, XDR strings are not null terminated.

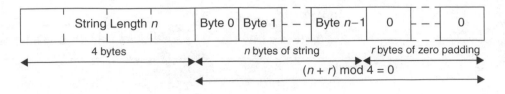

2.5   Structured XDR Data Types

The XDR standard includes encodings for structured types built from sets of primitive types.

2.5.1   Fixed-Length Array

A fixed-length array of n elements can be XDR encoded simply by encoding each element in order beginning with element 0 and ending with element $n-1$. It is assumed that the recipient of the array already knows the number of elements, n, that the array comprises. Each element must comprise an integral number of XDR units, though the elements themselves may have different sizes. For instance, in a fixed-length array of strings, all of the elements must be a string, but the strings themselves may vary in length.

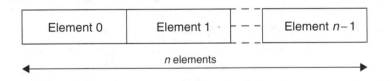

2.5.2   Variable-Length Array

A counted array can be used to encode an array of elements where the number of elements in the array is not known to the recipient. It is equivalent to a fixed-length array with a prepended integer that contains the element count.

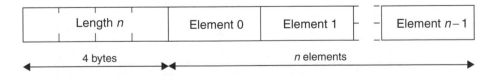

Note that there is no padding required between elements because each element is internally padded out to an integral number of XDR units.

2.5.3 Discriminated Union

While XDR does not require data items to have type tags, programs can insert integer or boolean values into the XDR sequence to describe the data that follow. A discriminated union is particularly useful where the data types that follow in the sequence cannot be predicted. For instance, a protocol reply message may contain a status code to indicate that a valid result follows, but if nonzero, the status indicates an error code and no result follows. Note the reference to discriminated unions in section 2.6.4.

Integer or Boolean Discriminant	Discriminant-dependent Values

2.5.4 Linked Lists

Data tags may also be used to encode linked list structures. Since a linked list is similar to a variable-size array, it may seem reasonable to use a variable-length array encoding by prepending a size value on a sequence of elements. However, this encoding assumes that the number of data elements is known in advance. The number of elements in a linked list cannot be known without first traversing the list and counting the elements. An XDR encoding of a linked list can be achieved in a single traverse of the list by including an XDR boolean value with each list element in the sequence that indicates whether there is a next element in the sequence.

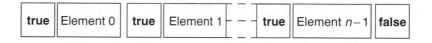

Linked list encoding can be reasonably efficient if the space occupied by the list elements is significantly larger than the space taken by the boolean tags. If the elements are relatively compact, then a variable-length array will provide a more space-efficient encoding.

This book uses a variant of the XDR language to describe a linked list. The list keyword introduces a structure that is replicated as a linked list. See section 2.6.6.

2.6 XDR Language

The XDR language is a notation for describing the sequence and types of XDR-encoded data. Although it is not a programming language, the XDR language can be used by "compilers" like Rpcgen[2] to convert an XDR language

---

2. The Rpcgen compiler is made available by vendors that support the ONC RPC toolkit. It is bundled with most versions of UNIX.

description into C or C++ data structures and functions to carry out the XDR encoding and decoding. It is no coincidence that the XDR language resembles the C language, since there is almost a one-to-one conversion of XDR language components to those of C and C++.

The language description in sections 2.6.1 through 2.6.5 is reproduced from Section 5 of RFC 1832, "XDR: External Data Representation Standard."

2.6.1   Notational Conventions

This specification uses an extended Backus-Naur Form notation for describing the XDR language. Here is a brief description of the notation:

- The characters |, (,), [,], ", and * are special.
- Terminal symbols are strings of any characters surrounded by double quotes.
- Nonterminal symbols are strings of nonspecial characters.
- Alternative items are separated by a vertical bar (|).
- Optional items are enclosed in brackets.
- Items are grouped together by parentheses.
- A * following an item means 0 or more occurrences of that item.

For example, consider the following pattern:

```
"a " "very" (", " "very")* [" cold " "and "] " rainy " ("day" |
"night")
```

An infinite number of strings match this pattern. A few of them are

```
"a very rainy day"
"a very, very rainy day"
"a very cold and rainy day"
"a very, very, very cold and rainy night"
```

2.6.2   Lexical Notes

- Comments begin with /* and terminate with */.
- White space serves to separate items and is otherwise ignored.
- An identifier is a letter followed by an optional sequence of letters, digits, or underbar (_). The case of identifiers is not ignored.
- A constant is a sequence of one or more decimal digits, optionally preceded by a minus sign (-).

2.6.3   Syntax Information

```
declaration:
      type_specifier identifier
    | type_specifier identifier "[" value "]"
    | type_specifier identifier "<" [ value ] ">"
    | "opaque" identifier "[" value "]"
    | "opaque" identifier "<" [ value ] ">"
    | "string" identifier "<" [ value ] ">"
    | type_specifier "*" identifier
    | "void"

value:
      constant
    | identifier

type_specifier:
      [ "unsigned" ] "int"
    | [ "unsigned" ] "hyper"
    | "float"
    | "double"
    | "quadruple"
    | "bool"
    | enum_type_spec
    | struct_type_spec
    | union_type_spec
    | identifier

enum_type_spec:
    "enum" enum_body

enum_body:
    "{"
        ( identifier "=" value )
        ( "," identifier "=" value )*
    "}"

struct_type_spec:
    "struct" struct_body

struct_body:
    "{"
        ( declaration ";" )
        ( declaration ";" )*
          "}"

union_type_spec:
    "union" union_body

union_body:
    "switch" "(" declaration ")" "{"
        ( "case" value ":" declaration ";" )
```

```
        ( "case" value ":" declaration ";" )*
        [ "default" ":" declaration ";" ]
      "}

constant_def:
    "const" identifier "=" constant ";"

type_def:
      "typedef" declaration ";"
    | "enum" identifier enum_body ";"
    | "struct" identifier struct_body ";"
    | "union" identifier union_body ";"

definition:
      type_def
    | constant_def

specification:
    definition *
```

2.6.4   Syntax Notes

- The following are keywords and cannot be used as identifiers: **bool**, **case**, **const**, **default**, **double**, **quadruple**, **enum**, **float**, **hyper**, **opaque**, **string**, **struct**, **switch**, **typedef**, **union**, **unsigned**, and **void**.

- Only unsigned constants may be used as size specifications for arrays. If an identifier is used, it must have been declared previously as an unsigned constant in a **const** definition.

- Constant and type identifiers within the scope of a specification are in the same namespace and must be declared uniquely within this scope.

- Similarly, variable identifiers must be unique within the scope of struct and union declarations. Nested struct and union declarations create new scopes.

- The discriminant of a union must be of a type that evaluates to an integer. That is, **int**, **unsigned int**, **bool**, an enumerated type, or any typedef type that evaluates one of these is legal. Also, the case values must be one of the legal values of the discriminant. Finally, a case value may not be specified more than once within the scope of a union declaration.

2.6.5   Example of an XDR Data Description

Here is a short XDR data description of a thing called a *file*, which might be used to transfer files from one machine to another.

```
const MAXUSERNAME = 32;      /* max length of a user name */
const MAXFILELEN  = 65535;   /* max length of a file      */
const MAXNAMELEN  = 255;     /* max length of a filename  */
```

```
/*
 * Types of files:
 */
enum filekind {
    TEXT = 0,        /* ascii data */
    DATA = 1,        /* raw data   */
    EXEC = 2         /* executable */
};

/*
 * File information, per kind of file:
 */
union filetype switch (filekind kind) {
case TEXT:
    void;                               /* no extra information*/
case DATA:
    string creator<MAXNAMELEN>;         /* data creator */
case EXEC:
    string interpretor<MAXNAMELEN>;  /* program interpretor*/
};

/*
 * A complete file:
 */
struct file {
    string filename<MAXNAMELEN>;  /* name of file    */
    filetype type;                /* info about file */
    string owner<MAXUSERNAME>;    /* owner of file   */
    opaque data<MAXFILELEN>;      /* file data       */
}
```

Suppose now that there is a user named "john" who wants to store his Lisp program "sillyprog" that contains just the data "(quit)." His file would be encoded as shown in Table 2.1.

2.6.6 XDR Language Variant in This Book

The XDR language was not designed with the goal of making XDR or RPC protocol descriptions easy to read. Because of its close association with C and C++ and the requirement that XDR data descriptions be readily converted into data structures for these languages, data descriptions in XDR language may appear somewhat long-winded. Any sequence of XDR fields must be represented by a named struct, even if the sequence comprises an unnamed sequence of parameters from a function call or the multiple items in the arm of a discriminated union. As a consequence, XDR language descriptions contain large numbers of named structures.

In this book I use a variant of the XDR language to describe XDR-based protocols. This variant makes protocol descriptions more compact and easier to comprehend.

TABLE 2.1 Lisp Program "sillyprog"

Offset	Hex bytes	ASCII	Comments
0	00 00 00 09	...	Length of filename = 9
4	73 69 6c 6c	sill	Filename characters
8	79 70 72 6f	ypro	. . . and more characters . . .
12	67 00 00 00	g...	. . . and 3 zero-bytes of padding
16	00 00 00 02	. . . .	Filekind is EXEC = 2
20	00 00 00 04	. . . .	Length of interpreter = 4
24	6c 69 73 70	lisp	Interpreter characters
28	00 00 00 04	. . . .	Length of owner = 4
32	6a 6f 68 6e	john	Owner characters
36	00 00 00 06	. . . .	Length of file data = 6
40	28 71 75 69	(qui	File data bytes . . .
44	74 29 00 00	t)..	. . . and 2 zero-bytes of padding

1. The keyword `int32` is used as a substitute for `int` and `uint32` for `unsigned int`.

2. The keyword `union` and the union name may be omitted from a union body:

```
union reply_body switch (uint32 msg_type) {
    case CALL:
        ...
    case REPLY:
        ...
}
```

3. Data items may be left unnamed if no name follows a type specifier. For instance, in a discriminant value,

```
switch (uint32) {
    case CALL:
        ...
    case REPLY:
        ...
}
```

4. A sequence of declarations may exist without an enclosing **struct**. For example, multiple declarations may appear in a discriminant arm:

```
switch (uint) {
    case CALL:
        uint32 rpcvers;
        uint32 prog;
        uint32 vers;
        uint32 proc;
        opaque_auth cred;
        opaque_auth verf;
```

```
        case REPLY:
            ...
    }
```

5. A case value may be associated with a variable name without the use of an **enum**:

```
switch (uint32) {
    case CALL = 0:
        ...
    case REPLY = 1:
        ...
}
```

6. The size of a counted array optionally follows the type specifier:

```
opaque[4] timestamp;
string<255> filename;
```

7. A list keyword may be used to introduce one or more items that constitute a "linked list." For instance, the declarations

```
struct *stringlist {
    string<> item1;
    uint32 item2;
    stringlist next;
};
    :
stringlist *names;
```

are replaced by

```
list {
    string<> item1;
    uint32 item2;
}
```

See descriptions of the NFS READDIR procedure in section 6.2.15 (version 2) and section 7.3.17 (version 3) for further examples of this simplified syntax.

Note: This language variant cannot be compiled with the XDR language compiler Rpcgen.

2.7 Summary

XDR is a data encoding method that represents data in a common format suitable for transfer between computers that represent the data differently. The XDR encoding does not include data description tags—programs that receive XDR data are assumed to know the expected sequence of data types. XDR defines encodings for primitive data types such as integers, floating point numbers, booleans, and strings. Each primitive type is represented in an integral number of 4-byte XDR units. Primitive types can be assembled into structured types such as arrays and linked lists.

The XDR language is used to describe streams of XDR encoded data. A program like Rpcgen can be used to "compile" an XDR description into C or C++ data structures and code to transfer data between these data structures and their XDR encoding.

Chapter 3
ONC RPC

The NFS protocol is independent of the type of operating system, network architecture, and transport protocols. This means that the NFS protocol is the same whether it is used between an IBM mainframe and an Apple iMac, whether it is using a TCP connection or UDP datagrams, whether it is running over an ethernet or a token ring network. This independence is due in part to the NFS protocol being an ONC RPC protocol. ONC is an acronym for Open Network Computing, the name Sun Microsystems gives to the RPC protocol described here. It is also known as "SunRPC." ONC RPC is now an Internet "standards track" protocol described in [RFC 1831] and [RFC 1832].

This chapter is not intended to be a complete description of ONC RPC. Enough of the RPC protocol is described so that you can understand how the protocol works for NFS and its associated RPC protocols: MOUNT, Network Lock Manager, PCNFSD, and so on. The C programming API is not described. If you would like details of the RPC programming interface, make note of the "RPC" *man* page on UNIX systems that support ONC, or refer to [Bloomer92].

3.1 Remote Procedure Call Model

A Remote Procedure Call is a message sent to a server with the expectation of a reply message, as shown in Figure 3.1. The call message identifies a server program and invokes a "procedure" within the program. Encoded along with the message are the parameters for the procedure. The reply message may be either an error code or reply data.

For instance, when an NFS client needs to read a file, it sends an RPC call to the server's NFS program to invoke the READ procedure and provides three arguments: the filehandle that identifies the file, an offset into the file, and the number of bytes that are to be read. The reply message contains the requested data from the file.

In a *local* procedure call there is one logical thread of execution; control is transferred to the procedure code and then back to the caller when execution

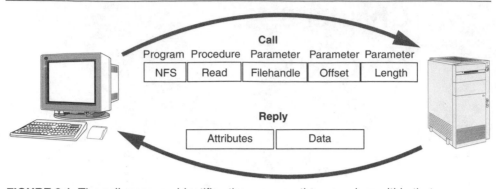

FIGURE 3.1 The call message identifies the program, the procedure within that program, and the parameters for the procedure. The reply message conveys the procedure results back to the caller.

of the procedure is complete. A *remote* procedure call is no different; the calling program waits until the remote procedure is complete and returns its reply. It is not a *requirement* that the calling program do nothing while it waits for the remote procedure—it could carry on with other work while waiting. The ability to work while waiting is usually expressed as some form of multi-threading within the client program, where the threads making an RPC call block until the remote call is complete.

The server program generally waits for a call message, decodes the arguments, dispatches them to the appropriate procedure, encodes the reply, and waits for another call message. A simple server program may process calls one at a time, though if the server is to handle concurrent calls from many clients (like an NFS server), then it may be necessary to have a more complex interface that can dispatch each call to a separate process or thread of execution.

While remote procedure calls are similar to local procedure calls, there are some important differences:

- *Error handling.* Failures of the remote server or network must be handled when using RPCs.

- *Global variables and side effects.* Since the server does not have access to the client's address space, hidden arguments cannot be passed as global variables or returned as side effects.

- *Performance.* Remote procedures usually operate one or more orders of magnitude slower than local procedure calls. There are notable exceptions: the first users of the NFS protocol sometimes saw better performance from their NFS mounted disks than from locally mounted disks, since the the file server disks had significantly faster seek time and I/O bandwidth.

- *Authentication.* Since remote procedure calls can be transported over unsecured networks, authentication may be necessary. Authentication prevents one entity from masquerading as some other entity.

The remote procedure call programming paradigm was introduced in a landmark paper by Andrew Birrell and Bruce Nelson, called "Implementing Remote Procedure Calls" [Birrell+84]. They were the first to create an operational RPC system while at the Computer Science Laboratory of the Xerox Palo Alto Research Center (PARC) in 1981. Their RPC made it possible for programs written in the Cedar language to communicate with each other over the Xerox datagram network via a simple procedure call interface. Their work was preceded by the release of Xerox Courier RPC, a standard intended to be used to build distributed applications. In 1994 Birrell and Nelson received the ACM Software System Award in recognition of their work.

ONC RPC is just one of several RPC systems that are based on the RPC work at Xerox PARC. The Open Group's DCE/RPC, Microsoft's DCOM, and the Java RMI are other RPC systems in common use. ONC RPC and XDR encoding were developed principally by Bob Lyon while at Sun. He informally referred to this RPC scheme as "Sun of Courier."

3.2 RPC Transport Independence and Semantics

The RPC protocol describes a standard for call and reply messages, but it does not require that the messages be conveyed between the client and server system over any particular transport protocol like TCP/IP. It would be possible, albeit slow, to move the messages back and forth using floppy disks!

While the RPC protocol itself does not assume any particular transport for conveying call and reply data, the initial C programming API for ONC RPC was based on Berkeley Sockets, which assumed some transport dependencies such as address size. In 1989, Sun developed a revised transport-independent API known as TI-RPC that rid the API of transport dependencies so that RPC could operate over other transports such as AT&T's Datakit, Novell Netware, or OSI. None of the TI-RPC changes affected the RPC protocol itself since the call and reply message formats had no transport dependencies in them. A new version of the Portmap protocol was added, which introduced the transport-independent *universal address* (section 3.8.1).

Although the RPC protocol is transport independent, it does not attempt to hide the limitations of the transport—a datagram transport like UDP will impose an absolute limit on the size of an RPC message (64 KB), while TCP will convey messages of any length. RPC does not guarantee any kind of *reliability*. If an application knows that it is using a reliable transport like TCP, then it can assume that the transport itself will handle reliable delivery of messages; however, if it is using an unreliable protocol like UDP, then it is possible that the call or reply message may be lost and the application will need to implement a time-out and retransmission policy.

Transport independence implies that RPC cannot attach specific semantics to the execution of remote procedures. For instance, if running over UDP where call or reply datagrams may be lost, the client will need to implement a retransmission policy (Figure 3.2). The use of a reliable transport like TCP does not completely remove the need for retransmissions. For instance, if the server drops the TCP connection because it crashed or is overloaded, then the client will need to reestablish the connection and retransmit any call messages that were pending when the connection was lost. If a client receives no reply from the server, it cannot assume that the remote procedure was not executed since it may be the reply that was lost. Additionally, if a client receives a reply after some number of retransmissions, it can assume only that the remote procedure was executed at least once.

For this reason it is preferable that remote procedures be *idempotent;* that is, if the procedure is repeatedly presented with the same arguments, it will always generate the same result. An example of a nonidempotent procedure would be one that takes a record in the call message and appends it to a file. If the call message is retransmitted, then the record may be appended more than once. The NFS READ request is a good example of an idempotent procedure; the call arguments specify the file offset and length so that the same file data are returned no matter how often the request is retransmitted.

Idempotent procedures are desirable but not always possible to implement. For instance, the NFS RENAME procedure is used to rename a file. If a RENAME request is retransmitted because the reply was lost, then the second request will attempt to rename the file again and the server will return a "no such entry" error. The client will be unable to tell whether the file was ever

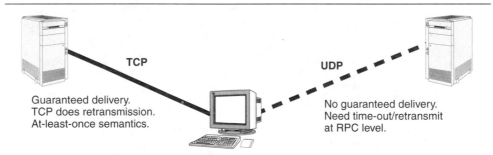

TCP   UDP

Guaranteed delivery.   No guaranteed delivery.
TCP does retransmission.   Need time-out/retransmit
At-least-once semantics.   at RPC level.

FIGURE 3.2 RPC transport independence does not insulate the protocol completely from the properties of the underlying transport. Since UDP does not guarantee message delivery, RPC uses a time-out/retransmission policy. Since TCP already provides its own time-out/retransmission, RPC utilizes it instead of its own. In practice, RPC does retransmit over TCP though with a longer time-out than it would use over TCP to handle the case of a broken TCP connection that must be reestablished.

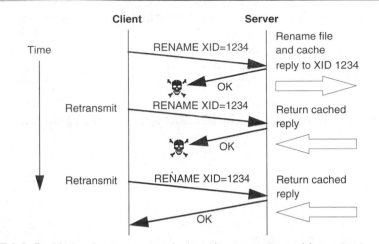

Client   **Server**

FIGURE 3.3 Problems due to retransmission of requests to nonidempotent procedures can be avoided by having the server cache reply to recent calls. In this example the server's reply is lost. If the server detects a retransmission (via the XID), then it can return the lost reply from the cache.

there. The server can mitigate the impact of retransmitted, nonidempotent requests by keeping a cache of recent requests (Figure 3.3). Each RPC request is distinguished by a transaction identifier (XID) that is kept constant across retransmissions. Using the XID, the server can check the cache for previous transmissions of the same request and send a cached reply to the client while taking no action.

Using a duplicate request cache, an RPC server can *approximate* "at most once" semantics, preventing a retransmitted RPC call from being executed twice. Since a duplicate request cache does not record all previous RPC calls, there is still a risk that an RPC call that is retransmitted after a long delay may miss the cache and be executed more than once. Additionally, if the cache is lost through a server reboot, RPC calls that were sent but not acknowledged before the reboot will not be detected as duplicate requests after the server reboot. For details on the duplicate request cache implemented by NFS servers, see section 8.9.

3.3 Program Numbers and Versioning

The RPC call message has three unsigned integer fields—remote program number, remote program version number, and remote procedure number—which uniquely identify the procedure to be called. Program numbers are administered by the Internet Assigned Numbers Authority—also known as IANA (iana@iana.org). Once implementors have a program number, they can implement their remote program. The first implementation would probably have the version number 1. Because most new protocols evolve, a version field of the call message identifies which version of the protocol the caller is using. Version numbers enable support of both old and new protocols through the same server process. The procedure number identifies the procedure to be called. These numbers are documented in the specific program's protocol specification. For example, a file service's protocol specification may state that its procedure number 5 is "read" and procedure number 12 is "write."

Just as remote program protocols may change over several versions, the actual RPC message protocol can also change. Therefore, the call message also has in it the RPC version number, which always equals 2 for the RPC described here. The version number of *the* RPC protocol should not be confused with the version number of *an* RPC protocol. The RPC call header contains both version numbers.

The reply message to a request message has enough information to distinguish the following error conditions:

- The remote implementation of RPC does not support protocol version 2. The lowest and highest supported RPC version numbers are returned. The RPC version error is not likely to be encountered since RPC version 2 is the only version of RPC and will be for the forseeable future.

- The remote program is not available on the remote system.

- The remote program does not support the requested version number. The lowest and highest supported remote program version numbers are returned.

- The requested procedure number does not exist. This is usually a client-side protocol or programming error.

- The parameters to the remote procedure appear to be garbage from the server's point of view. Again, this is usually caused by a disagreement about the protocol between client and service.

- The authentication flavor is invalid or unsupported.

3.4   Requirements of the RPC Protocol

The RPC protocol must provide for the following:

- Unique specification of a procedure to be called. Each procedure is assigned a unique number. Procedure 0 is reserved for the *null* procedure.

- Provisions for matching response messages to request messages. The transaction ID or XID is selected by the client to be a unique identifier for each call and response. The XID may also be used by the server to detect duplicate requests.

- Provisions for authenticating the caller to the service and vice versa. The use of credentials and verifiers in the RPC header is discussed in chapter 4.

Besides these requirements, features that detect the following are worth supporting because of protocol errors, implementation bugs, and user error:

- RPC protocol mismatches. Since there is (currently) only one version of the ONC RPC protocol (version 2), this is rarely a problem.
- Remote program protocol version mismatches. The client requests a version of the protocol that the server does not support. The server responds with the highest and lowest version numbers it supports.
- Protocol errors (such as invalid procedure parameters). For instance, on receiving an invalid NFS filehandle, the server will return an NFSERR_STALE error.
- Reasons the remote authentication failed, for example, where the client's credential is invalid or cannot be verified.
- Any other reasons the desired procedure was not called, for instance, if the server is out of memory.

3.5 RPC Call Message

RPC call and reply messages contain XDR-encoded parameters as required by the RPC protocol. The RPC call header is quite simple, requiring only six fields in addition to the credential and verifier (Figure 3.4).

The first value in both call and response messages is the XID, which uniquely identifies the RPC call and its response. The XID is useful to both the client and the server. Since the client may be waiting for several concurrent calls to the server, it needs the XID in the response to match it with the pending request. If the client needs to retransmit the request, it should use the same XID since a reply to the original transmission or retransmission will satisfy the request. The client must be careful to generate a unique XID for each new request; otherwise, an incorrect request-response matching is possible.

The easiest way to achieve uniqueness is to increment the XID value by 1 for each new request, beginning with a random number or a rapidly changing time value; otherwise, a client that crashes and restarts quickly could generate repeated XID sequences that would be confused with requests generated before the crash. The server is not required to do anything with the XID other than copy it from the request header to the response. Servers can use the XID to identify retransmitted requests and return a cached reply. Not only can the server avoid unnecessary work, but it can avoid problems resulting from retransmitted requests that are not idempotent, for instance, a request that appends a record to a log. Because the XID uniquely identifies a client request,

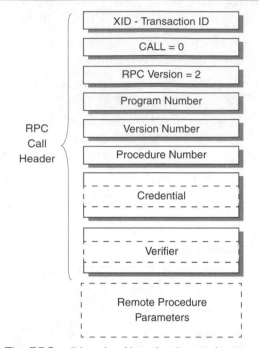

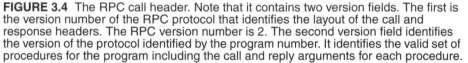

FIGURE 3.4 The RPC call header. Note that it contains two version fields. The first is the version number of the RPC protocol that identifies the layout of the call and response headers. The RPC version number is 2. The second version field identifies the version of the protocol identified by the program number. It identifies the valid set of procedures for the program including the call and reply arguments for each procedure.

the server can use it to approximate at-most-once semantics; that is, the RPC request will not be processed by the server more than one time even if the client retransmits it.

A discriminant value of zero after the XID value identifies an RPC call header. The RPC version identifies the layout of the RPC header. Currently there is only one version of the ONC RPC protocol—version 2. The RPC version number is followed by the program number, the version of this protocol for the program, and the number of the procedure to be called within the program. The credential and verifier are variable-length items that are used for authentication. The credential authenticates the client to the server, and the verifier validates the credential. The next chapter, dedicated to the RPC authentication, describes several authentication flavors that make use of the credential and verifier.

Immediately following the RPC call header are the parameters to the remote procedure.

3.6 RPC Reply Message

The RPC reply header is somewhat more complex than the call header. It has several variants, depending on the success or failure of the request (Figure 3.5).

The reply header begins with the XID the server has copied from the call header, followed by a value of 1 that identifies it as a reply. Unlike the call, there is nothing in the reply that identifies the program, version, or procedure number. This information is redundant since it is already present in the context that generated the request. The reply status indicates whether the server accepted or rejected the call.

The call can be rejected for two reasons: either the server is not running a compatible version of the RPC protocol (RPC MISMATCH), or the server rejects the identity of the caller (AUTH ERROR). In case of an RPC version mismatch error, the server returns the lowest and highest supported RPC version numbers. It is expected that the client will try another version that is in the version range low–high. Note that the RPC version number is distinct from the version number associated with the program. In case of invalid

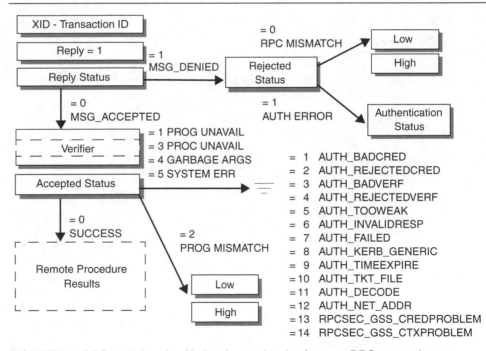

FIGURE 3.5 RPC reply header. Notice the two levels of errors: RPC protocol errors due to a protocol version error or an authentication error and errors where the server returns a verifier but indicates that it cannot invoke the requested program, program version, or procedure.

authentication, failure status is returned. The authentication failure errors appear in Table 3.1 .

Only if the accepted status indicates SUCCESS can the client proceed to decode the results from the remote procedure. If the reply status indicates that the call was accepted, the server returns an authentication verifier that the server uses to validate itself to the client. The accepted status field indicates whether the specified program, version, and procedure were invoked or whether an error occurred (Table 3.2).

An accepted status of SUCCESS indicates only that the remote procedure was successfully invoked. If the remote procedure detects some kind of error, then it will return a failure indication with the procedure results. If the server returns a PROG MISMATCH error, then the client should retry the request with a version of the protocol that is acceptable to the server, that is, within the low–high range. For instance, if an NFS client sends a version 3 request to a server that supports only version 2, then the server will return a PROG

TABLE 3.1 Authentication Failure Errors

Value	Name	Meaning
0	AUTH_OK	OK
Failure at Server		
1	AUTH_BADCRED	Bad credential
2	AUTH_REJECTEDCRED	Client must begin new session
3	AUTH_BADVERF	Bad verifier
4	AUTH_REJECTEDVERF	Verifier expired or replayed
5	AUTH_TOOWEAK	Rejected for security reasons
Failed Locally		
6	AUTH_INVALIDRESP	Bogus response verifier
7	AUTH_FAILED	Some unknown reason
Kerberos V4 Errors		
8	AUTH_KERB_GENERIC	Miscellaneous Kerberos error
9	AUTH_TIMEEXPIRE	Client's ticket has expired
10	AUTH_TKT_FILE	Server cannot locate ticket file
11	AUTH_DECODE	Client's ticket authenticator invalid
12	AUTH_NET_ADDR	Client's address and ticket address mismatch
RPCSEC_GSS Errors		
13	RPCSEC_GSS_CREDPROBLEM	Invalid context or credential
14	RPCSEC_GSS_CTXPROBLEM	Problem with context or credential

TABLE 3.2 Accepted Status Errors

Value	Name	Meaning
0	SUCCESS	The remote procedure was invoked successfully.
1	PROG UNAVAIL	The server does not recognize the program number.
2	PROG MISMATCH	The requested version of the program does not exist.
3	PROC UNAVAIL	The server does not recognize the procedure number.
4	GARBAGE ARGS	The arguments to the remote procedure cannot be XDR decoded.
5	SYSTEM_ERR	Unknown error on server

MISMATCH error with the low and high both set to 2. The client should retry that request (and all following requests to that server) using version 2 of the protocol.

The "extended" XDR Language definition of RPC call and reply headers follows:

```
struct rpc_msg {
    uint xid;                /* Transaction ID */
    switch (uint) {          /* message type */

case CALL = 0:
    uint rpcvers;            /* RPC version (=2) */
    uint prog;               /* Program number */
    uint vers;               /* Version number */
    uint proc;               /* Procedure number */
    opaque_auth cred;        /* Credential */
    opaque_auth verf;        /* Verifier
    /* Call parameters here */

case REPLY = 1:
    switch (uint reply_stat) {
        case MSG_ACCEPTED = 0:
            opaque_auth verf;
            switch (uint accept_stat) {
                case SUCCESS = 0:
                    /* Procedure Results */;
                case PROG_UNAVAIL = 1:;
                case PROG_MISMATCH = 2:
                    uint low;
                    uint high;
                case PROC_UNAVAIL = 3:
                case GARBAGE_ARGS = 4:
                case SYSTEM_ERR = 5:;
            }
        case MSG_DENIED = 1:
            switch (uint rejected_reply) {
                case RPC_MISMATCH = 0:
```

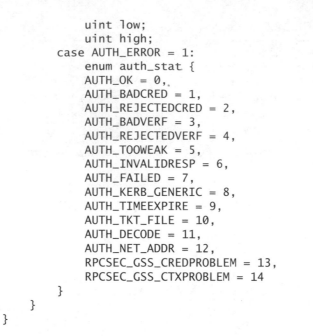

```
                             uint low;
                             uint high;
                    case AUTH_ERROR = 1:
                         enum auth_stat {
                         AUTH_OK = 0,
                         AUTH_BADCRED = 1,
                         AUTH_REJECTEDCRED = 2,
                         AUTH_BADVERF = 3,
                         AUTH_REJECTEDVERF = 4,
                         AUTH_TOOWEAK = 5,
                         AUTH_INVALIDRESP = 6,
                         AUTH_FAILED = 7,
                         AUTH_KERB_GENERIC = 8,
                         AUTH_TIMEEXPIRE = 9,
                         AUTH_TKT_FILE = 10,
                         AUTH_DECODE = 11,
                         AUTH_NET_ADDR = 12,
                         RPCSEC_GSS_CREDPROBLEM = 13,
                         RPCSEC_GSS_CTXPROBLEM = 14
                    }
                }
            }
        }
    }
```

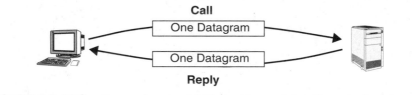

FIGURE 3.6 RPC call or reply using UDP must be contained in a single datagram.

3.7 Record-Marking Standard

RPC requests and replies conveyed on a datagram protocol like UDP use a single datagram for each request or reply (Figure 3.6), which may be further divided into packets according to the IP fragmentation requirements. In the case of UDP, the datagram size cannot exceed 64 KB of data.[1] If a protocol requires larger requests or replies, then a protocol such as TCP must be used.

---

1. Although in principle UDP can support 64-KB datagrams, in practice large datagrams will be fragmented according to the MTU (message transfer unit) size of the underlying medium. Ethernet, for instance, supports an MTU of about 1500 KB. So an 8-KB NFS READ will require 6 fragments. A 64-KB datagram on Ethernet will use 45 fragments!

Protocols such as TCP support a *stream* of data. Unlike a datagram protocol, there is no sure way to delimit one RPC request or reply from the next in the stream. If XDR encoding of requests and replies were followed strictly, then in theory it would be possible to determine the end of a request or reply and assume that the next byte in the stream is the beginning of the next. However, if the client or server runs afoul of a protocol encoding error (e.g., GARBAGE ARGS), then it can be extremely difficult to determine where the next valid request or response begins in the stream.

The RPC record-marking standard splits the data stream into a sequence of variable-length records. Each record is composed of one or more *record fragments* (Figure 3.7). A record fragment is a 4-byte header followed by 0 to $2^{31}-1$ bytes of fragment data. The bytes encode an unsigned binary number; as with XDR integers, the byte order is from highest to lowest. The number encodes two values—a boolean that indicates whether the fragment is the last fragment of the record (bit value 1 implies that the fragment is the last fragment) and a 31-bit unsigned binary value that is the length in bytes of the fragment's data. The boolean value is the highest-order bit of the header; the length is in the 31 low-order bits.

The RPC record-marking standard assumes that the data stream is reliable and error free. If for some reason the receiver of the data stream incorrectly computes the offset to the next record or if data are added to or missing from the record, there is no way for the receiver to resynchronize the record boundaries. For example, hardware devices often implement record-marking protocols that utilize a unique bit pattern that can be used to detect record boundaries if synchronization is lost.

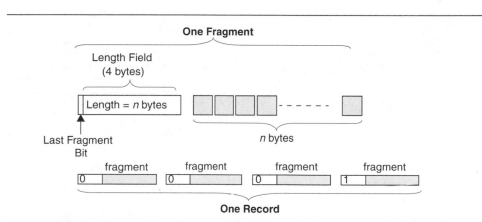

FIGURE 3.7 On a stream-based protocol like TCP, an RPC request or reply is contained in a record that consists of one or more variable-length fragments. The last fragment is flagged by the last fragment bit.

3.8 Portmapper and Rpcbind

The names *portmapper* and *Rpcbind* refer to different versions of the same RPC service (program number 100000). Portmapper refers to version 2, the most common implementation of the service, and Rpcbind refers to versions 3 and 4 (there is no version 1).

Each RPC protocol is uniquely identified by its program number and version. When a client needs to send a request to a server that supports that RPC protocol, it needs to know the server's network address (usually an IP address) as well as the *transport endpoint*—for UDP and TCP transports this is identified by the *port number*. If an RPC service has a well-known port number, then the client can send its requests to this port. For instance, NFS servers default to port 2049, so WebNFS clients automatically send requests to this port. However, it would be burdensome to require every RPC protocol to have a fixed port assignment. In addition, the TCP and UDP port number is constrained to an unsigned, 16-bit field, which limits the number of ports to 65,535.

The portmapper service allows an RPC service to listen for requests on any free port as long as it registers that port with the portmapper along with its program number, version, and transport protocol (Figure 3.8). Client programs that need to know the port assignment for a particular program number can then query the portmapper service. The portmapper service itself is registered on a well-known TCP and UDP port: 111. Port 111 is also a privileged port on UNIX systems. A privileged port is any port number less than

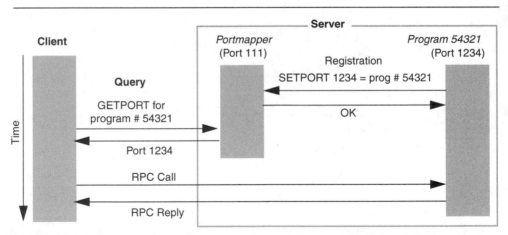

FIGURE 3.8 Clients use the portmapper to discover the port on which an RPC service is listening. An RPC service registers its TCP or UDP port using a local RPC call to the portmapper. A remote client can then query the portmapper for the port assignment and send RPC calls directly to the service.

1024 and can be used as a source port only by a UNIX superuser process. This restriction was intended to make it more difficult for a malicous UNIX process to masquerade as a portmapper service. The port restriction made sense when UNIX computers were large, expensive machines tended by system administrators. Modern networks include many non-UNIX servers and devices that have no notion of privileged ports, so the port restriction is almost worthless now as a security feature. RPC services can be registered on any available port (even on privileged ports if the process is authorized). NFS servers register on port 2049, which is not privileged.

3.8.1 Portmap Protocol

Version 2 of the Portmap protocol supports the following procedures:

0 PMAPPROC_NULL
This procedure does no work. By convention, procedure 0 of any RPC protocol is a "null" procedure that takes no arguments and returns no results.

1 PMAPPROC_SET
When an RPC service starts, it uses this call to register itself with the portmapper on the same machine. Along with the port number on which it is listening, it registers its program number, version, and the transport protocol number (6 for TCP, 17 for UDP). The reply is a boolean value that is true if the registration is successful, false if there is already a service registered with the same program, version, and protocol number. A correct implementation of the portmap protocol will allow a SET call only from a *local* client. Any attempt to register a port from a remote client must be rejected.

2 PMAPPROC_UNSET
Used by the RPC program to unregister the port assignment. The RPC service should do this before it exits, though this cannot always be done reliably if the service crashes. If the client should use a "stale" mapping, then it will receive an error when it tries to connect or send a request to the port. A correct implementation of the portmap protocol will allow an UNSET call only from a *local* client. Any attempt to unregister a port, from a remote client or from a local user different from the one that registered the port, will be rejected.

3 PMAPPROC_GETPORT
Used by an RPC client to obtain the port number for an RPC program. The parameters to this call are the program number, version, protocol number, and port, though the port argument is ignored. The portmapper returns the port on which the requested program, version, and protocol

are registered. If the mapping cannot be found, then a zero port number is returned. The return of a nonzero port number does not guarantee that the requested service is available since it may have crashed without calling PMAPPROC_UNSET. If the requested version number cannot be found, then the portmapper may return the port for another version of the same program and protocol number so that the client receives a "PROG MISMATCH" error including the high and low version numbers, which the client can then use to determine which versions of the program the server supports.

4 PMAPPROC_DUMP
   Returns a list of all the service registrations. This list is used by administrative commands like "rpcinfo" to determine the list of RPC services that are running on the server. There is some debate as to whether this procedure makes it too easy for hackers to determine if an RPC service worthy of attack is running on the server.

5 PMAPPROC_CALLIT
   This procedure allows the client to call a remote procedure on the server without knowing the port number. The portmapper simply forwards the remainder of the request to the procedure in the requested program. This portmap procedure is intended for use by clients using broadcast RPC, where a request is sent to a broadcast address using the portmapper's well-known port 111. To avoid the possibility of "network implosion," no errors or unsuccessful replies are returned, for instance, if the program is not available on the server. PMAPPROC_CALLIT has been exploited as a security hole since the redirection makes it appear that the caller is a "local" process on the server. Most portmappers now restrict the use of this procedure.

3.8.2 Rpcbind Protocol

Versions 3 and 4 of the portmap service are associated with transport-independent RPC (TI-RPC). TI-RPC was an effort to rid RPC of transport dependencies during the development of UNIX System V release 4 so that RPC could operate over other transports such as AT&T's Datakit, Novell Netware, and OSI. None of the TI-RPC changes affected the RPC protocol itself since the call and reply message formats had no transport dependencies in them. The Portmap protocol does have a transport dependency in its use of ports, since a "port" is considered to be a feature unique to IP-based protocols. These transport-independent versions of the protocol were renamed "Rpcbind."

In place of a PMAPPROC_GETPORT request, a TI-RPC client sends an RPCBPROC_GETATTR request that contains a program number and version. There is no longer a protocol number value since the transport protocol is assumed to be whatever is used for the RPCBPROC_GETATTR request.

Instead of a port number, the client receives a *universal address* for the RPC service. A Universal Address is a string representation of the transport address that designates a transport endpoint. In the case of UDP or TCP, this is just the dotted IP address with the port number appended. For instance, the NFS server running on port 2049 on the host 129.144.15.35 has the universal address 129.144.15.35.8.1, where the "8.1" are the high and low octets of port number 2049.

In practice, it's rare to see RPCBPROC_GETATTR calls on networks. When Sun engineers came to implement the RPC-based client services using the new Rpcbind request it was no surprise that no existing servers supported the new Rpcbind protocol. These servers would return a "version mismatch" error for Rpcbind and the client would revert to the previous version of the protocol, so the port number was eventually obtained but at the cost of additional network overhead and reduced performance. Eventually the decision was made to forego transport independence "temporarily" and stick with the TCP/IP dependency of PMAPPROC_GETPORT. This decision will be revisited now with the advent of version 6 of the IP protocol (IPv6) since PMAPPROC_GETPORT provides no indication of whether the service supports IPv6.

The RPCBPROC_GETTIME request returns the server's time in seconds relative to the 1970 epoch. This call is particularly useful for security schemes that require coordinated client and server clocks for validation of timestamps.

3.9 Summary

The remote procedure call model extends the well-known concept of procedure calls to a network where the call and response may transit a communications link between two computers. While ONC RPC insulates applications from the specifics of network transport protocols, it requires applications to consider message size limitations and unreliability of some transports.

An RPC message comprises a call or reply header followed by parameters or results. The call header contains a unique transaction ID followed by the program number and number of the procedure to be invoked within the program. The call header also includes a credential and verifier that can be used to identify the caller. The response header contains a matching transaction ID followed by the server verifier that can be used to authenticate the server to the client. The reply header may also contain error codes from the RPC service or the program. RPC messages that transit data stream protocols like TCP use a record-marking standard to separate one message from another.

The Portmap or Rpcbind protocol is an RPC service that is registered on port 111 and is used by clients to map an RPC program number to a server port or transport endpoint.

Chapter 4

RPC Authentication

How does an RPC service like NFS identify a client? Is the client's hostname sufficient if multiple users can log into the client computer? RPC authentication addresses this problem. It allows the server to identify the sender of each RPC request, which we will further refer to as a *principal*. A principal may identify some service on a client computer (such as a superuser or administrator) or a person (e.g., Bob or Alice).

This chapter describes several types of authentication credentials. By far the most commonly used for NFS is the easy-to-use but notoriously insecure AUTH_SYS credential. The secure Diffie-Hellman and Kerberos credentials are much less commonly used because they are more difficult to implement and require the administration of a security infrastructure on the network. The chapter concludes with an in-depth description of the RPCSEC_GSS, which is not a security mechanism itself but a framework into which other security mechanisms can be incorporated more easily.

4.1 RPC Credential and Verifier

The RPC protocol provides for the authentication of the caller to the server and vice versa. The call message has two authentication fields, the credential and the verifier (shown in Figure 3.4). The reply message has one authentication field, the response verifier. The RPC protocol specification defines all three fields to be the opaque type shown in Figure 4.1.

The *credential* field contains information that *identifies* the principal (e.g., a UNIX UID/GID or a Kerberos netname). The call and response *verifier* are used by the recipient to check whether the credential is *authentic*, that it truly represents the principal it claims to be from. You may wonder why there is an upper limit of 400 bytes imposed on the size of the RPC credential. Bob Lyon, the designer of the RPC protocol, insisted that excessively large credentials

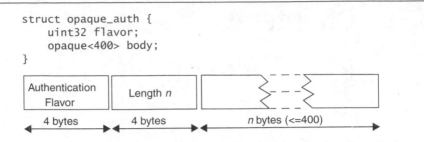

FIGURE 4.1 The RPC credential or verifier consists of an authentication *flavor* that identifies the type of authentication, followed by variable-length data specific to the flavor. The credential length field is implicit in the definition of body.

were an unnecessary overhead and that RPC flavor developers should be forced to think of compact, efficient ways to represent credential data.

4.2   Authentication Flavors

This chapter describes several *authentication flavors*. As originally designed, protocol developers are free to invent new authentication types, with the same rules of flavor number assignment as for program number assignment. The flavor of a credential or verifier refers to the value of the flavor field in the credential or verifier. Flavor numbers, like RPC program numbers, are administered centrally, and developers can assign new flavor numbers by applying through electronic mail to iana@iana.org.

The RPCSEC_GSS flavor signals a departure in the policy that determines the future direction of RPC authentication. RPCSEC_GSS provides not only an open-ended framework for dynamic inclusion of new security types, but also broadens the focus from authentication to include data integrity and privacy. These will be described in more depth in section 4.7. RPCSEC_GSS removes the need for a fixed set of centrally administered authentication flavors.

Now that RPCSEC_GSS offers more than just authentication, RPC authentication flavors are now referred to as *security* flavors. Credentials and verifiers are represented as variable length opaque data. The flavors currently assigned are listed in Table 4.1.

4.3   Null Authentication

Some services may not require authentication of client or server. In this case, the flavor of the RPC message's credential, verifier, and reply verifier can be set to AUTH_NONE. Opaque data associated with AUTH_NONE is undefined. The length of the opaque data should be zero.

TABLE 4.1 Authentication Flavors

Value	Name	Meaning
0	AUTH_NONE	Null authentication
1	AUTH_SYS	System authentication: UID, GID, groups. Also known as AUTH_UNIX.
2	AUTH_SHORT	Token authenticator for AUTH_SYS
3	AUTH_DH	Diffie-Hellman exchange of DES key. Also known as AUTH_DES.
4	AUTH_KERB4	Kerberos version 4 exchange of DES key. Also known as AUTH_KERB.
5	AUTH_RSA	(Never implemented)
6	RPCSEC_GSS	Generic security services API

AUTH_NONE is used by protocols that do not require user authentication. For instance the portmapper protocol as shown in the following snoop trace:

```
     :
RPC:    ----- SUN RPC Header -----
RPC:
RPC:    Transaction id = 881913697
RPC:    Type = 0 (Call)
RPC:    RPC version = 2
RPC:    Program = 100000 (PMAP), version = 2, procedure = 3
RPC:    Credentials: Flavor = 0 (None), len = 0 bytes
RPC:    Verifier    : Flavor = 0 (None), len = 0 bytes
RPC:
PMAP:   ----- Portmapper -----
PMAP:
PMAP:   Proc = 3 (Get port number)
PMAP:   Program = 100005 (MOUNT)
PMAP:   Version = 3
PMAP:   Protocol = 17 (UDP)
```

4.4 System Authentication

AUTH_SYS was originally labelled "AUTH_UNIX" authentication since it was based on the credential used by the UNIX operating system. To avoid trademark problems, it was changed to AUTH_SYS. A client can use the AUTH_SYS flavor if it needs to identify itself with a user ID (UID) and group ID (GID) as it is identified on a UNIX system. The opaque data of the credential contains the data shown in Figure 4.2.

```
struct authsys_cred {
    uint32 stamp;
    string<255> hostname;
    uint32 uid;
    uint32 gid;
    uint32<16> gids;
}
```

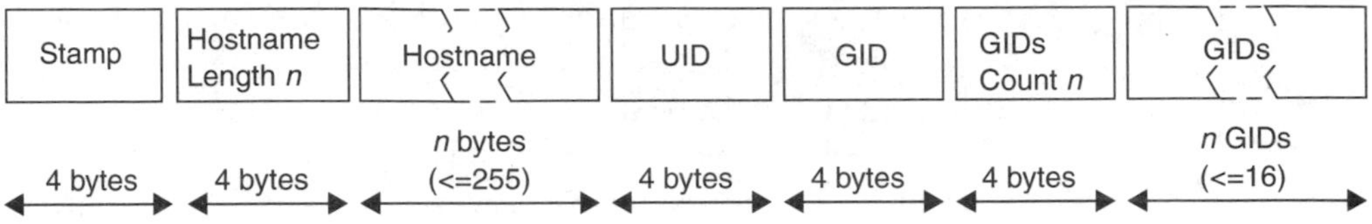

FIGURE 4.2 AUTH_SYS credential.

The *stamp* is an arbitrary value generated by the caller, generally a times-tamp. The *hostname* is the name of the caller's machine (like "krypton"). Nei-ther the timestamp nor the hostname are used by the server for any security purpose. Servers that need the hostname for some reason will usually ignore this field and obtain the hostname via the source IP address of the request.

The *UID* is the caller's effective user ID. The *GID* is the caller's effective group ID. The *GID* is a counted array of groups to which the caller belongs. The limit of 16 groups was problematic for some NFS implementations. Early versions of SunOS supported only 8 or 10 groups. Clients that used system credentials containing more than 10 groups would receive an authen-tication error. Solaris implementations now support the full 16 groups, yet there can still be problems when a 16-group client tries to communicate with an old 8- or 10-group server.

The verifier accompanying the *credential* should have AUTH_NONE fla-vor value (defined in section 4.3). Note that this credential is unique only within a particular domain of machine names, UIDs, and GIDs. The flavor value of the verifier received in the *reply* message from the server may be AUTH_NONE or AUTH_SHORT. The AUTH_SHORT verifier was intended to be a token created by the server that the client could use in place of the AUTH_SYS credential to save space; however, it is not widely supported. The following snoop trace shows a system credential in the RPC header from an NFS request:

```
RPC:  Transaction id = 881913699
RPC:  Type = 0 (Call)
RPC:  RPC version = 2
RPC:  Program = 100005 (MOUNT), version = 3, procedure = 1
RPC:  Credentials: Flavor = 1 (UNIX), len = 32 bytes
RPC:      Time = 18-Dec-98 02:01:39
```

```
RPC:      Hostname = terra
RPC:      Uid = 0, Gid = 10
RPC:      Groups = 10 15 259
RPC: Verifier    : Flavor = 0 (None), len = 0 bytes
```

The AUTH_SYS credential identifies a principal and his/her group membership, but since there is nothing in the verifier, the server cannot authenticate the credential. The client can enter any values for UID or GID and the server has no way of knowing whether the values are legitimate. The server trusts that the client machine has already authenticated the user by accepting a login with user name and password and that the user cannot forge another's credential. Some servers will accept NFS requests only from a *privileged port*. On UNIX clients, a privileged port is any port numbered lower than 1024 that can be used as a source port only by system processes with superuser credentials.

In a network of carefully administered UNIX systems, the server may enjoy some degree of assurance that requests from a privileged port are not from a user process using concocted AUTH_SYS credentials. Since TCP/IP stacks on PC operating systems (MacOS, DOS, Windows) do not have a privileged port restriction, a server's confidence in requests from privileged ports would be misplaced if the network environment includes systems running non-UNIX operating systems outside the system administrator's realm; there can be no assurance of secure AUTH_SYS credential use. Generally, the server will make a service available to a list of "trusted" clients. This trust may be misplaced, however, if the user has superuser access to the client (and can assume another's user ID without typing the password) or if the network is accessible to other clients that can spoof the IP addresses of the trusted clients.

Despite the weaknesses in the "trusted host" model of AUTH_SYS, it is the most commonly used authentication by NFS system administrators since it makes no assumption of a security infrastructure and is easy to administer (Figure 4.3). Corporate system administrators assume that employees are trustworthy and that their networks are secure. In environments where NFS-accessible data needs to be confidential, safe from unauthorized tampering, or where the network is not secure, one of the more secure authentication flavors, described in sections 4.5, 4.6, and 4.7, must be used.

AUTH_SHORT is a token-based variation on AUTH_SYS intended to reduce the header space requirement of AUTH_SYS. Consider that an AUTH_SYS credential with a hostname string and maximal group list could have a length up to 340 bytes. Rather than send a lengthy AUTH_SYS credential on every call, the server has the option of caching the credential and returning a variable length token in an AUTH_SHORT verifier. If the client sends this token in place of a full AUTH_SYS credential on subsequent calls, then the server can use the token to locate the cached credential. If the server crashes and loses the cached credential, or if it just flushes the credential cache

FIGURE 4.3 AUTH_SYS requires the server to trust the clients. The server may enumerate the clients it trusts in an access list enforced by checking the source IP address of RPC requests. Client A has validated the user's login and password and is given access by the server because it is in the server's access list. The user on client B has superuser access, which means that the user can easily assume the credential of the user on A without knowledge of his/her password. The user on client C has gained access to the network and has spoofed the IP address of A. RPC requests from C look like they come from A. Now C is trusted even though it isn't in the server's access list.

(as it is entitled to), then it will reject the client's use of an AUTH_SHORT token with an AUTH_REJECTEDCRED error. On receiving this error, the client must use the original AUTH_SYS credential. Clients are not obliged to use an AUTH_SHORT token and servers are not obliged to use them either. So in practice AUTH_SHORT is rarely used.

4.5   Diffie-Hellman Authentication

Diffie-Hellman authentication (AUTH_DH or just DH) was the first *secure* authentication flavor to be developed. Its developers, Sun engineers David Goldberg and Brad Taylor, intended DH to be the basis of what was then called *secure* NFS. As well as providing secure authentication, it was designed to overcome additional problems in system authentication. System authentication is very UNIX oriented. It assumes that the recipient of the credential can handle the UID representation of a user and can utilize the user's group and group list. The system credential can be easily faked, since the contents are not cryptographically secure. Diffie-Hellman authentication was created to address these problems. While the information provided here will be useful for implementors to ensure interoperability with existing applications that use DH authentication, it is strongly recommended that new applications use more secure authentication and that existing applications, which currently use DH authentication, migrate to more robust authentication mechanisms.

4.5.1   Naming

The client is identified by a simple string of characters instead of an operating system-specific integer. This string of up to 255 characters is known as the *network name* or *netname* of the client. The server is not allowed to interpret the contents of the client's name in any other way except to identify the client. Thus, netnames should be unique for every client in the Internet.

It is up to each operating system's implementation of DH authentication to generate netnames for its users that insure this uniqueness when they call on remote servers. Operating systems already know how to distinguish users local to their systems. It is usually a simple matter to extend this mechanism to the network. For example, a UNIX user at Sun with a user ID of 515 might be assigned the following netname:

```
unix.515@sun.com
```

This netname contains three items that serve to ensure its uniqueness: going backward, there is only one naming domain called `sun.com` in the Internet. Within this domain, there is only one UNIX user with user ID 515. However, there may be another user on another operating system, for example VMS, within the same naming domain that, by coincidence, happens to have the same user ID. To ensure that these two users can be distinguished, we add the operating system name. So one user is `unix.515@sun.com` and the other is `vms.515@sun.com`. The first field is actually a naming method rather than an operating system name. It happens that today there is almost a one-to-one correspondence between naming methods and operating systems. If the world could agree on a naming standard, the first field could be the name of the standard instead of an operating system name.

4.5.2   DH Authentication Verifiers

Unlike system authentication, DH authentication does have a verifier that allows the server to validate the client's credential (and vice versa). The contents of this verifier are primarily an encrypted timestamp. The server can decrypt this timestamp, and if it is within an accepted range relative to the current time, then the server knows that the client is authentic since only the client could have encrypted it correctly. The only way the client could encrypt it correctly is to know the *conversation key* of the RPC session, and if the client knows the conversation key, then it must be the real client. The conversation key is a DES [NBS77] key that the client generates and passes to the server in the first RPC call of a session. The conversation key is encrypted using a public key scheme in this first transaction. The particular public key scheme used in DH authentication is Diffie-Hellman [Diffie+76] with 192-bit keys. The details of this encryption method are described in section 4.5.8.

The client and the server need the same notion of the current time for all of this to work. There is risk in an assumption that clients and servers have the same notion of time. It is feasible for an adversary to manipulate the network so that clients and servers have an inconsistent view of the time. Although the client can obtain the server's time by using the RPCBPROC_ GETTIME procedure in Rpcbind versions 3 and 4, a more secure method is to use the Network Time Protocol version 3 using cryptographic authentication [Mills92] to reduce this risk. The way a server determines if a client's timestamp is valid is somewhat complicated. For any other transaction but the first, the server just checks for two things:

1. The timestamp is greater than the one previously seen from the same client. The timestamp check prevents the possibility of an attacker replaying a previously recorded client request.
2. The timestamp has not expired. The expiry check limits the possibility that a more determined attacker might crack the conversation key and hijack the session.

A timestamp is expired if the server's time is later than the sum of the client's timestamp plus what is known as the client's *TTL* (time-to-live—you can think of this as the lifetime for the client's credential). The TTL is a number the client passes (encrypted) to the server in its first transaction. In the first transaction, the server checks only that the timestamp has not expired. Also, as an added check, the client sends an encrypted item in the first transaction known as the *TTL verifier*, which must be equal to TTL-1 or the server will reject the credential. If either check fails, the server rejects the credential with an authentication status of AUTH_BADCRED. However, if the timestamp is earlier than the previous one seen, the server returns an authentication status of AUTH_REJECTEDCRED. The client too must check the verifier returned from the server to be sure it is legitimate. The server sends back to the client the timestamp it received from the client, minus one second, encrypted with the conversation key. If the client gets anything different than this, it will reject it, returning an AUTH_INVALIDRESP authentication status to the user.

Timestamp checking can be problematic if the client or server uses multiple threads of execution (Figure 4.4). If multiple client threads share the same credential (an NFS client using read-ahead), then the asynchronous use of timestamps can cause problems if the order in which RPC requests are executed by the server is different from the order in which they were sent by the client.

4.5.3 Nicknames and Clock Synchronization

After the first transaction, the server's DH authentication system returns a verifier to the client. In the verifier is an integer *nickname*, which the client may use in its further transactions instead of passing its netname. Not only will the nickname be shorter than the netname, but it could be an index into a table on the

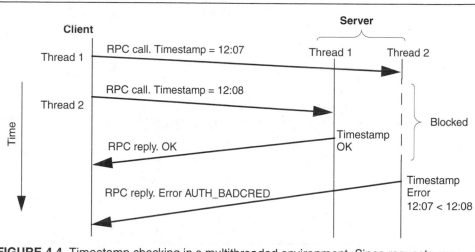

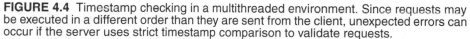

FIGURE 4.4 Timestamp checking in a multithreaded environment. Since requests may be executed in a different order than they are sent from the client, unexpected errors can occur if the server uses strict timestamp comparison to validate requests.

server that stores for each client its netname, decrypted conversation key, and TTL. Though they originally were synchronized, the client's and server's clocks can get out of synchronization again. When this happens, the server returns to the client an authentication status of AUTH_REJECTEDVERF, at which point the client should attempt to resynchronize. A client may also get an AUTH_BADCRED error when using a nickname that was previously valid. The reason is that the server's nickname table is limited in size, and it may flush entries whenever it wants. A client should resend its original fullname credential in this case and the server will give it a new nickname. If a server crashes, the entire nickname table gets flushed, and all clients have to resend their original credentials.

4.5.4 DH Authentication Protocol

There are two kinds of credentials: one in which the client uses its full network name and one in which it uses the nickname (just an unsigned integer) given to it by the server. The client must use its fullname in its first transaction with the server, in which the server will return to the client its nickname. The client may use its nickname in all further transactions with the server. There is no requirement to use the nickname, but it is wise to use it for performance reasons.

4.5.5 DH Full Network Name Credential and Verifier

The client first creates a conversation key for the session, then fills out the following structure:

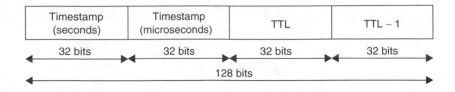

The fields are stored in XDR format. The timestamp encodes the time since midnight, January 1, 1970. These 128 bits of data are then encrypted in the DES CBC (cipher block chaining) mode,[1] using the conversation key for the session, with an initialization vector of 0, which yields

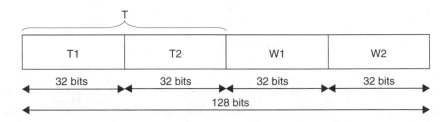

where T1, T2, W1, and W2 are all 32-bit quantities and have some correspondence to the original quantities occupying their positions but are now interdependent on each other for proper decryption. The 64-bit sequence comprising T1 and T2 is denoted by T (Figure 4.5).

The conversation key is encrypted with the "common key" using the ECB (Electronic Code Book) mode. The common key is a DES key that is derived from the Diffie-Hellman public and private keys, and is described in section

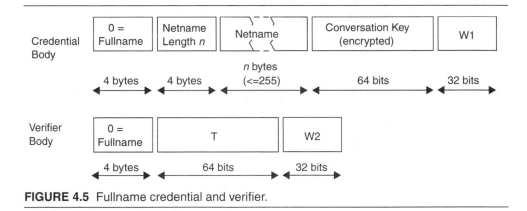

FIGURE 4.5 Fullname credential and verifier.

---

1. Both CBC and ECB are methods for encrypting blocks of information. These standards are documented in ANSI X3.106 [ANSI83].

4.5.8. Note that all of the encrypted quantities (key, w1, w2, timestamp) in Figure 4.5 are opaque. The fullname credential and its associated verifier together contain the network name of the client, an encrypted conversation key, the TTL, a timestamp, and a TTL verifier that is one less than the TTL. The TTL is actually the lifetime for the credential. The server will accept the credential if the current server time is "within" the time indicated in the timestamp plus the TTL. Otherwise, the server rejects the credential with an authentication status of AUTH_BADCRED. One way to ensure that requests are not replayed would be for the server to insist that timestamps are greater than the previous one seen, unless it is the first transaction. If the timestamp is earlier than the previous one seen, the server returns an authentication status of AUTH_REJECTEDCRED. The server returns a verifier that contains a nickname that may be used for subsequent requests in the current conversation.

4.5.6 DH Nickname Credential and Verifier

In transactions following the first, the client may use the shorter nickname credential and verifier for efficiency. First, the client fills out the following structure:

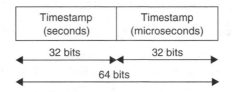

The fields are stored in XDR (external data representation) format. These 64 bits of data are then encrypted in the DES ECB mode, using the conversation key for the session, which yields

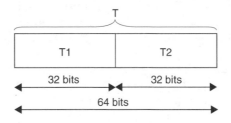

The nickname credential is represented as in Figure 4.6.

The nickname credential may be rejected by the server for several reasons. An authentication status of AUTH_BADCRED indicates that the nickname is no longer valid. The client should retry the request using the fullname credential. AUTH_REJECTEDVERF indicates that the nickname verifier is not valid. Again the client should retry the request using the fullname credential.

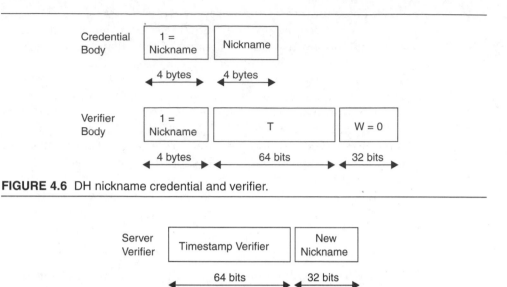

FIGURE 4.6 DH nickname credential and verifier.

FIGURE 4.7 DH verifier from server.

4.5.7   Server Verifier

The server never returns a credential. It returns only one kind of verifier, i.e., the nickname verifier. The server verifier has the XDR representation shown in Figure 4.7.

The timestamp verifier is constructed in exactly the same way as the client nickname credential. The server sets the timestamp value to the value the client sent minus one second and encrypts it in DES ECB mode using the conversation key. The server also sends the client a nickname to be used in future transactions (unencrypted). The complete XDR language description of the AUTH_DH credential and verifiers is as follows:

```
struct authdh_cred {
    switch (uint32) {
    case ADN_FULLNAME = 0:
        string<255> netname;
        opaque[8] key;
        opaque[8] w1;
    case ADN_NICKNAME = 1:
        uint32 nickname;
    }
}

struct authdh_verf {
    switch (uint32) {
    case ADN_FULLNAME = 0:
        opaque[8] timestamp;
```

```
            opaque[4] w2;
        case ADN_NICKNAME = 1:
            opaque[8] timestamp;
            opaque[4] w;
        }
}

struct authdh_server_verf {
    opaque[8] timestamp;
    uint32 nickname;
}
```

The initial exchange of fullname and nickname credentials is illustrated in the
following snoop trace:

Initial call to the server with fullname credential:

```
RPC:  ----- SUN RPC Header -----
RPC:
RPC:  Record Mark: last fragment, length = 128
RPC:  Transaction id = 882191572
RPC:  Type = 0 (Call)
RPC:  RPC version = 2
RPC:  Program = 100300 (NIS+), version = 3, procedure = 1
RPC:  Credentials: Flavor = 3 (DES), len = 48 bytes
RPC:     Name kind = 0 (fullname)
RPC:     Network name = unix.34186@mpk17.eng.sun.com
RPC:     Conversation key = 0x838D303DCC2E59D9 (DES encrypted)
RPC:     Window = 0x8A895653 (DES encrypted)
RPC:  Verifier   : Flavor = 3 (DES), len = 12 bytes
RPC:     Timestamp = 0x237320D91277C897 (DES encrypted)
RPC:     Window    = 0xA1058323 (DES encrypted)
```

Response from server containing nickname

```
RPC:  ----- SUN RPC Header -----
RPC:
RPC:  Record Mark: last fragment, length = 2460
RPC:  Transaction id = 882191572
RPC:  Type = 1 (Reply)
RPC:  This is a reply to frame 15
RPC:  Status = 0 (Accepted)
RPC:  Verifier   : Flavor = 3 (DES), len = 12 bytes
RPC:     Timestamp = 0x70C94BCEF5D467D1 (DES encrypted)
RPC:     Nickname  = 0x50000000
RPC:  Accept status = 0 (Success)
```

Client's next request uses nickname credential

```
RPC:  ----- SUN RPC Header -----
RPC:
RPC:  Record Mark: last fragment, length = 108
RPC:  Transaction id = 882191571
RPC:  Type = 0 (Call)
```

```
RPC:  RPC version = 2
RPC:  Program = 100300 (NIS+), version = 3, procedure = 5
RPC:  Credentials: Flavor = 3 (DES), len = 8 bytes
RPC:      Name kind = 1 (nickname)
RPC:      Nickname = 0x50000000
RPC:  Verifier   : Flavor = 3 (DES), len = 12 bytes
RPC:      Timestamp = 0x4FC3C38B93CADDA9 (DES encrypted)
RPC:      Window    = 0x00000000 (DES encrypted)
```

Figure 4.8 illustrates the use of fullname and nickname credentials in initial session setup and recovery after error.

4.5.8   Diffie-Hellman Encryption

In this scheme, there are two constants BASE and MODULUS [Diffie+76]. The particular values Sun has chosen for these constants for the DH authentication protocol are

```
BASE = 3
MODULUS = "d4a0ba0250b6fd2ec626e7efd637df76c716e22d0944b88b";
```

Note that the modulus is represented as a 192-bit hexadecimal string. The way this scheme works is best explained by an example. Suppose there are two people A and B who want to send encrypted messages to each other. A and B both generate at random "secret" keys that they do not reveal to anyone. Let

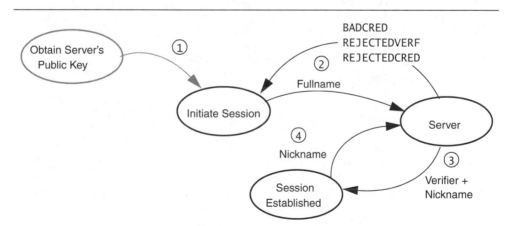

FIGURE 4.8 The client sends a fullname credential on the first request and receives a nickname credential from the server, which may be used in subsequent requests. If the credential or its verifier is rejected, then the client must send a new fullname credential to reestablish the session.

these keys be represented as SK_A and SK_B. They also publish in a public directory their public keys. These keys are computed as follows:

$$PK_A = BASE^{SK_A} \bmod MODULUS$$

$$PK_B = BASE^{SK_B} \bmod MODULUS$$

Now, both A and B can arrive at the "common" key between them, represented here as CK_{AB}, without revealing their secret keys. A computes

$$CK_{AB} = (PK_B{}^{SK_A}) \bmod MODULUS$$

while B computes

$$CK_{AB} = (PK_A{}^{SK_B}) \bmod MODULUS$$

To show that these are the same; in other words, that

$$(PK_B{}^{SK_A}) \bmod MODULUS = (PK_A{}^{SK_B}) \bmod MODULUS$$

We drop the $MODULUS$ parts and assume modulo arithmetic to simplify things:

$$PK_B{}^{SK_A} = PK_A{}^{SK_B}$$

Then we replace PK_B by what B computed earlier and likewise for PK_A:

$$(BASE^{SK_B})^{SK_A} = (BASE^{SK_A})^{SK_B}$$

which leads to

$$BASE^{SK_A SK_B} = BASE^{SK_A SK_B}$$

The common key CK_{AB} is not used to encrypt the timestamps used in the protocol. Rather, it is used only to encrypt a conversation key, which is then used to encrypt the timestamps. The reason for doing this is to use the common key as little as possible for fear that it could be broken. Breaking the conversation key is far less damaging, since conversations are relatively short-lived. The conversation key is encrypted using 56-bit DES keys, yet the common key is 192 bits. To reduce the number of bits, 56 bits are selected from the common key as follows. The middle 8 bytes are selected from the common key, and then parity is added to the lower-order bit of each byte, producing a 56-bit key with 8 bits of parity. Only 48 bits of the 8-byte conversation key is used in the DH authentication scheme. The least and most significant bits of each byte of the conversation key are unused.

4.5.9 Weaknesses of DH Authentication

DH authentication does not describe a secure method to obtain the server's public key. While it would be reasonably secure to obtain public keys from a local file, it would be burdensome to keep the file up to date and distributed securely to a large number of clients. The first implementation of DH authentication obtained server public keys from an NIS netname map. Since the NIS name service is not itself secure, it would be easy for an attacker to spoof the NIS server and distribute bogus public keys. The lack of a secure name service was an obstacle to the deployment of DH authentication.

While the arrival of the NIS+ name service, which uses DH authentication, provided a secure name service, the implementation of DH authentication has been shown to be weak due to the selection of a small key (192 bits). While a larger modulus provides better security, it takes longer to compute the common key. Originally Goldberg and Taylor chose 256 bits, but this was too large for the then-current processor technology (Motorola M68010) to handle within a reasonable time. The 192-bit key length was a compromise between speed and security. In 1991, Brian LaMacchia and Andrew Odlyzko at AT&T Bell Laboratories [LaMacchia+91] discovered a technique that for a given Diffie-Hellman system with a common BASE and modulus could generate a table that could be used to derive the private key from any public key. The cost of generating this table was trivial for a 192-bit modulus. Using this technique, a moderately powerful computer could compute a database for a particular user that would allow any AUTH_DH key for that user to be obtained within a few minutes.

While the information provided here will be useful for implementors to ensure interoperability with existing applications that use DH authentication, it is strongly recommended that new applications use more secure authentication and that existing applications that currently use DH authentication migrate to more robust authentication mechanisms. While the use of a fullname credential piggybacked on the first RPC request is an economical way to establish a security context by eliminating unnecessary messages, there is an implicit risk that sensitive data within the call arguments, for instance a credit card number, may be delivered to a server that is not authenticated. Establishing a security context via dataless control messages, as in RPCSEC_GSS security (see section 4.7.1), is more secure.

4.6 Kerberos Version 4 Authentication

The Kerberos security model [Kohl+93] is based in part on Needham and Schroeder's trusted third-party authentication protocol [Needham+78] and on modifications suggested by Denning and Sacco [Denning+81] to detect replay. Conceptually, Kerberos-based authentication is very similar to DH authentication. The major difference is that Kerberos-based authentication takes advantage of the fact that Kerberos tickets have encoded in them the client name and the conversation key. This section does not describe Kerberos name syntax, protocols, and ticket formats. The reader is referred to [Miller+87] and [Steiner+88].

TABLE 4.2 Valid Kerberos Names

Kerberos version 4 name	Principal	Instance	Kerberos realm
billb	billb	(*null*)	(*use local realm*)
jis.admin	jis	admin	(*use local realm*)
srz@lcs.mit.edu	srz	(*null*)	lcs.mit.edu
treese.root@athena.mit.edu	treese	root	athena.mit.edu

4.6.1 Kerberos Naming

A Kerberos name contains three parts. The first is the *principal name*, which is usually a user's or service's name. The second is the *instance*, which in the case of a user is usually null. Some users may have privileged instances, however, such as root or admin. In the case of a service, the instance is the name of the machine on which it runs; that is, there can be an NFS service running on machine ABC, which is different from the NFS service running on machine XYZ. The third part of a Kerberos name is the *realm*. The realm corresponds to the Kerberos service providing authentication for the principal. When writing a Kerberos name, the principal name is separated from the instance (if not NULL) by a period, and the realm (if not the local realm) follows, preceded by an @ symbol. Examples of valid Kerberos names are given in Table 4.2.

4.6.2 Kerberos-Based Authentication Protocol Specification

The Kerberos-based authentication protocol described here is based on Kerberos version 4 and uses the fullname/nickname credential scheme of the AUTH_DH protocol that preceded it.

4.6.3 Kerberos Full Network Name Credential and Verifier

First, the client must obtain a Kerberos ticket from the Kerberos server. The ticket contains a Kerberos session key, which will become the conversation key. Next, the client fills out the following structure:

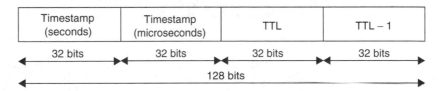

The fields are stored in XDR (external data representation) format. The timestamp encodes the time since midnight, January 1, 1970. TTL is identical in meaning to the corresponding field in Diffie-Hellman authentication, the credential "time-to-live" for the conversation being initiated. These 128 bits of data are then encrypted in the DES CBC mode, using the conversation key, and with an initialization vector of 0, which yields

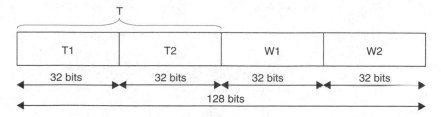

where T1, T2, W1, and W2 are all 32-bit quantities and have some correspondence to the original quantities occupying their positions but are now interdependent on each other for proper decryption. The 64-bit sequence comprising T1 and T2 is denoted by T.

Note that all the client-encrypted quantities (W1, W2, and timestamp T) in the structures are opaque. The client does not encrypt the Kerberos ticket for the server. The fullname credential and its associated verifier together contain the Kerberos ticket (which contains the client name and the conversation key), the TTL, a timestamp, and a TTL verifier that is one less than the TTL (Figure 4.9). The TTL is actually the lifetime for the credential. The server will accept the credential if the current server time is "within" the time indicated in the timestamp plus the TTL. Otherwise, the server rejects the credential with an authentication status of AUTH_BADCRED. One way to ensure that requests are not replayed would be for the server to insist that timestamps are greater than the previous one seen, unless it is the first transaction. If the timestamp is earlier than the previous one seen, the server returns an authentication status of AUTH_REJECTEDCRED. As in Diffie-Hellman authentication, the server returns a verifier, which is described in the next section. The verifier structure contains a nickname, which may be used for subsequent requests in the current session.

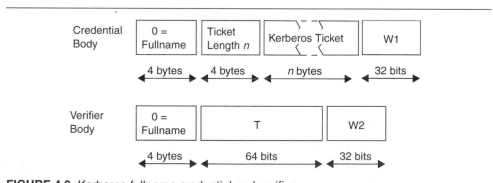

FIGURE 4.9 Kerberos fullname credential and verifier.

4.6.4 Kerberos Nickname Credential and Verifier

In transactions following the first, the client may use the shorter nickname credential and verifier for efficiency. First, the client fills out the following structure:

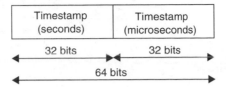

The fields are stored in XDR (external data representation) format. These 64 bits of data are then encrypted in the DES ECB mode, using the conversation key for the session, which yields

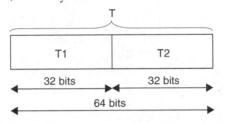

The nickname credential is represented in Figure 4.10.

The nickname credential may be rejected by the server for several reasons. An authentication status of AUTH_BADCRED indicates that the nickname is no longer valid. The client should retry the request using the fullname credential. AUTH_REJECTEDVERF indicates that the nickname verifier is not valid. Again, the client should retry the request using the fullname credential. AUTH_TIMEEXPIRE indicates that the session's Kerberos ticket has expired. The client should initiate a new session by obtaining a new Kerberos ticket.

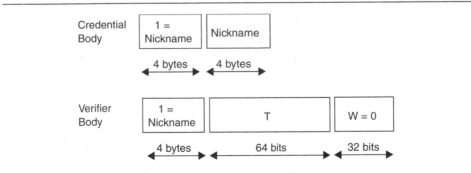

FIGURE 4.10 Kerberos nickname credential and verifier.

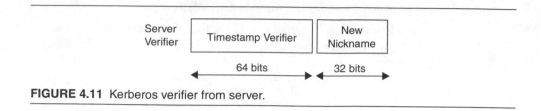

FIGURE 4.11 Kerberos verifier from server.

4.6.5   Server Verifier

The server never returns a credential. It returns only one kind of verifier, i.e., the nickname verifier. The verifier has the XDR representation shown in Figure 4.11. The timestamp verifier is constructed in exactly the same way as the client nickname credential. The server sets the timestamp value to the value the client sent minus one second and encrypts it in DES ECB mode using the conversation key. The server also sends the client a nickname to be used in future transactions (unencrypted).

The complete XDR language description of the AUTH_KERB4 credential and verifiers follows:

```
struct authkerb4_cred {
    switch (uint32) {
    case AKN_FULLNAME = 0:
        opaque<> ticket;          /* Kerberos ticket for server */
        opaque[8] w1;
    case AKN_NICKNAME = 1:
        uint32 nickname;          /* Nickname returned by server */
    }
}

struct authkerb4_verf {
    switch (uint32) {
    case AKN_FULLNAME = 0:
        opaque[8] timestamp;   /* T */
        opaque[4] w2;
    case AKN_NICKNAME = 1:
        opaque[8] timestamp;   /* T */
        opaque[4] w;           /* set to 0 */
    }
}

struct authkerb4_server_verf {
    opaque[8] timestamp;       /* timestamp verifier (encrypted) */
    uint32 nickname;           /* new nickname (unencrypted) */
}
```

4.6.6   Kerberos-Specific Authentication Status Values

The server may return to the client one of the errors listed in Table 4.3 in the authentication status field. The client's actions are illustrated in Figure 4.12.

TABLE 4.3 Kerberos-Specific Authentication Errors

Value	Name	Meaning
6	AUTH_DECODE	The server is unable to decode the authenticator of the client's ticket.
7	AUTH_TIMEEXPIRE	The client's ticket has expired.
8	AUTH_TKT_FILE	The server was unable to find the ticket file. The client should create a new session by obtaining a new ticket.
9	AUTH_NET_ADDR	The network address of the client does not match the address contained in the ticket.
10	AUTH_KERB_GENERIC	Any other Kerberos-specific error.

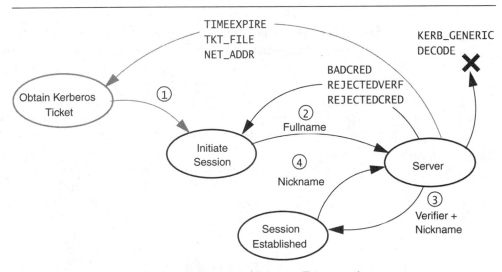

FIGURE 4.12 Kerberos authentication state diagram. Errors such as AUTH_TIMEEXPIRE can be resolved by obtaining a new Kerberos ticket, though unresolvable errors like AUTH_KERB_GENERIC may require the session to be terminated.

4.6.7 Weaknesses of Kerberos Authentication

As with AUTH_DH authentication, there is a risk that sensitive data in the call arguments might be delivered via a message with the fullname credential to a server that is not authenticated. Kerberos version 4 can also run into problems with multihomed hosts that have an IP address for each of many interfaces. The Kerberos ticket acknowledges only one IP address per host.

Weaknesses of the Kerberos authentication protocol itself are beyond the scope of this chapter but are well documented in a paper by Steven Bellovin and Michael Merrit [Bellovin+91].

4.7 RPCSEC_GSS Authentication

The RPCSEC_GSS security flavor is a radical departure from previous authentication flavor policy. It is referred to as a *security* flavor rather than an *authentication* flavor because it provides security not only for the credential but also for the data in the payload of the RPC call and reply. The RPCSEC_GSS specification was developed by the ONC RPC Working Group of the IETF and is described in [RFC 2203]. Since it is a new standard, it is not widely deployed, though there is already an implementation in Solaris 7. This section assumes that you have knowledge of the Generic Security Services API (GSS-API), which is documented in [RFC 1508] and [RFC 1509]. Most of the text in sections 4.7.4 through 4.7.8 is adapted directly from [RFC 2203].

Using RPCSEC_GSS, a client or server can protect the *integrity* of the data in a call or reply with a secure checksum. This protection prevents the information from being changed as it travels across the network. The *privacy* of the data can be protected by the use of encryption schemes. Most important, RPCSEC_GSS is intended to be the *last* security flavor since it is an open-ended framework that can include many different security mechanisms such as Kerberos V5, RSA public key, Diffie-Hellman public key, PGP, and so on.

The authentication flavors previously described associate a specific security mechanism with a network representation. The RPCSEC_GSS flavor makes the security mechanism independent of the network representation, making it much easier to add new mechanisms without rewriting parts of the client or server RPC implementation. RPCSEC_GSS is designed to be used with the Generic Security Services API (GSS-API) [Linn93], which presents a common API to all security mechanisms (Figure 4.13). The GSS-API provides

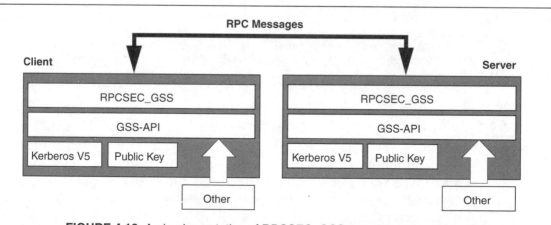

FIGURE 4.13 An implementation of RPCSEC_GSS security can accommodate any security mechanism that is compatible with the GSS-API interface. These mechanisms can be "plugged in" without requiring changes to the RPC implementation or the network protocol.

TABLE 4.4 GSS-API Functions

Function	Sender	Receiver
Establish security context	GSS_Init_sec_context()	GSS_Accept_sec_context()
Message integrity checksum	GSS_GetMIC()	GSS_VerifyMIC()
Message data encryption	GSS_Wrap()	GSS_Unwrap()

functions that allow principals (machines, programs, or people) to establish a security context that can then be used to authenticate messages between them or protect the message integrity or privacy. The version of the API for the C language described in [RFC 2078] contains many functions, but in this description I refer only to the ones in Table 4.4.

4.7.1 RPCSEC_GSS Security Protocol

An RPC session based on the RPCSEC_GSS security flavor consists of three phases:

1. Context creation
2. RPC data exchange
3. Context destruction

The *context* of a session is information shared by both client and server, for example, the full identity of the client and server, initial sequence numbers, session keys, and so on. The creation of a context usually includes the mutual authentication of client and server. The AUTH_DH and AUTH_KERB4 authentication protocols combine context creation within the RPC data exchange by the use of fullname and nickname credentials. A fullname credential is used to establish context and a nickname credential utilizes the context. However, not all security mechanisms can conveniently combine context creation and data exchange. In some cases the amount of context creation data may not fit within the 400-byte limit of the RPC credential. To support these mechanisms, RPCSEC_GSS embeds control messages within the null procedure call of the RPC protocol to convey context information. All RPC protocols support a null procedure (procedure 0) that normally takes no arguments and returns no results (Figure 4.14).

These control messages are not dispatched to service procedures registered by an RPC server, even though the program and version numbers used in these control messages are the same as the RPC service's program and version numbers. A field in the RPCSEC_GSS credential information specifies whether a message is to be interpreted as a control message or a regular RPC message. If this field is set to RPCSEC_GSS_DATA, no control action is implied—it is a regular data message. If this field is set to any other value, a control action is implied. Just as with normal RPC data exchange messages,

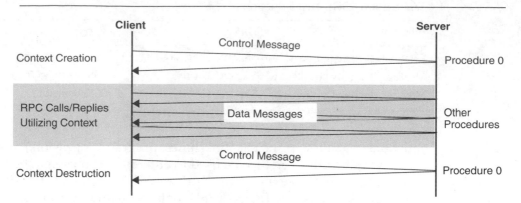

FIGURE 4.14 RPCSEC_GSS context can be created and destroyed by the use of control messages sent to procedure 0 of the service. Control messages need be used only if the security mechanism requires them and may require more than one message to establish context creation or destruction.

the RPC transaction identifier (XID) should be set to unique values on each call for context creation and destruction.

4.7.2 RPCSEC_GSS Credential

The first field in the credential is the RPCSEC_GSS version number (Figure 4.15). The client should assume that the server supports version 1 credentials when it issues a context creation message.

4.7.3 Context Creation

Before RPC data are exchanged on a session using the RPCSEC_GSS flavor, the client and server must agree on a security mechanism and a quality of protection (QOP) to be used. Applications can specify the QOP (cryptographic algorithms to be used in conjunction with integrity or privacy service) for each RPC exchange. There is no facility in the RPCSEC_GSS protocol to negotiate GSS-API mechanism identifiers or QOP values. Applications may depend on negotiation schemes constructed as pseudomechanisms under the GSS-API, such as the SPNEGO mechanism [RFC 2478]. Because such schemes are below the GSS-API layer, the RPCSEC_GSS protocol can make use of them.

The first RPC request from the client to the server may be a control message for context creation (Figure 4.16). The GSS procedure field must be set to 1 (RPCSEC_GSS_INIT) for the first creation request and 2 (RPCSEC_GSS_CONTINUE_INIT) in any subsequent requests in a creation sequence. In a creation request, the sequence number and service fields are not set. In the first creation request, the handle field is null (opaque data of zero length). In subsequent creation requests, the context handle must be equal to the value

```
struct rpc_gss_cred {
    switch (uint32 version) {/* version of RPCSEC_GSS */
        case RPCSEC_GSS_VERS_1 = 1:
            enum gss_proc {/* control procedure */
                RPCSEC_GSS_DATA = 0,
                RPCSEC_GSS_INIT = 1,
                RPCSEC_GSS_CONTINUE_INIT = 2,
                RPCSEC_GSS_DESTROY = 3
                };
            uint32 seq_num;/* sequence number */
            enum service {/* service used */
                RPCSEC_GSS_SVC_NONE = 1,
                RPCSEC_GSS_SVC_INTEGRITY = 2,
                RPCSEC_GSS_SVC_PRIVACY = 3
                };
            opaque<> handle;/* context handle */
    }
}
```

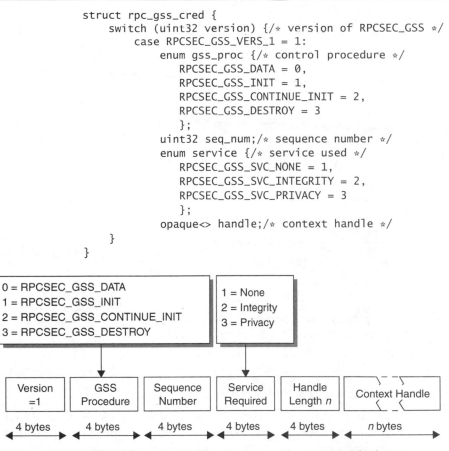

FIGURE 4.15 RPCSEC_GSS credential. The version number provides for future revision of the credential format. The GSS procedure field indicates whether the message constitutes context creation or destruction control message or a data exchange message. The sequence number is used to detect duplicate or replayed credentials. The service field allows the client to change the data protection from call to call. The variable-length context handle contains data that is private to the security scheme in use.

returned by the server. The context handle field serves as the identifier for the context and does not change for the duration of the context, including responses to "Continue Init" calls. All context creation requests have a null verifier (AUTH_NONE flavor with zero-length opaque data).

Normally a null procedure call takes no arguments, but an RPCSEC_GSS context creation request requires an opaque token obtained from the security mechanism via the GSS-API interface. Since version 2 of the RPC protocol limits the size of the credential to 400 bytes, the token cannot reliably be packed into the credential; hence it is provided instead as an argument to the null procedure call.

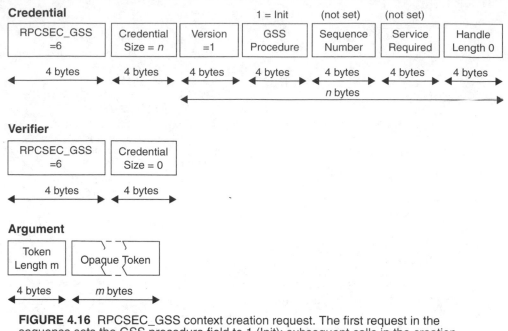

FIGURE 4.16 RPCSEC_GSS context creation request. The first request in the sequence sets the GSS procedure field to 1 (Init); subsequent calls in the creation sequence set this field to 2 (Continue Init).

4.7.4   Successful Creation Response

The response to a successful creation request is MSG_ACCEPTED with a status of SUCCESS. The results field encodes a response with the structure shown in Figure 4.17.

The returned context handle must be used in all subsequent requests whether control or otherwise. The gss_major and gss_minor fields contain the results of the call to GSS_Accept_sec_context() executed by the server. The values for gss_major are defined in [Eisler+96]. The values for the gss_minor field are GSS-API mechanism specific and are defined in the mechanism's specification. If gss_major is not 0 (GSS_S_COMPLETE) or 1 (GSS_S_CONTINUE _NEEDED), the context setup has failed; in this case the handle and token will be set to NULL by the server. The value of the gss_minor field is dependent on the value of gss_major and the security mechanism used. The gss_token field contains any token returned by the GSS_ accept_sec_context() call executed by the server. A token may be returned for both successful values of gss_major. If the value is GSS_S_COMPLETE, it indicates that the server is not expecting any more tokens, and the RPC data exchange phase must begin on the subsequent request from the client. If the value is GSS_S_CONTINUE_NEEDED, the server is expecting another token. Hence the client must send at least one

```
struct rpc_gss_init_res {
    opaque<> handle;
    uint32 gss_major;
    uint32 gss_minor;
    uint32 seq_window;
    opaque<> gss_token;
}
```

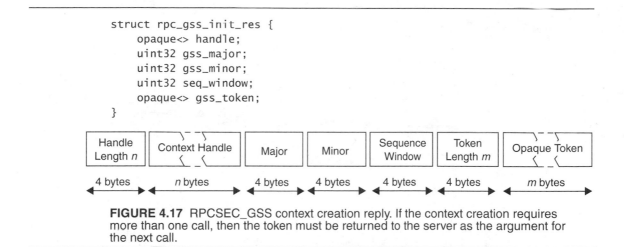

FIGURE 4.17 RPCSEC_GSS context creation reply. If the context creation requires more than one call, then the token must be returned to the server as the argument for the next call.

more creation request (with gss_proc set to RPCSEC_GSS_CONTINUE_INIT in the request's credential) carrying the required token.

In a successful response, the seq_window field is set to the sequence window length supported by the server for this context (see Figure 4.22 on page 74). This window specifies the maximum number of client requests that may be outstanding for this context. The server will accept seq_window number of requests at a time, and these may be out of order. The client may use this number to determine the number of threads that can simultaneously send requests on this context.

If gss_major is GSS_S_COMPLETE, the flavor field of the verifier (the verf element in the response) is set to RPCSEC_GSS and the body field set to the checksum of the seq_window (in network order). The QOP used for this checksum is 0 (zero), which is the default QOP. For all other values of gss_major, a NULL verifier (AUTH_NONE flavor with zero-length opaque data) is used.

If the value of gss_major in the response is GSS_S_CONTINUE_NEEDED, then the client, per the GSS-API specification, must invoke GSS_init_sec_context() using the token returned in gss_token in the context creation response. The client must then generate a context creation request, with gss_proc set to RPCSEC_GSS_CONTINUE_INIT.

If the value of gss_major in the response is GSS_S_COMPLETE, and if client's previous invocation of GSS_init_sec_context() returned a gss_major value of GSS_S_CONTINUE_NEEDED, then the client, per GSS-API specification, must invoke GSSi_init_sec_context() using the token returned in gss_token in the context creation response (Figure 4.18). If GSS_init_sec_context() returns GSS_S_COMPLETE, the context is successfully set up, and the RPC data exchange phase must begin on the subsequent request from the client.

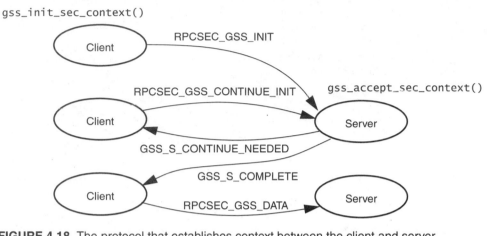

gss_init_sec_context()

RPCSEC_GSS_INIT

gss_accept_sec_context()

RPCSEC_GSS_CONTINUE_INIT

GSS_S_CONTINUE_NEEDED

GSS_S_COMPLETE

RPCSEC_GSS_DATA

FIGURE 4.18 The protocol that establishes context between the client and server is controlled by the chosen security mechanism via the client's GSS-API calls to gss_init_sec_context() and the server's calls to gss_accept_sec_context(). The gss_token contains information private to the security mechanism.

4.7.5 Unsuccessful Context Creation

An MSG_ACCEPTED reply (to a creation request) with an acceptance status of other than SUCCESS has a NULL verifier (flavor set to AUTH_NONE, zero-length opaque data in body field) and is formulated as usual for different status values.

A MSG_DENIED reply (to a creation request) is also formulated as usual. Note that MSG_DENIED could be returned because the server's RPC implementation does not recognize the RPCSEC_GSS security flavor. RFC 1831 (Remote Procedure Call Protocol Version 2) does not specify the appropriate reply status in this instance, but common implementation practice appears to be to return a rejection status of AUTH_ERROR with an auth_stat of AUTH_REJECTEDCRED. Even though two new values (RPCSEC_GSS_ CREDPROBLEM and RPCSEC_GSS_CTXPROBLEM) have been defined for the auth_stat type, neither can be returned in responses to context creation requests. The auth_stat new values can be used for responses to normal (data) requests. These are described in section 4.7.11.

MSG_DENIED might also be returned if the RPCSEC_GSS version number in the credential is not supported on the server. In that case, the server returns a rejection status of AUTH_ERROR with an auth_stat of AUTH_REJECTED_CRED.

4.7.6 RPC Data Exchange

Once the context phase is complete, the client and server can exchange normal RPC calls and responses using the procedure numbers defined for the RPC

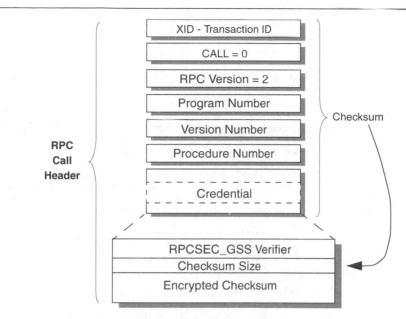

FIGURE 4.19 The RPCSEC_GSS verifier used in RPC data calls contains an encrypted checksum of the RPC header. The verifier not only authenticates the user (since only an authenticated principal can know the key) but also protects the header from modification.

protocol in use. RPCSEC_GSS provides three services: message authentication, data integrity, and data privacy. For all three services, the RPCSEC_GSS credential has the format shown in Figure 4.15.

The gss_proc field is set to RPCSEC_GSS_DATA. The service field is set to indicate the desired service: none, integrity, or privacy. The handle field is set to the context handle value received from the RPC server during context creation. The seq_num value must be incremented for successive requests. Use of sequence numbers is described in detail when server processing of the request is discussed.

The RPCSEC_GSS verifier contains a checksum of the RPC header (up to and including the credential) computed using the GSS_GetMIC() call with the desired QOP (Figure 4.19). This returns the checksum as an opaque octet stream and its length. Note that the QOP is not explicitly specified anywhere in the request. It is implicit in the checksum or encrypted data. The same QOP value as is used for the header checksum must also be used for the data if it is to be checksummed for integrity or encrypted for privacy.

4.7.7 Data Integrity Protection

If the data integrity protection service is chosen, the procedure arguments and results are protected with a secure checksum that depends on the chosen security mechanism (Figure 4.20). The request data are represented as follows:

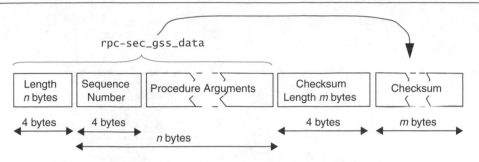

FIGURE 4.20 The procedure arguments are integrity protected within the rpcsec_gss_integ_data structure. The sequence number prevents the arguments from being separated from the header since it must match the sequence number in the header. The procedure arguments cannot be modified without invalidating the checksum.

```
struct rpc_gss_integ_data {
    opaque<> databody_integ;
    opaque<> checksum;
}
```

The databody_integ field is created as follows. A structure consisting of a sequence number followed by the procedure arguments is constructed. This structure is shown as the type rpc_gss_data:

```
struct rpc_gss_data {
    uint32 seq_num;
    proc_req_arg arg;
}
```

Here, seq_num must have the same value it has in the credential. The type proc_req_arg is the procedure-specific XDR type describing the procedure arguments (and so is not specified here). The octet stream corresponding to the XDR-encoded rpc_gss_data structure and its length are placed in the databody_integ field. Note that because the XDR type of databody_integ is opaque, the XDR encoding of databody_integ will include an initial four-octet length field, followed by the XDR-encoded octet stream of rpc_gss_data.

The checksum field represents the checksum of the XDR-encoded octet stream corresponding to the XDR-encoded rpc_gss_data structure (note: this is not the checksum of the databody_integ field). This is obtained using the GSS_GetMIC() call, with the same QOP as was used to compute the header checksum (in the verifier). The GSS_GetMIC() call returns the checksum as an opaque octet stream and its length. The checksum field of struct rpc_gss_integ_data has an XDR type of opaque. Thus the checksum length from GSS_GetMIC() is encoded as a four-octet length field, followed by the checksum, padded to a multiple of four octets.

4.7.8   Data Privacy

When data privacy is used (Figure 4.21), the request data are represented as follows:

```
struct rpc_gss_priv_data {
    opaque<> databody_priv;
}
```

The databody_priv field is created as follows: The rpc_gss_data structure described earlier is constructed again in the same way as for data integrity. Next, the GSS_Wrap() call is invoked to encrypt the octet stream corresponding to the rpc_gss_data structure, using the same value for QOP (argument qop_req to GSS_Wrap()) as was used for the header checksum (in the verifier) and conf_req_flag (an argument to GSS_Wrap()) of TRUE. The GSS_Wrap() call returns an opaque octet stream (representing the encrypted rpc_gss_data structure) and its length, and this is encoded as the databody_priv field. Since databody_priv has an XDR type of opaque, the length returned by GSS_Wrap() is encoded as the four-octet length, followed by the encrypted octet stream (padded to a multiple of four octets).

The privacy option encrypts only the call arguments and results. Information about the application in the form of RPC program number, version number, and procedure number is transmitted in the clear. Encrypting these fields in the RPC call header would have changed the size and format of the call header. A change in the layout of the RPC call header would have required revising the RPC protocol, which was not considered desirable by the designers of RPCSEC_GSS.

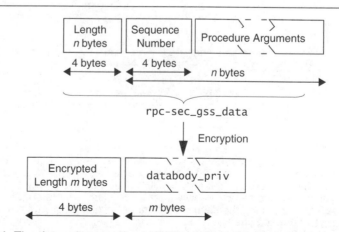

FIGURE 4.21 The data privacy option is similar to that of data integrity: a sequence number that matches a counterpart in the RPC header is encrypted along with the arguments. The sequence number prevents the encrypted data from being separated and recombined with another header.

4.7.9 Server Processing of RPC Data Requests

When a request is received by the server, it checks the version number, service, and context handle in the credential. In addition, the header checksum in the verifier is checked to make sure that the RPC header that contains the credential has not been changed.

Finally, the `seq_num` sequence number is checked. The server maintains a window of `seq_window` sequence numbers, starting with the last sequence number seen and extending backwards (Figure 4.22). Whenever a sequence number higher than the last number seen is received, the window is moved forward to the new sequence number. Requests with sequence numbers within the window can be received in any order, but if a sequence number has already been seen or if it is below the limit of the window, then it is silently discarded. The server should select a `seq_window` value based on the number of concurrent requests it is prepared to handle. Instead of returning an error, duplicate or out-of-range requests are discarded silently because the server cannot know whether the erroneous request is due to a replay attack or a network problem. A client can recover from a dropped request by retransmitting it, although it must take care to increment the sequence number to remain within `seq_window`.

Note that the sequence number algorithm requires that the client increment the sequence number even if it is retrying a request with the same RPC transaction identifier (XID); otherwise the server will silently discard the retransmitted request rather than resend a cached reply. It is not infrequent for clients to get into a situation where they send two or more attempts and a slow server sends the reply for the first attempt. With RPCSEC_GSS, each request and reply has a unique sequence number.

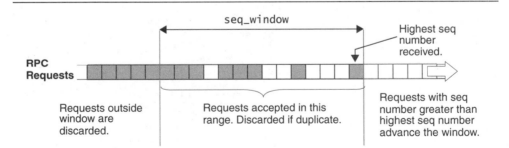

FIGURE 4.22 Within a given security context, the server associates a window within which it will accept requests with a given sequence number. Sequence numbering of requests makes it difficult for an attacker to replay requests. Rather than require a strict ordering of requests, the server will accept requests in any order within the window, which provides some flexibility for multithreaded clients. An attacker cannot coax the server into raising the sequence number beyond the range the legitimate client is aware of (and thus engineer a denial of service attack) without constructing an RPC request that will pass the header checksum.

Following the sequence number check, the request arguments are decoded according to the service specified in the credential. If no integrity or privacy was specified, then no decoding is necessary. If integrity checking was requested, then the server will verify the request argument checksum. If privacy was requested, then the server will decrypt the arguments. For both integrity and privacy, the embedded sequence number will be compared with its counterpart in the credential. The embedded sequence number prevents an attacker from simply separating the request arguments from the header and splicing them with another header. If the integrity or privacy check does not pass, then the server will return a GARBAGE_ARGS error.

4.7.10 Server's Reply

The server's verifier in the reply header contains a checksum (the output of GSS_GetMIC()) of the sequence number from the client's request (Figure 4.23). If data integrity or privacy was requested, the results are encoded in the reply as the parameters were in the corresponding request.

4.7.11 RPCSEC_GSS Errors

The authentication errors, as shown in Table 3.1, include two new values, RPCSEC_GSS_CREDPROBLEM and RPCSEC_GSS_CTXPROBLEM. If the server loses the client's context information set up during the control messages

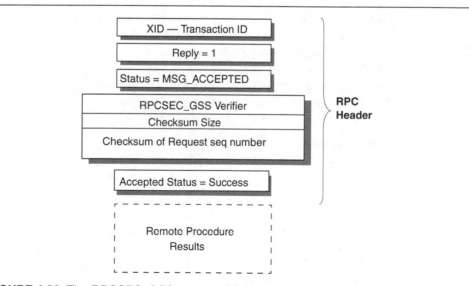

FIGURE 4.23 The RPCSEC_GSS server verifier returned in the RPC reply contains a checksum of the sequence number that came with the client's request.

(perhaps because the server rebooted or needed to reclaim some memory), then the server will reject the request with RPCSEC_GSS_CREDPROBLEM. The client can recover from this by destroying the context and reestablishing it with more control messages. This error is also returned if the GSS_VerifyMIC() call on the header checksum (contained in the verifier) fails to return GSS_S_COMPLETE. The RPCSEC_GSS_CTXPROBLEM is returned if the credential is invalid due to some mechanism-specific reason, for instance, if a Kerberos V5 ticket expires. The client can recover by fixing the mechanism-specific problem, for instance, obtaining a new Kerberos ticket. For other errors, retrying will not fix the problem, and the client cannot refresh the context until the problem is rectified.

4.7.12   Performance of RPCSEC_GSS

The computation of integrity checksums and data encryption requires additional computation on the client and server, depending on the security mechanism used. Computation of the header checksum adds a small, fixed overhead to an RPC transaction that should be barely noticeable to an application or end user. The use of integrity and privacy protection of the request and reply data can add considerable computational overhead that increases in proportion to the amount of data in the request or reply. An end user or application will perceive this overhead as additional latency on the RPC transaction—it might be large enough to require an application developer to recalculate RPC request time-outs. An end user or system administrator will have to consider the trade-off between data security and network throughput and server loading. As a rule of thumb, data integrity will increase client and server latency 50 percent and data privacy will increase latency by 300 percent [Eisler+96]. These factors will vary depending on the processor speed, bus bandwidth, and computational requirements of the cryptographic algorithm. We can expect the performance cost of data integrity and privacy to drop with the steady improvement of computer performance.

4.7.13   Snoop Trace of Session

A detailed snoop trace of an NFS session using Kerberos V5 as the authentication mechanism demonstrates the use of RPCSEC_GSS to establish and use a security context. This trace shows just the RPC headers.

First the client sends the Kerberos ticket to the server within the argument to the NFS null procedure call using an RPCSEC_GSS credential indicating a control request of RPCSEC_GSS_INIT.

```
RPC:   ----- SUN RPC Header -----
RPC:
RPC:   Record Mark: last fragment, length = 568
RPC:   Transaction id = 3733815415
```

```
RPC:   Type = 0 (Call)
RPC:   RPC version = 2
RPC:   Program = 100003 (NFS), version = 3, procedure = 0
RPC:   Credentials: Flavor = 6 (RPCSEC_GSS), len = 20 bytes
RPC:      version = 1
RPC:      gss control procedure = 1 (RPCSEC_GSS_INIT)
RPC:      sequence num = 0
RPC:      service = 1 (none)
RPC:      handle: length = 0, data = []
RPC:   Verifier   : Flavor = 0 (None), len = 0 bytes
RPC:
RPC:   RPCSEC_GSS_INIT args:
RPC:      gss token: length = 502 bytes
RPC:      ... (context information) ...
RPC:
```

The server responds with a control message indicating that it has accepted the client's Kerberos ticket and includes a context handle [00000003] that the client will use in the following data requests.

```
RPC:   ----- SUN RPC Header -----
RPC:
RPC:   Record Mark: last fragment, length = 196
RPC:   Transaction id = 3733815415
RPC:   Type = 1 (Reply)
RPC:   This is a reply to frame 26
RPC:   Status = 0 (Accepted)
RPC:   Verifier   : Flavor = 6 (RPCSEC_GSS), len = 37 bytes
RPC:      ... checksum of seq_window ...
RPC:   Accept status = 0 (Success)
RPC:
RPC:   RPCSEC_GSS_INIT result:
RPC:      handle: length = 4, data = [00000003]
RPC:      gss_major status = 0
RPC:      gss_minor status = 0
RPC:      sequence window  = 128
RPC:      gss token: length = 106 bytes
RPC:         ... gss token data ...
```

The gss_major status in the result indicates that the context creation is complete. The client can now send a data request to the server. In this case it is an NFS version 3 FSINFO call. The RPCSEC_GSS credential contains a sequence number and a context handle [00000003] that identifies the security context set up in the prior control request.

```
RPC:   ----- SUN RPC Header -----
RPC:
RPC:   Record Mark: last fragment, length = 140
RPC:   Transaction id = 3733815418
RPC:   Type = 0 (Call)
RPC:   RPC version = 2
```

```
RPC:   Program = 100003 (NFS), version = 3, procedure = 19
RPC:   Credentials: Flavor = 6 (RPCSEC_GSS), len = 24 bytes
RPC:     version = 1
RPC:     gss control procedure = 0 (RPCSEC_GSS_DATA)
RPC:     sequence num = 2
RPC:     service = 1 (none)
RPC:     handle: length = 4, data = [00000003]
RPC:   Verifier   : Flavor = 6 (RPCSEC_GSS), len = 37 bytes
RPC:       ... checksum of seq_num ...
RPC:
NFS:   ----- Sun NFS -----
NFS:
NFS:   Proc = 19 (Get filesystem information)
NFS:   File handle = 0080000800000002000A000000001700
NFS:                     3D83CDE1000A0000000017003D83CDE1
```

The verifier in the server's reply contains a checksum of the sequence number from the client's request.

```
RPC:   ----- SUN RPC Header -----
RPC:
RPC:   Record Mark: last fragment, length = 204
RPC:   Transaction id = 3733815418
RPC:   Type = 1 (Reply)
RPC:   This is a reply to frame 29
RPC:   Status = 0 (Accepted)
RPC:   Verifier   : Flavor = 6 (RPCSEC_GSS), len = 37 bytes
RPC:          ... encrypted seq_no ...
RPC:   Accept status = 0 (Success)
RPC:
NFS:   ----- Sun NFS -----
NFS:
NFS:   Proc = 19 (Get filesystem information)
NFS:   Status = 0 (OK)
NFS:   Post-operation attributes:
NFS:     File type = 2 (Directory)
NFS:     Mode = 0755
NFS:       Setuid = 0, Setgid = 0, Sticky = 0
NFS:       Owner's permissions = rwx
NFS::
NFS::
```

4.8 Connection-Based Security

So far, this chapter has presented the various flavors of security built into the RPC protocol. Security can also be provided outside the RPC protocol in the connection layer. The most common use of secure communication today is via secure TCP connections on the Internet.

The Secure Shell (ssh) provides strong authentication, data privacy, and data integrity protection for remote login sessions. The transport layer of the

Secure Shell can be used independently to provide a secure data stream for other network protocols. For instance, an X-window session can be tunneled through a Secure Shell connection.

The most common use of secure connections is through the SSL protocol when used to protect transactions over the HTTP protocol with the "https" URL. The SSL protocol also provides authentication, data privacy, and integrity. The SSL protocol is now described as *transport layer security* (TLS) by an IETF working group [RFC 2246]. Connection-based security will be available at the IP layer via IPsec, another Internet protocol developed initially for IPv6 and to be made available also for IPv4 [RFC 2401].

RPC-based protocols can utilize these secure connections by making sure that the protocol is run over a secure connection (Figure 4.24). With a credential of AUTH_NONE, the task of authenticating the user and guaranteeing privacy and data integrity can be left entirely up to the secure connection. This option is particularly attractive where implementations of RPC-based security are not implemented or not available. If for other reasons the RPC protocol is tunneled over a secure connection, it makes no sense to further authenticate or protect the data, so it's appropriate to be able to disable the RPC-based security.

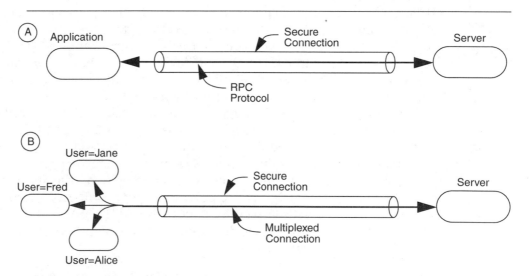

FIGURE 4.24 (A) An RPC-based protocol using a secure connection can delegate its security to that of the connection. This delegation is fine if the connection is dedicated to a single user. (B) RPC-based security must be used for authentication if the connection is shared by multiple users because the connection-based security cannot distinguish the call and response data of each user. The secure connection may still be useful if it provides privacy and data integrity.

The RPC protocol can be used to multiplex the requests and replies of several users onto a single connection. Some NFS clients, for instance, set up a single connection to the server for all users or on a per-mount basis. In this case the requests and replies of several users may be intermixed on the same connection. A connection-based security scheme will not be able to distinguish the RPC calls of each user. In this situation it is more appropriate to use the RPC-based security. The secure connection may still be useful if it provides privacy and data integrity.

RPC can also use UDP datagrams rather than a TCP stream to transport requests and responses. Connection-based security that assumes a persistent, stateful connection between the client and server cannot be used over UDP. Again, NFS is a good example. Although many NFS products support TCP connections, UDP is still widely used. RPC-based security must be used over UDP.

4.9 Summary

RPC authentication was designed as an open-ended framework to allow clients and servers to be able to authenticate each other through the use of credential and verifier information embedded in the RPC header. The flavor of RPC authentication is determined by the application or service and may vary from no authentication at all (AUTH_NONE), to unverified authentication (AUTH_SYS) or one of the secure forms of authentication (AUTH_DH and AUTH_KERB4). Both AUTH_DH and AUTH_KERB4 have shortcomings that have limited their deployment. RPCSEC_GSS is called the "final" authentication flavor because it provides a framework that allows any GSS-API-based security mechanism to be plugged in dynamically. As improved security mechanisms are developed, they can be used by existing RPCSEC_GSS implementations without modification of the RPC code. RPCSEC_GSS not only provides secure authentication but also supports integrity protection and privacy of call arguments and results. Connection-based security mechanisms like SSL and IPsec may be used to provide security for RPC protocols in some situations. More detail on security issues with AUTH_SYS, AUTH_DH, and AUTH_KERB4, as well as a description of RPCSEC_GSS implementation using Kerberos V5, can be found in [RFC 2623].

Chapter 5

NFS Filesystem Model

The NFS protocol supports the common model of a hierarchically organized filesystem comprising named directories that group related files
and directories. Each file or directory has a string name that is unique within
the directory. Although this common model appears to be heavily biased
toward the UNIX filesystem model, it encompasses many filesystems implemented on UNIX and other operating systems. The common filesystem
model of NFS is largely responsible for the success of NFS as an *interoperable*
protocol.

5.1 Filesystem and Filesystem Objects

A *filesystem* is a tree on a single server (usually a single disk or physical partition) with a specified "root" (Figure 5.1). UNIX operating systems provide a
mount operation to make all file systems appear as a single tree, while DOS,
Windows, and Windows NT assign filesystems to disk letters or top-level
names. The NFS file attribute *fsid* uniquely identifies a filesystem on a server
and the *fileid* attribute identifies a file or directory within that filesystem. NFS
clients assume that the *fsid/fileid* pair are unique for each file on a particular
server. NFS requests, like STATFS (version 2) and FSSTAT (version 3), return
filesystem attributes such as the amount of available space left in the filesystem.

Although files and directories are similar objects in many ways, different
procedures are used to read directories and files. The NFS READDIR procedure provides a network standard format for representing directories. NFS
provides access to several different kinds of filesystem *objects*:

1. *Files* are assumed to be uninterpreted byte sequences. The client and
server are not expected to translate file data in any way. For instance, UNIX
text files delimit lines of text with a single newline character, whereas DOS

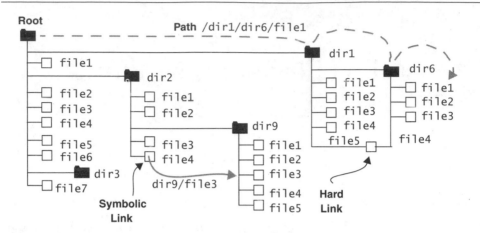

FIGURE 5.1 A filesystem is a hierarchy of directories containing files or subdirectories. Any file or directory can be named uniquely by a series of names forming a path from the root directory. A symbolic link contains a path that references another file or directory. A hard link allows a single file to have multiple names.

text files delimit text lines with a pair of characters: carriage return followed by newline. An application on a DOS client reading a text file from a UNIX server is expected to handle the different line delimiter conventions. Similarly, NFS clients and servers are not expected to translate character encodings like ASCII, EBCDIC, or Unicode.

An NFS file may have multiple names or *hard links* indicated by the *nlinks* file attribute. These additional links are created with the LINK request.

2. *Directories* are assumed to be lists of simple file names. NFS provides READDIR and READDIRPLUS (version 3) requests to read these lists of names. If the size of a directory is larger than the maximum size of an NFS reply, then the client can continue a partial list using the cookie value associated with each entry in a subsequent READDIR request. An NFS directory can have only one name—its *nlinks* attribute cannot be greater than 1.

3. *Symbolic links* are assumed to contain a text pathname that can be read and interpreted by the client and are assumed to be an indirect reference to another file or directory. A symbolic link has properties distinct from those of a hard link: it may refer to either a file or a directory and the referenced object is not required to exist. The requirement for the client to interpret the pathname contained in a symbolic link is rather a strange dichotomy for the NFS protocol: NFS clients are not required to know of server pathname syntax, yet a symbolic link implies knowledge of some pathname syntax. WebNFS clients assume that symbolic links contain either base or relative URLs (see section 16.5.5).

4. *Special files.* NFS appears to provide access to a number of *special* files or *device* types: block special, character special, socket, and named pipes. However, these filetypes are just place holders and provide no real remote access to these file types. The device major and minor attributes for these types refer to special files on the *client*—not the server.

In contrast to the RFS protocol (described at the beginning of chapter 13), the NFS protocol designers made a conscious decision *not* to support direct access to remote data *devices* such as tape drives or printers. It is possible to fit file access into a generalized model that can be used to provide interoperability between different kinds of clients and servers. It is much harder to generalize access to the much larger variety of data devices. The RFS protocol provided device access through UNIX ioctl calls, but only between UNIX clients and servers and for a very limited set of devices.

5.2 Filehandles

An NFS filehandle is a reference to a file or directory that is independent of the filename. All NFS operations use a filehandle to identify the file or directory to which the operation applies. An NFS filehandle is opaque to the client. The server creates filehandles and only the server can interpret the data contained within them. The opaque nature of filehandles gives servers a lot of flexibility in determining the most efficient way to reference a file. UNIX servers, for instance, typically identify a file or directory by its filesystem identifier and inode number.

An NFS version 2 filehandle is 32 bytes long and the length is fixed (Figure 5.2). NFS version 3 allowed the filehandle to be of variable length up to 64 bytes. Variable length allows a server to use a much smaller filehandle if it chooses. The increase in maximum size to 64 bytes makes life a bit easier for servers that cannot easily cram a complete file reference into the smaller NFS

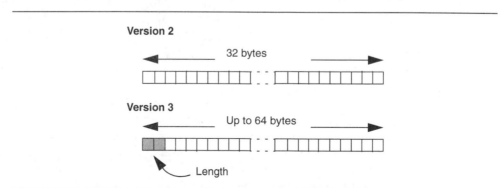

FIGURE 5.2 NFS version 2 filehandles are a 32-byte fixed-length quantity. Version 3 filehandles can be variable length up to a maximum of 64 bytes.

version 2 filehandle. NFS version 3 set a limit of 64 bytes to facilitate server memory management—for instance, a server could preallocate 64-byte buffers knowing that any version 3 filehandle would fit. The WebNFS extensions to both versions of the protocol included a public filehandle (see section 16.4) that defines a reserved value for the filehandle: all-zero bytes for a version 2 filehandle, zero-length for a version 3 filehandle.

The reference that the server places in the filehandle to reference the file or directory must meet a couple of important criteria:

1. *Persistence*. Clients will assume that the filehandle is a persistent reference to the file or directory. An NFS client will cache filehandles expecting them to be valid until the file or directory is removed from the server. The client's assumption of persistent filehandles means that a filehandle value must survive a crash and reboot of the server, whether the server is implemented as a kernel module or as a user-level process. This property precludes the use of a filehandle as an index into a table of file descriptors, unless the table and the assignment of filehandles to files can be stored in a file.

2. *Pathname independence*. The most obvious way to create a persistent reference is to store the pathname to the file or directory in the filehandle. That's a tight fit for NFS version 2 filehandles, since pathnames would be limited to just 32 bytes; even the NFS version 3 filehandle would limit pathnames to 64 bytes. Although pathnames are indeed persistent, NFS requires a reference to the file or directory that is *independent of the pathname*. If the pathname to a file is changed through a RENAME operation (perhaps by another client) or if the pathname is removed, the filehandle must continue to be a valid reference to the file. This property reflects a requirement of UNIX filesystems: once a file is open, it can be renamed or unlinked without affecting access to the file.

The dual requirement for filehandle persistence and pathname independence creates a problem for NFS servers implemented as a user-level process. A UNIX kernel server can identify a file or directory by its device and inode numbers and meet the persistence and pathname independence requirements. However, a UNIX process cannot open a file identified by a device and inode number. Only a pathname will suffice as a persistent reference for the file. For example, the Linux user-level server, unfs, stores a compressed pathname in the filehandle. Each pathname component is hashed into an 8-bit quantity and the file inode number is included as a check. The filehandle becomes invalid if the file is renamed.

The server will return a new filehandle in response to several procedures. The LOOKUP procedure is used sequentially to evaluate pathnames, and filehandles are returned when new objects are created by CREATE, MKDIR, LINK, SYMLINK. The READDIRPLUS procedure in version 3 will return a filehandle for each directory entry. Each of these procedures assumes that the client already has a filehandle for the parent directory. Until WebNFS (chapter 16) provided the public filehandle, there was no way to obtain an *initial* filehandle within the NFS protocol itself. The NFS design team intended that the MOUNT protocol (chapter 9) be used to obtain an initial filehandle from a server pathname.

5.3 Pathnames

A *pathname* is a sequence of component names that uniquely names a file or directory within the hierarchy. Different operating systems may have restrictions on the depth of the tree or the names used, as well as using different syntax to represent the *pathname*, which is the concatenation of all the *components* (directory and file names) in the name. For instance, UNIX pathname components are separated with a slash character, Windows uses a backslash, and the Macintosh uses a colon.

5.3.1 Filename Component Handling

Servers frequently impose restrictions on the names that can be created. The maximum length of a component name may vary: UNIX components can be up to 255 characters in length, whereas DOS components are limited to 8 characters with a 3-character extension. Although the XDR standard limits the characters of a string to 7-bit ASCII characters, common usage is to allow any ISO Latin-1 (8-bit) character to be encoded in a filename.

Many servers also forbid the use of names that contain certain characters, such as the path component separator used by the server operating system. For example, the UNIX operating system will reject a name that contains /, while . and .. are distinguished in UNIX and may not be specified as the name when creating a filesystem object. Windows short names will be restricted to an 8-character name with a 3-character extension and names cannot contain any of the characters "./\[]:+|<>=;,*?. If the server receives a filename containing characters that it cannot handle, the error NFSERR_EACCES (version 2) or NFS3ERR_EACCES (version 3) should be returned. Client implementations should be prepared to handle this side effect of heterogeneity.

The following comments apply to all NFS filenames.

■ The filename must not be null, nor may it be the null string. The server should return the error NFSERR_ACCES (version 2) or NFS3ERR_ACCES (version 3) if it receives such a filename. On some clients, the filename, "", or a null string is assumed to be an alias for the current directory. Clients that require this functionality must implement it for themselves and not depend on the server to support such semantics.

- A filename having the value of . is assumed to be an alias for the current directory. Clients that require this functionality should implement it for themselves and not depend on the server to support such semantics. However, the server should be able to handle such a filename correctly.

- A filename having the value of .. is assumed to be an alias for the parent of the current directory, i.e., the directory that contains the current directory. The server should be prepared to handle this semantic, if it supports directories, even if those directories do not contain UNIX-style . or .. entries.

If the filename is longer than the maximum for the filesystem, the result depends on the value of the PATHCONF flag, no_trunc. NFS version 2 clients must obtain this field using the MOUNTPROC_PATHCONF procedure from version 2 of the MOUNT protocol. NFS version 3 clients can use the PATH-CONF procedure in the protocol itself (see section 7.3.21). If no_trunc is FALSE, the filename will be silently truncated to name_max bytes. If no_trunc is TRUE and the filename exceeds the server's filesystem maximum filename length, the operation will fail with the error NFSERR_NAMETOOLONG (version 2) or NFS3ERR_NAMETOOLONG (version 3).

5.3.2   Pathname Evaluation

The NFS LOOKUP operation evaluates only one pathname component at a time. At first this seems a rather pedestrian way to evaluate a long pathname; why not just send the entire pathname to the server for evaluation? There are several reasons:

1. *Pathname syntax.* One-component-at-a-time evaluation makes it easier for clients and servers with different pathname conventions to evaluate pathnames. It doesn't matter if the client's pathname component separator character is different from the server's because the separator is never sent over the wire.

2. *Client namespace.* UNIX clients typically evaluate pathnames one component at a time so that filesystem mountpoints on the client can be detected and crossed (Figure 5.3).

3. *Caching and latency.* At first glance the component-at-a-time requirement would seem to be expensive in network requests and latency. For instance, the path /a/b/c/d/e would require five LOOKUP requests to the server. Most UNIX clients use a directory name lookup cache (DNLC) to cache previous pathname evaluations. In practice, the hit rate on this cache is very high (typically > 98 percent) since naming operations exhibit a high degree of directory locality. Thanks to the caching of the DNLC, it's rare that pathnames with many components are evaluated with multiple LOOKUP requests. In

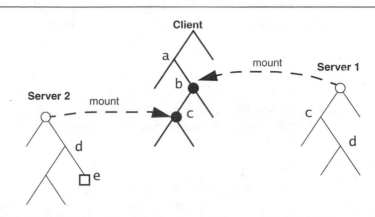

FIGURE 5.3 Mountpoint crossing. A client must take mountpoints into account when evaluating pathnames. Here the pathname /a/b/c/d/e crosses two mountpoints that take the evaluation path first into the filesystem on server 1 then into server 2. Neither server is aware of the mountpoints on the client.

addition, the NFS protocol was designed with an assumption of low latency. Typically an NFS LOOKUP request receives a response within a couple of milliseconds on a LAN.

The design team for NFS version 3 considered a multicomponent LOOKUP operation but rejected it due to the additional complexity of implementation and negligible benefit—multicomponent LOOKUP operations appeared to be rare, thanks to the effectiveness of the client's DNLC cache. Subsequently, the WebNFS extensions to NFS versions 2 and 3 (see chapter 16) added multicomponent LOOKUP support via a pathname with slash-separated components relative to the public filehandle with the intent that it be used to replace the MOUNT request of the MOUNT protocol.

5.4 Stateless Server

An initial goal of the NFS protocol design was to make each request stand-alone so that a server would not be required to preserve any client state from one NFS request to the next. The "stateless" server feature is often mistakenly quoted as a "requirement" of the protocol. In practice, most NFS servers do maintain some client state to improve performance, but the protocol itself does not require it. In practice, it can be argued that the protocol *should* require some state to preserve at-most-once semantics, which can be approximated by a duplicate request cache (see section 8.9). The Network Lock Manager protocol, which handles all the file locking for NFS, is, by necessity, highly stateful.

The most obvious manifestation of statelessness in the protocol is the lack of a file OPEN or CLOSE request. An NFS server does not need to know which clients have open files. When a client is reading a file the server is not required to retain a "current" file offset since each READ request specifies the offset to be used. The NFS server expects the client to retain all necessary state information.

The statelessness of the NFS protocol may become a historical artifact when version 4 of the NFS protocol (chapter 17) is complete. Drafts of version 4 include a file locking protocol that is inherently stateful. Further statefulness may be introduced with support for more aggressive caching.

5.4.1   Server Recovery

The NFS protocol was intended to be as stateless as possible. That is, a server should not need to maintain any protocol state information about any of its clients in order to function correctly. Stateless servers have a distinct advantage over stateful servers in the event of a failure. With stateless servers, a client need only retry a request until the server responds; it does not even need to know that the server has crashed or the network temporarily went down. The client of a stateful server, on the other hand, needs to either detect a server failure and rebuild the server's state when it comes back up or cause client operations to fail.

In practice, the NFS protocol does not meet the ideal of a completely stateless protocol. Since the underlying RPC protocol does not provide at-most-once semantics, an NFS server must implement a duplicate request cache if it is to respond correctly to retransmitted requests (see section 8.9). Some RPC authentication flavors require context state to be maintained on the server, and programs that require file locking must use the very stateful Network Lock Manager protocol, described in chapter 10.

5.4.2   Idempotent Operations

The NFS protocol simplifies server recovery by making many operations *idempotent*. An idempotent operation is one that returns the same result if it is repeated. If an NFS client does not receive a response to a request within a reasonable time, it will retransmit the request periodically until the server responds. If the client retransmits because the server's response was lost, then the server may receive the same request multiple times. If the request is idempotent, then the effect will be the same no matter how many times the server receives the request. If the request is not idempotent, then the client may receive an error if the request is retransmitted. For example, the READ request is idempotent (Figure 5.4), but a REMOVE request is not (Figure 5.5).

The failure of a server or network is more likely to occur between a client's NFS requests, not between the server's receipt of a request and the transmission of a response—retransmissions due to lost responses are relatively rare. Hence, errors resulting from retransmissions of nonidempotent requests

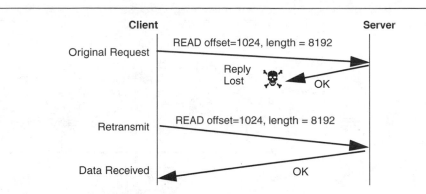

FIGURE 5.4 Retransmission of the idempotent READ request produces the same result no matter how many times it is retransmitted.

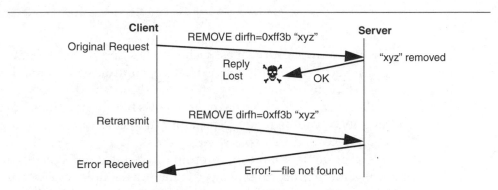

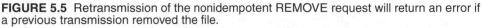

FIGURE 5.5 Retransmission of the nonidempotent REMOVE request will return an error if a previous transmission removed the file.

are rare. These rare circumstances can be almost completely eliminated by the server's use of a duplicate request cache (section 8.9).

5.4.3 Statelessness and High Availability

While the stateless server feature was intended to facilitate server recovery in the event of a server crash due to a software or hardware problem, in subsequent years this design feature has paid dividends in the straightforward implementation of highly available servers and clients (Figure 5.6). Highly available NFS servers (HA-NFS) consist of two or more NFS servers connected to a common set of disk drives. The drive sets are configured so that each server is solely responsible for a subset of the drives but can take over the other server's drives if it detects that the other server is no longer providing access. Since there is little NFS client state to be transferred from one server to the other, it is easy for one server to assume the other server's functions. If the

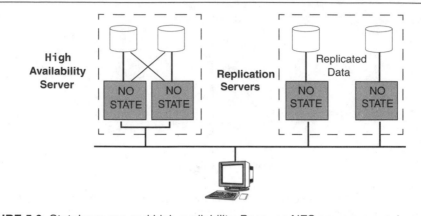

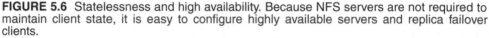

FIGURE 5.6 Statelessness and high availability. Because NFS servers are not required to maintain client state, it is easy to configure highly available servers and replica failover clients.

server uses a duplicate request cache (see section 8.9), then data in the cache should be accessible to the server taking control. One method, exploited in [Bhide+91], is to maintain the cache as log records within a logging filesystem. Since the Network Lock Manager protocol is highly stateful, failover for clients holding locks can be made transparent (invisible to clients) only if all client locks are recorded in stable storage accessible to the standby server. Rather than rely on stable storage for recording lock state (and affecting server performance), a more practical scheme is to handle the failover as a fast server crash and recovery (to standby server) so that clients will reclaim their locks [Bhide+92].

Client-side failover allows a client to switch its NFS requests from one server that is no longer responding to another replica server. Once the client has obtained filehandles for the new server, it can retransmit any unanswered requests to the new server. A failover client does not have to reestablish state on the new server.

5.5 Summary

The NFS protocol assumes a hierarchically organized filesystem with a single root. Files are located relative to an initial filehandle by a sequence of LOOKUP operations. NFS has no formal pathname representation. The protocol recognizes directories, files, symbolic links, and a small number of "special" file types. Since the protocol does not require the server to maintain client state, recovery following a server crash is simple, and highly available server configurations featuring failover are easy to configure.

Chapter 6

NFS Version 2

Despite its designation as "version 2" of the protocol, NFS version 2 was the first published version of the NFS protocol. Version 1 of the protocol existed briefly at Sun as a prototype that was deployed on a few clients and servers within the development group. When substantial changes were made to the version 1 protocol, the development group decided to apply the changes as a new version number to verify the ability of the server to support multiple versions concurrently and to verify the RPC version fallback of the prototype clients. NFS version 1 was never published.

Implementation of NFS version 2 began at Sun in March 1984. It was based on the SunOS UNIX kernel, which was based on BSD 4.2. In 1985, NFS version 2 became a product in SunOS 3.2. This implementation was first described in a paper presented at the Usenix conference later that year [Sandberg+85]. Soon after, Geoff Arnold in Sun's East Coast engineering labs, built the first PC version of NFS. At that time, PC-NFS was constrained to be run within the 640-KB DOS memory limit.

NFS version 2 was received well by customers. Its good performance made it practical to take data scattered around the disks of individual workstations and move them to centralized servers, promoting data sharing, easier file backup, cheaper disk storage, and in some cases better performance from server disks.

Although NFS version 2 has been superseded in recent years by NFS version 3, system administrators are slow to upgrade the operating systems of their clients and servers, so NFS version 2 use is not only widespread, it is still by far the most popular version of NFS.

The following description of the NFS version 2 protocol follows RFC 1094 (the first public specification of the protocol) in explaining the data types used in the protocol and the semantics of the procedures that make up the protocol. The description is designed to suit the needs of a protocol implementor or a person interested in the details of the protocol.

6.1 Common Data Types

The following XDR definitions are common structures and types used in the arguments and results of several protocol procedures. First, the sizes, given in decimal bytes, of various XDR structures used in the protocol:

```
const MAXDATA = 8192;     /* Max size of a READ or WRITE request */
const MAXPATHLEN = 1024;  /* Max length of a pathname argument */
const MAXNAMLEN = 255;    /* Max length of a file name argument */
const COOKIESIZE  = 4;    /* Size of READDIR cookie*/
const FHSIZE = 32;        /* Size of file handle */
```

The following structures are used as arguments or results by many procedures in the protocol. Procedure descriptions refer to these structures.

stat

```
enum stat {
    NFS_OK = 0,
    NFSERR_PERM=1,
    NFSERR_NOENT=2,
    NFSERR_IO=5,
    NFSERR_NXIO=6,
    NFSERR_ACCES=13,
    NFSERR_EXIST=17,
    NFSERR_NODEV=19,
    NFSERR_NOTDIR=20,
    NFSERR_ISDIR=21,
    NFSERR_FBIG=27,
    NFSERR_NOSPC=28,
    NFSERR_ROFS=30,
    NFSERR_NAMETOOLONG=63,
    NFSERR_NOTEMPTY=66,
    NFSERR_DQUOT=69,
    NFSERR_STALE=70,
    NFSERR_WFLUSH=99
}
```

The stat type is returned with every procedure's results. A value of NFS_OK indicates that the call completed successfully and the results are valid. The other values indicate that some kind of error occurred on the server side during the servicing of the procedure (Table 6.1). The error values are derived from UNIX error numbers.

TABLE 6.1 NFS Errors

Error name	Value	Meaning
NFS_OK	0	Indicates that the call completed successfully.
NFSERR_PERM	1	Not owner. The caller does not have correct ownership to perform the requested operation.
NFSERR_NOENT	2	No such file or directory. The file or directory specified does not exist.
NFSERR_IO	5	Some sort of hard error occurred when the operation was in progress—a disk error, for example.
NFSERR_NXIO	6	No such device or address.
NFSERR_ACCES	13	Permission denied. The caller does not have the correct permission to perform the requested operation.
NFSERR_EXIST	17	File exists. The file specified already exists.
NFSERR_NODEV	19	No such device.
NFSERR_NOTDIR	20	Is not a directory. The caller specified a nondirectory in a directory operation.
NFSERR_ISDIR	21	Is a directory. The caller specified a directory in a nondirectory operation.
NFSERR_FBIG	27	File too large. The operation caused a file to grow beyond the server's limit.
NFSERR_NOSPC	28	No space left on device. The operation caused the server's filesystem to reach its limit.
NFSERR_ROFS	30	Read-only filesystem. Write attempted on a read-only filesystem.
NFSERR_NAMETOOLONG	63	Filename too long. The filename in an operation was too long.
NFSERR_NOTEMPTY	66	Directory not empty. Attempted to remove a directory that was not empty.
NFSERR_DQUOT	69	Disk quota exceeded. The client's disk quota on the server has been exceeded.
NFSERR_STALE	70	The filehandle given in the arguments was invalid. That is, the file referred to by that filehandle no longer exists, or access to it has been revoked.
NFSERR_WFLUSH	99	The server's write cache used in the WRITECACHE call was flushed to disk. This error will never be encountered since the WRITECACHE procedure was never fully defined or implemented.

ftype

```
enum ftype {
    NFNON    = 0,    /* Non-file */
    NFREG    = 1,    /* Regular file */
    NFDIR    = 2,    /* Directory */
    NFBLK    = 3,    /* Block-special device */
    NFCHR    = 4,    /* Character-special device */
    NFLNK    = 5     /* Symbolic link */
    NFSOCK   = 6,    /* Socket */
    NFFIFO   = 7     /* Named pipe */
}
```

The enumeration ftype gives the type of a file. The type NFNON indicates a nonfile, NFREG is a regular file, NFDIR is a directory, and NFLNK is a symbolic link.

The remaining types are special types intended for use by diskless UNIX clients. NFBLK is a block-special device, NFCHR is a character-special device, NFSOCK is a UNIX domain socket, and NFFIFO is a named pipe. While there are no procedures within the NFS protocol that operate on these special objects directly, the protocol does allow these objects to be created. NFS version 2 implementations support an overloaded form of CREATE (section 6.2.8) and NFS version 3 provides a MKNOD procedure (section 7.3.12).

fhandle

```
typedef opaque fhandle[FHSIZE];
```

The fhandle is the filehandle passed between the server and the client. All file operations are done using filehandles to refer to a file or directory. The filehandle is defined as an opaque sequence of bytes. This means that the contents of a filehandle are not defined by the protocol. The server can put anything in the filehandle that will reliably and persistently identify a file or directory. For additional information on filehandles see section 5.2.

timeval

```
struct timeval {
    uint32 seconds;
    uint32 useconds;
}
```

The timeval structure is the number of seconds and microseconds since midnight Greenwich Mean Time January 1, 1970. It is used to pass time and date information. There are some limitations on the times and dates that can be represented with this format; since the seconds value is unsigned it is impossible to represent dates prior to 1970 and the 32-bit seconds value overflows after 136 years, on February 5, 2106. A more immediate problem exists for

UNIX clients since their system time uses the same epoch (1970) with a signed 32-bit seconds value that will overflow in 2038.

fattr

```
struct fattr {
    ftypetype;              /* Type of file */
    uint32mode;             /* Permission bits */
    uint32nlink;            /* Number of hard links (names)*/
    uint32uid;              /* User identification number */
    uint32gid;              /* Group identification number */
    uint32size;             /* Size of file in bytes */
    uint32blocksize;        /* Size of a disk block in bytes */
    uint32rdev;             /* Device number of a file */
    uint32blocks;           /* Number of disk blocks used */
    uint32fsid;             /* Identifier of filesystem */
    uint32fileid;           /* Identifier of file in filesystem */
    timevalatime;           /* Last access time */
    timevalmtime;           /* Last modification time */
    timevalctime;           /* Attribute modification time */
}
```

The `fattr` structure contains the attributes of a file (Table 6.2).

TABLE 6.2 File Attributes in `fattr` Structure

Attribute	Description
type	Type of the file
mode	Protection mode bits (see Table 6.3)
nlink	Number of hard links to the file—that is, the number of different names for the same file
uid	User ID of the owner of the file
gid	Group ID of the group of the file
size	Size of the file in bytes
blocksize	Size in bytes of a file block
rdev	Identifies the device file if the file type is NFCHR or NFBLK
blocks	Number of blocks the file takes up on disk
fsid	Filesystem identifier for the filesystem containing the file
fileid	Number that uniquely identifies the file within its filesystem (on UNIX this would be the inode number)
atime	The time when the file data were last accessed for read or write
mtime	The time when the file data were last modified (written)
ctime	The time when the attributes of the file were last changed. Writing to the file changes the `ctime` in addition to the `mtime`.

Mode is the access mode encoded as a set of bits. Notice that the file type is specified both in the mode bits and in the file type, which duplicates the specification of mode in the POSIX stat structure. This redundancy was removed in version 3 of the protocol. The descriptions in Table 6.3 use the UNIX convention of representing the bit positions with octal numbers.

The collection of file attributes supported by NFS version 2 closely follows the POSIX stat structure that is implemented by UNIX operating systems (Table 6.4). Although this close correspondence of file attributes has been criticized as unduly favoring UNIX clients and servers, the attributes in the fattr structure have served the needs of implementations on other operating systems.

TABLE 6.3 fattr Structure Access Modes

Mode Bit	Description
0040000	This is a directory; "type" field should be NFDIR.
0020000	This is a character special file; "type" field should be NFCHR.
0060000	This is a block special file; "type" field should be NFBLK.
0100000	This is a regular file; "type" field should be NFREG.
0120000	This is a symbolic link file; "type" field should be NFLNK.
0140000	This is a named socket; "type" field should be NFNON.
0004000	Set user id on execution.
0002000	Set group id on execution.
0001000	On directories, restricted deletion flag. On regular files, do-not-cache flag.
0000400	Read permission for owner.
0000200	Write permission for owner.
0000100	Execute and search permission for owner.
0000040	Read permission for group.
0000020	Write permission for group.
0000010	Execute and search permission for group.
0000004	Read permission for others.
0000002	Write permission for others.
0000001	Execute and search permission for others.

TABLE 6.4 POSIX stat and NFS Version 2 File Attributes

POSIX stat structure	NFS version 2 file attributes
st_type	type
st_mode	mode
st_ino	fileid
st_dev	fsid
st_rdev	rdev
st_nlink	nlink
st_uid	uid
st_gid	gid
st_size	size
st_atime	atime
st_mtime	mtime
st_ctime	ctime
st_blksize	blocks
st_blocks	blocksize

sattr

The sattr structure contains the file attributes that can be set from the client. The fields are the same as for fattr. A value of −1 indicates a field that should be ignored.

```
struct sattr {
    uint32   mode;
    uint32   uid;
    uint32   gid;
    uint32   size;
    timeval  atime;
    timeval  mtime;
}
```

UNIX clients will restrict change of file ownership (uid) to the superuser or the current owner of the file. The client may apply further restrictions to prevent a user "giving away" a file or changing its group (gid) if "restricted chown" semantics apply (see chown_restricted on page 219). If the file ownership or group is changed, then the client will probably reset the setuid and setgid bits in the file mode attribute to avoid any security problems.

Setting of the size field controls the size of the file on the server. A size of zero means that the file should be truncated. The client should take care to flush any cached writes to the server before setting the size to preserve the correct ordering of operations. Some servers may refuse to increase the size of the file through a change in the size field and return no error. The client can work around this problem by unconditionally writing a byte of data at the maximum offset.

If the useconds field of the mtime is set to 1 million, it is a signal to the server to set the atime and mtime to the current time on the server. The client may be unable to set an accurate time in these fields because of clock skew between the client's and the server's clock or because the server's clock has more precision that the client's. This overloading of the mtime.useconds field is eliminated in version 3 with an explicit indication of whether client or server time is to be used.

filename

```
typedef string<MAXNAMLEN> filename;
```

The type filename is used for passing filenames or pathname components. The protocol makes no restrictions on the characters that can appear in a filename though the server's operating system, or the filesystem on the server may reject names that contain "illegal" characters (NFSERR_IO) or if the name is too long (NFSERR_NAMETOOLONG). Although the XDR standard limits the characters of a string to 7-bit ASCII characters, common usage is to allow any ISO Latin-1 (8-bit) character to be encoded in a filename. Refer to section 5.3.1 for more information on pathnames.

path

```
typedef string<MAXPATHLEN> path;
```

The type path is a pathname. The server considers it as a string with no internal structure, but to the client it is the name of a node in a filesystem tree. The path is used only to set or return the text in a symbolic link (SYMLINK and READLINK).

6.2 Server Procedures

The following sections define the RPC procedures that are supplied by an NFS version 2 protocol server (Table 6.5). The RPC procedure number is followed by its name. The **Description** part of each section details the XDR format of the procedure arguments and results and tells what the procedure is expected to do and how its arguments and results are used. The **Implementation** part gives information about how the procedure is expected to work and how it should be used by clients. The **Errors** part lists the errors returned for specific types of failures. These lists are intended not as the definitive statement of all of the errors that can be returned by any specific procedure but as a guide for the more common errors that may be returned.

TABLE 6.5 Summary of NFS Version 2 Procedures

Number	Name	Description	Section
0	NFSPROC_NULL	Null procedure	6.2.1, page 99
1	NFSPROC_GETATTR	Get file attributes	6.2.2, page 100
2	NFSPROC_SETATTR	Set file attributes	6.2.3, page 102
3	NFSPROC_ROOT	*Not implemented*	
4	NFSPROC_LOOKUP	Lookup file name	6.2.4, page 104
5	NFSPROC_READLINK	Read from symbolic link	6.2.5, page 106
6	NFSPROC_READ	Read from file	6.2.6, page 107
7	NFSPROC_WRITECACHE	*Not implemented*	
8	NFSPROC_WRITE	Write to file	6.2.7, page 109
9	NFSPROC_CREATE	Create file	6.2.8, page 112
10	NFSPROC_REMOVE	Remove file	6.2.9, page 115
11	NFSPROC_RENAME	Rename file	6.2.10, page 116
12	NFSPROC_LINK	Create ink to file	6.2.11, page 119
13	NFSPROC_SYMLINK	Create symbolic link	6.2.12, page 120
14	NFSPROC_MKDIR	Create directory	6.2.13, page 122
15	NFSPROC_RMDIR	Remove directory	6.2.14, page 124
16	NFSPROC_READDIR	Read directory	6.2.15, page 126
17	NFSPROC_STATFS	Get file systems attributes	6.2.16, page 128

Client implementations should be prepared to deal with unexpected errors coming from a server. Finally, a **Snoop Trace** of the procedure is included to show a typical call and response.

6.2.1   Procedure 0: NULL—Do Nothing

Description

This procedure does no work. It is made available in all RPC services to allow server response testing and timing.

Arguments	*Results*
void	void

Arguments

None.

Results

None.

Implementation

It is important that this procedure do no work at all so that it can be used to measure the overhead of processing a service request. By convention, the NULL procedure should never require any authentication. A server may choose to ignore this convention, in a more secure implementation, where responding to the NULL procedure call acknowledges the existence of a resource to an unauthenticated client. The null procedure call is most commonly used to establish whether the NFS service is available and responding.

The null procedure is also used to establish an RPCSEC_GSS security context. Security information is exchanged as arguments and results on the null procedure call. For more information see section 4.7.2.

Errors

Since the NULL procedure takes no arguments and returns nothing, it cannot return an error except where it is used to establish an RPCSEC_GSS context.

6.2.2   Procedure 1: GETATTR—Get File Attributes

Description

Retrieves the attributes of a specified filesystem object.

```
Arguments                        Results
fhandle    file;                 switch (uint32 status) {
                                     case NFS_OK = 0:
                                         fattr attributes;
                                     default:
                                         void;
                                 }
```

Arguments

file

The filehandle of an object whose attributes are to be retrieved.

Results

status

NFS_OK if successful, otherwise an error code.

attributes

The attributes for the object. The file attribute structure is described in Table 6.2.

Implementation

The attributes of filesystem objects are a point of major disagreement between different operating systems. Servers should make a best attempt to support all the attributes in the fattr structure so that clients can count on it as common ground. Some mapping may be required to map local attributes to those in the fattr structure.

Most client NFS protocol implementations implement a time-bounded attribute caching scheme to reduce over-the-wire attribute checks. In addition, NFS version 3 returns attributes on almost all calls, further reducing the number of GETATTR requests. If the client is using a large memory cache or a disk cache then the GETATTR call may be the most common NFS call from these clients—simply checking whether cached objects have changed on the server.

Clients that cache writes to the file should flush any cached data before sending a GETATTR request so that the file mtime attribute will return a sane value that will not surprise an application that expects to see a recent modification time due to recent writes.

Errors

NFSERR_IO	5	Some sort of hard error occurred when the operation was in progress—a disk error, for example.
NFSERR_STALE	70	The filehandle given in the arguments was invalid. That is, the file referred to by that filehandle no longer exists, or access to it has been revoked.

Snoop Trace of GETATTR

```
NFS:   Proc = 1 (Get file attributes)
NFS:   File handle = 0080001800000002000A00000001CE8C
NFS:               0E1FB8A2000A00000001CE8C0E1FB8A2
```

⇩

```
NFS:   Proc = 1 (Get file attributes)
NFS:   Status = 0 (OK)
NFS:   File type = 2 (Directory)
NFS:   Mode = 040777
NFS:    Type = Directory
NFS:    Setuid = 0, Setgid = 0, Sticky = 0
NFS:    Owner's permissions = rwx
NFS:    Group's permissions = rwx
NFS:    Other's permissions = rwx
NFS:   Link count = 17, UID = 0, GID = 1
NFS:   File size = 1536, Block size = 8192, No. of blocks = 4
NFS:   File system id = 8388632, File id = 118412
NFS:   Access time       = 10-Aug-98 18:31:41.570007 GMT
NFS:   Modification time = 10-Aug-98 18:32:16.770002 GMT
NFS:   Inode change time = 10-Aug-98 18:32:16.770002 GMT
```

6.2.3   Procedure 2: SETATTR—Set File Attributes

Description

Procedure SETATTR changes one or more of the attributes of a file system object on the server. The new attributes are specified by a sattr structure.

Arguments		*Results*
fhandle	file;	```switch (uint32 status) {```
sattr	attributes;	``` case NFS_OK = 0:```
		``` fattr attributes;```
		``` default:```
		``` void;```
		```}```

Arguments

file

> The filehandle for the object.

attributes

> The attributes argument contains fields which are either −1 or are the new value for the attribute of file.

Results

status

> NFS_OK if successful, otherwise an error code.

attributes

> A fattr structure containing the new attributes for the object.

Implementation

The size field is used to request changes to the size of a file. A value of 0 causes the file to be truncated, a value less than the current size of the file causes data from new size to the end of the file to be discarded, and a size greater than the current size of the file causes logically zeroed data bytes to be added to the end of the file. Servers are free to implement this using holes or actual zero data bytes. Clients should not make any assumptions regarding a server's implementation of this feature, beyond that the bytes returned will be zeroed. Servers must support extending the file size via SETATTR.

   SETATTR is not guaranteed atomic. A failed SETATTR may partially change a file's attributes. Changing the size of a file with SETATTR indirectly changes the mtime. A client must account for this, as size changes can result in data deletion. If server and client times differ, programs that compare client time to file times can break.

Errors

NFSERR_PERM	1	Not owner. The caller does not have correct owner-ship to perform the requested operation.
NFSERR_IO	5	Some sort of hard error occurred when the operation was in progress—a disk error, for example.
NFSERR_ACCES	13	Permission denied. The caller does not have the correct permission to perform the requested operation.
NFSERR_ISDIR	21	Is a directory. The caller specified a directory in a nondirectory operation.
NFSERR_ROFS	30	Read-only filesystem. Write was attempted on a read-only filesystem.
NFSERR_STALE	70	The filehandle given in the arguments was invalid. That is, the file referred to by that filehandle no longer exists, or access to it has been revoked.

Snoop Trace of SETATTR

```
NFS:   Proc = 2 (Set file attributes)
NFS:   File handle = 00800018000000002000A00000001CE95
NFS:                 4C87FC5B000A00000001CE8C0E1FB8A2
NFS:   Mode = 037777777777
NFS:    Type = ?
NFS:    Setuid = 1, Setgid = 1, Sticky = 1
NFS:    Owner's permissions = rwx
NFS:    Group's permissions = rwx
NFS:    Other's permissions = rwx
NFS:   UID = -1
NFS:   GID = -1
NFS:   Size = -1
NFS:   Access time       = 10-Aug-98 18:31:26.000000 GMT
NFS:   Modification time = 10-Aug-98 18:31:26.1000000 GMT
```

⬇

```
NFS:   Proc = 2 (Set file attributes)
NFS:   Status = 0 (OK)
NFS:   File type = 1 (Regular File)
NFS:   Mode = 0100664
NFS:    Type = Regular file
NFS:    Setuid = 0, Setgid = 0, Sticky = 0
NFS:    Owner's permissions = rw-
NFS:    Group's permissions = rw-
NFS:    Other's permissions = r--
NFS:   Link count = 1, UID = 3497, GID = 10
NFS:   File size = 0, Block size = 8192, No. of blocks = 0
NFS:   File system id = 8388632, File id = 118421
NFS:   Access time       = 10-Aug-98 18:34:37.280001 GMT
NFS:   Modification time = 10-Aug-98 18:34:37.280001 GMT
NFS:   Inode change time = 10-Aug-98 18:34:37.280001 GMT
```

6.2.4   Procedure 4: LOOKUP—Look Up File Name

Description

Procedure LOOKUP searches a directory for a specific name and returns the filehandle and attributes for the corresponding filesystem object.

Arguments	*Results*
| ```
fhandle    dir;
filename   name;
``` | ```
switch (uint32 status) {
    case NFS_OK = 0:
        fhandle file;
        fattr attributes;
    default:
        void;
}
``` |

Arguments

`dir`

The filehandle for the directory to search.

`name`

The name of the object to find.

Results

`status`

NFS_OK if successful, otherwise an error code.

`file`

The filehandle of the object corresponding to `name`.

`attributes`

The attributes of the object corresponding to `name`.

Implementation

At first glance, in the case where `name` refers to a mountpoint on the server, two different replies seem possible. The server can return either the filehandle for the underlying directory it is mounted on or the filehandle of the root of the mounted directory. This ambiguity is resolved simply. A server will not allow a LOOKUP operation to cross a mountpoint to the root of a different filesystem, even if the filesystem is exported. This does not prevent a client from accessing a hierarchy of filesystems exported by a server, but the client must mount each of the filesystems individually so that the mountpoint crossing takes place on the client. A given server implementation may refine these rules, given capabilities or limitations particular to that implementation. See section 5.3.2 for further description of pathname evaluation and section 8.5 for a discussion of mountpoint crossing issues.

Two filenames are distinguished: . is an alias for the current directory, and the name .. is an alias for the parent directory, that is, the directory that includes the specified directory as a member. There is no facility for dealing with a multiparented directory, and the NFS protocol assumes a hierarchy organized as a single-rooted tree. If the name represents a symbolic link, the server will return the filehandle for the symbolic link—not the file it points to. Except in the case of multicomponent lookup, the client is responsible for all parsing of filenames, including filenames that are modified by symbolic links encountered during the lookup process.

Normally the filename is a single pathname component, but if a public filehandle is used, then the filename may contain an entire pathname limited to 255 bytes in size. For more details of WebNFS lookups, see section 16.5.

Errors

NFSERR_PERM	1	Not owner. The caller does not have correct ownership to perform the requested operation.
NFSERR_NOENT	2	No such file or directory. The file or directory specified does not exist.
NFSERR_IO	5	Some sort of hard error occurred when the operation was in progress—a disk error, for example.
NFSERR_ACCES	13	Permission denied. The caller does not have the correct permission to perform the requested operation.
NFSERR_NOTDIR	20	Not a directory. The caller specified a nondirectory in a directory operation.
NFSERR_NAMETOOLONG	63	Filename too long. The filename in an operation was too long.
NFSERR_STALE	70	The filehandle given in the arguments was invalid. That is, the file referred to by that filehandle no longer exists, or access to it has been revoked.

Snoop Trace of LOOKUP

```
NFS:   Proc = 4 (Look up file name)
NFS:   File handle = 00800018000000002000A00000001CE8C
NFS:                 0E1FB8A2000A00000001CE8C0E1FB8A2
NFS:   File name = newfile

            ⇩

NFS:   Proc = 4 (Look up file name)
NFS:   Status = 0 (OK)
NFS:   File handle = 00800018000000002000A00000001CE95
NFS:                 4C87FC5B000A00000001CE8C0E1FB8A2
NFS:   File type = 1 (Regular File)
NFS:   Mode = 0100664
```

```
NFS:    Type = Regular file
NFS:    Setuid = 0, Setgid = 0, Sticky = 0
NFS:    Owner's permissions = rw-
NFS:    Group's permissions = rw-
NFS:    Other's permissions = r--
NFS:    Link count = 1, UID = 3497, GID = 10
NFS:    File size = 0, Block size = 8192, No. of blocks = 0
NFS:    File system id = 8388632, File id = 118421
NFS:    Access time        = 10-Aug-98 18:34:37.280001 GMT
NFS:    Modification time  = 10-Aug-98 18:34:37.280001 GMT
NFS:    Inode change time  = 10-Aug-98 18:34:37.280001 GMT
```

6.2.5   Procedure 5: READLINK—Read from Symbolic Link

Description

Procedure READLINK reads the pathname stored in a symbolic link. The pathname is an ASCII string that is opaque to the server. Whether created by the client or created locally on the server, the data in a symbolic link are not interpreted when created; they are simply stored. Since NFS normally parses pathnames on the client, the pathname in a symbolic link may mean something different (or be meaningless) on a different client or on the server if a different pathname syntax is used.

Arguments	*Results*

`fhandle    symlink;`	`switch (uint32 status) {`
	`    case NFS_OK = 0:`
	`        path data;`
	`    default:`
	`        void;`
	`}`

Arguments

`symlink`

   The filehandle for a symbolic link (filesystem object of type NFLNK).

Results

`status`

   NFS_OK if successful, otherwise an error code.

`data`

   The data associated with the symbolic link.

Implementation

A symbolic link is nominally a reference to another file. The data are not necessarily interpreted by the server; they are just stored in the file. It is possible for a client implementation to store a pathname that is not meaningful to the server operating system in a symbolic link. A READLINK operation returns the data to the client for interpretation. If different implementations want to share access to symbolic links, then they must agree on the interpretation of the data in the symbolic link.

The READLINK operation is allowed only on objects of type NFLNK. The server should return the error NFS3ERR_INVAL if the object is not of type NFLNK. (Note: The X/Open XNFS Specification for the NFS version 2 protocol defined the error status in this case as NFSERR_NXIO. This is inconsistent with existing server practice.)

The server may be required to interpret the text in a symbolic link if a WebNFS client sends a multicomponent lookup pathname that names a symbolic link as an intermediate (not final) component. For more details, see section 16.5.5.

Errors

NFSERR_IO	5	Some sort of hard error occurred when the operation was in progress—a disk error, for example.
NFSERR_NXIO	6	No such device or address.
NFSERR_STALE	70	The filehandle given in the arguments was invalid. That is, the file referred to by that filehandle no longer exists, or access to it has been revoked.

Snoop Trace of READLINK

```
NFS:  Proc = 5 (Read from symbolic link)
NFS:  File handle = 00800018000000002000A00000001CE95
NFS:                4C886EDB000A00000001CE8C0E1FB8A2
```

⇩

```
NFS:  Proc = 5 (Read from symbolic link)
NFS:  Status = 0 (OK)
NFS:  Path = /export/home/data
```

6.2.6 Procedure 6: READ—Read from File

Description

Reads the data from a given offset in a file returning the data and the file attributes.

Arguments

```
fhandle file;
uint32 offset;
uint32 count;
uint32 totalcount;
```

Results

```
switch (uint32 status) {
   case NFS_OK = 0:
      fattr attributes;
      opaque<MAXDATA> data;
   default:
      void;
}
```

Arguments

file

The filehandle of the file from which data are to be read. It must identify a file system object of type NFREG.

offset

The position within the file at which the read is to begin. An offset of 0 means to read data starting at the beginning of the file. If the offset is greater than or equal to the size of the file, the status NFS_OK is returned but the data field is zero length.

count

The number of bytes of data that are to be read. If the count is 0, the READ will succeed and return 0 bytes of data, subject to access permissions checking. The count must be less than or equal to the value of the tsize field in the STATFS reply structure for the file system that contains file. If it is greater, the server may return only tsize bytes, resulting in a short read.

totalcount

Unused. Removed in version 3.

Results

status

NFS_OK if successful, otherwise an error code.

attributes

The attributes of the file on completion of the read.

data

The counted data read from the file.

Implementation

If the server returns a "short read," (i.e., fewer than count bytes of data) to the client, the client will assume that the last byte of data is the end of file. The MAXDATA value of 8,912 bytes limits the absolute size of a read request, though the server may require a smaller transfer size as indicated by the tsize attribute of the STATFS request in section 6.2.16. NFS version 3 adds a more positive indication of end-of-file allowing a server to return less data than requested without implying end-of-file.

Errors

NFSERR_IO	5	Some sort of hard error occurred when the operation was in progress—a disk error, for example.
NFSERR_ACCES	13	Permission denied. The caller does not have the correct permission to perform the requested operation.
NFSERR_ISDIR	21	Is a directory. The caller specified a directory in a nondirectory operation.
NFSERR_STALE	70	The filehandle given in the arguments was invalid. That is, the file referred to by that filehandle no longer exists, or access to it has been revoked.

Snoop Trace of READ

```
NFS:   Proc = 6 (Read from file)
NFS:   File handle = 0080001800000002000A00000001CE8F
NFS:                 73135A03000A00000001CE8C0E1FB8A2
NFS:   Offset = 0
NFS:   Count = 8192
```

⇩

```
NFS:   Proc = 6 (Read from file)
NFS:   Status = 0 (OK)
NFS:   File type = 1 (Regular File)
NFS:   Mode = 0100644
NFS:    Type = Regular file
NFS:    Setuid = 0, Setgid = 0, Sticky = 0
NFS:    Owner's permissions = rw-
NFS:    Group's permissions = r--
NFS:    Other's permissions = r--
NFS:   Link count = 1, UID = 0, GID = 1
NFS:   File size = 29, Block size = 8192, No. of blocks = 2
NFS:   File system id = 8388632, File id = 118415
NFS:   Access time       = 10-Aug-98 18:36:26.459999 GMT
NFS:   Modification time = 13-Aug-97 21:05:17.000000 GMT
NFS:   Inode change time = 10-Aug-98 18:35:44.800000 GMT
NFS:   (29 byte(s) of data)
```

6.2.7 Procedure 8: WRITE—Write to File

Description

Writes data beginning offset bytes from the beginning of file. The first byte of the file is at offset zero. If the reply status is NFS_OK, then the reply attributes contains the attributes of the file after the write is complete. The write operation is atomic. Data from this WRITE will not be mixed with data from another client's WRITE. The arguments beginoffset and totalcount are ignored and are removed in version 3.

Arguments	Results
| ```
fhandle file;
uint32 beginoffset;
uint32 offset;
uint32 totalcount;
opaque<MAXDATA> data;
``` | ```
switch (uint32 status) {
  case NFS_OK = 0:
    fattr attributes;
  default:
    void;
}
``` |

Arguments

file

The filehandle for the file to which data are to be written. This must identify a filesystem object of type NFREG.

beginoffset

Not used. Eliminated in version 3.

offset

The position within the file at which the write is to begin. An offset of 0 means to write data starting at the beginning of the file.

totalcount

Not used. Eliminated in version 3.

data

The data to be written to the file. If the size of the opaque data is 0, the WRITE will succeed and return a count of 0, barring errors due to permissions checking. The size of data must be less than or equal to the value of the tsize field in the STATFS reply structure for the file system that contains file. If greater, the server may write only tsize bytes, resulting in a short write.

Results

status

NFS_OK if successful, otherwise an error code.

attributes

The attributes of the file at completion of the write.

Implementation

It is assumed that the act of writing data to a file will cause the mtime of the file to be updated. However, the mtime of the file should not be changed unless the contents of the file are changed. Thus, a WRITE request with no data should not cause the mtime of the file to be updated.

The server must write all data in the write request. If the write cannot be completed in its entirety, then an error must be returned. Additionally, the data must be written to stable storage. The definition of stable storage has been historically a point of contention. The following expected properties of stable storage may help in resolving design issues in the implementation. Stable storage is persistent storage that survives (1) repeated power failures; (2) hardware failures (of any board, power supply, and so on); (3) repeated software crashes, including reboot cycle.

This definition does not address failure of the stable storage module itself. Some implementations may return NFSERR_NOSPC instead of NFSERR_DQUOT when a user's quota is exceeded.

Errors

NFSERR_IO	5	Some sort of hard error occurred when the operation was in progress—a disk error, for example.
NFSERR_ACCES	13	Permission denied. The caller does not have the correct permission to perform the requested operation.
NFSERR_ISDIR	21	Is a directory. The caller specified a directory in a nondirectory operation.
NFSERR_FBIG	27	File too large. The operation caused a file to grow beyond the server's limit.
NFSERR_NOSPC	28	No space left on device. The operation caused the server's filesystem to reach its limit.
NFSERR_ROFS	30	Read-only filesystem. Write was attempted on a read-only filesystem.
NFSERR_DQUOT	69	Disk quota exceeded. The client's disk quota on the server has been exceeded.
NFSERR_STALE	70	The filehandle given in the arguments was invalid. That is, the file referred to by that filehandle no longer exists, or access to it has been revoked.

Snoop Trace of WRITE

```
NFS:   Proc = 8 (Write to file)
NFS:   File handle = 00800018000000002000A00000001CE95
NFS:                 4C892188000A00000001CE8C0E1FB8A2
NFS:   Offset = 0
NFS:   (29 bytes(s) of data)
```
                    ⬇

```
NFS:  Proc = 8 (Write to file)
NFS:  Status = 0 (OK)
NFS:  File type = 1 (Regular File)
NFS:  Mode = 0100644
NFS:   Type = Regular file
NFS:   Setuid = 0, Setgid = 0, Sticky = 0
NFS:   Owner's permissions = rw-
NFS:   Group's permissions = r--
NFS:   Other's permissions = r--
NFS:  Link count = 1, UID = 3497, GID = 10
NFS:  File size = 29, Block size = 8192, No. of blocks = 2
NFS:  File system id = 8388632, File id = 118421
NFS:  Access time        = 10-Aug-98 18:36:26.410001 GMT
NFS:  Modification time = 10-Aug-98 18:36:26.470000 GMT
NFS:  Inode change time = 10-Aug-98 18:36:26.470000 GMT
```

6.2.8   Procedure 9: CREATE—Create File

Description

Creates a regular file.

Arguments		Results

`fhandle` `dir;`
`filename` `name;`
`sattr` `attributes;`
		`switch (uint32 status) {`
		`    case NFS_OK = 0:`
		`        fhandle file;`
		`        fattr attributes;`
		`    default:`
		`        void;`
		`}`

Arguments

`dir`

The file handle for the directory in which the file is to be created.

`name`

The name that is to be associated with the created file.

`attributes`

The initial attributes assigned to the file.

Results

`status`

NFS_OK if successful, otherwise an error code.

`file`

The filehandle of the newly created regular file.

attributes

The attributes of the regular file just created.

Implementation

The create request does not support "exclusive create" semantics; i.e., it does not create the file only if it doesn't already exist. Clients can approximate this feature by use of a prior LOOKUP request to establish the file's existence, though this leaves open the possibility that another client or process might create the file between the LOOKUP and CREATE request. Exclusive create is supported by version 3.

As well as creating regular files (NFREG), the semantics of the CREATE request are overloaded to permit the creation of devices nodes (NFCHR, NFBLK, NFSOCK, and NFFIFO). These device nodes are just "place holder" nodes intended to be used by diskless NFS clients that need to be able to create device entries in their NFS-mounted /dev directory. These filetypes are indicated by setting of the mode bits to indicate the file type. The device *major* and *minor* numbers require additional arguments to be set. These parameters are compressed and inserted into the size attribute. The major and minor attributes for these types refer to devices on the *client*, not the server. The device overloading of the version 2 CREATE is not a formal part of the protocol and is not intended to be interoperable between different client and server implementations. NFS version 3 adds an explicit MKNOD operation to create these nodes (see section 7.3.12).

Errors

NFSERR_IO	5	Some sort of hard error occurred when the operation was in progress—a disk error, for example.
NFSERR_ACCES	13	Permission denied. The caller does not have the correct permission to perform the requested operation.
NFSERR_ISDIR	21	Is a directory. The caller specified a directory in a nondirectory operation.
NFSERR_NOSPC	28	No space left on device. The operation caused the server's filesystem to reach its limit.
NFSERR_ROFS	30	Read-only filesystem. Write was attempted on a read-only filesystem.
NFSERR_NAMETOOLONG	63	Filename too long. The filename in an operation was too long.

continued

| NFSERR_DQUOT | 69 | Disk quota exceeded. The client's disk quota on the server has been exceeded. |
| NFSERR_STALE | 70 | The filehandle given in the arguments was invalid. That is, the file referred to by that filehandle no longer exists, or access to it has been revoked. |

Snoop Trace of CREATE

```
NFS:   Proc = 9 (Create file)
NFS:   File handle = 00800018000000002000A00000001CE8C
NFS:                 0E1FB8A2000A00000001CE8C0E1FB8A2
NFS:   File name = newfile
NFS:   Mode = 0664
NFS:    Type = ?
NFS:    Setuid = 0, Setgid = 0, Sticky = 0
NFS:    Owner's permissions = rw-
NFS:    Group's permissions = rw-
NFS:    Other's permissions = r--
NFS:   UID = -1
NFS:   GID = 10
NFS:   Size = 0
NFS:   Access time       = -1
NFS:   Modification time = -1
```

⇩

```
NFS:   Proc = 9 (Create file)
NFS:   Status = 0 (OK)
NFS:   File handle = 00800018000000002000A00000001CE95
NFS:                 4C87FC5B000A00000001CE8C0E1FB8A2
NFS:   File type = 1 (Regular File)
NFS:   Mode = 0100664
NFS:    Type = Regular file
NFS:    Setuid = 0, Setgid = 0, Sticky = 0
NFS:    Owner's permissions = rw-
NFS:    Group's permissions = rw-
NFS:    Other's permissions = r--
NFS:   Link count = 1, UID = 3497, GID = 10
NFS:   File size = 0, Block size = 8192, No. of blocks = 0
NFS:   File system id = 8388632, File id = 118421
NFS:   Access time       = 10-Aug-98 18:34:37.230001 GMT
NFS:   Modification time = 10-Aug-98 18:34:37.230001 GMT
NFS:   Inode change time = 10-Aug-98 18:34:37.230001 GMT
```

6.2.9   Procedure 10: REMOVE—Remove File

Description

Procedure REMOVE removes (deletes) an entry from a directory. If the entry in the directory was the last reference to the corresponding filesystem object, the object may be destroyed.

Arguments		*Results*
fhandle	dir;	uint32 status;
filename	name;	

Arguments

dir

   The filehandle for the directory from which the entry is to be removed.

name

   The name of the entry to be removed.

Results

status

   NFS_OK if successful, otherwise an error code.

Implementation

In general, REMOVE is intended to remove nondirectory file objects and RMDIR is to be used to remove directories. However, REMOVE can be used to remove directories, subject to restrictions imposed by either the client or server interfaces.

   Since a file may have multiple names (as indicated by the nlinks file attribute), the remove request may have no effect on the file data since another valid name may still exist. Since a filehandle refers to the content of a file (not its name), the filehandle for the file may continue to be valid after the remove is complete.

   If two processes on a UNIX client are accessing an NFS file and one client removes (unlinks) the file, the other process must continue to have access to the file data until it closes the file. This feature is implemented by having the first process check the nlinks attribute. If it is greater than 1 (more than one name), then the REMOVE request can be issued secure in the knowledge that the filehandle will continue to be valid for the other process. If the nlinks attribute is 1, a REMOVE cannot be sent since it would delete the file data from under the other process and invalidate the filehandle. Instead, the first process can issue a RENAME request to change the name to a hidden name. Solaris clients use the name .nfsxxxx, where the x's are digits intended to make the name unique within the directory. These hidden files are deleted later by the server when it has determined that they are no longer in use. For more details, see section 8.4.

Errors

NFSERR_NOENT	2	No such file or directory. The file or directory specified does not exist.
NFSERR_IO	5	Some sort of hard error occurred when the operation was in progress—a disk error, for example.
NFSERR_ACCES	13	Permission denied. The caller does not have the correct permission to perform the requested operation.
NFSERR_NOTDIR	20	Is not a directory. The caller specified a nondirectory in a directory operation.
NFSERR_ISDIR	21	Is a directory. The caller specified a directory in a nondirectory operation.
NFSERR_ROFS	30	Read-only filesystem. Write was attempted on a read-only filesystem.
NFSERR_NAMETOOLONG	63	Filename too long. The filename in an operation was too long.
NFSERR_STALE	70	The filehandle given in the arguments was invalid. That is, the file referred to by that filehandle no longer exists, or access to it has been revoked.

Snoop Trace of REMOVE

```
NFS:   Proc = 10 (Remove file)
NFS:   File handle = 0080001800000002000A00000001CE8C
NFS:                 0E1FB8A2000A00000001CE8C0E1FB8A2
NFS:   File name = newfile
```

⇩

```
NFS:   Proc = 10 (Remove file)
NFS:   Status = 0 (OK)
```

6.2.10   Procedure 11: RENAME—Rename File

Description

Procedure RENAME renames the directory entry identified by fromname in the directory fromdir to toname in the directory todir. The operation is required to be atomic to the client; it cannot be interrupted in the middle or leave a partial result on failure. Todir and fromdir must reside on the same filesystem and server.

Arguments		*Results*
fhandle	fromdir;	uint32 status;
filename	fromname;	
fhandle	todir;	
filename	toname;	

Arguments

fromdir

The filehandle for the directory from which the entry is to be renamed.

fromname

The name of the entry that identifies the object to be renamed.

todir

The filehandle for the directory to which the object is to be renamed.

toname

The new name for the object.

If the directory todir already contains an entry with the name toname, the source object must be compatible with the target: either both are nondirectories or both are directories and the target must be empty. If compatible, the existing target is removed before the rename occurs. If they are not compatible or if the target is a directory but not empty, the server should return the error NFSERR_EXIST.

Results

status

NFS_OK if successful, otherwise an error code.

Implementation

The RENAME operation must be atomic to the client. This means that the RENAME operation must not fail in a way that leaves a directory entry in a partially renamed state nor should a client be able to detect any partially renamed state on the server. If the fromdir and todir directories do not reside on the same filesystem (fsid attributes are the same), then the server may return an undetermined error. NFS version 3 servers will return NFS3ERR_XDEV.

A filehandle may or may not become stale on a rename. However, server implementors are strongly encouraged to attempt to keep filehandles from becoming stale in this fashion.

On some servers, the filenames . and .. are illegal as either fromname or toname. In addition, neither fromname nor toname can be an alias for fromdir. If fromdir/fromname and todir/toname both refer to the same file (they might be hard links of each other), then RENAME should perform no action and return NFS_OK.

Errors

NFSERR_NOENT	2	No such file or directory. The file or directory specified does not exist.
NFSERR_IO	5	Some sort of hard error occurred when the operation was in progress—a disk error, for example.
NFSERR_ACCES	13	Permission denied. The caller does not have the correct permission to perform the requested operation.
NFSERR_EXIST	17	File exists. The file specified already exists.
NFSERR_NOTDIR	20	Is not a directory. The caller specified a nondirectory in a directory operation.
NFSERR_ISDIR	21	Is a directory. The caller specified a directory in a nondirectory operation.
NFSERR_NOSPC	28	No space left on device. The operation caused the server's filesystem to reach its limit.
NFSERR_ROFS	30	Read-only filesystem. Write was attempted on a read-only filesystem.
NFSERR_NAMETOOLONG	63	Filename too long. The filename in an operation was too long.
NFSERR_NOTEMPTY	66	Directory not empty. Attempted to remove a directory that was not empty.
NFSERR_DQUOT	69	Disk quota exceeded. The client's disk quota on the server has been exceeded.
NFSERR_STALE	70	The filehandle given in the arguments was invalid. That is, the file referred to by that filehandle no longer exists, or access to it has been revoked.

Snoop Trace of RENAME

```
NFS:  Proc = 11 (Rename)
NFS:  File handle = 00800018000000002000A00000001CE8C
NFS:                0E1FB8A2000A00000001CE8C0E1FB8A2
NFS:  File name = oldname.txt
NFS:  File handle = 00800018000000002000A00000001CE8C
NFS:                0E1FB8A2000A00000001CE8C0E1FB8A2
NFS:  File name = newname.txt

          ⬇

NFS:  Proc = 11 (Rename)
NFS:  Status = 0 (OK)
```

6.2.11   Procedure 12: LINK—Create Link to File

Description

Creates the file `toname` in the directory given by `todir`, which is a hard link to the existing file given by `fromfile`. A hard link should have the property that changes to either of the linked files as reflected in both files. When a hard link is made to a file, the attributes for the file should have a value for `nlink` that is one greater than the value before the link.

Arguments		Results
fhandle	fromfile;	uint32 status;
fhandle	todir;	
filename	toname;	

Arguments

`fromfile`

The filehandle for the existing filesystem object.

`todir`

The filehandle for the directory in which the link is to be created.

`toname`

The name that is to be associated with the created link.

Results

`status`

NFS_OK if successful, otherwise an error code.

Implementation

Changes to any property of the hard-linked files are reflected in all the linked files. When a hard link is made to a file, the attributes for the file should have a value for `nlink` that is one greater than the value before the LINK.

The comments under RENAME regarding object and target residing on the same file system apply here as well. The comments regarding the target name apply as well.

Errors

NFSERR_PERM	1	Not owner. The caller does not have correct ownership to perform the requested operation.
NFSERR_IO	5	Some sort of hard error occurred when the operation was in progress (e.g., could be a disk error).
NFSERR_ACCES	13	Permission denied. The caller does not have the correct permission to perform requested operation.
NFSERR_EXIST	17	File exists. The file specified already exists.
NFSERR_NOTDIR	20	Not a directory. The caller specified a nondirectory in a directory operation.
NFSERR_NOSPC	28	No space left on device. The operation caused the server's filesystem to reach its limit.
NFSERR_ROFS	30	Read-only filesystem. Write was attempted on a read-only filesystem.
NFSERR_NAMETOOLONG	63	Filename too long. The filename in an operation was too long.
NFSERR_DQUOT	69	Disk quota exceeded. The client's disk quota on the server has been exceeded.
NFSERR_STALE	70	The filehandle given in the arguments was invalid. That is, the file referred to by that filehandle no longer exists, or access to it has been revoked.

Snoop Trace of LINK

```
NFS:  Proc = 12 (Link)
NFS:  File handle = 00800018000000002000A00000001CE8F
NFS:                73135A03000A00000001CE8C0E1FB8A2
NFS:  File handle = 00800018000000002000A00000001CE8C
NFS:                0E1FB8A2000A00000001CE8C0E1FB8A2
NFS:  File name = hardlink

NFS:  Proc = 12 (Link)
NFS:  Status = 0 (OK)
```

6.2.12   Procedure 13: SYMLINK—Create Symbolic Link

Description

Creates a new symbolic link.

```
Arguments                        Results
fhandle    fromdir;              uint32 status;
filename   fromname;
path       linktext;
sattr      attributes;
```

Arguments

fromdir

The filehandle for the directory in which the symbolic link is to be created.

fromname

The name that is to be associated with the created symbolic link.

linktext

The string containing the symbolic link data.

attributes

The initial attributes for the symbolic link. On UNIX servers the attributes are never used, since symbolic links always have mode 0777.

Results

status

NFS_OK if successful, otherwise an error code.

Implementation

A symbolic link is a reference to another file. The name given in to is not interpreted by the server; it is only stored in the newly created file. When the client references a file that is a symbolic link, the contents of the symbolic link are normally transparently reinterpreted as a pathname to substitute. A READLINK operation returns the data to the client for interpretation.

For symbolic links, the actual filesystem node and its contents must be created in a single atomic operation. That is, once the symbolic link is visible, there must not be a window where a READLINK would fail or return incorrect data.

Errors

NFSERR_IO	5	Some sort of hard error occurred when the operation was in progress—a disk error, for example.
NFSERR_ACCES	13	Permission denied. The caller does not have the correct permission to perform the requested operation.
NFSERR_EXIST	17	File exists. The file specified already exists.
NFSERR_NOTDIR	20	Not a directory. The caller specified a nondirectory in a directory operation.
NFSERR_NOSPC	28	No space left on device. The operation caused the server's filesystem to reach its limit.
NFSERR_ROFS	30	Read-only filesystem. Write was attempted on a read-only filesystem.

continued

NFSERR_NAMETOOLO NG	63	Filename too long. The filename in an operation was too long.
NFSERR_DQUOT	69	Disk quota exceeded. The client's disk quota on the server has been exceeded.
NFSERR_STALE	70	The filehandle given in the arguments was invalid. That is, the file referred to by that filehandle no longer exists, or access to it has been revoked.

Snoop Trace of SYMLINK

```
NFS:  Proc = 13 (Make symbolic link)
NFS:  File handle = 0080001800000002000A00000001CE8C
NFS:                0E1FB8A2000A00000001CE8C0E1FB8A2
NFS:  File name = symlink
NFS:  Path = pathname
NFS:  Mode = 0777
NFS:   Type = ?
NFS:   Setuid = 0, Setgid = 0, Sticky = 0
NFS:   Owner's permissions = rwx
NFS:   Group's permissions = rwx
NFS:   Other's permissions = rwx
NFS:  UID = -1
NFS:  GID = -1
NFS:  Size = -1
NFS:  Access time        = -1
NFS:  Modification time = -1
```

⬇

```
NFS:  Proc = 13 (Make symbolic link)
NFS:  Status = 0 (OK)
```

6.2.13   Procedure 14: MKDIR—Create Directory

Description

Creates a new directory.

Arguments		*Results*
fhandle dir;		```switch (uint32 status) {```
filename dirname;		``` case NFS_OK = 0:```
sattr attributes;		``` fhandle newdir;```
		``` fattr attributes;```
		``` default:```
		``` void;```
		```}```

Arguments

`dir`

The filehandle for the directory in which the new directory is to be created.

`dirname`

The name that is to be associated with the new directory.

`attributes`

The initial attributes for the new directory.

Results

`status`

NFS_OK if successful, otherwise an error code.

`newdir`

The filehandle for the new directory.

`attributes`

The attributes for the new directory.

Implementation

Many server implementations will not allow the filenames . or .. to be used as targets in a MKDIR operation. In this case, the server should return NFSERR_EXIST.

Errors

NFSERR_IO	5	Some sort of hard error occurred when the operation was in progress—a disk error, for example.
NFSERR_ACCES	13	Permission denied. The caller does not have the correct permission to perform the requested operation.
NFSERR_EXIST	17	File exists. The file specified already exists.
NFSERR_NOTDIR	20	Not a directory. The caller specified a nondirectory in a directory operation.
NFSERR_NOSPC	28	No space left on device. The operation caused the server's filesystem to reach its limit.
NFSERR_ROFS	30	Read-only filesystem. Write was attempted on a read-only filesystem.
NFSERR_NAMETOOLONG	63	Filename too long. The filename in an operation was too long.

continued

NFSERR_DQUOT   69   Disk quota exceeded. The client's disk quota on
                           the server has been exceeded.

NFSERR_STALE   70   The filehandle given in the arguments was in-
                           valid. That is, the file referred to by that filehandle
                           no longer exists, or access to it has been revoked.

Snoop Trace of MKDIR

```
NFS:   Proc = 14 (Make directory)
NFS:   File handle = 00800018000000002000A00000001CE8C
NFS:                 0E1FB8A2000A00000001CE8C0E1FB8A2
NFS:   File name = newdir
NFS:   Mode = 0775
NFS:    Type = ?
NFS:    Setuid = 0, Setgid = 0, Sticky = 0
NFS:    Owner's permissions = rwx
NFS:    Group's permissions = rwx
NFS:    Other's permissions = r-x
NFS:   UID = -1
NFS:   GID = 10
NFS:   Size = -1
NFS:   Access time       = -1
NFS:   Modification time = -1
```

⇩

```
NFS:   Proc = 14 (Make directory)
NFS:   Status = 0 (OK)
NFS:   File handle = 00800018000000002000A00000000D32A
NFS:                 6078F015000A00000001CE8C0E1FB8A2
NFS:   File type = 2 (Directory)
NFS:   Mode = 040775
NFS:    Type = Directory
NFS:    Setuid = 0, Setgid = 0, Sticky = 0
NFS:    Owner's permissions = rwx
NFS:    Group's permissions = rwx
NFS:    Other's permissions = r-x
NFS:   Link count = 2, UID = 3497, GID = 10
NFS:   File size = 512, Block size = 8192, No. of blocks = 2
NFS:   File system id = 8388632, File id = 54058
NFS:   Access time       = 10-Aug-98 18:34:47.510000 GMT
NFS:   Modification time = 10-Aug-98 18:34:47.510000 GMT
NFS:   Inode change time = 10-Aug-98 18:34:47.510000 GMT
```

6.2.14   Procedure 15: RMDIR—Remove Directory

Description

Removes a subdirectory from a directory.

Arguments		*Results*
fhandle	dir;	uint32 status;
filename	dirname;	

Arguments

dir

The filehandle for the directory from which subdirectory is to be removed.

dirname

The name of the subdirectory to be removed.

Results

status

NFS_OK if successful, otherwise an error code.

Implementation

Note that on some servers, removal of a non-empty directory is disallowed. The client should not rely on the resources (disk space, directory entry, and so on) formerly associated with the directory becoming immediately available.

Errors

NFSERR_NOENT	2	No such file or directory. The file or directory specified does not exist.
NFSERR_IO	5	Some sort of hard error occurred when the operation was in progress—a disk error, for example.
NFSERR_ACCES	13	Permission denied. The caller does not have the correct permission to perform the requested operation.
NFSERR_NOTDIR	20	Not a directory. The caller specified a non-directory in a directory operation.
NFSERR_ROFS	30	Read-only filesystem. Write was attempted on a read-only filesystem.
NFSERR_NAMETOOLONG	63	Filename too long. The filename in an operation was too long.
NFSERR_NOTEMPTY	66	Directory not empty. Attempted to remove a directory that was not empty.
NFSERR_STALE	70	The filehandle given in the arguments was invalid. That is, the file referred to by that file handle no longer exists, or access to it has been revoked.

Snoop Trace of RMDIR

```
NFS:  Proc = 15 (Remove directory)
NFS:  File handle = 00800018000000002000A00000001CE8C
NFS:                0E1FB8A2000A00000001CE8C0E1FB8A2
NFS:  File name = newdir
```

⇩

```
NFS:  Proc = 15 (Remove directory)
NFS:  Status = 0 (OK)
```

6.2.15   Procedure 16: READDIR—Read from Directory

Description

Procedure READDIR retrieves a variable number of entries, in sequence, from a directory and returns the name and file identifier for each, with information to allow the client to request additional directory entries in a subsequent READDIR request.

Arguments	*Results*

`fhandle    dir;`
`nfscookie  cookie;`
`uint32     count;`
	`switch (uint32 status) {`
	`    case NFS_OK = 0:`
	`        list {`
	`            uint32     fileid;`
	`            filename   name;`
	`            nfscookie  cookie;`
	`        }`
	`        bool  eof;`
	` `
	`    default:`
	`        void;`
	`}`

Arguments

`dir`

The filehandle for the directory to be read.

`cookie`

This should be set to 0 in the first request to read the directory. On subsequent requests, it should be the cookie as returned by the server from the last entry returned by the previous READDIR call.

`count`

The maximum size of the results in bytes. The size must include all XDR overhead. The server is free to return fewer than count bytes of data.

Results

status

NFS_OK if successful, otherwise an error code.

entries

A list of directory entries consisting of

fileid

The fileid attribute of each entry.

name

The name of the directory entry.

cookie

An opaque reference to the next entry in the directory. The cookie is used in the next READDIR call to get more entries starting at a given point in the directory.

eof

TRUE if the last entry in the list is the last entry in the directory or the list is empty and the cookie corresponded to the end of the directory. If FALSE, there may be more entries to read.

Implementation

A cookie can become invalid if two READDIRs are separated by one or more operations that change the directory in some way (for example, reordering or compressing it). On some servers a rename or unlink operation will invalidate cookie values, for instance if the cookie represents the ordinal value of the directory entry. It is possible that the second or subsequent READDIR could miss entries or process entries more than once. Version 3 adds a *cookie verifier* that allows the client to detect whether the cookie is still valid.

The server may return fewer than count bytes of XDR-encoded entries. The count specified by the client in the request should be greater than or equal to STATFS tsize.

Since UNIX clients give a special meaning to the fileid value zero, UNIX clients should be careful to map zero fileid values to some other value and servers should try to avoid sending a zero fileid.

Errors

NFSERR_NOENT	2	No such file or directory. The file or directory specified does not exist.
NFSERR_IO	5	Some sort of hard error occurred when the operation was in progress—a disk error, for example.

continued

NFSERR_ACCES	13	Permission denied. The caller does not have the correct permission to perform the requested operation.
NFSERR_NOTDIR	20	Not a directory. The caller specified a nondirectory in a directory operation.
NFSERR_STALE	70	The fileandle given in the arguments was invalid. That is, the file referred to by that file handle no longer exists, or access to it has been revoked.

Snoop Trace of READDIR

```
NFS:   Proc = 16 (Read from directory)
NFS:   File handle = 00800018000000002000A00000001EDD7
NFS:                 3834CD03000A00000001CE8C0E1FB8A2
NFS:   Cookie = 0
NFS:   Count = 1048
```

⇩

```
NFS:   Proc = 16 (Read from directory)
NFS:   Status = 0 (OK)
NFS:    File id  Cookie Name
NFS:    126423      12 .
NFS:    118412      24 ..
NFS:    126424      44 index.html
NFS:    126425     512 hostname.pl
NFS:    4 entries
NFS:   EOF = 1
```

6.2.16   Procedure 17: STATFS—Get Filesystem Attributes

Description

Returns the attributes of a filesystem.

Arguments	*Results*

`fhandle    file;`	`switch (uint32 status) {`
	`    case NFS_OK = 0:`
	`        uint32 tsize;`
	`        uint32 bsize;`
	`        uint32 blocks;`
	`        uint32 bfree;`
	`        uint32 bavail;`
	
	`    default:`
	`        void;`
	`}`

Arguments

file

A filehandle that identifies an object within the filesystem.

Results

status

NFS_OK if successful, otherwise an error code.

tsize

The optimum transfer size of the server in bytes. This is the number of bytes the server would like to have in the data part of READ and WRITE requests.

bsize

The block size in bytes of the filesystem.

blocks

The total number of *bsize* blocks on the filesystem.

bfree

The number of free *bsize* blocks on the filesystem.

bavail

The number of *bsize* blocks available to nonprivileged users.

Implementation

Not all implementations can support the entire list of attributes. It is expected that servers will make a best effort at supporting all the attributes. Note: This call does not work well if a filesystem has variable size blocks.

Errors

NFSERR_IO	5	Some sort of hard error occurred when the operation was in progress—a disk error, for example.
NFSERR_STALE	70	The filehandle given in the arguments was invalid. That is, the file referred to by that filehandle no longer exists, or access to it has been revoked.

Snoop Trace of STATFS

```
NFS:  Proc = 17 (Get filesystem attributes)
NFS:  File handle = 0080001800000002000A00000001CE8C
NFS:                  0E1FB8A2000A00000001CE8C0E1FB8A2
```

⇩

```
NFS:  Proc = 17 (Get filesystem attributes)
NFS:  Status = 0 (OK)
NFS:  Transfer size = 8192
NFS:  Block size = 1024
NFS:  Total blocks = 292015
NFS:  Free blocks = 115552
NFS:  Available blocks = 86352
```

Chapter 7

NFS Version 3

Although NFS version 2 has been successfully implemented on many different operating systems and filesystems, its UNIX orientation and simplicity made it difficult or impossible for the protocol to provide complete access to all the features offered by the operating systems on which it was implemented. The NFS engineers at Sun received many requests for protocol enhancements that might be incorporated into a future version of the protocol:

- File versioning
- Record-oriented I/O
- Macintosh file formats
- Extensible file types
- Extended attributes
- and many more . . .

The draft version 3 protocol specification became a "kitchen sink" of features that evolved from one draft to another over several years. Eventually it became clear that in trying to please everybody, the complexity of the protocol precluded any practical implementation. It pleased nobody.

Meanwhile, the need for changes did not relent. Most notable was the need for access to large files. The NFS version 2 protocol allowed only 32-bit unsigned file offsets, which limited accessible file size to 4 GB. Several vendors were upgrading their operating systems to support 64-bit memory addresses and file offsets, and the NFS file offset field needed a corresponding increase; however, this could not be done without creating a new version of the protocol. At the February 1992 Connectathon event in San Jose, a group of NFS vendors met and resolved to empty the kitchen sink and get NFS version 3 on the road with support for 64-bit file offsets and a modest collection of other protocol fixes and improvements. The utility of some of these fixes had been demonstrated already in an NFS variant called NQNFS in the 4.4BSD implementation of NFS (described in section 12.2). NQNFS included 64-bit file offsets, procedures similar to ACCESS and READDIRPLUS, and caching hints similar to version 3 weak cache consistency.

Engineers from Auspex, Inc., Cray Research, Digital Equipment Corporation, Data General, Hewlett Packard, IBM, Legato, Network Appliance, the Open Software Foundation, and Sun Microsystems formed a mailing list and designed the NFS version 3 protocol cooperatively by e-mail. With an agreed goal of completing the design and first implementations of the protocol within a year, guiding principles of the protocol design effort were to keep it simple and throw out any controversial proposals. The effort was low key and described as a "minor rev" consisting of some field extensions (64-bit offsets), protocol "fixes" (remove field overloading), and performance improvements (speed up writes and reduce the number of GETATTR calls). The first protocol draft followed a week-long Boston meeting in July 1992, and the first implementations by Peter Staubach of Sun and Chet Juczcak of Digital were interoperating several months later and tested at Connectathon in 1993.

Much of the text in this section is adapted directly from [RFC 1813].

7.1   Changes from the NFS Version 2 Protocol

As an evolutionary revision of the NFS protocol, NFS version 3 is best understood in relation to NFS version 2. This section describes these changes.

7.1.1   Deleted Procedures

The ROOT and WRITECACHE procedures were removed. These were never described or implemented in the version 2 protocol.

7.1.2   Modified Procedures

LOOKUP

The LOOKUP return structure now includes the attributes for the directory searched.

READ

The reply structure includes a boolean that is TRUE if the end-of-file was encountered during the READ. This allows the client to detect end-of-file correctly.

WRITE

The `beginoffset` and `totalcount` fields were removed from the WRITE arguments. These fields were never described or used by the NFS version 2 protocol. The reply now includes a count so that the server can write less than the requested amount of data, if required. An indicator was added to the arguments to instruct the server as to the level of cache synchronization that is required by the client.

CREATE

An exclusive flag and a create verifier were added for the exclusive creation of regular files. An exclusive create is forced by the O_EXCL flag to the POSIX open() call and requires an error to be returned if the file already exists. Although NFS version 2 clients could approximate the semantic via a LOOKUP call before the CREATE, there was nothing to prevent another client or server process from creating the file between the LOOKUP and the CREATE requests.

READDIR

The READDIR arguments now include a verifier to allow the server to validate the cookie. The cookie is now a 64-bit unsigned integer instead of the 4-byte array that was used in the NFS version 2 protocol. This will help to reduce interoperability problems.

7.1.3 New Procedures

ACCESS

Provides an explicit over-the-wire permissions check, which addresses known problems with the superuser ID mapping feature in many server implementations (where, due to mapping of root user, unexpected permission-denied errors could occur while reading from or writing to a file). ACCESS also provides correct results where file access is controlled by an ACL (access control list). It removes the assumption, which was made in the NFS version 2 protocol, that access to files was controlled by UNIX-style mode bits.

MKNOD

Supports the creation of special files, which avoids overloading fields of CREATE as was done in some NFS version 2 protocol implementations.

READDIRPLUS

Extends the functionality of READDIR by returning not only filenames and file IDs, but also filehandles and attributes for each entry in a directory.

FSINFO

Provides nonvolatile information about a file system. The reply includes preferred and maximum read transfer size, preferred and maximum write transfer size, and flags stating whether hard links or symbolic links are supported. Also returned are preferred transfer size for READDIR procedure replies, server time granularity, and whether times can be set in a SETATTR request.

FSSTAT

Replaces the NFS version 2 STATFS procedure, providing volatile information about a file system for use by utilities such as the UNIX *df* command. The reply includes the total size and free space in the filesystem specified in bytes, the total number of files and number of free file slots in the filesystem, and an estimate of time between filesystem modifications (for use in cache consistency checking algorithms).

PATHCONF

Returns information on filesystem characteristics necessary to support the POSIX *pathconf* call.

COMMIT

Commits buffered data on the server to stable storage. Used in conjunction with the new asynchronous WRITE modes.

7.1.4   Filehandle Size

The NFS version 2 filehandle was a fixed-length opaque array of 32 bytes. Version 3 changed this to a variable length array with an upper limit of 64 bytes. The filehandle was converted from fixed length to variable length to reduce local storage and network bandwidth requirements for systems that do not utilize the full 64 bytes of length.

7.1.5   Maximum Data Sizes

NFS version 2 limited the amount of data that could be transferred in a single READ or WRITE request to 8192 bytes. NFS version 3 sets the maximum size of a data transfer to values in the FSINFO return structure. In addition, preferred transfer sizes are returned by FSINFO. The protocol does not place any artificial limits on the maximum transfer sizes; clients and server can use whatever transfer size is mutually acceptable. Version 2 filenames and pathnames were limited to 255 and 1024 characters. Version 3 specifies these as strings of variable length. The actual length restrictions are determined by the client and server implementations as appropriate. The error NFS3ERR_ NAMETOOLONG is provided to allow the server to return an indication to the client that it received a pathname that was too long for it to handle.

7.1.6   Error Return

Error returns in some instances now return data (for example, postoperation attributes). The `nfsstat3` enumeration now defines the full set of errors that can be returned by a server. No other values are allowed.

7.1.7 File Type

The version 3 file type includes NF3CHR and NF3BLK for special files. Attributes for these types include subfields for UNIX major and minor devices numbers. NF3SOCK and NF3FIFO are now defined for sockets and fifos in the file system.

7.1.8 File Attributes

The `blocksize` (the size in bytes of a block in the file) field was removed and the mode field no longer contains file type information. The `size` and `fileid` fields were widened to 64-bit unsigned integers from 32-bit integers. Major and minor device information is presented in a distinct structure. The `blocks` field name was changed to `used` and contains the total number of bytes used by the file. It is also a 64-bit unsigned integer.

NFS version 2 returned file attributes only for the following seven operations: GETATTR, SETATTR, LOOKUP, READ, WRITE, CREATE, and MKDIR. NFS version 3 returns file attributes in the results of all procedures to preempt the need for the client to make explicit GETATTR calls to update cached attributes. In addition, directory operations like CREATE, MKDIR, MKNOD, LINK and SYMLINK return not only the attributes of the new directory entry but also the attributes of the directory.

NFS version 3 introduced a new subset of the file attributes that are used to implement *weak cache consistency*. This subset, consisting of the file `size`, `mtime`, and `ctime`, can be used by the client to detect any changes in attributes on the server that would have been masked by the client's own request. For instance, when the client creates a new file, it can detect whether the directory was already modified before the server created the client's file. The client can then invalidate any cached directory information.

7.1.9 Set File Attributes

In the NFS version 2 protocol, the settable attributes were represented by a subset of the file attributes structure; the client indicated attributes that were not to be modified by setting the corresponding field to –1, overloading some unsigned fields. The `sattr3` structure uses a discriminated union for each field to tell whether or how to set that field. In addition, the `atime` and `mtime` fields can be set to either the server's current time or a time supplied by the client.

7.1.10 32-Bit Clients/Servers and 64-Bit Clients/Servers

The 64-bit nature of the NFS version 3 protocol introduced several compatibility problems. The most notable emerged from mismatched clients and servers, that is, a 32-bit client and a 64-bit server or a 64-bit client and a 32-bit server.

The problems of a 64-bit client and a 32-bit server are easy to handle. The client will never encounter a file it cannot handle. If it sends a request to the server that the server cannot handle, the server should reject the request with an appropriate error.

The problems of a 32-bit client and a 64-bit server are much harder to handle. In this situation, the server does not have a problem because it can handle anything the client can generate. However, the client may encounter a file it cannot handle. The client will not be able to handle a file whose size cannot be expressed in 32 bits. Thus, the client will not be able to properly decode the size of the file into its local attributes structure. Also, a file can grow beyond the limit of the client while the client is accessing the file.

The solutions to these problems are left up to the individual implementor. However, there are two common approaches used to resolve this situation. The implementor can choose between them or even can invent a new solution altogether. The most common solution is for the client to deny access to any file whose size cannot be expressed in 32 bits. This is probably the safest, but it does introduce some strange semantics when the file grows beyond the limit of the client while it is being accessed by that client. The file becomes inaccessible even while it is being accessed.

The second solution is for the client to map any size greater than it can handle to the maximum size it can handle. Effectively, it is lying to the application program. This allows the application access to as much of the file as possible given the 32-bit offset restriction. This eliminates the strange semantic of the file effectively disappearing after it has been accessed, but it does introduce other problems. The client will not be able to access the entire file. Currently, the first solution is the recommended solution. However, client implementors are encouraged to do the best they can to reduce the effects of this situation.

A different kind of problem exists with the NFS version 3 directory cookies. These cookie values (section 7.3.17) were extended from a 32-bit quantity in NFS version 2 to 64 bits in NFS version 3. Operating systems that use a 32-bit directory offset can run into difficulties if they receive 64-bit cookie values.

7.2   Basic Data Types

This section describes data structures used as arguments and results by the protocol procedures.

7.2.1   Sizes

These are the sizes of various XDR structures used in the following protocol description:

```
const NFS3_FHSIZE = 64;
            /* Max size in bytes of a file handle */

const NFS3_COOKIEVERFSIZE = 8;
            /* Max size in bytes of cookie verifier
             * used by READDIR and READDIRPLUS */

const NFS3_CREATEVERFSIZE = 8;
            /* The size in bytes of the opaque verifier
             * used for exclusive CREATE */

const NFS3_WRITEVERFSIZE = 8;
            /* The size in bytes of the opaque verifier used
             * for asynchronous WRITE */
```

7.2.2 Basic Data Types

The following XDR definitions are basic definitions that are used in other structures.

filename3

```
typedef string<> filename3;
```

Refer to section 5.3.1 for a description of allowable filenames.

nfspath3

```
typedef string<> nfspath3;
```

Pathnames are used only to contain symbolic link text in the procedures SYMLINK and READLINK.

cookieverf3

```
typedef opaque[NFS3_COOKIEVERFSIZE] cookieverf3;
```

A cookie verifier returned in the response to READDIR and READDIRPLUS calls to verify that the cookie is still valid (sections 7.3.17 and 7.3.18).

createverf3

```
typedef opaque[NFS3_CREATEVERFSIZE] createverf3;
```

An opaque verifier supplied by the client and checked by the server to support exclusive CREATE semantics (section 7.3.9).

writeverf3

```
typedef opaque[NFS3_WRITEVERFSIZE] writeverf3;
```

A verifier provided by the server that allows the client to check whether the server has rebooted and lost pending asynchronous writes (section 7.3.8).

nfsstat3

```
enum nfsstat3 {
    NFS3_OK              = 0,      /* Successful call */
    NFS3ERR_PERM         = 1,      /* Not owner */
    NFS3ERR_NOENT        = 2,      /* No such file or directory */
    NFS3ERR_IO           = 5,      /* I/O Error */
    NFS3ERR_NXIO         = 6,      /* I/O Error - no such device */
    NFS3ERR_ACCES        = 13,     /* Permission denied */
    NFS3ERR_EXIST        = 17,     /* File already exists */
    NFS3ERR_XDEV         = 18,     /* Invalid cross device link */
    NFS3ERR_NODEV        = 19,     /* No such device */
    NFS3ERR_NOTDIR       = 20,     /* Not a directory */
    NFS3ERR_ISDIR        = 21,     /* Is a directory */
    NFS3ERR_INVAL        = 22,     /* Invalid argument */
    NFS3ERR_FBIG         = 27,     /* File too big */
    NFS3ERR_NOSPC        = 28,     /* No space left on device */
    NFS3ERR_ROFS         = 30,     /* Read-only filesystem */
    NFS3ERR_MLINK        = 31,     /* Too many hard links */
    NFS3ERR_NAMETOOLONG  = 63,     /* Filename is too long */
    NFS3ERR_NOTEMPTY     = 66,     /* Directory is not empty */
    NFS3ERR_DQUOT        = 69,     /* Resource quota exceeded */
    NFS3ERR_STALE        = 70,     /* Invalid filehandle */
    NFS3ERR_REMOTE       = 71,     /* Filehandle not server local */
    NFS3ERR_BADHANDLE    = 10001,  /* Illegal filehandle */
    NFS3ERR_NOT_SYNC     = 10002,  /* Setattr update problem */
    NFS3ERR_BAD_COOKIE   = 10003,  /* Bad readdir cookie */
    NFS3ERR_NOTSUPP      = 10004,  /* Operation not supported */
    NFS3ERR_TOOSMALL     = 10005,  /* Buffer is too small */
    NFS3ERR_SERVERFAULT  = 10006,  /* Unknown server error */
    NFS3ERR_BADTYPE      = 10007,  /* Invalid filetype */
    NFS3ERR_JUKEBOX      = 10008   /* Server operation pending */
}
```

The nfsstat3 type is returned with every procedure's results except for the NULL procedure. A value of NFS3_OK indicates that the call completed successfully. Any other value indicates that some error occurred on the call, as identified by the error code. Note that the precise numeric encoding must be followed. No other values may be returned by a server. Servers are expected to make a best effort mapping of error conditions to the set of error codes defined. In addition, no error precedences are specified. Error precedences determine the error value that should be returned when more than one error applies in a given situation. The error precedence will be determined by the individual server implementation. If the client requires specific error precedences, it should check for the specific errors for itself. A description of each defined error appears in Table 7.1.

TABLE 7.1 NFS Version 3 Errors

Error name	Value	Meaning
NFS3_OK	0	Indicates that the call completed successfully.
NFS3ERR_PERM	1	Not owner. The operation was not allowed because the caller is either not a privileged user (root) or not the owner of the target of the operation.
NFS3ERR_NOENT	2	No such file or directory. The file or directory name specified does not exist.
NFS3ERR_IO	5	I/O error. A hard error (for example, a disk error) occurred while processing the requested operation.
NFS3ERR_NXIO	6	I/O error. No such device or address.
NFS3ERR_ACCES	13	Permission denied. The caller does not have the correct permission to perform the requested operation. Contrast this with NFS3ERR_PERM, which restricts itself to owner or privileged user permission failures.
NFS3ERR_EXIST	17	File exists. The file specified already exists.
NFS3ERR_XDEV	18	Attempt to do a cross-device hard link.
NFS3ERR_NODEV	19	No such device.
NFS3ERR_NOTDIR	20	Not a directory. The caller specified a nondirectory in a directory operation.
NFS3ERR_ISDIR	21	Is a directory. The caller specified a directory in a nondirectory operation.
NFS3ERR_INVAL	22	Invalid argument or unsupported argument for an operation. Two examples are attempting a READLINK on an object other than a symbolic link and attempting to SETATTR a time field on a server that does not support this operation.
NFS3ERR_FBIG	27	File too large. The operation would have caused a file to grow beyond the server's limit.
NFS3ERR_NOSPC	28	No space left on device. The operation would have caused the server's filesystem to exceed its limit.
NFS3ERR_ROFS	30	Read-only filesystem. A modifying operation was attempted on a read-only filesystem.
NFS3ERR_MLINK	31	Too many hard links.
NFS3ERR_NAMETOOLONG	63	The filename in an operation was too long.
NFS3ERR_NOTEMPTY	66	An attempt was made to remove a directory that was not empty.
NFS3ERR_DQUOT	69	Resource (quota) hard limit exceeded. The user's resource limit on the server has been exceeded.

continued

TABLE 7.1 NFS Version 3 Errors

Error name	Value	Meaning
NFS3ERR_STALE	70	Invalid filehandle. The filehandle given in the arguments was invalid. The file referred to by that filehandle no longer exists, or access to it has been revoked.
NFS3ERR_REMOTE	71	Too many levels of remote in path. The file handle given in the arguments referred to a file on a nonlocal file system on the server.
NFS3ERR_BADHANDLE	10001	Illegal NFS filehandle. The filehandle failed internal consistency checks.
NFS3ERR_NOT_SYNC	10002	Update synchronization mismatch was detected during a SETATTR operation.
NFS3ERR_BAD_COOKIE	10003	READDIR or READDIRPLUS cookie is stale.
NFS3ERR_NOTSUPP	10004	Operation is not supported.
NFS3ERR_TOOSMALL	10005	Buffer or request is too small.
NFS3ERR_SERVERFAULT	10006	An error occurred on the server that does not map to any legal NFS version 3 protocol error values. Client should translate this into an appropriate error. UNIX clients may choose to translate this to EIO.
NFS3ERR_BADTYPE	10007	An attempt was made to create an object of a type not supported by the server.
NFS3ERR_JUKEBOX	10008	Server initiated the request but was not able to complete it in a timely fashion. Client should wait and then try the request with a new RPC transaction ID. For example, this error should be returned from a server that supports hierarchical storage and receives a request to process a file that has been migrated. In this case, server should start the immigration process and respond to client with this error.

ftype3

The enumeration ftype3 gives the type of a file. The type NF3REG is a regular file, NF3DIR is a directory, and NF3LNK is a symbolic link.

The remaining types are special types intended for use by diskless UNIX clients. NF3BLK is a block special device, NF3CHR is a character special device, NF3SOCK is a UNIX domain socket, and NF3FIFO is a named pipe. While there are no procedures within the NFS protocol that operate on these special objects directly, the protocol does allow these objects to be created via the MKNOD procedure (section 7.3.12).

```
enum ftype3 {
    NF3REG= 1,     /* Regular file */
    NF3DIR= 2,     /* Directory */
    NF3BLK= 3,     /* Block special device */
    NF3CHR= 4,     /* Character special device */
    NF3LNK= 5,     /* Symbolic link */
    NF3SOCK= 6,    /* Socket */
    NF3FIFO= 7     /* Named pipe */
}
```

specdata3

```
struct specdata3 {
    uint32  specdata1;
    uint32  specdata2;
}
```

The interpretation of the specdata fields depends on the type of filesystem object. For a block special (NF3BLK) or character special (NF3CHR) file, specdata1 and specdata2 are the major and minor device numbers, respectively (this is obviously a UNIX-specific interpretation). For all other file types, these two elements should either be set to 0 or the values should be agreed on by the client and server. If the client and server do not agree on the values, the client should treat these fields as if they are set to 0. This data field is returned as part of the fattr3 structure and so is available from all replies returning attributes. Since these fields are otherwise unused for objects that are not devices, out-of-band information can be passed from the server to the client. However, once again, both the server and the client must agree on the values passed.

nfs_fh3

```
struct nfs_fh3 {
    opaque<NFS3_FHSIZE>data;
}
```

The nfs_fh3 filehandle is the variable-length opaque object that is returned by the server on LOOKUP, CREATE, MKDIR, SYMLINK, MKNOD, LINK, or READDIRPLUS operations, which is used by the client on subsequent operations to reference a filesystem object such as a file or directory. The filehandle contains all the information the server needs to distinguish an individual file. To the client, the filehandle is opaque. The client stores filehandles for use in a later request and can compare two filehandles from the same server for equal-ity by doing a byte-by-byte comparison but cannot otherwise interpret the contents of filehandles. If two filehandles from the same server are equal, they must refer to the same file, but if they are not equal, no conclusions can be drawn. Servers should try to maintain a one-to-one correspondence between filehandles and files, but this is not required. Clients should use filehandle comparisons only to improve performance, not for correct behavior.

Servers can revoke the access provided by a filehandle at any time. If the filehandle passed in a call refers to a filesystem object that no longer exists on the server or access for that filehandle has been revoked, the error NFS3ERR_STALE should be returned.

WebNFS clients and servers recognize a public filehandle as one that has zero length (see section 16.4).

nfstime3

The nfstime3 structure gives the number of seconds and nanoseconds since midnight, Greenwich Mean Time, January 1, 1970. It is used to pass time and date information.

```
struct nfstime3 {
    uint32  seconds;     /* Time in sec since midnight 1/1/70 */
    uint32  nseconds;    /* Fractional nanoseconds */
}
```

Since negative values are not permitted, it cannot be used to refer to files older than 1970. The times associated with files are all server times except in the case of a SETATTR operation where the client can explicitly set the file time. A server converts to and from local time when processing time values, preserv-ing as much accuracy as possible.

fattr3

The file attribute structure defines the attributes of a filesystem object (Table 7.2). It is returned by most operations on an object; in the case of operations that affect two objects (for example, a MKDIR that modifies the target direc-tory attributes and defines new attributes for the newly created directory), the attributes for both are returned.

```
struct fattr3 {
    ftype3      type;    /* The file type */
    uint32      mode;    /* File permission bits */
    uint32      nlink;   /* Number of hard links */
    uint32      uid;     /* File user ID (owner) */
    uint32      gid;     /* File group ID */
    uint64      size;    /* File size in bytes */
    uint64      used;    /* Disk space used */
```

```
        specdata3      rdev;    /* File device information */
        uint64         fsid;    /* Filesystem identifier */
        uint64         fileid;  /* File number within filesystem */
        nfstime3       atime;   /* Last access time */
        nfstime3       mtime;   /* Last modify time */
        nfstime3       ctime;   /* Last attribute change time */
    }
```

TABLE 7.2 `fattr3` File Attributes

Attribute	Description
type	Type of the file
mode	Protection mode bits (see Table 7.3)
nlink	Number of hard links to file—that is, number of different names for same file
uid	User ID of the owner of the file
gid	Group ID of the group of the file
size	Size of the file in bytes
used	Number of bytes of disk space that the file actually uses (which can be smaller than the `size` because the file may have holes or it may be larger due to fragmentation)
rdev	Identifies the device file if the file type is NF3CHR or NF3BLK (see `specdata3` on page 141)
fsid	Filesystem identifier for the filesystem
fileid	Number that uniquely identifies the file within its filesystem (on UNIX this would be the inode number)
atime	The time when the file data were last accessed
mtime	The time when the file data were last modified
ctime	The time when the attributes of the file were last changed. Writing to the file changes the `ctime` in addition to the `mtime`.

In some cases, the attributes are returned in the structure `wcc_data`, which is defined later; in other cases the attributes are returned alone. The main changes from the NFS version 2 protocol are that many of the fields have been widened and the major/minor device information is now presented in a distinct structure rather than being packed into a 32-bit field. All servers should support this set of attributes even if they have to simulate some of the fields. The mode bits are defined in Table 7.3.

post_op_attr

This structure is used for returning attributes in operations that are not directly involved with manipulating attributes. One of the principles of the

TABLE 7.3 `fattr3` Structure Access Modes

Mode Bit (octal)	Description
0004000	Set user ID on execution.
0002000	Set group ID on execution.
0001000	On directories, restricted deletion flag. On regular files, do-not-cache flag (not defined in POSIX).
0000400	Read permission for owner.
0000200	Write permission for owner.
0000100	Execute permission for owner on a file. Or lookup (search) permission for owner in directory.
0000040	Read permission for group.
0000020	Write permission for group.
0000010	Execute permission for group on a file. Or lookup (search) permission for group in directory.
0000004	Read permission for others.
0000002	Write permission for others.
0000001	Execute permission for others on a file. Or lookup (search) permission for others in directory.

NFS version 3 protocol is to return the real value from the indicated operation and not an error from an incidental operation. The `post_op_attr` structure was designed to allow the server to recover from errors encountered while getting attributes.

```
union post_op_attr switch (boolean) {
    case TRUE:
        fattr3  attributes;
    case FALSE:
        void;
}
```

This structure appears to make returning attributes optional. However, server implementors are strongly encouraged to make their best effort to return attributes whenever possible, even when returning an error. In returning attributes in the results of all version 3 procedures, the protocol provides clients with a frequent supply of fresh attributes, precluding the need for additional GETATTR requests to restore stale, cached attributes.

pre_op_attr

This is the subset of preoperation attributes needed to better support the weak cache consistency semantics.

```
union pre_op_attr switch (boolean) {
    case TRUE:
        uint64      size;  /* File size in bytes */
        nfstime3    mtime; /* File modification time */
        nfstime3    ctime; /* Attribute modification time */
    case FALSE:
        void;
}
```

The `size` is the file size in bytes of the object before the operation; `mtime` is the time of last modification of the object before the operation; `ctime` is the time of last change to the attributes of the object before the operation.

The use of `mtime` by clients to detect changes to filesystem objects residing on a server is dependent on the granularity of the time base on the server.

wcc_data

When a client performs an operation that modifies the state of a file or directory on the server, it cannot immediately determine from the postoperation attributes whether the operation just performed was the only operation on the object since the last time the client received the attributes for the object. This is important, since if an intervening operation has changed the object, the client will need to invalidate any cached data for the object (except for the data that it just wrote).

To deal with this, the notion of weak cache consistency data or `wcc_data` is introduced. A `wcc_data` structure consists of certain key fields from the object attributes before the operation, together with the object attributes after the operation. This information allows the client to manage its cache more accurately than in NFS version 2 protocol implementations. The term *weak cache consistency* emphasizes the fact that this mechanism does not provide the strict server-client consistency that a strong cache consistency protocol would provide.

```
struct wcc_data {
    pre_op_attr     before;
    post_op_attr    after;
}
```

To support the weak cache consistency model, the server needs to be able to get the preoperation attributes of the object, perform the intended modify operation, and then get the postoperation attributes *atomically*. If there is a window for the object to be modified between the operation and either of the get attributes operations, then the client will not be able to determine whether it was the only entity to modify the object. Some information will have been lost, thus weakening the weak cache consistency guarantees.

For those procedures that return either `post_op_attr` or `wcc_data` structures on failure, the discriminated union may contain the preoperation attributes of the object or object parent directory. This depends on the error encountered and may also depend on the particular server implementation. Implementors are strongly encouraged to return as much attribute data as possible on failure, but client implementors need to be aware that their implementation must correctly handle the variant return instance where no attributes or consistency data is returned.

post_op_fh3

The `post_op_fh3` structure is designed to allow the server to recover from errors encountered while constructing a file handle.

```
union post_op_fh3 switch (boolean) {
    case TRUE:
        nfs_fh3  handle;
    case FALSE:
        void;
}
```

This is the structure used to return a filehandle from the CREATE, MKDIR, SYMLINK, MKNOD, and READDIRPLUS requests. In each case, the client can get the file handle by issuing a LOOKUP request after a successful return from one of the listed operations. Returning the filehandle is an optimization so that the client is not forced to immediately issue a LOOKUP request to get the filehandle.

sattr3

The `sattr3` structure contains the file attributes that can be set from the client. The fields are the same as the similarly named fields in the `fattr3` structure. In the NFS version 3 protocol, the settable attributes are described by a structure containing a set of discriminated unions. Each union indicates whether the corresponding attribute is to be updated, and if so, how.

```
struct sattr3 {
    switch (boolean) {
        case TRUE:
            uint32  mode;
        case FALSE:
            void;
    };
```

```
            switch (boolean) {
                case TRUE:
                    uint32  uid;
                case FALSE:
                    void;
            };
            switch (boolean) {
                case TRUE:
                    uint32  gid;
                case FALSE:
                    void;
            };
            switch (boolean) {
                case TRUE:
                    uint64  size;
                case FALSE:
                    void;
            };
            switch (uint32) {
                case DONT_CHANGE      = 0:
                case SET_TO_SERVER_TIME = 1:
                    void;
                case SET_TO_CLIENT_TIME = 2:
                    nfstime3  atime;
            };
            switch (uint32) {
                case DONT_CHANGE      = 0:
                case SET_TO_SERVER_TIME = 1:
                    void;
                case SET_TO_CLIENT_TIME = 2:
                    nfstime3 mtime;
            }
        }
```

There are two forms of discriminated unions used. In setting the mode, uid, gid, or size, the discriminated union is switched on a boolean, set_it; if it is TRUE, a value of the appropriate type is then encoded.

In setting the atime or mtime, the union is switched on an enumeration type, set_it. If set_it has the value DONT_CHANGE, the corresponding attribute is unchanged. If it has the value SET_TO_SERVER_TIME, the corresponding attribute is set by the server to its local time; no data is provided by the client. Finally, if set_it has the value SET_TO_CLIENT_TIME, the attribute is set to the time passed by the client in an nfstime3 structure.

7.3 Server Procedures

The following sections define the RPC procedures that are supplied by an NFS version 3 protocol server (Table 7.4). The RPC procedure number and name head each section. The **Description** part details the XDR format of the procedure arguments and results and tells what the procedure is expected to do and how its arguments and results are used. The **Implementation** part gives information about how the procedure is expected to work and how it should be used by clients. The **Errors** part lists the errors returned for specific types of failures. These lists are intended not as the definitive statement of all of the errors that can be returned by any specific procedure but as a guide for the more common errors that may be returned. Client implementations should be prepared to deal with unexpected errors coming from a server. Finally, a **Snoop Trace** of the procedure shows a typical call and response.

TABLE 7.4 Summary of NFS Version 3 Procedures

Number	Name	Description	Section
0	NFSPROC3_NULL	Null procedure	7.3.1, page 149
1	NFSPROC3_GETATTR	Get file attributes	7.3.2, page 149
2	NFSPROC3_SETATTR	Set file attributes	7.3.3, page 151
3	NFSPROC3_LOOKUP	Look up filename	7.3.4, page 155
4	NFSPROC3_ACCESS	Check access permission	7.3.5, page 158
5	NFSPROC3_READLINK	Read from symbolic link	7.3.6, page 162
6	NFSPROC3_READ	Read from file	7.3.7, page 164
7	NFSPROC3_WRITE	Write to file	7.3.8, page 168
8	NFSPROC3_CREATE	Create file	7.3.9, page 174
9	NFSPROC3_MKDIR	Create directory	7.3.10, page 179
10	NFSPROC3_SYMLINK	Create symbolic link	7.3.11, page 182
11	NFSPROC3_MKNOD	Create a special device	7.3.12, page 186
12	NFSPROC3_REMOVE	Remove file	7.3.13, page 190
13	NFSPROC3_RMDIR	Remove directory	7.3.14, page 192
14	NFSPROC3_RENAME	Rename file or directory	7.3.15, page 195
15	NFSPROC3_LINK	Create link to file	7.3.16, page 199
16	NFSPROC3_READDIR	Read directory	7.3.17, page 202
17	NFSPROC3_READDIRPLUS	Extended read from directory	7.3.18, page 205
18	NFSPROC3_FSSTAT	Get file systems attributes	7.3.19, page 212
19	NFSPROC3_FSINFO	Get static file system information	7.3.20, page 214
20	NFSPROC3_PATHCONF	Retrieve POSIX information	7.3.21, page 218
21	NFSPROC3_COMMIT	Commit cached data on a server to stable storage	7.3.22, page 221

7.3.1 Procedure 0: NULL—Do Nothing

Description

Although the null procedure does nothing, it is useful for testing the availability and responsiveness of the server. It is also used to establish a security context by RPCSEC_GSS security (see section 4.7).

Arguments	*Results*
void	void

Arguments

None

Results

None

Implementation

It is important that this procedure do no work at all so that it can be used to measure the overhead of processing a service request. By convention, the null procedure should never require any authentication. A server may choose to ignore this convention, in a more secure implementation, where responding to the NULL procedure call acknowledges the existence of a resource to an unauthenticated client. The NULL procedure call is most commonly used to establish whether the NFS service is available and responding.

  The null procedure is also used to establish an RPCSEC_GSS security context. Security information is exchanged as arguments and results on the NULL procedure call. For more information see section 4.7.2.

Errors

Since the null procedure takes no arguments and returns nothing, it cannot return an error except where it is used to establish an RPCSEC_GSS context.

7.3.2 Procedure 1: GETATTR—Get File Attributes

Description

GETATTR retrieves the attributes for a specified filesystem object.

Arguments	*Results*

nfs_fh3 object;	switch (nfsstat3 status) {
	    case NFS3_OK = 0:
	        fattr3 obj_attr;
	    default:
	        void;
	}

Arguments

`object`

The filehandle of an object for which the attributes are to be retrieved.

Results

`status`

NFS3_OK if successful, otherwise an error code.

`obj_attr`

The attributes for the object. The `fattr3` attribute structure was described before.

Implementation

The attributes of filesystem objects are a point of major disagreement between different operating systems. Servers should make a best attempt to support all the attributes in the `fattr3` structure so that clients can count on it as common ground. Some mapping may be required to map local attributes to those in the `fattr3` structure.

Since almost all the NFS version 3 procedures return file attributes that are used to update cached attributes, GETATTR operations are not common from version 3 clients. Generally, a client will issue a GETATTR request when opening a file that is already cached to guarantee close-to-open cache consistency (section 8.14.2).

Errors

NFS3ERR_IO	5	I/O error. A hard error (for example, a disk error) occurred while processing the requested operation.
NFS3ERR_STALE	70	Invalid filehandle. The filehandle given in the arguments was invalid. The file referred to by that filehandle no longer exists, or access to it has been revoked.
NFS3ERR_BADHANDLE	10001	Illegal NFS filehandle. The filehandle failed internal consistency checks.
NFS3ERR_SERVERFAULT	10006	An error occurred on the server that does not map to any of the legal NFS version 3 protocol error values. The client should translate this into an appropriate error. UNIX clients may choose to translate this to EIO.

Snoop Trace of GETATTR

```
NFS:  Proc = 1 (Get file attributes)
NFS:  File handle = 0080000180000000002000A00000000DD0A
NFS:                    50295369000A00000000DD0A50295369
```

$$\Downarrow$$

```
NFS:  Proc = 1 (Get file attributes)
NFS:  Status = 0 (OK)
NFS:    File type = 2 (Directory)
NFS:    Mode = 0777
NFS:     Setuid = 0, Setgid = 0, Sticky = 0
NFS:     Owner's permissions = rwx
NFS:     Group's permissions = rwx
NFS:     Other's permissions = rwx
NFS:    Link count = 3, User ID = 0, Group ID = 3
NFS:    File size = 512, Used = 1024
NFS:    Special: Major = 0, Minor = 0
NFS:    File system id = 8388632, File id = 56586
NFS:    Last access time    = 11-Jul-98 10:15:00.835416000 GMT
NFS:    Modification time   = 24-Apr-98 03:55:41.840716000 GMT
NFS:    Attribute change time = 24-Apr-98 03:55:41.840716000 GMT
```

7.3.3 Procedure 2: SETATTR—Set File Attributes

Description

Procedure SETATTR changes one or more of the attributes of a file system object on the server. The new attributes are specified by a sattr3 structure.

Arguments	Results

`nfs_fh3   obj_fh;`
`sattr3    new_attr;`
`switch (boolean check) {`
`  case TRUE:`
`    nfstime3 obj_ctime;`
`  case FALSE:`
`    void;`
`}`
	`nfsstat3   status;`
	`wcc_data   obj_wcc;`

Arguments

`obj_fh`

The filehandle for the object.

`new_attr`

A sattr3 structure (described earlier) containing booleans and enumerations describing the attributes to be set and the new values for those attributes.

check

> TRUE if the server is to verify that obj_ctime matches the ctime for the object.
>
> A client may request that the server check that the object is in an expected state before performing the SETATTR operation. To do this, it sets the argument check to TRUE and the client passes a time value in obj_ctime. If check is TRUE, the server must compare the value of obj_ctime to the current ctime of the object. If the values are different, the server must preserve the object attributes and must return a status of NFS3ERR_NOT_SYNC. If check is FALSE, the server will not perform this check.

Results

obj_wcc

> A wcc_data structure containing the old and new attributes for the object.

Implementation

The check mechanism allows the client to avoid changing the attributes of an object on the basis of stale attributes. It does not guarantee exactly-once semantics. In particular, if a reply is lost and the server does not detect the retransmission of the request, the procedure can fail with the error NFS3ERR_NOT_SYNC, even though the attribute setting was previously performed successfully. The client can attempt to recover from this error by getting fresh attributes from the server and sending a new SETATTR request using the new ctime. The client can optionally check the attributes to avoid the second SETATTR request if the new attributes show that the attributes have already been set as desired (though it may not have been the issuing client that set the attributes).

The new_attr.size field is used to request changes to the size of a file. A value of 0 causes the file to be truncated, a value less than the current size of the file causes data from new size to the end of the file to be discarded, and a size greater than the current size of the file causes logically zeroed data bytes to be added to the end of the file. Servers are free to implement this size change using holes or actual zero data bytes. Clients should not make any assumptions regarding a server's implementation of this feature, other than the added bytes being zeroed.[1]

SETATTR is not guaranteed atomic. A failed SETATTR may partially change a file's attributes. Changing the size of a file with SETATTR indirectly

---

1. Although servers are expected to support extending the file size this way, experience indicates that some do not.

changes the mtime. A client must account for this, as size changes can result in data deletion. If server and client times differ, programs that compare client time to file times can break. A time maintenance protocol should be used to limit client/server time skew. In a heterogeneous environment, it is quite possible that the server will not be able to support the full range of SETATTR requests. The error NFS3ERR_INVAL may be returned if the server cannot store a uid or gid in its own representation of uids or gids, respectively. If the server can support only 32-bit offsets and sizes, a SETATTR request to set the size of a file to larger than can be represented in 32 bits will be rejected with this same error.

UNIX clients will restrict change of file ownership (uid) to the superuser or the current owner of the file. The client may apply further restrictions to prevent a user from "giving away" a file or changing its group (gid) if "restricted chown" semantics apply (see chown_restricted in section 7.3.21). If the file ownership or group is changed, then the client will probably reset the setuid and setgid bits in the file mode attribute to avoid any security problems.

To change either the atime or mtime of a file on a UNIX server, the request must come from either the owner of the file or the superuser (UID 0), or the client must have write permission on the file.

The client should take care to flush any cached writes to the server before setting the size to preserve the correct ordering of operations. Some servers may refuse to increase the size of the file through a change in the size field and return no error. The client can work around this problem by unconditionally writing a byte of data at the maximum offset.

Errors

NFS3ERR_PERM	1	Not owner. The operation was not allowed because the caller is either not a privileged user (root) or not the owner of the target of the operation.
NFS3ERR_IO	5	I/O error. A hard error (for example, a disk error) occurred while processing the requested operation.
NFS3ERR_ACCES	13	Permission denied. The caller does not have the correct permission to perform the requested operation. Contrast this with NFS3ERR_PERM, which restricts itself to owner or privileged-user permission failures.
NFS3ERR_INVAL	22	Invalid argument or unsupported argument for an operation.
NFS3ERR_NOSPC	28	No space left on device. The operation would have caused the server's file system to exceed its limit.

continued

NFS3ERR_ROFS	30	Read-only filesystem. A modifying operation was attempted on a read-only filesystem.
NFS3ERR_DQUOT	69	Resource (quota) hard limit exceeded. The user's resource limit on the server has been exceeded.
NFS3ERR_STALE	70	Invalid filehandle. The filehandle given in the arguments was invalid. The file referred to by that filehandle no longer exists, or access to it has been revoked.
NFS3ERR_BADHANDLE	10001	Illegal NFS filehandle. The filehandle failed internal consistency checks.
NFS3ERR_NOT_SYNC	10002	Update synchronization mismatch was detected during a SETATTR operation.
NFS3ERR_SERVERFAULT	10006	An error occurred on the server that does not map to any of the legal NFS version 3 protocol error values. The client should translate this into an appropriate error. UNIX clients may choose to translate this to EIO.

Snoop Trace of SETATTR

```
NFS:  Proc = 2 (Set file attributes)
NFS:  File handle = 0080001800000002000A000000011183
NFS:                5511F045000A00000000DD0A50295369
NFS:    Mode = 0666
NFS:      Setuid = 0, Setgid = 0, Sticky = 0
NFS:      Owner's permissions = rw-
NFS:      Group's permissions = rw-
NFS:      Other's permissions = rw-
NFS:  User ID = (not set)
NFS:  Group ID = (not set)
NFS:  Size = (not set)
NFS:  Access time = (do not set)
NFS:  Modification time = (do not set)

              ⇩

NFS:  Proc = 2 (Set file attributes)
NFS:  Status = 0 (OK)
NFS:  Pre-operation attributes:
NFS:    Size = 3499 bytes
NFS:    Modification time     = 12-Jul-98 00:59:11.051125000 GMT
NFS:    Attribute change time = 12-Jul-98 00:59:11.051125000 GMT
NFS:
NFS:  Post-operation attributes:
NFS:    File type = 1 (Regular File)
NFS:    Mode = 0666
NFS:      Setuid = 0, Setgid = 0, Sticky = 0
```

```
NFS:      Owner's permissions = rw-
NFS:      Group's permissions = rw-
NFS:      Other's permissions = rw-
NFS:      Link count = 1, User ID = 3497, Group ID = 10
NFS:      File size = 3499, Used = 4096
NFS:      Special: Major = 0, Minor = 0
NFS:      File system id = 8388632, File id = 70019
NFS:      Last access time    = 12-Jul-98 00:59:09.091125000 GMT
NFS:      Modification time   = 12-Jul-98 00:59:11.051125000 GMT
NFS:      Attribute change time = 12-Jul-98 00:59:11.071125000 GMT
```

7.3.4   Procedure 3: LOOKUP—Look Up Filename

Description

Procedure LOOKUP searches a directory for a specific name and returns the filehandle for the corresponding filesystem object.

Arguments	*Results*
`nfs_fh3    dir;` `filename3  name;`	```switch (nfsstat3 status) {` ` case NFS3_OK = 0:` ` nfs_fh3 obj_fh;` ` post_op_attr obj_attr;` ` post_op_attr dir_attr;` ` default:` ` post_op_attr dir_attr;` `}```

Arguments

`dir`

The filehandle for the directory to search.

`name`

The filename to find.

Results

`status`

NFS3_OK if successful, otherwise an error code.

`obj_fh`

The filehandle of the object corresponding to `name`.

`obj_attr`

The postoperation attributes of the object corresponding to `name`.

`dir_attr`

The postoperation attributes of the directory `dir`.

Results on Failure

status

  Error code.

dir_attr

  The postoperation attributes for the directory di r.

Implementation

At first glance, in the case where name refers to a mountpoint on the server, two different replies seem possible. The server can return either the filehandle for the underlying directory it is mounted on or the filehandle of the root of the mounted directory. This ambiguity is simply resolved. A server will not allow a LOOKUP operation to cross a mountpoint to the root of a different filesystem, even if the filesystem is exported. This does not prevent a client from accessing a hierarchy of filesystems exported by a server, but the client must mount each of the filesystems individually so that the mountpoint crossing takes place on the client. A given server implementation may refine these rules given capabilities or limitations particular to that implementation. See section 5.3.2 for further description of pathname evaluation and section 8.5 for a discussion of mountpoint crossing issues.

    Two filenames are distinguished, as in the NFS version 2 protocol. The name . is an alias for the current directory and the name .. is an alias for the parent directory, that is, the directory that includes the specified directory as a member. There is no facility for dealing with a multiparented directory, and the NFS filesystem model assumes a hierarchy organized as a single-rooted tree. Note that this procedure does not follow symbolic links on the server. The client is responsible for all parsing of filenames, including filenames that are modified by symbolic links encountered during the lookup process.

    Normally, the filename is a single pathname component, but if a public filehandle is used, then the filename may contain an entire pathname. For more details of WebNFS lookups, see section 16.5.

    UNIX clients cache the results of previous LOOKUP operations in a directory name lookup cache (DNLC). Cache entries are addressed by the filehandle of the directory and the name to be looked up. If the cache entry exists, then the client can obtain the required filehandle and file attributes from the cache. The DNLC cache is very effective; hit rates above 90 percent are typical. The client must take some care to keep the DNLC cache consistent; for instance, if the client detects that a directory has changed on the server, then it must purge any entries from the cache for that directory. Similarly, if the client removes or renames a directory entry, then it must update the cache accordingly. The DNLC does not do any *negative* caching. If the client frequently looks up a name that does not exist, as is common when a UNIX client is searching a sequence of directories in a PATH, then it can benefit from a negative cache that precludes unproductive LOOKUPs. One way to implement negative caching is to cache all the names in a directory. If the required name does not exist in the cached directory, then it can be assumed not to exist. Alternatively, the client could record the results of negative LOOKUPs in the DNLC. To maintain some reasonable level of consistency with the server's directory, the cached directory validity must be time-bounded and verified with a GETATTR request to the server to check that the server's directory has not changed.

Errors

NFS3ERR_NOENT	2	No such file or directory. The file or directory name specified does not exist.
NFS3ERR_IO	5	I/O error. A hard error (for example, a disk error) occurred while processing the requested operation.
NFS3ERR_ACCES	13	Permission denied. The caller does not have the correct permission to perform the requested operation. Contrast this with NFS3ERR_PERM, which restricts itself to owner or privileged-user permission failures.
NFS3ERR_NOTDIR	20	Not a directory. The caller specified a non-directory in a directory operation.
NFS3ERR_NAMETOOLONG	63	The filename in an operation was too long.
NFS3ERR_STALE	70	Invalid filehandle. The filehandle given in the arguments was invalid. The file referred to by that filehandle no longer exists or access to it has been revoked.
NFS3ERR_BADHANDLE	10001	Illegal NFS filehandle. The filehandle failed internal consistency checks.
NFS3ERR_SERVERFAULT	10006	An error occurred on the server that does not map to any of the legal NFS version 3 protocol error values. The client should translate this into an appropriate error. UNIX clients may choose to translate this to EIO.

Snoop Trace of LOOKUP

```
NFS:    Proc = 3 (Look up file name)
NFS:    File handle = 0080001800000002000A00000000DD0A
NFS:                       50295369000A00000000DD0A50295369
NFS:    File name = test
```

⇩

```
NFS:    Proc = 3 (Look up file name)
NFS:    Status = 0 (OK)
NFS:    File handle = 0080001800000002000A000000011168
NFS:                       102754F8000A00000000DD0A50295369
NFS:    Post-operation attributes: (object)
NFS:      File type = 2 (Directory)
NFS:      Mode = 0777
NFS:       Setuid = 0, Setgid = 0, Sticky = 0
NFS:       Owner's permissions = rwx
NFS:       Group's permissions = rwx
NFS:       Other's permissions = rwx
NFS:      Link count = 9, User ID = 3497, Group ID = 1
NFS:      File size = 1024, Used = 1024
NFS:      Special: Major = 0, Minor = 0
NFS:      File system id = 8388632, File id = 69992
NFS:      Last access time     = 11-Jul-98 10:15:00.835417000 GMT
NFS:      Modification time    = 08-Jul-98 20:49:23.011564000 GMT
NFS:      Attribute change time = 08-Jul-98 20:49:23.011564000 GMT
NFS:
NFS:    Post-operation attributes: (directory)
NFS:      File type = 2 (Directory)
NFS:      Mode = 0777
NFS:       Setuid = 0, Setgid = 0, Sticky = 0
NFS:       Owner's permissions = rwx
NFS:       Group's permissions = rwx
NFS:       Other's permissions = rwx
NFS:      Link count = 3, User ID = 0, Group ID = 3
NFS:      File size = 512, Used = 1024
NFS:      Special: Major = 0, Minor = 0
NFS:      File system id = 8388632, File id = 56586
NFS:      Last access time     = 11-Jul-98 10:15:00.835416000 GMT
NFS:      Modification time    = 24-Apr-98 03:55:41.840716000 GMT
NFS:      Attribute change time = 24-Apr-98 03:55:41.840716000 GMT
```

7.3.5   Procedure 4: ACCESS—Check Access Permission

Description

Procedure ACCESS determines the access rights that a user, as identified by the credentials in the request, has with respect to a filesystem object. The client encodes the set of permissions that are to be checked in a bit mask. The server checks the permissions encoded in the bit mask and returns a bit mask encoded with the permissions that the client is allowed.

The results of this procedure are necessarily advisory in nature. That is, the result does not imply that such access will be allowed to the filesystem object in the future, as access rights can be revoked by the server at any time.

Arguments	*Results*

`nfs_fh3 object;`
`uint32  accessbits;`
	`switch (nfsstat3 status) {`
	`   case NFS3_OK = 0:`
	`      post_op_attr  obj_attr;`
	`      uint32        accessbits;`
	`   default:`
	`      post_op_attr  obj_attr;`
	`}`

Arguments

`object`

The file handle for the file system object to which access is to be checked.

`accessbits`

A bit mask of access permissions to check. The access permissions in Table 7.5 may be requested. The server should return a `status` of NFS3_OK if no errors occurred that prevented the server from making the required access checks.

Results

`status`

NFS3_OK.

`obj_attr`

The postoperation attributes of the `object`.

TABLE 7.5 Access Permissions

Bit Value	Name	Type of Access
0x01	ACCESS3_READ	Read data from file or read a directory.
0x02	ACCESS3_LOOKUP	Look up a name in a directory (no meaning for nondirectory objects).
0x04	ACCESS3_MODIFY	Rewrite existing file data or modify existing directory entries.
0x08	ACCESS3_EXTEND	Write new data or add directory entries.
0x10	ACCESS3_DELETE	Delete an existing directory entry.
0x20	ACCESS3_EXECUTE	Executable file (no meaning for a directory).

`accessbits`

A bit mask of access permissions indicating access rights for the authentication credentials provided with the request.

Results on Failure

`status`

Error code.

`obj_attr`

The attributes of `object`, if access to attributes is permitted.

Implementation

In general, it is not sufficient for the client to attempt to deduce access permissions by inspecting the `uid`, `gid`, and `mode` fields in the file attributes, since the server may perform uid or gid mapping or enforce additional access control restrictions. It is also possible that the server may not be in the same ID space as the client. In these cases (and perhaps others), the client cannot reliably perform an access check with only current file attributes.

In the NFS version 2 protocol, the only reliable way to determine whether an operation was allowed was to try it and see if it succeeded or failed. Using the ACCESS procedure, the client can ask the server to indicate whether or not one or more classes of operations are permitted. The ACCESS operation is provided to allow clients to check before doing a series of operations. This is useful in operating systems (such as UNIX) where permission checking is done only when a file or directory is opened. The intent is to make the behavior of opening a remote file more consistent with the behavior of opening a local file.

The information returned by the server in response to an ACCESS call is not permanent. It was correct at the exact time the server performed the checks, but not necessarily afterwards. The server can revoke access permission at any time.

The client should use the effective credentials of the user to build the authentication information in the ACCESS request used to determine access rights. It is the effective user and group credentials that are used in subsequent read and write operations. See the comments in section 8.7 for more information on this topic.

Many implementations do not directly support the ACCESS3_DELETE permission. Operating systems like UNIX will ignore the ACCESS3_DELETE bit if set on an access request on a nondirectory object. In these systems, delete permission on a file is determined by the access permissions on the directory in which the file resides instead of being determined by the permissions of the file itself. Thus, the bit mask returned for such a request will have the

ACCESS3_DELETE bit set to 0, indicating that the client does not have this permission.

Clients can cache the returned access information and avoid the need for frequent access calls for the same file from the same user. Since the cache entries are valid only for a single user, a multiuser client may require multiple cache entries for a single file if multiple users are accessing the same file. To maintain a reasonable level of consistency with the server's access control, the cached access information must be time-bounded and checked against the modification time of the file or directory either through postoperations attributes or an explicit GETATTR or ACCESS call. The cached access information for a file must be purged if the file owner, group, or permission bits are changed by the client.

Errors

NFS3ERR_IO	5	I/O error. A hard error (for example, a disk error) occurred while processing the requested operation.
NFS3ERR_STALE	70	Invalid filehandle. The filehandle given in the arguments was invalid. The file referred to by that filehandle no longer exists, or access to it has been revoked.
NFS3ERR_BADHANDLE	10001	Illegal NFS filehandle. The filehandle failed internal consistency checks.
NFS3ERR_SERVERFAULT	10006	An error occurred on the server that does not map to any of the legal NFS version 3 protocol error values. The client should translate this into an appropriate error. UNIX clients may choose to translate this to EIO.

Snoop Trace of ACCESS

```
NFS:  Proc = 4 (Check access permission)
NFS:  File handle = 0080001800000002000A00000001117F
NFS:              5E585378000A00000000DD0A50295369
NFS:  Access bits = 0x0000000c
NFS:  .... ...0 = (no read)
NFS:  .... ..0. = (no lookup)
NFS:  .... .1.. = Modify
NFS:  .... 1... = Extend
NFS:  ...0 .... = (no delete)
NFS:  ..0. .... = (no execute)

NFS:  Proc = 4 (Check access permission)
NFS:  Status = 0 (OK)
```

```
NFS:  Post-operation attributes:
NFS:    File type = 1 (Regular File)
NFS:    Mode = 0777
NFS:     Setuid = 0, Setgid = 0, Sticky = 0
NFS:     Owner's permissions = rwx
NFS:     Group's permissions = rwx
NFS:     Other's permissions = rwx
NFS:    Link count = 1, User ID = 3497, Group ID = 10
NFS:    File size = 10, Used = 1024
NFS:    Special: Major = 0, Minor = 0
NFS:    File system id = 8388632, File id = 70015
NFS:    Last access time     = 08-Jul-98 20:50:21.981577000 GMT
NFS:    Modification time    = 08-Jul-98 20:50:18.221565000 GMT
NFS:    Attribute change time = 08-Jul-98 20:50:18.221565000 GMT
NFS:
NFS:  Access = modify,extend
```

7.3.6   Procedure 5: READLINK—Read from Symbolic Link

Description

Procedure READLINK reads the pathname stored in a symbolic link. The pathname is an ASCII string that is opaque to the server. That is, whether created by the NFS version 3 protocol software from a client or created locally on the server, the data in a symbolic link are not interpreted when created but are simply stored.

Arguments	Results

`nfs_fh3 symlink;`	`switch (nfsstat3 status) {`
	`   case NFS3_OK = 0:`
	`      post_op_attr sym_attr;`
	`      nfspath3     data;`
	`   default:`
	`      post_op_attr sym_attr;`
	`}`

Arguments

`symlink`

The filehandle for a symbolic link (filesystem object of type NF3LNK).

Results

`status`

NFS3_OK.

`sym_attr`

The postoperation attributes for the symbolic link.

data

The data associated with the symbolic link.

Results on Failure

status

Error code.

sym_attr

The postoperation attributes for the symbolic link.

Implementation

A symbolic link is nominally a reference to another file. The data are not necessarily interpreted by the server; they are just stored in the link object. It is possible for a client implementation to store a pathname that is not meaningful to the server operating system in a symbolic link; for instance, WebNFS clients may store a URL in a symbolic link. A READLINK operation returns the data to the client for interpretation. If different implementations want to share access to symbolic links, then they must agree on the interpretation of the data in the symbolic link.

The READLINK operation is allowed only on objects of type NF3LNK. The server should return the error NFS3ERR_INVAL if the object is not of type NF3LNK.

Client implementations can cache symbolic link text just as they do file data. This avoids unnecessary READLINK calls. As with cached data, the cached symbolic link text must be time-bounded, and the link mtime must be compared with the server's link mtime periodically.

Errors

NFS3ERR_IO	5	I/O error. A hard error (for example, a disk error) occurred while processing the requested operation.
NFS3ERR_ACCES	13	Permission denied. The caller does not have the correct permission to perform the requested operation. Contrast this with NFS3ERR_PERM, which restricts itself to owner or privileged-user permission failures.
NFS3ERR_INVAL	22	Invalid argument or unsupported argument for an operation.
NFS3ERR_STALE	70	Invalid filehandle. The filehandle given in the arguments was invalid. The file referred to by that filehandle no longer exists or access to it has been revoked.

continued

NFS3ERR_BADHANDLE	10001	Illegal NFS filehandle. The filehandle failed internal consistency checks.
NFS3ERR_NOTSUPP	10004	Operation is not supported.
NFS3ERR_SERVERFAULT	10006	An error occurred on the server that does not map to any of the legal NFS version 3 protocol error values. The client should translate this into an appropriate error. UNIX clients may choose to translate this to EIO.

Snoop Trace of READLINK

```
NFS:   Proc = 5 (Read from symbolic link)
NFS:   File handle = 00800018000000002000A000000011181
NFS:                 13761BA9000A00000000DD0A50295369
```

⇩

```
NFS:   Proc = 5 (Read from symbolic link)
NFS:   Status = 0 (OK)
NFS:   Post-operation attributes:
NFS:     File type = 5 (Symbolic Link)
NFS:     Mode = 0777
NFS:      Setuid = 0, Setgid = 0, Sticky = 0
NFS:      Owner's permissions = rwx
NFS:      Group's permissions = rwx
NFS:      Other's permissions = rwx
NFS:     Link count = 1, User ID = 3497, Group ID = 10
NFS:     File size = 8, Used = 1024
NFS:     Special: Major = 0, Minor = 0
NFS:     File system id = 8388632, File id = 70017
NFS:     Last access time      = 10-Aug-98 21:50:31.573290000 GMT
NFS:     Modification time     = 12-Jul-98 00:45:35.766869000 GMT
NFS:     Attribute change time = 12-Jul-98 00:45:35.766869000 GMT
NFS:
NFS:   Path = linktext
```

7.3.7   Procedure 6: READ—Read from File

Description

Procedure READ reads data from a file.

Arguments		*Results*
nfs_fh3	file;	```
uint64	offset;	switch (nfsstat3 status) {
uint32	count;	case NFS3_OK = 0:

```
Arguments                    Results
nfs_fh3    file;             switch (nfsstat3 status) {
uint64     offset;              case NFS3_OK = 0:
uint32     count;                  post_op_attr file_attr;
                                   uint32       count;
                                   boolean      eof;
                                   opaque<>     data;
                               default:
                                   post_op_attr file_attr;
                             }
```

Arguments

file

The filehandle of the file from which data are to be read. It must identify a file system object of type NF3REG.

offset

The position within the file at which the read is to begin. An offset of 0 means to read data starting at the beginning of the file. If the offset is greater than or equal to the size of the file, the status NFS3_OK is returned with count set to 0 and eof set to TRUE, subject to access permissions checking.

count

The number of bytes of data that are to be read. If the count is 0, the READ will succeed and return 0 bytes of data, subject to access permissions checking. The count must be less than or equal to the value of the rtmax field in the FSINFO reply structure for the file system that contains file. If it is greater, the server may return only rtmax bytes, resulting in a short read.

Results

status

NFS3_OK.

file_attr

The attributes of the file on completion of the read.

count

The number of bytes of data returned by the read.

eof

If the read ended at the end-of-file (formally, in a correctly formed READ request, if offset plus count is equal to the size of the file), eof is returned as TRUE; otherwise it is FALSE. A successful READ of an empty file will always return eof as TRUE.

data

The counted data read from the file.

Results on Failure

status

Error code.

file_attr

The postoperation attributes of the file.

Implementation

The nfsdata type used for the READ and WRITE operations in the NFS version 2 protocol defining the data portion of a request or reply was changed to a variable-length opaque byte array. The maximum size allowed by the NFS version 3 protocol is limited by what XDR and underlying transports will allow. There are no artificial limits imposed by the NFS version 3 protocol. See section 7.3.20 for details of transfer size.

It is possible for the server to return fewer than count bytes of data. If the server returns fewer than the count requested and eof set to FALSE, the client should issue another READ to get the remaining data. A server may return fewer data than requested under several circumstances. The file may have been truncated by another client or perhaps on the server itself, changing the file size from what the requesting client believes to be the case. This would reduce the actual quantity of data available to the client. It is possible, through server resource exhaustion, that the server may back off the transfer size and reduce the quantity of data returned.

Some NFS version 2 protocol client implementations chose to interpret a short read response as indicating EOF. The addition of the eof flag in the NFS version 3 protocol provides a correct way of handling EOF.

Some NFS version 2 protocol server implementations incorrectly returned NFSERR_ISDIR where the file system object type was not a regular file. The correct return value for the NFS version 3 protocol is NFS3ERR_INVAL.

Errors

NFS3ERR_IO	5	I/O error. A hard error (for example, a disk error) occurred while processing the requested operation.
NFS3ERR_NXIO	6	I/O error. No such device or address.
NFS3ERR_ACCES	13	Permission denied. The caller does not have the correct permission to perform the requested operation. Contrast this with NFS3ERR_PERM, which restricts itself to owner or privileged-user permission failures.

continued

NFS3ERR_INVAL	22	Invalid argument or unsupported argument for an operation.
NFS3ERR_STALE	70	Invalid filehandle. The filehandle given in the arguments was invalid. The file referred to by that filehandle no longer exists or access to it has been revoked.
NFS3ERR_BADHANDLE	10001	Illegal NFS filehandle. The filehandle failed internal consistency checks.
NFS3ERR_SERVERFAULT	10006	An error occurred on the server that does not map to any of the legal NFS version 3 protocol error values. The client should translate this into an appropriate error. UNIX clients may choose to translate this to EIO.

Snoop Trace of READ

```
NFS:  Proc = 6 (Read from file)
NFS:  File handle = 00800018000000002000A000000011169
NFS:               6D7FBD47000A00000000DD0A50295369
NFS:  Offset = 0
NFS:  Count = 32768
```

⇩

```
NFS:  Proc = 6 (Read from file)
NFS:  Status = 0 (OK)
NFS:  Post-operation attributes:
NFS:    File type = 1 (Regular File)
NFS:    Mode = 0644
NFS:     Setuid = 0, Setgid = 0, Sticky = 0
NFS:     Owner's permissions = rw-
NFS:     Group's permissions = r--
NFS:     Other's permissions = r--
NFS:    Link count = 1, User ID = 3497, Group ID = 10
NFS:    File size = 4352096, Used = 4366336
NFS:    Special: Major = 0, Minor = 0
NFS:    File system id = 8388632, File id = 69993
NFS:    Last access time    = 12-Jul-98 00:43:27.496866000 GMT
NFS:    Modification time   = 18-Sep-97 01:52:06.525313000 GMT
NFS:    Attribute change time = 10-Oct-97 06:52:29.747375000 GMT
NFS:
NFS:  Count = 32768 bytes read
NFS:  End of file = False
```

7.3.8   Procedure 7: WRITE—Write to File

Description

Procedure WRITE writes data to a file.

Arguments	*Results*
| ```
nfs_fh3    file;
uint64    offset;
uint32    count;
enum stable_how {
   UNSTABLE   = 0,
   DATA_SYNC  = 1,
   FILE_SYNC  = 2
};
opaque<>  data;
``` | ```
switch (nfsstat3 status) {
   case NFS3_OK = 0:
      wcc_data    file_wcc;
      uint32      count;
      stable_how  committed;
      writeverf3  verf;
   default:
      wcc_data    file_wcc;
}
``` |

Arguments

`file`

> The filehandle for the file to which data is to be written. It must identify a filesystem object of type NF3REG.

`offset`

> The position within the file at which the write is to begin. An offset of 0 means to write data starting at the beginning of the file.

`count`

> The number of bytes of data to be written. If the `count` is 0, the WRITE will succeed and return a `count` of 0, barring errors due to permissions checking. The size of data must be less than or equal to the value of the `wtmax` field in the FSINFO reply structure for the filesystem that contains the file. If greater, the server may write only `wtmax` bytes, resulting in a short write.

`stable_how`

> If `stable_how` is UNSTABLE, the server is free to commit any part of the data and the metadata to stable storage, including all or none, before returning a reply to the client. There is no guarantee whether or when any uncommitted data will subsequently be committed to stable storage. The only guarantees made by the server are that it will not destroy any data without changing the value of `verf` and that it will not commit the data and metadata at a level lower than that requested by the client.
>
> If `stable_how` is DATA_SYNC, then the server must commit all the data to stable storage and enough of the metadata to retrieve the data before returning.The server implementor is free to implement DATA_SYNC in the same fashion as FILE_SYNC, but with a possible performance drop.

If `stable_how` is FILE_SYNC, the server must commit the data written plus all filesystem metadata to stable storage before returning results. This corresponds to the NFS version 2 protocol semantics. Any other behavior constitutes a protocol violation.

See section 7.3.22 for more information about the transfer of data to stable storage.

Value	Name	Requirement
0	UNSTABLE	Server is free to commit any of the data and the metadata to stable storage, including all or none, before returning a reply to the client.
1	DATA_SYNC	The server must commit all the data to stable storage and enough of the metadata to retrieve the data before replying.
2	FILE_SYNC	Version 2 requirement: the server must commit the data written plus all filesystem metadata to stable storage before replying.

`data`

The data to be written to the file.

Results

`status`

NFS3_OK.

`file_wcc`

Weak cache consistency data for the file. For a client that requires only the postwrite file attributes, the attributes can be found in `wcc_data.after` (page 145).

`count`

The number of bytes of data written to the file. The server may write fewer bytes than requested. If so, the actual number of bytes written starting at location `offset` is returned.

`committed`

The server should return an indication of the level of commitment of the data and metadata via `committed`.

If the server committed all data and metadata to stable storage, `committed` should be set to FILE_SYNC. If the level of commitment was at least as strong as DATA_SYNC, then `committed` should be set to DATA_SYNC. Otherwise, `committed` must be returned as UNSTABLE. If `stable_how` was FILE_SYNC, then `committed` must also be FILE_SYNC: anything else constitutes a protocol violation. If `stable_how` was DATA_SYNC, then `committed` may be FILE_SYNC or DATA_SYNC: anything else constitutes a protocol violation. If `stable_how` was UNSTABLE, then `committed` may be either FILE_SYNC, DATA_SYNC, or UNSTABLE.

`verf`

This is a cookie that the client can use to determine whether the server has changed state between a call to WRITE and a subsequent call to either WRITE or COMMIT. This cookie must be consistent during a single invocation of the NFS version 3 protocol service and must be unique between instances of the NFS version 3 protocol server, where uncommitted data may be lost.

Results on Failure

`status`

Error code.

`file_wcc`

Weak cache consistency data for the file. For a client that requires only the postwrite file attributes, the attributes can be found in `file_wcc`. Even though the write failed, full `wcc_data` is returned to allow the client to determine whether the failed write resulted in any change to the file.

If a client writes data to the server with the `stable` argument set to UNSTABLE and the reply yields a committed response of DATA_SYNC or UNSTABLE, the client will follow up some time in the future with a COMMIT operation to synchronize outstanding asynchronous data and metadata with the server's stable storage, barring client error. It is possible that due to client crash or other error, a subsequent COMMIT will not be received by the server.

Implementation

The `nfsdata` type used for the READ and WRITE operations in the NFS version 2 protocol defining the data portion of a request or reply has been changed to a variable-length opaque byte array. The maximum size allowed by the protocol is now limited by what XDR and underlying transports will allow. There are no artificial limits imposed by the NFS version 3 protocol. Consult the FSINFO procedure description for details.

It is possible for the server to write fewer than `count` bytes of data. In this case, the server should not return an error unless no data was written at all. If the server writes less than `count` bytes, the client should issue another WRITE to write the remaining data.

Writing of data to a file will have the side effect of updating the file `mtime`; however, the `mtime` of the file should not be changed unless the contents of the file are changed. Thus, a WRITE request with count set to 0 should not cause the mtime of the file to be updated.

The NFS version 3 protocol introduces safe asynchronous writes. The combination of WRITE with stable set to UNSTABLE followed by a COMMIT addresses the performance bottleneck found in the NFS version 2 protocol, the need to synchronously commit all writes to stable storage.

Historically, the definition of stable storage has been a point of contention. The following expected properties of stable storage may help in resolving design issues in the implementation. Stable storage is persistent storage that survives repeated power failures; hardware failures (of any board, power supply, and so on); repeated software crashes, including reboot cycle.

This definition does not address failure of the stable storage module itself. A cookie, verf, is defined to allow a client to detect different invocations of a server over which cached, uncommitted data may be lost. In the most likely case, the verf allows the client to detect server reboots. This information is required so that the client can safely determine whether the server could have lost cached data. If the server fails unexpectedly and the client has uncommitted data from previous WRITE requests (done with the stable_how argument set to UNSTABLE and in which the result committed was returned as UNSTABLE as well), it may not have flushed cached data to stable storage. The burden of recovery is on the client, and the client will need to retransmit the data to the server. A suggested verf cookie would be to use the time that the server was booted or the time the server was last started (if restarting the server without a reboot results in lost buffers).

The committed field in the results allows the client to do more effective caching. If the server is committing all WRITE requests to stable storage, then it should return with committed set to FILE_SYNC, regardless of the value of the stable_how field in the arguments. A server that uses an NVRAM accelerator may choose to implement this policy. The client can use this choice to increase the effectiveness of the cache by discarding cached data that have already been committed on the server.

Some implementations may return NFS3ERR_NOSPC instead of NFS3ERR_DQUOT when a user's quota is exceeded. Some version 2 server implementations incorrectly returned NFSERR_ISDIR if the filesystem object type was not a regular file. The correct return value for the version 3 protocol is NFS3ERR_INVAL.

Stable vs. Unstable Writes

The setting of the stable field in the WRITE arguments, that is, whether or not to do asynchronous WRITE requests, is straightforward on a UNIX client. If the version 3 protocol client receives a write request that is not marked as being asynchronous, it should generate the WRITE with `stable` set to TRUE. If the request is marked as being asynchronous, the WRITE should be generated with `stable` set to FALSE. If the response comes back with the `committed` field set to TRUE, the client should just mark the write request as done and no further action is required. If `committed` is set to FALSE, indicating that the buffer was not synchronized with the server's disk, the client will need to mark the buffer in some way that indicates that a copy of the buffer lives on the server and that a new copy does not need to be sent to the server but that a COMMIT is required.

Note that this algorithm introduces a new state for buffers; thus there are now three states for buffers: (1) dirty, (2) done but needs to be committed, and (3) done. This extra state on the client will probably require modifications to the system outside the version 3 client.

One proposal that was rejected was the addition of a boolean commit argument to the WRITE operation. It would have been used to indicate whether the server should do a full file commit after doing the write. This seems as if it could be useful if the client knew that it was doing the last write on the file. It is difficult, though, to see how it could be used, given existing client architectures.

The asynchronous write opens up the window of problems associated with write sharing. For example: client A writes some data asynchronously. Client A is still holding the buffers cached, waiting to commit them later. Client B reads the modified data and writes it back to the server. The server then crashes. When it comes back up, client A issues a COMMIT operation, which returns with a different cookie as well as changed attributes. In this case, the correct action may or may not be to retransmit the cached buffers. Unfortunately, client A can't tell for sure, so it will need to retransmit the buffers, thus overwriting the changes from client B. Fortunately, write sharing is rare, and the solution matches the current write-sharing situation. Without using locking for synchronization, the behavior will be indeterminate.

In a high-availability (redundant system) server implementation, two cases exist that relate to the `verf` changing. If the high-availability server implementation does not use a shared-memory scheme, then the `verf` should change on failover, since the unsynchronized data are not available to the second processor and there is no guarantee that the system that had the data cached was able to flush it to stable storage before going down. The client will need to retransmit the data to be safe. In a shared-memory high-availability server implementation, the `verf` would not need to change because the server would still have the cached data available to be flushed. The exact policy regarding the `verf` in a shared-memory high-availability implementation, however, is up to the server implementor.

Errors

NFS3ERR_IO	5	I/O error. A hard error (for example, a disk error) occurred while processing the requested operation.
NFS3ERR_ACCES	13	Permission denied. The caller does not have the correct permission to perform the requested operation. Contrast this with NFS3ERR_PERM, which restricts itself to owner or privileged-user permission failures.
NFS3ERR_INVAL	22	Invalid argument or unsupported argument for an operation.
NFS3ERR_FBIG	27	File too large. The operation would have caused a file to grow beyond the server's limit.
NFS3ERR_NOSPC	28	No space left on device. The operation would have caused the server's filesystem to exceed its limit.
NFS3ERR_ROFS	30	Read-only filesystem. A modifying operation was attempted on a read-only filesystem.
NFS3ERR_DQUOT	69	Resource (quota) hard limit exceeded. The user's resource limit on the server has been exceeded.
NFS3ERR_STALE	70	Invalid filehandle. The filehandle given in the arguments was invalid. The file referred to by that filehandle no longer exists or access to it has been revoked.
NFS3ERR_BADHANDLE	10001	Illegal NFS filehandle. The filehandle failed internal consistency checks.
NFS3ERR_SERVERFAULT	10006	An error occurred on the server that does not map to any of the legal NFS version 3 protocol error values. The client should translate this into an appropriate error. UNIX clients may choose to translate this to EIO.

Snoop Trace of WRITE

```
NFS:   Proc = 7 (Write to file)
NFS:   File handle = 00800018000000002000A000000011182
NFS:                 56CB152E000A00000000DD0A50295369
NFS:   Offset = 0
NFS:   Size   = 32768
NFS:   Stable = ASYNC

                ⇓

NFS:   Proc = 7 (Write to file)
NFS:   Status = 0 (OK)
NFS:   Pre-operation attributes:
```

```
NFS:    Size = 0 bytes
NFS:    Modification time      = 12-Jul-98 00:56:47.701127000 GMT
NFS:    Attribute change time  = 12-Jul-98 00:56:47.701127000 GMT
NFS:
NFS:  Post-operation attributes:
NFS:    File type = 1 (Regular File)
NFS:    Mode = 0664
NFS:     Setuid = 0, Setgid = 0, Sticky = 0
NFS:     Owner's permissions = rw-
NFS:     Group's permissions = rw-
NFS:     Other's permissions = r--
NFS:    Link count = 1, User ID = 3497, Group ID = 10
NFS:    File size = 32768, Used = 32768
NFS:    Special: Major = 0, Minor = 0
NFS:    File system id = 8388632, File id = 70018
NFS:    Last access time       = 12-Jul-98 00:56:47.701127000 GMT
NFS:    Modification time      = 12-Jul-98 00:56:47.891129000 GMT
NFS:    Attribute change time  = 12-Jul-98 00:56:47.891129000 GMT
NFS:
NFS:  Count = 32768 bytes written
NFS:  Stable = ASYNC
NFS:  Verifier = 72602A263369254D
```

7.3.9   Procedure 8: CREATE—Create a File

Description

Procedure CREATE creates a regular file.

Arguments	Results

```nfs_fh3   dir;```
```filename3 name;```
```switch (enum mode) {```
```   case UNCHECKED = 0:```
```   case GUARDED = 1:```
```   sattr3   obj_attr;```
```   case EXCLUSIVE = 2:```
```   createverf3   verf;```
```}```
	```switch (nfsstat3 status) {```
	``` case NFS3_OK = 0:```
	``` switch (boolean) {```
	``` case TRUE:```
	``` nfs_fh3 obj_fh;```
	``` case FALSE:```
	``` void;```
	``` };```
	``` post_op_attr obj_attr;```
	``` wcc_data dir_wcc;```
	``` default:```
	``` wcc_data dir_wcc;```
	```}```

Arguments

dir

   The filehandle for the directory in which the file is to be created.

name

The name that is to be associated with the created file. Refer to section 5.3.1 for a description of allowable names.

mode

Controls the conditions under which the file is created.

- UNCHECKED   The file is created without checking for the existence of a duplicate file in the same directory. In this case, obj_attr is a sattr3 describing the initial attributes for the file.
- GUARDED   The server checks for the presence of a duplicate file before performing the create and must fail the request with NFS3ERR_EXIST if a duplicate file exists. If the file does not exist, the request is performed as described for UNCHECKED.
- EXCLUSIVE   The server follows exclusive creation semantics, using the verifier to ensure exclusive creation of the target. No attributes may be provided in this case, since the server may use the target file metadata to store the createverf3 verifier.

Results

status

NFS3_OK.

obj_fh

The file handle of the newly created regular file.

obj_attr

The attributes of the regular file just created (page 144).

dir_wcc

Weak cache consistency data for the directory dir. For a client that requires only the post-CREATE directory attributes, the attributes can be found in wcc_data.after (page 145).

Results (on Failure)

status

Error code.

dir_wcc

Weak cache consistency data for the directory dir. For a client that requires only the post-CREATE directory attributes, the attributes can be found in wcc_data.after. Even though the CREATE failed, full wcc_data is returned to allow the client to determine whether the failing CREATE resulted in any change to the directory.

Implementation

Unlike the NFS version 2 protocol, in which certain fields in the initial attributes structure were overloaded to indicate creation of devices and FIFOs in addition to regular files, this procedure supports only the creation of regular files. The MKNOD procedure was introduced in the NFS version 3 protocol to handle creation of devices and FIFOs. Implementations should have no reason in the NFS version 3 protocol to overload CREATE semantics.

The UNIX open and `create` system calls support an *exclusive* option. The call must fail if the file already exists. Some applications use the exclusive create option to implement lock files—prior to using some resource, a program attempts to create a lock file with exclusive create. If the call fails, indicating that the file already exists, the program can infer that the resource is already in use. The NFS version 2 CREATE procedure did not support exclusive create semantics directly. To approximate exclusive semantics, version 2 clients had to first check for the existence of the file via a LOOKUP request, then follow that with a CREATE request if the LOOKUP failed. This was unsatisfactory because it left a window of opportunity for another client to create the file between the LOOKUP and CREATE calls. NFS version 3 solved the problem by adding exclusive create semantics to the CREATE call.

An NFS version 3 client can set `mode` to EXCLUSIVE. In this case, `verf` contains a verifier that can reasonably be expected to be unique. A combination of a client identifier, perhaps the client network address, and a unique number generated by the client, perhaps the RPC transaction identifier, may be appropriate. If the file does not exist, the server creates the file and stores the verifier in stable storage. For filesystems that do not provide a mechanism for the storage of arbitrary file attributes, the server may use one or more elements of the file metadata to store the verifier. The verifier must be stored in stable storage to prevent erroneous failure on retransmission of the request. It is assumed that an exclusive `create` is being performed because exclusive semantics are critical to the application. Because of the expected usage, exclusive CREATE does not rely solely on the normally volatile duplicate request cache for storage of the verifier. The duplicate request cache in volatile storage does not survive a crash and may actually flush on a long network partition, opening failure windows. In the UNIX local filesystem environment, the expected storage location for the verifier on creation is the metadata (timestamps) of the file. For this reason, an exclusive file `create` may not include initial attributes because the server would have nowhere to store the verifier. The use of a file timestamp for verifier storage (the file `mtime` is most commonly used) can cause difficulties if the client sends a 64-bit verifier value that exceeds the capacity of the server's time attribute.

If the server cannot support these exclusive create semantics, possibly because of the requirement to commit the verifier to stable storage, it should fail the CREATE request with the error NFS3ERR_NOTSUPP.

During an exclusive CREATE request, if the file already exists, the server reconstructs the file's verifier and compares it with the verifier in the request. If they match, the server treats the request as a success. The request is presumed to be a duplicate of an earlier, successful request for which the reply was lost and that the server duplicate request cache mechanism did not detect. If the verifiers do not match, the request is rejected with the status NFS3ERR_EXIST. Once the client has performed a successful exclusive create, it must issue a SETATTR to set the correct file attributes. Until it does so, it should not rely on any of the file attributes, since the server implementation may need to overload file metadata to store the verifier.

Use of the GUARDED attribute does not provide exactly-once semantics. In particular, if a reply is lost and the server does not detect the retransmission of the request, the procedure can fail with NFS3ERR_EXIST, even though the create was performed successfully.

Errors

NFS3ERR_IO	5	I/O error. A hard error (for example, a disk error) occurred while processing the requested operation.
NFS3ERR_ACCES	13	Permission denied. The caller does not have the correct permission to perform the requested operation. Contrast this with NFS3ERR_PERM, which restricts itself to owner or privileged-user permission failures.
NFS3ERR_EXIST	17	File exists. The file specified already exists.
NFS3ERR_NOTDIR	20	Not a directory. The caller specified a non-directory in a directory operation.
NFS3ERR_NOSPC	28	No space left on device. The operation would have caused the server's filesystem to exceed its limit.
NFS3ERR_ROFS	30	Read-only filesystem. A modifying operation was attempted on a read-only filesystem.
NFS3ERR_NAMETOOLONG	63	The filename in an operation was too long.
NFS3ERR_DQUOT	69	Resource (quota) hard limit exceeded. The user's resource limit on the server has been exceeded.
NFS3ERR_STALE	70	Invalid filehandle. The filehandle given in the arguments was invalid. The file referred to by that filehandle no longer exists or access to it has been revoked.
NFS3ERR_BADHANDLE	10001	Illegal NFS file handle. The filehandle failed internal consistency checks.

continued

NFS3ERR_NOTSUPP	10004	Operation is not supported.
NFS3ERR_SERVERFAULT	10006	An error occurred on the server that does not map to any of the legal NFS version 3 protocol error values. The client should translate this into an appropriate error. UNIX clients may choose to translate this to EIO.

Snoop Trace of CREATE

```
NFS:   Proc = 8 (Create file)
NFS:   File handle = 00800018000000002000A000000011168
NFS:                 102754F8000A00000000DD0A50295369
NFS:   File name = foofile
NFS:   Method = Guarded
NFS:     Mode = 0644
NFS:       Setuid = 0, Setgid = 0, Sticky = 0
NFS:       Owner's permissions = rw-
NFS:       Group's permissions = r--
NFS:       Other's permissions = r--
NFS:   User ID = (not set)
NFS:   Group ID = 10
NFS:   Size = 0
NFS:   Access time = (do not set)
NFS:   Modification time = (do not set)


NFS:   Proc = 8 (Create file)
NFS:   Status = 0 (OK)
NFS:   File handle = 00800018000000002000A00000001117F
NFS:                 5E58E82F000A00000000DD0A50295369
NFS:   Post-operation attributes:
NFS:     File type = 1 (Regular File)
NFS:     Mode = 0644
NFS:       Setuid = 0, Setgid = 0, Sticky = 0
NFS:       Owner's permissions = rw-
NFS:       Group's permissions = r--
NFS:       Other's permissions = r--
NFS:     Link count = 1, User ID = 3497, Group ID = 10
NFS:     File size = 0, Used = 0
NFS:     Special: Major = 0, Minor = 0
NFS:     File system id = 8388632, File id = 70015
NFS:     Last access time     = 12-Jul-98 00:43:56.746868000 GMT
NFS:     Modification time    = 12-Jul-98 00:43:56.746868000 GMT
NFS:     Attribute change time = 12-Jul-98 00:43:56.746868000 GMT
NFS:
NFS:   Pre-operation attributes:
NFS:     Size = 1024 bytes
NFS:     Modification time    = 12-Jul-98 00:43:09.676869000 GMT
NFS:     Attribute change time = 12-Jul-98 00:43:09.676869000 GMT
```

```
NFS:
NFS:   Post-operation attributes:
NFS:     File type = 2 (Directory)
NFS:     Mode = 0777
NFS:      Setuid = 0, Setgid = 0, Sticky = 0
NFS:      Owner's permissions = rwx
NFS:      Group's permissions = rwx
NFS:      Other's permissions = rwx
NFS:     Link count = 8, User ID = 3497, Group ID = 1
NFS:     File size = 1024, Used = 1024
NFS:     Special: Major = 0, Minor = 0
NFS:     File system id = 8388632, File id = 69992
NFS:     Last access time     = 12-Jul-98 00:42:20.586866000 GMT
NFS:     Modification time    = 12-Jul-98 00:43:56.776866000 GMT
NFS:     Attribute change time = 12-Jul-98 00:43:56.776866000 GMT
```

7.3.10   Procedure 9: MKDIR—Create a Directory

Description

Procedure MKDIR creates a new subdirectory.

Arguments	*Results*

`nfs_fh3    dir;`
`filename3  name;`
`sattr3     attr;`
	`switch (nfsstat3 status) {`
	`  case NFS3_OK = 0:`
	`      post_op_fh3  obj_fh;`
	`      post_op_attr obj_attr;`
	`      wcc_data       dir_wcc;`
	`  default:`
	`      wcc_data   dir_wcc;`
	`}`

Arguments

`dir`

The filehandle for the directory in which the subdirectory is to be created.

`name`

The name that is to be associated with the created subdirectory. Refer to section 5.3.1 for a description of allowable filenames.

`attr`

The initial attributes for the subdirectory. See page 146.

Results

`status`

NFS3_OK.

`obj_fh`

The filehandle for the newly created directory.

`obj_attr`

The attributes for the newly created subdirectory (page 144).

`dir_wcc`

Weak cache consistency data for the directory `dir`. For a client that requires only the post-MKDIR directory attributes, the attributes can be found in `wcc_data.after` (page 145).

Results on Failure

`status`

Error code.

`dir_wcc`

Weak cache consistency data for the directory `dir`. For a client that requires only the post-MKDIR directory attributes, the attributes can be found in `dir_wcc.after`. Even though the MKDIR failed, full `wcc_data` is returned to allow the client to determine whether the failing MKDIR resulted in any change to the directory.

Implementation

Many server implementations will not allow the filenames `.` or `..` to be used as targets in a MKDIR operation. In this case, the server should return NFS3ERR_EXIST. Refer to section 5.3.1 for a description of allowable filenames.

Errors

NFS3ERR_IO	5	I/O error. A hard error (for example, a disk error) occurred while processing the requested operation.
NFS3ERR_ACCES	13	Permission denied. The caller does not have the correct permission to perform the requested operation. Contrast this with NFS3ERR_PERM, which restricts itself to owner or privileged user permission failures.
NFS3ERR_EXIST	17	File exists. The file specified already exists.
NFS3ERR_NOTDIR	20	Not a directory. The caller specified a non-directory in a directory operation.

continued

NFS3ERR_NOSPC	28	No space left on device. The operation would have caused the server's filesystem to exceed its limit.
NFS3ERR_ROFS	30	Read-only filesystem. A modifying operation was attempted on a read-only filesystem.
NFS3ERR_NAMETOOLONG	63	The filename in an operation was too long.
NFS3ERR_DQUOT	69	Resource (quota) hard limit exceeded. The user's resource limit on the server has been exceeded.
NFS3ERR_STALE	70	Invalid filehandle. The filehandle given in the arguments was invalid. The file referred to by that filehandle no longer exists or access to it has been revoked.
NFS3ERR_BADHANDLE	10001	Illegal NFS filehandle. The filehandle failed internal consistency checks.
NFS3ERR_NOTSUPP	10004	Operation is not supported.
NFS3ERR_SERVERFAULT	10006	An error occurred on the server that does not map to any of the legal NFS version 3 protocol error values. The client should translate this into an appropriate error. UNIX clients may choose to translate this to EIO.

Snoop Trace of MKDIR

```
NFS:  Proc = 9 (Make directory)
NFS:  File handle = 0080000180000000002000A000000011168
NFS:               102754F8000A00000000DD0A50295369
NFS:  File name = newdir
NFS:    Mode = 0775
NFS:      Setuid = 0, Setgid = 0, Sticky = 0
NFS:      Owner's permissions = rwx
NFS:      Group's permissions = rwx
NFS:      Other's permissions = r-x
NFS:  User ID = (not set)
NFS:  Group ID = 10
NFS:  Size = (not set)
NFS:  Access time = (do not set)
NFS:  Modification time = (do not set)
```

⬇

```
NFS:  Proc = 9 (Make directory)
NFS:  Status = 0 (OK)
NFS:  File handle = 0080000180000000002000A000000016FD4
NFS:               4508B8F1000A00000000DD0A50295369
NFS:  Post-operation attributes:
```

```
NFS:      File type = 2 (Directory)
NFS:      Mode = 0775
NFS:       Setuid = 0, Setgid = 0, Sticky = 0
NFS:       Owner's permissions = rwx
NFS:       Group's permissions = rwx
NFS:       Other's permissions = r-x
NFS:      Link count = 2, User ID = 3497, Group ID = 10
NFS:      File size = 512, Used = 1024
NFS:      Special: Major = 0, Minor = 0
NFS:      File system id = 8388632, File id = 94164
NFS:      Last access time     = 12-Jul-98 00:56:08.111121000 GMT
NFS:      Modification time    = 12-Jul-98 00:56:08.111121000 GMT
NFS:      Attribute change time = 12-Jul-98 00:56:08.111121000 GMT
NFS:
NFS:   Pre-operation attributes:
NFS:      Size = 1024 bytes
NFS:      Modification time    = 12-Jul-98 00:55:55.211121000 GMT
NFS:      Attribute change time = 12-Jul-98 00:55:55.211121000 GMT
NFS:
NFS:   Post-operation attributes:
NFS:      File type = 2 (Directory)
NFS:      Mode = 0777
NFS:       Setuid = 0, Setgid = 0, Sticky = 0
NFS:       Owner's permissions = rwx
NFS:       Group's permissions = rwx
NFS:       Other's permissions = rwx
NFS:      Link count = 9, User ID = 3497, Group ID = 1
NFS:      File size = 1024, Used = 1024
NFS:      Special: Major = 0, Minor = 0
NFS:      File system id = 8388632, File id = 69992
NFS:      Last access time     = 12-Jul-98 00:55:34.961134000 GMT
NFS:      Modification time    = 12-Jul-98 00:56:08.151121000 GMT
NFS:      Attribute change time = 12-Jul-98 00:56:08.151121000 GMT
```

7.3.11   Procedure 10: SYMLINK—Create a Symbolic Link

Description

Procedure SYMLINK creates a new symbolic link.

```
Arguments                          Results

nfs_fh3     dir;                   switch (nfsstat3 status) {
filename3   name;                     case NFS3_OK = 0:
sattr3      sym_attr;                    post_op_fh3  obj_fh;
nfspath3    sym_data;                    post_op_attr obj_attr;
                                         wcc_data     dir_wcc;
                                      default:
                                         wcc_data     dir_wcc;
                                   }
```

Arguments

dir

The filehandle for the directory in which the symbolic link is to be created.

name

The name that is to be associated with the created symbolic link. Refer to section 5.3.1 for a description of allowable filenames.

sym_attr

The initial attributes for the symbolic link. On UNIX servers the attributes are never used, since symbolic links always have mode 0777.

sym_data

The string containing the symbolic link data.

Results

status

NFS3_OK.

obj_fh

The filehandle for the newly created symbolic link.

obj_attr

The attributes for the newly created symbolic link (page 143).

dir_wcc

Weak cache consistency data for the directory dir. For a client that requires only the post-SYMLINK directory attributes, the attributes can be found in dir_wcc.after.

Results on Failure

status

Error code.

dir_wcc

Weak cache consistency data for the directory dir. For a client that requires only the post-SYMLINK directory attributes, the attributes can be found in wcc_data.after (page 145). Even though the SYMLINK failed, full wcc_data is returned to allow the client to determine whether the failing SYMLINK changed the directory.

Implementation

For symbolic links, the actual filesystem node and its contents are expected to be created in a single atomic operation. That is, once the symbolic link is visible, there must not be a window where a READLINK would fail or return incorrect data.

Errors

NFS3ERR_IO	5	I/O error. A hard error (for example, a disk error) occurred while processing the requested operation.
NFS3ERR_ACCES	13	Permission denied. The caller does not have the correct permission to perform the requested operation. Contrast this with NFS3ERR_PERM, which restricts itself to owner or privileged-user permission failures.
NFS3ERR_EXIST	17	File exists. The file specified already exists.
NFS3ERR_NOTDIR	20	Not a directory. The caller specified a nondirectory in a directory operation.
NFS3ERR_NOSPC	28	No space left on device. The operation would have caused the server's filesystem to exceed its limit.
NFS3ERR_ROFS	30	Read-only filesystem. A modifying operation was attempted on a read-only filesystem.
NFS3ERR_NAMETOOLONG	63	The filename in an operation was too long.
NFS3ERR_DQUOT	69	Resource (quota) hard limit exceeded. The user's resource limit on the server has been exceeded.
NFS3ERR_STALE	70	Invalid filehandle. The filehandle given in the arguments was invalid. The file referred to by that filehandle no longer exists, or access to it has been revoked.
NFS3ERR_BADHANDLE	10001	Illegal NFS filehandle. The filehandle failed internal consistency checks.
NFS3ERR_NOTSUPP	10004	Operation is not supported.
NFS3ERR_SERVERFAULT	10006	An error occurred on the server that does not map to any of the legal NFS version 3 protocol error values. The client should translate this into an appropriate error. UNIX clients may choose to translate this to EIO.

Snoop Trace of SYMLINK

```
NFS:   Proc = 10 (Make symbolic link)
NFS:   File handle = 00800018000000002000A000000011168
NFS:                 102754F8000A00000000DD0A50295369
NFS:   File name = symlink
```

```
NFS:      Mode = 0777
NFS:        Setuid = 0, Setgid = 0, Sticky = 0
NFS:        Owner's permissions = rwx
NFS:        Group's permissions = rwx
NFS:        Other's permissions = rwx
NFS:   User ID = (not set)
NFS:   Group ID = (not set)
NFS:   Size = (not set)
NFS:   Access time = (do not set)
NFS:   Modification time = (do not set)
NFS:
NFS:   Path = linktext
```

⇩

```
NFS:   Proc = 10 (Make symbolic link)
NFS:   Status = 0 (OK)
NFS:   File handle = 0080001800000002000A000000011181
NFS:                 13761BA9000A00000000DD0A50295369
NFS:   Post-operation attributes:
NFS:     File type = 5 (Symbolic Link)
NFS:     Mode = 0777
NFS:        Setuid = 0, Setgid = 0, Sticky = 0
NFS:        Owner's permissions = rwx
NFS:        Group's permissions = rwx
NFS:        Other's permissions = rwx
NFS:     Link count = 1, User ID = 3497, Group ID = 10
NFS:     File size = 8, Used = 1024
NFS:     Special: Major = 0, Minor = 0
NFS:     File system id = 8388632, File id = 70017
NFS:     Last access time     = 12-Jul-98 00:45:35.736869000 GMT
NFS:     Modification time    = 12-Jul-98 00:45:35.766869000 GMT
NFS:     Attribute change time = 12-Jul-98 00:45:35.766869000 GMT
NFS:
NFS:   Pre-operation attributes:
NFS:     Size = 1024 bytes
NFS:     Modification time    = 12-Jul-98 00:45:26.516867000 GMT
NFS:     Attribute change time = 12-Jul-98 00:45:26.516867000 GMT
NFS:
NFS:   Post-operation attributes:
NFS:     File type = 2 (Directory)
NFS:     Mode = 0777
NFS:        Setuid = 0, Setgid = 0, Sticky = 0
NFS:        Owner's permissions = rwx
NFS:        Group's permissions = rwx
NFS:        Other's permissions = rwx
NFS:     Link count = 8, User ID = 3497, Group ID = 1
NFS:     File size = 1024, Used = 1024
NFS:     Special: Major = 0, Minor = 0
NFS:     File system id = 8388632, File id = 69992
NFS:     Last access time     = 12-Jul-98 00:42:20.586866000 GMT
NFS:     Modification time    = 12-Jul-98 00:45:35.766868000 GMT
NFS:     Attribute change time = 12-Jul-98 00:45:35.766868000 GMT
```

7.3.12   Procedure 11: MKNOD—Create a Special Device

Description

Procedure MKNOD creates a new special file. Special files can be device files, sockets, or named pipes.

```
Arguments

nfs_fh3    dir;
filename3 name;
switch (ftype3 type) {
  case NF3CHR:
  case NF3BLK:
     sattr3    dev_attr;
     specdata3 spec;
  case NF3SOCK:
  case NF3FIFO:
     sattr3  pipe_attr;
  default:
     void;
}
```

```
Results

switch (nfsstat3 status) {
  case NFS3_OK = 0:
     post_op_fh3  obj_fh;
     post_op_attr obj_attr;
     wcc_data      dir_wcc;
  default:
     wcc_data    dir_wcc;
}
```

Arguments

`dir`

The filehandle for the directory in which the special file is to be created.

`name`

The name that is to be associated with the created special file. Refer to section 5.3.1 for a description of allowable filenames.

`type`

The type of the object to be created.

When creating a character special file (`type` is NF3CHR) or a block special file (`type` is NF3BLK), the following arguments are included:

`dev_attr`

The initial attributes for a character or block device.

`spec`

The major and minor device number (see `specdata3` on page 141).

When creating a socket (`type` is NF3SOCK) or a FIFO (`type` is NF3FIFO), the following argument is included:

`pipe_attr`

The initial attributes for the special file.

Results

status

NFS3_OK.

obj_fh

The filehandle for the newly created special file.

obj_attr

The attributes for the newly created special file (page 144).

dir_wcc

Weak cache consistency data for the directory dir. For a client that requires only the post-MKNOD directory attributes, the attributes can be found in wcc_data.after (page 145).

Results on Failure

status

Error code.

dir_wcc

Weak cache consistency data for the directory dir. For a client that requires only the post-MKNOD directory attributes, the attributes can be found in dir_wcc.after. Even though the MKNOD failed, full wcc_data is returned to allow the client to determine whether the failing MKNOD changed the directory.

Implementation

Without explicit support for special filetype creation in the NFS version 2 protocol, fields in the CREATE arguments were overloaded to indicate creation of certain types of objects. This overloading is not necessary in the version 3 protocol.

If the server does not support any of the defined types, the error NFS3ERR_NOTSUPP should be returned. Otherwise, if the server does not support the target type or the target type is illegal, the error NFS3ERR_BADTYPE should be returned. Note that NF3REG, NF3DIR, and NF3LNK are illegal types for MKNOD. The procedures CREATE, MKDIR, and SYMLINK should be used to create these file types, respectively, instead of MKNOD.

Errors

NFS3ERR_IO	5	I/O error. A hard error (e.g., a disk error) occurred while processing the requested operation.
NFS3ERR_ACCES	13	Permission denied. The caller does not have the correct permission to perform the requested operation. Contrast this with NFS3ERR_PERM, which restricts itself to owner or privileged-user permission failures.
NFS3ERR_EXIST	17	File exists. The file specified already exists.
NFS3ERR_NOTDIR	20	Not a directory. The caller specified a non-directory in a directory operation.
NFS3ERR_INVAL	22	Invalid argument or unsupported argument for an operation.
NFS3ERR_NOSPC	28	No space left on device. Operation would have caused server's filesystem to exceed its limit.
NFS3ERR_ROFS	30	Read-only filesystem. A modifying operation was attempted on a read-only filesystem.
NFS3ERR_NAMETOOLONG	63	The filename in an operation was too long.
NFS3ERR_DQUOT	69	Resource (quota) hard limit exceeded. User's resource limit on the server has been exceeded.
NFS3ERR_STALE	70	Invalid filehandle. The filehandle given in the arguments was invalid. The file referred to by that filehandle no longer exists or access to it has been revoked.
NFS3ERR_BADHANDLE	10001	Illegal NFS filehandle. The filehandle failed internal consistency checks.
NFS3ERR_NOTSUPP	10004	Operation is not supported.
NFS3ERR_SERVERFAULT	10006	An error occurred on the server that does not map to any of the legal NFS version 3 protocol error values. The client should translate this into an appropriate error. UNIX clients may choose to translate this to EIO.
NFS3ERR_BADTYPE	10007	An attempt was made to create an object of a type not supported by the server.

Snoop Trace of MKNOD

```
NFS:   Proc = 11 (Make special file)
NFS:   File handle = [0082]
NFS:    0080000000000002000A000000000002
        3B72A359000A0000000000023B72A359
NFS:   File name = foo
```

```
NFS:  File type = Block special
NFS:    Mode - 0664
NFS:     Setuid = 0, Setgid = 0, Sticky = 0
NFS:     Owner's permissions = rw-
NFS:     Group's permissions = rw-
NFS:     Other's permissions = r--
NFS:  User ID = (not set)
NFS:  Group ID = 0
NFS:  Size = (not set)
NFS:  Access time = (do not set)
NFS:  Modification time = (do not set)
NFS:
NFS:  Major = 1943
NFS:  Minor = 224
NFS:
```

⬇

```
NFS:  Proc = 11 (Make special file)
NFS:  Status = 0 (OK)
NFS:  File handle = [896F]
NFS:  0080000000000002000A0000000000F6
      46B35781000A0000000000023B72A359
NFS:  Post-operation attributes:
NFS:    File type = 3 (Block special)
NFS:    Mode = 0664
NFS:     Setuid = 0, Setgid = 0, Sticky = 0
NFS:     Owner's permissions = rw-
NFS:     Group's permissions = rw-
NFS:     Other's permissions = r--
NFS:    Link count = 1, User ID = 0, Group ID = 0
NFS:    File size = 2147483647, Used = 0
NFS:    Special: Major = 1943, Minor = 224
NFS:    File system id = 8388608, File id = 246
NFS:    Last access time      = 21-Jun-99 07:16:48.000000000 GMT
NFS:    Modification time      = 21-Jun-99 07:16:48.000000000 GMT
NFS:    Attribute change time = 21-Jun-99 07:16:48.000000000 GMT
NFS:
NFS:  Pre-operation attributes:
NFS:    Size = 512 bytes
NFS:    Modification time      = 21-Jun-99 07:16:23.877293000 GMT
NFS:    Attribute change time  = 21-Jun-99 07:16:23.877293000 GMT
NFS:
NFS:  Post-operation attributes:
NFS:    File type = 2 (Directory)
NFS:    Mode = 0755
NFS:     Setuid = 0, Setgid = 0, Sticky = 0
NFS:     Owner's permissions = rwx
NFS:     Group's permissions = r-x
NFS:     Other's permissions = r-x
NFS:    Link count = 29, User ID = 0, Group ID = 0
NFS:    File size = 512, Used = 1024
NFS:
```

```
NFS:     Special: Major = 0, Minor = 0
NFS:     File system id = 8388608, File id = 2
NFS:     Last access time      = 21-Jun-99 07:13:54.555393000 GMT
NFS:     Modification time     = 21-Jun-99 07:16:48.057573000 GMT
NFS:     Attribute change time = 21-Jun-99 07:16:48.057573000 GMT
```

7.3.13   Procedure 12: REMOVE—Remove a File

Description

Procedure REMOVE removes (deletes) an entry from a directory. If the entry in the directory was the last reference to the corresponding filesystem object, the object may be destroyed.

Arguments		*Results*	
nfs_fh3	dir;	nfsstat3 status;	
filename3	name;	wcc_data dir_wcc;	

Arguments

dir

The filehandle for the directory from which the entry is to be removed.

name

The name of the entry to be removed. Refer to section 5.3.1 for a description of allowable filenames.

Results

status

NFS3_OK.

dir_wcc

Weak cache consistency data for the directory dir. For a client that requires only the post-REMOVE directory attributes, the attributes can be found in wcc_data.after (page 145).

Results on Failure

status

Error code.

dir_wcc

Weak cache consistency data for the directory dir. For a client that requires only the post-REMOVE directory attributes, the attributes can be found in dir_wcc.after. Even though the REMOVE failed, full wcc_data is returned to allow the client to determine whether the failing REMOVE changed the directory.

Implementation

In general, REMOVE is intended to remove nondirectory file objects and RMDIR is to be used to remove directories. However, REMOVE can be used to remove directories, subject to restrictions imposed by either the client or server interfaces. This had been a source of confusion in the NFS version 2 protocol.

The concept of last reference is server specific. However, if the nlink field in the previous attributes of the object had the value 1, the client should not rely on referring to the object via a filehandle. Likewise, the client should not rely on the resources (disk space, directory entry, and so on) formerly associated with the object becoming immediately available. Thus, if a client needs to be able to continue to access a file after using REMOVE to remove it, the client should take steps to make sure that the file will still be accessible. The usual mechanism used is to use RENAME to rename the file from its old name to a new hidden name. For more details see section 8.4.

Errors

NFS3ERR_NOENT	2	No such file or directory. The file or directory name specified does not exist.
NFS3ERR_IO	5	I/O error. A hard error (for example, a disk error) occurred while processing the requested operation.
NFS3ERR_ACCES	13	Permission denied. The caller does not have the correct permission to perform the requested operation. Contrast this with NFS3ERR_PERM, which restricts itself to owner or privileged-user permission failures.
NFS3ERR_NOTDIR	20	Not a directory. The caller specified a non-directory in a directory operation.
NFS3ERR_ROFS	30	Read-only filesystem. A modifying operation was attempted on a read-only filesystem.
NFS3ERR_NAMETOOLONG	63	The filename in an operation was too long.
NFS3ERR_STALE	70	Invalid filehandle. The filehandle given in the arguments was invalid. The file referred to by that filehandle no longer exists or access to it has been revoked.
NFS3ERR_BADHANDLE	10001	Illegal NFS filehandle. The filehandle failed internal consistency checks.

continued

NFS3ERR_SERVERFAULT   10006   An error occurred on the server that does not map to any of the legal NFS version 3 protocol error values. The client should translate this into an appropriate error. UNIX clients may choose to translate this to EIO.

Snoop Trace of REMOVE

```
NFS:  Proc = 12 (Remove file)
NFS:  File handle = 008000180000000002000A000000017A40
NFS:                09BD9D63000A00000000DD0A50295369
NFS:  File name = subfile
```

⬇

```
NFS:  Proc = 12 (Remove file)
NFS:  Status = 0 (OK)
NFS:  Pre-operation attributes:
NFS:    Size = 512 bytes
NFS:    Modification time    = 13-Nov-97 23:04:50.261264000 GMT
NFS:    Attribute change time = 13-Nov-97 23:04:50.261264000 GMT
NFS:
NFS:  Post-operation attributes:
NFS:    File type = 2 (Directory)
NFS:    Mode = 0775
NFS:     Setuid = 0, Setgid = 0, Sticky = 0
NFS:     Owner's permissions = rwx
NFS:     Group's permissions = rwx
NFS:     Other's permissions = r-x
NFS:    Link count = 2, User ID = 3497, Group ID = 10
NFS:    File size = 512, Used = 1024
NFS:    Special: Major = 0, Minor = 0
NFS:    File system id = 8388632, File id = 96832
NFS:    Last access time     = 12-Jul-98 00:42:58.986867000 GMT
NFS:    Modification time    = 12-Jul-98 00:42:59.006869000 GMT
NFS:    Attribute change time = 12-Jul-98 00:42:59.006869000 GMT
```

7.3.14   Procedure 13: RMDIR—Remove Directory

Description

Procedure RMDIR removes (deletes) a subdirectory from a directory. If the directory entry of the subdirectory is the last reference to the subdirectory, the subdirectory may be destroyed.

```
Arguments                    Results
nfs_fh3   dir;               nfsstat3 status;
filename3 name;              wcc_data dir_wcc;
```

Arguments

dir

The filehandle for the directory from which the subdirectory is to be removed.

name

The name of the subdirectory to be removed. Refer to section 5.3.1 for a description of allowable filenames.

Results

status

NFS3_OK.

dir_wcc

Weak cache consistency data for the directory dir. For a client that requires only the post-RMDIR directory attributes, the attributes can be found in wcc_data.after (page 145).

Results on Failure

status

Error code.

dir_wcc

Weak cache consistency data for the directory dir. For a client that requires only the post-RMDIR directory attributes, the attributes can be found in dir_wcc.after. Note that even though the RMDIR failed, full wcc_data is returned to allow the client to determine whether the failing RMDIR changed the directory.

Implementation

On some servers, removal of a nonempty directory is disallowed. The client should not rely on the resources (disk space, directory entry, and so on) formerly associated with the directory becoming immediately available.

Errors

NFS3ERR_NOENT	2	No such file or directory. The file or directory name specified does not exist.
NFS3ERR_IO	5	I/O error. A hard error (e.g., a disk error) occurred while processing the requested operation.

continued

NFS3ERR_ACCES	13	Permission denied. The caller does not have the correct permission to perform the requested operation. Contrast this with NFS3ERR_PERM, which restricts itself to owner or privileged-user permission failures.
NFS3ERR_EXIST	17	File exists. The file specified already exists.
NFS3ERR_NOTDIR	20	Not a directory. The caller specified a non-directory in a directory operation.
NFS3ERR_INVAL	22	Invalid argument or unsupported argument for an operation.
NFS3ERR_ROFS	30	Read-only filesystem. A modifying operation was attempted on a read-only filesystem.
NFS3ERR_NAMETOOLONG	31	The filename in an operation was too long.
NFS3ERR_NOTEMPTY	66	An attempt was made to remove a directory that was not empty.
NFS3ERR_STALE	70	Invalid filehandle. The filehandle given in the arguments was invalid. The file referred to by that filehandle no longer exists or access to it has been revoked.
NFS3ERR_BADHANDLE	10001	Illegal NFS filehandle. The filehandle failed internal consistency checks.
NFS3ERR_NOTSUPP	10004	Operation is not supported.
NFS3ERR_SERVERFAULT	10006	An error occurred on the server that does not map to any of the legal NFS version 3 protocol error values. The client should translate this into an appropriate error. UNIX clients may choose to translate this to EIO.

Snoop Trace of RMDIR

```
NFS:   Proc = 13 (Remove directory)
NFS:   File handle = 00800018000000002000A000000016FD4
NFS:                     4507FA55000A00000000DD0A50295369
NFS:   File name = subdir
```

⇩

```
NFS:   Proc = 13 (Remove directory)
NFS:   Status = 0 (OK)
NFS:   Pre-operation attributes:
NFS:     Size = 512 bytes
NFS:     Modification time      = 13-Nov-97 23:04:39.201266000 GMT
NFS:     Attribute change time  = 13-Nov-97 23:04:39.201266000 GMT
NFS:
```

```
NFS:  Post-operation attributes:
NFS:    File type = 2 (Directory)
NFS:    Mode = 0775
NFS:     Setuid = 0, Setgid = 0, Sticky = 0
NFS:     Owner's permissions = rwx
NFS:     Group's permissions = rwx
NFS:     Other's permissions = r-x
NFS:    Link count = 2, User ID = 3497, Group ID = 10
NFS:    File size = 512, Used = 1024
NFS:    Special: Major = 0, Minor = 0
NFS:    File system id = 8388632, File id = 94164
NFS:    Last access time    = 12-Jul-98 00:42:58.956866000 GMT
NFS:    Modification time   = 12-Jul-98 00:42:59.066867000 GMT
NFS:    Attribute change time = 12-Jul-98 00:42:59.066867000 GMT
```

7.3.15   Procedure 14: RENAME—Rename File or Directory

Description

Procedure RENAME renames the file identified by fromname in the directory fromdir to toname in the directory todir. The operation is required to be atomic to the client. The directories todir and fromdir must reside on the same filesystem and server.

Arguments		*Results*	
nfs_fh3	fromdir;	nfsstat3	status;
filename3	fromname;	wcc_data	fromdir_wcc;
nfs_fh3	todir;	wcc_data	todir_wcc;
filename3	toname;		

Arguments

fromdir

The filehandle for the directory from which the entry is to be renamed.

fromname

The name of the entry that identifies the object to be renamed. Refer to section 5.3.1 for a description of allowable filenames.

todir

The filehandle for the directory to which the object is to be renamed. It is commonly the same as fromdir.

toname

The new name for the object. Refer to section 5.3.1 for a description of allowable filenames. If the directory todir already contains an entry with the name toname, the source object must be compatible with the target: either both are nondirectories or both are directories and the target must be empty. If compatible, the existing target is removed before the rename occurs. If they are not compatible or if the target is a directory but not empty, the server should return the error NFS3ERR_EXIST.

Results

status

NFS3_OK if successful, otherwise an error code.

fromdir_wcc

Weak cache consistency data for the directory fromdir.

todir_wcc

Weak cache consistency data for the directory todir.

Implementation

The RENAME operation must be atomic to the client. This means that the RENAME operation must not fail in a way that leaves a directory entry in a partially renamed state nor should a client be able to detect any partially renamed state on the server. The phrase "todir and fromdir must reside on the same filesystem on the server [or the operation will fail]" means that the fsid fields in the attributes for the directories are the same. If they reside on different filesystems, the error NFS3ERR_XDEV is returned. Even though the operation is atomic, the status NFS3ERR_MLINK may be returned if the server used an "unlink/link/unlink" sequence internally.

A filehandle may or may not become stale on a rename. However, server implementors are strongly encouraged to attempt to keep filehandles from becoming stale in this fashion.

If fromdir/fromname and todir/toname both refer to the same file (they might be hard links of each other), then RENAME should perform no action and return NFS3_OK.

Errors

NFS3ERR_NOENT	2	No such file or directory. The file or directory name specified does not exist.	
NFS3ERR_IO	5	I/O error. A hard error (e.g., a disk error) occurred while processing the requested operation.	
NFS3ERR_ACCES	13	Permission denied. The caller does not have the correct permission to perform the requested operation. Contrast this with NFS3ERR_PERM, which restricts itself to owner or privileged-user permission failures.	

continued

NFS3ERR_EXIST	17	File exists. The file specified already exists.
NFS3ERR_XDEV	19	Attempt to do a cross-device hard link.
NFS3ERR_NOTDIR	20	Not a directory. The caller specified a non-directory in a directory operation.
NFS3ERR_ISDIR	21	Is a directory. The caller specified a directory in a nondirectory operation.
NFS3ERR_INVAL	22	Invalid argument or unsupported argument for an operation.
NFS3ERR_NOSPC	28	No space left on device. The operation would have caused the server's filesystem to exceed its limit.
NFS3ERR_ROFS	30	Read-only filesystem. A modifying operation was attempted on a read-only filesystem.
NFS3ERR_MLINK	31	Too many hard links.
NFS3ERR_NAMETOOLONG	63	The filename in an operation was too long.
NFS3ERR_NOTEMPTY	66	An attempt was made to remove a directory that was not empty.
NFS3ERR_DQUOT	69	Resource (quota) hard limit exceeded. The user's resource limit on the server has been exceeded.
NFS3ERR_STALE	70	Invalid filehandle. The filehandle given in the arguments was invalid. The file referred to by that filehandle no longer exists or access to it has been revoked.
NFS3ERR_BADHANDLE	10001	Illegal NFS filehandle. The filehandle failed internal consistency checks.
NFS3ERR_NOTSUPP	10004	Operation is not supported.
NFS3ERR_SERVERFAULT	10006	An error occurred on the server that does not map to any of the legal NFS version 3 protocol error values. The client should translate this into an appropriate error. UNIX clients may choose to translate this to EIO.

Snoop Trace of RENAME

```
NFS:  Proc = 14 (Rename)
NFS:  File handle = 008000180000000002000A000000011168
NFS:              102754F8000A00000000DD0A50295369
NFS:  File name = fubar
```

```
NFS:   File handle = 008000180000002000A000000011168
NFS:                 102754F8000A00000000DD0A50295369
NFS:   File name = barfu
```

⇩

```
NFS:   Proc = 14 (Rename)
NFS:   Status = 0 (OK)
NFS:   Pre-operation attributes: (from directory)
NFS:      Size = 1024 bytes
NFS:      Modification time      = 12-Jul-98 00:46:00.246866000 GMT
NFS:      Attribute change time  = 12-Jul-98 00:46:00.246866000 GMT
NFS:
NFS:   Post-operation attributes: (from directory)
NFS:      File type = 2 (Directory)
NFS:      Mode = 0777
NFS:       Setuid = 0, Setgid = 0, Sticky = 0
NFS:       Owner's permissions = rwx
NFS:       Group's permissions = rwx
NFS:       Other's permissions = rwx
NFS:      Link count = 8, User ID = 3497, Group ID = 1
NFS:      File size = 1024, Used = 1024
NFS:      Special: Major = 0, Minor = 0
NFS:      File system id = 8388632, File id = 69992
NFS:      Last access time      = 12-Jul-98 00:55:34.961134000 GMT
NFS:      Modification time     = 12-Jul-98 00:55:55.211121000 GMT
NFS:      Attribute change time = 12-Jul-98 00:55:55.211121000 GMT
NFS:
NFS:   Pre-operation attributes: (to directory)
NFS:      Size = 1024 bytes
NFS:      Modification time      = 12-Jul-98 00:46:00.246866000 GMT
NFS:      Attribute change time  = 12-Jul-98 00:46:00.246866000 GMT
NFS:
NFS:   Post-operation attributes: (to directory)
NFS:      File type = 2 (Directory)
NFS:      Mode = 0777
NFS:       Setuid = 0, Setgid = 0, Sticky = 0
NFS:       Owner's permissions = rwx
NFS:       Group's permissions = rwx
NFS:       Other's permissions = rwx
NFS:      Link count = 8, User ID = 3497, Group ID = 1
NFS:      File size = 1024, Used = 1024
NFS:      Special: Major = 0, Minor = 0
NFS:      File system id = 8388632, File id = 69992
NFS:      Last access time      = 12-Jul-98 00:55:34.961134000 GMT
NFS:      Modification time     = 12-Jul-98 00:55:55.211121000 GMT
NFS:      Attribute change time = 12-Jul-98 00:55:55.211121000 GMT
```

7.3.16   Procedure 15: LINK—Create Link to an Object

Description
Procedure LINK creates a hard link fromname in the directory fromdir for file. The file and its hard link must reside on the same filesystem and server.

Arguments		*Results*	
nfs_fh3	file;	nfsstat3	status;
nfs_fh3	fromdir;	post_op_attr	fromdir_wcc;
filename3	fromname;	wcc_data	linkdir_wcc;

Arguments
file

The filehandle for the existing filesystem object.

fromdir

The filehandle for the directory in which the link is to be created.

fromname

The name that is to be associated with the created link. Refer to section 5.3.1 for a description of allowable filenames.

Results
status

NFS3_OK if successful, otherwise an error code.

fromdir_wcc

The postoperation attributes of the filesystem object identified by file (page 144).

linkdir_wcc

Weak cache consistency data for the directory fromdir (page 145).

Implementation
Changes to any property of the hard-linked files are reflected in all the linked files. When a hard link is made to a file, the attributes for the file should have a value for nlink that is one greater than the value before the LINK.

The comments under RENAME regarding object and target residing on the same filesystem apply here as well. The comments regarding the target name apply as well.

Errors

NFS3ERR_IO	5	I/O error. A hard error (for example, a disk error) occurred while processing the requested operation.
NFS3ERR_ACCES	13	Permission denied. The caller does not have the correct permission to perform the requested operation. Contrast this with NFS3ERR_PERM, which restricts itself to owner or privileged-user permission failures.
NFS3ERR_EXIST	17	File exists. The file specified already exists.
NFS3ERR_XDEV	18	Attempt to do a cross-device hard link.
NFS3ERR_NOTDIR	20	Not a directory. The caller specified a non-directory in a directory operation.
NFS3ERR_INVAL	22	Invalid argument or unsupported argument for an operation.
NFS3ERR_NOSPC	28	No space left on device. The operation would have caused the server's filesystem to exceed its limit.
NFS3ERR_ROFS	30	Read-only filesystem. A modifying operation was attempted on a read-only filesystem.
NFS3ERR_MLINK	31	Too many hard links.
NFS3ERR_NAMETOOLONG	63	The filename in an operation was too long.
NFS3ERR_DQUOT	69	Resource (quota) hard limit exceeded. The user's resource limit on the server has been exceeded.
NFS3ERR_STALE	70	Invalid filehandle. The filehandle given in the arguments was invalid. The file referred to by that filehandle no longer exists, or access to it has been revoked.
NFS3ERR_BADHANDLE	10001	Illegal NFS filehandle. The filehandle failed internal consistency checks.
NFS3ERR_NOTSUPP	10004	Operation is not supported.
NFS3ERR_SERVERFAULT	10006	An error occurred on the server that does not map to any of the legal NFS version 3 protocol error values. The client should translate this into an appropriate error. UNIX clients may choose to translate this to EIO.

Snoop Trace of LINK

```
NFS:  Proc = 15 (Link)
NFS:  File handle = 00800018000000002000A00000001117F
NFS:              5E58E82F000A00000000DD0A50295369
NFS:  File handle = 00800018000000002000A000000011168
NFS:              102754F8000A00000000DD0A50295369
NFS:  File name = hardlink
```

⇩

```
NFS:  Proc = 15 (Link)
NFS:  Status = 0 (OK)
NFS:  Post-operation attributes:
NFS:    File type = 1 (Regular File)
NFS:    Mode = 0644
NFS:     Setuid = 0, Setgid = 0, Sticky = 0
NFS:     Owner's permissions = rw-
NFS:     Group's permissions = r--
NFS:     Other's permissions = r--
NFS:    Link count = 2, User ID = 3497, Group ID = 10
NFS:    File size = 445, Used = 1024
NFS:    Special: Major = 0, Minor = 0
NFS:    File system id = 8388632, File id = 70015
NFS:    Last access time    = 12-Jul-98 00:43:56.746868000 GMT
NFS:    Modification time   = 12-Jul-98 00:43:56.806866000 GMT
NFS:    Attribute change time = 12-Jul-98 00:46:00.216871000 GMT
NFS:
NFS:  Pre-operation attributes:
NFS:    Size = 1024 bytes
NFS:    Modification time   = 12-Jul-98 00:45:35.766868000 GMT
NFS:    Attribute change time = 12-Jul-98 00:45:35.766868000 GMT
NFS:
NFS:  Post-operation attributes:
NFS:    File type = 2 (Directory)
NFS:    Mode = 0777
NFS:     Setuid = 0, Setgid = 0, Sticky = 0
NFS:     Owner's permissions = rwx
NFS:     Group's permissions = rwx
NFS:     Other's permissions = rwx
NFS:    Link count = 8, User ID = 3497, Group ID = 1
NFS:    File size = 1024, Used = 1024
NFS:    Special: Major = 0, Minor = 0
NFS:    File system id = 8388632, File id = 69992
NFS:    Last access time    = 12-Jul-98 00:42:20.586866000 GMT
NFS:    Modification time   = 12-Jul-98 00:46:00.246866000 GMT
NFS:    Attribute change time = 12-Jul-98 00:46:00.246866000 GMT
```

7.3.17   Procedure 16: READDIR—Read from Directory

Description

Procedure READDIR retrieves a variable number of entries, in sequence, from a directory and returns the name and file identifier for each, with information to allow the client to request additional directory entries in a subsequent READDIR request.

Arguments		*Results*
nfs_fh3	dir;	```switch (nfsstat3 status) {```

```
Arguments

nfs_fh3      dir;
uint64       cookie;
cookieverf3  cookieverf;
uint32       count;
```

```
Results

switch (nfsstat3 status) {
   case NFS3_OK = 0:
      post_op_attr dir_attr;
      cookieverf3  cookieverf;
      list {
         uint64     fileid;
         filename3 name;
         uint64     cookie;
      };
      boolean  eof;
   default:
      post_op_attr dir_attr;
}
```

Arguments

`dir`

The filehandle for the directory to be read.

`cookie`

This should be set to 0 in the first request to read the directory. On subsequent requests, it should be a cookie as returned by the server.

`cookieverf`

This should be set to 0 in the first request to read the directory. On subsequent requests, it should be a `cookieverf` as returned by the server. The `cookieverf` must match that returned by the READDIR in which the cookie was acquired.

`count`

The maximum size of the reply arguments, in bytes. The size must include all XDR overhead. The server is free to return fewer than `count` bytes of data.

Results

`status`

NFS3_OK.

dir_attr

The attributes of the directory dir.

cookieverf

The cookie verifier.

entries

A list of directory entries, each containing

fileid

The fileid attribute of each entry.

name

The name of the directory entry.

cookie

An opaque reference to the next entry in the directory. The cookie is used in the next READDIR call to get more entries starting at a given point in the directory dir.

eof

TRUE if the last member of entry list is the last entry in the directory or the list of entries is empty and the cookie corresponded to the end of the directory. If FALSE, there may be more entries to read.

Results on Failure

status

Error code.

dir_attr

The attributes of the directory dir (page 144).

Implementation

In the NFS version 2 protocol, each directory entry returned included a cookie identifying a point in the directory. By including this cookie in a subsequent READDIR, the client could resume the directory read at any point in the directory. One problem with this scheme was that there was no easy way for a server to verify that a cookie was valid. If two READDIRs were separated by one or more operations that changed the directory in some way (for example, reordering or compressing it), it was possible that the second READDIR could miss entries or process entries more than once. If the cookie was no longer usable, for example, pointing into the middle of a directory entry, the server would have to either round the cookie down to the cookie of the previous entry or round it up to the cookie of the next entry in the directory. Either way would possibly lead to incorrect results and the client would be unaware that any problem existed.

In the NFS version 3 protocol, each READDIR request includes both a cookie and a cookie verifier. For the first call, both are set to 0. The response includes a new cookie verifier, with a cookie per entry. For subsequent READ-DIRs, the client must present both the cookie and the corresponding cookie verifier. If the server detects that the cookie is no longer valid, the server will reject the READDIR request with the status NFS3ERR_BAD_COOKIE. The client should be careful to avoid holding directory entry cookies across operations that modify the directory contents, such as REMOVE and CREATE.

One implementation of the cookie-verifier mechanism might be for the server to use the modification time of the directory. This might be overly restrictive, however. A better approach would be to record the time of the last directory modification that changed the directory organization in a way that would make it impossible to reliably interpret a cookie. Servers in which directory cookies are always valid are free to use zero as the verifier always.

The server may return fewer than count bytes of XDR-encoded entries. The count specified by the client in the request should be greater than or equal to FSINFO dtpref. Since UNIX clients give a special meaning to the fileid value zero, UNIX clients should be careful to map zero fileid values to some other value, and servers should try to avoid sending a zero fileid.

Errors

NFS3ERR_IO	5	I/O error. A hard error (for example, a disk error) occurred while processing the requested operation.
NFS3ERR_ACCES	13	Permission denied. The caller does not have the correct permission to perform the requested operation. Contrast this with NFS3ERR_PERM, which restricts itself to owner or privileged-user permission failures.
NFS3ERR_NOTDIR	20	Not a directory. The caller specified a nondirectory in a directory operation.
NFS3ERR_STALE	70	Invalid filehandle. The filehandle given in the arguments was invalid. The file referred to by that filehandle no longer exists or access to it has been revoked.
NFS3ERR_BADHANDLE	10001	Illegal NFS filehandle. The filehandle failed internal consistency checks.
NFS3ERR_BAD_COOKIE	10003	READDIR or READDIRPLUS cookie is stale.

continued

NFS3ERR_TOOSMALL	10005	Buffer or request is too small.
NFS3ERR_SERVERFAULT	10006	An error occurred on the server that does not map to any of the legal NFS version 3 protocol error values. The client should translate this into an appropriate error. UNIX clients may choose to translate this to EIO.

Snoop Trace of READDIR

```
NFS:  Proc = 16 (Read from directory)
NFS:  File handle = 008000180000000002000A000000017A40
NFS:                09BD9D63000A00000000DD0A50295369
NFS:  Cookie   = 512
NFS:  Verifier = 0000000000000000
NFS:  Count = 1048
```

⇩

```
NFS:  Proc = 16 (Read from directory)
NFS:  Status = 0 (OK)
NFS:  Post-operation attributes:
NFS:    File type = 2 (Directory)
NFS:    Mode = 0775
NFS:     Setuid = 0, Setgid = 0, Sticky = 0
NFS:     Owner's permissions = rwx
NFS:     Group's permissions = rwx
NFS:     Other's permissions = r-x
NFS:    Link count = 2, User ID = 3497, Group ID = 10
NFS:    File size = 512, Used = 1024
NFS:    Special: Major = 0, Minor = 0
NFS:    File system id = 8388632, File id = 94164
NFS:    Last access time    = 12-Jul-98 00:42:58.956866000 GMT
NFS:    Modification time   = 12-Jul-98 00:42:59.126872000 GMT
NFS:    Attribute change time = 12-Jul-98 00:42:59.126872000 GMT
NFS:
NFS:  Cookie verifier = 0000000000000000
NFS:
NFS:   File id  Cookie Name
NFS:    0 entries
NFS:  EOF = True
```

7.3.18   Procedure 17: READDIRPLUS—Extended Read from Directory

Description

Procedure READDIRPLUS retrieves a variable number of entries from a filesystem directory and returns complete information about each entry along with information to allow the client to request additional directory entries in a subsequent READDIRPLUS. READDIRPLUS differs from READDIR only in the amount of information returned for each entry. In READDIR, each entry returns the filename and the `fileid`. In READDIRPLUS, each entry returns the name, the `fileid`, attributes (including the `fileid`), and filehandle.

Arguments		*Results*

```
Arguments                          Results
nfs_fh3     dir;                    switch (nfsstat3 status) {
uint64      cookie;                    case NFS3_OK = 0:
cookieverf3 cookieverf;                   post_op_attr dir_attr;
uint32      dircount;                     cookieverf3  cookieverf;
uint32      maxcount;                     list {
                                              uint64     fileid;
                                              filename3 name;
                                              uint64     cookie;
                                              post_op_attr  name_attr;
                                              switch (boolean) {
                                                  case TRUE:
                                                      nfs_fh3 obj_fh;
                                                  case FALSE:
                                                      void;
                                              }
                                          };
                                          boolean  eof;
                                       default:
                                          post_op_attr dir_attr;
                                    }
```

Arguments

dir

The filehandle for the directory to be read.

cookie

This should be set to 0 on the first request to read a directory. On subsequent requests, it should be a cookie as returned by the server.

cookieverf

This should be set to 0 on the first request to read a directory. On subsequent requests, it should be a cookieverf as returned by the server. The cookieverf must match that returned by the READDIRPLUS call in which the cookie was acquired.

dircount

The maximum number of bytes of directory information returned. This number should not include the size of the attributes and filehandle portions of the result.

maxcount

The maximum size of the READDIRPLUS3 reply in bytes. The size must include all XDR overhead. The server is free to return fewer than maxcount bytes of data.

Results

status

  ,   NFS3_OK.

dir_attr

The attributes of the directory, dir (page 144).

cookieverf

The cookie verifier.

entries

A list of directory entries, each containing

    fileid

      The fileid attribute of each entry.

    name

      The name of the directory entry.

    cookie

      An opaque reference to the next entry in the directory. The cookie is used in the next READDIR call to get more entries starting at a given point in the directory dir.

    name_attr

      File attributes for the entry returned in a post_op_attr structure, giving the server the option of not returning attributes.

    obj_fh

      Filehandle for the entry.

eof

TRUE if the last member of the entries list is the last entry in the directory or the list is empty and the cookie corresponded to the end of the directory. If FALSE, there may be more entries to read.

Results on Failure

status

Error code.

`dir_attr`

The attributes of the directory `dir`.

Implementation

Issues that need to be understood for this procedure include increased cache flushing activity on the client (as new filehandles are returned with names that are entered into caches) and over-the-wire overhead versus expected subsequent LOOKUP elimination. The intent of this procedure is to improve performance for directory browsing where attributes are always required, as when navigating a file tree with a graphical file browser.

The `dircount` and `maxcount` fields are included as an optimization. Consider a READDIRPLUS call on a UNIX operating system implementation for 1048 bytes: the reply does not contain many entries because of the overhead due to attributes and filehandles. An alternative is to issue a READDIRPLUS call for 8192 bytes and then only use the first 1048 bytes of directory information. However, the server doesn't know that all that is needed is 1048 bytes of directory information (as would be returned by READDIR). It sees the 8192 byte request and issues a VOP_READDIR for 8192 bytes. It then steps through all those directory entries, obtaining attributes and filehandles for each entry. When it encodes the result, the server encodes only until it gets 8192 bytes of results, which include the attributes and filehandles. Thus, it has done a larger VOP_READDIR and many more attribute fetches than it needed to. The ratio of the directory entry size to the size of the attributes plus the size of the filehandle is usually at least 8 to 1. The server has done much more work than it needed to.

The solution to this problem is for the client to provide two counts to the server. The first is the number of bytes of directory information the client really wants, `dircount`. The second is the maximum number of bytes in the result, including the attributes and file handles, `maxcount`. Thus, the server will issue a VOP_READDIR for only the number of bytes that the client really wants to get, not an inflated number. This should help to reduce the size of VOP_READDIR requests on the server, thus reducing the amount of work done there, and to reduce the number of VOP_LOOKUP, VOP_GETATTR, and other calls done by the server to construct attributes and filehandles.

The server may return fewer than `maxcount` bytes of XDR-encoded entries. The `maxcount` specified by the client in the request should be greater than or equal to FSINFO `dtpref`. Since UNIX clients give a special meaning to the `fileid` value zero, UNIX clients should be careful to map zero `fileid` values to some other value, and servers should try to avoid sending a zero `fileid`.

Errors

NFS3ERR_IO	5	I/O error. A hard error (for example, a disk error) occurred while processing the requested operation.
NFS3ERR_ACCES	13	Permission denied. The caller does not have the correct permission to perform the requested operation. Contrast this with NFS3ERR_PERM, which restricts itself to owner or privileged-user permission failures.
NFS3ERR_NOTDIR	20	Not a directory. The caller specified a nondirectory in a directory operation.
NFS3ERR_STALE	70	Invalid filehandle. The filehandle given in the arguments was invalid. The file referred to by that filehandle no longer exists, or access to it has been revoked.
NFS3ERR_BADHANDLE	10001	Illegal NFS file handle. The file handle failed internal consistency checks.
NFS3ERR_BAD_COOKIE	10003	READDIR or READDIRPLUS cookie is stale.
NFS3ERR_NOTSUPP	10004	Operation is not supported.
NFS3ERR_TOOSMALL	10005	Buffer or request is too small.
NFS3ERR_SERVERFAULT	10006	An error occurred on the server that does not map to any of the legal NFS version 3 protocol error values. The client should translate this into an appropriate error. UNIX clients may choose to translate this to EIO.

Snoop Trace of READDIRPLUS

```
NFS:  Proc = 17 (Read from directory - plus)
NFS:  File handle = 0080001800000002000A000000016FD4
NFS:              4507FA55000A00000000DD0A50295369
NFS:  Cookie   = 0
NFS:  Verifier = 0000000000000000
NFS:  Dircount = 1048
NFS:  Maxcount = 8192

              ⬇

NFS:  Proc = 17 (Read from directory - plus)
NFS:  Status = 0 (OK)
NFS:  Post-operation attributes:
NFS:     File type = 2 (Directory)
NFS:     Mode = 0775
NFS:      Setuid = 0, Setgid = 0, Sticky = 0
NFS:      Owner's permissions = rwx
NFS:      Group's permissions = rwx
```

```
NFS:    Other's permissions = r-x
NFS:    Link count = 3, User ID = 3497, Group ID = 10
NFS:    File size = 512, Used = 1024
NFS:    Special: Major = 0, Minor = 0
NFS:    File system id = 8388632, File id = 94164
NFS:    Last access time    = 12-Jul-98 00:42:58.956866000 GMT
NFS:    Modification time    = 13-Nov-97 23:04:39.201266000 GMT
NFS:    Attribute change time = 13-Nov-97 23:04:39.201266000 GMT
NFS:
NFS: Cookie verifier = 0000000000000000
NFS:
NFS: ----------------- entry #1
NFS: File ID = 94164
NFS: Name = .
NFS: Cookie = 12
NFS: Post-operation attributes:
NFS:    File type = 2 (Directory)
NFS:    Mode = 0775
NFS:     Setuid = 0, Setgid = 0, Sticky = 0
NFS:     Owner's permissions = rwx
NFS:     Group's permissions = rwx
NFS:     Other's permissions = r-x
NFS:    Link count = 3, User ID = 3497, Group ID = 10
NFS:    File size = 512, Used = 1024
NFS:    Special: Major = 0, Minor = 0
NFS:    File system id = 8388632, File id = 94164
NFS:    Last access time    = 12-Jul-98 00:42:58.956866000 GMT
NFS:    Modification time    = 13-Nov-97 23:04:39.201266000 GMT
NFS:    Attribute change time = 13-Nov-97 23:04:39.201266000 GMT
NFS:
NFS: File handle = 0080001800000002000A000000016FD4
NFS:                4507FA55000A00000000DD0A50295369
NFS: ----------------- entry #2
NFS: File ID = 69992
NFS: Name = ..
NFS: Cookie = 24
NFS: Post-operation attributes:
NFS:    File type = 2 (Directory)
NFS:    Mode = 0777
NFS:     Setuid = 0, Setgid = 0, Sticky = 0
NFS:     Owner's permissions = rwx
NFS:     Group's permissions = rwx
NFS:     Other's permissions = rwx
NFS:    Link count = 9, User ID = 3497, Group ID = 1
NFS:    File size = 1024, Used = 1024
NFS:    Special: Major = 0, Minor = 0
NFS:    File system id = 8388632, File id = 69992
NFS:    Last access time    = 12-Jul-98 00:42:20.586866000 GMT
NFS:    Modification time    = 08-Jul-98 20:49:23.011564000 GMT
NFS:    Attribute change time = 08-Jul-98 20:49:23.011564000 GMT
NFS:
```

```
NFS:    File handle = 00800018000000002000A000000011168
NFS:                  102754F8000A00000000DD0A50295369
NFS:    ------------------ entry #3
NFS:    File ID = 96832
NFS:    Name = subdir
NFS:    Cookie = 40
NFS:    Post-operation attributes:
NFS:      File type = 2 (Directory)
NFS:      Mode = 0775
NFS:       Setuid = 0, Setgid = 0, Sticky = 0
NFS:       Owner's permissions = rwx
NFS:       Group's permissions = rwx
NFS:       Other's permissions = r-x
NFS:      Link count = 2, User ID = 3497, Group ID = 10
NFS:      File size = 512, Used = 1024
NFS:      Special: Major = 0, Minor = 0
NFS:      File system id = 8388632, File id = 96832
NFS:      Last access time     = 11-Jul-98 10:15:00.835423000 GMT
NFS:      Modification time    = 13-Nov-97 23:04:50.261264000 GMT
NFS:      Attribute change time = 13-Nov-97 23:04:50.261264000 GMT
NFS:
NFS:    File handle = 00800018000000002000A000000017A40
NFS:                  09BD9D63000A00000000DD0A50295369
NFS:    ------------------ entry #4
NFS:    File ID = 94165
NFS:    Name = afile
NFS:    Cookie = 512
NFS:    Post-operation attributes:
NFS:      File type = 1 (Regular File)
NFS:      Mode = 0664
NFS:       Setuid = 0, Setgid = 0, Sticky = 0
NFS:       Owner's permissions = rw-
NFS:       Group's permissions = rw-
NFS:       Other's permissions = r--
NFS:      Link count = 1, User ID = 3497, Group ID = 10
NFS:      File size = 11, Used = 1024
NFS:      Special: Major = 0, Minor = 0
NFS:      File system id = 8388632, File id = 94165
NFS:      Last access time     = 26-May-98 23:24:34.037944000 GMT
NFS:      Modification time    = 13-Nov-97 23:04:39.201268000 GMT
NFS:      Attribute change time = 13-Nov-97 23:04:39.201268000 GMT
NFS:
NFS:    File handle = 00800018000000002000A000000016FD5
NFS:                  1AB7F898000A00000000DD0A50295369
NFS:
NFS:    4 entries
NFS:    EOF = True
```

7.3.19   Procedure 18: FSSTAT—Get Dynamic Filesystem Information

Description

Procedure FSSTAT retrieves volatile filesystem state information.

Arguments	*Results*

nfs_fh3 obj_fh;	switch (nfsstat3 status) {
	    case NFS3_OK = 0:
	        post_op_attr obj_attr;
	        uint64 tbytes;
	        uint64 fbytes;
	        uint64 abytes;
	        uint64 tfiles;
	        uint64 ffiles;
	        uint64 afiles;
	        uint32 invarsec;
	    default:
	        post_op_attr obj_attr;
	}

Arguments

obj_fh

A filehandle identifying an object in the filesystem. This is normally a file-handle for a mountpoint for a filesystem, as originally obtained from the MOUNT service on the server.

Results

status

NFS3_OK.

obj_attr

The attributes of the filesystem object specified in obj_fh (page 144).

tbytes

The total size, in bytes, of the filesystem.

fbytes

The amount of free space, in bytes, in the filesystem.

abytes

The amount of free space, in bytes, available to the user identified by the authentication information in the RPC. (This reflects space that is reserved by the filesystem; it does not reflect any quota system implemented by the server.)

tfiles

The total number of file slots in the filesystem. (On a UNIX server, this often corresponds to the number of inodes configured.)

ffiles

The number of free file slots in the filesystem.

afiles

The number of free file slots that are available to the user corresponding to the authentication information in the RPC. (This reflects slots that are reserved by the filesystem; it does not reflect any quota system implemented by the server.)

invarsec

A measure of filesystem volatility: this is the number of seconds for which the filesystem is not expected to change. For a volatile, frequently updated filesystem, this will be 0. For an immutable filesystem, such as a CD-ROM, this would be the largest unsigned integer. For filesystems that are infrequently modified, for example, one containing local executable programs and on-line documentation, a value corresponding to a few hours or days might be used. The client may use this as a hint in tuning its cache management. Note, however, that this measure is assumed to be dynamic and may change at any time.

Results on Failure

status

Error code.

obj_attr

The attributes of the filesystem object specified in obj_fh (page 144).

Implementation

Not all implementations can support the entire list of attributes. It is expected that servers will make a best effort at supporting all the attributes.

Errors

NFS3ERR_IO	I/O error. A hard error (e.g., a disk error) occurred while processing the requested operation.
NFS3ERR_STALE	Invalid filehandle. The filehandle given in the arguments was invalid. The file referred to by that filehandle no longer exists, or access to it has been revoked.

continued

NFS3ERR_BADHANDLE   Illegal NFS filehandle. The filehandle failed internal consistency checks.

NFS3ERR_SERVERFAULT   An error occurred on the server that does not map to any of the legal NFS version 3 protocol error values. The client should translate this into an appropriate error. UNIX clients may choose to translate this to EIO.

Snoop Trace of FSSTAT

```
NFS:  Proc = 18 (Get filesystem statistics)
NFS:  File handle = 0080001800000002000A00000000DD0A
NFS:                50295369000A00000000DD0A50295369
```

⇩

```
NFS:  Proc = 18 (Get filesystem statistics)
NFS:  Status = 0 (OK)
NFS:  Post-operation attributes:
NFS:    File type = 2 (Directory)
NFS:    Mode = 0777
NFS:     Setuid = 0, Setgid = 0, Sticky = 0
NFS:     Owner's permissions = rwx
NFS:     Group's permissions = rwx
NFS:     Other's permissions = rwx
NFS:    Link count = 3, User ID = 0, Group ID = 3
NFS:    File size = 512, Used = 1024
NFS:    Special: Major = 0, Minor = 0
NFS:    File system id = 8388632, File id = 56586
NFS:    Last access time     = 11-Jul-98 10:15:00.835416000 GMT
NFS:    Modification time    = 24-Apr-98 03:55:41.840716000 GMT
NFS:    Attribute change time = 24-Apr-98 03:55:41.840716000 GMT
NFS:
NFS:  Total space = 334838784 bytes
NFS:  Available space = 34195456 bytes
NFS:  Available space - this user = 720896 bytes
NFS:  Total file slots = 163968
NFS:  Available file slots = 153028
NFS:  Available file slots - this user = 153028
NFS:  Invariant time = 0 sec
```

7.3.20   Procedure 19: FSINFO—Get Static Filesystem Information

Description

Procedure FSINFO retrieves nonvolatile filesystem state information and general information about the NFS version 3 protocol server implementation.

```
Arguments                          Results
nfs_fh3        obj_fh;             switch (nfsstat3 status) {
                                     case NFS3_OK = 0:
                                       post_op_attr obj_attr;
                                       uint32        rtmax;
                                       uint32        rtpref;
                                       uint32        rtmult;
                                       uint32        wtmax;
                                       uint32        wtpref;
                                       uint32        wtmult;
                                       uint32        dtpref;
                                       uint64        maxfilesize;
                                       nfstime3      time_delta;
                                       uint32        properties;
                                     default:
                                       post_op_attr obj_attr;
                                   }
```

Arguments

obj_fh

A filehandle identifying a file object. Normal usage is to provide a filehandle for a mountpoint for a filesystem, as originally obtained from the MOUNT service on the server.

Results

status

NFS3_OK.

obj_attr

The attributes of the filesystem object specified in obj_fh (page 144).

rtmax

The maximum size in bytes of a READ request supported by the server. Any READ with a number greater than rtmax will result in a short read of rtmax bytes or less.

rtpref

The preferred size in bytes of a READ request. This should be the same as rtmax unless there is a clear benefit in performance or efficiency.

rtmult

The suggested multiple for the size of a READ request.

wtmax

The maximum size in bytes of a WRITE request supported by the server. In general, the client is limited by wtmax since there is no guarantee that a server can handle a larger write. Any WRITE with a count greater than `wtmax` will result in a short write of at most `wtmax` bytes.

`wtpref`

The preferred size in bytes of a WRITE request. This should be the same as `wtmax` unless there is a clear benefit in performance or efficiency.

`wtmult`

The suggested multiple for the size of a WRITE request.

`dtpref`

The preferred size in bytes of a READDIR request.

`maxfilesize`

The maximum size in bytes of a file on the filesystem.

`time_delta`

The server time granularity. When setting a file time using SETATTR, the server guarantees only to preserve times to this accuracy. If this is {0, 1}, the server can support nanosecond times; {0, 1000000} denotes millisecond precision, and {1, 0} indicates that times are accurate only to the nearest second.

`properties`

A bit mask of filesystem properties. The following values are defined.

Value	Name	Property if bit is set
0x0001	FSF3_LINK	The file system supports hard links.
0x0002	FSF3_SYMLINK	The file system supports symbolic links.
0x0008	FSF3_HOMOGENEOUS	The information returned by PATHCONF is identical for every file and directory in the filesystem. If not set, the client should retrieve PATHCONF information for each file and directory as required.
0x0010	FSF3_CANSETTIME	The server will set the times for a file via SETATTR if requested (to the accuracy indicated by `time_delta`). If not set, the server cannot set times as requested.

Results on Failure

`status`

Error code.

`attributes`

The attributes of the filesystem object specified in `obj_fh`.

Implementation

Not all implementations can support the entire list of attributes. It is expected that a server will make a best effort at supporting all the attributes.

The filehandle provided is expected to be the filehandle of the filesystem root, as returned to the MOUNT operation. Since mounts may occur anywhere within an exported tree, the server should expect FSINFO requests specifying filehandles within the exported filesystem. A server may export different types of filesystems with different attributes returned to the FSINFO call. The client should retrieve FSINFO information for each mount completed. Though a server may return different FSINFO information for different files within a filesystem, there is no requirement that a client obtain FSINFO information for other than the filehandle returned at mount.

The `maxfilesize` field determines whether a server's particular filesystem uses 32-bit sizes and offsets or 64-bit file sizes and offsets. This may affect a client's processing.

The preferred sizes for requests are nominally tied to an exported filesystem mounted by a client. A surmountable issue arises in that the transfer size for an NFS version 3 protocol request depends not only on characteristics of the filesystem but also on characteristics of the network interface, particularly the maximum transfer unit (MTU). A server implementation can advertise different transfer sizes (for the fields `rtmax`, `rtpref`, `wtmax`, `wtpref`, and `dtpref`) depending on the interface on which the FSINFO request is received. This is an implementation issue.

Errors

NFS3ERR_STALE	70	Invalid filehandle. The filehandle given in the arguments was invalid. The file referred to by that filehandle no longer exists, or access to it has been revoked.
NFS3ERR_BADHANDLE	10001	Illegal NFS filehandle. The filehandle failed internal consistency checks.
NFS3ERR_SERVERFAULT	10006	An error occurred on the server that does not map to any of the legal NFS version 3 protocol error values. The client should translate this into an appropriate error. UNIX clients may choose to translate this to EIO.

Snoop Trace of FSINFO

```
NFS:  Proc = 19 (Get filesystem information)
NFS:  File handle = 00800018000000002000A00000000DD0A
NFS:                50295369000A00000000DD0A50295369
```

```
NFS:   Proc = 19 (Get filesystem information)
NFS:   Status = 0 (OK)
NFS:   Post-operation attributes:
NFS:     File type = 2 (Directory)
NFS:     Mode = 0777
NFS:       Setuid = 0, Setgid = 0, Sticky = 0
NFS:       Owner's permissions = rwx
NFS:       Group's permissions = rwx
NFS:       Other's permissions = rwx
NFS:     Link count = 3, User ID = 0, Group ID = 3
NFS:     File size = 512, Used = 1024
NFS:     Special: Major = 0, Minor = 0
NFS:     File system id = 8388632, File id = 56586
NFS:     Last access time    = 11-Jul-98 10:15:00.835416000 GMT
NFS:     Modification time     = 24-Apr-98 03:55:41.840716000 GMT
NFS:     Attribute change time = 24-Apr-98 03:55:41.840716000 GMT
NFS:
NFS:   Read transfer sizes:
NFS:       Maximum = 32768 bytes
NFS:       Preferred = 32768 bytes
NFS:       Suggested multiple = 512 bytes
NFS:   Write transfer sizes:
NFS:       Maximum = 32768 bytes
NFS:       Preferred = 32768 bytes
NFS:       Suggested multiple = 512 bytes
NFS:   Directory read size:
NFS:       Preferred = 8192 bytes
NFS:   File system limits:
NFS:       Max file size = 1099511627775 bytes
NFS:       Server minimum time discrimination = 0.001000 sec
NFS:   Properties = 0x1b
NFS:   .... ...1 = Hard links supported
NFS:   .... ..1. = Symbolic links supported
NFS:   .... 1... = Pathconf cannot vary per file
NFS:   ...1 .... = Server can always set file times
```

7.3.21   Procedure 20: PATHCONF—Retrieve POSIX Information

Description

Procedure PATHCONF retrieves the pathconf information for a file or directory. If the FSF_HOMOGENEOUS bit is set in FSFINFO3resok.properties, the pathconf information will be the same for all files and directories in the exported filesystem in which this file or directory resides.

```
    Arguments                           Results
    nfs_fh3        obj_fh;              switch (nfsstat3 status) {
                                            case NFS3_OK = 0:
                                                post_op_attr obj_attr;
                                                uint32       linkmax;
                                                uint32       name_max;
                                                boolean      no_trunc;
                                                boolean      chown_restricted;
                                                boolean      case_insensitive;
                                                boolean      case_preserving;
                                            default:
                                                post_op_attr obj_attr;
                                        }
```

Arguments

obj_fh

The filehandle for the filesystem object.

Results

status

NFS3_OK.

obj_attr

The attributes of the object specified by object (page 144).

linkmax

The maximum number of hard links to an object.

name_max

The maximum length of a component of a filename.

no_trunc

If TRUE, the server will reject any request that includes a name longer than name_max with the error NFS3ERR_NAMETOOLONG. If FALSE, any length name over name_max bytes will be silently truncated to name_max bytes.

chown_restricted

If TRUE, the server will reject any request to change either the owner or the group associated with a file if the caller is not the privileged user (uid 0).

case_insensitive

If TRUE, the server filesystem does not distinguish case when interpreting filenames.

case_preserving

If TRUE, the server filesystem will preserve the case of a name during a CREATE, MKDIR, MKNOD, SYMLINK, RENAME, or LINK operation.

Results on Failure

status

Error code.

obj_attr

The attributes of the object specified by object.

Implementation

In some implementations of the NFS version 2 protocol, pathconf information was obtained at mount time through the MOUNT protocol. The proper place to obtain it is as here, in the NFS version 3 protocol itself.

Errors

NFS3ERR_STALE	70	Invalid filehandle. The filehandle given in the arguments was invalid. The file referred to by that filehandle no longer exists, or access to it has been revoked.
NFS3ERR_BADHANDLE	10001	Illegal NFS filehandle. The filehandle failed internal consistency checks.
NFS3ERR_SERVERFAULT	10006	An error occurred on the server that does not map to any of the legal NFS version 3 protocol error values. The client should translate this into an appropriate error. UNIX clients may choose to translate this to EIO.

Snoop Trace of PATHCONF

```
NFS:  Proc = 20 (Get POSIX information)
NFS:  File handle = 00800018000000002000A000000011171
NFS:                   3FAF141C000A00000000DD0A50295369

            ⇩

NFS:  Proc = 20 (Get POSIX information)
NFS:  Status = 0 (OK)
NFS:  Post-operation attributes:
NFS:    File type = 1 (Regular File)
NFS:    Mode = 0666
NFS:     Setuid = 0, Setgid = 0, Sticky = 0
NFS:     Owner's permissions = rw-
NFS:     Group's permissions = rw-
```

```
NFS:     Other's permissions = rw-
NFS:     Link count = 1, User ID = 4294967294, Group ID = 429496729
NFS:     File size = 398520, Used = 409600
NFS:     Special: Major = 0, Minor = 0
NFS:     File system id = 8388632, File id = 70001
NFS:     Last access time     = 21-Apr-98 03:55:19.883238000 GMT
NFS:     Modification time    = 21-Apr-98 03:54:51.853236000 GMT
NFS:     Attribute change time = 24-Apr-98 00:07:36.737699000 GMT
NFS:
NFS: Link max = 32767
NFS: Name max = 255
NFS: No trunc         = True
NFS: Chown restricted = True
NFS: Case insensitive = False
NFS: Case preserving  = True
```

7.3.22 Procedure 21: COMMIT—Commit Cached Data on a Server to Stable Storage

Description

Procedure COMMIT forces or flushes data to stable storage that was previously written with a WRITE procedure call with the stable field set to UNSTABLE.

Arguments		*Results*

`nfs_fh3`
`uint64`
`uint32`
	`file;`
	`offset;`
	`count;`
		`switch (nfsstat3 status) {`
		`    case NFS3_OK = 0:`
		`        wcc_data    file_wcc;`
		`        writeverf3 verf;`
		`    default:`
		`        wcc_data    file_wcc;`
		`}`

Arguments

`file`

The filehandle for the file to which data is to be flushed (committed). This must identify a filesystem object of type NF3REG.

`offset`

The position within the file at which the flush is to begin. An offset of 0 means to flush data starting at the beginning of the file.

`count`

The number of bytes of data to flush. If `count` is 0, a flush from offset to the end of the file is done.

Results

status

NFS3_OK.

file_wcc

Weak cache consistency data for the file. For a client that requires only the postoperation file attributes, the attributes can be found in wcc_data.after (page 145).

verf

This is a cookie that the client can use to determine whether the server has rebooted between a call to WRITE and a subsequent call to COMMIT. This cookie must be consistent during a single boot session and must be unique between instances of the NFS version 3 protocol server where uncommitted data may be lost.

Results on Failure

status

Error code.

file_wcc

Weak cache consistency data for the file. For a client that requires only the postwrite file attributes, the attributes can be found in wcc_data.after. Even though the COMMIT failed, full wcc_data is returned to allow the client to determine whether the file changed on the server between calls to WRITE and COMMIT.

Implementation

Procedure COMMIT is similar in operation and semantics to the POSIX fsync(2) system call that synchronizes a file's state with the disk; that is, it flushes the file's data and metadata to disk. COMMIT performs the same operation for a client, flushing any unsynchronized data and metadata on the server to the server's disk for the specified file. Like fsync(2), it may be that there is some modified data or no modified data to synchronize. The data may have been synchronized by the server's normal periodic buffer synchronization activity. COMMIT will return NFS3_OK unless there has been an unexpected error.

COMMIT differs from fsync(2) in that it is possible for the client to flush a range of the file (most likely triggered by a buffer-reclamation scheme on the client before file has been completely written).

The server implementation of COMMIT is reasonably simple. If the server receives a full file COMMIT request, that is, starting at offset 0 and count 0, it should do the equivalent of fsync()-ing the file. Otherwise, it should arrange to have the cached data in the range specified by the offset and count to be flushed to stable storage. In both cases, any metadata associated with the file must be flushed to stable storage before returning. It is not an error for there to be nothing to flush on the server. This means that the data and metadata that needed to be flushed have already been flushed or lost during the last server failure.

The client implementation of COMMIT is a little more complex. There are two reasons for wanting to commit a client buffer to stable storage. The first is that the client wants to reuse a buffer. In this case, the offset and count of the buffer are sent to the server in the COMMIT request. The server then flushes any cached data based on the `offset` and `count` and flushes any metadata associated with the file. It then returns the status of the flush and the `verf` verifier. The other reason for the client to generate a COMMIT is for a full file flush, such as may be done at close. In this case, the client would gather all the buffers for this file that contain uncommitted data, do the COMMIT operation with an offset of 0 and count of 0, and then free all of those buffers. Any other dirty buffers would be sent to the server in the normal fashion.

This implementation will require some modifications to the buffer cache on the client. After a buffer is written with stable UNSTABLE, it must be considered as dirty by the client system until it is either flushed via a COMMIT operation or written via a WRITE operation with stable set to FILE_SYNC or DATA_SYNC. This is done to prevent the buffer from being freed and reused before the data can be flushed to stable storage on the server.

When a response comes back from either a WRITE or a COMMIT operation that contains an unexpected `verf`, the client will need to retransmit all the buffers containing uncommitted cached data to the server. How this is to be done is up to the implementor. If there is only one buffer of interest, then it should probably be sent back over in a WRITE request with the appropriate stable flag. If there are more than one, it might be worthwhile to retransmit all the buffers in WRITE requests with stable set to UNSTABLE and then retransmit the COMMIT operation to flush all the data on the server to stable storage. The timing of these retransmissions is left to the implementor.

This description applies to page-cache-based systems as well as buffer-cache-based systems. In page-cache-based systems, the virtual memory system will need to be modified instead of the buffer cache.

Errors

NFS3ERR_IO	5	I/O error. A hard error (for example, a disk error) occurred while processing the requested operation.
NFS3ERR_STALE	70	Invalid filehandle. The filehandle given in the arguments was invalid. The file referred to by that filehandle no longer exists, or access to it has been revoked.

continued

NFS3ERR_BADHANDLE   10001   Illegal NFS filehandle. The filehandle failed internal consistency checks.

NFS3ERR_SERVERFAULT   10006   An error occurred on the server that does not map to any of the legal NFS version 3 protocol error values. The client should translate this into an appropriate error. UNIX clients may choose to translate this to EIO.

Snoop Trace of COMMIT

```
NFS:   Proc = 21 (Commit to stable storage)
NFS:   File handle = 00800018000000002000A000000011182
NFS:                 56CB152E000A00000000DD0A50295369
NFS:   Offset = 0
NFS:   Count = 98304
```

⇩

```
NFS:   Proc = 21 (Commit to stable storage)
NFS:   Status = 0 (OK)
NFS:   Pre-operation attributes:
NFS:     Size = 100000 bytes
NFS:     Modification time      = 12-Jul-98 00:56:48.091126000 GMT
NFS:     Attribute change time  = 12-Jul-98 00:56:48.091126000 GMT
NFS:
NFS:   Post-operation attributes:
NFS:     File type = 1 (Regular File)
NFS:     Mode = 0664
NFS:      Setuid = 0, Setgid = 0, Sticky = 0
NFS:      Owner's permissions = rw-
NFS:      Group's permissions = rw-
NFS:      Other's permissions = r--
NFS:     Link count = 1, User ID = 3497, Group ID = 10
NFS:     File size = 100000, Used = 114688
NFS:     Special: Major = 0, Minor = 0
NFS:     File system id = 8388632, File id = 70018
NFS:     Last access time       = 12-Jul-98 00:56:47.701127000 GMT
NFS:     Modification time      = 12-Jul-98 00:56:48.091126000 GMT
NFS:     Attribute change time  = 12-Jul-98 00:56:48.091126000 GMT
NFS:
NFS:   Verifier = 72602A263369254D
```

Chapter 8

NFS Implementation

Although this book focuses on the NFS protocol and filesystem model, it would be incomplete if it did not discuss issues that are common to all implementations. Most of the material in this chapter applies to both versions 2 and 3 of the protocol.

8.1 File Attributes

The NFS filesystem model has strong similarities to the POSIX 1003.1 specification. Some might say that the two are almost indistinguishable, a conclusion that is borne out by a comparison of the supported file attributes. Table 8.1 compares some of the file attributes supported by POSIX, NFS versions 2 and 3, DOS FAT filesystem, and Windows NTFS.

In some cases, a server can support most of the semantics described by the protocol but not all. For example, the ctime file attribute gives the time that a file's attributes were last modified. Many filesystems do not keep this information. In this case, rather than not support the GETATTR operation, a server could simulate it by returning the last modified time (mtime) in place of ctime. Servers must be careful when simulating attribute information because of possible side effects on clients. For example, many clients use file modification times as a basis for their cache consistency scheme.

8.2 Unsupported Procedures

The NFS filesystem model contains many procedures that are common to all popular filesystem types, for instance, directory lookup, file read and write, and operations to get and set file attributes. However, there are some operations that cannot be supported by some servers or filesystems. The server will return a "not supported" error for any request that cannot be supported directly or approximated. There are many servers that cannot support symbolic links or

TABLE 8.17 Comparison of File Attributes Supported by POSIX, NFS Versions 2 and 3, DOS FAT, and Windows NTFS

POSIX	NFS v2	NFS v3	FAT	NTFS	Description
	type	type			File type
st_mode	mode	mode	readonly	ACL	Permission bits
st_ino	fileid	fileid			File ID
st_dev	fsid	fsid			Filesystem ID
st_rdev	rdev	rdev			Device ID
st_nlink	nlink	nlink		names	Number of links
st_uid	uid	uid		owner	Owner ID
st_gid	gid	gid		group	Group ID
st_size	size	size	size	size	File size
		used			Space used
st_atime	atime	atime			Last access time
st_mtime	mtime	mtime	mtime	mtime	Last modification time
st_ctime	ctime	ctime			Metadata modification time
st_blksize	blocks				Number of file blocks
st_blocks	blocksize				File block size

hard links, that is, the SYMLINK, READLINK, and LINK requests. There is no reliable way to predict in advance which procedures a server will support, though in NFS version 3 the FSINFO procedure can be used to determine if symbolic or hard links are supported.

8.3 Multiple Version Support

The RPC protocol provides support for explicit versioning of a service. Both client and server might support multiple versions of a protocol. The client should use the highest version number that is supported by both it and the server (Figure 8.1).

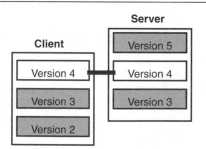

FIGURE 8.1 Client and server should use highest mutually supported version.

8.4   Last Close Problem

The statelessness of the NFS server can be a challenge when implementing POSIX clients that allow removal of open files. A process can open a file and, while it is open, remove it from the directory. The file can be read and written as long as the process keeps it open, even though the file has no name in the filesystem. The filesystem must maintain a count of all processes that currently have the unnamed file open and remove the file when the last process closes the file (otherwise the filesystem would become polluted with invisible, unreachable files). Since an NFS server has no knowledge of file opens, it cannot implement this "last close" requirement. The client can approximate the requirement by renaming the file to a hidden name (e.g., .nfs*xxxx*, where *xxxx* is the process's ID) and only physically removing it after the last close (Figure 8.2).

Since it's possible for a client to crash or otherwise neglect to remove the hidden file, the server may need to periodically remove accumulated hidden files. Solaris servers have a daily *cron* script that searches writeable, exported filesystems for hidden files that haven't been accessed for more than a week and deletes them with the assumption that they are no longer in use. The script presumes that all clients use the same convention for naming hidden files (name starts with .nfs).

There is no general solution for the situation where processes on other clients have the file open. They will continue to have access on the renamed file since the filehandle is independent of the filename, but they will receive a "stale filehandle" error when they attempt to access the file after it is removed from the server.

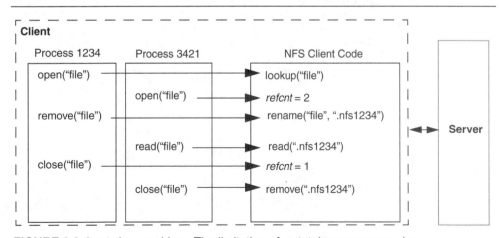

FIGURE 8.2 Last close problem. The limitation of a stateless server can be overcome by renaming the file. The name seems to disappear from the directory but the file data are preserved. The client removes the renamed file from the server after the last close.

8.5   Crossing of Server Mountpoints

An NFS client can also be a server, with remote and local mounted filesystems freely mixed. The mounting of remote filesystems within local filesystems (and vice versa) leads to some problems when a client travels down the directory tree of a remote filesystem and reaches the mountpoint on the server for another filesystem.

1. *Filesystem identification.* The crossing of a server mountpoint implies a change in the filesystem ID (*fsid*) for the files and directories in the new filesystem. UNIX clients require each filesystem ID to have a corresponding mounted filesystem that has previously been configured with a mount system call and recorded in associated system files.

2. *Filehandle limitations.* NFS filehandles have a finite size: 32 bytes in version 2 and up to 64 bytes in version 3. If the server mountpoint represents another NFS mount, then it would seem easy just to pass these NFS filehandles back to the client. However, the server in the middle cannot reliably distinguish the remote NFS server filehandles from the filehandles for its own exported filesystems. The remote filehandles could be tagged with additional data, but this will not work for fixed-length version 2 filehandles, nor will it work indefinitely for version 3 filehandles. The server could set up a filehandle mapping table, though making it persistent across a server crash would be difficult.

3. *Namespace cycles.* If the remote NFS server is the client itself or some NFS server that mounts from a server earlier in a chain of references, then the risk of a namespace cycle exists (Figure 8.3). Generally, client operating systems are unprepared for such cycles; a client application that encountered a

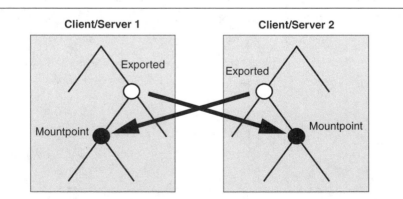

FIGURE 8.3 A namespace cycle caused by clients and servers mounting each other. A program that attempts to walk this file tree will become stuck in this cycle crossing mountpoints from one server to the other.

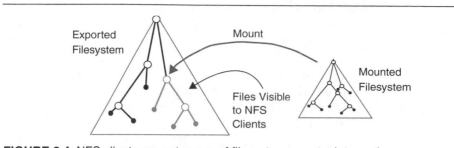

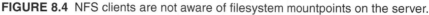

FIGURE 8.4 NFS clients are not aware of filesystem mountpoints on the server.

cycle during a file tree walk (e.g., UNIX find command) would never terminate. To prevent these problems from being encountered, NFS servers prevent NFS client LOOKUPs from crossing server mountpoints. The client sees the directory underlying the server's mountpoint instead of the mounted directory (Figure 8.4).

For example, if a server with a filesystem called /usr mounts another filesystem on /usr/src and a client mounts /usr, it does not see the mounted version of /usr/src.

Clients solve the mountpoint crossing problem by replicating the server's mounts to be consistent with the server's view (Figure 8.5). For instance, in the preceding example the client would mount /usr/src in addition to /usr.

Mount replication is commonly encountered when a client uses the automounter to gain access to a hierarchy of filesystems mounted from a server (see section 11.6). The automounter queries the server's mount service to obtain a list of exported filesystems, then mounts each exported filesystem in an identical hierarchy.

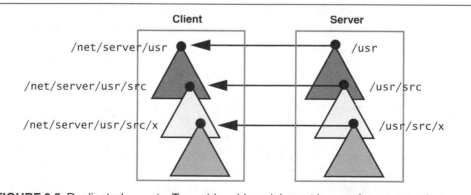

FIGURE 8.5 Replicated mounts. To avoid problems inherent in crossing mountpoints on the server, NFS clients replicate the server's mounts so that the mountpoint crossing is performed on the client instead.

The Silicon Graphics Inc. Irix implementation of NFS supports a "nohide" export option that allows a client LOOKUP from an exported mounted-on filesystem to cross into the "nohide" exported filesystem. The Linux *unfsd* server also permits client LOOKUP requests to cross mountpoints on the server. The nohide option provides some convenience for clients since a single "mount" from the server may provide access to a number of server filesystems mounted within that filesystem. The downside is that the client is unaware that it is crossing into a new filesystem that has its own file ID namespace. There is a risk that file IDs for files in the mounted and mounted-on filesystems may be identical, creating unpredictable effects on the client.

8.6   Problems with Hierarchical Mounts

The previous section illustrates the use of hierarchical mounts to replicate a server's namespace. There is no requirement that all the mounts in a hierarchy come from the same server, though that is the most common case. Hierarchical NFS mounts from the same server can present some unique problems at both mount time and unmount time.

1. *Namespace gaps.* If the server did not export the filesystem /usr/src in Figure 8.5, then the client would be unable to mount /usr/src/x because the required mountpoint would be missing. The client may not be permitted to create the missing mountpoint since it may have read-only access to the mounted-on filesystem /usr. The server administrator must be careful to export these intermediate filesystems if clients are expected to mount the server hierarchy.

2. *Unmount from dead server.* If a client has hierarchical mounts from a server that is not responding, then it may not be possible for the client to unmount the filesystems. Normally a client does not have to communicate with a server to unmount a filesystem from it, but a hierarchical mount presents a situation where the client is required to span inaccessible directories to reach a mountpoint. For example, if the server in Figure 8.5 is down, the mountpoints /net/server/usr/src and /net/server/usr/src/x are inaccessible and cannot be unmounted. The top-level mount, /net/server/usr, cannot be unmounted either because the submounts keep the filesystem "busy." The problem cannot be resolved until the dead server comes back to life.

8.7   Permission Issues

The NFS protocol defines neither the method used by the server to *authenticate* users nor the mechanism used by the server to *authorize access* to files and directories. The server relies on the RPC authentication contained in the credential of every request. The most commonly used method of authentication is via the AUTH_SYS credential, discussed in section 4.4. AUTH_SYS requires the server to *trust* the client not to forge the credential. Servers that accept AUTH_SYS credentials generally associate an *access list* with each exported filesystem. The access list is a list of client hostnames from which the server will accept credentials as well as determine which clients will have read-only access and which clients will have read-write access. For authorization at the filesystem level, the server delegates responsibility to the policy of the exported filesystem. The access control policy could be a simple model, such as that of the DOS FAT filesystem, which has no concept of file ownership, or more complex, like that of Windows NTFS, which controls file access through access control lists (ACLs).

8.7.1   Identifying Users

Despite its lack of security, most implementations use AUTH_SYS authentication, described in section 4.4. Its popularity is due to its easy integration with existing UNIX environments and simple administration compared with more secure private key or public key schemes that require a management infrastructure to maintain security keys. With AUTH_SYS authentication, the server gets the client's UID, GID, and group list on each call and uses them to check permission. Additionally, when a client receives file attributes from a server, it must convert the UID and GID attributes into usernames and group names for display. Using UID and GID implies that the client and server share the same UID assignments. Every server and client pair must have the same mapping from username to UID and from group name to GID. Since every client can also be a server, this tends to imply that the whole network shares the same UID/GID space. If this is not the case, then it usually falls to the server to perform some custom mapping of credentials from one authentication domain into another. The requirement for a consistent UID/GID mapping across many clients and servers drove the development of the NIS name service. NIS is a simple protocol that provides access from many clients to a single database containing the username to UID and group name to GID mappings.

AUTH_DES and AUTH_KERB use a network name, or *netname*, as the basis for identification. Again, it is assumed that the client and server both have access to a common service that will map the netname to and from the local credentials. For example, a UNIX server will convert the netname to a username from which it will derive the user's UID, GID, and group list.

8.7.2   Access to Open Files

Most operating systems check permission to access a file only when the file is opened. Subsequently access is granted based on the file permissions at open time, even if they change after the open. With stateless servers, the server cannot detect that the file is open and must do permission checking on each read and write call. A UNIX process can open a file, then change the permissions so that one is not allowed to touch it but will still be granted access to the file because it is open. If the process is accessing an NFS file, it would be denied access because the server does not know that the "client has opened the file." To get around this problem, the server's permission-checking algorithm has to allow the owner of a file access for READ or WRITE calls regardless of the permission setting.

8.7.3   UID/GID Mapping

On UNIX servers, the *superuser* has access to all files, no matter what permission and ownership they have. UNIX servers are configured not to allow superuser access from NFS clients, since anyone who can become superuser on their client could gain access to all files on the server. A UNIX server by default maps the superuser or superuser's group (UID or GID of 0) to a distinguished value (generally −2 or 60001) before doing its access checking. A server implementation may provide a mechanism to change this mapping on a per-export basis; for instance, a diskless client may need superuser access to its root filesystem, which is exported from the server. In this case the server may allow superuser access (no mapping) for the diskless client.

8.7.4   Checking File Access

The NFS client's view of the server's access control is provided by the *mode* field of the file attributes. The mode field determines file access based on three identities (owner, group, and other) and three capabilities (read, write, and execute). These match the mode field defined by the POSIX standard commonly implemented in UNIX filesystems. These permissions are presented as a bit map laid out as follows:

```
        Owner          Group          Other
       ┌──┴──┐        ┌──┴──┐        ┌──┴──┐
       r  w  x        r  w  x        r  w  x
  Bit  8  7  6        5  4  3        2  1  0
```

For example, the following bit values in the mode field give the owner of the file read and write permission, read access only to any user with a group that matches the file GID, and no access to any other users.

```
        Owner          Group          Other
       ┌──┴──┐        ┌──┴──┐        ┌──┴──┐
       r  w  -        r  -  -        -  -  -
```

Since the permission bits in the mode field are grouped into triples, it is convenient to represent the field as an octal value. The field could be represented by the value 0640.

A UNIX client will use these permission bits to determine whether the user can perform some operation on the file or directory. If the user's UID matches that of the file, then the "Owner" bits are checked. If the UID does not match (or if access is not granted), then the "Group" bits are checked if the user's GID matches the file's GID. If the GID does not match (or if access is not granted), the "Other" bits are checked.

There are cases where the permission bits might give a false indication of access resulting in an unexpected error from the server when the operation is attempted.

1. *UID/GID mapping.* Unknown to the client, the server may map the user's UID or GID to another value. The most common instance is where the user is the UNIX *superuser* (UID = 0), which the server will map to user nobody (UID = 60001 or –2) to prevent the client from having superuser access to all the files on the server.

2. *Access control lists.* The mode field may be viewed as containing a small access control list with three entries. Some servers can associate an access control list with a file or directory that may contain entries for users or groups in addition to owner, group, and other. Since it is not possible to map the information in a large ACL into the mode field accurately, the server will make a best-effort approximation of the ACL in the permission bits that may give the user a false indication of access or nonaccess.

NFS version 3 resolved the problem of false permission indications by providing a new ACCESS procedure that allows the client to request permission information from the server directly rather than attempting to elicit the information from the mode field.

8.7.5 Executable Files

A similar problem has to do with paging in an executable program over the network. The operating system usually checks for execute permission before opening a file for demand paging and then reads blocks from the open file. In a local UNIX file system, an executable file does not need read permission to execute. An NFS server cannot tell the difference between a normal file read (where the "r" permission bit is meaningful) and a demand pagein read (where the server should allow access to the executable file if the execute bit is set for that user or group or public). To make this work, the server allows reading of files if the UID given in the call has either execute or read permission on the file through ownership, group membership, or public access. Again, this departs from correct local UNIX filesystem semantics.

8.8   Concurrent RPC Calls

Until now, we've discussed the use of the NFS protocol only in regard to a single client thread or process calling a single server thread or process. According to the RPC model, execution of the client thread is blocked while a reply to the remote procedure call is pending. We've assumed that the server is a single thread or process that handles one remote procedure call at a time. While it is possible to implement a single-threaded NFS client or server, in practice most implementations are highly parallel.

If an NFS server is to provide good service to a large number of clients, it must be able to service concurrent NFS requests. The first UNIX kernel implementations of NFS achieved this concurrency via the use of multiple process contexts within the UNIX kernel. Each process context was provided by an *nfsd* daemon. An nfsd process made a system call into the kernel from which it never returned. The process context provided the kernel with a thread of execution for NFS requests. Typically, an NFS server would run with 8 to 16 nfsd processes, though system administrators have many rules of thumb to determine the optimal number of nfsd processes. More recently, as UNIX vendors have included multithreading support within their UNIX kernels to support symmetric multiprocessing, the need for a process context has disappeared. NFS requests can be handled by UNIX kernel threads managed in a thread pool.

An NFS server may get concurrent NFS requests from multiple clients. It can also get multiple requests from a single client that is able to run multiple processes, each performing NFS file access independently. In this case, one or more threads within the process will generate NFS requests. Even a single-threaded process on a client can generate multiple NFS I/O calls through the use of read-ahead and write-behind (section 8.12). UNIX client implementations have used *biod* daemons to provide a kernel context for generating read-ahead and write-behind calls (Figure 8.6). Symmetric multiprocessing kernels that support native kernel threads dispense with the process context provided by biod daemons and implement the read-ahead and write-behind threads directly in the kernel.

8.9   Duplicate Request Cache

If an NFS client does not receive a response to a request in a reasonable time, then it retransmits the request. What constitutes a "reasonable" time is an implementation detail. A client may assign time-out values that depend on the specific NFS procedure. A READ or WRITE request will generally take longer for the server to execute than a GETATTR (GET ATTRibutes) request. Also, the server's response time may depend on the server's load, its CPU, disk, and network bandwidth, its remoteness on the network, and the bandwidth of the network.

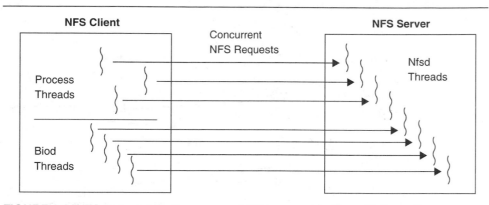

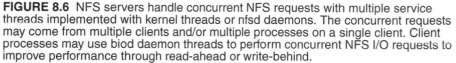

FIGURE 8.6 NFS servers handle concurrent NFS requests with multiple service threads implemented with kernel threads or nfsd daemons. The concurrent requests may come from multiple clients and/or multiple processes on a single client. Client processes may use biod daemon threads to perform concurrent NFS I/O requests to improve performance through read-ahead or write-behind.

Some of the NFS procedures are idempotent. An idempotent procedure can be repeated with equivalent results (see section 5.4.2). Although idempotent procedures can be repeated safely, the server is burdened with the repetition of a previously completed request. The protocol does contain some nonidempotent operations that may return an error if repeated. For instance, a REMOVE procedure will fail if repeated since a file can be removed only once. This bogus error might lead the client to believe, erroneously, that the file never existed. Retransmitted nonidempotent operations may even cause corrupted or lost file data. For instance, consider the scenario in Figure 8.7, where a server that supports two *nfsd* processes truncates data written by a client because one nfsd process servicing a CREATE request became blocked.

These problems can be prevented through the use of a duplicate request cache. Each RPC request from a client has a unique transaction ID (XID) in the RPC header. If the server maintains a cache of recent requests keyed by the XID, then it can identify retransmitted requests from a client. The server can use this cache to avoid unnecessary work and errors or data corruption from nonidempotent requests.

- If the cache entry indicates that the request is "in progress" and has not been replied to, then the server can just ignore the request.
- If the cache entry indicates that the server replied to the client recently (within the last few seconds), then it is likely that the retransmitted request and its reply crossed in transit. Again, the server ignores the request. If the assumption is wrong (perhaps the reply was lost in transit) then the client will eventually retransmit the request.
- If the cache entry indicates that the reply was sent, but not recently, then the server can send the cached reply to the client.

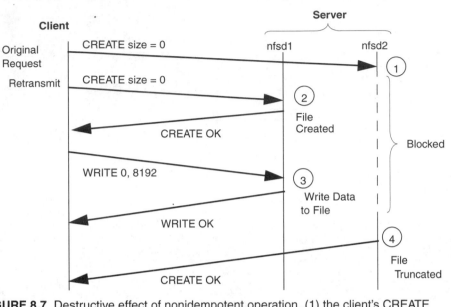

FIGURE 8.7 Destructive effect of nonidempotent operation. (1) the client's CREATE request is received by nfsd 2, which becomes blocked. (2) The retransmitted CREATE request is received by another nfsd, which creates the file. (3) The client writes data to the new file. (4) The blocked nfsd resumes and recreates the file, effectively truncating the data written at (3).

The duplicate request cache is typically implemented in RAM with a fixed size (Figure 8.8). As new entries are added, old entries are deleted. It's possible that on a busy server the cache could lose its effectiveness if old entries in the cache are reused so quickly that duplicate requests are not recognized. Additionally, a memory-based cache will be lost if the server reboots—retransmission of requests that were completed just before the server crashed will not be detected. Loss of the cache can be avoided in some highly available configurations by storing the cache entries in NVRAM (nonvolatile RAM) or in a disk file. A good description of the implementation and use of a duplicate request cache can be found in [Juszczak89].

8.10 Synchronous Operations and Stable Storage

Data-modifying operations in the NFS protocol must be synchronous. When the server replies to the client, the client can assume that the operation has completed and any data associated with the request are now on stable storage (Figure 8.9).

The term *stable storage* refers to a storage medium that will protect the integrity of its data from an operating system crash or an unexpected power

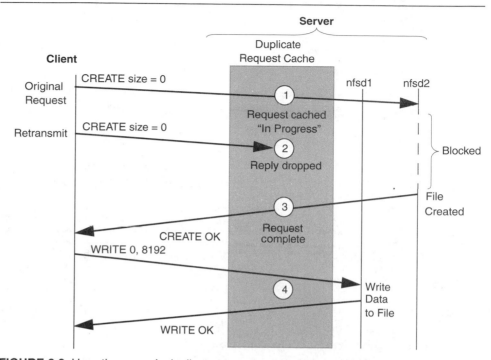

FIGURE 8.8 Here the server's duplicate request cache prevents the file truncation problem. (1) The CREATE request is cached "in progress." (2) The duplicate request is detected, and because it is "in progress" the request is dropped. (3) The blocked nfsd process creates the file and replies. Any further retransmissions of the CREATE request after this point will be detected and the cached CREATE OK reply will be sent. (4) The WRITE proceeds without risk of data loss from a pending CREATE operation.

failure. A disk is assumed to be stable storage assuming that the disk medium itself does not fail. Servers can guard against data loss due to media failure by employing mirrored disks or RAID protection. Some disk drives may utilize one or more track buffers to store modified data so that the data might be more efficiently written to the disk. A track buffer lets the disk respond to the server more quickly since it doesn't have to wait for the data to be written to the disk platter. These disks are stable only if the track buffers are NVRAM or the disk is protected by a UPS (uninterruptible power supply).

The server itself may buffer the changes in memory, but to be considered stable storage, the memory must be protected against power failure or crash and reboot of the server's operating system. After a server reboot the server must be able to locate and account for all data in the protected memory. Generally this memory is provided via a small memory card with attached batteries, such as Legato's PrestoServe™, or the server's memory is protected with a UPS.

Most data-modifying operations in the NFS protocol are synchronous. That is, when a data-modifying procedure returns to the client, the client can assume

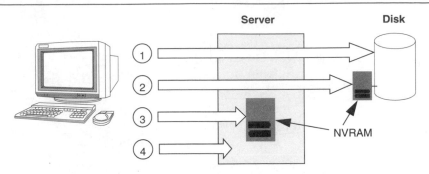

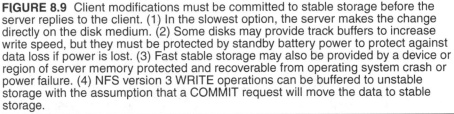

FIGURE 8.9 Client modifications must be committed to stable storage before the server replies to the client. (1) In the slowest option, the server makes the change directly on the disk medium. (2) Some disks may provide track buffers to increase write speed, but they must be protected by standby battery power to protect against data loss if power is lost. (3) Fast stable storage may also be provided by a device or region of server memory protected and recoverable from operating system crash or power failure. (4) NFS version 3 WRITE operations can be buffered to unstable storage with the assumption that a COMMIT request will move the data to stable storage.

that the operation has completed and any modified data associated with the request is now on stable storage. For example, a synchronous client WRITE request may cause the server to update data blocks, filesystem information blocks, and file attribute information (metadata[1]). Operations that modify directory contents (MKDIR, CREATE, LINK, SYMLINK, MKNOD, RENAME, REMOVE, RMDIR) must be synchronous as well as operations that modify attributes (SETATTR). When the WRITE operation completes, the client can assume that the write data are safe and discard them. The guaranteed safety of client modifications is a very important part of the stateless nature of the server. If the server did not save client modifications in stable storage, the client would have no way of knowing when it was safe to discard modified data.

The requirement for synchronous operations on the server can have a significant impact on the performance of these operations if the server has no stable buffering available (NVRAM). When compared with other protocols that do not make the stable storage requirement, NFS version 2 write performance was poor. Some implementations of NFS version 2 offer asynchronous server operations as an option to improve performance. But although performance is improved, there is a risk of silent data loss. If the server crashes after it has replied to a client's WRITE request but before the data have been written to the disk, then the client's data will be lost. The client will receive no

---

1. File metadata is information that is not directly read or written. For instance, file attributes (owner, modification time, permissions, etc.) and structures within the filesystem that organize the file data blocks, such as indirect blocks.

error message that would give it an opportunity to recover from the data loss. The issue of asynchronous writes has been debated for many years by NFS engineers. Those in favor argue that it is wrong to deny a substantial performance improvement to customers who are willing to accept the risk of data loss. Those against asynchronous writes call them "unsafe" writes and argue that the use of unsafe writes exposes customers to an unnecessary risk of data corruption or loss.

The NFS version 3 protocol has settled the debate with its introduction of *safe* asynchronous writes on the server, when asynchronous WRITE requests are followed with a COMMIT request. The COMMIT procedure provides a way for the client to flush data from previous asynchronous WRITE requests on the server to stable storage and to detect whether it is necessary to retransmit the data. Servers have the option of performing synchronous or asynchronous operations but with the full knowledge of the client.

The requirement for changes to be committed to stable storage is relaxed by some implementations where the changes are made to file metadata (file attributes). Explicit changes to attributes like the file owner and group, file permissions, or file size should certainly be committed to stable storage. However, an implicit change to the file access time (atime) occurs on the server whenever the file is read. Flushing of the updated atime to stable storage on every file read would have a significant impact on read performance, while an up-to-date atime following a server crash would provide little benefit for client applications. Hence server implementations typically relax the stable storage requirement in this instance.

8.11 Adaptive Retransmission for UDP

NFS client implementations that use UDP generally use an exponential back-off strategy when retransmitting requests that have timed out. An initial time-out value is chosen that is then doubled after each retransmission to some maximum value.

Most client implementations use an exponential back-off strategy that doubles or quadruples the time-out after each retransmission up to some preset limit (Figure 8.10). Although a short time-out allows the client to recover quickly from a lost request or reply, if the server is responding slowly because it is heavily loaded or if the network is congested, then frequent retransmissions can aggravate the problem. The retransmission back-off avoids this problem.

The initial time-out must be chosen carefully. If it is too short, the client will retransmit before the server has had a chance to respond, making more work for the server if it does not have a duplicate request cache. If the time-out is too long, the client may be unnecessarily idle waiting for a lost reply. For instance, if a client's READ requests are each being handled in 100 msec,

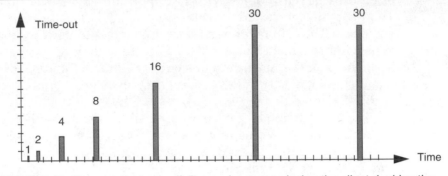

FIGURE 8.10 Exponential back-off. For each retransmission the client doubles the time-out up to a preset limit—in this case 30 seconds. This strategy allows the client to recover quickly from a lost request or response while it avoids burdening an overloaded server or network with a barrage of retransmissions.

then a time-out that is 500 msec too long implies a loss of five READ requests. If the time-outs are frequent, the drop in throughput will be noticeable.

An initial guess at an appropriate time-out can be based on the knowledge that some NFS requests typically take longer than others. A LOOKUP request and response exchanges only a small amount of data across the network and is handled quickly by the server, whereas a READ or WRITE request generally takes longer. Solaris clients divide NFS requests into three categories each with an initial time-out estimate (Table 8.2). This time-out estimate is then revised based on a running average of the observed response time of each procedure for the specific server. For instance, if the client observes that the READDIR requests take between 1200 and 1300 msec, then it might adjust the time-out up to 1400 msec. The category time-outs are also minimums, so if a server that consistently responds much more quickly for some procedure than its minimum time-out, the procedure time-out will not be adjusted down. The minimum timeout avoids problems with the client trimming its time-outs too aggressively and risking unnecessary retransmissions because the server is temporarily indisposed.

TABLE 8.18 Solaris NFS Request Categories

Category	Initial time-out (msec)	Operations
LOOKUP	750	GETATTR, LOOKUP, ACCESS, READLINK, FSSTAT, STATFS, FSINFO, PATHCONF
READ	875	SETATTR, READ, READDIR
WRITE	1250	WRITE, CREATE, MKDIR, SYMLINK, MKNOD, REMOVE, RMDIR, RENAME, LINK, READDIRPLUS, COMMIT

8.12   Read-ahead and Write-behind

An NFS client implementation can exploit the parallelism in an NFS server to improve performance through the use of read-ahead and write-behind techniques, when reading or writing a file (Figure 8.11). These techniques have been known for many years to operating system designers as a way to speed up sequential access to file data, whether reading or writing. Most programs tend to read a file beginning with the first byte and proceeding down the file in byte order until the end of the file is reached. Similarly, programs tend to write files from beginning to end in sequence. An operating system can take advantage of a sequential reading pattern by issuing I/O calls for blocks of the file not yet read in anticipation of the program's need. For instance, if the program issues a call for block n of a file, the operating system will issue an I/O request to the disk for block n and block $n+1$. If the operating system can support multiple I/O channels and striped disks, then it may issue I/O requests several blocks ahead. The operating system can also speed up sequential writes by allowing the program to write several blocks of data ahead of the data that the disk has written.

These techniques can be used to speed up sequential reading and writing of NFS files. When a multithreaded NFS client detects sequential I/O on a file, it can assign NFS READ or WRITE calls to individual threads. Each of these threads can issue an RPC call to the server independently and in parallel. Even if the server's I/O subsystem can service only one call at a time, the client still receives a net benefit through an overlap in network latency (Figure 8.12).

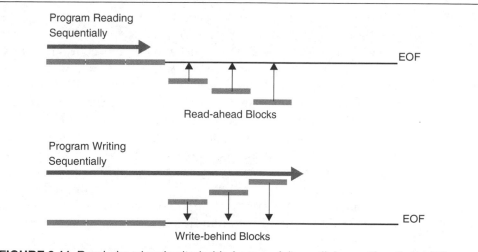

FIGURE 8.11 Read-ahead and write-behind can exploit parallel operations in the I/O system to improve sequential read or write performance.

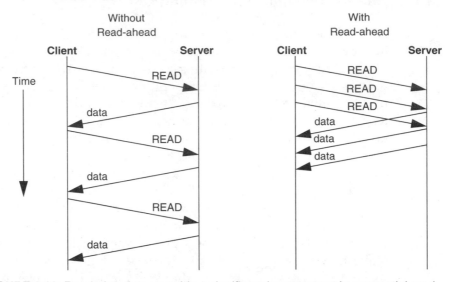

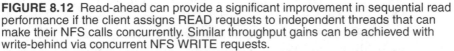

FIGURE 8.12 Read-ahead can provide a significant improvement in sequential read performance if the client assigns READ requests to independent threads that can make their NFS calls concurrently. Similar throughput gains can be achieved with write-behind via concurrent NFS WRITE requests.

The first UNIX reference implementations of NFS used user-level dae-mons on the client and the server to implement concurrent I/O threads. On the client these were called *biod* processes. Each biod process would make a single, nonreturning system call that would block and provide the kernel with an execution thread in the form of a process context. By increasing the number of biod processes on the client, an administrator could increase the amount of NFS I/O concurrency. Similarly, on the server concurrent NFS requests were handled by *nfsd* processes. Each nfsd process would make a nonreturning sys-tem call to provide the server's kernel with an execution context. The number of concurrent NFS requests that the server could handle scaled with the num-ber of nfsd processes that were run. More recent UNIX kernels support multi-ple threads of execution without the need for a user context. For example, the Solaris client and server use kernel threads. The client has no biod processes and the kernel has only a single nfsd process that exists to accept TCP connec-tions. One of the more common questions asked by NFS server administrators was "How many nfsds should I run on my server for best throughput?" The answer depended very much on the server's configuration—setting up too many nfsd processes could make the server accept more NFS requests than it had the I/O bandwidth to handle—and too few could result in excess I/O bandwidth inaccessible to clients.

On the client side, read-ahead and write-behind throughput increases as the number of concurrent read-ahead and write-behind threads is increased

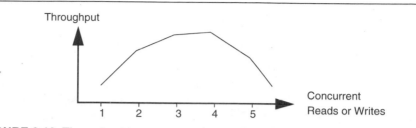

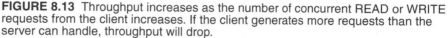

FIGURE 8.13 Throughput increases as the number of concurrent READ or WRITE requests from the client increases. If the client generates more requests than the server can handle, throughput will drop.

(Figure 8.13). At some point the client will generate concurrent READ or WRITE requests faster than the server (or network) can absorb them, and the client will need to retransmit dropped requests, and throughput will suffer.

NFS write-behind has a secondary effect of delaying write errors. Because the write operation is no longer synchronous with the application thread, an error that results from an asynchronous write cannot be reported in the result of an application write call. In most client implementations, if a biod process gets a write error (perhaps because the disk is full), the error will be posted against the file so that it can be reported in the result of a subsequent write or close call. If the application that is doing the writing is diligent in checking the results of write and close calls, then it can detect the error and take some recovery action, for example, alert the user that a disk is full and then rewrite the data when more space is created. Unfortunately, there are many examples of poorly written programs that do not check the result of write or close calls and suffer data loss when unexpected I/O errors occur.

8.13 Write Gathering

Write gathering [Juszczak94] describes a server procedure for writing NFS data to disk that takes advantage of write-behind behavior on multithreaded NFS clients. An NFS version 2 WRITE operation is an expensive procedure on the server. The protocol requires the server to commit the client's data to stable storage. If the server is fitted with fast stable storage like NVRAM, then writes can be quite fast—but most NFS servers make do with synchronous writes to disk. Not only is the write to disk inherently slow, but for each synchronous write of data to the disk, the server may have to perform several additional synchronous writes to write modified indirect blocks and the file attributes in the inode to update the file modification time (*mtime*). The server suffers this per I/O overhead for each synchronous write request—no matter how many data are written. The server may be capable of writing up to 64 KB of data in a single I/O request to the disk, yet a version 2 NFS client is limited

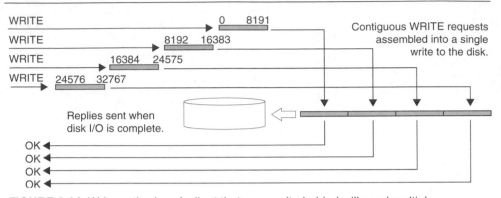

FIGURE 8.14 Write gathering. A client that uses write-behind will send multiple WRITE requests. If the server delays these small WRITE requests, it can assemble them into a single large WRITE request that completes more quickly due to lower I/O overhead. When the single I/O is complete, individual replies are returned to the client's write-behind threads.

to a maximum WRITE size of 8 KB. Write gathering allows the server to accumulate a sequence of smaller 8-KB WRITE requests into a single block of data that can be written with the overhead of a write to the disk.

On receiving the first WRITE request, a server thread sleeps for some optimal number of milliseconds in case a contiguous write to the same file follows (Figure 8.14). If no further writes are received during this sleep period, the accumulated writes are written to the disk in a single I/O. If a contiguous write is received, then it is accumulated with previously received WRITE requests. The sleep period for additional writes can negatively affect throughput if the writes are random or if the client is single-threaded and does not use write-behind (early PC-NFS clients are in this category), but overall write throughput is improved.

An alternative write-gathering algorithm is used in the Solaris server. Instead of delaying the write thread while waiting for additional writes, it allows the first write to go synchronously to the disk. If additional writes for the file arrive while the synchronous write is pending, they are accumulated. When the initial synchronous write is completed, the accumulated WRITEs are written. Although slightly less data are accumulated in the I/O, the effect on random I/O or nonwrite-behind clients is less serious.

8.14 Caching Policies

All NFS clients cache data returned from the server with the primary objective of providing faster access to the data and the secondary objective of reduction in network and server loading. Although file data are most often considered candidates for caching, there are significant performance benefits in caching attributes, results of directory lookups, entire directories, and filesystem information. The client's memory can be used for fast, short-term caching, and if the client has a disk it can be used for its greater capacity and persistence through client reboot.

8.14.1 Cached Objects

Although caching is most commonly thought of in terms of file data, NFS clients cache the result of any NFS operation if there's a chance that the cached item may preclude a future RPC request to the server. The following seven types of results are commonly cached.

1. *File data.* The data returned by READ requests, which are cached in memory pages. Data written to a file are also accumulated in memory pages and consolidated into larger and more efficient WRITE requests to the server.

2. *Lookup results.* The results of LOOKUP requests, the filehandle and attributes, are cached. UNIX clients cache these results in the directory name lookup cache (DNLC), which typically has hit rates above 90 percent. These DNLC entries are invalidated if the modification time of the directory changes. Directory changes initiated by the client can be problematic since the client's change may mask a previous, undetected change to the directory by another client. To avoid the risk of missing undetected changes, NFS version 2 clients invalidate all DNLC entries for the directory if the client changes the directory. The *pre-op* attributes of NFS version 3 allow the client to detect changes prior to its own, avoiding the need for preemptive purging of the DNLC.

3. *Directories.* The results of READDIR or READDIRPLUS requests can be cached, though the results of READDIR can be used only for negative caching. Since READDIR returns only a list of names (and their file IDs), the cached directory cannot be used in place of the DNLC, but it can provide an indication of whether a directory entry exists or does not exist—thereby avoiding a DNLC miss and unsuccessful LOOKUP call to the server. The benefit of this negative caching is best observed by the effect of PATH evaluations by UNIX clients. A UNIX PATH is a sequence of directories that must be searched for a program. Normally the program is in just one directory, and if that directory is near the end of the PATH sequence, then many unsuccessful LOOKUPs will precede the successful location of the program.

Since READDIRPLUS returns the file handle and attributes for each directory entry, the cached directory information can be used to preclude LOOKUP calls to the server, successful or not. The most common benefit of this caching is seen by programs that "walk" a file tree enumerating all directory entries, such as the UNIX find command or the "Find file" facility of Windows 95.

4. *Attributes.* The attributes of all objects are cached along with the object both to provide fast access to individual attributes like the permission bits, file

ID, and so on, and to record the state of the object to detect change. The modification time is the most accurate and widely used indicator of change, but the size of the object may also be used, particularly where the modification time is unreliable.

5. *Symbolic links.* The pathname that returns as the result of a READLINK request can be cached to avoid unnecessary READLINK calls to the server.

6. *File access.* The results of the ACCESS call in the NFS version 3 protocol can be cached for each user on the client. The ACCESS call is typically made when an NFS file is opened to determine the type of access to the file the user will have. Since a file may be opened and closed many times during the execution of a client program or script, the cached ACCESS information can preclude unnecessary calls to the server.

7. *Filesystem information.* NFS clients typically issue a STATFS or FSINFO call to the server when a filesystem is first mounted to obtain static filesystem information such as the maximum transfer sizes, pathname properties, and other invariant information. Filesystem information is assumed not to change for the duration of a mount.

8.14.2 Cache Consistency

Since data obtained from the server may be cached by many clients at different times, there is a possibility that the cached data may be inconsistent between the client and its server or other clients. The protocol provides no facility that will guarantee that cached data will always be consistent with the server—instead, clients are expected to make a best-effort attempt to keep their cached data in sync with the server.

The most commonly implemented caching scheme uses two times: a *cache time* and a *modification time*. When server data are cached, the server's modification time for the data is also cached (along with other attributes). A cache time associated with the data may vary depending on the type of data (file or directory). If the data is referenced within the cache time, then the cache data are used and the server is not consulted. If the cache time has been exceeded, the client will contact the server and verify that the cached modification time has not changed. If it is unchanged, then the cache time is reset and cache data are used. If the modification time is different, then the cached data are invalidated and fresh data are obtained from the server.

A client that uses the modification time attribute for caching is making an assumption that the server will update the modification time if the file or directory changes. The modification time can be an unreliable indication of change under the following conditions.

- The server doesn't update the modification time. This is more commonly observed with non-UNIX server operating systems that do not update the directory modification time for some directory operations, for example, RENAME.

- The server does not support a modification time attribute. The server may instead return an approximation to the file creation time or attribute change time.
- The server's clock or modification time value may not have sufficient resolution to distinguish two file or directory modifications that are almost simultaneous.

The cache time is a compromise that trades off cache consistency against server and network loading. If the cache time is small, then the cache consistency will be high, but the server will be consulted frequently to check if the modification time has changed. If the cache time is set to 0, then the server will be consulted whenever the cached data are accessed. If the cache time is long, then the server will be consulted infrequently, but there's a greater chance that the client may use stale cached data—consistency is low.

Cache time should be small for server data that is likely to change frequently and large if changes on the server are infrequent. Directory data typically change less frequently than file data since files are modified more frequently than they are created, deleted, or renamed. Hence it would be appropriate to assign a larger cache time to directories than to files.

Cache time can also be assigned based on the frequency at which a file or directory is observed to change on the server. A file that changes frequently can be assigned a smaller cache time than a file that does not change—making it more likely that the client will check the server's modification time and notice a change. If the client finds that the server's modification time has changed, then it computes a new cache time based on the difference between the old modification time and the new one. The computed cache time is then bounded by minimum and maximum values so that the cache time is not too small or too large. Solaris clients use the ranges in Table 8.3 for cache time.

TABLE 8.19 Solaris Cache Time Ranges

Object	Minimum cache time	Maximum cache time
File	3 seconds	30 seconds
Directory	30 seconds	60 seconds

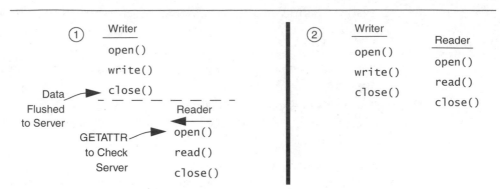

FIGURE 8.15 Close-to-open consistency. (1) All data written to a file are flushed to the server when the file is closed. If a reading program is started after the writing program completes, then a GETATTR call issued when the file is opened will detect the updated file on the server so that the read will retrieve the latest data from the server. Close-to-open consistency works only when the file open of one program follows the close of another. (2) It cannot help where the reader may not see the data written by the writer because the reader's open does not follow the writer's close.

8.14.3 Close-to-Open Consistency

Clients may implement a feature called *close-to-open* consistency (Figure 8.15). The time-bounded consistency used by most NFS clients provides no absolute cache consistency between client and server. It may be several seconds before the data written by an application are flushed to the server and several more seconds before the cache time is exceeded, allowing an application on another client to detect the file change. Close-to-open consistency provides a guarantee of cache consistency at the level of file opens and closes. When a file is closed by an application, the client flushes any cached changes to the server. When a file is opened, the client ignores any cache time remaining (if the file data are cached) and makes an explicit GETATTR call to the server to check the file modification time. The GETATTR on open provides a guarantee that after a file is closed, any application on the network that opens the file will see the latest changes. This close/open level of cache consistency meets the needs of many applications; for instance, at the completion of editing a source file on one client, a user can initiate a compile of that file on another client or on the server, knowing that the compiler will have the latest changes when it opens the file.

8.14.4 Read and Write Caching

The caching of data on the client for file reading makes it possible for the client to generate larger, more efficient READ requests to the server. For instance, an application that reads data in chunks of 512 bytes can obtain 16 of these chunks from a single 8-KB READ request. Similarly, an application that writes

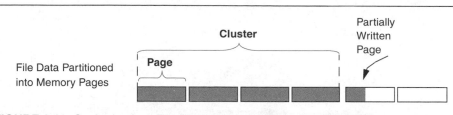

FIGURE 8.16 Cached writes. The file extent is partitioned into pages and cached in client memory. Sequential writes to the file progressively fill pages until a write fills a page or crosses a page boundary that comprises a *page cluster*—a collection of file pages that can be written efficiently to the server within the server's advertised transfer size.

file data in small chunks can benefit if these chunks are accumulated into a much larger chunk of data before they are written to the server (Figure 8.16).

Clients typically accumulate data written sequentially to a file in memory pages. When enough pages have been written to fill a cluster of pages that make up an efficient transfer to the server, the data are then written to the server via a WRITE request. Partially filled clusters or pages must be written to the server when the application closes the file. If the server returns an error that indicates it has no available disk, the application must be informed of the error either as a result of a write call (if the file is not closed) or when the file is closed so that the application can take action to prevent data loss.

Other data-modifying operations, such as attribute changes (SETATTR) or directory operations, are typically not buffered or delayed and are performed synchronously. There is little advantage in delaying or aggregating these operations, and recovery from asynchronous errors can be complicated.

8.14.5 Disk Caching

A disk on the client can be used to improve on memory-only caching in two ways: disk space is typically much cheaper and more plentiful than RAM memory and disk storage is persistent across client shutdown/restart or system crashes. On some UNIX clients the *CacheFS* is a disk cache that interposes itself between an application and its access to an NFS mounted filesystem. Data read from the server are cached in client memory and written to the disk cache, forming a *cache hierarchy*. First the memory cache is checked for cached data followed by the disk cache and finally a call to the server if the data are found in neither cache. The use of a disk cache must not weaken the cache consistency of the memory cache. The disk cache must use the same cache times as the memory cache (Figure 8.17).

The disk cache is particularly effective at caching read-only data that changes infrequently or not at all on the server. A good example is a /usr/local filesystem, common in many organizations, that contains packages, documents, and other files shared by a large number of people in the

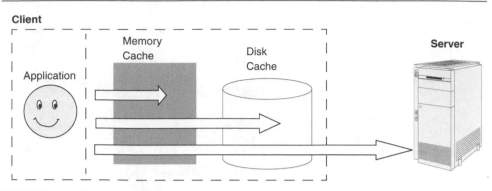

FIGURE 8.17 Disk cache forms a cache hierarchy. If data cannot be found in the memory cache, the disk cache is checked, followed by the NFS server.

organization. Once the disk cache of each client is populated with the files in common usage, the server receives only GETATTR requests from clients validating their cached data.

A "write-back" disk cache allows whole files to be written to the disk cache before being written to the server. Write-back is most beneficial if the file is removed soon after it is written, as is common with temporary files written by some applications like compilers. The file creation and deletion can be managed entirely on the client with no communication with the server at all. The utility of write-back caching is limited by the implications for error handling if the writes to the server fail due to lack of disk availability or other I/O problems. If the errors cannot be returned to the application that wrote the data, then the client is stuck with data that it cannot dispose of and errors that cannot be reported reliably to the end user. Consequently, the Solaris CacheFS uses *write-through* caching: data are written to the server first, then to the cache, if the server writes succeed. Alternatively, the client administrator can select *write-around* caching where data are written to the server but not to the cache and any cached data pages for the file are invalidated. Write-around has the advantage of avoiding unnecessary writes to the cache if the client is unlikely to read the data written.

8.14.6 Disconnection and Reconnection

A cache that can be disconnected from the server provides a client machine with some independence from the server. A disconnectable cache is useful if the server is temporarily unavailable because of a network or server problem or if the client is a laptop computer that the user has disconnected to take on the road.

Since the cache is usually not big enough to contain a complete copy of the data on the server, there is a chance that an application may try to access data that are not cached. If the cache is disconnected then a cache *miss* cannot be satisfied by data retrieval from the server. For this reason, a disconnectable cache like Sun's CacheFS or that of the Coda filesystem [Satyanarayanan90] will include a program that allows the user to select files that must be cached prior to disconnection. This process is known as *packing* or *hoarding*.

While a cache is disconnected, changes to cached data cannot be propagated back to the server. File creations, deletions, renames, or modifications must be recorded and replayed back to the server when the cache is reconnected. CacheFS records its changes in a log file. To control the size of the log file, some optimization is used; for instance, if the creation of a file is followed some time later by the deletion of the same file, then the file creation record in the log is deleted, too.

When the cache is reconnected, the accumulated changes in the log are replayed to the server. File changes are resolved by comparing the modification times of the cache copy with the server's copy. This dependence on file modification times can be risky if the client and server clocks are not well synchronized. If a file has been changed on the client but not on the server, then it is written back to the server. The reverse is also true—if a file has been changed on the server but not on the client, then the client's cache copy is invalidated. If a file has been changed both in the cache and on the server, then the conflict must be resolved. The caching policy can be configured to decide consistently in favor of the server's copy or of the client's copy of the file—depending on the user's preference. Alternatively, the cache software can notify the user to resolve the conflict.

In addition to the possibility of file modification conflict, reconnection raises more interesting issues. Write access to a cached file may be limited to one or more authorized users. The log replay process must be careful to propagate changes to the server using the credentials of the user that made the changes while disconnected. A cached file on a multiuser client may contain changes from several users yet be unable to distinguish which user made each change. The replay process must choose to use the credentials of one of the users and hope that access to the server's copy of the file has not been changed during disconnection. Alternatively, the client cache software could limit use of the cache to a single user (a reasonable assumption for desktop or laptop clients).

If a file or directory is created during disconnection, then it will be created on the server via log replay at reconnection. The server's copy of this new file or directory is unlikely to have the same inode number as the cached copy. The change in inode number could create a problem for some applications that assume the inode number is unchanging. The CacheFS maintains an inode mapping table that maintains the cache inode number even when new file attributes are fetched from the server's copy of the file.

8.15 Connectathon

No chapter that discusses the implementation of NFS would be complete without some mention of the annual Connectathon event. Connectathon is a testing event where implementors of the protocol bring their engineers, machines, and source code to a small network where they can test their client and server implementations against other client and server implementations (Figure 8.18). When implementing any protocol from a specification, it's possible to build a client and server implementation in which client and server communicate successfully with each other but with no other client or server implementation. Interoperability testing reveals bugs that originate with a misinterpretation of the specification or bugs that manifest themselves only when testing against an implementation that behaves in a subtly different way.

Connectathon events are hosted by Sun Microsystems Inc. and are usually held in San Jose, California, in February or March each year. The event extends over approximately 10 days and draws 40 to 60 participants. The first Connectathon (1985) was aimed exclusively at the NFS protocol, though in recent years other protocols, like NIS/NIS+, PPP, X-Windows and DHCP, have been included. Connectathon is well known for its relaxed and cooperative atmosphere. As bugs are discovered, engineers fix them on the spot and retest. The attending engineers have hotel rooms within walking distance and can work 24 hours a day if they choose. For more information on Connectathon, visit the Web site at www.connectathon.org.

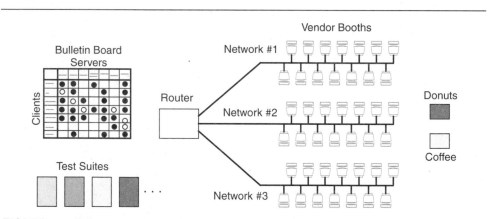

FIGURE 8.18 Elements of Connectathon. Each attendee brings their protocol implementation, source code, and client-server machines and connects to a common network at an assigned vendor booth. Test suites are made available for testing of clients against servers and servers against clients. Testing progress and results of the testing are monitored on a bulletin board.

8.16   **Summary**

Since the NFS protocol file attributes are modeled after those of POSIX, implementations of NFS on non-POSIX clients or servers must approximate equivalents of the POSIX attributes. Not all implementations can support all the NFS procedures; for example, servers that do not have symbolic links cannot support READLINK or SYMLINK procedures. As an RPC protocol, clients and servers should use the highest mutually supported version number of the NFS protocol. The "last close" problem refers to a UNIX filesystem semantic that cannot easily be supported on a stateless server: since an NFS server has no knowledge of a client opening or closing a file, it cannot delete an unlinked file after the last close. The protocol assumes that LOOKUP operations on a server filesystem will not cross server mountpoints. Hierarchical mounts can in some circumstances present namespace gaps and unmountable filesystems.

The AUTH_SYS authentication flavor assumes a consistent set of UID and GID values for all clients. The netnames used by other authentication flavors do not have this problem. NFS servers will map the superuser UID value 0 to a harmless "nobody" value.

Servers use a duplicate request cache to avoid problems caused by the retransmission of nonidempotent requests. The duplicate request cache also improves server performance by allowing the server to avoid unnecessary work. Clients use a time-out/retransmit scheme to increase reliability in the event that requests or replies are lost. NFS WRITE requests are committed to stable storage on the server to eliminate the risk of data loss in the event of a server crash. NFS version 3 improves write performance by allowing the client to control the commitment of data to stable storage.

NFS clients use extensive data caching with cache validation based on frequency of update and detection of changes on the server. Network and server loading is reduced by caching both READ and WRITE requests. A client's disk can be used to extend the space available for caching and to increase the persistence of cached data across client reboots.

The Connectathon event presents an annual opportunity for vendors of NFS implementations to test the interoperability of their products on a common network.

Chapter 9

NFS MOUNT Protocol

An NFS server provides a filchandle for each directory or file a client needs to access. It also provides a LOOKUP operation that lets a client name any directory entry and obtain its filehandle. An NFS client evaluates a pathname as a sequence of LOOKUP operations. It may seem strange, though, that the protocol provides no procedure to obtain an initial filehandle for the root of an exported filesystem.[1] The initial filehandle is obtained using the MOUNT protocol (Figure 9.1).

Why have a separate protocol from NFS? Why not integrate features of the MOUNT protocol with the NFS protocol? The team that designed the NFS protocol wanted these functions to remain outside the NFS protocol for two reasons.

1. *Checking access to exported filesystems.* On UNIX systems, the NFS server is implemented within the kernel. A kernel process can be more tightly integrated with the supported filesystems and does not suffer the context switch and data movement overheads of user-level processes. However, a kernel process cannot as easily access user-level services and files for checking access to exported filesystems. For instance, a UNIX kernel cannot easily make a call to a name service like NIS, NIS+, or LDAP to check for netgroup[2] membership. This explains why UNIX servers handle the NFS protocol in the kernel and implement the MOUNT protocol in a daemon (user-level) process.

2. *Alternative protocols.* The NFS protocol designers felt that to integrate a single pathname to filehandle mapping procedure into NFS would unnecessarily limit its implementation to UNIX systems. They imagined that file-

---

1. Until WebNFS provided the public filehandle and multicomponent LOOKUP (chapter 16).

2. A *netgroup* is a set of hostnames and other netgroups supported by NIS and NIS+ name services.

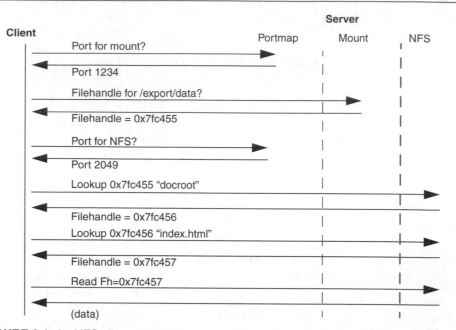

FIGURE 9.1 An NFS client cannot access any file on the server without first obtaining a filehandle via the MOUNT protocol. A client's NFS traffic to a server begins with a call to the portmapper to locate the UDP port for the MOUNT service. Once the initial filehandle is obtained, the client will again call the portmapper to verify the NFS port. Initial NFS traffic will probably be a series of LOOKUP calls to evaluate a pathname from the initial filehandle.

handles might be made available to clients by other MOUNT protocols or name services.

As it turned out, all NFS implementations use a common MOUNT protocol, driven by the need to interoperate with other implementations. Although the protocol has had two minor revisions, future revisions are unlikely. WebNFS clients and servers make the use of the MOUNT protocol optional, and NFS version 4 (chapter 17) seeks to avoid the need for a MOUNT protocol.

Since all three versions of the MOUNT protocol are so similar, this chapter presents a unified description of the protocol, with version differences pointed out as necessary.

9.1   Protocol Revisions

Version 1 of the protocol met the needs of most NFS version 2 implementations for many years. In 1990, seeking compliance with the IEEE POSIX 1003.1 standard, Sun created version 2 of the protocol, which added one additional procedure: MOUNTPROC_PATHCONF. It retrieves additional filesystem information from the server to make NFS filesystems comply with the needs of the POSIX-sanctioned *pathconf* procedure. It would have been more appropriate to add this procedure to the NFS protocol, but it was thought easier to add it to the MOUNT protocol rather than create industry upheaval with an NFS protocol revision.

The MOUNTPROC_MNT procedure of versions 1 and 2 of the protocol returned a fixed-length, 32-byte filehandle for NFS version 2. Since NFS version 3 required a variable-length filehandle with up to 64 bytes, version 3 of the MOUNT protocol was created. The MOUNTPROC_MNT procedure of this new version returned the larger NFS version 3 filehandle as well as an array of authentication flavors that allowed the client to determine the type of NFS authentication required by the server. Since NFS version 3 returned POSIX pathconf information in a new PATHCONF procedure built into the protocol, the MOUNTPROC_PATHCONF procedure was removed, as well as the unused MOUNTPROC_EXPORTALL procedure.

9.2 Transport

Most NFS servers provide access to the MOUNT protocol by both UDP and TCP transports. UDP is used in preference to TCP for the MOUNT call since it requires only a single RPC that conveys a small amount of data. The overhead in setting up a TCP connection cannot justify such a brief exchange. Clients will favor a TCP connection for calls like DUMP or EXPORT that may result in the transfer of a very large amount of information that could exceed the maximum size of a UDP datagram.

9.3 Authentication

Since the MOUNT protocol cannot be used to change state on the server (other than indirect modification of the MOUNT table), client authentication is not particularly important. Since MOUNT requests generally originate from a system mount process using superuser (UID = 0) credentials, there is no need to identify a particular user. Servers generally ignore the credential, permitting either AUTH_NONE or AUTH_SYS credentials. Digital UNIX servers require an AUTH_SYS credential and check that the UID is 0.

Some servers will use a *port monitoring* or *portmon* feature to check that a MOUNT request comes from a privileged port (< 1024). A program on a UNIX client cannot use a privileged port unless it has superuser credentials. For some system administrators this may provide some level of comfort that MOUNT requests from perhaps mischievous user-level processes will be ignored, though this does not prevent such processes being used on non-UNIX clients that do not enforce privileged ports.

9.4   Access Lists

Where the MOUNT daemon is controlling access to exported filesystems, the server uses the source IP address to identify the client. Although the source IP address can be spoofed, it is sufficient for the security needs of informal workgroups. A server administrator associates an access list with each exported filesystem. The access list enumerates the client machines that can access the filesystem. For instance:

```
share -o rw=lucy:charlie:snoopy,ro=linus  /export/data
```

If there is no list associated with an exported filesystem, then access to any client is allowed. The types of entries in the share access list vary from one implementation to another—those of a Solaris server can be any of the following:

1. *Client hostname.* This hostname must be in the same format as would be returned by the server's `gethostbyaddr()` function since the hostname to be matched is derived from the source IP address of the MOUNT PROC_MNT request. If the server is using DNS to map IP addresses to hostnames, then the access list should contain a fully qualified domain name (e.g., `myserver.corp.com`).

2. *Netgroup name.* A netgroup is a named list of client hostnames or other netgroup names that is stored in the NIS name service. Because a netgroup can be maintained in a single place (the NIS server) and can be organized hierarchically, it can be a labor-saving device for system administrators.

3. *Domain name.* A name beginning with a dot is assumed to represent a DNS domain suffix. Any client that has a fully qualified domain name with the same suffix is assumed to be a member of the domain. For instance, `wonderhog.eng.sun.com` is a member of the `.eng.sun.com` domain as well as the `.sun.com` domain.

4. *Network name or number.* A client might be identified by the network to which it belongs. For instance, a client that has a Class C IP address of 192.29.44.6 belongs to the network 192.29.44, which can have up to 253 other clients. The client's network number can be derived directly from its IP address. The network can be identified either by the network name (which maps to a network number in the NIS `networks.byname` map) or by the IP address, prefixed by an "@" sign. For instance, `@eng-net` or `@192.29.44`.

Access lists can also be used to assign different kinds of access to the client. For instance, an exported filesystem can be made read-only to one group of clients and read-write to another:

```
share -o ro=charlie:delta,rw=echo:foxtrot/export/data
```

The list of allowed security flavors might also be varied from one group of clients to another:

```
share -o auth=sys,ro=charlie:delta,\
        auth=krb5,rw=echo:foxtrot/export/data
```

means that clients `charlie` and `delta` must use AUTH_SYS credentials and get read-only access. Clients `echo` and `foxtrot` must use Kerberos version 5 credentials to get read-write access.

9.5 Server Procedures

The list of protocol procedures has changed over two protocol revisions (Table 9.1). Version 1 of the protocol supported procedures 1 through 6. Procedure 7 was added in version 2. Version 3 removed procedures 6 and 7.

9.5.1 Procedure 0: NULL—Do Nothing

Description

This procedure does no work. It is made available in all RPC services to allow server response testing and timing.

Arguments	Results
void;	void;

TABLE 9.1 Summary of MOUNT Procedures

Number	Name	Description	Mount versions	Section
0	MOUNTPROC_NULL	NULL procedure	1, 2, 3	9.5.1, page 259
1	MOUNTPROC_MNT	Add MOUNT entry	1, 2, 3	9.5.2, page 260
2	MOUNTPROC_DUMP	Return MOUNT entries	1, 2, 3	9.5.3, page 263
3	MOUNTPROC_UMNT	Remove MOUNT entry	1, 2, 3	9.5.4, page 264
4	MOUNTPROC_UMNTALL	Remove all MOUNT entries	1, 2, 3	9.5.5, page 265
5	MOUNTPROC_EXPORT	Return export list	1, 2, 3	9.5.6, page 265
6	MOUNTPROC_EXPORTALL	Same as MOUNTPROC_EXPORT	1, 2	9.5.7, page 267
7	MOUNTPROC_PATHCONF	POSIX pathconf information	2	9.5.8, page 267

Implementation

It is important that this procedure do no work at all so that it can be used to measure the overhead of processing a service request. By convention, the NULL procedure should never require any authentication. A server may choose to ignore this convention in a more secure implementation, where responding to the NULL procedure call acknowledges the existence of a resource to an unauthenticated client. The NULL procedure call is most commonly used to establish whether the NFS service is available and responding.

9.5.2   Procedure 1: MOUNTPROC_MNT—Add MOUNT Entry

Description

Given a pathname, it returns the corresponding filehandle.

Arguments	Results

`string<1024> pathname;`	`switch (unsigned status) {`
	`    case 0:`
	`        opaque[32] fhandle;`
	`            – or –`
	`        opaque<64> fhandle;`
	`        uint32<>     auth_flavors;`
	
	`    default:`
	`        void;`
	`}`

Arguments

`pathname`

   The filehandle of an object whose attributes are to be retrieved.

Results

`status`

   MNT_OK or an error code.

`fhandle`

   Versions 1 and 2 of the protocol return an NFS version 2 filehandle: an opaque, fixed-length array of 32 bytes. Version 3 of the protocol returns an NFS version 3 filehandle: a variable-length array of up to 64 bytes.

`auth_flavors`

   This list is returned only by version 3 of the protocol. It is a list of authentication flavor numbers that are acceptable to the server for NFS access to this filesystem. The list is presented in order of preference; that is, the client should examine each flavor in the list proceeding from left to right until it finds one it can support. Some security flavors may be limited to read-only

TABLE 9.2 Registered Entries for Kerberos Version 5 Security

Flavor number	Flavor name	Mechanism OID	Mechanism algorithm	RPCSEC_GSS aervice
390003	krb5	1.2.840.113554.1.2.2	DES, MAC, MD5	rpc_gss_svc_none
390004	krb5i	1.2.840.113554.1.2.2	DES, MAC, MD5	rpc_gss_svc_integrity
390005	krb5p	1.2.840.113554.1.2.2	DES, MAC, MD5	rpc_gss_svc_privacy

access. Generally, a server will arrange for these limited-access flavors to come later in the list. The list of acceptable flavors is presented in section 4.2.

RPCSEC_GSS security is not represented by a single flavor number since it is a security mechanism that encapsulates many different security mechanisms. RPCSEC_GSS security is assigned *pseudoflavors* that identify a security triple (mechanisms, algorithms, service) registered with the Internet Assigned Numbers Authority (IANA). For example, the registered entries for Kerberos version 5 security are given in Table 9.2.

Implementation

On UNIX systems this procedure is used by the `mount` command or auto-mounter to mount NFS filesystems. On DOS clients, the `net use` command is used to assign an NFS filesystem to a disk letter.

```
mount jurassic:/export/test/test  (UNIX)
net use d:   \\jurassic\export\test (DOS)
```

The pathname in the request `/export/test` is sent to the server to obtain a filehandle to be used for a mounted directory or disk letter. Note that DOS clients will change the backslashes to forward slashes assuming that the server is a UNIX system that understands only forward slashes. This path editing is not required by the protocol but makes it somewhat easier for DOS users who are mounting from UNIX servers and are unused to typing pathnames with forward slashes.

Although the pathname most commonly refers to a *directory* on the server, the protocol does not prevent a client from requesting the filehandle for a *regular file*. Diskless clients mount their swap space as a regular file from the server. WebNFS clients will also resort to using the MOUNT protocol to get filehandles for regular files.[3]

---

3. A pathname that is evaluated by the server's MOUNT daemon will cross server mount-points. The same cannot be said of the NFS LOOKUP procedure. WebNFS clients use the MOUNT protocol to convert the pathname part of an NFS URL to a filehandle if the server does not support public filehandles or multicomponent LOOKUP (Chapter 16).

Errors

MOUNTPROC_MNT is the only procedure in the protocol that returns error codes. Versions 1 and 2 of the protocol defined errors as "a UNIX error number." In practice, these were the same error codes as assigned to the version 2 NFS protocol. All versions of the MOUNT protocol share the same error numbers.

MNT_OK	0	Mount successful—filehandle follows.
NFSERR_PERM	1	Not owner. The caller does not have correct ownership to perform the requested operation.
NFSERR_NOENT	2	No such file or directory. The file or directory specified does not exist.
NFSERR_IO	5	Some sort of hard error occurred when the operation was in progress—a disk error, for example.
NFSERR_ACCES	13	Permission denied. The caller does not have the correct permission to perform the requested operation.
NFSERR_NOTDIR	20	Not a directory. The caller specified a nondirectory in a directory operation.
NFSERR_INVAL	22	Invalid argument.
NFSERR_NAMETOOLONG	63	Filename too long. The filename in an operation was too long.
NFSERR_NOTSUPP	10004	Operation not supported.
NFSERR_SERVERFAULT	10006	A failure on the server.

The most common errors are NFSERR_NOENT (no such file or directory) and NFSERR_ACCES (permission denied). Permission to access a filehandle may be denied if the client's hostname does not appear in an access list associated with the exported filesystem.

Snoop Trace

```
MOUNT:----- NFS MOUNT -----
MOUNT:
MOUNT:Proc = 1 (Add mount entry)
MOUNT:Directory = /export

        ⇩

MOUNT:----- NFS MOUNT -----
MOUNT:
MOUNT:Proc = 1 (Add mount entry)
MOUNT:Status = 0 (OK)
MOUNT:File handle = 0080001800000002000A00000000DD0A
MOUNT:              50295369000A00000000DD0A50295369
MOUNT:Authentication flavor = unix
```

9.5.3 Procedure 2: MOUNTPROC_DUMP—Return MOUNT Entries

Description

Returns a list of clients and the exported filesystems they have mounted.

Arguments	*Results*

void;	list entries {
	        string<255> hostname;
	        string<1024> pathname;
	}

Results

entries

> A list of MOUNT entries, each consisting of

> > hostname

> > > The hostname of the client that sent a MOUNTPROC_MNT request.

> > pathname

> > > The pathname that the client sent in the MOUNTPROC_MNT request.

Implementation

This procedure is used by the UNIX commands showmount and dfmounts to display the list of clients and the filesystems they have mounted from a selected server. Since the number of clients and mounted filesystems can be very long, clients should use this call via a TCP connection.

Errors

If any errors are encountered, a zero-length list is returned.

Snoop Trace

```
MOUNT:----- NFS MOUNT -----
MOUNT:
MOUNT:Proc = 2 (Return mount entries)
```

```
MOUNT:----- NFS MOUNT -----
MOUNT:
MOUNT:Proc = 2 (Return mount entries)
MOUNT:Mount list
MOUNT:    rahil:/export1
MOUNT:    krbsec6:/export1
MOUNT:    fileset6:/export2/krb5
MOUNT:    fileset7:/export1
MOUNT:    gandalf:/export1
MOUNT:    neptune:/export2/home
MOUNT:    paratu:/export1
```

```
MOUNT:     wonderhog:/export2/krb5
MOUNT:     firefly:/export2/home
MOUNT:     vishwas:/export2/home
MOUNT:     aqua:/export2/home
MOUNT: 11 entries.
```

9.5.4   Procedure 3: MOUNTPROC_UMNT—Remove MOUNT Entry

Description

Removes a MOUNT entry from the server's MOUNT list.

Arguments	Results
string<1024> pathname;	void;

Arguments

pathname

   The pathname that was used in a previous MOUNTPROC_MNT request.

Implementation

This procedure is an advisory call to the server as notification that the client has unmounted the filesystem and will no longer be using it. Since the call returns no results, the Solaris umount command sends the call and closes the UDP socket without waiting for a reply. To wait for a server reply risks an unnecessary client hang if the server is down.

   The server determines the client's hostname from the source IP address of the call, and with the pathname provided, attempts to locate a record of this mount within its MOUNT table. If the client sends this request while the server is unreachable or down, the call will not be retransmitted. The UNMOUNT request will be lost and a stale MOUNT entry will persist in the server's mount table.

   Web browsers and other NFS clients that use the MOUNT protocol to access filehandles without actually mounting a filesystem will send a MNTPROC_UMNT call immediately after a successful MNTPROC_MNT call to delete the MOUNT record from the server's MOUNT table.

Snoop Trace

```
MOUNT:----- NFS MOUNT -----
MOUNT:
MOUNT:Proc = 3 (Remove mount entry)
MOUNT:Directory = /export

        ⇩

MOUNT:----- NFS MOUNT -----
MOUNT:
MOUNT:Proc = 3 (Remove mount entry)
```

9.5.5   Procedure 4: MOUNTPROC_UMNTALL—Remove All MOUNT Entries

Description

Remove all MOUNT entries recorded for this client.

Arguments	*Results*
void;	void;

Implementation

This procedure is intended to be used as a broadcast RPC[4] when a client boots or reboots after a crash. It is supposed to prevent the problem of stale MOUNT entries remaining on a server if a client crashes before it can issue a MOUNTPROC_UMNT call. Any server that receives this request is to clear all entries for this client from its `/etc/rmtab` file.

In practice, the broadcast RPC is received only by servers on the same subnet or bridged network as the client. Stale MOUNT entries will persist on servers that must be reached by routers. Routers will usually not forward broadcast RPCs.

Snoop Trace

```
MOUNT:----- NFS MOUNT -----
MOUNT:
MOUNT:Proc = 3 (Remove all mount entries)
```

⇩

- no reply -

9.5.6   Procedure 5: MOUNTPROC_EXPORT—Return Export List

Description

Return a list of exported filesystems and their export information.

Arguments	*Results*
void;	list entries {
	string<1024> directory;
	list exportinfo {
	string<255> name;
	}
	}

---

4. A Remote Procedure Call that is sent to a broadcast IP address. The request is received by multiple servers.

Results

`entries`

A list of export entries consisting of

`directory`

The pathname of an exported directory.

`exportinfo`

A list of hostnames or netgroup names that can have access to the exported directory. A list with no entries implies unrestricted access.

Implementation

Since the export list can be large (perhaps hundreds of entries), a TCP connection should be used to retrieve this data.

When the protocol was first designed, the `exportinfo` strings represented hostnames or netgroup names that would be given access (via filehandle) to the exported filesystem. Netgroup names are indistinguishable from hostnames in the list. The SunOS `export` command allowed a directory to be exported read-only or read-write (the default). Access could be restricted to a list of hosts, for example:

```
share -o ro=dopey:sleepy:bashful  /export/dir
```

The `export` command was enhanced to allow some clients to have read-write access to a read-only filesystem—

```
share -o ro,rw=dopey /export/dir
```

—or to control access to both read-only *and* read-write modes—

```
share -o ro=happy:grumpy,rw=dopey /export/dir
```

Since the export list entry of the MOUNT protocol provides only a single hostname list, the SunOS server returned the concatenation of read-write and read-only lists. Not only is it impossible to tell whether a name in the list is a netgroup or a hostname, it is also impossible to tell whether it has read-only or read-write access. The situation has become even more complicated with the advent of Solaris 2.6, which provides not only additional lists attached to security flavors but increases the list entries to include domain name and network name suffixes. To summarize: clients should not attach any significance to the entries in an access list other than to note that the absence of a list implies no host-based restrictions on access.

This procedure is used by automounters that need to enumerate the list of mountable filesystems when a user references a */net/server* path. Early automounter implementations would attempt to mount all the exported filesystems. The Solaris 2.6 automounter records the list of exported filesystems but delays their mounting until the mountpoint is crossed on the client. On UNIX systems the showmount or dfshares command can be used to return the server's export list via this procedure.

Errors

If any errors are encountered, a zero-length list of entries is returned.

Snoop Trace

```
MOUNT:----- NFS MOUNT -----
MOUNT:
MOUNT:Proc = 5 (Return export list)
```

⇩

```
MOUNT:----- NFS MOUNT -----
MOUNT:
MOUNT:Proc = 5 (Return export list)
MOUNT:Directory = /export1
MOUNT:Directory = /export2/home
MOUNT:Directory = /export/util
MOUNT: Group = .west.sun.com
MOUNT: Group = .east.sun.com
MOUNT: Group = .corp.sun.com
MOUNT: Group = .central.sun.com
MOUNT: Group = engineering
MOUNT: Group = admin2
MOUNT:Directory = /export2/secure
MOUNT:Directory = /tmp
```

9.5.7   Procedure 6: MOUNTPROC_EXPORTALL—Return Export List

Description

Identical to MOUNTPROC_EXPORT. This procedure was eliminated in version 3 of the protocol.

9.5.8   Procedure 7: MOUNTPROC_PATHCONF—POSIX Pathconf Information

Description

Return filesystem information required by the *pathconf* procedure described in IEEE POSIX standard 1003.1.

Arguments	*Results*	
string<1024> pathname;	uint32	pc_link_max;
	uint32	pc_max_canon;
	uint32	pc_max_input;
	uint32	pc_name_max;
	uint32	pc_path_max;
	uint32	pc_pipe_buf;
	uint32	pc_vdisable;
	uint32	pc_xxx;
	uint32	pc_mask;

Results

pc_link_max

The maximum number of hard links allowed to a file. A hard link is created when an NFS client uses the LINK procedure. Most UNIX systems will return a value of 32,767.

pc_max_canon

The maximum line length for a terminal device. This field is valid only for NFS device files (NF3CHR).

pc_max_input

The number of input characters that can be buffered by a terminal device. This field is valid only for NFS device files (NFCHR).

pc_name_max

The maximum length of a pathname component. UNIX servers will usually set this to 255. A value greater than 255 is meaningless for NFS version 2 clients since the protocol imposes a limit of 255 characters.

pc_path_max

The maximum pathname length. UNIX servers will set this to 1024. The NFS version 2 protocol imposes an upper limit of 1024 characters.

pc_pipe_buf

The size of a pipe in bytes. This number is valid only for NFFIFO device files. A common value is 5120 bytes.

pc_vdisable

This attribute is valid only for NFCHR (terminal) devices. It represents the value of an ASCII control character that disables the recognition of control characters.

TABLE 9.3 Validity Bits of `pc_mask` Field

Bit	Meaning
0	If set, an error occurred and all fields are invalid.
1	If set, `pc_link_max` is valid.
2	If set, `pc_max_canon` is valid.
3	If set, `pc_max_input` is valid.
4	If set, `pc_name_max` is valid.
5	If set, `pc_path_max` is valid.
6	If set, `pc_pipe_buf` is valid.
7	`pc_chown_restricted`. If set, the server will reject any request to change either the owner or the group associated with a file if the caller is not the privileged user (uid 0).
8	`pc_no_trunc`. If set, the server will reject any request that includes a name longer than name_max with the error NAMETOOLONG. If not set, any length name over `pc_name_max` bytes will be silently truncated to `pc_name_max` bytes.
9	If set, `pc_vdisable` is valid.

`pc_xxx`

This field is unused. In a C version of the pathconf information, this field was used as alignment padding for the `pc_vdisable` character. XDR encoding makes this unnecessary, but the field was left in by mistake.

`pc_mask`

This field contains validity bits for previous fields, as well as some single-bit boolean values (Table 9.3).

Implementation

This procedure was added in version 2 of the MOUNT protocol to provide compliance with the POSIX *pathconf* procedure for NFS filesystems. Version 2 of the protocol is identical to version 1 except for this addition.

Since the pathconf information is not expected to change for the duration of the client's access to a filesystem, it is assumed that a client that needs pathconf information will make one call at mount time to retrieve the pathconf information and cache it. Demands for pathconf information from client processes will then be met from the cache. NFS version 3 clients are expected to use the *pathconf* procedure to obtain POSIX pathconf information (section 7.3.21).

Solaris clients will not use the *pathconf* procedure unless the `posix` mount option is used. The default is to use approximate values for pathconf information rather than incur the extra overhead of another MOUNT procedure call for each NFS mounted filesystem.

Errors

If any errors are encountered, the error bit of the pc_mask value is set and the returned values must be ignored.

Snoop Trace

Snoop has no code to interpret this procedure.

9.6 MOUNT Table

The MOUNT protocol assumes that the server will maintain a table that lists the clients that have mounted filesystems from the server and which exported filesystems they have mounted (Figure 9.2). By this assumption, the MOUNT protocol is certainly a stateful protocol. The entries in the table can be returned with the MOUNTPROC_DUMP procedure. An entry is added to the table whenever a filehandle is returned to the client via the MOUNTPROC_MNT request, and the entry is removed by a subsequent MOUNTPROC_UMNT or MOUNTPROC_UMNTALL request.

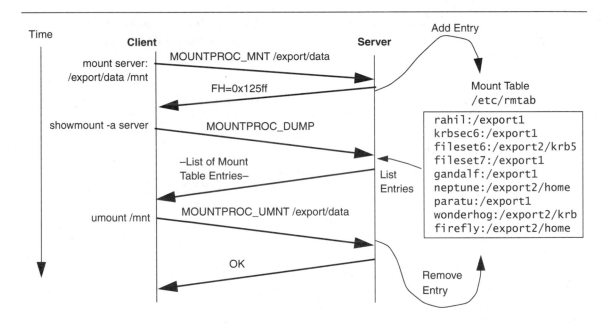

FIGURE 9.2 The server maintains a table of clients that have mounted filesystems (received filehandles). Each entry identifies the client and the filesystem it mounted. The MOUNTPROC_UMNT request serves only to notify the server that the client has unmounted the filesystem and should be removed from the MOUNT table.

The designers of the protocol intended this table to be a useful record of the server's clients. For instance, the Solaris shutdown command was configured to use the MOUNT table to send console messages to clients that had filesystems mounted from the server. The message was intended as a courtesy to warn users of the pending unavailability of an NFS filesystem mounted from the server.

In practice, the MOUNT table proved to be notoriously unreliable as an accurate indicator of the server's clients and the filesystems they were using. The chief difficulty was that clients would sometimes crash or be rebooted without having the opportunity to send a MOUNTPROC_UMNT request to the server. The missing MOUNTPROC_UMNT request would result in a "stale" entry in the MOUNT table. The MOUNTPROC_UMNTALL request was designed to flush stale entries from the table; when the client recovers it is supposed to broadcast the request to all NFS servers to remove stale entries before the client remounts its filesystems. Since the range of a broadcast RPC call is limited to the local Ethernet segment, servers on the other side of routers did not receive the request and the stale entries persisted.

Persistent stale entries could be quite annoying to clients. Whenever a server containing a stale entry was shut down, the shutdown command sent a message to the client warning of the shutdown. A client could receive shutdown requests from a server for a filesystem that it had mounted briefly some months ago. I remember writing a shell script called "silence" that took a server name as an argument. The script used the showmount command to obtain the MOUNT table. It removed the stale entries by mounting from the server followed immediately by an unmount of the same filesystem.

9.7 Submounts

The pathname a client sends in a MOUNTPROC_MNT request normally matches a pathname in the server's export list. The export list is a list of the directories the server has made available to NFS clients, for example:

```
/var/mail        rw=engineering
/export/home1    rw=engineering
/export/home2    rw=engineering
/export/home3    rw=engineering
/export/local    rw
```

The clients of this server mount their /var/mail directories using a command like this:

```
mount   server:/var/mail     /var/mail
```

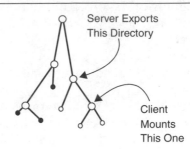
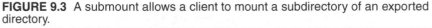

FIGURE 9.3 A submount allows a client to mount a subdirectory of an exported directory.

Clients that mount home directories from this server mount individual home directories as users log into the client. For instance, when user Larry logs in, the local automounter might issue a request equivalent to

```
mount  server:/export/home2/larry    /home/larry
```

Notice that the pathname sent to the server, /export/home2/larry, does not match the exported directory, /export/home2. Instead, it refers to a subdirectory of the exported directory. This is a nice feature, since it allows a server adminis-trator to export a disk partition as a single directory that may contain many users' home directories that are individually mountable (Figure 9.3).

There is a potential security problem with this feature. Since the pathname in the MOUNT request is evaluated by a user-level MOUNT daemon on the server that will be running with superuser permissions, it is possible for a cli-ent to obtain filehandles for directories that are normally protected from access (Figure 9.4). For example, a user might set the permissions of a direc-tory to prevent any access to subdirectories by anyone else. On UNIX servers, the MOUNT daemon runs with superuser permission, so it is allowed to eval-uate pathnames that pass through the restricted directory. The result is that an NFS client may get a filehandle and access to subdirectories that users logged into the server would not be able to see.

A workaround for this problem is to provide the system administrator with an option that restricts the ability of the MOUNT daemon to return file-handles for subdirectories of an exported directory. The Solaris share com-mand has a nosub option that requires the pathname in a MOUNT request to match exactly the exported pathname.

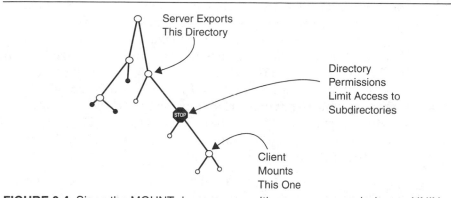

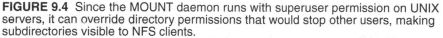

FIGURE 9.4 Since the MOUNT daemon runs with superuser permission on UNIX servers, it can override directory permissions that would stop other users, making subdirectories visible to NFS clients.

9.8 Export Limitations

Servers limit the directories that can be exported to NFS clients.

1. *No filehandle support.* Some filesystems will not be exportable at all if they do not provide a means to obtain a filehandle. The Solaris *procfs* filesystem is used to present a filesystem view of UNIX processes under a /proc directory. Since the information provided by this filesystem is mostly restricted to superuser processes and is not generally useful to NFS clients, procfs does not make filehandles available, so /proc cannot be exported.

2. *No reexporting.* NFS filesystems are generally not *reexportable* because the filehandle is generally large enough to contain only the information for one server unambiguously. For example, in Figure 9.5, server B cannot reex-

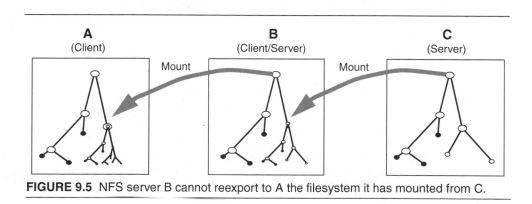

FIGURE 9.5 NFS server B cannot reexport to A the filesystem it has mounted from C.

port any NFS filesystem it has mounted from C. The filehandles obtained from server C cannot be used by client A because they might match other filehandles on B. A prefix added to C's filehandles by B could "uniquefy" the filehandles, but not within the constraints of filehandle size limitations (32 bytes for NFS version 2 and 64 bytes for version 3). Server B could issue its own filehandles that correspond to those from C, but this would require a filehandle mapping table that would need to persist across reboots of B.

Reexporting also presents problems for AUTH_SYS security based on server access lists. Server C may limit access to client B, but cannot prevent access from client A through client B.

3. *No hierarchical exports.* NFS servers use a fairly simple model when exporting directories: the client gets access to the directory and all directories below it (subject to directory permission checking). When an NFS server receives an NFS LOOKUP request, it checks the client's credential against the directory permissions, but it does not check the access list associated with the export. The access list is checked only by the MOUNT daemon when the client mounts the filesystem (Figure 9.6). The hierarchical export limitation is imposed by servers to avoid having to validate every client LOOKUP request against a potential access list associated with the directory.

This limitation may sometimes appear to be violated. For instance, it is not uncommon to have a server return an export list that looks like this

```
/export              rw
/export/data         ro
```

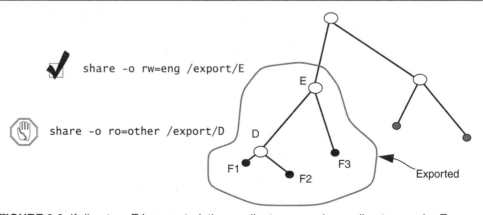

FIGURE 9.6 If directory E is exported, then a client can reach any directory under E without further access list checking. Directory D cannot be exported because clients descending from export E would not be checked against the access list for D.

which would appear to be a case of hierarchical exporting because /export/data is clearly a subdirectory of /export. However, further investigation would show that these directories are not in the same filesystem—/export/data is another filesystem mounted within /export. This hierarchical export is permissible because NFS LOOKUP request will not cross from a mountpoint from one filesystem to another on the server. If /export/data were mounted but not exported, NFS clients would not have access to the filesystem at all; instead, they would see "underneath" the filesystem mounted on the server (see section 8.5).

These exporting limitations are sometimes confusing to system administrators, but they are driven by a need for simple, high-performance implementation.

9.9 Summary

The MOUNT protocol is used to obtain an initial filehandle when a client mounts an NFS filesystem from a server. A server can use this request to validate the client against an access list before returning the filehandle. The MOUNT protocol can be used over a TCP connection or with UDP. The low overhead of UDP is preferred for short requests like MOUNTPROC_MNT, but TCP is better for requests that return a lot of information like MOUNT PROC_DUMP. The protocol has undergone two revisions; version 2 added the MOUNTPROC_PATHCONF request and version 3 extended the size of the filehandle to a limit of 64 bytes, as well as returning security flavor information. The server's MOUNT daemon maintains a MOUNT table that lists the server's clients and the exported filesystems that they have mounted. Most NFS servers allow clients to mount subdirectories of an exported directory. NFS servers apply some limitations on the kinds of filesystems that can be exported, and on hierarchical exports.

Chapter 10

NFS Lock Manager Protocol

The team that designed the NFS protocol consciously omitted file locking operations. Although simple file operations like READ and WRITE could be generalized across different operating systems, there was no clear consensus on what should constitute a general file and record locking protocol. In 1984, Bill Joy, one of the architects of the NFS protocol, replied to a question on the omission of file locking:

> When we started the company [Sun Microsystems, Inc.] I went around and talked to the people I respect the most who were doing databases, and asked them well, if I gave you this and I gave you that . . . first of all, what would you want and if I gave you this or that would you use it . . . and it was very discouraging because they just basically said just make the file system fast and we'll do the rest ourselves, and they almost didn't want anything that I thought of giving them.[1]

In addition, locking by its very nature implies a stateful server with additional complexity in recovering lock state following a server crash and reboot. As it turned out, there was a customer demand for file locking to be supported for not only the whole file locks of Berkeley UNIX clients but also the byte-range locking required by UNIX System V, Release 4 clients. File locking was added to SunOS clients and servers in the SunOS 3.2 release in 1986.

The Network Lock Manager protocol depends on another RPC protocol, the Network Status Monitor protocol, to notify clients and/or servers of loss of lock state resulting from a crash/reboot. The Status Monitor protocol is also described in this chapter.

The interaction of these protocols, the use of asynchronous RPC calls and callbacks, and the multiplicity of locking procedures (monitored vs. nonmonitored, record vs. share reservations, and so on) make this a difficult protocol to implement successfully. For this reason, some NFS server implementations

---

1. From the transcript of a talk given at a workshop on personal computing technology, at the Certosa di San Giacomo, Capri, Italy, in June 1984.

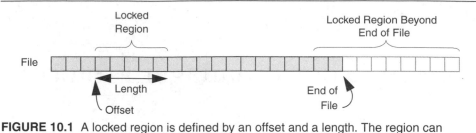

FIGURE 10.1 A locked region is defined by an offset and a length. The region can extend beyond the end of the file. The properties of a locked region are further defined by the shared or exclusive nature of the lock.

have neglected to support the Lock Manager protocol. NFS clients that encounter these servers must resort to local locking.

The Lock Manager protocol assumes a locking model that allows a client application to lock a region of a file defined by an offset and a length. A lock can span an entire file, starting with an offset of zero and with a length that extends to the last byte (Figure 10.1). A locked region can also extend beyond the last byte of a file. The extension of a range beyond the end-of-file is to allow additional data to be appended to the file within the protection of a lock. A locked region can be controlled by one of two different types of lock. A *shared* lock allows other applications to read the data in the region but not modify it. Multiple clients can hold shared locks on the same region of a file, or overlapping regions. An *exclusive* lock prevents other applications from reading or writing data in the region. Another client cannot establish any lock on a region that is covered by an exclusive lock.

10.1 Monitored Locking

A file locking protocol must provide a solution for two common scenarios that relate to the maintenance of lock state by the client and the server.

1. *Loss of server state.* When a server grants a lock to a client it must maintain a record of the lock: the owner of the lock, the offset and length of the locked byte range (if it is a record lock), the exclusivity of the lock, and so on. For performance reasons, this state is generally maintained in volatile storage, that is, the server's memory. If the server crashes and reboots, this lock state will be lost and the client may continue without the knowledge that it has lost the lock. The client needs to be notified of the server's crash/recovery so that it can reestablish the lock.

2. *Loss of client state.* If the client crashes, then its record of the locks assigned to various programs will be lost. The server, unaware that the client

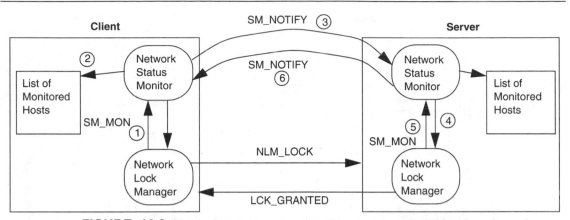

FIGURE 10.2 The lock manager uses the status monitor to notify it of any loss of lock state. While a file lock is held, the client monitors the server and the server monitors the client. (1) When the client is granted a lock, the client's lock manager sends an SM_MON request to the local status monitor to monitor the server. (2) The monitored hostname is recorded in a file. (3) If the client crashes and recovers, the status monitor will read the file of monitored hosts and send a notification to the server's status monitor. (4) The server's status monitor will then forward the information to the server's lock manager so that it can free the client's locks. (5) A reciprocal arrangement occurs on the server when it grants a lock: the server's lock manager asks the local status monitor to monitor the client so that (6) it will notify the client if it crashes and recovers.

has forgotten its locks, will maintain the locks and prevent other clients from establishing conflicting locks. It is important that the server learn of the client's loss of state so that it can remove the "forgotten" locks.

The Lock Manager protocol uses the Status Monitor protocol to provide a timely notification of client or server loss of lock state (Figure 10.2). The status monitor is a service that notifies other interested hosts if the status monitor host is restarted. In a reciprocal way, the interested hosts can be monitored by the status monitor, which receives a notification message if they are restarted.

The Status Monitor protocol is poorly named since it does no *active* monitoring of other machines. It *receives* a recovery notification only when a host recovers, but it cannot be used to signal that a host is down—but not yet recovered. Its only active role is to notify selected hosts when it recovers (Figure 10.3). The Status Monitor protocol is described in more detail in section 10.15.

Since DOS clients can support only single-threaded applications, a status monitor service that listens for status notifications may be difficult or impossi-

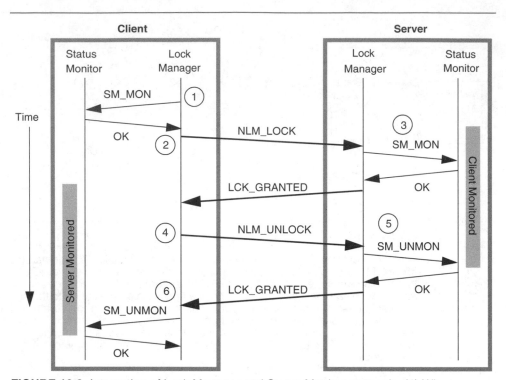

FIGURE 10.3 Interaction of Lock Manager and Status Monitor protocols. (1) When the client requests its first lock, it makes an SM_MON call to its status monitor so that the server will be notified if the client crashes while holding one or more locks. (2) On granting the first lock request from a client, the server makes an SM_MON call to its status monitor so that the client will be notified if the server reboots while the client is holding one or more locks. (4) When the client removes the last lock held on the server, (5) the server requests its status monitor to cease monitoring the client. (6) When the client receives confirmation that this last lock has been removed, it requests its status monitor to stop monitoring the server. The SM_MON and SM_UNMON messages are used only for the *first* and *last* lock held by the client.

ble to run concurrently with an application making LOCK requests. Acknowledging the limitations of these clients, the Lock Manager protocol provides a procedure that creates a *nonmonitored* lock. In addition, the file SHARE reservation request, which is used when a DOS or Windows application opens a file, is also nonmonitored. Without the state change service provided by the status monitor, clients that use nonmonitored locks cannot readily detect that a server has rebooted and lost its locks. Similarly, a server cannot easily recover locked files that remain after a client has crashed and forgotten its locks.

A client can create a nonmonitored lock by using the NLM_NM_LOCK variation of the NLM_LOCK procedure call (section 10.14.9) or by creating a SHARE reservation. Since these locks are not monitored, the client must be prepared to deal with errors that may result from the loss of locks on the server. It is possible that an unmonitored lock may become "stuck" if the client that is holding it crashes and does not recover or if it recovers without unlocking its locks. Clients that use unmonitored locks should issue an NLM_FREE_ALL call at reboot to any servers on which it may have held locked files prior to the crash.

10.2 Advisory vs. Mandatory Locks

The Network Lock Manager (NLM) protocol implements an *advisory* locking scheme (Figure 10.4). It assumes that programs running on clients will a lock a file (or region of a file) before attempting any reads or writes. An advisory locking scheme doesn't prevent noncooperating clients or applications from having read or write access to the file.

A *mandatory* locking scheme prevents noncooperating clients or applications from having read or write access to the file. The UNIX operating system has a tradition of supporting only *advisory* locking. Berkeley UNIX systems provided advisory locking only, whereas System V systems provided both advisory and mandatory locking. Since the NLM protocol supports only advisory locking, it does not completely meet the needs of DOS and Windows clients that assume a mandatory locking scheme. As long as the clients connected to a server are all UNIX or all DOS/Windows, there is no conflict. However, there is a possibility of data corruption if a file that is locked by a DOS/Windows application is updated by a noncooperating UNIX application. A mandatory locking scheme cannot easily be imposed on UNIX clients because the errors resulting from READ and WRITE requests would not be properly handled by the UNIX applications. Nor is there any support in the NFS protocol itself to identify the lock holder for a particular READ or WRITE request.[2]

10.3 Exclusive and Nonexclusive Locks

An *exclusive* lock is one that excludes other clients or programs from holding an overlapping lock on the same byte range. It is also referred to as a *write* lock because it is most commonly used when the data in the byte range are about to be updated or changed. It prevents other clients from reading out-of-date or partially written data.

A *nonexclusive* or *shared* lock is one that permits other clients to have their own nonexclusive locks on the same byte range. It is also referred to as a *read* lock because it is used to protect a byte range in the file from modification

---

2. NFS requests identify a user through the RPC credential, but a locking protocol needs to distinguish between multiple client threads or processes that all may be identified with the same user.

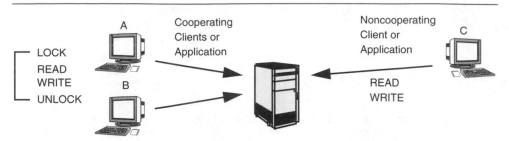

FIGURE 10.4 Advisory locking. Clients A and B use advisory locking to coordinate their changes to a file on the server. They will not proceed with a read or write on a file unless they successfully establish an advisory lock. The advisory locks do not prevent client C from ignoring the lock and reading or writing the locked file.

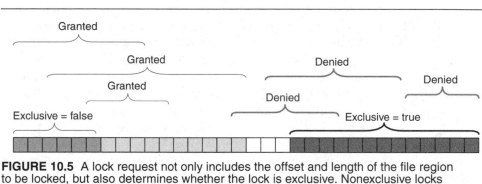

FIGURE 10.5 A lock request not only includes the offset and length of the file region to be locked, but also determines whether the lock is exclusive. Nonexclusive locks can share identical or overlapping regions of the file. If a region is covered by an exclusive lock, then other attempts to lock the same or overlapping regions will be denied. Similarly, an attempt to create an exclusive lock that overlaps a nonexclusively locked region will be denied.

while the data are being read. An exclusive lock cannot be established on an overlapping byte range while a nonexclusive lock is being held.

Each NLM lock request includes a flag to indicate whether the desired lock is to be exclusive or nonexclusive (Figure 10.5).

10.4 Asynchronous Procedures and Callback

The Network Lock Manager protocol is unusual in its use of optional asynchronous procedures and the use of a callback procedure for the granting of blocked locks. Each of the five basic locking operations TEST, LOCK, CANCEL, UNLOCK, and GRANTED has a corresponding pair of asynchronous procedures (Table 10.1). These procedures implement a message-passing scheme that was intended to make it easier for single-threaded platforms to

TABLE 10.1 Network Lock Manager's Asynchronous Procedures and Callback

Synchronous procedure	Asynchronous call	Asynchronous reply
NLM_TEST	NLM_TEST_MSG	NLM_TEST_RES
NLM_LOCK	NLM_LOCK_MSG	NLM_LOCK_RES
NLM_CANCEL	NLM_CANCEL_MSG	NLM_CANCEL_RES
NLM_UNLOCK	NLM_UNLOCK_MSG	NLM_UNLOCK_RES
NLM_GRANTED	NLM_GRANTED_MSG	NLM_GRANTED_RES

implement asynchronous handling of file locking and unlocking. Each asynchronous procedure handles either the call or reply arguments of its synchronous counterpart and expects no reply.

These asynchronous procedures have an interesting feature: they're redundant. There's no reason why they need to exist as distinct procedures within the protocol since the synchronous procedures could be implemented by an RPC library that supports nonblocking RPC calls.

Of the five basic locking procedures, NLM_GRANTED is interesting because, except for the asynchronous _MSG and _RES procedures, it is the only call that is initiated by the server as a *callback* RPC. Here the roles of client and server are reversed: the server must determine the network address and port of the client's network Lock Manager via the client's portmapper service. Because the client may have to wait for minutes or even hours for a callback, it is possible that the application that requested the lock might crash or be terminated, making the locking call unnecessary. Hence the protocol provides an NLM_CANCEL procedure that allows the client to cancel a pending lock request. The asynchronous nature of this callback creates timing problems when the calls are retransmitted (see Figure 10.14).

10.5 DOS/Windows File Sharing Procedures

The DOS/Windows file sharing procedures (described in section 10.14.7) were added to version 3 of the protocol to provide file locking for PC clients. When a DOS or Windows program opens a file, it also has the opportunity to lock the file, controlling access to the file by other applications while the file is open. The Win32 API uses the CreateFile system call to open existing files and create new ones:

```
CreateFile  ( LPCTSTR lpFileName,
              DWORD dwDesiredAccess,
              DWORD dwShareMode,
              LPSECURITY_ATTRIBUTES lpSecurityAttributes,
              DWORD dwCreationDistribution,
              DWORD dwFlagsAndAttributes,
              HANDLE hTemplateFile)
```

TABLE 10.2 Deny Mode Effect on Other Applications

Deny mode	Effect on other applications
Deny all	Cannot open the file.
Deny read	Can open for writing but not for reading.
Deny write	Can open the file for reading but not for writing
Deny none	Can open the file for reading or writing.

Of particular interest here are the dwDesiredAccess and dwShareMode arguments. With dwDesiredAccess, the application indicates its desired file usage: reading only, writing only, or both reading and writing. The dwShareMode, or deny mode, argument is used to control access to the file by other applications while the application has the file open. The deny modes have the values listed in Table 10.2.

When a PC client creates a file, it uses the NFS protocol to create the file and the NLM protocol to establish the lock. This process is illustrated in Figure 10.6. This SHARE-style file locking works well for PC clients—it protects applications from data corruption caused by concurrent access to files during update. Since the file locks are advisory within the NLM protocol, the NFS server will not prevent UNIX clients from reading or writing a file that is open with a share lock. Hence, data corruption is a risk where files are being accessed concurrently by PC and UNIX clients.

10.6   Server Crash Recovery

When an NFS server recovers from a crash, it restarts the NFS service (nfsd), the NLM server (lockd), and the status monitor (statd). The status monitor reads the list of monitored clients from disk and sends an SM_NOTIFY message to the status monitor on each client. Each client's status monitor will forward the notification to the client's lock manager. At this point the server will have entered a grace period where it will grant locks only to requests with the reclaim field set to true. The grace period gives all clients that were holding locks an opportunity to reclaim their locks before the server resumes normal operation.

There is no set duration for the grace period. It needs to be long enough that clients can receive the SM_NOTIFY message from the server's status monitor and recover all their locks by replaying LOCK requests with the reclaim argument set to true. If the grace period is too long, then clients will be unnecessarily delayed in their use of normal locking operations. Solaris servers use a grace period of 45 seconds.

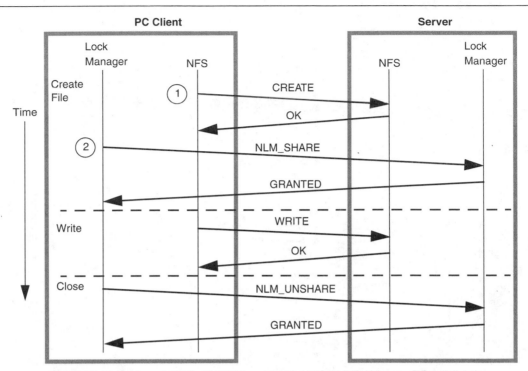

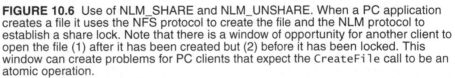

FIGURE 10.6 Use of NLM_SHARE and NLM_UNSHARE. When a PC application creates a file it uses the NFS protocol to create the file and the NLM protocol to establish a share lock. Note that there is a window of opportunity for another client to open the file (1) after it has been created but (2) before it has been locked. This window can create problems for PC clients that expect the CreateFile call to be an atomic operation.

One problem with a fixed grace period is that it doesn't take into account any problems that the status monitor may have in notifying all the monitored clients. If some of the clients do not respond, then the status monitor will take longer to notify all the clients. It is possible that some of the clients might be notified after the grace period has expired and not be able to reclaim their locks. A workaround for this problem is to use a multithreaded status monitor that can assign a thread to each client. In this way all clients can be notified almost simultaneously and only unresponsive clients will lose locks. Ideally, the status monitor would multicast the notification. A multicast notification was in the original status monitor design but never implemented.

In the rare circumstance that the server's status monitor (statd) crashes, but not the server itself, on restart it will behave as if the server had crashed and send an SM_NOTIFY message to all the monitored clients. The effect can be chaotic as clients proceed to reclaim locks that the server's lock manager rejects because it is not in the grace period.

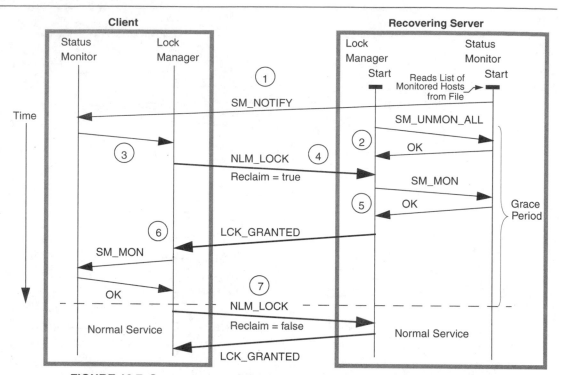

FIGURE 10.7 Server recovery following a crash. (1) When the server Status Monitor is restarted, it retrieves a list of the monitored clients from stable storage and notifies each client. (2) The server's Lock Manager sends a request to clear the monitor list. (3) When the client Status Monitor receives the notification, it calls the Lock Manager with the procedure registered in the SM_MON request. (4) On realizing that its locks have been lost, the client's Lock Manager sends a new LOCK request for each lock it was holding when the server crashed. During the grace period, the server will accept only LOCK requests with the reclaim field set to true. Nonreclaim requests are rejected with a LCK_DENIED_GRACE_PERIOD error. (5) On receiving the first lock reclaim request from a client, the server will again ask the Status Monitor to monitor it. (6) On receiving the server's granted reply, the client will again monitor the server if it is the first recovered lock. (7) At the conclusion of the grace period, normal service resumes.

In Figure 10.7 at step 5, the server requests its status monitor to monitor the client before responding to the client's first LOCK request. This request may be slow, since it requires the status monitor to record the client's hostname on stable storage. Server implementors, intent on improving server responsiveness, may be tempted to reply to the client before receiving confirmation from the status monitor. An early reply is risky, because if the server crashes before the status monitor has recorded the client in stable storage, the client will not be notified to reclaim its lock when the server recovers.

10.7 Lockd and Statd Implementation

Until now, we've have discussed the Lock Manager and Status Monitor protocol implementations rather abstractly. It is interesting to understand how
these services are implemented on top of an existing operating system that
supports file locking.

UNIX implementations typically implement the NLM protocol in a daemon called *lockd* and the Status Monitor protocol in a daemon called *statd*
(Figure 10.8). When an application on the client needs to lock or unlock a file,
it makes a system call to the kernel locking code in the kernel. If the kernel
locking code identifies the filesystem as an NFS filesystem, then it makes an
RPC call to the local lockd using a private Kernel Lock Manager RPC protocol. When the lockd receives this upcall from the kernel, it makes an NLM call
to the server's lockd, which makes a locking system call to the server's kernel.
The results of the locking call follow the reverse path back to the application
on the client through the server's lockd, the client's lockd, and the client's kernel. Because the lockd holds a great deal of locking state, it was difficult for
the client or server to recover if the lockd crashed or was killed and restarted
by a system administrator. The tortuous route of locking calls through each
daemon also added to the latency of locking calls, and the single-threaded
daemon limited the performance of both client and server locking. In Solaris
2.4, most of the lockd code was moved into the kernel and the private KLM
protocol was eliminated (Figure 10.9).

In the course of moving the lock manager code from the lockd into the kernel, the code was multithreaded, allowing the client's lock manager to handle
concurrent locking requests from multiple applications and allowing the
server's lock manager to handle concurrent locking requests from a large number of NFS clients. The failure semantics are much simpler in this configuration:

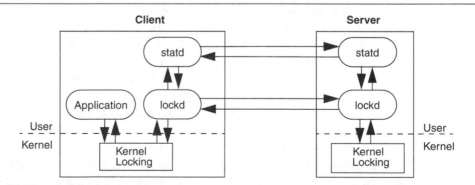
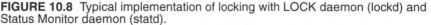

FIGURE 10.8 Typical implementation of locking with LOCK daemon (lockd) and
Status Monitor daemon (statd).

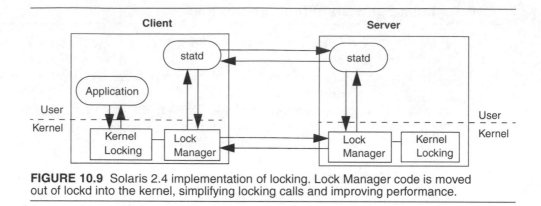

FIGURE 10.9 Solaris 2.4 implementation of locking. Lock Manager code is moved out of lockd into the kernel, simplifying locking calls and improving performance.

since all lock state is now held in the kernel, recovery of a crashed lockd is no longer an issue. In principle, the Status Monitor code could also be implemented in the kernel, though it would result in no significant performance or reliability advantages.

10.8 Client Crash Recovery

If an NFS client crashes, the server will continue to hold any locks that the client established before it crashed (Figure 10.10). There is no time-out on these locks—the server will hold them indefinitely. The persistence of locks is sometimes a problem if a client crashes and is disabled for some period of time (days or weeks) or if the client is disconnected from the network and removed. Normally, a client will recover within a few minutes and resume operation.

When the client's Status Monitor (statd) process restarts, it increments the client's state number to the next odd value (server up). The new state number is sent in an SM_NOTIFY message to each server recorded in its on-disk monitor list. Thanks to the monitor list, the client knows which servers were holding its locks, but it has no knowledge of which locks were held.

The client's entry in the server's monitor list was created prior to the client's crash in response to SM_MON calls from the server's lock manager when the client established its first lock. When the server's status monitor receives this notify message, it removes the client from its monitor list (since it is no longer holding any locks on the server) and passes on the client's identity and state number to the server's lock manager with a callback RPC registered by the SM_MON call. The server's lock manager compares the new value of the state variable to the state variable that was recorded with locks issued to the client before it crashed (each LOCK request includes the client's state variable). Any locks that are older than the new state value are removed.

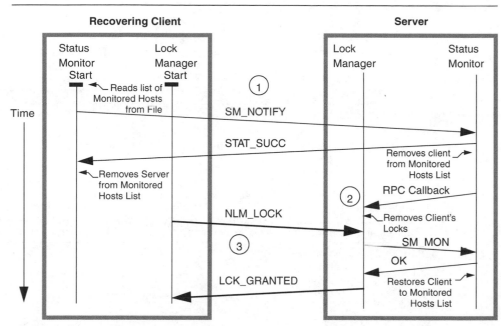

FIGURE 10.10 Client recovery following a crash. It's important that the server know when the client has crashed and recovered so that it can remove any stale locks established before the crash. (1) When the client status monitor is restarted, it retrieves a list of the monitored clients from stable storage and notifies each server. (2) When the server's status monitor receives the notification, it calls the lock manager with the procedure registered in the SM_MON request. The server's lock manager then removes the client's stale locks. (3) The server is ready to receive new LOCK requests from the recovered client. On receiving the first request, it will request the status monitor to restore the client to its list of monitored clients.

10.9 Deadlock Detection

A client can receive an NLM_DEADLCK error in response to a LOCK request. This error signals to the client that the server would create a deadlock if it granted the client's request. A deadlock situation exists if the LOCK requests of two or more processes are blocked because they are waiting for each other to release a lock. At least one of the processes must be attempting an exclusive lock or be holding an exclusive lock for a deadlock situation to occur (Figure 10.11). To detect deadlocks, the server maintains a dependency graph for all blocked LOCK requests that are waiting for locks (Figure 10.12). Any lock request that would create a cycle in the dependency graph is denied with an NLM_DEADLCK response.

Deadlocks are usually detected only for locks held on the same server. It is much more difficult to detect deadlocks between processes blocking on locks held on different servers; to do so requires servers to maintain a global dependency graph.

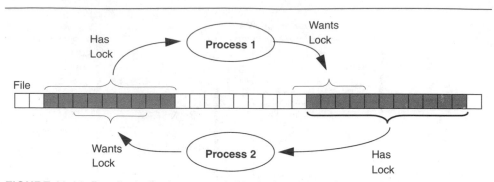

FIGURE 10.11 Deadlock. Each process is blocked on a lock that is held by the other process. An NLM server will detect a potential deadlock like this and deny any LOCK request that would result in a deadlock. Deadlock can occur where conflict exists between locked regions on the same file (as here) or across different files. A deadlock can result from any circular lock dependency among two or more processes.

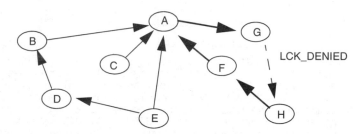

FIGURE 10.12 A lock dependency graph. The server uses a graph of lock dependencies to detect deadlocks. The nodes in the graph represent processes and the arrows represent dependencies; for example, the arrow from B to A indicates that B is blocked waiting for a lock held by A. Process G is not permitted to block on a lock held by process H because it would create a deadlock cycle: G, H, F, A, G.

10.10   Locking Cached or Mapped Files

Many NFS client implementations support the mapping of files into virtual memory. The most common incarnation of this is the *mmap* system call in Berkeley UNIX. It maps the data in a file to an area of virtual memory in the client. Rather than accessing the file in small buffer-sized chunks with read and write calls, the client sees the file data as an array of bytes in memory. The operating system will partition the mapped file into memory pages that are demand paged as the client touches them; the server sees these as page-size READ requests. Similarly, the client's operating system writes back any changes to the mapped file data in page-size WRITE requests.

Even if the client does not explicitly use file mapping, a similar page-size partitioning of the file may be performed by the client's virtual memory system to cache file data in page-size chunks. The effect is that small READ and WRITE requests act on the cached pages of data, and more efficient page-size READ and WRITE requests are sent to the server (see section 8.14.4).

Although the larger I/O requests that result from file caching and mapping are very good at boosting performance, they are not compatible with applications that need to update small regions of a file that are not page-aligned. For instance, an application on one machine may lock the first byte of a file and read the byte. The NFS client will attempt to optimize that single-byte I/O by reading an entire page of data from the server, perhaps, 8 kB. An application on another client may lock the second byte of the same file and also read a byte. This single-byte read will also be extended to an 8-kB READ request. The first client updates the first byte and writes it back. Since the client's operating system doesn't keep track of which cached parts of the file were updated, it will write back an entire 8-kB page when the application closes the file—even though only 1 byte was changed. However, this updated byte will be lost when the second client's program writes the second byte and closes the file. The second client's cached page will be written back, together with the unmodified first byte. The first client's update is lost (Figure 10.13).

Solaris client implementations avoid this problem by disabling all caching of file data and disallowing file mapping for any file that has a lock. It fixes the problem just described because each client's single-byte WRITE request will be sent directly to the server. Data outside the locked range will not be overwritten. The data corruption problem is fixed at the cost of poor performance through the loss of data caching. Files are more commonly locked in their entirety. If an application is performing small I/O requests (perhaps 512 bytes at a time) then it will suffer the overhead of an NFS call and response for every I/O request.

File mapping and caching could be made compatible with file locking if the client extended the range of a client's LOCK request to be page-aligned (see "Page 1" in Figure 10.13). For instance, if the client requested a lock just for the first byte of a file, the client's lock manager might extend this lock to cover the first page of a file (8 KB). This extended lock would prevent other clients from locking regions in the same cached page. Although the restoration of caching would boost performance and permit file mapping, there is a risk that the extended locks would cause unnecessary lock conflicts and potential deadlock. For instance, processes on separate clients attempting to update nonoverlapping, locked regions of the same file may be blocked if the regions lie within the same page covered by an extended lock.

10.11 Transport and Authentication

Lock Manager and Status Monitor protocols can be used over TCP or UDP transports. Most implementations support both protocols. Since the protocol

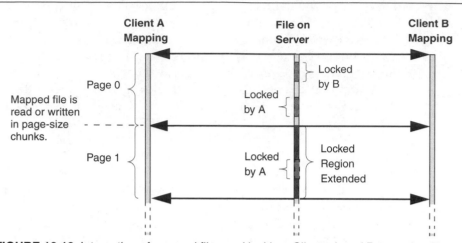

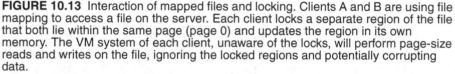

FIGURE 10.13 Interaction of mapped files and locking. Clients A and B are using file mapping to access a file on the server. Each client locks a separate region of the file that both lie within the same page (page 0) and updates the region in its own memory. The VM system of each client, unaware of the locks, will perform page-size reads and writes on the file, ignoring the locked regions and potentially corrupting data.

messages are short, there is no significant advantage in the ability of TCP to handle arbitrary-length RPC calls and replies, although there is some benefit in message sequencing and time-out/retransmission features that TCP provides.

Because the Lock Manager protocol is separate from that of NFS, the authentication of clients to servers and vice versa needs to be negotiated separately. The client should expect to use the same RPC authentication flavor as that used by the NFS traffic. If the NFS server accepts Kerberos version 5 credentials via RPCSEC_GSS security, then the client should attempt to use that when communicating with the server's LOCK daemon. If the NFS server accepts AUTH_SYS, then that is what should be used. Where RPCSEC_GSS security is used, the server must create an initial context with the client so that the NLM_GRANTED callback message can be sent.

10.12 Basic Data Types

The Lock Manager protocol has three data types that are used by all its procedure calls.

netobj

This object is used to identify an object, generally a transaction, owner, or file. A variable-length, opaque object, the contents and form of the netobj are defined by the client. Where the netobj identifies a file, the contents will be the filehandle.

```
opaque<1024> netobj;
```

nlm_stats

This value is returned when the lock manager indicates a successful result or an error. The zero result generally indicates that the call succeeded, though due to the generic nature of this result it would be more appropriately termed NLM_OK than NLM_GRANTED.

```
enum nlm_stats {
    NLM_GRANTED               = 0,
    NLM_DENIED                = 1,
    NLM_DENIED_NOLOCKS        = 2,
    NLM_BLOCKED               = 3,
    NLM_DENIED_GRACE_PERIOD   = 4,
    NLM_DEADLCK               = 5,
    NLM_ROFS                  = 6,
    NLM_STALE_FH              = 7,
    NLM_FBIG                  = 8,
    NLM_FAILED                = 9
}
```

nlm_lock

This structure identifies a particular lock. It is used by all five basic locking procedures: TEST, LOCK, CANCEL, UNLOCK, and GRANTED.

```
struct nlm_lock {
    string<1024>    caller_name;   /* name of client machine */
    netobj          fh;            /* identify the file */
    netobj          oh;            /* identify the lock owner */
    int32           svid;          /* unique process id */
    uint32/64       l_offset;      /* offset of locked region */
    uint32/64       l_len;         /* extent of locked region */
}
```

The caller_name field identifies the host that is making the request. Where possible, this name should be a fully qualified domain name so that a unique name is guaranteed in a multidomain organization.

The fh field contains the filehandle of the file to be locked. In the NLM version 3 protocol, the filehandle is a fixed-length NFS version 2 protocol filehandle, which is encoded as a byte count followed by a byte array. In the NFS version 3 protocol, the filehandle is already variable-length, so it is copied directly into the fh field. That is, the first four bytes of the fh field are the same as the byte count in an NFS version 3 filehandle. The rest of the fh field contains the byte array from the NFS version 3 filehandle.

The oh field is an opaque object that identifies the host or process that is making the request. Most commonly the client puts its IP address or hostname in this netobj. Early Solaris implementations encoded a timestamp into the oh field so that it could be used to detect retransmitted requests. The encoded timestamp created a problem with some servers that rejected UNLOCK requests because the oh field didn't match that of the LOCK request, so the timestamp was removed.The svid field identifies the process that is making the request.

The l_offset and l_len fields identify the region of the file that the lock controls. A l_len of 0 means "to the end of the file." In the NLM version 3 protocol, the length and offset are 32 bits wide, while they are 64 bits wide in the NLM version 4 protocol.

Since byte-range locking is supported as an atomic operation on DOS clients, locks have been used by some DOS applications to synchronize multiple processes. To flag these special locks, these applications set the high bit in the 32-bit offset—a value that would presumably "never" occur because it indicates an offset beyond 2 GB. The flag bit caused some problems with UNIX implementations that use the *fcntl* function, which assumes that lock offsets are a 32-bit *signed* value. The server would reject these special offsets as illegal negative values. To work around this problem, the server was modified to detect negative offsets and set bit 31 instead—a large positive value.

10.13 Errors

The Lock Manager protocol error returns are returned in the nlm_stat return argument (Table 10.3). The errors are not described individually for each procedure; they are described just once in Table 10.3. Any procedure may return any of these errors.

10.14 Lock Manager Procedures

The following sections define the RPC procedures that are supplied by an NFS version 3 protocol server (Table 10.4). The RPC procedure number and the name are followed by the **Description** part, which details the XDR format of the procedure arguments and results and tells what the procedure is expected to do and how its arguments and results are used. The **Asynchronous Procedures** part names the asynchronous procedures that correspond to the call and response for each synchronous procedure. The **Implementation** part gives information about how the procedure is expected to work and how it should be used by clients. Finally, a **Snoop Trace** for some procedures is included to show a typical call and response.

TABLE 10.3 Network Lock Manager Protocol Errors

Error name	Value	Meaning
NLM_GRANTED	0	The lock was granted.
NLM_DENIED	1	The lock was not granted, most likely due to a conflicting lock.
NLM_DENIED_NOLOCKS	2	The lock was not granted because the server's lock manager could not allocate the resources needed to process the request.
NLM_BLOCKED	3	The request cannot be granted immediately. The server will make a callback to the client with an NLM_GRANTED procedure call when the lock can be granted.
NLM_DENIED_GRACE_PERIOD	4	The procedure call failed because the server has recently been rebooted and the server is reestablishing existing locks, and is not yet ready to receive normal service requests.
NLM_DEADLCK	5	The request could not be granted and blocking would cause a deadlock.
NLM_ROFS	6	The remote file system is read-only. For example, some server implementations might not support exclusive locks on read-only file systems.
NLM_STALE_FH	7	The filehandle is invalid. This can happen if the file has been removed or if access to the file has been revoked on the server.
NLM_BIG	8	An offset or length was used that exceeds the range supported by the server.
NLM_FAILED	9	The failure is for some reason not already listed. The client should take this status as a strong hint not to retry the request.

10.14.1 Procedure 0: NULL—Do Nothing

Description

This procedure does no work. It is made available in all RPC services to allow server response testing and timing.

Arguments	Results
void;	void;

Implementation

It is important that this procedure do no work at all so that it can be used to measure the overhead of processing a service request. By convention, the

TABLE 10.4 Summary of Lock Manager Procedures

Number	Name	Description	Section
Synchronous procedures			
0	NLM_NULL	Do nothing	10.14.1, page 295
1	NLM_TEST	Test for a lock	10.14.2, page 296
2	NLM_LOCK	Create a lock	10.14.3, page 299
3	NLM_CANCEL	Cancel a lock	10.14.4, page 302
4	NLM_UNLOCK	Remove a lock	10.14.5, page 304
5	NLM_GRANTED	Lock granted	10.14.6, page 305
Asynchronous requests and responses			
6	NLM_TEST_MSG	Test lock message	10.14.2, page 296
7	NLM_LOCK_MSG	Create a lock message	10.14.3, page 299
8	NLM_CANCEL_MSG	Cancel a lock message	10.14.4, page 302
9	NLM_UNLOCK_MSG	Unlock message	10.14.5, page 304
10	NLM_GRANTED_MSG	Lock granted message	10.14.6, page 305
11	NLM_TEST_RES	Test lock result	10.14.2, page 296
12	NLM_LOCK_RES	Create a lock result	10.14.3, page 299
13	NLM_CANCEL_RES	Cancel a lock result	10.14.4, page 302
14	NLM_UNLOCK_RES	Unlock result	10.14.5, page 304
15	NLM_GRANTED_RES	Lock granted result	10.14.6, page 305
16–19	*(not assigned)*		
DOS file sharing and nonmonitored locks (added in version 3)			
20	NLM_SHARE	Share a file	10.14.7, page 308
21	NLM_UNSHARE	Unshare a file	10.14.8, page 310
22	NLM_NM_LOCK	Nonmonitored lock	10.14.9, page 311
23	NLM_FREE_ALL	Free all locks	10.14.10, page 311

NULL procedure should never require any authentication. This procedure was not described in versions 1 through 3 of the protocol—it was formally added in version 4.

10.14.2 Procedure 1: NLM_TEST—Test for a Lock

Description

This procedure checks whether a lock is available to the client.

```
Arguments                          Results
netobj     cookie;                 netobj       cookie;
bool       exclusive;              switch (nlm_stats stat) {
nlm_lock   alock;                     case LCK_DENIED = 1:
                                          bool    exclusive;
                                          int32   svid;
                                          netobj  oh;
                                          uint32/64 l_offset;
                                          uint32/64 l_len;
                                       default:
                                          void;
                                   }
```

Arguments

cookie

An opaque value determined by the client that is used to match an asynchronous response with a request.

exclusive

Set to true if testing whether the client could get access to the lock.

alock

Identifies the monitored lock that is being tested.

Results

cookie

An opaque value determined by the client that is used to match an asynchronous response with a request.

stat

The status returned by the operation. If NLM_DENIED is returned, then the following results that identify the conflicting lock and its holder are returned:

exclusive

True if the lock is exclusively held by the current holder.

svid

Identifies the process ID of the lock holder.

oh

An opaque quantity that identifies the host or process on the host that holds the lock.

l_offset

The byte offset of the lock held by the holder. The offset may not be the same as the lock identified by the alock argument, but it can be assumed that the locked region overlaps alock. Version 4 of the protocol increases the offset value from a 32-bit to a 64-bit quantity.

l_len

The length, in bytes, of the region locked by the holder. The length may not be the same as the lock identified by the alock argument, but it can be assumed that the locked region overlaps alock. Version 4 of the protocol increases the length value from a 32-bit to a 64-bit quantity.

Asynchronous Procedures

NLM_TEST_MSG (procedure 6) calls the server with the arguments described. NLM_TEST_RES (procedure 11) returns the results.

Implementation

This procedure is used by UNIX clients that need to implement the POSIX *fcntl* procedure with the F_GETLCK flag and the *lockf* procedure with the F_TLOCK and F_TEST flags. The procedure result is transient. A result that indicates that a lock is held may not be true when the client receives the reply, since the lock holder may have released the lock soon after the result was transmitted to the client. Similarly, a result that indicates that a lock is not held may not be true when the client receives it.

Snoop Trace of NLM_TEST

```
NLM:   ----- Network Lock Manager -----
NLM:
NLM:   Proc = 1 (Test)
NLM:   Cookie = 00000078
NLM:   Exclusive = True
NLM:   Caller = terra
NLM:   Filehandle = 0154026200000002000A0000003B491B
NLM:                A8BBB5FA000A0000003B46D40C39CF83
NLM:
NLM:   Lock owner = 000006BE74657272
NLM:   Svid = 1726 (process id)
NLM:   Offset = 0 bytes
NLM:   Length = 1 bytes

                ⇩

NLM:   ----- Network Lock Manager -----
NLM:
NLM:   Proc = 1 (Test)
NLM:   Cookie = 00000078
NLM:   Status = 0 (granted)
```

10.14.3   Procedure 2: NLM_LOCK—Create a Lock

Description

This procedure creates a locked byte range on a file.

Arguments		Results	
netobj	cookie;	netobj	cookie;
bool	block;	nlm_stat	stat;
bool	exclusive;		
nlm_lock	alock;		
bool	reclaim;		
int32	state;		

Arguments

cookie

An opaque value determined by the client that is used to match an asynchronous response with a request.

block

A LOCK request cannot be granted if a conflicting lock is already held. If block is set to *true* the client indicates that it expects the call to block on the server until the request can be granted. The server will first return a LCK_BLOCKED result, which indicates that the client should expect an asynchronous NLM_GRANTED callback when the lock is granted. If block is set to *false*, the call will return immediately with a LCK_DENIED error if a conflict is detected.

exclusive

Set to *true* if exclusive access to the locked region of the file is required. An exclusive lock blocks other conflicting lock requests. A nonexclusive lock allows other clients to establish nonexclusive locks on the same locked region or overlapping regions.

alock

Identifies the file, lock owner, and process as well as the locked region in the file.

reclaim

Set to true only if the client is attempting to reestablish a lock during the server's grace period following a server crash.

state

The current value of the client's Status Monitor state number. This number is recorded along with the lock information so that the server can determine which locks can be discarded if the client crashes and recovers. It is possible that a recovering client may be granted locks before the server has received and acted on the SM_NOTIFY message from the client's Status Monitor. In this case, the server needs to be able to distinguish the old, precrash locks from the new locks.

Results

cookie

> An opaque value determined by the client that is used to match an asynchronous response with a request.

stat

> The status returned by the operation. A LCK_GRANTED status indicates that the lock was granted and the client is now the lock holder. LCK_DENIED is returned only if the client set the block argument to false and the LOCK request conflicted with an existing lock. If the block argument is true then LCK_BLOCKED will be returned and the client must wait for a callback NLM_GRANTED from the server when the lock is ready.

Asynchronous Procedures

NLM_LOCK_MSG (procedure 7) calls the server with the same arguments. NLM_LOCK_RES (procedure 12) returns the results.

Implementation

This procedure is used by UNIX clients that implement the POSIX *fcntl* and *lockf* procedure and by Windows clients that use the *LockFile* and *LockFileEx* procedures.

The Lock Manager protocol implements an advisory locking scheme. The server will prevent other clients from creating conflicting locks, but it will not prevent other clients from reading or writing the locked region of the file.

The client can revoke a blocked LOCK request by sending an NLM_ CANCEL request (section 10.14.4).

The implementation of blocking LOCK requests is buggy in some implementations of the Lock Manager. The asynchronous nature of the NLM_ GRANTED callback can be a problem if the client does not receive the callback for some reason. Some servers will not retransmit the NLM_GRANTED request, so the client may retransmit the blocking NLM_LOCK call in case the NLM_GRANTED message was missed. If the client uses a new RPC XID for the retransmissions, the server has no way to tell whether the retransmissions are new requests.

Implementation of a duplicate request cache on the server could fix some duplicate transmission problems, though the size of the cache would have to be quite large because LOCK requests can be blocked for long periods of time. Additionally, the server must be able to handle asynchronous calls that have unvarying XID values across retransmissions. A duplicate request cache

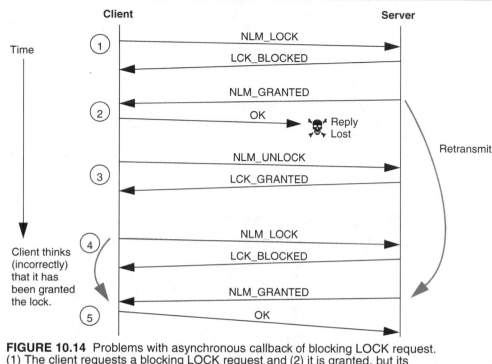

FIGURE 10.14 Problems with asynchronous callback of blocking LOCK request. (1) The client requests a blocking LOCK request and (2) it is granted, but its acknowledgment of the lock is lost. (3) It unlocks the file and (4) attempts to lock it again. (5) It receives the retransmitted grant message and incorrectly assumes that it has the lock.

would need to base its detection of duplicates on the netobj identifiers as well as on the offset and length.

When locking activity is heavy and the client is locking and unlocking the same file repeatedly, it may associate a retransmitted NLM_GRANTED from an old LOCK request with a new LOCK request. As Figure 10.14 demonstrates, the client might be led to assume that it is holding a lock that the server has not yet granted.

Snoop Trace of NLM_LOCK

```
NLM:    ----- Network Lock Manager -----
NLM:
NLM:    Proc = 2 (Lock)
NLM:    Cookie = 0000184E
NLM:    Block = False
NLM:    Exclusive = True
NLM:    Caller = terra
NLM:    Filehandle = 0154026200000002000A0000003B491B
NLM:                 A8BBB5FA000A0000003B46D40C39CF83
NLM:
```

```
NLM:  Lock owner = 000006BE74657272
NLM:  Svid = 1726 (process id)
NLM:  Offset = 0 bytes
NLM:  Length = 0 bytes
NLM:  Reclaim = False
NLM:  State = 1
```

⇩

```
NLM:  ----- Network Lock Manager -----
NLM:
NLM:  Proc = 2 (Lock)
NLM:  Cookie = 0000184E
NLM:  Status = 0 (granted)
```

10.14.4   Procedure 3: NLM_CANCEL—Cancel a Lock

Description

This procedure cancels a blocked LOCK request.

Arguments		*Results*	
netobj	cookie;	netobj	cookie;
bool	block;	nlm_stat	stat;
bool	exclusive;		
nlm_lock	alock;		

Arguments

cookie

An opaque value determined by the client that is used to match an asynchronous response with a request.

block

This argument must match the block argument of the pending NLM_LOCK request that is to be canceled (i.e., it must be set to true).

exclusive

This argument must match the exclusive argument of the pending NLM_LOCK request.

alock

Identifies the lock that the pending request was attempting to create. It must match the alock argument of the pending NLM_LOCK request.

Results

cookie

An opaque value determined by the client that is used to match an asynchronous response with a request.

```
stat
```
The status returned by the operation.

Asynchronous Procedures

NLM_CANCEL_MSG (procedure 8) calls the server with the same arguments. NLM_CANCEL_RES (procedure 13) returns the results.

Implementation

On receiving this request, the server should attempt to locate the blocked LOCK request and cancel it (Figure 10.15). The server should return a LCK_DENIED error if there was no matching lock to cancel. Some server implementations may return a LCK_GRANTED response even if there was no pending LOCK request to cancel.

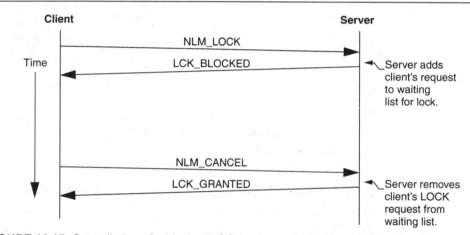

FIGURE 10.15 Cancellation of a blocked LOCK request. A blocking LOCK request might block for an indefinite amount of time. The NLM_CANCEL message allows an impatient user on the client to abandon the transaction and notify the server that the lock is no longer required.

Snoop Trace of NLM_CANCEL

```
NLM:   ----- Network Lock Manager -----
NLM:
NLM:   Proc = 3 (Cancel)
NLM:   Cookie = 0000184E
NLM:   Block = False
NLM:   Exclusive = True
NLM:   Caller = terra
NLM:   Filehandle = 0154026200000002000A0000003B491B
NLM:                A8BBB5FA000A0000003B46D40C39CF83
```

```
NLM:
NLM:  Lock owner = 000006BE74657272
NLM:  Svid = 1726 (process id)
NLM:  Offset = 0 bytes
NLM:  Length = 0 bytes
```

⇩

```
NLM:  ----- Network Lock Manager -----
NLM:
NLM:  Proc = 3 (Cancel)
NLM:  Cookie = 0000184E
NLM:  Status = 0 (granted)
```

10.14.5   Procedure 4: NLM_UNLOCK—Remove a Lock

Description

This procedure unlocks a locked region of a file.

Arguments		Results	
netobj	cookie;	netobj	cookie;
nlm_lock	alock;	nlm_stat	stat;

Arguments

cookie

> An opaque value determined by the client that is used to match an asynchronous response with a request.

alock

> Identifies the lock that is to be removed. The l_offset and l_len fields must identify a region of the file that is already covered by a lock held by the lock owner.

Results

cookie

> An opaque value determined by the client that is used to match an asynchronous response with a request.

stat

> The status returned by the operation.

Asynchronous Procedures

NLM_UNLOCK_MSG (procedure 9) calls the server with the same arguments. NLM_UNLOCK_RES (procedure 14) returns the results.

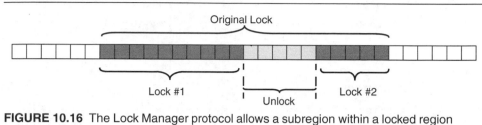

FIGURE 10.16 The Lock Manager protocol allows a subregion within a locked region to be unlocked.

Implementation

The NLM protocol follows the semantics of POSIX file locking, which allows a subrange of a previously locked region in a file to be unlocked (Figure 10.16). The subrange can be anywhere within the locked range. Unlocking a subrange entirely contained within a locked range may leave two locked ranges. The server may return a LCK_GRANTED result even if the lock could not be found.

Snoop Trace of NLM_UNLOCK

```
NLM:    ----- Network Lock Manager -----
NLM:
NLM:    Proc = 4 (Unlock)
NLM:    Cookie = 0000184F
NLM:    Caller = terra
NLM:    Filehandle = 0154026200000002000A0000003B491B
NLM:                 A8BBB5FA000A0000003B46D40C39CF83
NLM:
NLM:    Lock owner = 000006BE74657272
NLM:    Svid = 1726 (process id)
NLM:    Offset = 1124860 bytes
NLM:    Length = 0 bytes

            ⇩

NLM:    ----- Network Lock Manager -----
NLM:
NLM:    Proc = 4 (Unlock)
NLM:    Cookie = 0000184F
NLM:    Status = 0 (granted)
```

10.14.6 Procedure 5: NLM_GRANTED—Lock Is Granted

Description

This is a callback procedure from the server to the client that indicates that a blocked LOCK request has been granted.

Arguments		Results	
netobj	cookie;	netobj	cookie;
bool	exclusive;	nlm_stat	stat;
nlm_lock	alock;		

Arguments

cookie

An opaque value that is normally the same as the client sent in the LOCK request, though the client cannot depend on it.

block

The value from the blocked LOCK request—true.

exclusive

The value from the blocked LOCK request.

alock

The value from the blocked LOCK request.

Results

cookie

An opaque value determined by the server (in this case) that is returned by the client from the request.

stat

The status returned to the server by the client.

Asynchronous Procedures

NLM_GRANTED_MSG (procedure 10) calls the client with the arguments described. NLM_GRANTED_RES (procedure 15) returns the result from the client.

Implementation

This callback procedure is unusual in that it reverses the roles of client and server at the RPC level. The server must use the client's portmapper to obtain a callback port for the client's lock service.

If a client makes a LOCK request with the block argument set to true, then the server will return a LCK_BLOCKED error if there is a conflicting lock (Figure 10.17). This result indicates to the client that it should wait for an NLM_GRANTED request from the server when the lock is granted. The client must reply to this callback with a result that indicates whether it has accepted the granted lock: LCK_GRANTED if it has accepted the lock, LCK_DENIED if for some reason it cannot accept the lock.

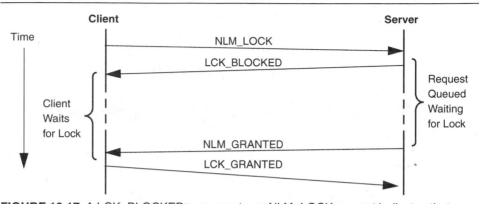

FIGURE 10.17 A LCK_BLOCKED response to an NLM_LOCK request indicates that the client will need to wait some period of time for the requested lock to become available. The NLM_GRANTED message from the server indicates that the client has been granted the lock. The client must acknowledge this call with a LCK_GRANTED result.

When a client receives a LCK_BLOCKED response, it should request the local status monitor to add the server to its notification list (if it has not done so already). If the client crashes and recovers while a LOCK request is pending on the server, then the server will receive a notification and cancel the pending request.

If the server gets no response from the NLM_GRANTED callback, it should continue to retransmit the call until it gets a reply from the client. The client may have accepted the lock but may be unable, for some reason, to respond to the server.

Snoop Trace of NLM_GRANTED

```
NLM:    ----- Network Lock Manager -----
NLM:
NLM:    Proc = 5 (Granted)
NLM:    Cookie = 00000014
NLM:    Exclusive = True
NLM:    Caller = swoop
NLM:    Filehandle = 0154026200000002000A0000003B491B
NLM:                 A8BBB5FA000A0000003B46D40C39CF83
NLM:
NLM:    Lock owner = 000006BE74657272
NLM:    Svid = 1726 (process id)
NLM:    Offset = 0 bytes
NLM:    Length = 4 bytes

NLM:    ----- Network Lock Manager -----
NLM:
```

```
NLM:  Proc = 5 (Granted)
NLM:  Cookie = 00000014
NLM:  Status = 0 (granted)
```

10.14.7   Procedure 20: NLM_SHARE—Share a File

Description

This procedure is used by PC clients to create a SHARE reservation on a given file.

Arguments		Results	
netobj	cookie;	netobj	cookie;
string<1024>	caller_name;	nlm_stat	stat;
netobj	fh;	int32	sequence;
netobj	oh;		
fsh_mode	mode;		
fsh_access	access;		
bool	reclaim;		

Arguments

cookie

An opaque value determined by the client that is used to match an asynchronous response with a request.

caller_name

A string that uniquely identifies the caller (e.g., the caller's hostname).

fh

The filehandle for the file to which the SHARE reservation applies.

oh

An opaque object that identifies the owner of the SHARE reservation.

mode

Indicates the file sharing mode. The mode determines the access that another client will be permitted when it attempts to share the file. A *deny none* value indicates that other clients can open the file for any kind of access. A *deny read and write* value indicates that no other client can share the file for read or write access.

```
enum fsh_mode {
    fsm_DN   = 0,    /* Deny none */
    fsn_DR   = 1,    /* Deny read */
    fsm_DW   = 2,    /* Deny write */
    fsm_DRW  = 3     /* Deny read and write */
}
```

access

Indicates the kind of access to the file that the client requires. The SHARE request may be denied if the desired access is not compatible with the deny mode of an existing share.

```
enum fsh_access {
    fsa_NONE = 0,    /* No access */
    fsa_R = 1,       /* Read only */
    fsa_W = 2,       /* Write only */
    fsa_RW = 3       /* Read and write */
}
```

reclaim

Set to *true* if the client is attempting to reestablish a SHARE reservation during the grace period following a server crash and reboot. During the grace period, the server will accept only SHARE reservations with reclaim set to *true*.

Results

cookie

An opaque value determined by the client that is used to match an asynchronous response with a request.

stat

The status returned by the operation.

sequence

Unused. Set to zero.

Implementation

A SHARE reservation is created by DOS or Windows clients whenever a file is opened. SHARE reservations are not monitored by the status monitor. If a client crashes and reboots while it holds SHARE reservations on server files, it should issue an NLM_FREE_ALL call to the server to release stale shares.

The server can evaluate a share conflict using a simple formula that performs a bitwise AND operation of the request mode against an established share access and the request access against the established share mode. If both AND operations yield a zero result, then the SHARE request is granted. This formula is illustrated by the following C code:

```
granted = (request_mode  & share_access == 0 &&
           (request_access& share_mode)  == 0;
```

A matrix (Figure 10.18) represents this comparison; the figure shows whether a SHARE request will be granted (indicated by a Y) based on the mode

			Second and Subsequent SHARE Reservations on Same File											
			Deny All			Deny Write			Deny Read			Deny None		
			R	W	RW	R	W	RW	R	W	RW	R	W	RW
First SHARE Reservation of a File	Deny All	R	N	N	N	N	N	N	N	N	N	N	N	N
		W	N	N	N	N	N	N	N	N	N	N	N	N
		RW	N	N	N	N	N	N	N	N	N	N	N	N
	Deny Write	R	N	N	N	Y	N	N	N	N	N	Y	N	N
		W	N	N	N	N	N	N	Y	N	N	Y	N	N
		RW	N	N	N	N	N	N	N	N	N	Y	N	N
	Deny Read	R	N	N	N	N	Y	N	N	N	N	N	Y	N
		W	N	N	N	N	N	N	N	Y	N	N	Y	N
		RW	N	N	N	N	N	N	N	N	N	N	Y	N
	Deny None	R	N	N	N	Y	Y	Y	N	N	N	Y	Y	Y
		W	N	N	N	N	N	N	Y	Y	Y	Y	Y	Y
		RW	N	N	N	N	N	N	N	N	N	Y	Y	Y

FIGURE 10.18 A Share Conflict Matrix

and access of the request against the mode and access of an established SHARE reservation on the file.

10.14.8   Procedure 21: NLM_UNSHARE—Unshare a File

Description

This procedure releases a SHARE reservation.

Arguments	*Results*
– same as NLM_SHARE _	– same as NLM_SHARE _

Arguments

Same as NLM_SHARE.

Results

Same as NLM_SHARE.

Implementation

This procedure is called by DOS or Windows clients when closing a file. Most server implementations will return a GRANTED status whether or not the SHARE reservation exists.

10.14.9   Procedure 22: NLM_NM_LOCK—Establish a Nonmonitored Lock

Description

This procedure creates a nonmonitored byte-range lock on a file.

Arguments			Results	
netobj	cookie;		netobj	cookie;
bool	block;		nlm_stat	stat;
bool	exclusive;			
nlm_lock	alock;			
bool	reclaim;			
int32	state;			

Arguments

The arguments are the same as NLM_LOCK. Since the lock is not monitored by the Status Monitor, the state argument should be set to 0. Since the procedure does not block, the block argument should be set to *false*.

Results

The results are the same as for NLM_LOCK. Since a nonmonitored LOCK request will not block, a LCK_DENIED error will be returned if another lock conflicts.

Implementation

A nonmonitored lock is used by clients that do not use the Network Status Monitor service. For instance, operating systems like DOS that support only a single-threaded process model cannot easily support a concurrent status monitor process that must respond to state notifications from servers. The use of a nonmonitored lock imposes a responsibility on the client to ensure that the lock is removed from the server if the client crashes and reboots, losing the lock state. In this case the client should send an NLM_FREE_ALL request to the server on recovery to make sure that stale locks are removed. There is also a risk that the server may crash and lose the client's lock state. Since the client is not running a Status Monitor, the server will not notify the client of the change of state (loss of lock) when the server has rebooted.

The NLM_UNLOCK procedure must be used to remove nonmonitored locks.

10.14.10   Procedure 23: NLM_FREE_ALL—Free All Locks

Description

This procedure notifies the server that the client has lost lock state and all server locks owned by this client should be freed.

Arguments	Results
string<1024> name; uint32 state;	- no results -

Arguments

name

A string that identifies the client uniquely (e.g., the client's hostname).

state

Unused. Set to 0.

Implementation

This procedure is used by clients that have nonmonitored locks, either NLM_SHARE or NLM_NM_LOCK. On recovery, the client sends this request to the server to free any locks that were established before the client crashed and lost the lock state. The client does not expect a response from the server.

10.15   Network Status Monitor Protocol

The Network Status Monitor (NSM) protocol was originally designed as a general-purpose service for monitoring the state of selected hosts on a network. It was first described in a USENIX paper [Chang85] as a component of a "SunNet" architecture. The protocol was designed to be useful to any RPC protocol that needed to monitor state on a remote host. In practice, the NLM protocol is the only known protocol that uses NSM.

In the SunNet architecture, the status monitor was a program that actively monitored other network hosts by probing their network status monitors with a multicast status request message (SM_STAT) (Table 10.5). Each monitored host would return its state; a monotonically increasing number that is incremented anytime the host crashes or recovers. An even value for the state indicates that the host is down, while an odd value indicates that it is up:

```
...   127     128     129     130     131     ...
      Up      Down    Up      Down    Up
```

The intent of the state number was to allow the status monitor to detect a change in state of a monitored host (crash followed by recovery) no matter how quickly the monitored host recovered. Even if a host crashed and recovered between two successive probes, its incremented state number would record the fact of a crash. In theory, an odd state (server down) should never come back in a response to an SM_STAT probe. The SunNet architecture organized status monitors into a hierarchy that had servers monitoring clients and servers monitoring each other. If a client failed to respond to an SM_STAT

TABLE 10.5 Summary of Status Monitor Procedures

Proc#	Name	Description	Section
0	SM_NULL	Do nothing	10.15.1, page 313
1	SM_STAT	Check status	10.15.2, page 313
2	SM_MON	Monitor a host	10.15.3, page 314
3	SM_UNMON	Unmonitor a host	10.15.4, page 316
4	SM_UNMON_ALL	Unmonitor all hosts	10.15.5, page 317
5	SM_SIMU_CRASH	Simulate a crash	10.15.6, page 317
6	SM_NOTIFY	Notify a host	10.15.7, page 318

probe within a reasonable time-out, the server assigned an odd status value to the client, which it would then pass on, if requested, to other hosts' queries.

The SunNet architecture was never realized, and the nature of the Status Monitor protocol changed. Instead of actively monitoring hosts with SM_STAT requests, a passive SM_NOTIFY message was added that was invoked when a host recovered from a crash. With current implementations of the protocol, even values (server is down) are never seen and cannot be communicated. Obviously, a host cannot notify others that it is down (even value). If an RPC service maintains state on a host and the state number of the host has changed since the state was established, then the service can assume that the host has rebooted and information (like locks) maintained in the host's RAM memory has been lost.

10.15.1 Procedure 0: SM_NULL—Do Nothing

Description

This procedure does no work. It is made available in all RPC services to allow server response testing and timing.

Arguments	Results
void;	void;

Implementation

It is important that this procedure do no work at all so that it can be used to measure the overhead of processing a service request.

10.15.2 Procedure 1: SM_STAT—Check Status

Description

This procedure checks whether the status monitor is monitoring the given host.

Arguments	*Results*
`string<1024> mon_name;`	`uint32  res;`
	`uint32  state;`

Arguments

`mon_name`

> The name of the host to be monitored.

Results

`res`

> The return status of the call.

`state`

> The state number of the status monitor.

Implementation

This procedure is a remnant of the original active monitoring architecture for the status monitor. Do not depend on this procedure being implemented. Many status monitor implementations will always return STAT_FAIL.

Errors

STAT_SUCC	0	Status monitor agrees to monitor.
STAT_FAIL	1	Status monitor cannot monitor.

10.15.3   Procedure 2: SM_MON—Monitor a Host

Description

Establish monitoring of a given host.

Arguments		*Results*	
`string<1024>`	`mon_name;`	`uint32`	`res;`
`string<1024>`	`my_name;`	`uint32`	`state;`
`uint32`	`my_prog;`		
`uint32`	`my_vers;`		
`uint32`	`my_proc;`		
`opaque[16]`	`priv;`		

Arguments

`mon_name`

> The name of the host to be monitored. This name should be that received in the LOCK request (`caller_name`), though the server may choose to reverse-

map the client's IP address through DNS to guarantee a fully qualified domain name that will handle locking properly across multiple domains.

my_name

The client's hostname. For the lock manager, it passes the name of the host it is running on.

my_prog

The callback RPC program number. In this context, it will usually be that of the lock manager, 100021, but need not be.

my_vers

The callback program's version number. One of the version numbers supported by the lock manager.

my_proc

The callback program's procedure number. Each implementation of the lock manager can choose its own procedure number, though it should not conflict with possible future procedure numbers added to the protocol. There is a gap in the protocol procedure numbers (16–19) that provides good candidates. The Solaris lock manager uses procedure 18.

priv

Private information returned as arguments to the callback. Again, each implementation can choose whether or not to use private data. Solaris does not use this feature.

Results

res

The return status of the call.

state

The state number of the status monitor. The Solaris NLM ignores it.

Implementation

This call is most commonly made from the lock manager to the status monitor when the lock manager receives the first lock request from a client. Before granting the lock, the client needs to be monitored by the status monitor so that if the server crashes, the client will be notified to reclaim its lock. The same call is also made on the client before it requests its first lock from the server: the server must be monitored so that if the client crashes and recovers, it will notify the server to remove stale locks.

The status monitor must record the client's hostname on stable storage so that it can survive a server crash and recovery. The most common method is to create a directory or zero-length file with the name of the client (mon_name) under a well-known directory, for example, /var/sm/. This technique is simple and efficient because directory operations are atomic on most operating systems. Maintaining a list of hostnames in a single file is more complex because each change to the file must be covered by a lock, and deletion of a hostname may require the entire file to be locked and rewritten.

The callback information (my_name, my_prog, etc.) does not need to be stored in stable storage because it is used only when the status monitor receives an SM_NOTIFY message from a monitored host that is recovering. The RPC information for the callback could, in theory, represent any RPC service, but in general my_prog is set to 100021 (program number for lock manager) and the version to any version supported by the lock manager (versions 1 through 4). The Solaris lock manager defines an unpublished procedure (procedure 18) to receive the callback notification.

Errors

STAT_SUCC	0	Status monitor agrees to monitor.
STAT_FAIL	1	Status monitor cannot monitor.

10.15.4   Procedure 3: SM_UNMON—Unmonitor a Host

Description

Stop monitoring the given host.

Arguments		Results	
string<1024>	mon_name;	int32	state;
string<1024>	my_name;		
uint32	my_prog;		
uint32	my_vers;		
uint32	my_proc;		

Arguments

mon_name

> The name of the host for which monitoring is to cease. It should be identical to the mon_name supplied in the SM_MON request.

my_name, my_vers, my_proc

> These must match the arguments supplied in the corresponding SM_MON request.

Results

state

> The state number of the status monitor. Solaris ignores this.

Implementation

The server's lock manager may request the Lock Manager protocol to cease monitoring a client that has released its last lock. As a performance enhancement, some lock managers may never issue SM_UNMON requests, which avoids repeated monitor/unmonitor calls for a client that repeatedly locks and unlocks a file. Although this may cause the list of monitored hosts to be longer than it needs to be, a notification sent to a host that holds no locks will be ignored.

10.15.5 Procedure 4: SM_UNMON_ALL—Unmonitor All Hosts

Description

Stop monitoring all hosts.

```
Arguments                          Results
string<1024>   my_name;            int32    state;
uint32         my_prog;
uint32         my_vers;
uint32         my_proc;
```

Arguments

`my_name`

Not used.

`my_name`, `my_vers`, `my_proc`

These must match the arguments supplied in the corresponding SM_MON requests.

Results

`state`

The state number of the status monitor.

Implementation

The Solaris status monitor implements this procedure, but the lock manager does not use it.

10.15.6 Procedure 5: SM_SIMU_CRASH—Simulate a Crash

Description

This procedure simulates a crash.

```
Arguments                          Results
void;                              void;
```

Implementation

This procedure is useful to client-side lock managers that are implemented as a user-level process. If the Lock Manager daemon crashes, then it will lose the state of all the client's locks. On restart, it uses this procedure to inform the status monitor that lock state has been lost. The status monitor will then send a notification to all servers on which locks were held so that they can remove the client's locks.

10.15.7   Procedure 6: SM_NOTIFY—Notify a Host

Description

Notify of state change.

```
Arguments                              Results
string<1024>   mon_name;               void;
uint32         state;
```

Arguments

mon_name

  The name of the host from which the request is sent.

state

  The new state number of the host.

Implementation

When a status monitor restarts after a crash, it examines its list of monitored hosts from stable storage (recorded by SM_MON requests before the crash) and sends an SM_NOTIFY call to each host in the list. The status monitor should make a reasonable effort to retransmit the notification to clients that do not respond.

On receiving an SM_NOTIFY request, a status monitor is expected to invoke the callback procedure registered with a previous SM_MON request.

10.16   Summary

File locking service for NFS is provided by two cooperating protocols, the Network Lock Manager protocol and the Network Status Monitor protocol. The status monitor allows clients and servers to detect a loss of state following a crash and initiate timely recovery.

Due to the complexity of these two protocols, some NFS servers do not support file locking at all. Some clients cannot support the asynchronous notifications of the Status Monitor protocol, so the Lock Manager protocol makes nonmonitored locks available for these clients. NLM locks are advisory: an NFS server will not prevent a client that does not hold a lock from reading or writing a locked file. The NLM protocol supports both exclusive (or non-shared) locks and nonexclusive (or shared) locks. In addition, share reservations are supported for DOS clients.

The NLM and Status Monitor protocols are unusual in their use of asynchronous procedures and callbacks. Vague protocol specifications have made it difficult to build interoperable implementations of these protocols. In addition, timing problems inherent in some of the asynchronous procedures make these protocols unreliable on busy or congested networks.

Chapter 11

Automounting

The NFS protocol does not require the use of a *global* or *shared* namespace. A global namespace is a feature supported by other distributed filesystems, such as the Andrew File System [Morris+86]. AFS provides a consistent pathname to any remote file from any client machine. AFS servers and their exported filesystems are grouped into cells that are named under an /afs directory. These invariant paths to shared data make it easy to locate files from any client on a network.

The team at Sun Microsystems, Inc., that designed the NFS protocol and built its first implementation had a more basic requirement: that a *remote* filesystem be managed as if it were a *local* filesystem. Since filesystems on local disks are mounted using a mount command, remote filesystems accessed with NFS should also be mountable with a mount command.

```
mount /dev/dsk/c0t0d0s2 /usr/local          (local filesystem)
mount jurassic:/export/home/jane /home/jane  (NFS filesystem)
```

This simple *remote-as-local* paradigm made it easy for users to adapt to NFS. NFS mounts could be included with local filesystems in the /etc/fstab or /etc/vfstab files of UNIX clients so that they would be mounted automatically when the client booted. The following example shows a simple /etc/vfstab file that lists the filesystems to be mounted at boot time for a particular UNIX client. It includes two NFS mounts for the client's user: her e-mail and her own "home" directory.

```
# Filesystem                    Mountpoint     Type
/dev/dsk/c0t0d0s0               /              ufs
/proc                          /proc          proc
jurassic:/var/mail             /var/mail      nfs
jurassic:/export/home/jane     /home/jane     nfs
```

Having each NFS client determine its own set of mounts works well for small numbers of clients in well-organized workgroups, but as the use of NFS gained hold in larger organizations, it became clear that the enumeration of all a client's NFS mounts in a local file would not scale to hundreds or thousands of clients. The problems were numerous, including the following three:

1. *Inconsistent naming.* Since each client determined where a filesystem was mounted in its own namespace, shared files could have inconsistent names from client to client. For instance, a shared filesystem of commonly used packages might be mounted on some clients under the name /usr/local and on others as /local. Programs and scripts that worked fine on one client could fail when run on another client because the packages could not be located.

2. *Unavailable mounts.* The example vfstab file above shows Jane's home directory being mounted on a particular client. If Jane needs to access files in another user's home directory, then she must locate the server that holds the home directory and issue a mount command as the superuser. If the number of users is small, then a mount for the home directory of each user could be included in the vfstab file. Mounting in advance is impractical, however, if there are hundreds or thousands of users.

3. *Administration overhead.* If the server administrator needs to relocate a filesystem on the server or move it to another server, then the administrator needs to notify all clients that are mounting that filesystem so that they can edit their vfstab files to account for the new location. Having the location of each filesystem embedded in each client creates enormous system administration problems.

These problems can be fixed by implementing a global namespace for NFS access to files that supports consistent naming of files across all clients and centralizes the location information so that filesystems can be relocated from one server to another without having to notify all the clients. An automounter is a service that implements this global namespace by obtaining name-to-location information from a name service and performing mounts automatically—hence the name *automounter.*

This chapter explains how an automounter creates a global namespace for NFS filesystems.

11.1 Automounter as NFS Server

An automounter creates the illusion of a large number of continuously mounted NFS filesystems by mounting filesystems on demand and unmounting them when they are no longer needed. To mount a filesystem on demand, an automounter needs to be able to detect access to a filesystem that is not yet mounted, mount the filesystem, then redirect any further access to the mounted filesystem (Figure 11.1).

The first automounters on UNIX systems were implemented as user-level NFS servers. The first user-level NFS server was implemented by Bradley Taylor of the Sun NFS group in 1986. He created an NFS server in a daemon process that implemented a memory filesystem. The daemon created a socket to receive NFS RPC calls, then called the mount system call to create an NFS mount, providing its own address for the NFS server and the name of a directory to act at the mountpoint. Then, when any program attempted to access the directory, the NFS client code in the UNIX kernel sent NFS calls to the daemon (see Figure 11.2). The memory filesystem was a simple prototype to demonstrate the utility of the technique: that new types of filesystems could be implemented by local daemon programs posing as NFS servers. Among filesystems that have been implemented this way are a caching filesystem called the Autocacher [Minnich93], an encrypting filesystem [Blaze94], a backup filesystem [Moran+93], and a translucent filesystem [Hendricks 88].

Tom Lyon, in the NFS group at Sun, implemented the first automounter as a user-level NFS daemon. His intent was to create an automatic mounting service for NFS clients that would obtain its global namespace information from a name service like NIS. Using this information, the automounter daemon would automatically mount and unmount NFS filesystems as needed. This service was first made available in SunOS 4.0. Another automounter called Amd was made available in source form and ported to a large number of UNIX operating systems (section 11.10). Figure 11.2 shows how a daemon can mount itself as an NFS server. An automounter daemon provides service by mounting itself on directories that are to receive automounting service. The daemon reads a list of these directories when it starts up and issues a mount

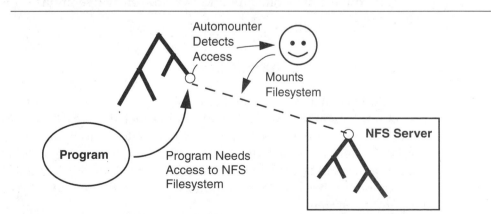

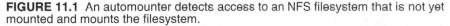

FIGURE 11.1 An automounter detects access to an NFS filesystem that is not yet mounted and mounts the filesystem.

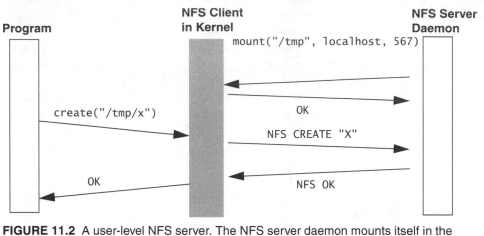

FIGURE 11.2 A user-level NFS server. The NFS server daemon mounts itself in the client's namespace as an NFS server using a local address (localhost) and port number (in this case, 567). Any access to the daemon's mountpoint (here it's /tmp) will be forwarded as an NFS request to the daemon.

system call for each directory. The UNIX kernel will then notify the automounter with an NFS LOOKUP call if any program attempts to access an entry in any of these directories.

The automounter daemon is needed to mount and unmount filesystems, but it need not be involved in every access to the filesystem once it is mounted. To have the automounter forwarding data-intensive operations like NFS READ and WRITE requests would hurt performance, so the NFS mounts are done in a temporary directory and the daemon returns a symbolic link in response to any LOOKUP request. This deft sidestep allows the automounter to remove itself from data-intensive operations; the NFS client in the kernel will follow the symbolic link and perform those operations on the real NFS mountpoint.

11.2   Problems with Symbolic Links

An automounter implemented as a user-level NFS server is attractive because it is implemented entirely outside the kernel (Figure 11.3). Since no kernel modifications are necessary, it is easy to port to a variety of other UNIX operating systems. The Solaris automounter has been licensed to several other companies and is available in Irix, HP-UX, Digital UNIX, and AIX. The Amd automounter has been ported to more than 20 different versions of the UNIX operating system.

An important measure of the success of an automounter is its ability to create the illusion of continuously available NFS filesystems. Users should not

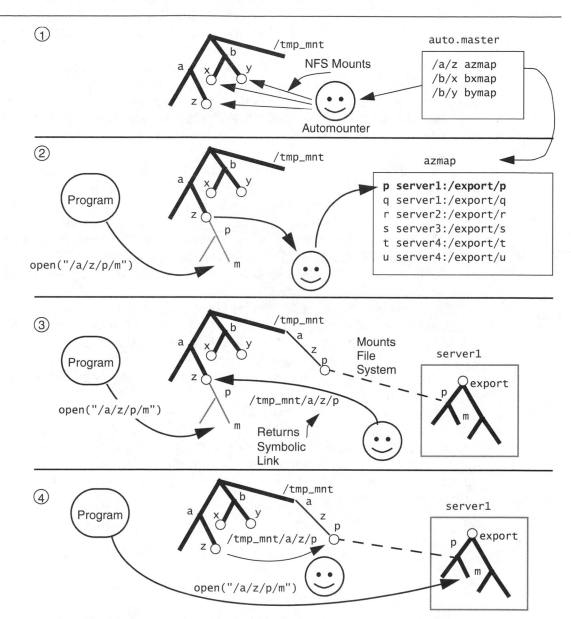

FIGURE 11.3 Automounter operation. (1) At start-up the automounter daemon reads the auto.master map, mounts itself at each directory, and associates a map with each directory. (2) A program attempts to open a file in an NFS filesystem that isn't mounted. The automounter finds the mount information in the map associated with the directory. (3) It mounts the filesystem in a temporary directory and returns a symbolic link to the mountpoint. (4) The program opens the file in the NFS filesystem. The automounter is not involved in READ or WRITE operations.

be aware that an automounter is mounting and unmounting filesystems. It must do its work quickly and unobtrusively. Automounters are pretty good at mounting quickly. However, the symbolic link that redirects access to the temporary mountpoint directory (/tmp_mnt) can create problems. When a UNIX program needs to determine its current directory, it invokes a function called *getwd* that determines the path to the current directory by walking up the directory hierarchy with lookups of the .. entry at each directory level (Figure 11.4). A program that does this within an automounted directory will receive a path that has /tmp_mnt prepended.

This pathname change can be disconcerting to users with automounted home directories. When user Jane logs in, she expects her current directory to be /home/jane—not /tmp_mnt/home/jane. The problem is not just an aesthetic one; some programs, like the UNIX *at* command, record the current directory in a file and expect the directory to be available at a later time. If the automounter has unmounted the filesystem, then the program will find that the recorded path is invalid. References to /tmp_mnt paths do not trigger automatic mounting.

Relative pathnames do not work as expected, either. For instance, if Jane has /home/jane as her current directory, she should reasonably expect to use the path ../fred to refer to Fred's home directory. Because Jane's home directory is mounted under the /tmp_mnt directory, the path ../fred will be equivalent to the path /tmp_mnt/home/fred, which, if not already mounted, will appear to be missing.

One workaround is to modify the UNIX *getwd* function to remove the prepended /tmp_mnt directory if it appears at the front of a path. However, this is not a complete solution: both the Solaris automounter and the Amd automounter can be configured to use a directory different from /tmp_mnt, not all programs use *getwd* to determine the current directory, and the relative pathname problem remains.

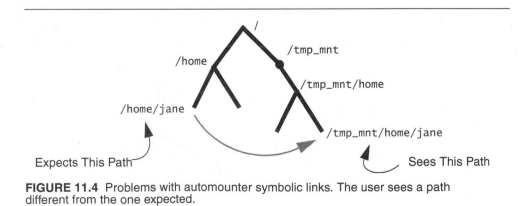

FIGURE 11.4 Problems with automounter symbolic links. The user sees a path different from the one expected.

The temporary mountpoint problem can be solved by implementing a kernel-based filesystem that works with the automounter daemon to perform in-place mounts: the *autofs*.

11.3 Automounting with Autofs

The autofs is a kernel-based filesystem that supports in-place mounting by the automount daemon. When the automounter starts up, it mounts the autofs at each directory that needs automounter service (as determined by the master map). When the autofs at one of these directories detects access to a filesystem that is not yet mounted, it sends an RPC call to the automounter daemon requesting that the missing filesystem be mounted. This automount daemon is not an NFS server. The autofs communicates with the daemon using a simple RPC protocol that has only two requests: MOUNT and UNMOUNT. The MOUNT request contains the name of the directory that needs to be mounted and the name of the map that contains the mount information. The daemon gets the mount information from the map and performs one or more mounts in place; if there is an autofs mount at /home and a program tries to access /home/jane, then the automounter daemon will mount the filesystem at /home/jane. This process of in-place mounting is illustrated in Figure 11.5.

As well as eliminating the temporary mountpoint problem, the autofs automounter has a number of additional features, including the three that follow.

1. *Better performance.* Although the NFS-server automounter successfully avoided heavyweight I/O operations via redirection to the NFS mountpoint with a symbolic link, it still needed to return the link whenever a program opened an automounted file. The overhead of this redirection was noticeable for programs that opened files frequently.

2. *Stateless daemon.* Since each autofs mount retains the association between the directory and the associated map, the daemon receives all the information it needs to perform a mount or unmount in the RPC request from the autofs. If the daemon crashes, programs continue to have access to existing mounts, but cannot access new mounts until the daemon is restarted.

3. *Changes to autofs mounts.* Autofs mounts can be added or removed without restarting the automounter daemon or affecting existing mounts. The Solaris automount command compares the desired set of autofs mounts in the auto.master map with the actual set of autofs mounts from the system MOUNT table (/etc/mnttab) and adds or removes autofs mounts to resolve any differences.

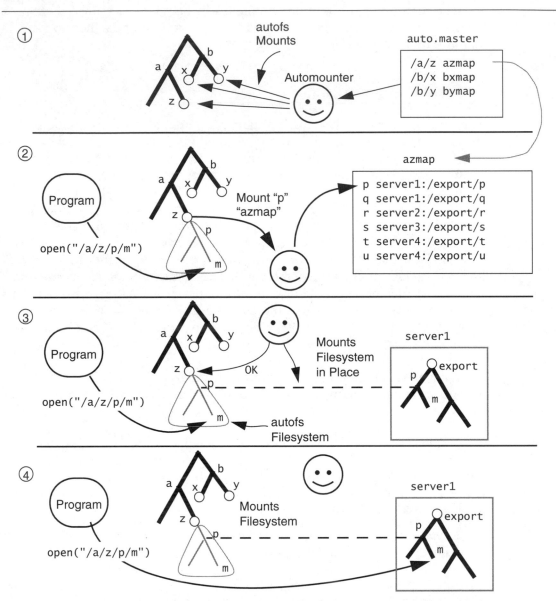

FIGURE 11.5 Autofs operation. (1) At start-up the automounter reads the auto.master map and mounts an autofs at each directory that associates a map with each directory. (2) A program attempts to open a file in an NFS filesystem that isn't mounted. The autofs makes an RPC call to the daemon to mount the filesystem. (3) It mounts the filesystem in place and responds to the autofs. (4) The autofs unblocks the program, which then opens the file in the NFS filesystem. The automounter daemon is not involved in further READ, WRITE, or pathname operations.

11.4   Automounter Maps

An automounter *map* is a database that describes the layout of the global
namespace. A map can be represented by a local text file, where each entry in
the map is a line of text, but this has all the disadvantages of the `/etc/vfstab`
or `/etc/fstab` file that the automounter makes redundant for NFS mounts. It
is difficult to keep local files synchronized across a large number of clients.
More commonly, a map is an NIS or NIS+ map that is visible to all clients (see
Figure 11.5).

11.4.1   Master Map

The master map lists the directories that will receive automounter service and
associates each directory with an indirect map that describes the mounts that
will comprise the directory entries. The following master map is typical. The
first two fields in each entry are the directory to receive automounter service
and the name of the map to be used with this directory. The third field is
optional; it provides default `mount` options to be used for map entries that do
not have `mount` options. The first entry, `/net`, uses a special `-hosts` map that is
built in to the automounter and provides access to all the exported directories
of an NFS server.

```
#Directory    Map                 Mount options
/net          -hosts              -rw
/home         auto_home           -nosuid
/shared       auto_shared
/ws           auto_ws
/-            auto_direct
```

The final entry uses a dummy directory name, `/-`, that indicates that the
map `auto_direct` is a *direct* map that is not associated with a single directory.
Except for the built-in `-hosts` map, the other maps are located first by checking for a file with that name under the client's `/etc` directory. If the file doesn't
exist, then the automounter looks for an NIS or NIS+ map with that name.

11.4.2   Direct Map

A direct map is the simplest and most intuitive kind of map (Figure 11.6).
Each entry associates the pathname for a directory with a filesystem to be
mounted at that directory. In this sense, it resembles an `/etc/vfstab` file,
which describes filesystems to be mounted when a UNIX client is booted. The
direct map is read in its entirety when the automounter starts up and automount service is established for the directory named in each entry.

Each map entry identifies one or more remote filesystems to be mounted
at the directory. When the autofs filesystem mounted at the directory detects

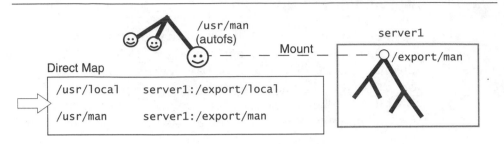

FIGURE 11.6 Direct map. Each entry in a direct map has the pathname of a directory to be automounted and the location of a filesystem to be mounted there when referenced.

access by a program, it sends a MOUNT call to the automount daemon requesting a mount. When the mount is complete, the application that triggered the mount is given access to the NFS filesystem. The NFS mount covers the autofs mountpoint until the filesystem is unmounted and the autofs mountpoint is again exposed, ready to trigger another mount.

Although direct maps appear to be a useful and general solution, they do not scale very well. When the automounter starts, it must read the entire map and issue an autofs mount for every entry in the map. These mounts are a significant start-up overhead for maps that contain a large number of entries. Some home directory maps can hold thousands of entries. Additionally, if entries are added to or deleted from the map by the system administrator, the automounter on each client will have to be signaled to reread the direct map.

11.4.3   Indirect Map

An indirect map is equivalent to the entries in a directory (Figure 11.7). Each entry in a direct map represents an entry in a directory controlled by the automounter. An indirect map is almost identical in layout to a direct map except for the first field. Instead of a full pathname, the field is a simple name representing a name in the automounter-controlled directory. When the autofs filesystem receives a LOOKUP request for a name in the directory that is not already mounted, it sends a MOUNT request to the automounter daemon. The daemon finds the entry for the name in the map associated with the directory and uses the mount location information to mount the filesystem, having first created an entry in the autofs directory to use as a mountpoint. Having the automounter daemon process create the mountpoint carries the risk that the daemon's request will be blocked by the autofs—as it would be for other processes. The first autofs implementation simply tagged the pathname with a trailing space character. Although space-terminated names are rare, there is the risk that some other application might also use space-terminated names.

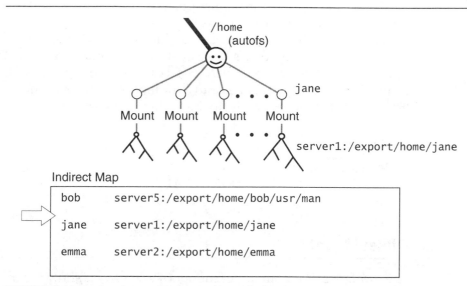

Indirect Map

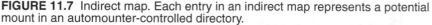

bob	server5:/export/home/bob/usr/man
jane	server1:/export/home/jane
emma	server2:/export/home/emma

FIGURE 11.7 Indirect map. Each entry in an indirect map represents a potential mount in an automounter-controlled directory.

More recently, the autofs was changed to create mountpoints internally, rather than from the automount daemon.

A big advantage of the indirect map is its scalability. The map does not need to be read when the automounter starts up. Entries are located individually, as needed. A UNIX *readdir* request to list the entries in the directory will require the entire map to be read, though this is a less common operation. The autofs must exercise caution in enumerating the directory lest it be forced to mount every entry.[1] The Solaris automounter succeeds in avoiding this problem by mounting a directory entry only when a directory LOOKUP request is issued against the entry.

11.4.4 Executable Map

An executable map has its entries generated dynamically by a program or script. If the automounter daemon locates a map as a local file under the /etc directory and its *execute* bit is set, then instead of opening the file and searching for an entry, the daemon executes the file as a program and passes the key to be located within the map as an argument. The program or script is expected to generate a map entry on its *stdout* I/O stream. An executable map

---

1. This event is referred to as a *mount storm*.

can obtain the data that make up a map entry from some other database and construct the map entry on the fly.

For example, the following executable map, implemented as a shell script, emulates the automounter's built-in -hosts map for /net. It obtains a list of exported filesystems from an NFS server (its name given as the key argument), formats the pathnames into a multiple-mount map entry, and sorts the list to order the mounts correctly into a top-down hierarchy.

```
#!/bin/sh
SERVER=$1
dfshares -h $1 |
awk '{print $1 "\t'$SERVER':" $1 "\\"}' |
sort
```

11.5 Offset Mounts

The examples of automounter mounts shown so far show the in-place mount at the autofs mountpoint (direct mount) or one level below (indirect mount). These are *zero offset* mounts (Figure 11.8). An *offset* is some number of directory levels that separate the autofs *trigger* directory from the actual mountpoint. Offset paths are most commonly used when the automounter is creating multiple mounts below a trigger directory. When a map entry with an offset is located, the daemon will create the offset directories, if required. In the trivial and common example where no offset is necessary, it need not be specified in the map; a default offset of "/" is assumed.

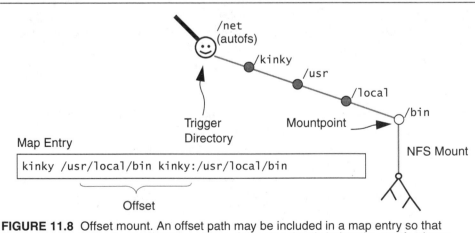

FIGURE 11.8 Offset mount. An offset path may be included in a map entry so that the mount can be performed some number of directory levels below the autofs trigger directory.

11.6 Multiple Mounts

To satisfy a MOUNT request, the automounter may need to mount more than one filesystem. A common example of this is the /net directory that uses the built-in -hosts map. When /net/*servername* is accessed, the automounter attempts to mount all the exported filesystems of the named server below the directory /net/*servername*. A map entry can specify multiple mounts, each with an offset path that creates a unique mountpoint below the autofs trigger. The general form of a multiple MOUNT entry is

```
key offset location { offset location } ...
```

Following the entry key (in a direct map it is a pathname, in an indirect map it is the name of a directory entry) is a series of one or more mounts, each comprising an offset pathname that names the mountpoint and the location of the filesystem to be mounted.

Using the /net example, if the server kinky exports the following filesystems

```
/tmp
/usr/local
/usr/local/bin
```

then with the built-in -hosts feature, the automounter would build the following multiple-mount map entry:

```
kinky \
    /tmp            kinky:/tmp \
    /usr/local      kinky:/usr/local \
    /usr/local/bin  kinky:/usr/local/bin
```

The map entry is represented here on several lines; the backslash is used to indicate a continuation onto the next line. An access to this map entry via the /net directory would yield the mounts shown in Figure 11.9. For some mounts the daemon may need to create directories in the offset path within the autofs filesystem, for instance, the directories in the subpath kinky/usr/local. Where one filesystem is mounted on a directory in another, the required mountpoint may already exist. For instance, the path kinky/usr/local/bin already exists within the filesystem mounted at kinky/usr/local. When constructing multiple mount entries that have dependencies like these (one filesystem mounted within a previously mounted filesystem), it is important that the automounter do the mounts in the right order. The -hosts facility achieves this with a simple lexicographic sort of the pathnames from the server's export list so that a top-down hierarchy of mounts is presented as a left-to-right ordering of mountpoints and locations in the map entry.

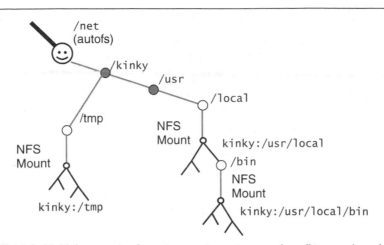

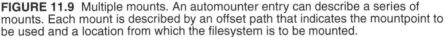

FIGURE 11.9 Multiple mounts. An automounter entry can describe a series of mounts. Each mount is described by an offset path that indicates the mountpoint to be used and a location from which the filesystem is to be mounted.

11.7 Replica Servers

The automounter's map syntax allows multiple locations to be listed for each mount. The locations in the list are expected to represent replica servers. In large networks, servers that hold packages and data files that are shared by many clients are often replicated one per subnet. These replicas not only spread the load over a larger number of machines, they also keep NFS traffic off network backbones and provide a greater level of redundancy (the loss of a server will inconvenience a smaller set of clients). The existence of replica filesystems can be acknowledged in an automounter map. For instance, a filesystem containing shared packages that is replicated on three servers could be described by the following map entry:

```
packages    server1:/pkg    server2:/pkgserver3:/pkg
```

If some of the servers in the replica list use the same pathname to the filesystem, then a comma-separated list of servers can be used. The example can be shortened to

```
packages    server1,server2,server3:/pkg
```

When confronted with a choice of locations, the automounter will choose the *nearest available* server. In the network shown in Figure 11.10 the system administrator would like to have a single automounter map for all clients but have each group of clients mount the replica server on their own subnet. The

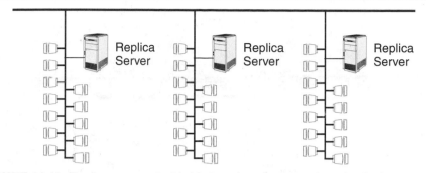

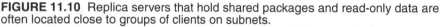

FIGURE 11.10 Replica servers that hold shared packages and read-only data are often located close to groups of clients on subnets.

nearest server is considered to be the one that is reachable with the least number of network hops. The automounter figures out the nearest server by obtaining the network address(es)[2] of its own host and comparing them with the network addresses of the replicas. Preference is given in the following order (Figure 11.11).

1. *Same host.* It's possible that the automounter that's attempting the mount is running on one of the replica machines. In that case the filesystem can be accessed locally—no NFS mount is required. The old NFS-server automounter would redirect access with a symbolic link to the local filesystem. An autofs automounter does a *loopback* mount instead of an NFS mount.

2. *Same subnet.* If a server resides on the same subnet as the automounter's host, then it will be preferred over a server that is on a different subnet. As part of the address comparison, the *netmasks* must be obtained from the name service for all addresses.

3. *Same network.* If a server resides on the same network as the automounter's host, then it will be preferred over a server that is on a different network.

The address filtering process may eliminate some unsuitable replica servers, but there may still be some candidate servers left that are equally near. As a tiebreaker, the automounter *pings* each server with an RPC call to the NULL procedure of its NFS server. There is no preference implied by the order in which the replicas are listed in the map; the pings are transmitted in parallel and the automounter then waits for the responses. As each reply is received, the round-trip times are compared and the server that responds most quickly

---

2. A client may have several network interfaces, each with its own IP address.

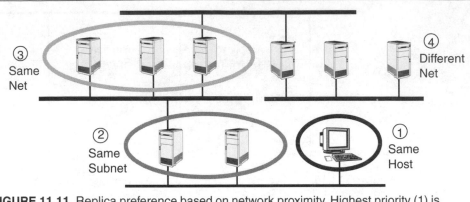

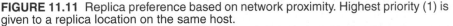

FIGURE 11.11 Replica preference based on network proximity. Highest priority (1) is given to a replica location on the same host.

is chosen, since it is assumed to be either the nearest or the most lightly loaded. The NULL procedure ping handily eliminates replicas that have crashed or are unreachable, since they won't respond at all. If no replies to the ping are received from any replica, then the list of candidates will be expanded to include replicas that may have been eliminated through address inspection and the ping repeated—looking for *any* replica server that will respond.

A system administrator may have a need to control the outcome of the tie-breaker ping. For example, a dedicated NFS server may be backed up by a replica server that is dedicated to other activities such as routing or providing CPU cycles to X terminals. The administrator might prefer that clients use the dedicated server and keep the load off the backup server until the primary server is unavailable. Each replica server can be assigned a weighting value that indicates its preference. The value is appended to the hostname as an integer in parentheses. The integer is used as a multiplier for a time penalty value that is added to the round-trip time measured for the server ping. If no weighting value is assigned, then the weighting value defaults to zero (no penalty). The larger the weighting value, the lower the preference. For example, to illustrate the case of `primary` and `backup` replicas described before,

```
images primary,backup(1):/export/images
```

which is equivalent to

```
images primary(0),backup(1):/export/images
```

Weighting values affect only the tie-breaker ping. A replica with a large weighting value will be chosen in preference to a server with a small weighting value if its address indicates that it is "closer" on the network.

11.8   Map Variables and Key Substitution

Map variables allow a system administrator to deploy a single map that refers to different locations depending on some characteristic of the client. The most common example is in mounting a directory that contains programs specific to a particular client architecture or operating system. For instance, the following map entry might be used to mount a directory containing software packages:

```
bin    central:/export/packages/bin
```

This entry is sufficient if all the clients run the same CPU and operating system, but not if the client population is a mix of different architectures (e.g., Solaris running on Sparc, Solaris on x86, Digital UNIX on Alpha, Linux on x86, and so on). The automounter supports a list of map variables that map to a different kind of string value depending on the kind of client (Table 11.1). A map variable is introduced with a dollar sign, $. The derived string results from the output of the UNIX uname command.

For instance, the CPU variable becomes sparc on a Sparc machine, and i386 on an Intel machine. If the server administrator exports different filesystems each containing executable files specific to the architecture of each type of client, and it names these directories with strings returned by map variables, then each client will get to mount the directory it needs if the map variable is used in the location pathname of the map entry. For example, if the server administrator exports two directories containing programs for Sparc clients and Intel clients, then he or she might export the paths

```
/export/pkgs/sparc
/export/pkgs/i386
```

TABLE 11.28 Automounter Map Variables

Variable	Meaning	Derived from	Example
$ARCH	Architecture type	uname -m	i86pc
$CPU	Processor type	uname -p	i386
$HOST	Hostname	uname -n	dinky
$OSNAME	Operating system name	uname -s	SunOS
$OSREL	Operating system release	uname -r	5.7
$OSVERS	Operating system version	uname -v	Generic

and if the map entry contains the CPU map variable

```
bin   server:/export/pkgs/$CPU
```

then the Sparc clients will evaluate the entry as

```
bin   server:/export/pkgs/sparc
```

and the Intel clients will see

```
bin   server:/export/pkgs/i386
```

Automounter maps interpret the ampersand character as a *key substitution* character. This abbreviation is most useful in maps that repeat the map key in the body of the entry. For example, the list of home directory entries

```
mary     donald:/export/home/mary
bill     mickey:/export/home/bill
ken      mickey:/export/home/ken
jane     mickey:/export/home/jane
angela   mickey:/export/home/angela
```

can be expressed more compactly by

```
mary     donald:/export/home/&
bill     mickey:/export/home/&
ken      mickey:/export/home/&
jane     mickey:/export/home/&
angela   mickey:/export/home/&
```

An asterisk can be used as a wildcard key to match any key that has not been previously matched by an explicit key. The asterisk is sometimes useful when used in conjunction with the key substitution character. For example, the map entries given in the example above could be replaced by

```
mary     donald:/export/home/&
*        mickey:/export/home/&
```

Wildcarded replica entries have been used by some system administrators with the expectation that the entry will be evaluated as a "search" path in hopes that the automounter will check each location looking for a successful mount. For instance:

```
*        donald,mickey:/export/home/&   (Don't do this!)
```

In practice, this does not work. The automounter assumes that each location is a valid mount. If the directory specified in the location is missing, the automounter will return an error. It won't check alternative locations. Even if the automounter did support this kind of searching for a successful mount, it would become very inefficient as the number of alternative locations grows.

11.9 MOUNT Options

An automounter uses a default set of options that satisfy the needs of most NFS mounts. NFS MOUNT options are rarely needed in map entries, though it is common practice for some system administrators to add MOUNT options anyway. For instance, rw, hard, and intr are commonly included even though they are all default values. If options need to be set, then the most useful place to set them is in the *map defaults* field of the master map. The map default options apply to any entry in the map that does not have its own set of MOUNT options. MOUNT options can be included in a map entry at several places.

- *Entry options.* MOUNT options placed after the map key and before the first offset path or location will apply to any mount specified later in the map entry, unless overridden by options specified later in the entry.
- *Mountpoint options.* MOUNT options that are placed prior to an offset path will apply to any mount for that mountpoint that does not have mount options associated with the location.
- *Location options.* MOUNT options that are placed after an offset path but before any location for that path will apply just to any mount made from that location.

11.10 Amd Automounter

Amd (Auto-Mounter Daemon) was developed by Jan-Simon Pendry, at Imperial College, London [Pendry94]. Like the original SunOS automounter, Amd is a user-level NFS server that mounts NFS filesystems in a temporary directory and returns a symbolic link to the temporary mountpoint. Amd provided some unique features that were missing from early versions of the SunOS automounter (Figure 11.12).

11.10.1 Nonblocking Operation

When attempting to mount a filesystem from a slow server, the SunOS automounter would block attempts to mount other filesystems. Amd provided better service through its use of a separate process to perform potential block-

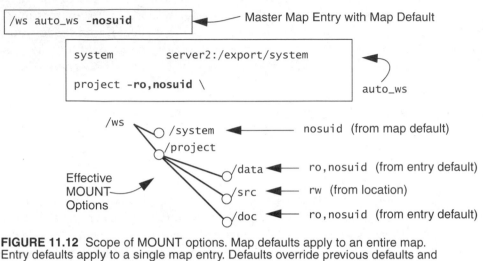

FIGURE 11.12 Scope of MOUNT options. Map defaults apply to an entire map. Entry defaults apply to a single map entry. Defaults override previous defaults and apply only to mounts with no explicit options.

ing operations like mounting. In more recent implementations, the autofs automounter resolved the blocking problem with a multithreaded daemon process.

11.10.2 Server Keepalives

When the Amd automounter completes a mount, it continues to monitor the server's responsiveness by pinging the NFS NULL procedure on the server. If the server crashes or is unreachable, the Amd automounter can mount a replica filesystem (if available) and redirect new processes to the new mount. The failover extends only to new file opens—a process blocked on I/O to a server that crashes after the file is opened would continue to be blocked. The Solaris 2.6 version of the autofs automounter integrated client-side failover capability implemented in the kernel.

11.10.3 Map Syntax

The Amd automounter uses a map syntax different from that of SunOS-derived automounters. Following the key in an Amd automounter entry is a series of mount locations that can each be controlled by a selector: a series of assertions that can be used to control whether the client uses the location or not. For example, the following Amd map contains two entries. The first is a default entry that specifies defaults for all entries in the map. The second entry is a regular map entry that contains two locations.

```
/defaults opts:=rw,intr,nosuid
spooky \
    host!=${key};type:=nfs;rhost:=${key};rfs:=/h/${key} \
    host==${key};type:=ufs;dev:=/dev/dsk/c0t0d0s2
```

The ${key} construct is equivalent to the SunOS automounter's key sub-stitution character &. In the example entry, it is replaced by the entry key spooky. The selector expression host!=${key} compares the current hostname with the entry key (spooky). If hostname is not spooky, then the NFS mount is used; server name is identified by rhost and the path to be mounted by rfs. The next selector handles the case where the hostname *is* spooky. In this case a local disk partition on spooky is mounted as a ufs filesystem.

Although the locator-based map entry syntax is powerful and flexible, its complexity makes it a challenge for novice system administrators to maintain large and varied maps. It is unfortunate that the SunOS-derived auto-mounters and Amd do not share the same map syntax. The 4.4BSD version of Amd comes with a collection of tools called *am-utils* that utilize the Amd auto-mounter. Among these is a *FSinfo*, a program that reads a single file describ-ing the mapping of an organization's disks, servers, and access options and produces a consistent set of Amd maps.

Perhaps the most attractive feature of Amd is its wide availability. Because it is distributed in source form, it has been ported to more than 20 dif-ferent versions of the UNIX operating system. The SunOS-derived auto-mounter has been licensed by Sun to the major UNIX vendors, but it is not as widely available as Amd. Additionally, because the SunOS automounter is bundled with the UNIX operating system, new versions are available only when a new version of the host OS is released. Amd is attractive to system administrators because a single version can be installed on a variety of machines each running different OS versions.

11.11 Summary

Automounting provides a global namespace for NFS filesystems. Using maps obtained from a name service like NIS or NIS+, a system administrator can centrally manage the mapping of the namespace across the exported file-systems on NFS servers in an organization. Automounter users are given the appearance of continuously available NFS mounts through on-demand mounting.

An automounting service can be provided by a user-level daemon process that mounts itself as an NFS server on the directories that need automounter service. The daemon intercepts requests to access NFS mounts, performs the required mount in a temporary directory, and returns a symbolic link to the temporary mountpoint. Once the symbolic link is returned, the automounter is no longer in the I/O path. NFS-server automounters, like the original SunOS automounter and the Amd automounter, can cause problems for users and applications through the unintended visibility of the temporary directory.

The autofs automounter avoids the use of a temporary mountpoint by its use of in-place mounts in cooperation with an autofs filesystem in the kernel. Although the kernel implementation limits portability of the service to other architectures, it provides superior service through in-place mounting and the additional benefits of a robust, stateless daemon and improved performance.

Automounter maps describe the mapping of the global namespace to specific mountpoints, servers, and filesystems. The master map describes the directories that are to be included in the global namespace and the maps to be associated with them. Direct or indirect maps describe the specific mounts that are to make up the namespace. Map information can be generated dynamically by executable maps.

An automounter map entry can describe a single mount as a server name followed by a pathname to be mounted from the server. This simple map entry syntax can be extended to describe multiple mounts in a hierarchy where each mountpoint can be specified by an offset path. An example is the built-in -hosts map that mounts the entire hierarchy of NFS filesystems exported from a server. Replicated filesystems can be described as a list of locations. The automounter chooses a replica server based on its network proximity and the server's reponsiveness to a NULL procedure ping. A weighting factor can be applied to replicas to favor one replica server over another. Map variables can be used to tailor map entries to vary the mounted location according to some characteristic of a client.

The Amd automounter is available in source form and has been ported to a large number of UNIX operating systems. It uses a map syntax that is different from the SunOS-based automounters.

Chapter 12

NFS Variants

The NFS protocol has been used as the basis for several variant protocols. It is often easier to begin with an existing and proven protocol and extend it than to design and implement a new distributed filesystem protocol from the ground up. This chapter gives a brief overview of several of these protocols.

12.1 Spritely NFS

The caching model used by most NFS clients (described in section 8.14) does not guarantee consistency across client caches. Because an NFS server cannot notify a client that its cached copy of file data has been modified, the client will not detect file changes on the server until it issues a GETATTR request or receives updated attributes attached to the response of a LOOKUP, READ, or WRITE request. A program may be reading stale cached data for several seconds before the client gets around to checking cache consistency. This caching model also imposes an overhead that degrades performance: the client must send periodic GETATTR calls even if the file is never changed on the server, and client writes must be sent directly to the server so that other clients can detect file modification. If a client can delay writes to the server, then it can detect and cancel unnecessary writes. If data in a file is overwritten one or more times in quick succession, then only the last write needs to be sent to the server. If the file is written, then removed, no writes at all need to be sent to the server. This behavior is common for programs that use files for temporary storage.

Spritely NFS was inspired by the Sprite project at the University of California, Berkeley [Nelson+88]. Sprite was a distributed operating system that utilized client caching with a consistency protocol that ensured that all clients were guaranteed *single-copy* semantics: clients could never have an inconsistent view of file or directory data. The Spritely NFS project borrowed on the Sprite caching model to provide cache consistency for NFS. As well as providing predictable, single-copy semantics (clients always see the latest modification to a file), the project hoped to realize some performance improvements through better cache management. Spritely NFS is described in a paper by V. Srinivasan and Jeffrey Mogul [Srinivasan+89]. The project first focused on investigating the cache consistency and performance benefits. A solution to the problem of stateful server recovery was described in a later paper [Mogul 94] along with some changes to the OPEN/CLOSE protocol to make it more reliable.

12.1.1   Stateful Server

The NFS protocol has no file OPEN or CLOSE call. An NFS server has no idea which clients or programs have files open on the server or whether clients are caching data. Such is the stateless nature of the NFS protocol that the server doesn't need to retain any client state from one RPC call to the next. Although this statelessness makes it easy for an NFS server to recover from a crash, it makes it impossible for the server to notify clients that a file has changed—a stateless server has no idea who its clients are or whether they're interested in the change.

Spritely NFS added an OPEN and CLOSE call to the protocol. Whenever a program opens a file, the client sends an OPEN call to the server that identifies the file along with two counts: the number of file opens for reading, and the number of file opens for writing. When a client program closes a file, a CLOSE call is sent to the server with adjusted read open and write open counts. For each file, the server knows which clients are caching the file for reading or writing.

12.1.2   Callback

When a Spritely NFS server receives an OPEN call, it checks for other clients that may have the same file open. The server's response indicates whether the client can cache file data. If no other client has the file open for writing, the OPEN response will give approval for file caching. If a client's OPEN call indicates that it wants to write to the file and other clients already have the file open for reading, then the server will send a callback RPC to each client. On receiving a callback, each client must invalidate its cached data for the file.

If a client's OPEN call indicates that it wants only to read the file, and some other client is writing to a cached copy, then the server will issue a CALLBACK request to the writing client to stop caching. If the client has any pending writes in the cache, then it must write any changes back to the server's copy of the file before responding to the callback. This process is illustrated in Figure 12.1. When the writing client has responded to the call-

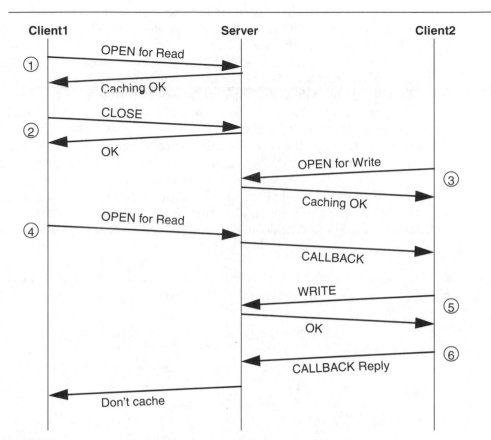

FIGURE 12.1 The Spritely NFS server controls client caching. The response to an OPEN request indicates whether the client can cache file data. (1) The server allows the client to cache a file it has opened for reading. (2) The file is closed. (3) Another client opens the file to write it. (4) When the first client opens the file again, the server sends a CALLBACK request to the write caching client requesting it to stop caching. (5) The client flushes pending writes from its cache and (6) replies to the callback. The server then responds to the client open request at (4).

back, the server will respond to the client that requested the open for write with an indication that it must not cache.

12.1.3 Write-behind

A conventional NFS client flushes any pending writes to the server when an application closes a file. The flushing of writes on close is necessary to preserve the *close-to-open* cache consistency model of conventional NFS caching (see section 8.14.3). Some programs use a file for temporary storage: the file exists briefly, is read, then is removed. If the NFS client can delay flushing writes to the server, then it may be able to avoid writing the data to the server altogether if the file is soon to be removed. The cache management of the Spritely NFS server allows the client to be more leisurely in writing file data back to the server (Figure 12.2).

Conventional NFS close-to-open cache consistency requires that the application's `close()` call be synchronous with the server; all pending writes must be completed before the application can continue past the `close()` call. An application on a Spritely NFS client can continue past the `close()` call before pending writes to the server are completed. The CLOSE call to the server will indicate whether the client has file changes that need to be written back to the server. If any other client needs to read the write-back data, then the server knows to send a CALLBACK request to the client to write back the changes.

Although write-behind can have performance benefits, it can introduce some complications that make implementation difficult. When the application issues a `close()` call, a conventional NFS client will flush any cached writes to

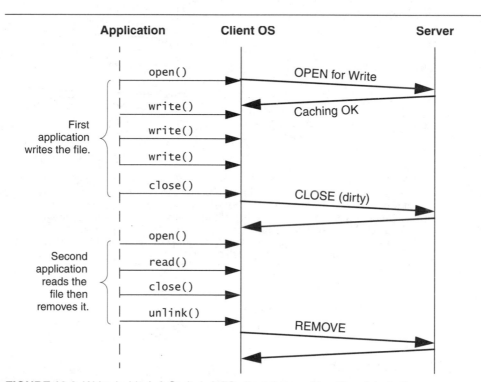

FIGURE 12.2 Write-behind. A Spritely NFS client can avoid writing data to the server by delaying writes to the server. The writes from the first application program are cached on the client. When the file is closed, the CLOSE call to the server indicates that the client has "dirty" data (changes that need to be written to the server). The second application reads the file from the client's cache and removes the file. The Spritely NFS client then issues a REMOVE call.

the server. At the completion of the file close() call, the application has an assurance that the data are safe on the server. Because a Spritely NFS client doesn't write data back immediately after the application closes the file, the data may be lost if the client crashes after the application exits.[1] If network or server errors prevent the data from being written back, the client application can no longer be notified via a close() result since it has already exited. The most common kind of write error occurs when the server runs out of disk space and reports a "no space" error. If the application were able to catch this error from a close() result, it would be able to notify the user, who could make some space available (by removing files) and then retry the operation. However, if the writes and the error are delayed until the application and the user have gone away, then the recovery action may not be as straightforward. Spritely NFS avoids this problem by requesting that the server reserve space for the pending writes when it issues the CLOSE call. If the server returns a "no space" error in response to the reservation request, the error can be returned through the application close() call. A client can cancel the space reservation (if it cancels the pending writes because the file is removed) by sending another CLOSE request with a zero space reservation.

12.1.4 Recovery

The OPEN and CLOSE calls require a Spritely NFS server to retain some state for each file that is open by one or more clients. Against each file, the server needs to record the list of clients that have it open and whether they have it open for reading or writing—indicating which clients are caching file data. If this state is stored in volatile memory and the server crashes, then it will be lost. To store all the state in a file would limit the performance of the server through the additional synchronous I/O to the state file.

Spritely NFS uses an elegant compromise: it stores the per-file state in volatile memory and keeps a list of clients that have opened a file at any time in a disk file. New clients are added to the on-disk list when they first open a file. During server recovery following a crash (Figure 12.3), the server reads the list of clients from the disk file and sends a "Begin recovery" callback to each client. The callback is a signal to clients that they should suspend normal operation and prepare for a recovery. To prevent the server from being overwhelmed by requests from recovering clients, each client waits until recovery is requested by the server. When the server is ready to recover the state from a client, it sends a "Request reopen" callback to the client. On receiving this request, the client uses one or more "Reopen" requests that tell the server which files are open. When the server has rebuilt its per-file open state, it

---

1. This kind of data loss is also possible for UNIX applications that write to local filesystems. Data can be held in memory for up to 30 seconds before being written to the disk.

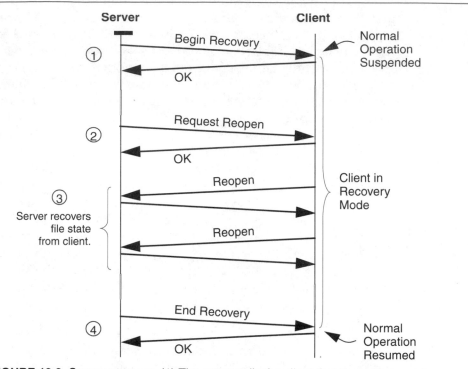

FIGURE 12.3 Server recovery. (1) The server tells the client that it must suspend normal operation because the server is recovering. (2) In turn, each client gets a "Request reopen" callback. The client then sends a series of "Reopen" requests to the server. Each request contains the state of several files. (3) When the server has recovered file open state from all clients, (4) it sends an "End recovery" callback to each client so that it will resume normal operation.

sends an "End recovery" callback to each client so that it can resume normal operation. Giving the server control over recovery helps avoid an "implosion" of simultaneous recovery requests from a large number of clients. This recovery technique is similar to that of the Network Lock Manager (see section 10.6).

12.1.5 Performance

As well as fixing the NFS cache consistency problem, one of the goals of the Spritely NFS project was to improve performance through more intelligent use of client caches. There would be little interest in Spritely NFS if its cache consistency feature was at the expense of lower performance. Performance could be hurt by the additional OPEN and CLOSE calls as well as the complex recovery procedure following a server crash.

Srinivasan and Mogul ran the Andrew benchmark [Howard+88] against a normal NFS client and server pair and a Spritely NFS client and server pair. The Andrew benchmark works on a large tree of directories and files of Make files and C source. The tree is first copied in its entirety. Then the tree is searched twice, first to obtain the file attributes for each file, then to read each file in its entirety. Finally, the benchmark compiles and links all the files in the hierarchy. Spritely NFS was measured to perform about 15 percent to 20 percent faster on the entire benchmark.

Although performance was significantly better, these results are not relevant to more recent implementations of NFS. A significant part of the speedup was observed in the make phase of the benchmark, where the compiler creates and deletes temporary work files. It is more recent practice to have compilers create temporary files outside the source hierarchy in a /tmp filesystem based in virtual memory. Although Spritely NFS reduced the number of WRITE operations to the server, the original benchmarking was based on NFS version 2, which was notorious for its slow, synchronous writes (see section 8.10). Much of this advantage was lost with the cached writes of NFS version 3. The NFS version 3 protocol also reduced the number of GETATTR calls. Since NFS version 3 implementations have become available, no further work has been done on Spritely NFS.

12.1.6   Summary

Although the Spritely NFS project was a useful investigation of a cache consistency protocol for NFS, the benefits were insufficient to generate market demand. Although the project did succeed in one of its primary goals—cache consistency for NFS—the demonstrated performance benefits have been eroded by the performance improvements of NFS version 3. In addition, the requirement for an elaborate and unproven client state recovery protocol on the server side did not ignite the enthusiasm of NFS vendors.

12.2   NQNFS

The NQNFS (Not Quite NFS) project had the same goals as the Spritely NFS project: to support cache consistency in the NFS protocol and to improve performance through better use of caching. NQNFS borrowed from the Spritely NFS work in adding procedures to the NFS protocol that allowed the server to maintain state indicating which files were open and cached on clients (Figure 12.4). NQNFS is notable for its use of leases [Gray+89] to solve the problem of server recovery of client state after a crash. NQNFS was investigated by Rick Macklem of the University of Guelph, who published his work in 1994 [Macklen94].

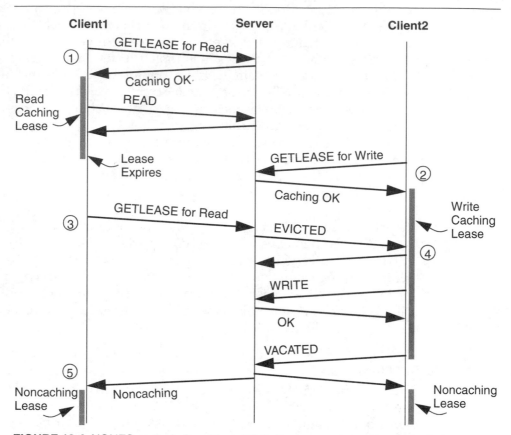

FIGURE 12.4 NQNFS control of caching. (1) A client requests and is granted a lease for reading the file. After the file is read, the client allows the lease to expire. (2) Another client then opens the file for writing with a GETLEASE call for writing. (3) The first client reopens the file for reading. (4) Because the second client is holding a WRITE lease, the server evicts this client from the lease. The second client writes back pending changes from its cache. From here on it must send WRITEs directly to the server. (5) When the server receives a VACATED call from the second client, it responds to the first client's LEASE request indicating that it must not cache because the file is open for writing by another client.

12.2.1   Leases

An NQNFS server maintains the same kind of file open state as a Spritely NFS server. When an NQNFS client needs to access file data on the server, it must hold a lease. A lease is a promise from the server that it will retain the client's file open state for a limited amount of time—determined by the *duration* of the lease. Before a client reads or writes file data, it issues a GETLEASE call that identifies the file, the type of access it needs (read-only or read-write), and the duration of the lease. If the file is already open for read-write on the server (perhaps by another client), then the server will return a "no cache" response, indicating that the client must not cache any data for this file and must send all READ or WRITE requests directly to the server.

Like Spritely NFS, NQNFS also features a callback RPC that is used when the server needs to stop the clients caching. If a client opens a file for writing that is cached with READ leases on other clients, the server sends an EVICTED callback to each client requesting that pending changes be written back to the server and that their leases should be given up. Clients respond to this EVICTED callback with a VACATED call to indicate that the lease has been given up. When all clients have responded, the server grants a WRITE lease to the client that requested it. If the number of clients that need to be evicted is large, there is a risk that some clients may not respond to the EVICTED callback. In this case the server just waits for their leases to expire before granting the WRITE lease to the original caller.

The server controls the lease period. If a client requests a lease period that is longer than the server desires, it will return a shorter lease period in the GETLEASE reply. If a client needs to retain a lease for a period longer than the initial lease period, then it must send additional GETLEASE requests periodically before the lease expires. NQNFS cleverly avoided the overhead of the OPEN/CLOSE calls of Spritely NFS by piggybacking the LEASE requests on other NQNFS RPC calls. NQNFS was based on NFS version 2, but it anticipated the ACCESS call of NFS version 3. The NQNFS ACCESS call included GETLEASE request arguments. GETLEASE responses could also be piggybacked on responses to any NQNFS call.

12.2.2   Recovery

Server recovery of client state is much simpler with NQNFS, thanks to its use of leases. The Spritely NFS protocol required the server to maintain a list of clients in stable storage so that it could notify them of recovery after a crash. The NQNFS server does not need to contact clients following recovery. It simply waits until all client leases have expired. When all leases have expired, there is no state to recover! If the maximum lease period that it will grant is one minute, then it simply waits a minute after recovery.

While it is waiting, it must handle WRITE requests from clients that were holding WRITE leases before the crash before issuing any new leases. If the server has numerous clients, then it could be overwhelmed by a deluge of WRITE requests from clients attempting write-backs from expired WRITE leases. The server can shed some of the nonwrite load by responding to other NFS calls with a "try later" error return. NFS version 3 implemented something similar with its NFS3ERR_JUKEBOX error (see Table 7.1). Clients that need to restore leases that expired while the server was down issue new GETLEASE requests.

Although the use of leases makes recovery much simpler, it introduces some cache consistency risk in scenarios where the lease expires before the client is able to completely flush modified data to a file and another client gets a lease on the file. The client may be prevented from flushing pending writes if the server is heavily loaded and drops the client's WRITE requests or if the network is partitioned, preventing writes or lease renewal requests from reaching the server.

12.2.3   Other Features

The NQNFS added some procedures to the NFS protocol unrelated to lease-based caching. Many of these features were later adopted in NFS version 3. File offsets in READ and WRITE calls and in file attributes were extended from 32 to 64 bits.[2] An *append* flag was added to the WRITE arguments to support append-mode writes. The resolution of file access and modification attributes was increased from milliseconds to nanoseconds. An ACCESS call allowed the client to reliably determine the type of file access allowed (read, write, or execute). A similar ACCESS call was added to NFS version 3. A READDIRLOOK procedure was added (similar to READDIRPLUS in NFS version 3) that allowed the client to obtain file attributes and filehandles in addition to the filenames in a directory. The new procedure was beneficial for programs that scanned directories, preempting the need for multiple LOOKUP calls. The cached directory entries could also be used to return negative LOOKUP results (i.e., "File not found").

12.2.4   Summary

NQNFS comes close to replicating the strong cache consistency and improved performance of Spritely NFS, while its use of server state controlled by leases made server recovery almost as simple as a completely stateless server. Although NQNFS was never used in a production environment, it demonstrated the use of some protocol features that were later adopted in NFS version 3. NQNFS has been used by users of 4.3BSD and 4.4BSD systems. It can be used in an environment that includes non-NQNFS systems. Clients and servers that use NQNFS benefit from the improved caching.

12.3   Trusted NFS

Trusted NFS (TNFS) was developed to support the requirements of the Trusted Computer System Evaluation Criteria (TCSEC). TNFS is a set of security requirements for operating systems and software used in computer sys-

---

2. While the READ and WRITE offset value was increased to 64 bits, the count value (size of READ or WRITE) was left at 32 bits.

tems that access classified material. The requirements are described in "Compartmented Mode Workstation Requirements" [Woodward87], a document published by the Defense Intelligence Agency of the U.S. government. TNFS was designed to support B1-level security, which assigns *security labels* to people and documents.

A security label identifies the security clearance level of a person or the security of information in a document (Figure 12.5). A person is not permitted access to information that has a higher security level than their own clearance. The control of access through security level is known as mandatory access control (MAC). TCSEC also provides discretionary access control (DAC) through the use of access lists. To implement these semantics at the level of file access through NFS, the protocol needed to be able to identify the security clearance level of a user and allow the user to read or modify the security information associated with a document on the server.

The protocol was developed by a team called the Trusted Systems Interoperability Group that included representatives from Digital Equipment Corporation, Sun Microsystems, Inc., SecureWare, Inc., and Silicon Graphics, Inc. These companies had each developed variants of NFS to support MLS (multi-level secure) security, but these protocols were not interoperable. The mission of the TSIG was to develop a common protocol. A draft of the protocol was published as an IETF Internet draft by a TSIG-inspired working group, but the specification was never completed. The TNFS described here is the one described in the incomplete specification.

12.3.1 AUTH_MLS Credential

TNFS defined a new RPC security flavor called AUTH_MLS and gave it a flavor number of 200,000 presumably as a temporary measure while the protocol

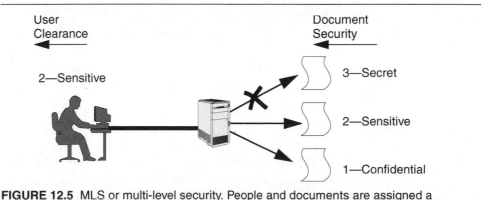

FIGURE 12.5 MLS or multi-level security. People and documents are assigned a sensitivity label that identifies a level of security. A person can read documents that have a sensitivity label that is equal to or lower than their own but cannot view documents with a higher sensitivity level.

was in development. The credential was based on the AUTH_SYS credential
(section 4.4) with added security tokens, among which was the user's clearance level. The TNFS server would map the credential into its own set of security policies for the user. These policies would then be considered against the
access control applied to the file to be accessed, governed by the sensitivity
label of the file.

The additional fields added to the credential and the file attributes took
the form of tokens. Instead of defining a common set of values for these fields,
the tokens would be references into a translation mechanism in a name service like NIS that would map each token to a value defined in the translation
mechanism. All would be well as long as the client and server agreed on a
common token translation mechanism.

The following pseudo-C code describes the AUTH_MLS credential. It is
taken from the draft specification.

```
#define AUTH_MLS 200000;      /* decimal */
#define MLS_TOKEN_SIZE 4;     /* 4 octets or 32 bits */
typedef opaque t_token[MLS_TOKEN_SIZE];/* tokens are opaque */

struct authmls_cred {
    u_long auc_stamp;         /* arbitrary id */
    char auc_machname<255>;   /* machine name */
    t_token auc_ids;          /* token for effective uid, gid gids */
    t_token auc_aid;          /* audit id token */
    t_token auc_privs;        /* subject privileges token */
    t_token auc_sens;         /* sensitivity token */
    t_token auc_info;         /* information token */
    t_token auc_integ;        /* integrity token */
    t_token auc_vend;         /* vendor specific policy token */
    t_token auc_clear;        /* subject clearance token */
    t_token auc_audinfo;      /* audit information token */
}
```

Like the NQNFS protocol, the TNFS protocol designers needed an ACCESS
operation that a client could use at file open time to check the kind of access
permitted to the file. Having the client check access using permission bits was
impossible since the client would not have access to the server's access control
policies or access control information.

12.3.2 Extended Attributes

The TNFS protocol extended the set of file attributes readable (SETATTR) and
settable (SETATTR) to include the MLS security attribute tokens. An MLS-
compliant operating system on the client would allow these security attributes to be displayed and changed, subject to the server's access control
policies for file attributes. The TNFS protocol simply appended the MLS secu-

rity tokens to the NFS version 2 file attributes structure, which follows in pseudo-C code. The additional fields are shown in **bold**.

```
struct fattr {
    ftype type;              /* file type */
    u_long mode;             /* encoded access mode */
    u_long nlink;            /* number of hard links */
    u_long uid;              /* file's owner id */
    u_long gid;              /* file's group id */
    u_long size;             /* file size in bytes */
    u_long blocksize;        /* number of bytes/block */
    u_long rdev;             /* device number of the file */
    u_long blocks;           /* current number of blocks */
    u_long fsid;             /* file system id */
    timeval atime;           /* time of file's last access */
    timeval mtime;           /* time last modified (written) */
    timeval ctime;           /* time of last attribute change */
    t_token privs;           /* file privileges token */
    t_token sens;            /* sensitivity token */
    t_token info;            /* information token */
    t_token integ;           /* integrity token */
    t_token acl;             /* access control list token */
    t_token vend;            /* vendor specific policy token */
    t_token udiinfo;         /* audit info token */
}
```

The NFS `setattr` structure was similarly extended for TNFS.

12.3.3 Filename Attributes

An unusual feature of TNFS security was the protection it afforded to filenames. An NFS version 2 filename can be as long as 255 characters. It can be regarded as a container of classified information. For instance, a document that described a plan for the invasion of Canada might have a top secret sensitivity label, but that would be of little good if the name of the file, PlanTo-InvadeCanada, were in plain view in the directory. TNFS allowed the *name* of a file, distinct from the *data* in the file, to have its own security attributes. The name attributes were included along with the file content attributes in the results of directory operations.

```
struct diropok {
    fhandle file;
    fattr attributes;
    t_token sens;
    t_token info;
    t_token vend;
}
```

12.3.4 TNFS Interoperability

The protocol designers wanted the TNFS protocol to have some backward compatibility with non-TNFS clients and servers. The protocol was assigned its own program number (390086) and version (1) so that a TNFS client could determine whether the server supported the TNFS protocol. If the server did not, then it would return a PROG_UNAVAIL RPC error and the client could then fall back to using the normal NFS protocol with program 10003.

The new security tokens in the file attributes were *appended* to the existing version 2 attributes. If a normal version 2 client received the extended attributes, then presumably it would ignore the appended security tokens. TNFS was intended to be run on the same port as the normal NFS service (port 2049).

12.3.5 Summary

The TNFS protocol was intended to be a common, interoperable protocol developed to meet federal government TCSEC requirements governing access by people with various levels of security clearance to files of varying sensitivity levels. The TNFS specification was never completed. TNFS included a new security flavor that included the user's security clearance information as well as additional file attributes encoded as security tokens that allowed the security labels of classified documents to be viewed and changed. Security labels could be attached not only to the content of a file but also to its name. A TNFS server used the new security flavor and the extended security file attributes to control access. TNFS included an ACCESS procedure to allow file access to be determined reliably at file open time.

12.4 NASD NFS

NASD (Network-Attached Secure Disks) is a project of the Parallel Data Laboratory at the Carnegie-Mellon University School of Computer Science [Gibson+98] (Figure 12.6). NASD aims to provide secure, high-bandwidth, low-latency access to data by supporting a direct path from a storage device to the client. With a conventional server configuration, the client sends a data access request to the server, which then locates the data on one of its attached disks and issues an SCSI command to the disk drive to read the data. The requested data are copied from the drive to the server's memory, then forwarded to the client. The server's intervention in storing and forwarding data between the client and the disk drive increases the time to transfer the data. In addition, the movement of data through the server limits the data bandwidth to that of the server's I/O system.

The NASD project observes that the server does not need any access to the data being written to or read from the drive. The server's role can be limited

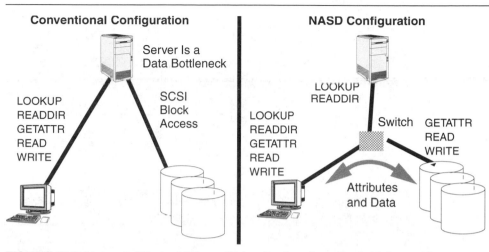

FIGURE 12.6 Network Attached Secure Disks give the client direct, high-speed access to storage devices. The server participates in directory operations and controls access. File attributes and READ and WRITE data are transferred directly between the client and storage device via a switch. Because file data are no longer transferred across the server's bus, access to data is faster and the server is more lightly loaded.

to location of data on a particular drive, authentication of a client's request, and checking the client's authorization to access the data. In an NASD configuration, file data are transferred directly between the client and the disk drive. Direct access to data reduces data latency (the time it takes to read or write the first byte of a file) and removes the server as a limit to the rate at which data can be transferred between the client and the drive.

Rather than invent an all-new file access protocol, the NASD team decided to make minor modifications to both the NFS and the AFS (Andrew File System) protocols. The modifications to the NFS protocol are described here.

12.4.1 NASD Storage

As the size and cost of powerful CPUs shrink along with that of DRAM and NVRAM memory, the computational power of disk drive electronics is increasing. Rather than respond to simple, block-access SCSI commands, a disk drive can provide a more sophisticated view of file data and exercise more efficient control over the placement of data blocks on the storage medium. The NASD project implemented an on-disk server that provides access to file data represented as variable-length objects. Each object has a unique name in a flat namespace along with a set of attributes. The on-disk server provides access to these storage objects via a small set of Remote Procedure Calls. For NFS clients, the server handles NFS READ, WRITE, and GETATTR calls directed to the storage objects (Figure 12.7).

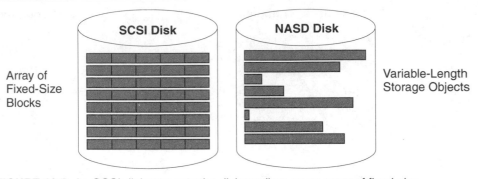

FIGURE 12.7 An SCSI disk presents the disk medium as an array of fixed-size storage blocks. The NASD disk presents storage as a number of variable-length storage objects.

12.4.2   Locating the Data

Before an NFS client can access a file, it needs to obtain its filehandle via a LOOKUP request. At first, the NASD NFS server, referred to as a *file manager*, performs the normal operations one would expect of an NFS server. It evaluates the LOOKUP operation and obtains a filehandle for the file. Then it checks the client's credential against the access permissions for the file. The NASD filehandle contains the disk drive identifier as a network address, along with the identifier for the file object. If the LOOKUP is successful, this filehandle is sent to the client in the LOOKUP reply. At this point the client behavior is quite different from that of a normal NFS server.

Normally, an NFS client would send the filehandle back to the server with a READ or WRITE request. A NASD client extracts the disk drive address from the filehandle and sends a READ, WRITE, or GETATTR request directly to the disk drive. Since the storage objects on an NASD drive correspond to NFS files, the NFS file offsets are used to locate data within a drive storage object (Figure 12.8).

12.4.3   Data Security

Connecting disk drives to a network is not without its security risks. The disk drive cannot accept READ or WRITE requests from any client on the network without authenticating the client and checking its authorization to access the data in a storage object. In a conventional storage configuration, where the disks are connected only to the server, the server handles all security. An NASD drive cannot grant access to a storage object unless it has some way of knowing that the server would grant access.

The NASD server and its disk drives share a secret key that is used to encrypt and decrypt a *capability*—data that authorize the operation. Because

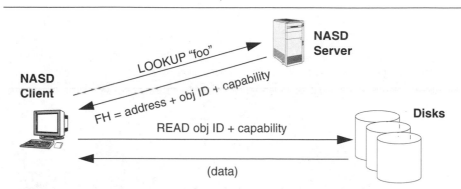

FIGURE 12.8 An NASD client obtains a filehandle from the server that contains the network address of the disk that contains a file along with the identifier of the object that represents the file. Also included in the filehandle is an encrypted capability that authorizes the client's access to the storage object. Requests that transfer file data or attributes are sent directly to the disk drive.

the capability is encrypted, the client cannot alter or forge the capability. The capability data are included in encrypted form in the filehandle returned by the LOOKUP request along with the drive address and storage object identifier. The filehandle containing the capability data is forwarded a READ, WRITE, or GETATTR request sent to the disk drive. The NFS protocol changes were limited to NFS version 3 because it supports a larger filehandle size (up to 64 bytes) that is needed to accommodate the drive and object information along with the encrypted capability.

12.4.4 Summary

The NASD project aims to improve the performance and scalability of file servers by removing the file server from the data path between the client and the storage device. An NASD disk drive is able to support a network protocol stack that provides access to variable-length storage objects. A client uses the server, or file manager, to locate a file and obtain a capability that authorizes its access to a storage object. To read file attributes or to transfer data to or from the file, the client communicates directly with the disk drive.

Chapter 13

Other Distributed Filesystems

I t is useful to take a look at some other distributed filesystems that compete with NFS. Each has a design philosophy and a feature set that is interesting to contrast with the NFS design philosophy and features. This chapter is not exhaustive in its overview—it does not mention some purely proprietary file access protocols like Appletalk and Novell's Netware. Instead, it focuses on protocols that are well documented and easy to describe in some detail.

13.1 Remote File Sharing

In the mid-1980s, the Remote File Sharing (RFS) feature of UNIX System V release 3 was AT&T's answer to remote file access. A design requirement for RFS was the *complete* preservation of UNIX filesystem semantics for remote file access. The NFS architects, in the pursuit of implementation simplicity and server statelessness, decided that a less than complete set of UNIX file-system semantics would be acceptable. For example, the last close problem (section 8.4) cannot be completely solved by an NFS implementation because it requires the server to keep track of the number of references to open files. RFS made no attempt to make its protocol useful to non-UNIX clients or servers.

With a stateful server and UNIX-only semantics as design assumptions, RFS provided some features that could not be supported by NFS. RFS extended remote access to devices such as tape drives and directly supported file locking.

13.1.1 Remote System Calls

RFS used a *remote system call* paradigm as a design framework (Figure 13.1). Each filesystem-related system call on the client *(open, close, read, write, fcntl, link,* and so on) was sent via Remote Procedure Call to the system call interface

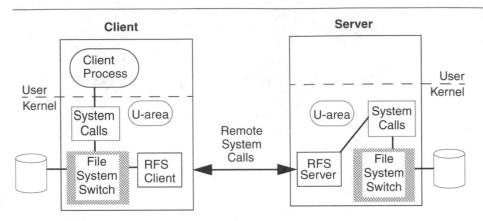

FIGURE 13.1 RFS remote system calls. System calls from a client process that referenced remote files or devices are redirected to the RFS client. It forwards the system call as an RPC to an RFS server. The RFS server impersonates the process on the client (setting up a shadow u-area) and makes a proxy system call.

in the kernel of the server. The arguments and results for each system call were marshaled into an RPC call and reply. XDR was used as a network data representation, but only if the client and server didn't recognize each other as "like" machines. UNIX system calls are evaluated within the context of a user process that includes its UID, GID, current directory, umask, and so on. This context needed to be set up on the remote machine so that the system calls could be executed there as if from a local process.

13.1.2   RFS Naming

Like NFS clients, an RFS client could mount a remote filesystem anywhere in its namespace. Although a shared namespace (like that of AFS or DCE/DFS) was not a goal of RFS, it did attempt to provide a measure of location independence. Instead of naming a remote filesystem with a hostname and pathname (as in an NFS mount command), an RFS server would *advertise* its filesystems with a *resource name* in a name server. An RFS client would mount a named resource, unaware of its precise location. An RFS filesystem could be relocated from one server to another without the need to change the *fstab* files on each client that mounts the filesystem. The following mount commands illustrate the use of a resource name. The first is an NFS mount using a server name and pathname. The second is an RFS mount using a resource name.

```
mount server:/export/home/jane /mnt
mount -d HOMEJANE /mnt
```

RFS used a dedicated name service protocol to map resource names to locations. When receiving an ADVERTISE request from an RFS server, the name server would verify the uniqueness of the resource name before registering the resource in its database. When a client queried a resource name, the name server would return the name of the server that had advertised it. To improve the scalability of the naming scheme for large organizations, clients, servers and name servers were organized into domains. A client could mount a resource from a server in another domain by naming the domain and the resource (e.g., SALES.HOMEJANE).

With an RFS filesystem mounted, a client path that crossed into an RFS filesystem would need special handling. The local system call that was evaluating the path would package the unevaluated remainder of the path and send it in a remote system call to the RFS server to complete the evaluation. The evaluation of an entire pathname is rather different from the one-component-at-a-time evaluation of NFS clients. Although pathname evaluation in a single call could be quite efficient, in practice it created some awkward implementation problems. A pathname that contains .. names might cross back into the client's namespace, requiring the RFS server to abort the evaluation. The *link* system call needed two pathnames, so it was split into two system calls with paths that could be evaluated separately. Since the RFS server could not see mounted filesystems on the client, it was not possible to mount other filesystems within an RFS filesystem.

13.1.3 Security and UID/GID Mapping

Like early versions of NFS, RFS provided no secure means to authenticate users. Access to advertised filesystems was controlled with an access list that enumerated the hostnames of client machines that were permitted to connect to the server. In addition, the server would require a password to be used (in the clear) at connection setup time. NFS used UNIX UID/GID values to identify individuals and assumed that NIS would be used to provide a consistent /etc/passwd database across all clients and servers. RFS allowed clients and servers to use different UID/GID assignments for users and used mapping tables to map UID and GID values back and forth between client and server. As with NFS, the superuser UID of 0 was normally mapped to an invalid value on the server.

13.1.4 Summary

RFS was not a commercial success. With its goal of preserving full UNIX file-system semantics for remote files, its designers chose a remote system call paradigm that presented some difficult problems. The implementation was complex and fragile. The lack of adequate caching of file data and attributes in its initial versions gave it a reputation as a poor performer. In contrast to the robust recovery built into NFS, an RFS server (or network outage) made itself known to clients with application error messages. RFS is no longer available and no longer supported.

13.2   Andrew File System

The Andrew[1] File System (AFS) [Kazar93] was developed at Carnegie-Mellon University to provide a distributed filesystem that would scale to provide file access to a very large number of clients across a university campus. AFS shared some of the NFS design considerations: support UNIX filesystem semantics and do it from within the client kernel so that applications would not need to be modified. AFS is notable for some additional design features. AFS clients cache file data aggressively and rely on server callbacks to maintain cache consistency. AFS supports a shared, location-independent namespace with a single root directory—clients do not mount filesystems individually. Since clients access data in a location-independent way through the shared namespace, system administrators are free to relocate storage volumes from one server to another while the volumes are in use. The location independence also makes it easier for AFS to support replication of read-only filesystems, making it possible to distribute server load and increase data availability. Emphasizing secure operation in a campus environment, AFS uses Kerberos authentication.

13.2.1   File Caching

When an AFS client opens a file for the first time, the client *cache manager* copies file data from the server to a local disk cache (Figure 13.2). Early versions of AFS needed to copy the entire file before the application could have access to it. The file transfer delayed application access to file data and limited the size of files that could fit into the client's cache. The whole file policy was later modified to allow files to be cached in chunks of 64 KB. As well as file data, AFS caches file attributes, directories, and symbolic links. This aggressive data caching is responsible, in a large part, for the scalability of AFS to support very large numbers of clients on a server. Once a file is cached locally, the client need contact the server only to write back changes.

When caching data from the server, the client's cache manager obtains a *callback* promise from the server. If a file or directory changes on the server, the server will send a callback message to each client that is holding a cached copy of the data, signaling that the cached data are no longer valid. The callback mechanism allows the client to operate on cached data for very long periods of time without contacting the server. Contrast this with the GETATTR consistency check at each NFS file open that is required for close-to-open cache consistency (section 8.14.3).

---

1. Named after the benefactors of Carnegie-Mellon University, Andrew Carnegie and Andrew Mellon.

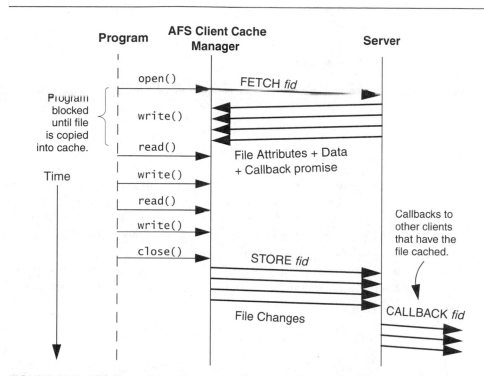

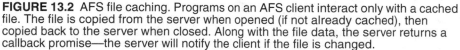

FIGURE 13.2 AFS file caching. Programs on an AFS client interact only with a cached file. The file is copied from the server when opened (if not already cached), then copied back to the server when closed. Along with the file data, the server returns a callback promise—the server will notify the client if the file is changed.

It is possible that during one of these extended periods a network problem might prevent callback messages from reaching one or more clients—leaving the client working on stale cached data. The client limits this period of potential inconsistency by sending a *probe* message to the server every 10 minutes. The reply to the probe allows the client to detect any missing callbacks and restore cache consistency. Since the AFS server needs to record client state—the per-file callback promises it has issued to each client—it keeps this state on stable storage so that it is not lost if the server crashes and reboots.

AFS file caching does not attempt to match the single-copy cache consistency semantics of Spritely NFS (section 12.1). After opening a file in the cache, an AFS client program can read and write the file with no server communication. Changes to a cached file are not transmitted to the server until after the file is closed. If several AFS clients concurrently update cached copies of the same file, the changes from the last client to close the file will overwrite changes from other clients. This policy is different from that of Spritely NFS or NQNFS, which allow only one client at a time to have write access to a file. AFS relaxes a strict one-copy cache consistency requirement to reduce client-server communication and increase the number of clients that can be supported by a server.

13.2.2   Shared Namespace

The NFS protocol itself enforces no shared namespace. Each client has its own namespace and is allowed to mount NFS filesystems anywhere in it. In practice, most NFS clients these days use an automounter to establish shared namespaces under directories like /home. All AFS clients access files in a shared namespace organized under a single directory: /afs (Figure 13.3). The first level of the AFS namespace names an AFS *cell,* a collection of AFS servers that are administered at a specific site. A cell is named with an Internet domain name, for instance, andrew.cmu.edu. The cell administrator maintains the namespace for each cell. The home directory for George at Stanford might be /afs/cs.stanford.edu/home/george, while Jane at Carnegie-Mellon might have /afs/andrew.cmu.edu/home/jane.

The directories and files in the Andrew shared namespace are collected into *volumes.* A volume is more flexible than a disk partition: it can be moved

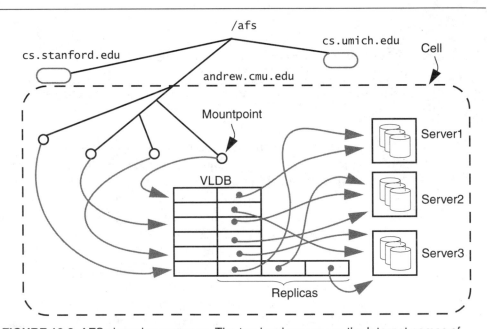

FIGURE 13.3 AFS shared namespace. The top-level names are the Internet names of cells, collections of clients, and servers administered independently at a site. Within a cell, volumes, located on AFS servers, are mounted by clients as their mountpoints are encountered in the namespace. The VLDB is a database that provides a mapping from volume numbers to server locations. A single VLDB is shown in the diagram, but in reality it is replicated across the servers. A VLDB entry for a replicated volume will have multiple locations.

from one server to another, and it can be easily cloned or replicated and changed in size. AFS directories and files are located with a 96-bit file identifier (fid).

```
        32 bits              32 bits              32 bits
   ┌─────────────┐      ┌─────────────┐      ┌─────────────┐
   │             │      │             │      │             │
┌──────────────────┬──────────────────┬──────────────────┐
│  Volume Number   ║   Inode Number   │    Uniquifier     │
└──────────────────┴──────────────────┴──────────────────┘
```

The fid serves the same purpose as the NFS filehandle. The AFS client performs component-by-component pathname evaluation and obtains a fid from the server. The fid is then used to perform operations on the file. The volume number identifies a volume with a number that is unique across all volumes in the cell. The inode number uniquely identifies a file entry in the volume equivalent to a UNIX inode number. Since inode numbers can be reused, the uniquifier serves the same purpose as the generation number that is embedded in some NFS filehandles—it identifies the instance of a file that is assigned to the inode.

Each AFS server has a volume location database (VLDB) that is replicated on each server. This database maps each volume to a server location somewhere in the cell. Clients keep cache entries from the VLDB so that references to recently used volumes can be evaluated without checking the server's VLDB. The AFS volumes are connected into the /afs namespace through the use of *mountpoints*, nodes in the shared namespace that contain a fid for the volume that is to be mounted there. When a client's cache manager encounters a mountpoint during pathname evaluation, it uses the fid at the mountpoint to locate the volume that is to be mounted there.

13.2.3 Volume Movement

Because an AFS volume is a self-contained, location-independent collection of files, it is mobile. AFS volumes support a *clone* operation that allows a *snapshot* of the file data to be taken and frozen. Cloning facilitates volume relocation: the snapshot data are moved first while the original volume remains accessible for READ and WRITE. Then the original volume is cloned again and frozen briefly for update while the remaining changes are moved. Finally, the VLDB entry for the volume is updated to reference the new location and the volume is made accessible at the new location. The callback promises associated with open files on the volume are not moved to the new location. Instead, the server at the old location sends a "break callback promises" message so that the client will reestablish callback promises with the server at the new location.

13.2.4   Read-only Replication

AFS supports read-only replication of volumes through volume cloning and the VLDB. A VLDB entry for a replicated volume can indicate the location of a read-write master volume and one or more read-only replicas. The replica volumes are created by multiple clones of the read-write master volume. As changes are made to the master volume, or at regular intervals (perhaps daily or weekly), volumes are cloned and distributed to multiple servers. If a replica volume becomes unavailable (because of server crash or network failure), the client can switch to another replica in its cached VLDB entry. Since the files in a replica volume are read-only to clients and are updated only by a clone of the entire volume, a single *volumewide* callback can be issued to clients of the volume.

13.2.5   Security

The AFS developers chose not to rely on a trusted host model, as used in NFS AUTH_SYS or RFS. Instead, Kerberos security [Steiner+88] is used to authenticate all client transactions with servers. With Kerberos, passwords are never transmitted between client and server. Instead, a secure *key distribution center* (KDC) server is used to hold passwords. When an AFS client needs to access a server for the first time, it first authenticates itself to the KDC to obtain a *ticket-granting ticket*, then contacts the KDC again to obtain a ticket for the server. With these tickets it can construct a *session key* that allows the server to authenticate the client. A similar procedure is used by NFS implementations of Kerberos security.

Rather than limit server access control to UNIX permission bits, the AFS server can associate an access control list with selected directories to assign access permissions to individual users or groups of users. An AFS ACL can be created, deleted, or modified by any authorized client.

13.2.6   Summary

AFS was developed with the goal of providing remote filesystem access to very large numbers of clients. This scalability is achieved by aggressively caching files on client disks and minimizing client-server interaction. Each client has a consistent view of a shared namespace that provides location-independent access data in volumes that can be moved and replicated. Kerberos is used to authenticate users, and access to files is controlled with access control lists.

AFS has been deployed on a large scale at many sites and is available on many different versions of UNIX. Implementations are available also for non-UNIX clients such as DOS PC's and Macintosh. AFS also forms the basis of the Coda filesystem [Satyanaryanan+90]. Coda allows mobile clients to access cached data while disconnected from the network.

13.3 DCE/DFS

DCE/DFS (henceforth referred to as DFS) used AFS as the basis for an improved distributed filesystem and utilized the distributed computing technologies selected for use by the Open Software Foundation™ as the building blocks of its Distributed Computing Environment (DCE). AFS used an RPC mechanism called Rx that was developed specifically for AFS at Carnegie-Mellon University. DFS replaced this RPC mechanism with DCE/RPC, derived from Apollo Computer's NCS 2.0. DFS redesigned the server to provide a virtual filesystem interface called VFS+ that allowed a variety of filesystems to be accessible to DFS clients. A new filesystem called Episode™ provided enhancements that included fast recovery (through a transaction log), access control lists for files and directories, and *filesets* that supported data portability and cloning operations. The biggest change to the AFS model was the extension of callbacks to a token scheme that provided single-copy cache consistency.

13.3.1 Cache Consistency with Tokens

When an AFS client downloads a file into its cache, it receives a callback promise from the server. The server will notify the client if the server's copy of a file (or directory) is changed. Because a client's changes to cached file data are not written back to the server until the file is closed, other clients that are caching the same file will not see the changes immediately. This behavior is equivalent to the close-to-open consistency provided by NFS clients: there is no guarantee that clients will see the latest data written to a file.

DFS followed a strategy similar to that of Spritely NFS (section 12.1). It sought to improve the cache consistency of AFS by guaranteeing single-copy semantics: each client would see the most recent change to a file. A DFS server has a *token manager* that controls client caching by issuing or revoking tokens that grant permission to perform specific operations. When a client wishes to cache a file or directory, it issues a request to the server's token manager for a particular class of token that reflects the client's use of the file. Each token class comprises a number of types: a data token has *read* and *write* types. A client may need tokens of several classes to carry out a file operation; for instance, to append data to a file a client may need an open token to open the file, a data write token to write data to it, and a status token to change the size of the file (Table 13.1).

Tokens of any class are compatible with tokens of any other class, but tokens of the same class can be incompatible with each other. For instance, a conflict exists if two clients attempt to obtain data write tokens to the same range of bytes in a file. When the server's token manager detects that a token request conflicts with one or more tokens that have already been issued, it sends a revocation request to clients that are holding conflicting tokens. If the

TABLE 13.29 Token Classes

Token class	Client capability
Data	Cache some range of bytes in the file. A read data token allows read-only access to the data. A write data token allows the client to update the range of bytes without writing it back from the cache.
Status	Change a file attribute such as the owner. If a client appends data to a file, increasing its size, then it needs a status token because it is changing the size attribute.
Lock	Lock or unlock some range of bytes within a file.
Open	Open a file for a particular use. If a file is open for executing, the server will prevent another client from opening the file for writing.

clients are holding data write tokens and have cached writes pending, then they will flush those writes back to the server before responding to the token revocation request.

When a server issues a token, it associates a *lifetime* value for which the token is valid. If the lifetime limit is reached, the token expires and the server need not call back to the client to revoke the token if a conflict arises. The token lifetime ensures that a client crash will not indefinitely deny access to a file. The server also associates a *host lifetime* with each client that is holding tokens. If the server receives no messages from the client for a period bound by the host lifetime, then it will assume that the client is dead and invalidate its tokens. This requirement for the client to contact the server within the host lifetime interval is useful for server recovery. If the server crashes and loses all knowledge of the tokens it has issued, it enters a *grace period* on restart where it denies access for new tokens, accepting only attempts by clients to recover token state for those tokens issued before the crash. The grace period is long enough (a few minutes) to allow clients to detect the crashed server through their keep-alive poll for host lifetime and recover their token state.

13.3.2   DFS Namespace

In common with AFS, DFS uses a shared namespace implemented through a cell directory service (CDS). Rather than using /afs as the root, CDS names begin with /... (three dots). With a few exceptions, the rest of the namespace is managed in a way similar to that of AFS. The next component in a shared pathname identifies the namespace of a particular cell, followed by an fs component that identifies the DFS *filespace*—names of DFS files and directories. Various nodes within the namespace are junctions that link to *filesets* via a fileset location database (FLDB) table. A fileset is equivalent to an AFS volume and the FLDB is similar to the AFS VLDB. For instance, a user's home directory in the company abc.com might be named by the path

```
/.../abc.com/fs/usr/george
```

When referencing these names from within a cell, a shorthand form can be used; for example,

```
/:/usr/george
```

The cache manager shares a common feature with the automounter in its handling of variables within names (section 11.8). The names @sys and @host are translated into strings that vary according to features of the client's operating system and hostname. In an environment with different kinds of clients, each client can mount a volume containing files that are specific to its architecture. For instance, executable files under the directory /usr/local might be mapped via a symbolic link to an @sys directory; for example,

```
/usr/local -> /:/fs/@sys/usr/local
```

13.3.3 Episode File System

The Episode File System [Chutani+92] was designed to support features of DFS. It supports UNIX filesystem semantics with the addition of POSIX-style access control lists and features logging techniques to reduce recovery time after server crash. Episode organizes file trees into *filesets*, which are equivalent to AFS volumes. The data in a fileset are organized so that they can be moved easily from one disk to another or to a different machine. An Episode disk partition can accommodate multiple filesets. Filesets support the cloning operation familiar to AFS users, which allows a snapshot of the data to be taken through a *copy-on-write* facility. Fileset cloning is used to support the *lazy replication* feature of DFS, which automatically updates replicas of a writable volume at regular intervals.

DFS is designed to provide access to non-Episode filesystems through the VFS+ interface on the server. However, without Episode, DFS loses many features: access control through ACLs, fileset relocation, and fileset replication.

13.3.4 Summary

DFS is an enhancement to AFS. It preserves the efficient use of client caching to relieve servers and networks from filesystem traffic while supporting single-copy cache consistency through a token scheme. DFS roots its shared namespace in a cell directory service that gives a view of files under a /... directory. Like AFS, Kerberos security is used to authenticate users. The Episode filesystem supports fileset movement and replication and features fast recovery after a server crash.

It is interesting to note that AFS users have been slow to migrate to DFS. Both filesystems continue to be developed and sold by the same company, Transarc, Inc. DFS requires AFS system administrators to learn new administrative commands and copy server data into Episode filesystems. DFS dependency on other DCE components such as the time service and name service imposed an installation overhead in non-DCE environments. Although DFS clients experience single-copy cache consistency, the AFS users seem comfortable with its close-to-open consistency.

13.4   SMB File Access

Server message block (SMB) file access is now commonly referred to as the Common Internet File System protocol (CIFS). SMB is an RPC mechanism that was designed for access of file and print services from a variety of clients and servers. The protocol was developed in the early 1980s by several vendors of PC-based operating systems that included OS/2, Windows NT, Windows 95, and Windows for Workgroups. SMB runs over a NetBIOS session. NetBIOS defines a set of networking services for data across a network. Initially NetBIOS was designed to run over a nonroutable transport layer called NETBEUI, but NetBIOS, and with it SMB, was later adapted to run over TCP/IP [RFC 1001, 1002]. I will refer to CIFS as the file access operations within SMB.

13.4.1   Namespace

A CIFS server periodically broadcasts its offering of shared directories and printers to the local subnet. These broadcasts are monitored by a "master browser" machine that can be queried by users to determine the resources available on the network. There is no location-independent namespace provided directly by CIFS—files are located relative to a particular server. However, an extension to CIFS, the *Dfs* facility on NT 4.0 servers, allows a server to connect together CIFS filesystems from a number of different servers into a single namespace at specific junction points, similar to those of AFS or DCE/DFS. If a CIFS/DFS server receives an OPEN request for a pathname that crosses a junction point, the CIFS/DFS server will return an error. The client will follow up with a GET_DFS_REFERRAL request, and the server will respond with information associated with the junction—the name of a server and its share path as well as the unresolved components in the path. If the filesystem is replicated, then a list of servers and share names will be returned. The client then selects another server from the list and resubmits the original path lookup (Figure 13.4).

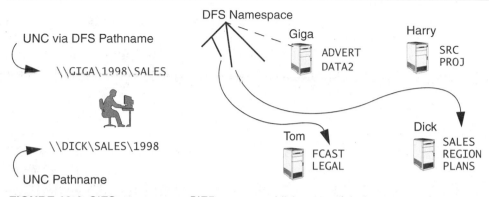

FIGURE 13.4 CIFS namespace. CIFS servers publish parts of their namespace as *shares*. A CIFS client can refer to them directly with UNC names. Alternatively, a DFS server can assemble the shares on a network into a DFS namespace. Clients can use location-independent names through the DFS server, which redirects them to the actual server and share.

13.4.2 Session Setup

On setting up a TCP connection with the server, a CIFS client must first determine which dialect of the protocol the server supports. It sends a NEGPROT command to the server that enumerates the dialects that the client is willing to use and the server returns a list of the dialects it will use with the client. The client then "logs on" to the server with a SessionsetupX command. It either sends a plaintext password or follows a Challenge/Response protocol—the client receives a challenge from the server and returns it encrypted with a secret key.

Once a session is set up, all client state is associated with the session. If the connection breaks, then the server assumes that the client is gone and closes any files it had open. If the server reboots, then all client state is lost and cannot be recovered. Clients must return an error to applications that had files open and begin new sessions. The server records a great deal of client state, not only which files the client has open but also the current file offset.

13.4.3 PC File Semantics

The CIFS filesystem model is strongly tied to that of the DOS/FAT filesystem model. Its DOS-style pathnames must have backslash file separators. Some CIFS calls support only DOS "8.3" names (8-character name plus 3-character extension). File names are looked up by case-insensitive search, and a large number of characters (such as, . / \ [ ] : + | < > = ; , * ?) are reserved for "wildcard" searching. More recent CIFS dialects support the more liberal naming of the NTFS filesystem. Names can be Unicode strings and have as many as 255 characters.

13.4.4   Batched Requests

An interesting feature of CIFS is its use of request batching through an AndX mechanism. Some CIFS requests can be batched into a single message to reduce round-trip time on the network. The individual requests in a batch can depend on results from preceding requests. A file can be looked up, read, and closed in a single transaction.

13.4.5   File Locking

DOS and Windows programs are unique in their association of file locks with all file access. When a DOS or Windows program opens or creates a file, it must specify the kind of access it needs (read or write) as well as a "deny mode," the kind of access that other programs will have while the file is open. For instance, a program can open a file for read-write and deny all other access—effectively an exclusive lock over the entire file. The lock is removed when the file is closed. The CIFS server records the type of access and deny mode for every open file and rejects OPEN or CREATE requests if they would conflict with another program's use of the file.

In addition to these whole-file locks associated with open files, the CIFS protocol supports the locking of byte ranges within a file. Both shared locks (nonexclusive) and exclusive locks are recognized.

13.4.6   Opportunistic Locks

A CIFS client that wishes to cache file data must request an *opportunistic lock* (*oplock*) when the file is opened (Figure 13.5). An *exclusive* oplock will be granted if no other client has the file open. If another client already has the file open, then the exclusive oplock will not be granted and the client must perform all file operations synchronously with the server.

While the oplock is held, applications on the client can read data from the cache, change the file, or apply locks. An exclusive oplock is equivalent to an AFS callback promise—if another client attempts to open the file while the oplock is held, the server will send an *oplock break* callback to break the oplock. If the client no longer needs to cache the file, then it can respond by closing the file. If the file is still in use, then the client must forward any file locks to the server as well as any pending writes in the cache. When the client has completed the oplock break processing, it acknowledges the oplock break to the server so that it can grant access to the file from the other client.

A *batch* oplock allows the client to cache the file for longer periods of time, through multiple file opens and closes. When an exclusive oplock is held, the client will notify the server with a CLOSE request when the application closes a file. If the file is reopened, a new oplock must be obtained. However, if the file is repeatedly opened and closed, then the server will receive a barrage of OPEN

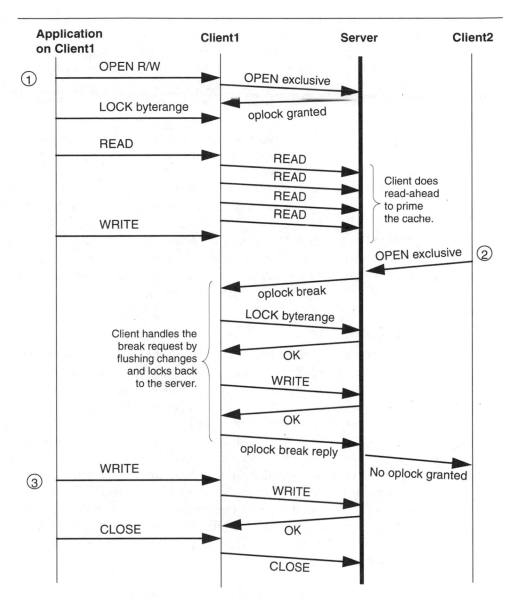

FIGURE 13.5 CIFS caching with an oplock. (1) An application opens a file and the client is granted an oplock. While the file is oplocked, file changes and lock operations can be cached on the client. (2) Another client attempts to oplock the file. The server sends an oplock break to the first client, which flushes its locks and changes back to the server. (3) Since multiple clients now have the file open, all file operations must be synchronous with the server.

and CLOSE requests. A batch oplock is like an exclusive oplock with the added feature that the client is not required to surrender the oplock when the file is closed. Since a batch oplock prevents file OPEN requests from going to the server, there is a risk that a file might be opened successfully but incorrectly if it has been renamed or removed on the server by another client. Hence, if a batch oplock is held, the server will report rename or delete events via an oplock break.

A *Level II* oplock can be shared by many clients for read-only access to a file. The most common example of this is a shared software package containing programs that are read (executed) by many clients but not changed. If a client requests an exclusive oplock while a Level II oplock is held by other clients, the server will send a BREAK request to each client that is holding an oplock on the file. Following the BREAK request, all clients must then cease caching (including the exclusive oplock requestor). If a client has an exclusive oplock and another client attempts to open the file for read, then the first client will receive a *break to Level II* oplock. Rather than cease caching completely, the client reverts to read-only caching.

13.4.7   The Samba Server

No description of the CIFS protocol would be complete without a mention of the Samba server [Blair98]. Samba is a suite of programs that can be run on a UNIX server to provide file and print services for PC clients using the CIFS protocol. The original Samba server was developed by Andrew Tridgell, a researcher in the Department of Computer Science, Australian National University. Because the CIFS protocol is not well documented, he reverse-engineered protocol traces to infer undocumented features of the protocol. Samba is popular because, like NFS, it allows a UNIX server to provide services for PC clients. While PC-NFS must be installed on each client, Samba needs to be installed in only one place: the UNIX server. Samba is available for free download for most UNIX platforms. The source code is also available under GNU Public License. For further information on Samba see www.samba.org.

13.4.8   Summary

CIFS was designed as a file access and printing protocol for DOS PC's. Initially it ran over a nonroutable transport called NetBEUI, but later it was adapted to run over TCP/IP networks. It uses a simple namespace model based on server shares published to browser servers. CIFS is a session-oriented protocol; a client is required to log on to a server using simple password authentication or a more secure cryptographic challenge. CIFS provides no recovery guarantees if the session is terminated through server or network outage. CIFS supports case-insensitive file lookup common to DOS or Windows clients as well as the locking semantics on file open that allow a client to assert "deny" modes. The most interesting feature of CIFS is its opportunistic locking, or oplock, mechanism that allows clients to cache directory and file data without compromising cache consistency. A server implementation for UNIX systems called Samba is popular and available for free download.

Chapter 14

PC NFS

The implementation of NFS by PC clients is an interesting case study in the success of NFS as a cross-platform protocol. The PC clients referred to in this chapter are assumed to be using DOS-derived operating systems: Windows 95, Windows NT, and OS/2. DOS and UNIX file accesses share many common features. Both organize their files and directories into one or more hierarchical trees where any file or directory in the tree can be referenced by a pathname. Files are generally considered to be uninterpreted byte sequences that support byte-range file locking. However, there are some significant differences in file naming and attributes that need to be resolved.

PC clients also make use of the PCNFSD protocol to provide authentication and file printing services that are not normally available on PC clients. Two versions of PCNFSD are described here, as well as an alternative protocol called BWNFSD—now called HCLNFSD.

14.1 File Naming

The NFS protocol allows files to be named by a sequence of names that make up a path. The protocol is careful not to require that pathnames be supported as entities within the protocol itself. A pathname is evaluated with a sequence of LOOKUP requests. Component-by-component evaluation makes it unnecessary for the protocol to reserve a character to separate the components in a pathname. It is fortunate for PC-UNIX interoperability because UNIX uses a forward slash separator, a/b/c, whereas PC clients use a backslash, a\b\c.

UNIX servers are *case-sensitive* and *case-preserving*. This means that a UNIX server sees ABC123 and abc123 as two different filenames—it is sensitive to differences in case. When a name is assigned to a new file, the UNIX server will preserve the cases of the characters in the filename; it will not map to uppercase or lowercase. DOS clients are *case-insensitive* and are not *case-preserving*. This means that a DOS client cannot distinguish the name ABC123 from abc123. If the file Abc123 is created, instead of preserving the cases, it will map all characters to uppercase—ABC123. A Windows client is *case-insensitive* and *case-preserving*. Like a DOS client, it cannot tell the difference between ABC123 and abc123, but it will preserve the cases in a filename—it will not map lowercase to uppercase.

The names within a UNIX or Windows path can be any sequence of up to 255 characters excluding the separator slash. DOS clients are restricted in their choice of names to an "8.3" format: the *name* is limited to 8 characters plus a dot and an *extension* of up to 3 characters. In addition, the characters .,+[]*?:\/;=<> are ruled illegal. These restrictions can create problems for DOS clients that access files on a UNIX or Windows server. How can long names be represented in 8.3 format and what can be done about the characters that are legal for UNIX but illegal for DOS or Windows? The DOS client uses an algorithm to map UNIX names to DOS equivalents, as follows:

1. The special names . and .. are not mapped.
2. Lowercase characters are mapped to uppercase characters and upper-case to lowercase: Abc123.txt becomes aBC123.TXT.
3. If the name is now a legal DOS name and has no lowercase characters, then no further mapping is required.
4. If the NFS name has a legal DOS extension (up to 3 characters, none illegal), the extension is preserved.
5. The NFS name is truncated to leave just the first 5 characters, and illegal DOS characters are mapped to tilde (~). If the name is shorter than 5 characters, it is extended to a full 5 characters by the addition of tildes.
6. The 5-character name is extended to 8 characters by adding a tilde and two legal DOS characters that are chosen to make the name unique within the directory (shown as *XX* in Table 14.1).
7. If the NFS name had a valid DOS extension, it is appended following a dot.

TABLE 14.1 Mapping Table

NFS name	DOS mapped name	Rules
abc123.txt	ABC123.TXT	2, 3
lengthyname	LENGT~*XX*	2, 5
CORE	CORE	2, 3
core	CORE~~*XX*	2, 5, 6
.cshrc	~CSHR~*XX*	2, 5, 6
whitepaper.ps	WHITE~*XX*.PS	2, 4, 5, 6, 7
index.html	INDEX~*XX*	2, 5, 6

The making of a unique name in step 6 through addition of *XX* characters presents an interesting challenge. The two uniqueness characters must not be randomly chosen because the name must persist from one day to the next, even if the client is rebooted and the mapping table is lost. The Beame and Whiteside (now Hummingbird, Inc.) PCNFS client solved the problem neatly by using the READDIR cookie value associated with the directory entry as the basis for generating the *XX* characters.

The DOS-mapped name and the NFS name are stored in a mapping table. If a user types a DOS-mapped name, the client will translate it to the NFS name via the mapping table before sending a LOOKUP request to the server. DOS clients allow the use of *wildcard* characters to assist in directory searches. For instance, one of the illegal DOS filename characters, the asterisk, can be used as a wildcard character to represent any sequence of characters in a DOS name. The name *.TXT will match all names in a directory that have an extension of .TXT. The NFS protocol does not acknowledge wildcard characters. A LOOKUP of a name containing one or more wildcard characters can return only a single filehandle—the server will not search the directory for multiple matches. A DOS client that needs to wildcard search a directory first copies the entire directory from the NFS server and searches it locally on the DOS client. UNIX shell programs conduct wildcard searches the same way.

14.2　File Attributes

DOS supports only a small set of file attributes compared with the POSIX set of 13 or so file attributes provided in the NFS `fattr` structure returned by the GETATTR request (Table 14.2). Some of the NFS attributes like file *size* and

TABLE 14.2 DOS File Attributes

DOS file attribute	NFS mapping
File size	`size`
Modification time	`mtime`
Read-only	Set if the write bit in the `mode` attribute is not set. The client needs to determine whether the user, group, or other write bit applies, depending on the file's owner and group. Server ACLs may make this determination unreliable. Reliable read-only indication can be returned by the NFS version 3 ACCESS procedure.
Hidden	If set, it indicates whether the file will appear in directory listings. The attribute is set if the NFS name begins with a dot, e.g., `.login`.
Archive	Used by DOS utilities to determine whether a file needs to be archived. The attribute is cleared (set to 0) when the file is archived and set back to 1 if the file is modified. Since there is no UNIX equivalent, it is set to 1 for all NFS files.
Directory	Set if the file `mode` attribute indicates that the file is a directory.
System	No NFS equivalent—not set.

mtime have DOS equivalents. Others have no mapping or an indirect mapping.

14.3   Text Files

The NFS protocol handles file content as an *uninterpreted* sequence of bytes. The insensitivity of NFS to file content is a desirable feature for most file formats. For ASCII text files, however, there are some minor differences in the representation of the end-of-line character that can have unexpected effects. DOS uses two characters to terminate each line: carriage return followed by newline <CR><LF>. UNIX uses only the newline character <LF>, and Macintosh computers use only the carriage return character <CR>.

A DOS program that displays a UNIX text file on an NFS filesystem mounted from a UNIX server may produce an unusual effect if it receives text lines that have only a single newline. The text

```
oneone was a racehorse
twotwo was one two
oneone won one race
twotwo won one too
```

might appear as:

```
oneeone was a racehorse
                    twotwo was one two
                                   oneone won one race
                                                  twotwo won one too
```

In practice, text-handling programs on both DOS/Windows and UNIX systems are normally tolerant of variations in end-of-line characters. For instance, a UNIX EMACS text editor will recognize a DOS file and provide the option of storing the edited file with DOS <CR><LF> or UNIX <LF>.

14.4   Symbolic Links

The NFS protocol supports UNIX style symbolic links. A symbolic link is a special file that contains only a pathname. Any process that attempts to access the symbolic link as a file or directory will be redirected automatically to the target of the pathname in the symbolic link. The pathname in a symbolic link can be any pathname that is valid on the server. A relative pathname will be evaluated relative to the directory that holds the symbolic link. For instance, the UNIX command

```
ln -s prog_version_3.2 /usr/bin/prog
```

creates a symbolic link. If a program attempts to open /usr/bin/prog, it will be redirected automatically to the file /usr/bin/prog_version_3.2. When a UNIX NFS client encounters a symbolic link, it will combine the link path-name with the original link path to form a new path, then evaluate the link path, as it does for any UNIX pathname, one component at a time with LOOKUP requests to the server.

Since UNIX symbolic links are not supported by PC operating systems like Windows, DOS, or OS/2, the PC-NFS client software must itself evaluate any symbolic links encountered on the server. To do this, it must follow the UNIX pathname convention of using a slash separator and handle the long names and case sensitivity. The client's evaluation must also allow for a link that crosses from one mounted filesystem to another. For instance, if the client has mounted the server's /usr/bin on D: and /usr/sbin on E:, then the sym-bolic link /usr/bin/prog -> /usr/sbin/prog must be followed by the client to the file on E:.

There still could be a difficulty if the destination filesystem for the sym-bolic link is not yet mounted by the client. The Hummingbird, Inc., NFS Mae-stro client takes a straightforward approach to symbolic link evaluation. It simply sends the link path back to the server via the MOUNT protocol. The MOUNT daemon on the server evaluates the path and returns a filehandle (Figure 14.1).

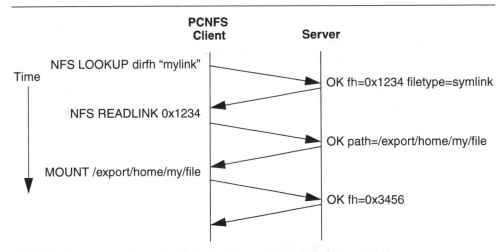

FIGURE 14.1 Evaluation of a symbolic link using the MOUNT protocol.

14.5   PCNFSD Protocol

The PCNFSD protocol provides some services for PC clients that are normally built into UNIX clients (Figure 14.2). If you walk up to a UNIX system, the first thing you do is authenticate yourself by logging in. You give your login name and password and the UNIX system obtains a UID and GID for you from a local /etc/passwd file or from a name service like NIS or NIS+. A PC client has no concept of an initial login step, though if connected to a network, it will pop up a network login prompt. With the PCNFSD protocol, a PC client can convert the login name and password from this network login prompt into a UID, GID, and group list that it can use to construct an AUTH_SYS credential to access an NFS server. For instance, if I log in as "brent" with password "zyzzygy" the PCNFSD protocol will return my UID and GID: 3497, 10.

The PCNFSD protocol provides another valuable service for PCs. The UNIX clients will use the 1p or 1pr commands to spool files to a local network printer server. Although products are now available that let PC clients print directly to these printers, PCNFSD provides a convenient way to spool files to network printers without installation of network printer software on the client. Version 1 of PCNFSD provides a couple of simple procedures to allow clients to submit printer jobs via the NFS server. Version 2 considerably expands this printing support by providing procedures to display and manage the printer queue.

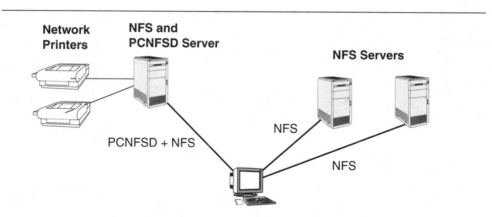

FIGURE 14.2 A PC client uses the PCNFSD protocol to obtain AUTH_SYS credential information from a server. Once the client has the credential set up, it can access any NFS server—the PCNFSD service does not have to be run on every NFS server. The PCNFSD protocol also provides access to printers through the PCNFSD server. The server must export an NFS filesystem writable to the client so that the client can create printer spool files on the server.

The protocol is unusual in that the server is distributed in source form ready to be compiled for whatever server it needs to be installed on. While the server implementation of the PCNFSD_AUTH procedure is easily managed with a call to a standard UNIX function like getpwnam(), the printer interfaces are less certain. Some systems may use the Berkeley UNIX lpr command for printing while others may use the System V lp command or something entirely different. The availability of server source gives a system integrator the ability to tailor the server to its environment.

14.5.1 Printing

PCNFSD provides a printing service that uses a combination of the PCNFSD protocol and the NFS protocol (Figure 14.3). The PC client first obtains the name of a spool directory on the server that is to be used to create printer output files.

The PCNFSD server exports this directory to the PC clients with write access. Each client establishes its own spool area within this export via the

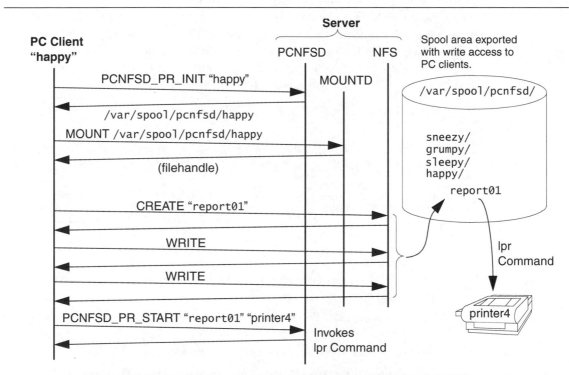

FIGURE 14.3 PCNFSD printing. The client uses the PCNFSD_PR_INIT procedure to obtain the name of the server's spool area which it then mounts. After creating a spool file on the server with NFS writes, it invokes PCNFSD_PR_START to print the spooled file.

PCNFSD_PR_INIT or PCNFSD2_PR_INIT procedure. The server returns the name of the client's private spool directory, which it then mounts. Thereafter, PC applications create spool files in the client's spool directory. When the client has established that printing is completed for each spool file, it calls the server's PCNFSD_PR_START procedure so that the server will hand off the spool file to the desired printer. When printing is complete, the server removes the spool file.

The PCNFSD printing protocol presents some dangers on an insecure network. The protocol uses no authentication, printing clients are assumed to have writable NFS access to the server's printer spool directory, and commands containing client-created filenames are invoked on the server. Evil clients could create files containing shell metacharacters that could be used to invoke unwanted actions on the server as superuser. The PCNFSD server checks all client-provided names for possible UNIX shell metacharacters. Any of the characters ; |&<>''!?*()[]^/". are considered to be suspicious and names containing them will be rejected.

In the descriptions for versions 1 and 2 of the protocol in sections 14.6 and 14.7, the type options is used for passing implementation-specific print control information. The option string is a set of printable ASCII characters. The first character should be ignored by the server; it is reserved for client use. The second character specifies the type of data in the print file. The types in Table 14.3 are defined (an implementation may define additional values).

If diablo data (type d) is specified, a formatting specification string will be appended. This specification has the form

```
ppnnnbbb
```

where pp is the pitch (10, 12, or 15), nnn is the normal font, and bbb is the bold font to be used—encoded as in Table 14.4. For example, the string nd10hrbcob

TABLE 14.3 Options Types

Option letter	Type of data in print file
p	PostScript data. The client will ensure that a valid PostScript header is included.
d	Diablo 630 data.
x	Generic printable ASCII text. The client will have filtered out all nonprintable characters other than CR, LF, TAB, BS, and VT.
r	Raw print data. The client performs no filtering.
u	User-defined. Reserved for custom extensions. A vanilla PCNFSD server will treat this as equivalent to r.

TABLE 14.4 Font Codes

Font	Code	Font	Code	Font	Code
Courier	crn	Helvetica	hrn	Times Roman	trn
Courier Bold	crb	Helvetica Bold	hrb	Times Bold	trb
Courier Oblique	con	Helvetica Oblique	hon	Times Italic	ton
Courier Bold Oblique	cob	Helvetica Bold Oblique	hob	Times Bold Italic	tob

specifies that the print data are in Diablo 630 format (d), it should be printed at 10 pitch, normal text should be printed in Helvetica-Bold (hrb), and bold text should be printed in Courier Bold Oblique (cob).

14.5.2 Comment Strings

Version 2 of the protocol includes a comment string with each set of call arguments and reply results. Generally, it is unused, but it may be used to pass an uninterpreted text string that may be displayed to a system administrator or end user or used for custom extensions to the PCNFSD protocol.

14.5.3 Transport and Authentication

PCNFSD uses a program number of 150001. The protocol can be used via UDP or TCP transports. Since call and reply messages are generally short and infrequent, the use of UDP is favored because it means that a server with a large number of clients does not have to maintain a large number of TCP connections. The protocol requires no specific RPC authentication—clients normally use AUTH_NONE. The lack of user authentication carries a risk of mischief for the printing procedures of version 2 where any user can manipulate the printer queue or cancel any print job.

14.6 PCNFSD Version 1

Version 1 of PCNFSD is notable for its simplicity (Table 14.5). The most commonly used procedure is PCNFSD_AUTH to authenticate the PC user and provide AUTH_SYS credential information. To use the printing procedures, the client uses PCNFSD_PR_INIT to obtain the spool directory to be used, creates the file to be printed in this directory using the NFS protocol, then calls PCNFSD_PR_START to print the file. There is no facility to examine or manage the printer queue. These features were added in version 2.

TABLE 14.5 Summary of PCNFSD Version 1 Procedures

Number	Name	Description	Section
0	PCNFSD_NULL	NULL procedure	
1	PCNFSD_AUTH	Perform user authentication	14.6.1, page 388
2	PCNFSD_PR_INIT	Prepare for remote printing	14.6.2, page 389
3	PCNFSD_PR_START	Submit job for printing	14.6.3, page 390

14.6.1   Procedure 1: PCNFSD_AUTH—Perform User Authentication

Description

Perform user authentication—map username and password into UID, GID.

```
Arguments                          Results
string<32>    ident;               uint32    status;
string<64>    passwd;              uint32    uid;
                                   uint32    gid;
```

Arguments

`ident`

> The encoded login name of the user to be authenticated. The name is obscured from casual viewers of network traffic by exclusive OR-ing each byte of the name with the value 0x5b and then AND-ing with 0x7f. The server reverses the process on the obscured name. Note that this process works only for 7-bit ASCII names.

`passwd`

> An encoded password for authentication. The server should decode the password as described for the `ident` argument.

Results

`status`

> See Errors.

`uid`

> The UID of the authenticated user. The UID is expected to be a number in the range 101 to 60,002. UID values up to 100 are assumed reserved for system processes.

`gid`

> The GID value assigned to the user by the server.

Implementation

This procedure is used to obtain an AUTH_SYS credential for NFS use. Although the login name and password are obscured with an exclusive OR pattern, it is trivial for a network sniffer program to collect login names and passwords off the network. The PCNFSD protocol should be used only on secure networks.

This procedure does not return all the information required to build a complete AUTH_SYS credential. As well as a UID and GID, the credential includes a group list, a list of the groups that the user belongs to—in addition to GID. This omission was corrected in version 2.

Errors

AUTH_RES_OK	0	Indicates that the server was able to verify the ident and password successfully.
AUTH_RES_FAKE	1	The server wishes to indicate that the verification failed but the server has synthesized acceptable values for UID and GID that the client may use if it wishes.
AUTH_RES_FAIL	2	A verification failure occurred.

14.6.2 Procedure 2: PCNFSD_PR_INIT—Prepare for Remote Printing

Description

Prepare for remote printing: identify exporting spool directory.

Arguments		*Results*	
string<64>	client;	uint32	status;
string<64>	printername;	string<64>	spoolname;

Arguments

client

This argument is the client's hostname that is used by the server in constructing a spool directory name for the client.

printername

The name of the printer the client wishes to use.

Results

status

See Errors.

`spoolname`

The directory that the server has assigned for the client's spool files.

Implementation

The server is expected to create a spool directory for the client. The client will then use this directory to create spool files for printing.

Errors

PI_RES_OK	0	The operation was performed successfully.
PI_RES_NO_SUCH_PRINTER	1	The printer name is not recognized.
PE_RES_FAIL	2	The printer name is valid but the operation cannot be performed.

14.6.3   Procedure 3: PCNFSD_PR_START—Submit Print Job

Description

Submit a spooled print job for printing: the print data are in a file created in the spool directory.

Arguments		*Results*	
string<64>	client;	uint32	status;
string<64>	printername;		
string<64>	username;		
string<64>	spoolname;		
string<64>	options;		

Arguments

`client`

The client's hostname, as used in the PCNFSD_PR_INIT call.

`printername`

The name of the printer to be used.

`username`

The name of the user who is printing the job.

`spoolname`

The name of the spool file in the client's spool directory.

`options`

See section 14.5.1.

Results

status

See Errors.

Errors

PS_RES_OK	0	The server has started printing the job.
PS_RES_ALREADY	1	Since it is possible that the reply to a PCNFSD_PR_START may be lost, a retransmitted request may return this error, indicating that the job has already begun printing.
PS_RES_NULL	2	The spool file was empty.
PS_RES_NO_FILE	3	The spool file cannot be found.
PS_RES_FAIL	4	A general failure.

14.7 PCNFSD Version 2

Version 2 adds a number of important improvements to the protocol (Table 14.6). The PCNFSD2_AUTH procedure includes a group list in the result. The list contains UNIX groups that the user belongs to and is a required part of the AUTH_SYS credential. The PCNFSD2_MAPID procedure was added to make it easier for clients to list usernames rather than UID numbers in directory listings. Most of the new procedures in version 2 were added to support printer management features of Windows 3.1 for NFS-attached printers. These procedures are implemented on the server by invoking a printer management command like the Berkeley lpr, lpq, and lprm commands.

14.7.1 Procedure 1: PCNFSD2_INFO—Determine Supported Services

Description

Determine which services are supported by this implementation of PCNFSD.

Arguments		Results	
string<255>	version;	string<255>	vers;
string<255>	comment;	string<255>	comment;
		int32<32>	facilities;

Arguments

version

The version of the protocol to be queried.

TABLE 14.6 Summary of PCNFSD Version 2 Procedures

Number	Name	Description	Section
0	PCNFSD2_NULL	Null procedure	
1	PCNFSD2_INFO	Determine supported services	14.7.1, page 391
2	PCNFSD2_PR_INIT	Prepare for remote printing	14.7.2, page 393
3	PCNFSD2_PR_START	Submit job for printing	14.7.3, page 394
4	PCNFSD2_PR_LIST	List printers on server	14.7.4, page 395
5	PCNFSD2_PR_QUEUE	List printer jobs queued	14.7.5, page 396
6	PCNFSD2_PR_STATUS	Determine printer status	14.7.6, page 398
7	PCNFSD2_PR_CANCEL	Cancel print job	14.7.7, page 399
8	PCNFSD2_PR_ADMIN	Printer administration	14.7.8, page 400
9	PCNFSD2_PR_REQUEUE	Change print job queue position	14.7.9, page 401
10	PCNFSD2_PR_HOLD	Hold print job in queue	14.7.10, page 403
11	PCNFSD2_PR_RELEASE	Release hold on print job	14.7.11, page 404
12	PCNFSD2_MAPID	Translate between username and ID	14.7.12, page 405
13	PCNFSD2_AUTH	Perform user authentication	14.7.13, page 407
14	PCNFSD2_ALERT	Send message to server administrator	14.7.14, page 408

comment

See section 14.5.2.

Results

vers

The version of the protocol for which the information is correct.

comment

See section 14.5.2.

facilities

An array of integers that is supposed to describe features of the protocol. Unfortunately, the list has no formal definition within the protocol. The Sun PCNFSD server uses the array to indicate the expected response times (in milliseconds) for various procedures in the protocol. For instance, the first element in the array is assigned to the NULL procedure and the fifteenth position is assigned to PCNFSD2_ALERT. Unsupported procedures are assigned values of −1; for instance, the Sun PCNFSD does not support PCNFSD2_ADMIN, PCNFSD2_REQUEUE, PCNFSD2_HOLD, or PCNFSD2_ RELEASE.

14.7.2   Procedure 2: PCNFSD2_PR_INIT—Prepare for Remote Printing

Description

Prepare for remote printing: identify exporting spool directory.

Arguments			Results	
string<64>	client;		uint32	status;
string<64>	printername;		string<64>	spoolname;
string<255>	comment;		uint32<255>	comment;

Arguments

client

The client's hostname.

printername

The name of the printer to be used.

comment

See section 14.5.2.

Results

status

See Errors.

spoolname

The directory the server has assigned for the client's spool files.

comment

See section 14.5.2.

Implementation

The server is expected to create a spool directory for the client. The client will then use this directory to create spool files for printing.

Errors

PI_RES_OK	0	The operation was performed successfully.
PI_RES_NO_SUCH_PRINTER	1	The printer name is not recognized.
PE_RES_FAIL	2	The printer name is valid but the operation cannot be performed.

14.7.3   Procedure 3: PCNFSD2_PR_START—Submit Job for Printing

Description

Submit a spooled print job for printing: the print data are in a file created in the spool directory.

Arguments		*Results*	
string<64>	client;	uint32	status;
string<64>	printername;	string<255>	printjobid;
string<64>	username;	string<255>	comment;
string<64>	spoolname;		
string<64>	options;		
int32	copies;		
string<255>	comment;		

Arguments

client

  The client's hostname.

printername

  The name of the printer to be used.

username

  The user's name to be assigned to this print job.

spoolname

  The name of the spool file in the client's spool directory.

options

  See section 14.5.1.

copies

  The number of copies to be printed.

comment

  See section 14.5.2.

Results

status

  See Errors.

printjobid

  The server-assigned identifier for the print job.

comment

  See section 14.5.2.

Errors

PS_RES_OK	0	The server has started printing the job.
PS_RES_ALREADY	1	Since it is possible that the reply to a PCNFSD2_PR_START may be lost, a retransmitted request may return this error, indicating that the job has already begun printing.
PS_RES_NULL	2	The spool file was empty.
PS_RES_NO_FILE	3	The spool file cannot be found.
PS_RES_FAIL	4	A general failure.

14.7.4 Procedure 4: PCNFSD2_PR_LIST—List Printers on Server

Description

List all printers known on the server.

Arguments	*Results*	
void;	string<255>	comment;
	list {	
	string<64>	printername;
	string<64>	device;
	string<64>	remhost;
	string<255>	comment;
	}	

Results

comment

   See section 14.5.2.

printers

   A list of printer entries consisting of

     printername

     The name of the printer.

     device

     The device to which the printer is attached (e.g., /dev/lp0).

     remhost

     The hostname of the machine to which the printer is attached. If the printer is attached to the PCNFSD host, then this string is null.

     comment

     See section 14.5.2.

Implementation

The Sun PCNFSD service uses the output of the command `lpstat -v` to obtain this information.

14.7.5   Procedure 5: PCNFSD2_PR_QUEUE—List Printer Jobs Queued

Description

List all or part of the queued jobs for a printer.

Arguments		Results	
string<64>	printername;	uint32	status;
string<64>	system;	string<255>	comment;
string<64>	user;	boolean	just_yours;
boolean	just_mine;	int32	queue_len;
string<64>	comment;	int32	queue_shown;
		list {	
		int32	position;
		string<255>	printjobid;
		string<255>	size;
		string<255>	status;
		string<64>	system;
		string<64>	user;
		string<64>	spoolname;
		string<255>	comment;
		}	

Arguments

`printername`

The name of the printer for which the queue is to be displayed.

`system`

The system to which the printer is attached. Null if it is local to the PCNFSD server.

`user`

The user that owns the job when the listing is restricted to `just_mine`.

`just_mine`

If true, then limit the listing to include only jobs that are owned by the specified `user`.

`comment`

See section 14.5.2.

Results

status

  See Errors.

comment

  See section 14.5.2.

just_yours

  Set to the just_mine argument.

queue_len

  Total number of entries in the print queue, including jobs that are not owned by the user.

queue_shown

  Number of entries in the print queue that are owned by user. If just_mine is not set, then it has the same value as queue_len.

jobs

  A list of print jobs consisting of

  position

  The position in the print queue. The first job is at position 1.

  printjobid

  The identifier for the print job assigned by the print server.

  size

  The size of the print job in bytes.

  status

  A status string assigned by the server (e.g., "waiting").

  system

  The name of the print server.

  user

  The name of the user who owns the print job.

  spoolname

  The name of the spool file to be printed.

  comment

  See section 14.5.2.

Implementation

The Sun PCNFSD obtains this queue information from the `lpstat -P` command for UNIX System V systems and the `lpq -P` command for Berkeley-based UNIX systems. Windows 3.1 clients may call this procedure frequently (every 30 seconds or so), leading to heavy use of the corresponding `lpstat` or `lpq` command on the server if hundreds of clients are connected. The BWNFSD server avoids this problem by running the server command less frequently and caching the results.

Errors

PI_RES_OK	0	The operation was performed successfully.
PI_RES_NO_SUCH_PRINTER	1	The printer name is not recognized.
PE_RES_FAIL	2	The printer name is valid but the operation cannot be performed.

14.7.6   Procedure 6: PCNFSD2_PR_STATUS—Determine Printer Status

Description

Determine the status of a printer.

```
Arguments                              Results
string<64>     printername;            uint32        status;
string<64>     comment;                boolean       avail;
                                       boolean       printing;
                                       int32         queue_len;
                                       boolean       needs_operator;
                                       string<255>   status
                                       string<255>   comment;
```

Arguments

`printername`

  The name of the printer for which status is needed.

`comment`

  See section 14.5.2.

Results

`status`

  See Errors.

`avail`

  True if the printer is available for printing. False if not.

`printing`

True if the printer is currently printing. False if it is idle.

`queue_len`

Number of jobs queued for this printer.

`needs_operator`

True if the printer needs operator attention, for instance, if the printer is out of paper.

`status`

If `needs_operator` is set, then this is the status string that indicates the reason for the problem.

`comment`

See section 14.5.2.

Implementation

The Sun PCNFSD obtains this information from the `lpstat -a` command. For BSD-based systems, it uses the `lpc status` command.

Errors

PI_RES_OK	0	The operation was performed successfully.
PI_RES_NO_SUCH_PRINTER	1	The printer name is not recognized.
PE_RES_FAIL	2	The printer name is valid but the operation cannot be performed.

14.7.7   Procedure 7: PCNFSD2_PR_CANCEL—Cancel a Print Job

Description

```
Arguments                              Results
string<64>    printername;             uint32       status;
string<64>    system;                  string<255>  comment;
string<64>    username;
string<255>   printjobid;
string<64>    comment;
```

Arguments

`printername`

The printer for which the enqueued job is to be canceled.

system

The server that manages the printer.

username

The owner of the job to be canceled.

printjobid

The server-assigned job identifier for the job to be canceled.

comment

See section 14.5.2.

Results

status

See Errors.

comment

See section 14.5.2.

Implementation

On UNIX System Vr4 systems, the Sun PCNFSD uses the /usr/bin/cancel command. On BSD-based systems, it uses the lprm command.

Errors

PC_RES_OK	0	The operation was performed successfully.
PC_RES_NO_SUCH_PRINTER	1	The printer name is not recognized.
PC_RES_NO_SUCH_JOB	2	The job does not exist or is not associated with the specified printer.
PC_RES_NOT_OWNER	3	The user does not have permission to cancel the job.
PC_RES_FAIL	4	The job could not be canceled for an unknown reason.

14.7.8   Procedure 8: PCNFSD2_PR_ADMIN—Printer Administration

Description

```
Arguments                              Results
string<64>    client                   uint32        status;
string<64>    username;                string<255>   comment;
string<64>    printername;
string<64>    comment;
```

Arguments

`system`

The hostname of the system to which the printer is attached.

`username`

The username on whose behalf the administration will be performed.

`printername`

The printer that will be administered.

`comment`

See section 14.5.2.

Implementation

The Sun PCNFSD does not implement this procedure. There is no way to protect the server from printer administration requests submitted by bogus usernames.

Results

`status`

See Errors.

`comment`

See section 14.5.2.

Errors

PI_RES_OK	0	The operation was performed successfully.
PI_RES_NO_SUCH_PRINTER	1	The printer name is not recognized.
PE_RES_FAIL	2	The printer name is valid but the operation cannot be performed.

14.7.9 Procedure 9: PCNFSD2_PR_REQUEUE—Change Print Job Queue Position

Description

```
Arguments                              Results
string<64>    printername              uint32       status;
string<64>    system;                  string<255>  comment;
string<64>    user;
string<255>   printjobid
int32         queue_pos;
string<255>   comment;
```

Arguments

printername

  The name of the printer for which the queue is to be manipulated.

system

  The hostname of the system to which the printer is attached.

user

  The owner of the job that is to be requeued.

printjobid

  The print job identifier assigned by the print server.

queue_pos

  The queue position to which the job is to be moved.

comment

  See section 14.5.2.

Implementation

This procedure is not implemented by the Sun PCNFSD.

Results

status

  See Errors.

comment

  See section 14.5.2.

Errors

PC_RES_OK	0	The operation was performed successfully.
PC_RES_NO_SUCH_PRINTER	1	The printer name is not recognized.
PC_RES_NO_SUCH_JOB	2	The job does not exist or is not associated with the specified printer.
PC_RES_NOT_OWNER	3	The user does not have permission to requeue the job.
PC_RES_FAIL	4	The job could not be requeued for an unknown reason.

14.7.10　Procedure 10: PCNFSD2_PR_HOLD—Hold a Print Job in the Queue

Description

Arguments		*Results*	
string<64>	printername	uint32	status;
string<64>	system;	string<255>	comment;
string<64>	user;		
string<255>	printjobid;		
string<255>	comment;		

Arguments

printername

　The printer for which the job is queued.

system

　The hostname of the system to which the printer is attached.

user

　The owner of the job to be held.

printjobid

　The print job identifier assigned by the print server.

comment

　See section 14.5.2.

Results

status

　See Errors.

comment

　See section 14.5.2.

Implementation

This procedure is not implemented by the Sun PCNFSD.

Errors

PC_RES_OK	0	The operation was performed successfully.
PC_RES_NO_SUCH_PRINTER	1	The printer name is not recognized.
PC_RES_NO_SUCH_JOB	2	The job does not exist or is not associated with the specified printer.

continued

| PC_RES_NOT_OWNER | 3 | The user does not have permission to hold the job. |
| PC_RES_FAIL | 4 | The job could not be canceled for an unknown reason. |

14.7.11   Procedure 11: PCNFSD2_PR_RELEASE—Release Hold on a Print Job

Description

Arguments			Results	
string<64>	printername		uint32	status;
string<64>	system;		string<255>	comment;
string<64>	user;			
string<255>	printjobid;			
string<255>	comment;			

Arguments

printername

   The printer for which the job is queued.

system

   The hostname of the system to which the printer is attached.

user

   The owner of the job to be released.

printjobid

   The print job identifier assigned by the print server.

comment

   See section 14.5.2.

Results

status

   See Errors.

comment

   See section 14.5.2.

Implementation

This procedure is not implemented by the Sun PCNFSD.

Errors

PC_RES_OK	0	The operation was performed successfully.
PC_RES_NO_SUCH_PRINTER	1	The printer name is not recognized.
PC_RES_NO_SUCH_JOB	2	The job does not exist or is not associated with the specified printer.
PC_RES_NOT_OWNER	3	The user does not have permission to release the job.
PC_RES_FAIL	4	The job could not be canceled for an unknown reason.

14.7.12   Procedure 12: PCNFSD2_MAPID—Translate Between Username and ID

Description

```
Arguments                          Results
string<255>   comment              string<255>   comment;
list {                             list {
   uint32     mapreq;                 uint32     mapreq;
   int32      id;                     uint32     maprstat;
   string<64> username;               int32      id;
}                                     string<64> name;
                                   }
```

Arguments

comment

    See section 14.5.2.

mappings

    A list of entries to be mapped consisting of

        mapreq

    Identifies the type of a mapping request.

MAP_REQ_UID	0	Map the UID in the id field to a username in name.
MAP_REQ_GID	1	Map the GID in the id field to a groupname in name.
MAP_REQ_UNAME	2	Map the username in name to a UID in id.
MAP_REQ_GNAME	3	Map the group name in name to a GID in id.

`id`

Holds a UID or GID for MAP_REQ_UID or MAP_REQ_GID mappings.

`name`

Holds a username or group name for MAP_REQ_UNAME or MAP_REQ_GNAME mappings.

Results

`comment`

See section 14.5.2.

`mappings`

A list of mapped entries consisting of

`mapreq`

The type of mapping—taken from the request.

`maprstat`

The result of the mapping request.

MAP_RES_OK	0	Successful mapping.
MAP_RES_UNKNOWN	1	The name or ID to be mapped does not exist.
MAP_RES_DENIED	2	The caller does not have permission to do the mapping.

`id`

A mapped UID or GID.

`name`

A mapped username or group name.

Implementation

This procedure is used by PCNFSD clients that wish to display directory listings that indicate the owner of each file in string form. The NFS file attributes that are returned as the result of GETATTR, LOOKUP, or READDIRPLUS requests contain only a numeric UID or GID value to identify the owner or group of a directory entry. With a single MAPID call, the client can obtain the strings corresponding to these numeric IDs. The reverse mappings (from name to ID) are less useful but are included for completeness.

The Sun PCNFSD uses the `getpwuid()`, `getgrgid()`, `getpwnam()`, and `getgrnam()` functions in the C library to carry out these mappings.

14.7.13 Procedure 13: PCNFSD2_AUTH—Perform User Authentication

Description

Arguments			Results	
string<64>	client		uint32	status;
string<32>	ident;		uint32	uid;
string<64>	password;		uint32	gid;
string<255>	comment;		uint32<16>	gids;
			string<255>	homedir;
			int32	def_umask;
			string<255>	comment;

Arguments

client

The hostname of the client requesting the authentication.

ident

The encoded login name of the user to be authenticated. The name is obscured from casual viewers of network traffic by exclusive OR-ing each byte of the name with the value 0x5b and then AND-ing with 0x7f. The server reverses the process on the obscured name. Note that this process works only for 7-bit ASCII names.

password

The password of the user to be authenticated. This string is also obscured.

comment

See section 14.5.2.

Results

status

See Errors.

uid

The UID of the authenticated user. The UID is expected to be a number in the range 101 to 60,002. UID values up to 100 are assumed reserved for system processes.

gid

The GID of the authenticated user.

gids

An array of up to 16 groups to which the user may belong.

homedir

The user's home directory. If this string is returned, it will be in the form *servername : path,* which may be used to mount the user's home directory on the PC client.

def_umask

The is the default umask value to be used in determining the permissions of new files or directories. The umask is applied to file mode bits such that any bit that is set in the umask value will turn off the corresponding bit in the file mode. For instance, if a program attempts to create a file with a file mode of octal 777 (read, write, and execute permission for owner, group, and others), then a umask value of octal 033 will turn off write and execute permissions for group and others.

comment

See section 14.5.2.

Errors

AUTH_RES_OK	0	Indicates that the server was able to verify the ID and password successfully.
AUTH_RES_FAKE	1	The server wishes to indicate that the verification failed but the server has synthesized acceptable values for UID and GID that the client may use if it wishes.
AUTH_RES_FAIL	2	A verification failure occurred.

14.7.14   Procedure 14: PCNFSD2_ALERT—Send Message to Server Administrator

Description

```
Arguments                          Results
string<64>    system               uint32      status;
string<64>    printername;         string<255> comment;
string<64>    username;
string<512>   message;
```

Arguments

system

The hostname of the server to which the printer is attached.

printername

The name of the printer to which the alert message relates.

username

The identity of the user that generated the alert message.

message

Text of the message to be sent to the system administrator. Up to 512 characters may be sent. Newlines are permitted in this string.

Results

status

See Errors.

comment

See section 14.5.2.

Implementation

This procedure is not implemented by the Sun PCNFSD.

Errors

ALERT_RES_OK	0	The PCNFSD was able to pass the message to the system operator.
ALERT_RES_FAIL	2	The system operator was not notified.

14.8 BWNFSD/HCLNFSD Protocol

The HCLNFSD protocol is an alternative to PCNFSD. First called BWNFSD, it was developed by Beame and Whiteside Software, Inc., now Hummingbird Communications Ltd. (hence the name change to HCLNFSD). The HCLNFSD procedures are not documented, nor are they presented in an rpcgen file. A reading of the HCLNFSD source code does disclose the function of many procedures in the protocol, described in Table 14.7.

HCLNFSD added many of the same features that were added to version 2 of PCNFSD: a group list in the authentication result, a procedure to map UID and GID values to readable names, and improved printer support. The most significant addition to HCLNFSD was a set of procedures to support PC-style locking and file sharing.

Early implementations of the Network Lock Manager protocol (chapter 10) did not support DOS file locking procedures (NLM_SHARE and NLM_UNSHARE) or nonmonitored byte-range locks (NLM_NM_LOCK). In addition, implementations based on user-level LOCK daemons were notoriously unreliable. This unreliability created severe problems for some PC

TABLE 14.7 Summary of HCLNFSD Procedures

Number	Name	Description	NLM or PCNFSD equivalent
0	NULL	Null procedure	
1	SPOOL_INQUIRE	Return filehandle of spool directory	PCNFSD2_PR_INIT
2	SPOOL_FILE	Spool file to printer	PCNFSD2_PR_START
3	AUTHORIZE	Authorize and return UID and GIDs	PCNFSD2_AUTH
4	GRP_NAME_TO_NUM	Convert group name to number	PCNFSD2_MAPID
5	GRP_TO_NUMBER	Convert group number(s) to name(s)	PCNFSD2_MAPID
6	RETURN_HOST	Convert IP address to hostname	None
7	UID_TO_NAME	Convert UID(s) to name(s)	PCNFSD2_MAPID
8	NAME_TO_UID	Convert name(s) to UID(s)	PCNFSD2_MAPID
20	SHARE	DOS share function	NLM_SHARE
21	UNSHARE	DOS unshare function	NLM_UNSHARE
22	LOCK	DOS lock request	NLM_NM_LOCK
23	REMOVE	Remove all locks/shares for client	NLM_FREE_ALL
24	UNLOCK	DOS unlock request	NLM_UNLOCK
30	GET_PRINTERS	Get a list of printers	PCNFSD_PR_LIST
31	GET_PRINTQ	Get print queue entries and status	PCNFSD2_PR_QUEUE
32	CANCEL_PRJOB	Cancel a print job	PCNFSD2_PR_CANCEL
105	ZAP_LOCKS	Remove locks on file by process	None

applications that used byte-range locking heavily. Most of the features that were implemented in HCLNFSD were later incorporated into PCNFSD version 2 and NLM version 3.

14.9　Summary

The operating systems that run on PC clients (DOS, Windows, OS/2) have some unique requirements that present some interesting problems in their use of the NFS protocol. DOS in particular has a very restrictive 8.3 naming convention. The other OSs use a different pathname delimiter, assign some characters as illegal, need wildcard file searching, and have case-insensitive file lookup.

PC operating systems have a more limited set of file attributes than are supported on UNIX servers; some attributes, like archive, have no UNIX equivalent. Since PC clients have no native support for UNIX-style symbolic links, the NFS client software must evaluate symbolic links transparently. Text files differ in their use of an end-of-line marker: DOS uses two characters—carriage return, newline—whereas UNIX uses a single newline character.

The PCNFSD protocol provides an authentication procedure that takes a user's login name and password and returns the elements of an AUTH_SYS credential: UID, GID, and group list. In addition, the PCNFSD protocol provides printing features that allow a PC client to create printer spool files on the server with NFS and have them printed on a selected printer. Version 2 of the PCNFSD protocol added printer queue management procedures. The HCLNFSD protocol is an alternative to PCNFSD that provides many of the same features. The most notable feature of HCLNFSD is its incorporation of PC file sharing locks and byte-range file locking.

Chapter 15

NFS Benchmarks

When evaluating NFS client and server products, performance is one of the most important considerations for most customers. Selection of NFS client and server implementations is normally considered separately. For UNIX clients the NFS implementation normally comes bundled with the operating system, and its performance is secondary to other features of the client and its overall suitability for running the customer's applications. Since NFS is not normally included with PC clients, there is a choice of NFS products, though there are no standard industry benchmarks to evaluate those client implementations. Also, the performance of client NFS depends heavily on the power and efficiency of the NFS server.

The most accurate NFS performance benchmark would measure both client and server performance together—a suite of client applications, chosen to represent typical customer load, that access one or more filesystems on the server. The Andrew benchmark (see section 12.1.5) has been used this way to measure client and server implementations together when comparing one filesystem protocol, such as AFS, with another protocol, like NFS. While integrated client-server benchmarking is used by customers when making a final decision between closely competing products, an integrated benchmark is valid only for a particular client-server combination. A server vendor would have to publish benchmark results for each client the customer might choose to use with the server. Customers prefer a benchmark that delivers a *single number* that makes it easier to compare products.

In providing a well-defined, reproducible workload, a benchmark provides a useful tool for customers to use in comparing different products. It is also a useful tool for vendors to use in tuning their NFS implementation. Against a constant workload, a performance engineer can tweak the factors that affect performance. If the benchmark is sensitive enough, changes in server configuration will be reflected in benchmark results. The same reproducible workload is also useful for an engineer looking for performance bottlenecks in the server. There is a risk, though, that the server will become optimized to produce good results for the benchmark and neglect performance improvements that might benefit features that are not measured or considered important by the benchmark.

This chapter will focus on the evolution of NFS server benchmarks, from Nfsstone to SPEC SFS 2.0.

15.1 Factors Affecting Performance

An NFS client or server has many components that individually contribute to performance. Because the components are dependent on each other, performance analysis of a client or implementation must consider the client or server as an interrelated system of components.

15.1.1 Memory

NFS clients and servers use memory to cache file attributes and file data. If a client or server is lacking in performance, the first response from an NFS performance consultant is likely to be "add more memory." A large memory on the client means that it can cache recently retrieved files, directories, and file attributes. Rather than sending an expensive READ request to the server, a client with sufficient memory to cache a file can send a relatively cheap GETATTR request to the server. An NFS version 3 client can also write to the server more quickly because it can keep a large number of uncommitted data pages in memory before it needs to send a COMMIT request. A server with large amounts of memory can retrieve directory entries, attributes, and file data from its memory very quickly instead of waiting for an I/O request to the disk.

15.1.2 CPU

The CPU speed directly affects the rate at which the client or server can process NFS requests and responses (Figure 15.1). On most clients, the CPU can easily generate more write traffic than the network can handle. Generally, the client CPU spends most of its time twiddling its thumbs waiting for the network. On the server, the speed of the CPU directly affects the rate at which the server can process requests from clients. Clients benefit because the fast CPU not only lowers response time through faster processing of the client's request, it also moves more quickly to a request pending from another client—which means that the server can support a larger number of clients. The number of CPUs also has a significant benefit for a server because it means that the server can process client requests concurrently. NFS servers are typically overconfigured—they have idle CPUs waiting for disk I/O.

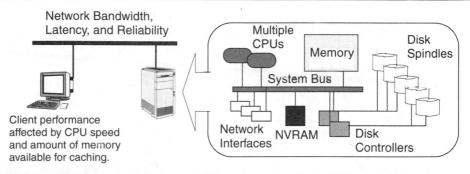

FIGURE 15.1 Factors contributing to NFS performance. Fast CPUs and plenty of memory for caching improve performance of clients and servers. On a system that is configured for good NFS performance, the server components are tuned to avoid bottlenecks while minimizing system cost.

15.1.3 Network

Clients that generate much READ or WRITE traffic are directly affected by network bandwidth. When an NFS version 3 client requests a 32-KB READ, it takes the server 20 milliseconds to transmit that data back to the client over a 10-MB Ethernet connection. With sufficient read-ahead threads, a client can generate 50 READ requests per second and use the whole bandwidth on the connection. On a poorly configured network that has many clients sharing the same Ethernet connection, the performance of a client may be severely affected by the activity of other clients on the same Ethernet segment—while the server is loafing.

The reliability of the network can have a significant effect on performance. While the NFS protocol is tolerant of lost packets (the client retransmits if it gets no response), the time-out and retransmission resulting from a lost UDP packet cause a big drop in throughput. In the time it takes a client to wait through a 1-second time-out, it could have read or written a megabyte of data on a 10-MB network and 10 megabytes of data on a 100-MB network. NFS over a TCP connection performs better over an unreliable network because the TCP transport itself handles retransmission more efficiently, through smaller retransmission units (TCP segments) and faster detection of packet loss through packet acknowledgments and accurate round-trip time (RTT) measurement.

Latency, the time it takes for a message to transit the connection between client and server, directly affects performance. Every NFS request and reply pays a latency penalty. The effect is most noticeable where many short messages are exchanged between client and server. A classic example is the NFS version 2 scenario of a client that issues a READDIR to retrieve directory entries, followed by a large number of LOOKUP requests to retrieve the file handles and attributes of the directory entries. If the processing time for a

LOOKUP request averages 2 msec and network round-trip time is 1 msec, then the LOOKUPs for a 100-entry directory on a server down the hallway will take 300 msec. However, if the server is in another state and the round-trip time is 50 msec, then the directory listing will take (2 + 50) * 100 = 5,200 msec—more than 5 seconds.

A feature unique to the use of UDP is the use of a checksum on the datagram payload. If the checksum field in the UDP header is nonzero, then it is assumed to contain a payload checksum. It was common in early implementations of NFS not to compute the checksum because its computation consumed enough CPU cycles to make a noticeable difference in performance. As long as UDP datagrams passed over Ethernet segments, data integrity was protected by the cyclic redundancy check (CRC) field in the Ethernet frame. However, if the datagram happened to be routed over a non-Ethernet link or via a router or other network hardware that corrupted bits in the datagram, then corrupted data could be read from or written to files. This error was serious because the corruption could be silent and hard to diagnose. If the UDP checksum was used, then network corruption could be detected quickly at the network level before corrupted data could reach files. As CPU development increased speed by orders of magnitude, vendors implemented UDP checksum protection in their NFS implementations. Now it is normal for UDP checksums to be set. The SFS benchmark (section 15.5) requires that servers check and compute UDP checksums.

15.1.4 Network Interfaces

In the mid-1980s, Ethernet and Token Ring network interface cards were dumb devices that performed a minimum of protocol processing and showered the host CPU with interrupts. The network interface was hampered by the speed of the server's main CPU. To overcome this, the idea of "smart" network interfaces became popular: speed up the server by off-loading the higher-level protocol processing (IP and TCP) from the host CPU to a CPU and memory on the network card itself—a *network processor*. When main CPU speeds increased by a hundredfold, the "dumb" network card looked more attractive. Improved protocol handling code came with each operating system upgrade and the server's ability to handle heavy loads scaled as more CPUs were added. Now it is the network's turn to increase again in speed—Ethernet has jumped quickly from 100 megabits/sec to 1,000 megabits/sec (gigabit). Although most higher-level protocol processing continues to be handled by the host CPUs, data-intensive operations like checksumming are now handled on some network cards.

Some network interface cards can handle multiple network connections, and larger servers can accept many network interface cards. If you scout around a large NFS server, you may find a dozen or more networks plugged into the back. A server that can handle multiple network interfaces has a distinct advantage over a server with just one network interface. Not only does it aggregate the bandwidth from the multiple networks to which it is connected, it also can transmit and receive concurrently on each of those interfaces.

15.1.5 Server Data Bus

The server data bus is a critical data path that connects the server's network interfaces to its CPU, memory, and disk channels. No increase in the server's CPUs, memory, or disk spindles will improve the server's performance if the data bus is already choked with data. Vendors generally configure the server's data bus to suit the scale of the machine—the bus bandwidth may determine the maximum number of CPUs, memory, or disk that can be plugged into the machine. A small server's bus may handle 50 or 100 MB per second, while a large server may have a bus that can transfer several gigabytes per second over a crossbar switch architecture.

15.1.6 NVRAM

Nonvolatile memory has been used on NFS servers to improve write performance (see section 8.10). NFS version 2 requires every write request to be committed to stable storage before the server can reply to the client. System memory cannot be used to cache these writes because it is volatile—if the server crashes, then data from cached writes in memory would be lost. The use of nonvolatile RAM allows the server to avoid a slow disk write and aggregate writes into larger I/O requests. Nonvolatile RAM may be provided on memory cards with built-in battery protection or at the system level with an uninterruptible power supply (UPS) and recovery software that retrieves buffered write data from system memory after an operating system crash. The size of the NVRAM available for caching must be scaled to allow for the maximum data throughput. If the server's I/O demands exceed the bandwidth of the NVRAM, then system throughput will drop quickly.

15.1.7 Disk Controllers

A server will have one or more disk controllers that handle I/O requests from the operating system to the disks attached to the system via a SCSI or fibre channel connection. Each disk controller has a CPU and a small amount of memory for buffering I/O requests to the set of disk spindles it manages. The controller may become a bottleneck if it cannot handle the I/O load. Additional disk controllers can be added to the server to share the load.

15.1.8 Disk Spindles

Large NFS servers are notable not for the physical size of the CPU and memory enclosure but for the large number of disk arrays that contain the data.

Disks are inherently slow devices—data cannot be read or written at a rate exceeding the rotational speed of the disk—and I/O requests to the disk suffer from both rotational latency (the time for the desired read or write location to move under the disk head) and the time required to move the disk head from one cylinder to the next. The physical limitations of the disk that affect performance can be overcome by spreading the server load over a larger number of disk *spindles*. By striping files over multiple disks, a server can increase the I/O bandwidth of the disk while reducing the disk latency.

15.2   Workload

To be useful to customers, a benchmark should measure performance against a workload that approximates the customer's workload. The most straightforward way to approximate a workload is to gather statistics from production sites using a command like nfsstat to determine the operation mix and survey the file sizes and distributions on real NFS servers.

15.2.1   Operation Mix

For NFS benchmarks, the most important consideration is the *mix* of operations generated by the client (Figure 15.2). Clients that mostly read files and execute programs from an NFS server will have a mix that is dominated by LOOKUP, GETATTR, and READ requests. Clients that use NFS for home directory mounting may have a mix of operations dominated by GETATTR and WRITE requests if they use large memory or disk caches.

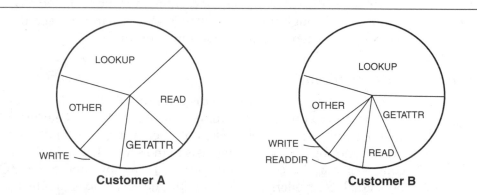

FIGURE 15.2 NFS operation mix. An important element of a benchmark workload is the mix of NFS operations. The mix may reflect the type of applications that the client is using, the type of data on the server, or whether the client is using a large cache. The pie charts show hypothetical mixes from two customers showing how their mixes may vary. The larger proportion of READs in customer A's mix may indicate that larger files are being read or that its clients have less memory for caching.

15.2.2 Working Set

The workload must also take into account the effect of caching on the client and server. If a client frequently accesses a small *working set* of files and directories, then cache hit rates will be high and performance will be good. However, if the workload is scattered randomly among a large number of directories and files, then cache misses will be higher and performance will be worse.

15.2.3 File and Directory Size

A benchmark needs to establish a representative set of files, directories, and symbolic links to be accessed on the server. Small files can be fetched from the server with a single READ operation and may be accessed more quickly on some servers that store pointers to data blocks in indirect blocks. Small files are also more likely to fit within the client or the server's cache. If the benchmark makes the client read or write some large files, then it can measure the client and server's prowess at read-ahead and write-behind techniques. Files must be distributed on the server so that directories contain a number of entries typical of a real server.

15.3 Nfsstone

Nfsstone was developed by Barry Shein of Software Tool & Die, Inc., and Mike Callahan and Paul Woodbury of Encore Computer Corporation and described in a 1989 paper [Shein+89]. The goals of nfsstone were to build a benchmark that could be ported easily to any UNIX client, and to produce a single number unit of NFS performance: the *nfsstone*. The desire for a single number was in line with other widely used performance benchmarks, such as the Whetstone and Dhrystone benchmark programs for measurement of floating point and integer performance.[1]

Nfsstone was a C program that performed a series of filesystem operations on a mounted NFS filesystem. The operations were carefully scaled to produce what was then considered to be a "typical" mix of NFS operations across the network (Table 15.1). The C program approximated the mix indirectly by generating fixed sequences of UNIX system calls directed at a mounted NFS filesystem: open, close, access, read, write, unlink, rename, and so on. File access included a mix of sequential read-writes with random reads.

---

1. Hence the derivation of benchmark program names with the suffix *-stone*.

TABLE 15.1 Nfsstone Filesystem Operations

NFS operation	Nfsstone percentage
LOOKUP	53.0
READ	32.0
READLINK	7.5
GETATTR	2.3
WRITE	3.2
CREATE	1.4

To provide a degree of concurrency to simulate NFS access from a multi-processing client, at startup the program would *fork* six child processes that would each run independently through the file access sequence. To simulate concurrent access from multiple clients, nfsstone employed a synchronization mechanism: a control program would lock a file on the server to be tested, then start the benchmark program on each client (Figure 15.3). Each invocation of the benchmark would block waiting to establish a lock on the same locked file. Once nfsstone was running on all clients, the control program would unlock the file, allowing each client's lock request to complete and the benchmark run to begin.

The nfsstone benchmark sought to produce a single number at the end of the benchmark run that would characterize the NFS throughput of the client and server. This number was reported in nfsstone units, defined as the total

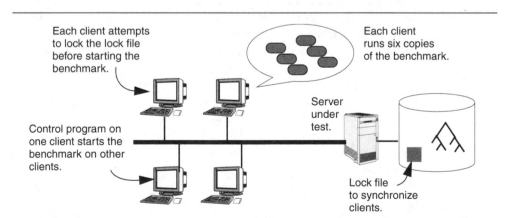

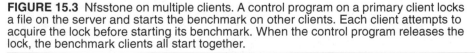

FIGURE 15.3 Nfsstone on multiple clients. A control program on a primary client locks a file on the server and starts the benchmark on other clients. Each client attempts to acquire the lock before starting its benchmark. When the control program releases the lock, the benchmark clients all start together.

number of NFS operations generated by the benchmark divided by the elapsed time of the benchmark run in seconds. With default parameters, the benchmark would generate approximately 45,522 operations—a 120-second run would be measured as 380 nfsstones. A higher nfsstone number indicates a better server.

A significant problem with the nfsstone benchmark was the unreliability of its workload, because each NFS client implementation varies in the way it generates NFS requests to the server. A larger client cache or more effective client caching could prevent some operations going to the server at all, which would give the server an unfairly high nfsstone number. The server might receive an unfairly low nfsstone rating if a slow client was used. The nfsstone benchmark was replaced by an improved benchmark: nhfsstone.

15.4 Nhfsstone

The nhfsstone (the "h" is silent, as in Dhrystone) was designed by Russell Sandberg of Legato Systems, Inc. Like its predecessor, nfsstone, this benchmark was a C program that approximated an NFS workload through the use of UNIX system calls to a mounted NFS filesystem, but nhfsstone was superior to nfsstone in its closer approximation to a chosen mix.

At startup, nhfsstone would read a mix file specifying the mix of NFS operations to be generated by the benchmark run (Figure 15.4). During the benchmark run, nhfsstone would obtain nfsstat statistics from the kernel to monitor its approximation to the desired mix. If it detected differences from the desired mix, the benchmark would adjust its selection of UNIX system

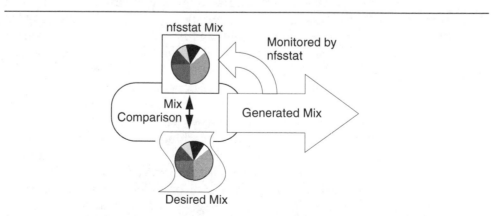

FIGURE 15.4 Nhfsstone operation mix. The benchmark monitors the generated mix as measured by the kernel's nfsstat reporting and adjusts the mix of UNIX system calls to maintain the desired read from the mix file.

calls to correct the error. In this way, nhfsstone provided a more accurate approximation to a predetermined mix.

As well as allowing the operation mix to be specified, nhfsstone provided parameters that allowed the load to be throttled to a specified number of NFS operations per second (default 30 ops/sec) as well as setting the total number of NFS calls (default 5000) and number of load-generating processes on the client (default 7). Rather than generate a single number (like nfsstone), nhfsstone reported the server's average response time in milliseconds per call along with the load in calls per second.

Although nhfsstone achieved a more accurate operation mix through nfsstat feedback, it needed to employ tricks to avoid caching effects. For instance, it used long file names that precluded the use of the client's directory name lookup cache (DNLC). The indirect method of generating NFS requests through UNIX system calls made it difficult to establish nhfsstone as a portable, industry-standard benchmark. Since the benchmark depended so heavily on the client's hardware configuration and on its implementation of NFS, change in the client's configuration or operating system could have significant effects on the benchmark result.

15.5 SFS 1.0 and 1.1

The System File Server (SFS) 1.0 benchmark [Watson+92; Wittle+93] was developed by SPEC (Standard Performance Evaluation Corporation), the consortium that developed the SPECint, SPECfp, and SPECweb benchmarks. SFS 1.0 was originally known as LADDIS, a name derived from the first letters of the companies that developed the benchmark: Legato Systems, Auspex Systems, Data General, Digital Equipment, Interphase, and Sun Microsystems. The LADDIS group was originally formed outside SPEC to improve the nhfsstone benchmark but joined SPEC shortly after development began. After two years of testing, the benchmark was released in March 1993 and was followed by a maintenance update, SFS 1.1, in November 1994.

The nfsstone and nhfsstone benchmark generated NFS calls indirectly through UNIX system calls to a mounted NFS filesystem. These programs suffered from inaccuracies due to variations in client hardware and NFS implementation effects such as caching. The SFS benchmark made the older nfsstone and nhfsstone benchmarks obsolete by generating the NFS calls *directly* from a C program that implements a user-level NFS client. The SFS client generates NFS RPC calls at a predetermined rate, measuring response time and handling the reply. By generating calls directly, the benchmark generates a precise and reproducible mix of NFS operations at a configurable load.

SFS not only introduced a stand-alone client, it also introduced strict run and report rules that constrain the client, network, and server configuration to make it easier to reproduce benchmark results. They also standardize the way in which results are reported, which makes it easier for customers to compare vendor offerings and harder for vendors to put marketing spin on the results.

15.5.1 Running the SFS Benchmark

The benchmark's operation is similar to that of the nfsstone and nhfsstone benchmarks. The benchmark forks a number of processes on each client machine to generate NFS load. The benchmark is run on a number of client machines that are spread across multiple networks—each network segment must have at least two load generator clients and a total of at least eight load-generating processes. If too many clients share a network segment, then the network itself may become a bottleneck through packet collisions and bandwidth limits. A single machine is designated the *prime client* and it is responsible for controlling the load-generating processes on the other client machines (Figure 15.5).

An SFS run is controlled by a control file on the prime client. The prime client gradually increases the generated load on all the client machines and tracks the server's average response time for the NFS requests (Figure 15.6). As the load increases, the server's response time increases. No results can be reported that exceed a response time of 50 milliseconds. The benchmark's *single figure of merit* is the maximum load the server can handle with a response time under 50 msec. To keep the reported response time at peak a small value, a vendor may elect to terminate the run before the response time gets anywhere near 50 msec.

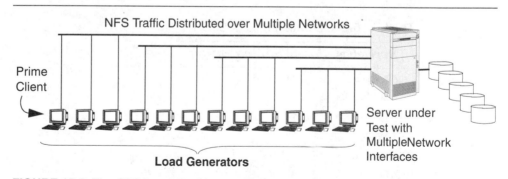

FIGURE 15.5 The SFS benchmark is commonly run with a large number of load generator clients under the control of a prime client. The load generators may be distributed over several networks connected to multiple network interfaces on the server so that the network will not reach maximum capacity before the load saturates the server under test. A 10-MB Ethernet segment is capable of supporting approximately 300 NFS ops/sec from the standard SFS 1.1 mix.

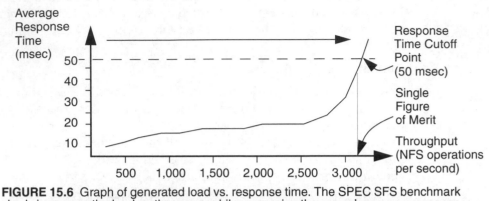

FIGURE 15.6 Graph of generated load vs. response time. The SPEC SFS benchmark slowly increases the load on the server while measuring the server's average response time. When the response time exceeds 50 msec, the run is terminated and the SPEC single figure of merit is the highest measured throughput under 50 msec.

15.5.2   Workload

The default SFS 1.1 workload is based on workload studies conducted at Sun in 1987 that collected nfsstat results from a large number of servers. The benchmark allows other mixes to be specified. For instance, a customer could specify that vendors competing on a bid run a mix that is representative of the customer's NFS usage (Table 15.2).

During the benchmark initialization, each load generator process sets up a directory on the server for its exclusive use and populates it with files, directories, and symbolic links to be accessed during the benchmark run. The

TABLE 15.2 Operation Mix for SFS 1.1

NFS operation	SFS 1.1 percentage
LOOKUP	34
READ	22
WRITE	15
GETATTR	13
READLINK	8
READDIR	3
CREATE	2
SETATTR	1
REMOVE	1
STATFS	1

benchmark requires that the server's filesystems be initialized to the state of an unused, empty filesystem via the use of *mkfs* or *newfs* on UNIX servers. Since each load-generating process has exclusive use of the contents of this directory during the run, there is no contention or file sharing between the load generators. The load-generating process creates 21 directories, 20 symbolic links, and 100 files, plus 40 additional files for each expected unit of load (Figure 15.7). Each file is initialized with 136-KB of data to ensure that there is sufficient disk capacity on the server to support the run. The 136-KB file size is chosen because on UNIX servers the filesystem must allocate indirect file index blocks to access data near the end of the file. Additionally, the file is of sufficient size to measure the server's handling of sequential reading and writing through read-ahead and write-behind threads.

The number of files created is adjusted according to the expected load level at which the server will reach saturation (response time exceeds 50 msec). The server is initialized with 5 megabytes of file data for each *unit of load* (1 NFS operation/second) plus an additional megabyte for fileset growth during the runs. For instance, if the server's expected figure of merit is 2000 NFS ops/sec, then 12 gigabytes of data would need to be created—spread across 87,500 136-KB files. This scaling of server storage size to expected throughput ensures that the server is able to support the storage requirements of a real client population at a customer site. During the benchmark run, not all the files created during the initialization phase are accessed. The benchmark randomly chooses just 20 percent of these files as a *working set* to be used during the benchmark. The working set models real-world experience; only a

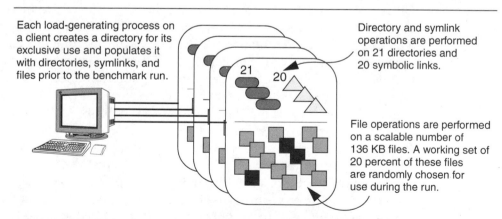

Each load-generating process on a client creates a directory for its exclusive use and populates it with directories, symlinks, and files prior to the benchmark run.

Directory and symlink operations are performed on 21 directories and 20 symbolic links.

File operations are performed on a scalable number of 136 KB files. A working set of 20 percent of these files are randomly chosen for use during the run.

FIGURE 15.7 SFS 1.1 server file setup. Each load generator creates an exclusive work area on the server. The number of directories and symbolic links is fixed. The number of 136-KB files is scaled according to the expected load limit: 100 files plus 40 files per unit of load. Only a 20-percent working set of files is accessed during the benchmark run.

small subset of files are accessed on a regular basis—the rest are accessed infrequently. The use of a working set also requires the server to support efficient file location and I/O within a much larger set of files.

15.5.3   Server Configuration

The SFS benchmark takes a "black box" approach to the server. It assumes nothing of the server's hardware or operating system—only that the server correctly implement version 2 of the NFS protocol. When the benchmark is started, it performs a simple validation check against the server to verify that it behaves correctly according to the protocol specification.

The validation check is not a complete verification of the server's conformance. In particular, some vendors provide an option that allows their server implementation to do *asynchronous* writes: NFS write requests are cached in server memory rather than being committed to disk or stable storage like NVRAM. Although asynchronous writes boost server performance, there is a risk of silent data loss if the server crashes and recovers while a client is writing to it. Because asynchronous writes violate the protocol specification, they are not permitted by the SPEC SFS run rules.

15.5.4   Cluster Challenge

The SPEC SFS run rules met an interesting challenge when several NFS server vendors reported benchmark results against cluster servers (Figure 15.8). As a server configuration grows in size, the hardware architects design an increasing level of parallelism into the system: multiple network interfaces, multiple CPUs, disk controllers, and power supplies. A *cluster server* takes parallelism to the extreme by its use of multiple smaller server computers assembled into a rack or as boards in a single chassis. Since each computer in a cluster runs its own copy of the operating system and is rebooted separately, a cluster can be highly reliable (the failure of one computer does not affect others in the cluster) and highly scalable (since there is no network, CPU, bus, memory, or I/O contention between computers). The almost infinite scalability of a cluster presented a problem for the black box approach taken by the SFS 1.1 Run Rules. Could a roomful of small servers qualify as a cluster server and receive an SFS figure of merit? The classification of cluster servers caused much debate within the SPEC consortium. It also raised a more general issue: Could a vendor contrive to partition the load generators to make optimal use of particular data paths within a highly parallel or clustered server—for instance, if the load generator clients on one network shared the same disk or disk controller?

The issue was resolved by extending a run rule that required uniform access by all clients of the server's filesystems. The extended rule required

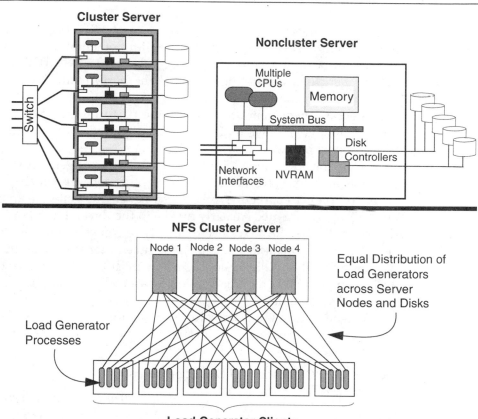

FIGURE 15.8 SFS benchmark and cluster servers. The top half of the diagram compares the architecture of a cluster server with a noncluster server. While a cluster server is more scalable, because there is little or no contention for resources between cluster nodes, a cluster server can be more difficult to configure and administer. The lower half of the diagram shows the application of the SFS run rule that requires load generator processes to be assigned uniformly across cluster nodes and disks. The network must be configured so that any load generator client can access any node in the cluster.

that each load-generating process, proceeding from client to client and network to network, be assigned to a different cluster processor (if the configuration is a cluster) and then to a different disk controller and then disk. This distribution of client load is intended to simulate more closely a real customer workload. In the extreme case of a "roomful of servers" cluster, the run rule does not prohibit the reporting of cluster results, but it does require that each load-generating client assign each of its load generators to a different cluster node—requiring some support from a high-speed switch or router in front of the cluster.

15.6   SFS 2.0

The SFS 1.1 benchmark was developed for NFS version 2. Shortly after its release, vendors began working on their implementations of NFS version 3 as well as supporting the use of both versions 2 and 3 over TCP connections. The SFS 1.1 benchmark could not measure the performance of version 3 servers, nor could it generate NFS requests over TCP connections. SFS 2.0 was designed as a benchmark to measure the performance of both NFS version 2 and version 3 over UDP or TCP. SFS 2.0 included a few improvements to the SFS 1.1 benchmark.

While the addition of TCP handling to the load generator client was relatively straightforward, the addition of NFS version 3 load generation was more complex. In particular, NFS version 3 clients generate an entirely different NFS operation mix. An early hurdle in the development of SFS 2.0 was the determination of the mix: since relatively few customers were using NFS version 3, it was difficult to assess a *typical* mix. After surveying the mix statistics of more than 1000 NFS version 2 servers in different customer environments, a representative mix for NFS version 3 was derived analytically from the NFS version 2 mix (Table 15.3).

As well as providing a mix for NFS version 3, the survey also updated the NFS version 2 mix for SFS 2.0. The most notable changes are a drop in the

TABLE 15.3 Comparison of Operation Mixes

NFS operation	SFS 1.1 mix NFS (%) v2	SFS 2.0 mix NFS (%) v2	SFS 2.0 mix NFS (%) v3
LOOKUP	34	36	27
READ	22	14	18
WRITE	15	7	9
GETATTR	13	26	11
READLINK	8	7	7
READDIR	3	6	2
CREATE	2	1	1
REMOVE	1	1	1
FSSTAT	1	1	1
SETATTR			1
READDIRPLUS			9
ACCESS			7
COMMIT			5

number of READ and WRITE operations and a large increase in the number of GETATTR operations. SFS 2.0 doubled the size of the file set from 5 MB per unit of workload to 10 MB, reflecting the general increase in NFS server disk capacity. The size of the working set of files and the percentage allowance for file growth was reduced from 20 percent in SFS 1.1 to 10 percent in SFS 2.0, no net change in the amount of file data accessed during a run.

The SFS 2.0 benchmark made some changes to the reporting rules (Figure 15.9). The cutoff response time was lowered from 50 milliseconds to 40 milliseconds to reflect the general improvement of NFS server response time across all vendors. The SFS 1.1 requirement for response time to be reported at peak throughput was changed to report an *overall* response time for the benchmark—derived by calculating the area under the curve divided by the peak throughput.

The SFS 2.0 benchmark makes some NFS protocol requirements that are unique to NFS version 3. WRITE requests with the *stable_how* bit set (section 7.3.8) and COMMIT requests must not be replied to unless the data is on stable storage. There are ten NFS version 3 procedures that return *wcc_data* (section 7.2.2, which allows optional attribute data to be returned. The server could opt to set the discriminant arm to FALSE for the data fields and reduce processing time for the request, but this behavior would not be normal for a server. So SFS 2.0 run rules require the server to return this attribute data.

The SFS 2.0 benchmark is now the official SPEC benchmark for both NFS version 2 and 3; it replaces the SFS 1.1 benchmark.

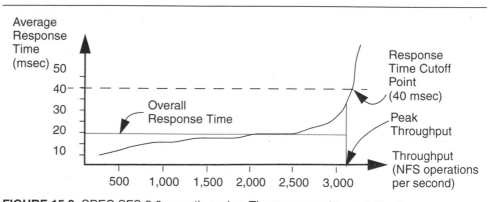

FIGURE 15.9 SPEC SFS 2.0 reporting rules. The response time cutoff value was lowered from 50 msec (SFS 1.1) to 40 msec. The response time, instead of being reported at peak throughput, is now reported as the overall response time for the entire run.

15.7 Summary

Nfsstone, the first widely available NFS benchmark, was a C program that generated NFS calls by performing filesystem operations on a mounted NFS filesystem. The benchmark contrived a set of file access operations to generate a mix of NFS operations that reflected typical server usage. The nfsstone figure of merit, the nfsstone, was computed as the total number of NFS operations (45,522) divided by the elapsed time in seconds. Consistent results were difficult to achieve with nfsstone because the benchmark was easily perturbed by features of the client's NFS implementation, such as caching.

The nhfsstone benchmark generated a more accurate mix by continuously monitoring the generated mix with the client kernel's nfsstat facility. Nhfsstone would adjust the system call mix to reduce any differences between the desired mix and the observed mix.

The SFS 1.1 benchmark (also known as LADDIS) was developed by the SPEC consortium. It eliminated the uncertainties of the NFS implementation on the load-generating client by making NFS calls directly to the server from the benchmark program. The SFS 1.1 benchmark also established strict *Run and Reporting Rules* that made it easier to reproduce and interpret benchmark results. The SFS 2.0 benchmark extended SFS 1.1 to measure NFS version 3 performance as well as NFS performance over TCP connections. SFS 2.0 provided a new operation mix for NFS version 3 measurement as well as updating the mix for NFS version 2 to reflect current usage of the protocol. SFS 2.0 has replaced the SFS 1.1 benchmark and is now the official SPEC benchmark for both NFS version 2 and version 3.

Chapter 16

WebNFS

This chapter describes WebNFS™, a feature that eliminates much of the overhead in connecting to an NFS server, making data on NFS servers more accessible to lightweight NFS clients like Web browsers and Java applications. Because WebNFS makes NFS server connection as easy as setting up a TCP connection to a well-known port, it is easier to configure a firewall to allow connections to Internet NFS servers. WebNFS is not a new version of the NFS protocol. It is just an enhancement to implementations of NFS versions 2 and 3 that improves the utility of NFS in the Internet realm.

16.1 Internet and NFS over TCP

While NFS is common on local area networks, it is almost unknown on the Internet. The lack of Internet use is in common with other popular PC-based file access protocols: Novell Netware and Microsoft's SMB/CIFS protocols are not used on the Internet, either, though the reasons are different: the PC protocols were implemented initially on non-IP transports, while NFS has always used the IP protocol on which the Internet is built.

NFS implementations most commonly use UDP as a transport. UDP was preferred initially because it performed well on high-bandwidth, local area networks and was faster than TCP. While UDP benefited from the high bandwidth and low latency typical of LANs, it performed poorly when subjected to the low bandwidth and high latency of WANs like the Internet. Excessive fragmentation requirements for the large transfers possible with NFS version 3 make UDP a poor choice over congested networks. Early experiences of NFS on the Internet were that the protocol was a bandwidth hog that used the network inefficiently. It is a characteristic of TCP connections that the client and server monitor the performance of the link and adjust the transmission rate accordingly. NFS over UDP takes no account of the link performance and transmits large data packets blindly even if the link is badly congested.

Improvements in hardware and TCP implementations have narrowed the LAN advantage of UDP enough that the performance of NFS over TCP is close to that of UDP. A growing number of NFS implementations now support TCP as well as UDP.

16.2   Internet and NFS Version 3

NFS version 2 limited the data transfer size to 8 kilobytes. No single read or write request could exceed 8 KB. NFS version 3 removed this limitation, leaving it up to the client and server to use a mutually agreeable transfer size (Figure 16.1). The transfer size over UDP is constrained by a 64-KB limit on the size of UDP datagrams. Since the NFS and RPC headers will be included in the 64-KB limit, the actual amount of NFS READ or WRITE data transferred will be fewer than 64 KB. The situation is different if TCP is used since the record marking protocol (section 3.7) permits RPC calls and replies to be of almost any size. A large file could be transferred by a single read request, but in practice the client and server will be bound by the size of buffers they are willing to allocate from available memory.

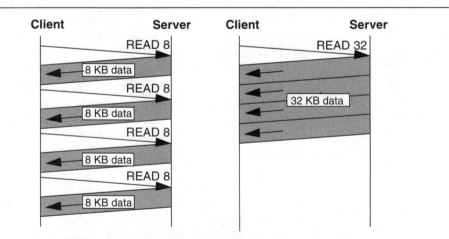

FIGURE 16.1 Transfer of larger chunks of file data is faster and makes more efficient use of network bandwidth. While the overlapped requests of a read-ahead policy would improve bandwidth use, there would still be some wastage due to the packet headers in additional requests/replies and additional load placed on the client and server by the processing of separate requests and responses.

16.3   Firewalls

Most NFS clients and servers are installed on private networks that are not directly connected to the Internet. The firewalls that are used to control traffic to the Internet provide an effective barrier to the use of NFS between clients and servers located on opposite sides of a firewall.

Packet-filtering firewalls and application proxies like SOCKS are relatively easy to configure for protocols that use TCP on well-known ports. UDP-based protocols are perceived as insecure because their lack of packet sequence numbers makes it easier for a "man in the middle" to insert datagrams or replay previously recorded datagrams. Today many NFS implementations can be run over a TCP connection.

Although port 2049 is used universally by NFS implementations and is registered with the Internet Assigned Numbers Authority (IANA) as the port for NFS, as an RPC-based protocol the NFS port is supposed to be determined via a portmap service (section 3.8.1). To communicate with an RPC service, a client is required first to submit the program number of the service to the server's Portmapper and receive the assigned port for the service. Although some sophisticated firewalls can track these port negotiations, it is not a common feature. Since all NFS implementations use port 2049, it would seem easy to permit firewall passage of NFS traffic by having clients avoid the Portmapper protocol and communicate directly with the server on port 2049. However, the client cannot communicate at all with an NFS server unless it has first obtained an initial filehandle using the MOUNT protocol.

16.4   Public Filehandle

Although the MOUNT service is an RPC-based protocol just like NFS, it does not have a well-known port. The server's portmapper must be used to locate the port for MOUNT. The MOUNT and Portmap protocols not only make it difficult to use NFS through a firewall, they also impose a binding overhead in additional network messages before the first NFS request can be transmitted. Since the MOUNT protocol provides the only way to obtain an initial filehandle to navigate an NFS server's namespace, an NFS server will be inaccessible if the MOUNT protocol cannot be used. WebNFS servers avoid this problem by providing access to a *public filehandle*.

The public filehandle is unique in having a value that is known (Figure 16.2). The client can use a public filehandle just like any other filehandle. Most commonly, the public filehandle is used in an NFS LOOKUP request to obtain the filehandle for a file or directory relative to the directory associated with the public filehandle. A LOOKUP with a public filehandle is similar to the "MOUNT" request of the MOUNT protocol, which names a directory on the server for which a filehandle is required. With the public filehandle the client can obtain the same information using the NFS protocol (Figure 16.3).

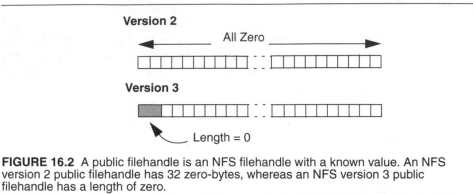

FIGURE 16.2 A public filehandle is an NFS filehandle with a known value. An NFS version 2 public filehandle has 32 zero-bytes, whereas an NFS version 3 public filehandle has a length of zero.

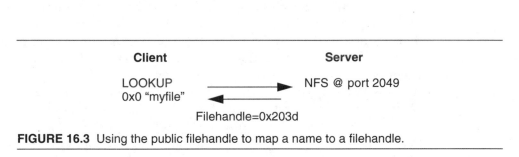

FIGURE 16.3 Using the public filehandle to map a name to a filehandle.

Avoidance of the MOUNT protocol not only allows the client to bind to the well-known NFS port 2049, but also bypasses the scalability limits of the MOUNT protocol. Most NFS servers implement the MOUNT server as a user-level daemon that was designed to handle a low volume of requests from a relatively small number of clients mounting filesystems. WebNFS servers may have thousands of clients making very brief connections for the purpose of downloading a single file. NFS servers are typically implemented as a part of the server's operating system, able to handle very high transaction loads.

16.5   Multicomponent LOOKUP

The availability of the public filehandle cannot completely replace the MOUNT protocol. In addition, the NFS server must be able to evaluate a pathname made up of component names. This section describes the features of multicomponent LOOKUP (MCL).

16.5.1   Pathname Evaluation and Latency

Wide Area Networks are noted for high latency. There is a minimum 30-msec round-trip latency imposed by the speed of light just to cross the United

States by the shortest path. On the Internet, packets rarely follow the shortest path between client and server. Routing delays can add tens or hundreds of milliseconds to packet transit time, and any route over a satellite link will add an additional half second per satellite. Protocols that require a high number of turnarounds (a request message followed by a reply) between client and server are particularly sensitive to latency effects.

16.5.2 Initialization Overhead

The NFS protocol was designed for Local Area Networks where latency is low and turnarounds are not a significant problem. A single read request requires a minimum of five turnarounds (portmap, mount, portmap, lookup, read). The public filehandle helps greatly in eliminating all this overhead; because the portmap and mount steps are eliminated, the very first message sent to the server can be an NFS operation (e.g., LOOKUP).

16.5.3 Pathname Evaluation

The process of evaluating a pathname using the NFS protocol is expensive in turnarounds. The NFS LOOKUP procedure normally evaluates only a single pathname component at a time, so a pathname evaluation requires a LOOKUP request to be transmitted to the server for every component in the pathname (Figure 16.4). It can be quite expensive to locate the filehandle for a file located several directory levels away from the public filehandle. This latency can become intolerable if the server is across the world. For instance, a client in California communicating with a server in Moscow incurs a 100-msec speed of light delay for one turnaround. Evaluation of a pathname with ten components would take a minimum of one second.

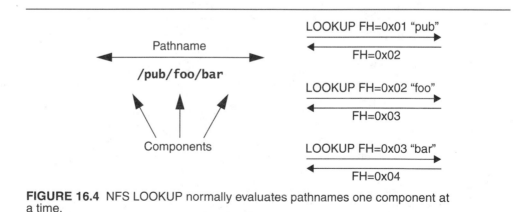

FIGURE 16.4 NFS LOOKUP normally evaluates pathnames one component at a time.

16.5.4   Server Evaluation of Pathname

A WebNFS server can evaluate an entire pathname in place of a component name when the LOOKUP is relative to the public filehandle. The NFS version 2 protocol limits this pathname to 255 characters, but UNIX pathnames can be as long as 1023 characters; however, pathnames longer than 255 characters are extremely rare. NFS version 3 does not limit the length of component names. This process of evaluating a pathname on the server is termed *multicomponent LOOKUP* (Figure 16.5).

A path that evaluates to a file or directory outside the NFS exported hierarchy may result in a "Not found" error from some servers, though this policy is completely up to the server implementation. Solaris WebNFS servers evaluate symbolic links that may cross from one exported filesystem to another, though the client's ability to use the resulting filehandle will depend on the server's access control policy for that filesystem.

16.5.5   Symbolic Links

When evaluating a multicomponent path, the server is responsible for the evaluation of any pathname components that represent symbolic links (Figure 16.6). This policy is different from the normal one-component-at-a-time evaluation process that requires the client to recognize symbolic links within the path and evaluate them with further LOOKUP requests. If the final component of the path is a symbolic link, then its evaluation will be left up to the client.

A multicomponent LOOKUP request that names a symbolic link will retrieve the filehandle for the symbolic link and the client must interpret the contents of the link. Although a symbolic link may contain any text at all, it is assumed to represent a pathname to another file or directory and the path is

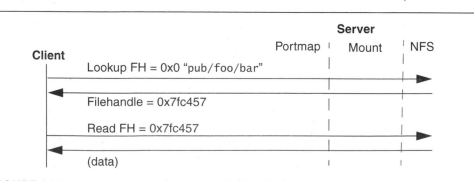

FIGURE 16.5 Use of the public filehandle combined with multicomponent lookup reduces the number of RPCs to access a file. Compare with Figure 9.1.

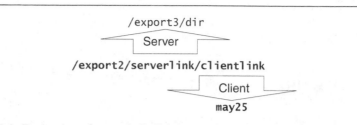

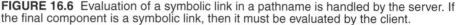

FIGURE 16.6 Evaluation of a symbolic link in a pathname is handled by the server. If the final component is a symbolic link, then it must be evaluated by the client.

assumed to follow UNIX pathname syntax. If the pathname starts with a slash, then it is an *absolute* name evaluated relative to the system root of the server. If the pathname begins with something other than a slash, then it is a *relative* name evaluated relative to the path that identified the symbolic link.

Symbolic link evaluation may present some problems for clients that do not share the same file namespace as the server. For instance, an absolute name is meaningless to a Windows or Macintosh client that has no concept of UNIX pathnames. Even UNIX clients may have difficulty evaluating an absolute symbolic link if the server does not provide NFS access to the system root directory. Rather than assuming properties of the client's namespace, a more reliable evaluation technique is to evaluate symbolic links as if they represent relative URLs.[1]

Relative URLs[2] are evaluated by combining the relative URL text with the original base URL to form a new URL. If we consider the original path to the symbolic link as a base URL and the link text as the relative URL, then we can combine the two to form a new pathname. For instance, given a multicomponent pathname of

```
/export/this/thing
```

then composition with the following symbolic links would yield new paths:

```
other            becomes   /export/this/other
../that/other    becomes   /export/that/other
/export2/dir     becomes   /export2/dir
```

---

1. Uniform resource locator.

2. Evaluation of relative URLs is described in RFC 1808: "Relative Uniform Resource Locators."

These new paths can then be returned to the server for further evaluation via multicomponent LOOKUP. It is possible that the link may contain an NFS URL. The client can determine this by checking for the prefix nfs://.

16.6   NFS URL

The NFS URL is the most visible feature of a WebNFS client or server. It has much in common with the more widely known HTTP URL.

16.6.1   URL Structure

The NFS uniform resource locator (URL) is a global name that can be used by any NFS client to identify a file or directory on any NFS server. Typical usage is from a Web browser or file browser that can handle URLs. The NFS URL structure follows the uniform resource locator specification described in RFC 1738. The general structure is.

```
nfs://server:port/path
```

If the :port is omitted, it defaults to 2049 (e.g., nfs://alpha:2001/x/y). The path is evaluated by the server using multicomponent LOOKUP relative to the public filehandle (section 16.4). The NFS URL has many desirable features common to all URL types, including:

- It is a global name that can be used to identify a file or directory on any NFS server accessible by the client.
- It is a filename that is portable across different operating and file systems. Since the format of the URL stays the same (slashes are always forward and there are no name length restrictions) it is safe to embed an NFS URL in a program, script, or symbolic link.
- The structure is simple and well known due to the ubiquity of the HTTP URL. In addition, there are rules that allow URLs to be combined with relative URLs to form new URLs, described in RFC 1808.

16.6.2   Absolute vs. Relative Paths

The pathname taken from an NFS URL should be evaluated relative to the public filehandle; the path should not begin with a slash unless it is intended to be a path relative to the server's root rather than the directory associated with the public filehandle. For instance, given a URL

```
nfs://server/a/b/c
```

the multicomponent path sent to the server will be a/b/c, but the URL

    nfs://server//a/b/c

will be evaluated with a multicomponent path of /a/b/c.

16.7 WebNFS Client Characteristics

The requirements of a WebNFS client are described in RFC 2054, detailing the use of the public filehandle and multicomponent LOOKUP to simplify access to WebNFS servers.

Ideally, a WebNFS client would be happy to find that it can make a TCP connection to the server and have public filehandle support with NFS version 3. In practice, it needs to handle the many NFS servers that do not yet support NFS version 3, TCP connections, or WebNFS access. The client needs to evaluate the kind of server it is connecting to with a minimum of network traffic. The server's portmapper should not be used, since requests to it may be blocked by a firewall, and calls to the NFS NULL procedure should be avoided because this introduces binding delay; so an optimistic approach like this is recommended:

- Make a TCP connection to the server. If the connection is refused, fall back to UDP.
- Request a version 3 LOOKUP for the path relative to the public filehandle.
- If the request is rejected with an NFSERR_STALE (or similar) error, then assume that there is no public filehandle support and use the MOUNT protocol to convert the pathname to a filehandle.
- If the request is rejected with a RPC program version mismatch error, then retry the request with NFS version 2. The client must also detect a broken connection and reestablish the connection if necessary.

If the server does not support public filehandles, the MOUNT protocol must be used to convert the path in the URL to a filehandle.

The following snoop trace shows protocol fallback of a WebNFS client attempting to access a directory via the URL nfs://server/home1 on a non-WebNFS version 2 server over UDP.

```
client-> server TCP D=2049 S=40061 Syn Seq=1365561478 Len=0
                          Win=8760
server-> client TCP D=40061 S=2049 Rst Ack=1365561479 Win=0
```

The client needs to obtain a filehandle for the pathname /home1 and determine from the file attributes whether /home1 represents a file or a directory. The first two packets show an attempt to set up a TCP connection. WebNFS clients prefer to use TCP because it is a more reliable transport than UDP and is handled more kindly by network firewalls.

It is not unusual that the connection is rejected. There are many old implementations of NFS that do not support the use of TCP. The client then must use UDP. First it tries an NFS version 3 multicomponent LOOKUP. This request is rejected by the server with a mismatch error because the server does not support NFS verson 3.

```
client  ->  server   NFS C LOOKUP3 FH=0000 /home1
server  ->  client   RPC R Program number mismatch (low=2, high=2)
```

Because the mismatch error indicated that the server does support NFS version 2 (low=2, high=2), the client then attempts an NFS version 2 multi-component LOOKUP, which fails with a "Stale Filehandle" error. This error indicates to the client that the server does not recognize public filehandles.

```
client  ->  server   NFS C LOOKUP2 FH=0000 /home1
server  ->  client   NFS R LOOKUP2 Stale NFS file handle
```

Since it is obvious that the server is not a WebNFS server, the client has no choice but to use the MOUNT protocol to obtain an initial filehandle for the path /home1. It requests the port for the MOUNT service and issues a MOUNT request to that port to obtain a filehandle for /home1.

```
client  ->  server   PORTMAP C GETPORT prog=100005 (MOUNT) vers=2
                        proto=UDP
server  ->  client   PORTMAP R GETPORT port=746
client  ->  server   MOUNT1 C Mount /home1
server  ->  client   MOUNT1 R Mount OK FH=072F
```

Having successfully received a filehandle for /home1, the client sends an UNMOUNT request to purge a record of the client's MOUNT from the server's /etc/rmtab log because the client is not considered to have *mounted* a filesystem.

```
client  ->  server   MOUNT1 C Unmount /home1
server  ->  client   MOUNT1 R Unmount reply
```

Finally, the client uses the filehandle to obtain the file attributes for /home1 so that it can determine whether the filehandle represents a regular file or a directory

```
client  ->  server   NFS C GETATTR2 FH=072F
server  ->  client   NFS R GETATTR2 OK
```

16.7.1 Mountpoint Crossing

An NFS LOOKUP request that does not use the public filehandle can look up only one component of a pathname at a time, and these lookups cannot cross mountpoints on the server (Figure 16.7). This subtlety of NFS lookups means that it is possible for NFS clients to see "underneath" mountpoints on the server and have access to files or directories that would normally be invisible to a user logged into the server.

It is tempting to consider allowing a WebNFS client that uses the MOUNT protocol to cache a filehandle associated with a directory and use normal NFS LOOKUP requests with this filehandle, since this would avoid the relatively slow MOUNT protocol. However, there's a danger that the client may unwittingly miss a server mountpoint and either receive a "Not found" error or access a file with the same name as a file in a filesystem mounted on top. For this reason it is desirable for WebNFS clients to use multicomponent lookup for all directory lookups and if the MOUNT protocol is being used, to use it to return every filehandle—albeit slowly.

16.7.2 Fetching a File

While HTTP clients obtain documents with a GET request, NFS clients must issue a LOOKUP request to obtain a filehandle for the document, followed by a READ request to download the data. The reply to the LOOKUP request includes the filehandle along with the file attributes. The client must check the file size in the attributes to decide whether to fetch the file with a single large READ request or, if limited by the server's transfer size, by a number of smaller READ requests. If the client is using the NFS version 2 protocol, then read requests must not exceed 8 KB. Version 3 does not specify a maximum read size, so the client could optimistically try a large read size of 32 KB or 64 KB—if the server does not support such large reads then it will return as much as it can. Solaris servers have a 32-KB limit.

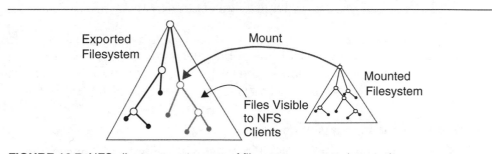

FIGURE 16.7 NFS clients are not aware of filesystem mountpoints on the server.

16.7.3   Fetching a Directory

If the attributes returned by the LOOKUP request indicate that the requested object is a directory, then a browser client must issue either a READDIR request (version 2) or a READDIRPLUS request (version 3). The READDIRPLUS request has the advantage that it returns filehandle and file attribute information along with the names of the directory entries. Version 2 clients must issue individual LOOKUP requests for every directory entry to retrieve this information. For large directories, the saving in network calls by READDIRPLUS is significant.

16.7.4   Fetching a Symbolic Link

If the attributes returned by a LOOKUP indicate that the requested object is a symbolic link, the browser should retrieve the link text with a READLINK request. It should then interpret the link text (see section 16.5.5).

16.7.5   Document Types

Documents retrieved by NFS do not arrive with MIME headers, so the client has to identify document types using file suffixes or other means. This identification is commonly done with reference to a ".mime.types" file that maps file suffixes to *mime* types.

16.8   WebNFS Server Requirements

A WebNFS server is just an NFS server that can recognize the public file-handle and evaluate multicomponent LOOKUP requests. The server administrator needs to be able to associate a directory with the public filehandle. On Solaris servers the "public" option of the NFS share command is used; for example,

```
# share -o ro,public /export/home/ftp
```

makes the directory tree below /export/home/ftp available to NFS clients and associates it with the public filehandle. Since NFS URL paths are relative to the public filehandle, the URL: http://server/pub would locate the server directory /export/home/ftp/pub.

16.8.1   Evaluating a Multicomponent LOOKUP

On receiving a LOOKUP request with a public filehandle, the server must be able to perform a multicomponent LOOKUP (Figure 16.8). On UNIX servers the slash-separated path can be passed to the server's namei or lookup_pn

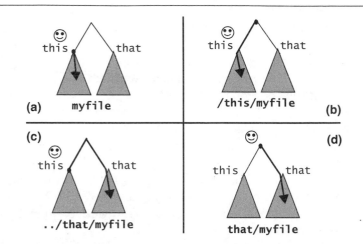

FIGURE 16.8 Interaction of the public filehandle location and multicomponent lookup. (a) The path identifies a file in a directory below the public directory (identified by the J). (b) The same file is identified with an absolute path that is independent of the public directory. (c) The path is relative to the public directory but names a file in another exported filesystem. (d) The public directory is the server's root (not exported) from which a relative path can name a file in any exported filesystem.

code, which routinely evaluates pathnames that may contain symbolic links or cross mountpoints. The resulting file or directory need only be checked to authorize the client's access depending on the server's access control policy. Many NFS servers control access to exported filesystems with the MOUNT daemon. Filehandles are given only to clients that have access to the filesystem. Since a WebNFS client does not use the MOUNT daemon, filehandle control exercised by the MOUNT daemon is useless for filesystems accessible with the public filehandle, so there is no point in using conventional client access restrictions for a public export.

Some servers not only control access through the MOUNT daemon but also check every use of a filehandle. This checking has the advantage that a client cannot gain any advantage via unauthorized use of a filehandle and the server can exercise control even for public exports. These servers have a further advantage that allows the client to specify a path that leads to another exported filesystem not associated with the public filehandle. The server will return a filehandle for any exported filesystem since it knows that every use of the filehandle will be checked. Solaris servers have a default location for the public filehandle at the server's root. Even though the root may not be exported to NFS clients, valid multicomponent LOOKUPs can be made relative to the server's root as long as the path names a file in an exported filesystem. Even if the public filehandle is associated with some nonroot directory, a multicomponent LOOKUP on an absolute path (starting with a slash) will be evaluated relative to the system root.

16.8.2   Canonical vs. Native Path

If the pathname in a multicomponent LOOKUP request begins with a printable ASCII character, then it must be a *canonical* path. A canonical path is a hierarchically related, slash-separated sequence of components: *directory/ directory/ . . . /name*. Any slashes within a component must be escaped using the escape code %2f. Nonprintable ASCII characters (with values in the range 00–1F and 7f hexadecimal) must also be escaped using the % character to introduce a two-digit hexadecimal code. Occurrences of the % character that do not introduce an encoded character must themselves be encoded with %25.

If the first character of the path is 0x80 (non-ASCII), then the following character is the first in a *native* path. A native path conforms to the natural pathname syntax of the server. The MOUNT protocol accepts only native paths, for example,

```
Lookup FH=0x0 "/a/b/c"      (Canonical path)
Lookup FH=0x0 0x80 "a:b:c"  (Native path)
```

In this example, the sequence 0x80 "a:b:c" represents the filename parameter of the LOOKUP request for NFS versions 2 or 3:

Length = 6	0x80	a	:	b	:	c

16.8.3   Client and Server Port

Some NFS servers accept requests only from reserved UDP or TCP ports (i.e., port numbers below 1024). These "privileged" ports are available only to UNIX processes with superuser permissions. Requests that do not originate from the range of reserved ports are rejected. Reserved port checking is an optimistic way of preventing direct access to the server from user processes that may attempt to spoof AUTH_UNIX RPC credentials. Since WebNFS clients are not required to use reserved ports, a WebNFS server must not check the originating port for requests to filesystems made available to Web-NFS clients.

As an RPC service, the NFS server is normally not required to listen for requests on a well-known port. In general, RPC servers can listen on any port as long as the port is registered with the Portmapper service on port 111. The NFS server is required to maintain its port assignment across server reboots, so in practice the server binds to a fixed port and all NFS servers use port 2049. WebNFS clients cannot rely on using the Portmap protocol to discover the NFS server port since the Portmap protocol is sometimes blocked by firewalls, and firewalls cannot easily be configured to filter protocols that are not assigned to fixed port numbers; a WebNFS client will assume that the server it is connecting to is listening on port 2049.

16.9   **WebNFS Security Negotiation**

When a WebNFS client attempts to contact a server, it needs to know what RPC security flavor the server supports. A client that uses version 3 of the MOUNT protocol can expect a list of the server's supported security flavors to be returned with the filehandle (see section 9.5.2). Since a WebNFS client does not use the MOUNT protocol, it must obtain the list of supported security flavors through the NFS protocol itself.

Internet servers that make public files accessible to anyone for read-only access are likely to support an AUTH_SYS credential with a UID and GID of "nobody." A good first attempt on contacting a server for the first time is to assume that this credential will work. If it does work, the client need not bother with any further security negotiation. If the server returns an authentication error, the client will need to determine the security flavor that the server will accept for the filesystem it is trying to access. A WebNFS client can query this list with a modified multicomponent LOOKUP request. If the first character of the pathname is the non-ASCII character 0x80, the path is assumed to be a native path. If the first character is the character 0x81 (non-ASCII), the LOOKUP is interpreted as a query for the security flavor list associated with the path. The following character is an index value into the server's security vector (one on the first call). The remaining pathname can be a canonical path (all ASCII) or a native path (prefixed with 0x80).

```
Lookup FH=0x0 0x81 0x0 "a/b/c"       (Query of canonical path)
Lookup FH=0x0 0x81 0x0 0x80 "a:b:c"  (Query of native path)
```

If the server does not support the security query LOOKUP, it will return a "No such file" error or "I/O error." If the server does understand the security query, it will return an overloaded filehandle that contains a list of the security flavors. The flavor numbers are encoded as a variable-length array of integers within the returned filehandle. This integer array is the same as would be returned with the filehandle if the client were able to use version 3 of the MOUNT protocol. Because the filehandle is of limited length (32 bytes for version 2 and up to 64 bytes for version 3), it is possible that the server may have a longer list of security flavors than can fit in a filehandle. The security negotiation protocol allows the server to return a long security list as a sequence of filehandles returned by a set of LOOKUP security queries that each specify an index into the list.

For example, if the client receives a security error for a multicomponent LOOKUP of the path a/b/c, then it will issue a security query LOOKUP string of

Length = 7	0 x 81	0 x 0	a	/	b	/	c

If the server supports security negotiation, then it will return a special file-handle that contains a list of security flavors arranged in preference order, just as it would be if returned by version 3 of the MOUNT protocol. For example, the first flavor in the list (most preferred) might give the client secure, read-write access—whereas the second flavor in the list may specify a less secure mechanism that is limited to read-only access (see Figure 16.9).

For version 2 of the protocol, the filehandle is a 32-byte opaque object. When used to return a list of security flavors, the first byte is a length byte that indicates the number of valid flavors in the filehandle. It is defined as 4 $*$ n, where n is the number of flavors. Thus, the length byte can vary between 4 (1 flavor returned) and 28 (7 flavors returned). The second byte in the filehandle is a status byte. A setting of 0 means that there are no more flavors to follow. A setting of 1 means that the flavor list is incomplete and the client should issue another query with the index value set to indicate the next series of flavors to be received. The third and fourth bytes are padding bytes, followed by one or more security flavors.

Since an NFS version 3 filehandle can be much larger, up to 64 bytes in size, it can carry up to 15 security flavors. Because a version 3 filehandle already has a pre-pended length word (it is defined as a variable-length opaque XDR object), it doesn't need a length byte. It has the value 4 $*$ $(n + 1)$ where n is the number of flavors. The length can vary between 8 (1 flavor returned) and 64 (15 flavors returned). The first byte following the length is the status byte that indicates whether more flavors are to come, followed by three bytes of padding.

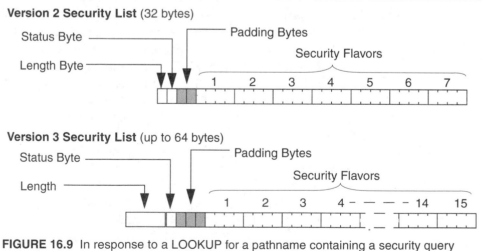

Version 2 Security List (32 bytes)

Version 3 Security List (up to 64 bytes)

FIGURE 16.9 In response to a LOOKUP for a pathname containing a security query code, the server returns a special filehandle that contains a list of security flavors.

16.10   Summary

The first implementations of the NFS protocol were limited to 8-KB transfers over UDP, which worked well on local area networks but not on the Internet. NFS version 3 features such Internet-friendly features as large transfer sizes, improved write performance, and an affinity for use of TCP connections. However, all versions of the protocol require the use of the MOUNT protocol to obtain an initial filehandle for an exported filesystem. Since the MOUNT protocol has no fixed port number, it cannot easily transit firewalls that identify protocols by port number.

Using WebNFS, a client can connect directly to the NFS server and obtain an initial filehandle via a LOOKUP request relative to the public filehandle. The public filehandle is identified as a filehandle filled with zeros (version 2) or zero length (version 3). If the LOOKUP request includes an entire slash-separated pathname, it is known as a multicomponent LOOKUP. The client can use a special form of the multicomponent LOOKUP to retrieve a list of valid security flavors from the server.

Chapter 17

NFS Version 4

Just as NFS version 3 is gaining in popularity, the NFS protocol is being revised again: NFS version 4. Why so soon after version 3? What is wrong with version 3? How will another protocol revision improve NFS? This chapter will explain the rationale for version 4.

NFS version 3, defined in 1992, was a limited protocol revision. There had been several attempts in prior years to fix the limitations of NFS version 2, but in each case the accretion of features made the protocol too unwieldy to implement. Mac users wanted a file model that would handle a data and resource fork. VAX/VMS users wanted operations for record-oriented files. DOS users wanted case-insensitive directory lookups.

The team that designed version 3 consciously avoided making large changes to the protocol and succeeded in completing the design within a year. Although version 3 incorporated a number of improvements (section 7.1.3), the protocol remained essentially a LAN protocol for UNIX clients and servers. In 1992, when NFS version 3 was developed, the Internet was not yet a household word. There was no World Wide Web or e-commerce or URLs displayed in magazines and billboards. Much has changed since 1992 that NFS version 3 does not acknowledge. WebNFS (chapter 16) brought some minor updates to the protocol to make it more Internet compatible. Yet WebNFS was limited in scope since it could not substantially change the protocol without a protocol revision.

As this book goes to press, an IETF working group is designing NFS version 4. Although the protocol exists only in draft, the requirements that drive the design have been discussed and published. In this chapter we will examine the NFS version 4 requirements and possible protocol enhancements to support them.

17.1 An IETF Protocol

NFS version 2 was developed, in house, by a team of Sun Microsystems engineers in 1984. NFS version 3 was developed in a more public forum by several companies that had shown an interest in participating in the development of the new protocol. The NFS version 3 protocol was hammered out over a mailing list with about 20 engineers on it.

NFS version 4 is being developed by an IETF working group (Figure 17.1). The Internet Engineering Task Force (IETF) is the engineering arm of the Internet Society. It is responsible for the development of networking standards that relate to the Internet.[1] The IETF is responsible for developing and standardizing transport protocols like IPv4, IPv6, UDP, and TCP, as well as higher-level protocols like FTP, DNS, and HTTP. The documents published by the IETF begin as Internet-Drafts, simple text documents that are made available for download via anonymous FTP. Documents that simply present information that does not constitute a "standard" can be published as informational RFCs (Requests for Comment). A document that describes a standard undergoes a more rigorous review process through a working group.

Most working group business is transacted on a mailing list moderated by a working group chair. Working groups can meet face to face three times a year at an IETF meeting. The IETF is organized as a management hierarchy: a number of working groups are organized into an area that is managed by a

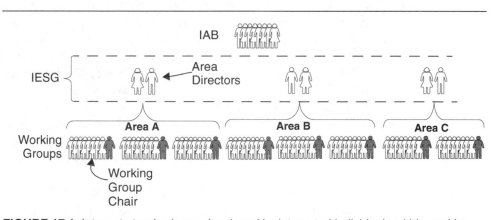

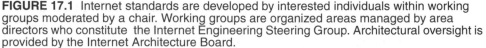

FIGURE 17.1 Internet standards are developed by interested individuals within working groups moderated by a chair. Working groups are organized areas managed by area directors who constitute the Internet Engineering Steering Group. Architectural oversight is provided by the Internet Architecture Board.

1. The Web site for the IETF can be found at *www.ietf.org*

couple of area directors. The area directors for the working groups constitute a committee called the Internet Engineering Steering Group (IESG), which reviews working group submissions for new standards and sets policy. Architectural oversight of the IESG is provided by the Internet Architecture Board (IAB).

The NFS version 4 working group began with a birds of a feather (BOF) meeting at the IETF meeting in San Jose in December 1996. The purpose of a BOF is to demonstrate interest in the working group's goals. Since Sun Microsystems, Inc., owns the NFS trademark, it controls any protocol specification that claims to be "NFS." So that NFS would be acceptable to the IETF as an open, Internet-standard protocol, Sun ceded change control of NFS version 4 to the Internet Society.[2] With this agreement signed, the NFS version 4 working group was formed in July 1997.

17.2 NFS Version 4 Working Group Charter

Every IETF working group has a charter statement that describes what it has been set up to do. The charter is an important guide that helps keep the working group on track. A working group will have as many different opinions as it has members. Each working group member will have a slightly different vision of the finished product. The charter helps the working group maintain focus on a coherent outcome. The NFS version 4 working group has the following draft charter.[3]

> The objective of this working group is to advance the state of NFS technology by producing a specification for NFS version 4 which will be submitted as an Internet standards track RFC. The first phase of the working group activity will produce a requirements document describing the limitations and deficiencies of NFS version 3, potential solutions for addressing these, and a cost/benefit analysis of the different solutions. Input for the development of this document will include experiences with other distributed file systems such as DCE/DFS and Coda. Following the publication of this document, the charter of the working group will be reassessed; however, it is anticipated that NFS version 4 will emphasize the following core features:
>
> - *Improved access and good performance on the Internet.*
>   The protocol will be designed to perform well where latency is high and bandwidth is low, to adapt to the presence of congestion, to scale to very large numbers of clients per server, and to transit firewalls easily.

---

2. Documented in RFC 2339, "An Agreement Between the Internet Society, the IETF, and Sun Microsystems, Inc., in the matter of NFS V.4 Protocols."

3. The NFS version 4 working group charter has not yet been formally approved by the IESG.

- *Strong security with negotiation built into the protocol.*
  The protocol may build on the work of the ONCRPC working group in supporting the RPCSEC_GSS protocol. The permission model needs to scale
  beyond the current flat integer UID space. Additionally, NFS version 4 will
  provide a mechanism to allow clients and servers to negotiate security and
  require clients and servers to support a minimal set of security schemes.
- *Better cross-platform interoperability.*
  The protocol will feature a filesystem model that provides a useful, common
  set of features that does not unduly favor one filesystem or operating system
  over another.
- *Designed for protocol extensions.*
  The protocol will be designed to accept standard extensions that do not compromise backward compatibility.

More detail on the design requirements for NFS version 4 can be found in
[RFC 2624]. The remainder of this chapter will discuss the protocol features
outlined in the charter—which deficiencies of previous NFS versions moti-
vated the features and how they should affect the design of NFS version 4.

17.3 Improved Access and Good Performance on the Internet

As a TCP/IP-based protocol, NFS has been used on the Internet—even
though the protocol was never designed for Internet use. A client cannot simply connect to an NFS version 2 or 3 server and use the protocol to access files
without an initial filehandle provided by the MOUNT protocol. The WebNFS
modifications to the NFS protocol (described in chapter 16) made the initial
connection to the server much faster and simpler by eliminating the requirement to use the MOUNT protocol. The WebNFS changes were limited in their
scope by the constraints of the protocol specifications. No new procedures
could be added and no procedures could be modified (by adding or rearrang-
ing call or reply fields) without a protocol revision. There is much more that
could be done to the protocol to make it work well on the Internet.

What are the characteristics of the Internet that make it different from a
local area network? What features of an Internet environment should a protocol designer take into account?

17.3.1 Protocol Integration

WebNFS made it possible to use the NFS protocol without using the Portmapper protocol or the MOUNT protocol. The integration of these protocols with
WebNFS made it possible to connect to a server through a single TCP connection—making it much easier to transit packet-filtering firewalls or application
proxies like SOCKS [RFC 1928]. Yet there are still other important protocols
for NFS that could not be integrated by WebNFS.

The NFS protocol itself provides no support for file locking. Locking functions are handled by the entirely separate Network Lock Manager protocol (chapter 10) that is registered on no fixed port, making it difficult to convey through a firewall or other application-level proxy. NFS version 4 can continue the protocol integration begun by WebNFS by defining locking operations within the NFS protocol itself (Figure 17.2).

PCNFS clients make use of the PCNFSD protocol (section 14.5) to obtain security credentials, map UIDs/GIDs to strings, and support printing functions. If features of the PCNFSD protocol could be integrated with the NFS protocol, as appropriate, then it would be possible for PC clients to connect to Internet NFS servers. There seems to be a clear consensus that NFS version 4 should not include the printing functions of the PCNFSD protocol, but it would be appropriate for NFS version 4 to assist PC-based clients in their handling of user or group identification via UIDs or GIDs (see section 17.5.2).

17.3.2   Latency

Network latency is a measurement of the time taken for a packet of data to transit the network from source to destination (Figure 17.3). Round-trip latency is the time it takes to receive a reply to an RPC call. Latency increases with distance. At the speed of light, it takes a message 15 milliseconds to travel from Los Angeles to New York (30-msec round-trip). On the Internet, messages don't normally travel in straight lines and may be held up briefly in routers between the source and destination. On average, messages may be slowed by ten times the speed of light delay. It may take between a hundred and several hundred milliseconds for a round-trip across 3000 miles.

A protocol designed for Internet use must economize on its use of messages or remote procedure calls if it is to avoid the cumulative effect of latency on each round-trip. NFS version 3 added some features that reduced the num-

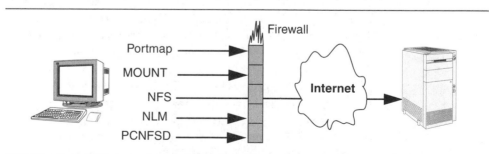

FIGURE 17.2 NFS through firewalls. NFS depends on other protocols that do not have well-known ports and cannot easily pass through firewalls. An NFS protocol that integrates the functions of these other protocols will be more compatible with Internet use.

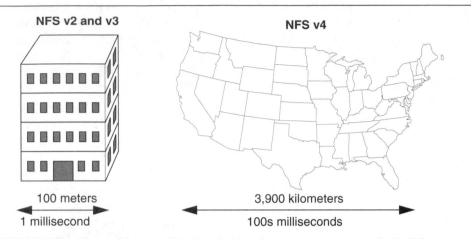

FIGURE 17.3 Network latency. The time it takes for a message to transit a building network is insignificant compared to the time it takes to travel across a continent. The NFS version 4 protocol must tackle the problem of network latency if it is to work well on the Internet.

ber of messages required to accomplish a task. Nearly all procedures return piggybacked file attributes, reducing the need to use additional GETATTR requests. A single READDIRPLUS request can return filehandle and attribute information for directory entries, while NFS version 2 clients must resort to a separate LOOKUP request for every directory entry to return the same information. The WebNFS changes eliminated the multiple round-trips required by NFS mounting (see chapter 9) with a single multicomponent LOOKUP request.

There are more opportunities for an NFS version 4 client to further reduce its use of RPC calls. Currently, an NFS client using the WebNFS changes must use at least two RPC calls to get data from a file: a multicomponent LOOKUP to return a filehandle for the file, then by a READ call to return the file data. If the protocol supported a combined LOOKUP and READ procedure, the client could retrieve file data with a single round-trip. A protocol designed for minimum use of messages could include a number of these integrated procedures that allow the client to accomplish more in a single message.

An alternative is to provide a mechanism that allows multiple procedures, or operations, to be combined into a single call and response. The CIFS protocol allows operations to be batched (section 13.4.4) into a single request (Figure 17.4). An NFS protocol that supports batched or compound requests could define simple LOOKUP and READ operations that could be combined into a single LOOKUP/READ request. Client implementations could build compound requests from these simple operations that map onto their API functions. For instance, a UNIX client might generate a LOOKUP/ACCESS/ GETATTR request from a file open( ) call.

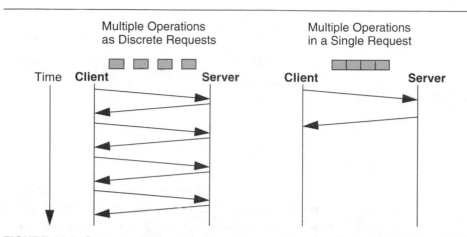

Multiple Operations
as Discrete Requests

Multiple Operations
in a Single Request

Time **Client**   **Server**   **Client**   **Server**

FIGURE 17.4 Compound request. Latency is an overhead on the round-trip for each RPC request and reply. A protocol that allows multiple operations to be combined into a compound request can avoid the cumulative latency of discrete requests.

A compound request can be particularly effective when an operation generates data that can be used by the next operation in the request, for instance, a LOOKUP operation that generates a filehandle that can be used by the following READ operation.

17.3.3 Bandwidth

The available network bandwidth between a client and server directly affects the rate at which data can be moved between the client and the server's disk. On a local area network typical of a home or office, high bandwidth is normal. Most offices and home networks have at least 10 megabits/second of bandwidth and many are now upgrading to 100-MB/sec networks. A 10-MB/sec network allows file data to be moved at slightly more than 1 megabyte per second and 10 megabytes per second over a 100-MB network. The NFS protocol was designed for this high bandwidth environment.

The Internet is notable for its comparatively low bandwidth (Table 17.1). Home users are familiar with the speed of modem access (56 KB/sec), ISDN (64–128 KB/sec) and DSL or cable modem (1–5 MB/sec). These bandwidths are in all cases slower than the type of network for which the NFS protocol was designed: 10 MB Ethernet or better. The network bandwidths are in all cases slower than the bandwidth to local disk storage. If an implementation of the NFS protocol is to provide performance comparable with that of local disks, then it must cache file data.

TABLE 17.40 Bandwidth Comparisions

Medium	Bandwidth	Relative to 10-Mb Ethernet
Modem	56 KB/sec	200 X slower
ISDN	128 KB/sec	100 X slower
DSL or cable	1–5 MB/sec	2–10 X slower
SCSI disk	5–40 MB/sec	5–40 X faster

17.3.4   Efficient Caching

As described in section 8.14, most NFS clients use main memory to cache file data and attributes, and there are examples of disk-based caches (e.g., CacheFS). On a high-bandwidth, low-latency LAN, the cost of a cache miss is quite low. To transfer 8 KB of data across a 10-MB Ethernet connection takes just 8 milliseconds. The same 8 KB of data across a modem connection would take 200 times longer—almost 2 seconds.

An NFS client that accesses a server across the Internet can enjoy a huge benefit from a cache if the cache is big enough to hold a "working set" of files. Although NFS versions 2 and 3 implementations can support large caches, the protocol provides no mechanism to support cache consistency. Beyond close-to-open consistency (section 8.14.3), NFS caching is probabilistic—the protocol cannot prevent the client from accessing stale data. Even close-to-open consistency cannot be supported efficiently; the requirement to check attributes with a GETATTR call on every file open will incur a latency cost if the server is far away.

NFS version 4 could support a more efficient caching model—perhaps lease-based as in NQNFS (section 12.2) or using callbacks as supported by AFS, DCE/DFS, and CIFS (see chapter 12). The caching schemes supported by these other distributed filesystems have the potential to reduce the amount of client/server interaction significantly. Efficient caching is particularly important on the Internet where a cache miss is so expensive. An efficient caching model in NFS version 4 would also help reduce the load on large Internet NFS servers that may have tens of thousands of clients.

17.3.5   Proxy Caching

NFS version 4 clients might also benefit from the use of proxy caching support. Currently, all NFS caching is done on the client. Web browsers also utilize large client caches for Web pages, but they also support the use of proxy caching. The HTTP protocol can route Web page queries indirectly through a proxy cache server (Figure 17.5).

The proxy cache server checks whether the page corresponding to the requested URL is already cached. If so, then it returns the page to the client

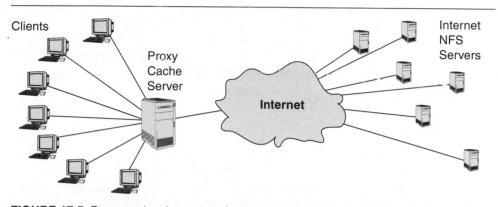

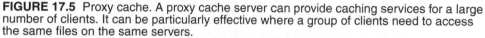

FIGURE 17.5 Proxy cache. A proxy cache server can provide caching services for a large number of clients. It can be particularly effective where a group of clients need to access the same files on the same servers.

without contacting the primary server at all. A proxy cache is particularly effective where there are pages commonly accessed by multiple clients. The NFS protocol does not support this redirection feature of HTTP. An NFS client cannot send an NFS request to a proxy cache server and specify its redirection to a target NFS server. A simple redirection capability in the NFS version 4 protocol could make this kind of caching available to NFS clients accessing NFS servers over the Internet.

17.3.6 Scalability

The NFS protocol was originally designed to provide a network file service for a work group. Despite some initial predictions that the protocol would not scale beyond 20 clients, improvements in network and server capacity have made it possible for a single NFS server to make files available, with good performance, to hundreds of client machines. Some problems can arise, however, as the scale of file service is increased further to the thousands or tens of thousands of clients that might be handled by an Internet service provider.

An efficient caching mechanism and the ability to proxy cache can go a long way toward off-loading the network and the server. The protocol should not require a server implementation to keep a lot of state about what a client is up to. An HTTP server, for instance, is stateless. If the server crashes and recovers, clients can continue operation with no recovery action needed. The statelessness of HTTP reflects the simplicity of a protocol for retrieving documents—the protocol supports neither file locking nor the kind of cache consistency expected of a distributed filesystem protocol. The caching and file locking features expected of NFS version 4 may demand the server to maintain some client state as to which files are cached or locked, but as long as the amount of state is small and easily recovered, it may not be a barrier to large-scale operation. The protocol must be careful to evaluate the scalability implications of some features. For instance, a callback feature that notifies interested clients of changes to a selected file or directory may work well in a small workgroup setting but be impractical in a much larger setting. Imagine 100,000 clients registering interest in changes to the /var/mail directory!

17.3.7   Availability

The expectations of file service availability change with scale. If a small NFS server crashes and puts a group of 20 clients out of action for an hour, the impact to an organization is an early coffee break. If the NFS server for an Internet service provider is down for an hour, the impact to 100,000 clients is a page one story.

If the protocol permits clients to keep the bulk of their file access directed to a cached working set of files, then the primary server may need to be contacted only a few times per hour or day. If a client does not miss the cache, it is possible that a server could crash and recover without the client being aware of it. The ability of a cache to mask a server outage depends very much on the pattern of file access on the client. Another way to provide higher availability is to install redundant paths to the data at the server side. Several NFS server vendors sell highly available NFS servers: a cluster of NFS servers with access to a common set of disks (see Figure 5.6). If a server crashes, another server in the cluster mounts its disks and adopts its IP address. Clients continue to access their data through the new server while the old server recovers or is repaired. If the data are read-only and infrequently updated, then the data can be replicated on multiple servers with no shared disk. An attractive feature of these replica servers is that they can be geographically dispersed to be in close proximity to the clients that use them. As long as a client knows the location of each replica server, it can switch if a server crashes.

The NFS requirement that filehandles be unchanging can hamper the switch from one server to another. An HA-NFS cluster must be configured to make sure that a standby server will recognize the filehandles used by the primary server. A client that can switch replicas will obtain new filehandles by reevaluating the path to each file. It assumes that the filehandles will change. Some within the working group have suggested that NFS version 4 support a *volatile* filehandle. A server would designate a filehandle as volatile if it cannot guarantee its indefinite validity. The client could then associate pathname information with the filehandle so that a new filehandle could be obtained if the filehandle becomes unusable. The volatile filehandle may make it easier to create HA clusters or replica configurations.

Service availability might also be increased if NFS version 4 could provide a graceful way for system administrators to load-balance servers by relocating disks or *filesets* (self-contained collections of files within a disk partition) from one server to another. The Andrew File System (AFS) provides a feature that allows a fileset to be moved while it is in use by clients (see section 13.2.3).

17.4 Strong Security with Negotiation Built into the Protocol

Most NFS clients and servers are configured with AUTH_SYS user authentication, notorious for its lack of secure user authentication. Although other more secure flavors have been available for some time (AUTH_DH and AUTH_KERB4), system administrators have been unwilling to set up the infrastructure required to maintain public or secret keys for each user. Since most NFS use has been within private corporate networks, the risk from unauthenticated users or from interception of NFS traffic is perceived as low. This laissez-faire security policy cannot exist outside the firewall on the Internet. No sane system administrator would expose their NFS server to the full onslaught of Internet hackers if sensitive data were at risk. It is the IETF's policy that all new protocols support strong security.

17.4.1 Connection-Based Security

One approach to providing secure access for Internet protocols is to set up a secure connection between the client and server. A good example of this is the secure sockets layer (SSL) security that is already widely used with the HTTP protocol. Since SSL[4] provides security for any TCP connection, it can provide security for any protocol that uses TCP, including NFS over TCP. Why not use SSL? The most obvious problem with connection-based security is that it cannot protect NFS traffic over a connectionless transport like UDP. Even when NFS is used over TCP, the same connection can be shared by multiple users on a multiuser client. Connection-based security cannot authenticate multiple users sharing the same connection. The same limitation applies to IP-based security such as IPSEC.

17.4.2 RPC-Based Security

The RPC protocol that supports all versions of NFS already provides a flexible security framework that can support strong security schemes. The RPCSEC_GSS security mechanism is described in section 4.7. RPCSEC_GSS can support not only private key schemes like Kerberos version 5, but also public key-based schemes. As well as secure authentication, RPCSEC_GSS provides functions that allow data to be protected for integrity or encrypted for privacy. Since RPCSEC_GSS is implemented at the RPC layer, it can be imple-

---

4. To become an Internet standard as the TLS protocol described in [RFC 2246].

mented for NFS versions 2 and 3 with no change to those protocols. What value can NFS version 4 add to NFS security?

The RPCSEC_GSS framework does not provide a way to negotiate security for an exported filesystem on the server. Although RPCSEC_GSS can support the simple and protected GSS-API negotiation mechanism (SPNEGO) described in [RFC 2478], it does not allow the choice of security mechanism to be negotiated on a per-export basis if, for instance, a system administrator makes all files under the /public directory open for public access with no security preference but insists that everything under /private be accessed with Kerberos version 5 security. The WebNFS security negotiation (section 16.9) layers a negotiation mechanism on the NFS version 2 and 3 protocols. It suggests a mechanism that NFS version 4 could support—allowing the client to query the security to be used for a particular directory hierarchy.

17.5   Better Cross-Platform Interoperability

Although the Sun engineers that designed the NFS protocol claimed it as a platform-independent protocol, it is clear that the protocol specification heavily favors the UNIX filesystem model. The clearest example is the set of file attributes returned by the fattr structure: it is almost exactly the set of UNIX file attributes.

17.5.1   File Attributes

Although PC FAT filesystems have attributes in common with NFS, such as the file size in bytes and the file modification time, there are DOS attributes such as *hidden* and *archive* attributes that had no direct counterpart in the UNIX file attributes. While new filesystems such as NTFS in Windows 2000 have added new file and filesystem attributes, the static set of file and filesystem attributes of NFS versions 2 and 3 cannot be extended to support them.

NFS version 4 will need to support an open-ended file attribute model that allows new file attributes to be defined and supported in a backward-compatible way (Figure 17.6). Rather than defining a fixed set of file attributes

FIGURE 17.6 Extensible attributes. NFS versions 2 and 3 define both file and filesystem attributes as a fixed set. A more flexible attribute framework in version 4 might allow attributes to be selected individually.

in a `fattr` structure, it would be more flexible to allow attributes to be read and set individually. For instance, it might assign a number to each attribute and have the client give a list of the attribute numbers it needs to set or read. A compact representation for a list of attribute numbers assigns each attribute a bit number in a bitmap. A bit set in the bitmap would indicate that the value is to be read (if a GETATTR request) or that its value follows (if a SETATTR request). The attribute values could then be marshaled in order of attribute number.

By allowing clients to be more selective in which file attributes are returned and servers to be more flexible in the file attributes they will support, NFS version 4 will be able to support a much larger set of file attributes and filesystem attributes.

17.5.2 Representing User and Group IDs

The representation of a file owner is another issue for cross-platform support. NFS follows the UNIX model of assigning a UID or GID value to a user or group. A single UID or GID space works well for UNIX clients and servers as long as they are in the same administrative domain. If the clients and servers are in different domains, then there may be no correspondence between these numbers. For instance "Bob" in the Finance domain and "Mary" in the Marketing domain may be assigned the same UID by their respective administrators. It may be possible on a small scale to set up a mapping scheme to translate the UID or GID values of one domain to a corresponding UID or GID of another domain, but mapping gets completely out of hand on an Internet scale. The assignment of UID values is also a platform issue: a user on a Windows NT system is represented by a security ID (SID) that is not a simple integer like the UNIX UID/GID values. Without employing complex mapping schemes, how are users and groups to be represented uniquely between platforms or across the Internet?

One possibility is to use a string to represent users and groups (see Figure 17.7). The string might resemble an e-mail address, taking the form *user@domain*. Each client or server would map its user or group representation into a string. Even if the mapping cannot be accomplished, a user still might view the unmapped string directly and be able to identify the user or group.

FIGURE 17.7 Representation of users and groups. The protocol could represent users and groups as a string with a format similar to an e-mail address. The string would be mapped to a local representation at the client and server.

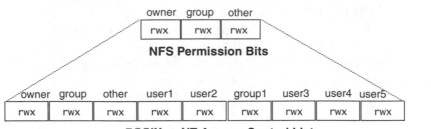

POSIX or NT Access Control List

FIGURE 17.8 Access control list. Many filesystems now support ACLs for file access control. Since NFS versions 2 and 3 have no ACL support, servers must make a best effort at mapping ACL information onto the UNIX permission bit model. ACL support in NFS version 4 would allow clients to create, modify, and view ACLs.

17.5.3   Access Control Lists

The NFS protocol has supported the UNIX permission bit model described in section 8.7. The sequence of bits defined in the *mode* field of the *fattr* structure is a simple ACL. Each group of three bits represents an access control entry. The permission bit ACL has three entries: *owner*, *group*, and *other*. Many UNIX filesystems and the Windows NT NFS filesystem support a more general form of ACL that has more permission bits per entry and a much larger number of entries that can represent individual users or groups. Since the NFS protocol does not support an ACL attribute, servers must make a best effort at mapping an ACL into a corresponding set of UNIX permission bits. An accurate mapping cannot always be achieved, yielding permission bits that are overly restrictive or permissive, depending on the mapping policy. Additionally, a client cannot view or manipulate an ACL through the protocol. A challenge for NFS version 4 is to support an ACL attribute that will suit the needs of diverse ACL models, for instance, POSIX style[5] on UNIX systems and NT style on Windows NT systems (Figure 17.8).

17.5.4   File Locking

There are no procedures for file locking in the NFS protocol. File locking has been handled by the Network Lock Manager (NLM) protocol described in chapter 10. To avoid the overhead in negotiating a separate protocol for file locking, NFS version 4 should include locking procedures. The NLM protocol follows the UNIX model of *advisory* locking. Participating applications can set and test for file locks, but nothing prevents a nonparticipating application from overriding a lock and reading or writing a locked region of a file.

---

5. Described in POSIX 1003.6, still a draft standard.

The advisory locking model contrasts with the *mandatory* locking model used by DOS and Windows applications—a file lock prevents other programs from reading and/or writing the file. DOS and Windows applications normally lock a file when it is first opened. The DOS `CreateFile()` function opens or creates a file and locks it in a single operation. The lack of NFS support for an atomic lock-on-open function can cause problems if two DOS programs attempt to create a file at the same time. A file locking protocol that meets the needs of and is interoperable with both UNIX and DOS/Windows systems is a difficult challenge for NFS version 4.

Some care must be taken in the design of the file locking functions in making them compatible with the Internet scale that is one of the design goals for NFS version 4. File locking implies that the server must keep a record of which files are locked and which clients have locked them. If an NLM client crashes while holding a lock, then the file will stay locked indefinitely or until the client recovers. An NFS version 4 server could put an upper bound on file unavailability by associating an expiration time with each lock. If the server crashes, then it will need a simple way to recover the lock state. The simplest way to do this may be to borrow the concept of a grace period from the NLM protocol: the server blocks file access for some period of time after recovery so that clients can reclaim their locks.

How is a client notified when a lock becomes available? The NLM protocol allows a client to wait for a server callback (NLM_GRANTED) if a lock request is blocked, but server callbacks will not work reliably across the Internet. Although a client may be able to contact a server, the reverse may be prevented by a firewall. An alternative is to have the client poll for a lock until it becomes available. Although polling is robust, it is also inefficient: if there is much contention for a lock, the server could be overwhelmed responding negatively to client polling. Also, if the lock becomes available, the client may wait unnecessarily for half the poll interval (on average).

17.5.5 Internationalization

The NFS protocol is somewhat unusual in its lack of strings as a component in the protocol. The only occurrence of an XDR string type in the protocol (version 2 or 3) is the filename string used in procedures like LOOKUP, CREATE, MKDIR, READDIR, and so on. In the XDR specification [RFC 1832], an XDR *string* type is defined as being composed of ASCII bytes. ASCII is a 7-bit character encoding that is adequate for most English characters but inadequate for 8-bit characters in the ISO Latin 1 character set[6] that is used by many Western

---

6. Also known as ISO 8859-1.

European languages. Nearly all NFS implementations are permissive, allowing 8-bit characters in their XDR strings, and ISO Latin 1 characters are used routinely. ISO Latin 1 is just one of several 8-bit character sets; there are others for Cyrillic, Arabic, Greek, and Hebrew. The NFS protocol provides no field that identifies the particular character set encoding that is used in a filename. An Italian attempting to view files on a Greek NFS server would assume that it is getting filenames encoded with ISO Latin 1. The result would not be pretty!

If NFS version 4 is to be an Internet protocol and span multiple languages, then it must name files in a way that preserves character sets. One possibility would be to provide a character set tag with each filename string. A problem with a string tag is that it wouldn't allow a filename to contain a mixture of character sets, for instance, an English name with a few Greek characters in it. A more commonly used option is to use the Unicode[7] character encoding. Unicode is a multibyte character set that acts as a superset for all other character sets (Figure 17.9). Since a character in any character set has a unique 16-bit Unicode encoding, this superset can hold more than 65,000 characters. The Unicode standard also defines a transformation format known as UTF-8, which provides some backward compatibility with existing software: the UTF-8 encoding for the ASCII character set is identical to the set of ASCII characters.

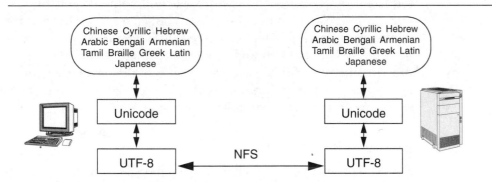

FIGURE 17.9 Filename encoding. The Unicode character set is large enough to encompass most of the world's unique character sets. The UTF-8 transformation format of the 16-bit Unicode encoding provides a measure of backward compatibility for ASCII characters.

7. The Unicode Consortium maintains an informative web site at *www.unicode.org*

17.6 Designed for Protocol Extensions

The NFS protocol was not designed to accept new features into the protocol in a backward-compatible way. The designers of the protocol assumed that changes to the protocol would be integrated in revisions designated by the RPC version number. This policy didn't acknowledge the incremental pressure for changes that accumulates over time. Since a small change on its own is not enough to justify a complete revision of the protocol, the other alternative is to implement the change by overloading the protocol or by adding the feature to another, less prominent protocol. For example, the NFS version 2 protocol did not support the creation of UNIX device nodes. The mode and size file attributes of the CREATE procedure (section 6.2.8) were overloaded to provide device information. These unpublished overloadings of the protocol are not interoperable between multiple vendor's implementations. When the POSIX 1003.1 standard included a new pathconf function to return filesystem information, it was found that the NFS protocol could not provide pathconf information for remote filesystems. It would have been logical to add a pathconf procedure to the NFS protocol, but an NFS protocol revision for this one procedure would have been too disruptive for this nonessential function (few applications used pathconf). Instead, a MOUNTPROC_PATHCONF procedure (section 9.5.8) was added to the MOUNT protocol. The addition of this procedure to the MOUNT protocol was judged acceptable because the pathconf data is relatively static and it would do no harm to retrieve it once at mount time and cache it on the client. The WebNFS changes to the protocol would have been more cleanly implemented by the addition of a new multicomponent LOOKUP procedure in a new revision of the protocol, but it was less disruptive to overload the existing LOOKUP procedure and maintain backward compatibility.

NFS version 4 needs to be able to accept new features without the overhead of a complete protocol revision. The most obvious area for extension would be file attributes. It should be possible to add a new file attribute to the protocol simply by the assignment of a new attribute number along with an XDR layout and a description of the attribute properties. Since NFS version 4 is destined to be an Internet standard controlled by the IETF, there is already a process in place for standardizing incremental changes through standards-track RFCs. The assignment of attribute numbers could be controlled by the Internet Assigned Numbers Authority. A client could determine the attributes that a server supports by querying a "supported attributes" attribute that returns a bitmap of all supported attributes. New file types and procedures might similarly be added to the protocol along with attributes that allow a client to determine what features the server supports.

A *minor version number* might also be used to codify a set of changes (Figure 17.10). Each standards document that incorporates minor changes to NFS version 4 through the addition of new attributes, file types, or procedures

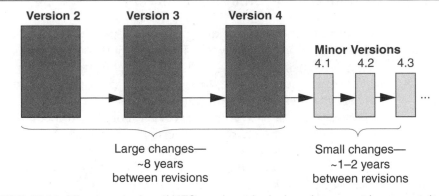

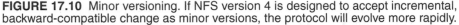

FIGURE 17.10 Minor versioning. If NFS version 4 is designed to accept incremental, backward-compatible change as minor versions, the protocol will evolve more rapidly.

could be identified through a minor version number. A minor version number that could be queried by a client could be used to identify protocol changes that cannot easily be codified by a bitmap of attribute or procedure numbers—for instance, a backward-compatible change to the semantics of an existing attribute or procedure.

17.7 Summary

NFS version 4 is being developed as an Internet standard through the IETF. The most prominent goal is to provide file access across the Internet, but the secondary goals are also important: strong security, interoperability between different platforms, and extensibility. In making the transition from local area networks to the Internet, the protocol must adjust to the Internet environment: firewalls, low bandwidth, high latency, and larger scale. NFS support for strong security has traditionally been weak, and motivation for security has been low on private networks. NFS will not be trusted on the Internet unless it provides strong authentication, data integrity, and data privacy. Security is best implemented at the RPC level by the RPCSEC_GSS security framework. If NFS is to be a lingua franca protocol for all platforms, independent of operating system or file system, then it must accommodate the features of these platforms in a way that allows them to interoperate. If NFS is to be an International protocol, then it must not surprise those who use different character sets. NFS version 4 must not be rigid in its definition. It must be designed to accommodate new features via minor versions in a way that preserves interoperability.

References

[ANSI83] American National Standards Institute, *American National Standard X.3106: Data Encryption Algorithm, Modes of Operation*, 1983.

[Bellovin+91] S. M. Bellovin, M. Merrit, "Limitations of the Kerberos Authentication System," *USENIX Conference Proceedings*, Dallas, Winter 1991.

[Bhide+91] A. K. Bhide, E. N. Elnozahy, S. P. Morgan, "A Highly Available Network File Server," *USENIX Conference Proceedings*, Dallas, Winter 1991: 199–205.

[Bhide+92] A. K. Bhide, S. Shepler, "A Highly Available Lock Manager for HA-NFS," *USENIX Conference Proceedings*, Summer 1992: 177–184.

[Birrell84] A. D. Birrell, B. J. Nelson, "Implementing Remote Procedure Calls," *ACM Transactions on Computer Systems*, 1984, 2: 39–59.

[Blair98] John D. Blair, "SAMBA, Integrating UNIX and Windows," Specialized Systems Consultants, Inc., 1998 (ISBN 1-57831-006-7).

[Blaze94] M. Blaze, "Key Management in an Encrypting Filesystem," *USENIX Conference Proceedings*, Boston, Summer 1994.

[Bloomer92] John Bloomer, "Power Programming with RPC." Sebastopol, CA: O'Reilly & Associates, Inc., 1992.

[Brownbridge+82] D. R. Brownbridge, L. F. Marshall, B. Randell, "The Newcastle Connection or UNIXes of the World Unite!," *Software–Practice and Experience*, Vol. 12 (pp. 1147–1162). New York: John Wiley and Sons Ltd., 1982.

[Chang85] J. M. Chang, "SunNet," *USENIX Conference Proceedings*, Summer 1985.

[Chutani+92] Sailesh Chutani, Owen T. Anderson, Michael L. Kazar, Bruce W. Leverett, W. Anthony Mason, Robert N. Sidebotham, "The Episode File System," *USENIX Conference Proceedings*, Winter 1992.

[Coulouris+96] George Coulouris, Jean Dollimore, Tim Kindberg, *Distributed Systems: Concepts and Design*. Reading, Mass.: Addison Wesley Longman, 1996.

[Denning+81] D. Denning, G. Sacco, "Time Stamps in Key Distribution Protocols," *Communications of the ACM*, 1981, 24(8): 533–536.

[Diffie+76] W. Diffie, M. E. Hellman, "New Directions in Cryptography," *IEEE
Transactions on Information Theory IT-22*, November 1976.

[Eisler+96] Mike Eisler, Roland J. Schemers, Raj Srinivasan, "Security Mechanism Independence in ONC RPC," *Sixth USENIX Security Symposium
Proceedings*, July 1996.

[Gibson+98] Garth A. Gibson, David F. Nagle, Khalil Amiri, Jeff Butler, Fay W.
Chang, Howard Gobioff, Charles Hardin, Erik Riedel, David Rochberg, Jim Zelenka, "A Cost-Effective, High-Bandwidth, Storage Architecture," *Proceedings of the 8th Conference on Architectural Support for
Programming Languages and Operating Systems*, 1998.

[Glover91] Glover, Fred, "TNFS Protocol Specification," Trusted System Interest Group (work in progress).

[Gray+89] Cary G. Gray, David R. Cheriton, "Leases: An Efficient Fault-
Tolerant Mechanism for Distributed File Cache Consistency," *Proceed-
ings of the Twelfth ACM Symposium on Operating Systems Principals*,
Litchfield Park, Arizona, December 1989.

[Hendricks88] D. Hendricks, "The Translucent File Service," *Proceedings European UNIX Users Group*, Cascais, Portugal, August 1988.

[Howard+88] John H. Howard, Michael L. Kazar, Sherri G. Menees, David A.
Nichols, M. Satyanarayanan, Robert N. Sidebotham, Michael J. West,
"Scale and Performance in a Distributed File System," *ACM Trans-
actions on Computer Systems*, February 1988: 51–88.

[Israel+89] Robert K. Israel, Sandra Jett, James Pownell, George M. Ericson,
"Eliminating Data Copies in UNIX-based NFS Servers," *Uniforum
Conference Proceedings*, San Francisco, February 27–March 2, 1989.
(Describes two methods for reducing data copies in NFS server code.)

[Jacobson88] V. Jacobson, "Congestion Control and Avoidance," *Proceedings
ACM SIGCOMM '88*, Stanford, CA, August 1988. (The paper describing improvements to TCP to allow use over Wide Area Networks
and through gateways connecting networks of varying capacity.
This work was a starting point for the NFS Dynamic Retransmission work.)

[Jaspan95] B. Jaspan, "GSS-API Security for ONC RPC," *'95 Proceedings of the
Internet Society Symposium on Network and Distributed System Security*,
1995: 144–151.

[Juszczak89] Chet Juszczak, "Improving the Performance and Correctness of
an NFS Server," *USENIX Conference Proceedings*, San Diego, Winter
1989.

[Juszczak94] Chet Juszczak, "Improving the Write Performance of an NFS
Server," *USENIX Conference Proceedings*, San Francisco, Winter 1994.

[Kazar93] Michael Leon Kazar, "Synchronization and Caching Issues in the Andrew File System," *USENIX Conference Proceedings*, Dallas, Winter 1988: 27–36. (A description of the cache consistency scheme in AFS. Contrasted with other distributed file systems.)

[Kohl+93] J. Kohl, C. Neuman, "The Kerberos Network Authentication Service (V5)." RFC 1510, 1993 (*ftp://ftp.isi.edu/in-notes/rfc1510.txt; see also* [RFC 1510].)

[LaMacchia+91] B. A. LaMacchia, A. M. Odlyzko, "Computation of Discrete Logarithms in Prime Fields," *AT&T Bell Laboratories*, 1991, (*http://www.research.att.com/~bal/papers/crypto/field/*—This paper shows that Diffie-Hellman authentication schemes, such as those used by the AUTH_DH security flavor in ONC RPC, are very insecure if the key length is less than 200 bits.)

[Linn96] J. Linn, "The Kerberos Version 5 GSS-API Mechanism," RFC 1964, 1996 (*ftp:// ftp.isi.edu/in-notes/rfc1964.txt*).

[Linn97] J. Linn, "Generic Security Service Application Program Interface, Version 2" RFC 2078, January 1997. (*ftp://ftp.isi.edu/in-notes/rfc2078.txt*).

[Macklem91] Rick Macklem, "Lessons Learned Tuning the 4.3BSD Reno Implementation of the NFS Protocol," *USENIX Conference Proceedings*, Dallas, Winter 1991.

[Macklem94] Rick Macklem, "Not Quite NFS, Soft Cache Consistency for NFS," *USENIX Conference Proceedings*, January 1994.

[McKusick+96] Marshall Kirk McKusick, Keith Bostic, Michael J. Karels, John Quarterman, *The Design and Implementation of the 4.4BSD UNIX Operating System* (Unix and Open Systems Series). Reading, Mass.: Addison-Wesley, 1996. (Chapter 9 has a good description of NFS as implemented in 4.4BSD.)

[Miller+87] S. Miller, C. Neuman, J. Schiller, J. Saltzer, "Section E.2.1: Kerberos Authentication and Authorization System," Cambridge, Mass.: M.I.T. Project Athena, December 21, 1987.

[Mills92] David L. Mills, "Network Time Protocol (Version 3)," RFC 1305, March 1992 (*ftp://ftp.isi.edu/in-notes/rfc1305.txt*—A description of the Network Time protocol. This version includes secure authentication of the time source.)

[Minnich93] R. G. Minnich, "The Autocacher: A File Cache Which Operates at the NFS Level," *USENIX Conference Proceedings*, San Diego, Winter 1993.

[Mogul94] Jeffrey C. Mogul, "Recovery in Spritely NFS," *Computing Systems,* Spring 1994: 7(2).

[Moran+93] Joe Moran, Bob Lyon, "The Restore-o-Mounter: The File Motel Revisited," *USENIX Conference Proceedings,* Cincinnati, Summer 1993.

[Morris+86] J. Morris, M. Satyanarayanan, M. H. Conner, J. H. Howard, D. S. Rosenthal, F. D. Smith, "Andrew: A Distributed Personal Computing Environment," *Communications of the ACM*, March 1986, 29(3): 184–201.

[NBS77] National Bureau of Standards, "Data Encryption Standard," Federal Information Processing Standards Publication 46, January 1977.

[Needham+78] R. Needham, M. Schroeder, "Using Encryption for Authentication in Large Networks of Computers," *Communications of the ACM*, December 1978, 21(12): 993–999.

[Nelson+88] Michael N. Nelson, Brent B. Welch, John K. Ousterhout. "Caching in the Sprite Network File System." *ACM Transactions on Computer Systems*, February, 1988, 6(1): 134–154.

[Neumann+94] C. Neumann, T. Ts'o, "Kerberos: An Authentication System for Computer Networks, *IEEE Communications*, 1994, 32(9): 33–38.

[Nowicki89] Bill Nowicki, "Transport Issues in the Network File System," *ACM SIGCOMM Newsletter Computer Communication Review*, April 1989. (A brief description of the basis for the dynamic retransmission work.)

[Pawlowski+89] Brian Pawlowski, Ron Hixon, Mark Stein, Joseph Tumminaro, "Network Computing in the UNIX and IBM Mainframe Environment," *Uniforum '89 Conference Proceeding*, 1989. (Description of an NFS server implementation for IBM's MVS operating system.)

[Pendry94] Jan-Simon Pendry, "4.4BSD Automounter Reference Manual," Document 13, System Manager's Manual, Sebastopol, CA: O'Reilly & Associates, Inc., April 1994.

[Popek+83] Bruce J. Walker, Gerald J. Popek, Robert English, Charles S. Kline, Greg Thiel, "The LOCUS Distributed Operating System," *9th Symposium on Operating Systems Principles*, Bretton Woods, NH, November 1983: 49–70.

[RFC 1094] Bill Nowicki, "NFS: Network Filesystem Specification," Sun Microsystems, Inc., March 1989. (*ftp://ftp.isi.edu/in-notes/rfc1094.txt*—the NFS version 2 protocol specification.)

[RFC 1508] J. Linn, "Generic Security Service Application Program Interface," September 1993. (*ftp://ftp.isi.edu/in-notes/rfc1508.txt*—description of the GSS-API security framework.)

[RFC 1509] J. Wray, "Generic Security Service API: C-bindings," September 1993. (*ftp://ftp.isi.edu/in-notes/rfc1509.txt*—C programming interface to the GSS-API.)

[RFC 1510] J. Kohl, C. Neuman, "The Kerberos Network Authentication Service (V5)," September 1993. (*ftp://ftp.isi.edu/in-notes/rfc1510.txt*—description of version 5 of the Kerberos network authentication protocol.)

[RFC 1808] Roy T. Fielding, "Relative Uniform Resource Locators." University of California–Irvine, June 1995. (*ftp://ftp.isi.edu/in-notes/rfc1808.txt*)

[RFC 1813] B. Callaghan, B. Pawlowski, P. Staubach, "NFS Version 3 Protocol Specification," June 1995. (*ftp://ftp.isi.edu/in-notes/rfc1813.txt*—the NFS version 3 protocol specification.)

[RFC 1831] R. Srinivasan, "Remote Procedure Call Protocol Version 2," August 1995. (*ftp://ftp.isi.edu/in-notes/rfc1831.txt*—the specification for ONC RPC messages.)

[RFC 1832] R. Srinivasan, "XDR: External Data Representation Standard," August 1995. (*ftp://ftp.isi.edu/in-notes/rfc1832.txt*—the specification for canonical format for data exchange, used with RPC.)

[RFC 1833] R. Srinivasan, "Binding Protocols for ONC RPC Version 2," August 1995. (*ftp://ftp.isi.edu/in-notes/rfc1833.txt*—the specification of portmap and rpcbind protocols.)

[RFC 1928] M. Leech, M. Ganis, Y. Lee, R. Kuris, D. Koblas, L. Jones, "SOCKS Protocol Version 5," March 1996. (*ftp://ftp.isi.edu/in-notes/rfc1928.txt*—an application layer protocol filter.)

[RFC 1964] *See* [Linn96].

[RFC 2054] B. Callaghan, "WebNFS Client Specification," October 1996. (*ftp://ftp.isi.edu/in-notes/rfc2054.txt*—describes WebNFS client use of NFS version 2 and 3 protocols including use of public filehandles and multicomponent LOOKUP.)

[RFC 2055] B. Callaghan, "WebNFS Server Specification," October 1996. (*ftp://ftp.isi.edu/in-notes/rfc2055.txt*—describes WebNFS server use of NFS version 2 and 3 protocols including handling of public filehandles and multicomponent LOOKUP.)

[RFC 2078] *See* [Linn97].

[RFC 2203] M. Eisler, A. Chiu, L. Ling, "RPCSEC_GSS Protocol Specification," September 1997. (*ftp://ftp.isi.edu/in-notes/rfc2203.txt*—describes the RPCSEC_GSS security framework for ONC RPC.)

[RFC 2246] T. Dierks, C. Allen, "The TLS Protocol, Version 1.0," January 1999. (*See ftp://ftp.isi.edu/in-notes/rfc2246.txt*—a protocol that provides communications privacy over the Internet.)

[RFC 2401] S. Kent, R. Atkinson, "Security Architecture for the Internet Protocol," November 1998. (*ftp://ftp.isi.edu/in-notes/rfc2401.txt*—a protocol for securing the payload of an IP datagram.)

[[RFC 2478] E. Baize, D. Pinkas, "The Simple and Protected GSS-API Negotiation Mechanism," December 1998. (*ftp://ftp.isi.edu/in-notes/rfc2478.txt*—describes a mechanism that allows the choice of a GSS-API based security mechanism to be negotiated.)

[RFC 2623] M. Eisler, "NFS Version 2 and Version 3 Security Issues and the NFS Protocol's Use of RPCSEC_GSS and Kerberos V5," June 1999. (*ftp://ftp.isi.edu/in-notes/rfc2623.txt*—describes some security issues with the use of authentication flavors AUTH_SYS, AUTH_DH, and

AUTH_KERB4. Then goes on to describe the use of RPCSEC_GSS security with Kerberos version 5 as an example.)

[RFC 2624] S. Shepler, "NFS Version 4 Design Considerations," RFC 2623, June 1999. (*ftp://ftp.isi.edu/in-notes/rfc2624.txt*—the design document for NFS version 4.)

[Sandberg+85] R. Sandberg, D. Goldberg, S. Kleiman, D. Walsh, B. Lyon, "Design and Implementation of the Sun Network Filesystem," *USENIX Conference Proceedings*, Summer 1985. (The basic paper that describes the SunOS implementation of the NFS version 2 protocol, and discusses the goals, protocol specification, and trade-offs.)

[Satyanarayanan+90] M. Satyanarayanan, J. J. Kistler, P. Kumar, M. I. Okasaki, E. H. Siegel, D. C. Steere, "Coda: A Highly Available File System for a Distributed Workstation Environment." *IEEE Transactions on Computers*, 1990, 39(4): 447–459.

[Shein+89] B. Shein, M. Callahan, P. Woodbury, "NFSSTONE: A Network File Server Performance Benchmark," *USENIX Conference Proceedings*, Summer 1989: 269–275.

[Srinivasan+89] V. Srinivasan, Jeffrey C. Mogul. "Spritely NFS: Experiments with Cache-Consistency Protocols," *Proceedings, Twelfth Symposium on Operating Systems Principles*, Litchfield Park, Arizona, December 1989: 45–57.

[Steiner+88] J. Steiner, C. Neuman, J. Schiller, "Kerberos: An Authentication Service for Open Network Systems," *Usenix Conference Proceedings*, Dallas, February 1988: 191–202.

[Stern91] Hal Stern, *Managing NFS and NIS*, Sebastopol, CA: O'Reilly & Associates, Inc., 1991.

[Stevens94] W. Richard Stevens, *TCP/IP Illustrated, Volume 1.* Reading, Mass.: Addison-Wesley, 1994.

[Taylor+88] Bradley Taylor, David Goldberg, "Secure Networking in the Sun Environment," Sun Microsystems, Inc., 1988. (This site explains the implementation of AUTH_DH security flavor for ONC RPC—*http://opcom.sun.ca/white-papers/secure-rpc.html*.)

[TCSEC85] U.S. Department of Defense, "Department of Defense Trusted Computer System Evaluation Criteria," DOD 5200.28-STD, National Computer Security Center, Fort Meade, MD, December 1985. (Available at: *http://www.disa.mil/MLS/info/orange/intro.html* or *http://csrc.nist.gov/secpubs/rainbow/std001.txt*)

[TOG-NFS96] The Open Group, "X/Open CAE Specification: Protocols for X/Open Interworking: XNFS, Version 3," 1996. (Apex Plaza, Forbury Road, Reading Berkshire, RG1 1AX, UK; *www.opengroup.org*—a reference for versions 2 and 3 of the NFS protocol and accompanying protocols, including the Lock Manager and the Portmap.)

[TOG-PCNFS96] The Open Group, "Developer's Specification, Protocols for X/Open PC Interworking: (PC)NFS," 1996. (Apex Plaza, Forbury Road, Reading Berkshire, RG1 1AX, UK; *www.opengroup.org*—a reference for version 2 of the NFS protocol and accompanying protocols, including the Lock Manager, Portmap, and PCNFSD.)

[Watson+92] Andy Watson, Bruce Nelson, "LADDIS: A Multi-Vendor and Vendor-Neutral SPEC NFS Benchmark," *Proceedings of the 6th USENIX Large Installation Systems Administration Conference (LISA VI)*, Long Beach, October 1992.

[Wittle+93] Mark Wittle, Bruce E. Keith, "LADDIS: The Next Generation in NFS File Server Benchmarking," *USENIX Conference Proceedings*, Cincinnati, June 1993.

[Woodward87] J. P. L. Woodward, "Security Requirements for System High and Compartmented Mode Workstations," Technical Report MTR 9992, Revision 1 (The MITRE Corporation, Bedford, MA), November 1987. (Also published by the Defense Intelligence Agency as Document DDS-2600-5502-87.)

[Wray93] J. Wray, "Generic Security Service API: C-bindings," RFC 1509, 1993 (*ftp://ftp.isi.edu/in-notes/rfc1509.txt; see also* [RFC 1509].)

[X/OpenNFS96] *See* [TOG-NFS96].

Index

32-bit clients/servers, vs. 64-bit clients/servers, compatibility issues in NFS Version 3; 135–136
64-bit clients/servers, vs. 32-bit clients/servers, compatibility issues in NFS Version 3; 135–136
absolute paths,
  See also namespace(s); pathnames; paths
  relative paths vs., in NFS URL; 438–439
access,
  See also authentication; locating
  checking, for exported filesystems, MOUNT protocol advantages; 255
  control lists,
    implementation issues; 231
    limitations as access control lists; 266
    military use; 353
    MOUNT protocol use of; 258–259
    as NFS Version 4 design consideration; 462
    RFS use; 363
    source of false access indication; 233
  data, in NASD NFS; 358
  file,
    access protocol, file transfer protocol vs.; 2–4
    access protocol, history; 4–6
    ACCESS results caching; 246
    open, as permission implementation issue; 231–232
    permissions, implementation issues; 230–233
  Internet, as NFS Version 4 design consideration; 452
  mode bits,
    `fattr` data type, NFS V.2 (reference description); 96
    `fattr3` data type, NFS V.3 (reference description); 144

file permission checking use, implementation issues; 232–233
permissions,
  checking, ACCESS procedure; 158–162
  checking for files, as permission implementation issue; 232–233
replica server, strategies for; 335–336
ACCESS procedure,
  NFS Version 3, description; 133
  NFS Version 3 (reference description); 158–162
  NQNFS; 352
  solution to false access indication problems, as; 233
  TNFS; 354
ACL (Access Control List),
  See also security
  ACL file attribute, comparison of support by different systems (table); 226
  Episode support of; 371
  implementation issues; 231
  military use; 353
  MOUNT protocol use; 258–259
  as NFS Version 4 design consideration; 462
  RFS use; 363
  source of false access indication; 233
adaptive, retransmission for UDP, implementation issues; 239–240
address,
  See also namespace(s); URL
  universal, term description; 40
ADMIN procedure,
  PCNFSD Version 2 (reference description); 400–401
administration,
  of printing, PR_ADMIN procedure, PCNFSD Version 2 (reference description); 400–401

administration *continued*
  server, sending a message to, ALERT procedure
      (PCNFSD Version 2); 408–409
advisory locking,
  (figure); 282
  LOCK procedure, Lock Manager protocol; 300
  mandatory locks vs.; 281
  term description; 281
AFS (Andrew File System); 364–368
  See also filesystem(s)
  Andrew benchmark,
      integrated client and server performance
          measurement; 413
      Spritely NFS performance on; 349
  cell, term description; 366
  as DFS basis; 369
  fileset use, NFS Version 4 consideration of; 459
  global namespace support; 321
ALERT procedure, PCNFSD Version 2 (reference
      description); 408–409
aliases,
  See also links
  hard links use as; 82
alignment, XDR data unit; 12
Allen, C.,
  [RFC 2246]; 79
      (footnote); 459
  security, TLS [RFC 2246]; 79
Amd (Auto-Mounter Daemon); 339–341
  as user-level NFS daemon; 323
American National Standards Institute, [ANSI83]; 467
Amiri, K., [Gibson+98]; 356, 468
Anderson, O. T., [Chutani+92]; 371, 467
Andrew File System (AFS), *See* AFS (Andrew File
      System)
ANSI standards, X3.106 [ANSI 83]; 52
Apollo, DOMAIN operating system, remote file access
      support; 4
append flag,
  See also writing
  NQNFS write extension; 352
arrays,
  See also data, types
  fixed-length, as structured XDR data type; 16
  variable-length, as structured XDR data type; 16
ASN.1 (Abstract Syntax Notation) standard, XDR
      compared with; 10
assignment, port, portmapper service use to
      determine; 38
asynchronous,
  See also synchronization

procedures, Lock Manager protocol use; 282–283
requests and responses, Lock Manager protocol
      (table); 296
writes,
  safe, COMMIT request use for; 239
  SFS benchmark prohibition of; 426
  verifying loss of, writeverf3, NFS V.3 (reference
      description); 137
  WRITE procedure, NFS V.3; 171–172
at-most-once semantics,
  See also semantics
  cache use; 87
  duplicate request cache use; 88
  RPC approximation of; 29
  XID use in implementing; 32
atime file attribute,
  comparison of support by different systems (table);
      226
  in fattr data type,
      POSIX stat comparison (table); 97
      (table); 95
  in fattr3 data type (table); 143
Atkinson, R., [RFC 2401]; 79
atomicity,
  See also lock(ing)
  not guaranteed by SETATTR procedure, NFS V.3;
      152
  requirement,
      RENAME; 196
      symbolic link creation; 183
attributes,
  See also data, types
  caching; 246
  file,
      caching of; 245
      client-settable, sattr, NFS V.2 (reference
          description); 97–98
      client-settable, sattr3 data type, NFS V.3
          (reference description); 146–147
      extensible, as NFS Version 4 design consideration;
          460–461
      fattr data type, NFS V.2 (reference description);
          95–97
      fattr3 data type, NFS V.3 (reference description);
          142–143
      fattr3 data type, NFS V.3 (table); 143
      implementation issues; 225
      mode fields use for permission checking,
          implementation issues; 232
      NFS Version 3 changes; 135
      in PC NFS; 381–382

in PC NFS (table); 381
retrieving, GETATTR procedure, NFS V.2;
    100–101
retrieving, GETATTR procedure, NFS V.3;
    149–151
returning, post_op_attr data type, NFS V.3
    (reference description); 143–144
setting, NFS Version 3 changes; 135
setting, SETATTR procedure, NFS V.2; 102–103
setting, SETATTR procedure, NFS V.3; 151–155
support comparison (table); 226
TNFS extensions; 354–355
TNFS extensions, filenames; 355
filesystem,
    NFS access; 81
    retrieving, STATFS procedure, NFS V.2; 128–130
AUTH_DES, netname use, for user identification; 231
AUTH_DH flavor, 48–58
    See also security
AUTH_KERB flavor, *See also* security
netname use, for user identification; 231
AUTH_MLS RPC security flavor; 353–354
    See also security
AUTH_NONE flavor; 44–45
    See also security
as AUTH_SYS credential verifier; 46
AUTH procedure,
    PCNFSD Version 1 (reference description); 388–389
    PCNFSD Version 2 (reference description); 407–408
AUTH_SHORT flavor; 46, 47–48
    See also security
AUTH_SYS flavor; 45–48
    See also security
credentials,
    implementation issues; 231
    obtaining, AUTH procedure (PCNFSD Version 1);
        388–389
AUTH_UNIX flavor, *See* AUTH_SYS flavor
AUTH_XXX authentication failure errors,
    See errors, Kerberos, authentication (table); errors,
        RPC, authentication (table)
authentication, *See also* security; verifiers
DH,
    naming; 49
    verifiers; 49–50
    verifiers, nickname credential; 53–54
    weaknesses; 57–58
flavors; 44
    DH; 48–58
    Kerberos; 58–63
    null; 44–45
    System; 45–48

(table); 45
    term description; 44
Kerberos,
    AFS use; 364
    Version 4; 58–63
    Version 5, registered entries (table); 261
local procedure call compared with RPCl; 27
Lock Manager protocol issues; 291
MOUNT protocol minimal need of; 257
network disk access issues; 358
in PCNFS; 387
PCNFSD protocol provision for; 384
RPC, errors (table); 34
RPC protocol; 43–65
RPCSEC_GSS; 64–78
Trusted NFS; 352–356
user,
    AUTH procedure (PCNFSD Version 1); 388–389
    AUTH procedure (PCNFSD Version 2); 407–408
    implementation issues; 230–233
verifier, in RPC reply; 34
authorization failure, as RPC call rejection cause; 33
Autocacher, as user-level NFS server [Minnich93]; 323
autofs filesystem,
    See also automounter; filesystem(s)
    automounting with; 327–328
    (figure); 328
    as temporary mountpoint problem solution; 327
automounter,
    See also MOUNT protocol
    Amd; 339–341
    autofs (figure); 328
    with autofs filesystem; 327–328
    (chapter); 321
    export list use; 267
    (figure); 325
    map variables,
        key substitution and; 337–339
        (table); 337
    maps; 329–332
        direct; 329–330
        executable; 331–332
        indirect; 330–331
        master; 329
        term description; 329
    symbolic link problems; 324–327
    term description; 322
availability,
    highly available NFS (HA-NFS) servers; 89–90
    lock, testing for, TEST procedure, Lock Manager
        protocol (reference description); 296–298
    as NFS Version 4 design consideration; 458–459

B1-level security,
    See also security
    as TNFS goal; 353
backoff, exponential, UDP use for retransmission; 239
backup, filesystem [Moran+93]; 323
Baize, E., [RFC 2478]; 66, 460, 471
bandwidth,
    comparisons (table); 456
    high, as NASD NFS goal; 356
    as NFS Version 4 design consideration; 455–456
basic data types,
    See also data, types
    in Lock Manager protocol; 292–294
    XDR; 13–16
batched requests, with CIFS; 374
Bellovin, S., [Bellovin+91]; 63, 467
benchmarks,
    See also performance
    NFS (chapter); 413
    nfsstone; 419–421
    nhfsstone; 421
    SFS,
        UDP checksum calculation requirement; 416
        Version 2.0; 428–429
        Versions 1.0 and 1.1; 422–427
Berkeley Sockets, ONC RPC influenced by; 27
Bhide, A. K., [Bhide+91+92]; 90, 467
big-endian,
    term description; 11
    XDR integer byte order; 11
        little-endian encoding relationship issues; 12
binary data,
    See also data types
    XDR encoding of; 10
biod daemon,
    I/O thread handling; 242–243
    RPC call handling; 234
        (figure); 235
Birds of a Feather (BOF); 451
Birrell, A. D., [Birrell84]; 467
Blair, J. D., [Blair98]; 376
Blaze, M., [Blaze94]; 323
block(ing),
    avoidance of, with Amd; 339–340
    lock requests,
        canceling, CANCEL procedure, Lock
            Manager protocol (reference description);
            302–304
        canceling (figure); 303
        implementation issues; 300, (figure); 301
blocks file attribute,
    comparison of support by different systems (table);
        226

in fattr data type,
    POSIX stat comparison (table); 97
    (table); 95
blocksize file attribute,
    comparison of support by different systems (table);
        226
    in fattr data type,
        POSIX stat comparison (table); 97
        (table); 95
Bloomer, J., [Bloomer92]; 9, 25
BNF (Backus-Naur Form), XDR specification use; 18
BOF (Birds of a Feather); 451
boolean,
    See also data, types
    as primitive XDR data type; 14
Bostic, K., [McKusick+96]; 469
broadcast,
    CIFS, namespace issues; 372
    RPC,
        term description (footnote); 265
        UMNTALL procedure use; 265
Brownbridge, D. R., [Brownbridge+82]; 4
browsers, WebNFS use with (chapter); 431–447
buffers,
    client, COMMIT impact; 223
    states, in WRITE procedure, NFS V.3; 172
    track, term description; 237
bus server data, performance impact; 417
Butler, J., [Gibson+98]; 356
BWNFSD protocol; 409–410

C language data structures, Rpcgen translation of XDR
        into; 17
C++ language data structures, Rpcgen translation of
        XDR into; 17
cache(ing),
    See also performance
    avoidance, nhfsstone tactics; 422
    CacheFS,
        disconnectable cache in; 251
        term description; 249–250
    CIFS (figure); 375
    client,
        COMMIT impact; 223
        as performance enhancer, in Spritely NFS;
            348–349
    consistency; 349
        AFS; 364
        client file attribute use for; 225
        close-to-open DFS equivalents; 369
        close-to-open implementation issues; 248
        close-to-open, Spritely NFS modifications; 346
        implementation issues; 246–248

as NFS Version 4 design goal; 456
NQNFS; 349
Spritely NFS; 343
with tokens, in DFS; 369–370
disconnection, implementation issues; 250–251
disk, implementation issues; 249–250
DNLC; 86–87
NSF V.3 LOOKUP use; 156–157
duplicate request, implementation issues; 234–236
efficient, as NFS Version 4 design consideration; 456
file,
in AFS; 364–366, 365
in AFS (figure); 365
locking of, Lock Manager protocol; 290–291
filesystem, Autocacher; 323
flushing cached data, to storage, COMMIT (reference description); 221–224
hierarchy,
(figure); 250
term description; 249
negative, implementation issues; 156–157
objects, implementation issues; 245–246
policies, implementation issues; 244–251
proxy, as NFS Version 4 design consideration; 456–457
read, implementation issues; 248–249
READDIRPLUS requirements; 208
reconnection, implementation issues; 250–251
of symbolic links, READLINK (reference description); 163
time, consistency maintenance use; 246
weak cache consistency semantics,
support for, pre_op_attr data type, NFS V.3 (reference description); 145
support for, wcc_data data type, NFS V.3 (reference description); 145–146
write,
(figure); 249
implementation issues; 248–249
write-around, term description; 250
write-back, term description; 250
write-through, term description; 250
call, messages, RPC protocol; 31–32
Callaghan, B.,
[RFC 1813]; 471
[RFC 2054]; 439
[RFC 2055]; 471
Callahan, M., [Shein+89]; 419
callbacks,
See also procedures
AFS,
cache manager use; 364–366

extensions in DFS; 369
volume movement impact on; 367, 368
breaking an oplock with; 374
client crash recovery use; 288
Lock Manager protocol use; 282–283
as model for NFS Version 4; 456
RPC,
GRANTED procedure as; 283
GRANTED procedure (reference description); 306
in Spritely NFS; 344–345
CALLIT procedure, Portmap protocol (reference description); 40
CANCEL procedure,
Lock Manager protocol (reference description); 302–304
PCNFSD Version 2 (reference description); 399–400
canceling,
See also removing
blocked locks, CANCEL procedure, Lock Manager protocol (reference description); 302–304
print jobs, PR_CANCEL procedure, PCNFSD Version 2 (reference description); 399–400
canonical,
paths,
vs. native paths, in WebNFS; 444
term description; 444
standard,
term description; 11
XDR as; 11
capability, data, term description; 358
case sensitivity and preservation, DOS vs. UNIX; 379
CBC (cipher block chaining) mode,
DH credential encryption use; 52
Kerberos credential encryption use; 60
Cedar language, RPC use; 27
cell, AFS, term description; 366
Chang, F. W., [Gibson+98]; 356
Chang, J. M., [Chang85]; 312,
change(ing),
printer job queue position, PR_REQUEUE procedure, PCNFSD Version 2 (reference description); 401–402
state, notifying hosts of, NOTIFY procedure, Status Monitor protocol (reference description); 318
character(s),
case sensitivity and preservation, DOS vs. UNIX; 379
delimiters, operating system differences; 81
international character sets, NFS Version 4 support goal; 463
key substitution, automounter; 338
protocol element representation as, advantages and disadvantages; 10
UNICODE, CIFS support; 373

checking,
    See also authentication
    access permissions, ACCESS procedure; 158–162
    monitoring status, STAT procedure, Status Monitor
        protocol (reference description); 313–314
checksums, UDP, SDS benchmark requirement for; 416
Cheriton, D. R., [Gray+89]; 349
Chiu, A., [RFC 2203]; 471
Chutani, S., [Chutani+92]; 371
CIFS (Common Internet File System) protocol; 372–377
    Samba server; 376
clients,
    See also servers
    32-bit clients/servers vs. 64-bit clients/servers,
        compatibility issues in NFS Version 3;
        135–136
    COMMIT implementation issues; 223
    crash recovery,
        Lock Manager protocol; 288–289
        (figure); 289
    failover in; 90
    file attribute use, server precautions; 225
    file attributes that can be set from,
        sattr, NFS V.2 (reference description); 97–98
        sattr3 data type, NFS V.3 (reference description);
            146–147
    hostname, ACL use, in MOUNT protocol; 258
    lightweight, WebNFS use with (chapter); 431–447
    server port and; 444
    state,
        loss of, lock manager handling; 279
        server recovery of, NQNFS; 351
    WebNFS; 439–442
clock,
    See also time
    synchronization, DH authentication; 50–51
cloning volume, in AFS; 368
CLOSE request, lack of, as stateless indication; 87
close-to-open cache consistency,
    DFS equivalents; 369
    implementation issues; 248
    Spritely NFS modifications; 346
closing files, implementation issues; 227
cluster,
    as benchmark challenge, SFS, Versions 1.0 and 1.1;
        426–427
    server,
        (figure); 426
        term description; 426
Coda filesystem,
    See also filesystem(s)
    AFS as basis of; 368

disconnectable cache in; 251
Colouris, G., [Coulouris+96]; 1
comments, in PCNFS; 387
COMMIT procedure,
    asynchronous write use; 171–172, 239
    NFS Version 3,
        description; 134
        (reference description); 221–224
compatibility, 64-bit vs. 32-bit clients/servers; 135–136
components,
    pathname,
        filename handling, in NFS protocol; 85–86
        term description; 85
concurrency,
    See also lock(ing); multithreading
    nfsstone benchmark simulation; 420
    RPC calls, implementation issues; 234
configuration,
    path, retrieving, PATHCONF procedure; 218–221
    server, SFS, Versions 1.0 and 1.1; 426
Connectathon,
    (figure); 252
    history and use; 252
connection-based security,
    See also security
    as NFS Version 4 design consideration; 459
    as RPC-based security alternative; 78–80
Conner, M. H., [Morris+86]; 321
consistency, *See* cache(ing), consistency
context,
    creation of,
        RPCSEC_GSS (figure); 68, 69
        RPCSEC_GSS, successful; 68–70
        RPCSEC_GSS, unsuccessful; 70
    RPCSEC_GSS-based RPC session,
        creation; 66–68
        (figure); 66
        term description; 65
    state, required by some RPC authentication flavors; 88
controllers, disk, performance impact; 417
conventions,
    lexical, XDR language; 18
    notation, XDR language; 18
cookies,
    cookieverf3 data type, NFS V.3 (reference
        description); 137
    validation issues; 203–204
cookieverf3 data type,
    NFS Version 3 (reference description); 137
Courier RPC standard, as early RPC system, RPC use;
    27
CPU speed, performance impact; 414–415

crash,
  recovery,
    client (figure); 289
    client, Lock Manager protocol; 288–289
    server, Lock Manager protocol; 284–286
    simulating, SIMU_CRASH procedure, Status
        Monitor protocol (reference description);
        317–318
  system, stable storage protection against; 237
CREATE procedure,
  NFS Version 2 (reference description); 112–114
  NFS Version 2, Version 3 changes; 133
  NFS Version 3 (reference description); 174–179
creation,
  context,
    RPCSEC_GSS; 66–68
    RPCSEC_GSS (figure); 68, 69
    RPCSEC_GSS, successful; 68–70
    RPCSEC_GSS, unsuccessful; 70
  createverf3 data type, NFS Version 3 (reference
      description); 137
  directories,
    MKDIR procedure, NFS V.2; 122–124
    MKDIR procedure, NFS V.3; 179–182
  files,
    CREATE procedure, NFS V.2; 112–114
    CREATE procedure, NFS V.3; 174–179
    special, MKNOD procedure; 186–190
  links,
    hard, LINK procedure, NFS V.2; 119–120
    hard, LINK procedure, NFS V.3; 199–201
    symbolic, SYMLINK procedure, NFS V.2; 120–122
    symbolic, SYMLINK procedure, NFS V.3; 182–185
  locks,
    LOCK procedure, Lock Manager protocol
        (reference description); 299–302
    unmonitored, NM_LOCK procedure, Lock
        Manager protocol (reference description); 311
credentials,
  AUTH_MLS; 353–354
  AUTH_SYS,
    (figure); 46
    implementation issues; 231
    obtaining, AUTH procedure (PCNFSD Version 1);
        388–38
    WebNFS use; 445
  full network name,
    DH authentication; 51–53
    Kerberos authentication; 59–60
  Kerberos, XDR description (code); 62
  lifetime, in Network Time protocol use; 50
  nickname,
    DH authentication; 53–54
    Kerberos authentication; 61–63
  RPC, as authentication field; 43–44
  RPCSEC_GSS; 66
    (figure); 67
cross-platform protocol,
  See also interoperability
  NFS, PC as example; 379
crossing,
  of filesystem mountpoints, implementation issues;
      228–230
  of server mountpoints,
    implementation issues; 228–230
    prohibited, LOOKUP procedure, NFS V.3; 156
    in WebNFS; 441
ctime file attribute,
  comparison of support by different systems (table);
      226
  in fattr data type,
    POSIX stat comparison (table); 97
    (table); 95
  in fattr3 data type (table); 143
cycles,
  namespace, remote filesystem mounting,
      implementation issues; 228

DAC (discretionary access control), as military access
    control mechanism; 353
daemon,
  automounter implementation as (figure); 323–324
  lockd, implementation; 287–288
  statd, implementation; 287
  stateless, autofs; 327
data,
  cached, flushing to storage, COMMIT (reference
      description); 221–224
  capability, term description; 358
  exchange, RPC, RPCSEC_GSS; 70–71
  integrity, protection, RPCSEC_GSS; 71–72
  locating, in NASD NFS; 358
  loss, write-behind issues; 347
  opaque,
    fixed-length, as XDR primitive data type; 15
    variable-length, as XDR primitive data type; 15
  privacy, RPCSEC_GSS; 73
  representation, XDR protocol (chapter); 9–24
  requests,
    maximum size, NFS Version 3 changes; 134
    server processing of, RPCSEC_GSS; 74–75
  security,
    in NASD NFS; 358–359
    RPCSEC_GSS flavor use; 64

data *continued*
  server data bus, performance impact; 417
  special, specdata3, NFS V.3 (reference description); 141
  stale, avoidance as file access protocol advantage; 3
  transport, protocols and; 9–11
  types,
    cookieverf3, NFS V.3 (reference description); 137
    createverf3, NFS V.3 (reference description); 137
    fattr, NFS V.2; 95–97
    fattr3, NFS V.3 (reference description); 142–143
    fattr3, NFS V.3 (table); 143
    fhandle, NFS V.2 (reference description); 94
    filename, NFS V.2 (reference description); 98
    filename3, NFS V.3 (reference description); 137
    ftype, NFS V.2 (reference description); 94
    ftype3, NFS V.3 (reference description); 140–141
    implicit, XDR use of; 10
    in Lock Manager protocol; 292–294
    netobj, Lock Manager protocol (reference description); 292–293
    nfs_fh3, NFS V.3 (reference description); 141–142
    in NFS Version 2; 92
    in NFS Version 3; 136–147
    in NFS Version 3, descriptions; 137–147
    nfspath3, NFS V.3 (reference description); 137
    nfsstat3, NFS V.3 (reference description); 138
    nfstime3, NFS V.3 (reference description); 142
    nlm_lock, Lock Manager protocol (reference description); 293–294
    nlm_stats, Lock Manager protocol (reference description); 293
    path, NFS V.2 (reference description); 98
    post_op_attr, NFS V.3 (reference description); 143–144
    post_op_fh3, NFS V.3 (reference description); 146
    pre_op_attr, NFS V.3 (reference description); 145
    primitive, XDR; 13–16
    sattr, NFS V.2 (reference description); 97–98
    sattr3, NFS V.3 (reference description); 146–147
    specdata3, NFS V.3 (reference description); 141
    stat, NFS V.2 (reference description); 92
    strings; 15
    structured, XDR; 16–17
    timeval, NFS V.2 (reference description); 94
    wcc_data, NFS V.3 (reference description); 145–146
    writeverf3, NFS V.3 (reference description); 137
  unit, XDR; 12–13
  XDR, example; 20
Data Encryption Standard, *See* DES (Data Encryption Standard)

datagrams,
  UDP, size limitations; 36
  Xerox network, RPC use; 27
DCE (Distributed Computing Environment),
  DFS; 369–372
  RPC,
    data encoding; 11
    Xerox PARC RPC work influence on; 27
DCOM, Xerox PARC RPC work influence on; 27
deadlock,
  See also lock(ing); synchronization
  detection, Lock Manager protocol; 289–290
  (figure); 290
  term description; 289
deleting,
  directories,
    RMDIR procedure, NFS V.2; 124–126
    RMDIR procedure, NFS V.3; 192–195
  file sharing, UNSHARE procedure, Lock Manager protocol (reference description); 310–311
  files,
    REMOVE procedure, NFS V.2; 115–116
    REMOVE procedure, NFS V.3; 190–192
  locks, UNLOCK procedure, Lock Manager protocol (reference description); 304–305
delimiters,
  TCP data stream; 36
  text, operating system differences; 81
demand,
  mounting on, automounter use; 322
  paging, executable files, permission implementation issues; 233
Denning, D., [Denning+81]; 58
deny mode, impact on other applications (table); 284
dependency,
  graph,
    deadlock detection use; 289
    (figure); 290
  in multiple mounts, automounter ordering; 333
DES (Data Encryption Standard),
  CBC,
    DH credential encryption use; 52
    Kerberos credential encryption use; 60
  ECB,
    DH conversation key encryption use; 52
    Kerberos conversation key encryption use; 61
  key, in DH authentication; 57
  NBS key, DH authentication use; 49
detection,
  deadlock, Lock Manager protocol; 289–290

mountpoint,
    as LOOKUP pathname evaluation advantage;
      86
    LOOKUP procedure, NFS V.3; 156
device,
    See also attributes
    files, creating, MKNOD procedure; 186–190
    support, NFS compared with RFS; 83
    types,
      ftype3 data type, NFS V.3 (reference description);
        140–141
      term description; 83
DFS (Distributed FileSystem); 369–372
    See also filesystem(s)
DH, *See* Diffie-Hellman
    flavor, *See* AUTH_DH flavor
Dierks, T.,
    [RFC 2246]; 79
      (footnote); 459
    security, TLS [RFC 2246]; 79
Diffie, W., [Diffie+76]; 49, 56–57
Diffie-Hellman,
    See also authentication
    authentication; 48–58
      clock synchronization; 50–51
      Kerberos authentication compared with; 58–63
      naming; 49
      nicknames; 50–51
      protocol; 51
      verifiers; 49–50
      weaknesses; 57–58
    credentials,
      full network name; 51–53
      nickname; 53–54
    encryption; 56–57
    public key scheme, DH flavor use; 49
    verifiers,
      full network name credential; 51–53
      nickname credential; 53–54
      server; 54–56
direct, automounter maps; 329–330
directories,
    See also file(s)
    caching of; 245
    creating,
      MKDIR procedure, NFS V.2; 122–124
      MKDIR procedure, NFS V.3; 179–182
    DNLC; 86–87
      filehandles and file attributes cached in; 245
      NSF V.3 LOOKUP use; 156–157
    fetching, in WebNFS; 442
    inaccessible, as hierarchical mount issue; 230

multiparent, not supported by NFS filesystem
    model; 156
reading, READDIRPLUS procedure; 205–211
reading from,
    READDIR procedure, NFS V.2; 126–128
    READDIR procedure, NFS V.3; 202–205
removing,
    RMDIR procedure, NFS V.2; 124–126
    RMDIR procedure, NFS V.3; 192–195
size, in benchmark workload; 419
subdirectories, MOUNT protocol handling; 271–273
term description; 82
disconnecting caches, implementation issues; 250–251
discriminated union, as structured XDR data type; 17
diskless client, file access protocol advantages for; 3
disks,
    caching, implementation issues; 249–250
    controllers, performance impact; 417
    NASD; 357
      (figure); 358
    NASD (Network-Attached Secure Disks) NFS;
      356–359
    spindles, performance impact; 417
distributed,
    See also NFS (Network File System) protocol
    filesystems,
      Andrew; 364–368
      (chapter); 361–377
      CIFS; 372–377
      DFS; 369–372
      Episode File System; 371–372
      protocol, *See* NFS (Network File System) protocol
      RFS; 361–363
    locks, deadlock detection issues; 289
    operating system,
      LOCUS, remote file access support; 4
      Sprite; 343
    systems; 1
DNLC (directory name lookup cache),
    filehandles and file attributes cached in; 245
    NSF V.3 LOOKUP use; 156–157
    performance enhancement; 86–87
document types, in WebNFS; 442
Dollimore, J., [Coulouris+96]; 1, 467
domain name, ACL use, in MOUNT protocol; 258
DOMAIN operating system, remote file access
    support; 4
DOS,
    FAT filesystem model, CIFS relationship to;
      373
    file attribute support, comparison with other
      systems (table); 226

DOS *continued*
  file sharing procedures,
    Lock Manager protocol, overview; 283–284
    Lock Manager protocol (table); 296
  unmonitored lock procedures, Lock Manager
      protocol (table); 296
DUMP procedure,
  MOUNT protocol (reference description); 263–264
  Portmap protocol (reference description); 40
duplicate request cache,
  implementation issues; 234–236
  RPC server use; 29
dynamic,
  automounter map generation; 331
  mounting, autofs use; 327

ECB (Electronic Code Book) mode,
  DH conversation key encryption use; 52
  Kerberos conversation key encryption use; 61
Eisler, M.,
  [Eisler+96]; 68, 76
  [RFC 2203]; 471
  [RFC 2623]; 80
  [RFC 2624]; 452
Elnozahy, E. N., [Bhide+91]; 90
encoding,
  character, operating system differences; 82
  data, XDR protocol (chapter); 9–24
encryption,
  See also authentication; DES
  Diffie-Hellman; 56–57
    CBC and ECB use; 52
  filesystem [Blaze94]; 323
  Kerberos, ECB use; 61
  RPCSEC_GSS data privacy weaknesses; 73
English, R., [Popek+83]; 4
EOF (end of file), handling issues; 166
Episode File System; 371–372
  DFS use; 369
Ericson, G. M., [Israel+89]; 468
errors,
  See also status
  conditions identified by RPC reply message (list);
    30
  filename construction; 85
  handling, local procedure call compared with RPC;
    26
  Kerberos, authentication (table); 63
  Kerberos authentication; 62–63
  in Lock Manager protocol; 294
  Lock Manager protocol (table); 295
  MOUNT protocol, MNT procedure; 262

NFS,
  in stat data type; 92
  Version 2 (table); 93
  Version 3 (table); 139–140
NFS Version 3 (table); 139–140
nfsstat3 data type, NFS V.3 (reference description);
    138
return, NFS Version 3 changes; 134
RPC,
  accepted status (table); 35
  authentication (table); 34
RPC call; 33
RPCSEC_GSS; 75–76
stat data type, NFS V.2 (reference description); 92
write, write-behind impact on; 243
evaluation,
  See also performance
  of multicomponent LOOKUP; 442–443
  pathname,
    latency and; 434–435
    NFS protocol; 86–87
    by server; 436
    WebNFS handling; 435
exactly-once semantics,
  See also semantics
  GUARDED attribute not sufficent for, in CREATE
    procedure, NFS V.3; 177
  not guaranteed by SETATTR procedure, NFS V.3;
    152
exchange of data, RPC, RPCSEC_GSS; 70–71
exclusive,
  exclusive create semantics,
    createverf3 data type, NFS V.3 (reference
      description); 137
    support for, CREATE procedure, NFS V.3;
      176–177
  locks; 281–282
    term description; 278, 281
executable,
  automounter maps; 331–332
  files, as permission implementation issue;
    233
exponential backoff,
  (figure); 240
  UDP use for retransmission; 239–240
export(ing),
  limitations, in MOUNT protocol; 273–275
  lists, limitations as access control lists; 266
EXPORT procedure, MOUNT protocol (reference
    description); 265–267
EXPORTALL procedure, MOUNT protocol (reference
    description); 267

extensibility,
　　See also interoperability; open(ing), systems
　　file attribute, as NFS Version 4 design consideration;
　　　　460–461
　　protocol, as NFS Version 4 design consideration;
　　　　465–466
　　RPCSEC_GSS flavor; 64
External Data Representation, *See* XDR

failover,
　　See also errors
　　with Amd; 340
　　client-side; 90
　　in highly available NFS servers; 90
failure,
　　See also errors
　　recovery from, stateless server advantages; 88
　　semantics, kernel-based file locking; 287
　　stable storage module, handling; 171
fattr data type,
　　NFS Version 2,
　　　　(reference description); 95–97
　　　　(table); 95
fattr3 data type,
　　NFS Version 3,
　　　　(reference description); 142–143
　　　　(table); 143
fetching, *See* retrieving
fhandle data type, NFS Version 2 (reference
　　　　description); 94
fid (file identifier),
　　AFS, filehandle compared with; 367
　　term description; 367
file(s),
　　See also directories
　　access,
　　　　ACCESS results caching; 246
　　　　permission checking, as permission imple-
　　　　　　mentation issue; 232–233
　　　　permissions, implementation issues; 230–233
　　　　protocol, file transfer protocol vs.; 2–4
　　　　protocol, history of; 4–6
　　AFS fid, filehandle compared with; 367
　　attributes,
　　　　client-settable, sattr, NFS V.2 (reference
　　　　　　description); 97–98
　　　　client-settable, sattr3 data type, NFS V.3
　　　　　　(reference description); 146–147
　　　　extensible, as NFS Version 4 design consideration;
　　　　　　460–461
　　　　fattr data type, NFS V.2 (reference description);
　　　　　　95–97
　　　　fattr data type, NFS V.2 (table); 95

fattr3 data type, NFS V.3 (reference description);
　　　　142–143
fattr3 data type, NFS V.3 (table); 143
implementation issues; 225
NFS Version 3 changes; 135
in PC NFS; 381–382
in PC NFS (table); 381
retrieving, GETATTR procedure, NFS V.2;
　　　　100–101
retrieving, GETATTR procedure, NFS V.3;
　　　　149–151
returning, post_op_attr data type, NFS V.3
　　　　(reference description); 143–144
setting, NFS Version 3 changes; 135
setting, SETATTR procedure, NFS V.2; 102–103
setting, SETATTR procedure, NFS V.3; 151–155
support comparison (table); 226
TNFS extensions; 354–355
TNFS extensions, filenames; 355
caching,
　　in AFS; 364–366
　　in AFS (figure); 365
creating,
　　CREATE procedure, NFS V.2; 112–114
　　CREATE procedure, NFS V.3; 174–179
　　links to, LINK procedure, NFS V.2; 119–120
　　links to, LINK procedure, NFS V.3; 199–201
data, caching of; 245
device, creating, MKNOD procedure; 186–190
executable, as permission implementation issue;
　　　　233
fetching, in WebNFS; 441
filesystems, *See* filesystem(s)
invisible, implementation issues; 227
last close problem, implementation issues; 227
locking,
　　cached, Lock Manager protocol; 290–291
　　with CIFS; 374
　　Lock Manager protocol (chapter); 277–319
　　Lock Manager protocol implementation;
　　　　287
　　mapped, Lock Manager protocol; 290–291
　　as NFS Version 4 design consideration; 462–463
　　as NFS Version 4 design goal; 453
　　reasons for omission in NFS; 277
　　stateful nature of; 88
　　Status Monitor protocol implementation;
　　　　287
metadata, term description (footnote); 238
names,
　　DOS vs. UNIX; 379–381
　　See filenames
offsets, NQNFS extension; 352

file(s) *continued*
    open,
        accessing, as permission implementation issue;
            231–232
        removal implementation issues; 227
    opening, ACCESS procedure impact; 160
    path configuration, retrieving, PATHCONF
            procedure; 218–221
    reading,
        READ procedure, NFS V.2; 107–109
        READ procedure, NFS V.3; 164–167
    regular, retrieving, with MNT procedure; 261
    removing,
        REMOVE procedure, NFS V.2; 115–116
        REMOVE procedure, NFS V.3; 190–192
    renaming, RENAME (reference description);
            116–118, 195–198
    semantics, CIFS; 373
    sharing,
        DOS procedures, Lock Manager protocol (table);
            296
        DOS/Windows, Lock Manager procedures
            overview; 283–284
        HCLNFSD protocol support of; 409
        removing, UNSHARE procedure, Lock Manager
            protocol (reference description); 310–311
        SHARE procedure, Lock Manager protocol
            (reference description); 308–310
    size,
        in benchmark workload; 419
        extending, SETATTR procedure, NFS V.3; 152
    special,
        creating, MKNOD procedure; 186–190
        term description; 83
    symbolic links,
        creating, SYMLINK procedure, NFS V.2; 120–122
        creating, SYMLINK procedure, NFS V.3; 182–185
    synchronization, COMMIT use; 222
    term description; 81–82
    text, in PC NFS; 382
    transfer protocol, file access protocol vs.; 2–4
    types,
        ftype data type, NFS V.2; 94
        ftype3 data type, NFS V.3 (reference description);
            140–141
        NFS Version 3 changes; 135
    unreachable, implementation issues; 227
    writing to,
        WRITE procedure, NFS V.2; 109–112
        WRITE procedure, NFS V.3; 168–174
filehandles,
    access, MOUNT protocol use; 264

    AFS fid compared with; 367
    caching of; 245
    construction failure recovery, support
            for, post_op_fh3 data type, NFS V.3
            (reference description);
            146
    export requirements; 273
    fhandle data type (reference description); 94
    FSINFO requirements; 217
    initial, obtaining, MOUNT protocol use; 255
    limitations, remote filesystem mounting,
            implementation issues; 228
    nfs_fh3 data type, NFS V.3 (reference description);
            141–142
    in NFS protocol; 83–85
    overloading with security flavors, in WebNFS;
            445–446
    public,
        advantages; 85
        handling, LOOKUP procedure, NFS V.3;
            156
        WebNFS use; 433
    RENAME issues; 196
    retrieving, MNT procedure, MOUNT protocol
            (reference description); 260–262
    as RPC call argument; 25
    size, NFS Version 3 changes; 134
    term description; 83
fileid, term description; 81
fileid file attribute,
    comparison of support by different systems (table);
            226
    in fattr data type,
        POSIX stat comparison (table); 97
        (table); 95
    in fattr3 data type (table); 143
filename data type, NFS Version 2 (reference
            description); 98
filename3 data type, NFS Version 3 (reference
            description); 137
filenames,
    filename data type, NFS V.2 (reference description);
            98
    filename3 data type, NFS V.3 (reference
            description); 137
    looking up,
        LOOKUP procedure, NFS V.2; 104–106
        LOOKUP procedure, NFS V.3; 155–158
    as pathname components, handling of, in NFS
            protocol; 85–86
    restrictions on; 85
    TNFS attribute extensions; 355

filesets,
  NFS Version 4 consideration of; 458–459
  term description; 370, 371
filespace, term description; 370
filesystem(s),
  attributes, retrieving, STATFS procedure, NFS V.2;
      128–130
  autofs,
    automounting with; 327–328
    as temporary mountpoint problem solution;
        327
  backup [Moran+93]; 323
  caching, Autocacher; 323
  Coda,
    AFS as basis of; 368
    disconnectable cache in; 251
  DFS; 369–372
  distributed,
    Andrew; 364–368
    (chapter); 361–377
    CIFS; 372–377
    DFS; 369–372
    Episode File System; 371–372
    NFS distinguishing characteristic; 4
    RFS; 361–363
  encrypting [Blaze94]; 323
  exported,
    access checking, MOUNT protocol advantages;
        255
    retrieving list of, EXPORT procedure, MOUNT
        protocol (reference description); 265–267
  (figure); 82
  identification,
    fsid; 81
    remote filesystem mounting, implementation
        issues; 228
  information, caching of; 246
  local, remote filesystem mounting, implementation
      issues; 228
  model,
    CIFS; 373
    NFS (chapter); 81–90
  mounted, retrieving a list of, DUMP procedure,
      MOUNT protocol (reference description);
      263–264
  mounting,
    MNT procedure, MOUNT protocol (reference
        description); 260–262
    multiple; 333–334
    without blocking, with Amd; 339–340
  mountpoints, crossing, implementation issues;
      228–230

  in NFS protocol; 81–83
  objects, in NFS protocol; 81–83
  RFS, as early file access system; 4
  state,
    static, retrieving, FSINFO procedure; 214–218
    volatile, retrieving, FSSTAT procedure; 212–214
  term description; 81
  translucent [Hendricks88]; 323
  unmounting,
    all entries, UMNTALL procedure, MOUNT
        protocol (reference description); 265
    UMNT procedure, MOUNT protocol (reference
        description); 264
firewalls,
  See also authentication
  NFS issues; 433
fixed-length,
  arrays, as structured XDR data type; 16
  opaque data, as primitive XDR data type; 15
flavors,
  See also security
  AUTH_DH; 48–58
  AUTH_NONE; 44–45
    as AUTH_SYS credential verifier; 46
  AUTH_SHORT; 46, 47–48
  AUTH_SYS; 45–48
  authentication; 44
    DH; 48–58
    Kerberos; 58–63
    null; 44–45
    system; 45–48
    (table); 45
    term description; 44
  overloading filehandles with, in WebNFS; 445–446
  RPCSEC_GSS, as extensible authentication
      framework; 44
  security,
    AUTH_MLS; 353–354
    RPCSEC_GSS; 64–78
flushing, cached data to storage, COMMIT (reference
      description); 221–224
FREE_ALL procedure, Lock Manager protocol
      (reference description); 311–312
freeing, locks, FREE_ALL procedure, Lock Manager
      protocol (reference description); 311–312
fsid file attribute,
  comparison of support by different systems
      (table); 226
  in fattr data type,
    POSIX stat comparison (table); 97
    (table); 95
  in fattr3 data type (table); 143

fsid (filesystem ID),
    change, remote filesystem mounting, implementa-
        tion issues; 228
    term description; 81
FSINFO procedure,
    NFS Version 3,
        description; 133
        (reference description); 214–218
FSSTAT procedure,
    NFS Version 3,
        description; 134
        (reference description); 212–214
fsync(2) POSIX system call, COMMIT semantics
    compared with; 222
FTP (File Transfer Protocol), characteristics and
    limitations; 2
ftype data type, NFS Version 2 (reference description);
    94
ftype3 data type, NFS Version 3 (reference
    description); 140–141

Ganis, M., [RFC 1928]; 452, 470
gathering, write gathering; 243–244
GETATTR procedure,
    NFS Version 2 (reference description); 100–101
    NFS Version 3 (reference description); 149–151
GETPORT procedure, Portmap protocol (reference
    description); 39
Gibson, G. A., [Gibson+98]; 356
gid file attribute,
    comparison of support by different systems (table);
        226
    in fattr data type,
        POSIX stat comparison (table); 97
        (table); 95
    in fattr3 data type (table); 143
GID (Group ID),
    representation, as NFS Version 4 design
        consideration; 461
    UID mapping,
        MAPID procedure (PCNFSD Version 2); 405–406
        as permission implementation issue; 232
        in RFS; 363
global,
    namespace,
        automounter creation of (chapter); 321
        layout, automounter maps use; 329
        remote-as-local paradigm problems; 322
    variables, local procedure call compared with RPC;
        26
Glover, F., [Glover91]; 468

GNU Public License, Samba server source code
    available under; 376
Gobioff, H., [Gibson+98]; 356
Goldberg, D.,
    [Sandberg+85]; 91
    [Taylor+88]; 472
government security requirements,
    TCSEC, TNFS support of; 352–356
grace period,
    DFS cache recovery use; 370
    server crash recovery; 284
GRANTED procedure,
    Lock Manager protocol (reference description);
        305–308
    as RPC callback; 283
granting, locks, GRANTED procedure, Lock Manager
        protocol (reference description); 305–308
graph dependency,
    deadlock detection use; 289
    (figure); 290
Gray, C. G., [Gray+89]; 349
group file attribute, comparison of support by different
    systems (table); 226
groups, UID/GID mapping, as permission
    implementation issue; 232
GSS (Generic Security Services) API,
    See also security
    RPCSEC_GSS flavor based on; 64

HA-NFS (highly available NFS) servers; 89–90
    as NFS Version 4 model; 458
hard links,
    See also links; RENAME procedure
    creating,
        LINK procedure, NFS V.2; 119–120
        LINK procedure, NFS V.3; 199
    symbolic links compared with; 82
    term description; 82
Hardin, C., [Gibson+98]; 356
HCLNFSD protocol; 409–410
    See also PCNFSD protocol
    procedures (table); 410
Hellman, M. E., [Diffie+76]; 49, 56–57
Hendricks, D., [Hendricks88]; 323
heterogeneity, as MOUNT protocol separation from
    NFS protocol rationale; 255
hierarchy,
    cache,
        (figure); 250
        term description; 249
    export restrictions; 274–275

mount, implementation issues; 230
highly available NFS (HA-NFS) servers; 89–90
   as NFS Version 4 model; 458
   WRITE procedure impact; 172
history,
   automounters; 323
   IETF; 450
   network interface cards; 416
   NFS,
     Version 2; 91
     Version 3; 131–132
     Version 4; 449, 450
   SMB; 372
   Spritely NFS; 343
Hixon, R., [Pawlowski+89]; 469
hoarding, term description; 251
HOLD procedure, PCNFSD Version 2 (reference
        description); 403–404
host(s),
   See also clients; servers
   monitoring,
     starting the, MON procedure, Status Monitor
       protocol (reference description); 314–316
     stopping all, UNMON_ALL procedure, Status
       Monitor protocol (reference description); 317
     stopping the, UNMON procedure, Status Monitor
       protocol (reference description); 316–317
   notifying, of a state change, NOTIFY procedure,
     Status Monitor protocol (reference
     description); 318
Howard, J. H.,
   [Howard+88]; 349
   [Morris+86]; 321
HTTP protocol,
   See also Internet; WebNFS
   connection-based security protocols that use; 79
   proxy cache server use; 456
HTTPS protocol URLs, SSL protocol; 79
hyper integers, as primitive XDR data type; 15

IAB (Internet Architecture Board); 450
IANA (Internet Assigned Numbers Authority),
   email address; 29
   NFS port assignment; 433
   program numbers assigned by; 29
   pseudoflavor registration with; 261
idempotent,
   operations,
     in NFS protocol; 88–89
     vs. nonidempotent operations (figure); 89
   procedures, retransmission impact; 235
   remote procedure advantages; 28

term description; 28, 88, 235
identification,
   file, fid term description; 367
   filesystem,
     fsid; 81
     remote filesystem mounting, implementation
       issues; 228
   UID/GID mapping, as permission implementation
     issue; 232
   of users, as permission implementation issue; 231
   users and groups, as NFS Version 4 design
     consideration; 453, 461
   XID, RPC requests distinguished by; 29
IEEE POSIX standard 1003.1, *See* POSIX
IESG (Internet Engineering Steering Group); 450
IETF (Internet Engineering Task Force); 450
   NFS Version 4,
     relationship to; 450
     working group charter; 451
   RPCSEC_GSS flavor; 64
   TLS; 79
implementation,
   See also each reference description for
       implementation issues specific to the
       procedure or data type
   NFS (chapter); 225–253
independence,
   pathname, as filehandle criterion; 84
   server, disconnectable cache advantages; 250
   transport,
     impact on remote procedure semantics; 28
     as RPC protocol characteristic; 27–29
     TI-RPC support of; 40
indirect, automounter maps; 330–331
INFO procedure, PCNFSD Version 2 (reference
       description); 391–392
information, obtaining, about supported services,
     INFO procedure (PCNFSD Version 2);
     391–392
INIT procedure,
   PCNFSD Version 1 (reference description); 389–390
   PCNFSD Version 2 (reference description); 393
initialization overhead, WebNFS handling; 435
integer(s),
   See also data, types
   hyper, as primitive XDR data type; 15
   signed, as primitive XDR data type; 13–14
   unsigned, as primitive XDR data type; 14
integration protocol, as NFS Version 4 design
     consideration; 452
integrity data, protection, RPCSEC_GSS; 71–72
interfaces, network, performance impact; 416–417

internationalization, as NFS Version 4 design
        consideration; 463–464
Internet,
    See also TCP/IP protocol
    Internet Architecture Board (IAB); 450
    Internet Engineering Steering Group (IESG); 450
    Internet Engineering Task Force, *See* IETF (Internet
        Engineering Task Force)
    Internet Society; 450
    NFS Version 3 and; 432
    NFS Version 4 design considerations relative to; 452
    WebNFS (chapter); 431–447
interoperability,
    See also open(ing), systems
    as DH flavor advantage; 48
    improved, as NFS Version 4 design consideration;
        460
    as LOOKUP pathname evaluation advantage; 86
    as MOUNT protocol separation from NFS protocol
        rationale; 255
    NFS, PC as example; 379
    NFS filesystem model impact on; 81
    nhfsstone issues; 422
    of RPC protocol; 25
    TNFS; 356
    XDR binary data format; 10
    XDR data unit support of; 12
IP protocol,
    IPsec connection-based security protocol [RFC
        2401]; 79
    Version 6, transport independence considerations;
        41
ISO, Abstract Syntax Notation (ASN.1 X.209), XDR
        compared with; 10
Israel, R. K., [Israel+89]; 468

Jacobson, V., [Jacobson88]; 468
Jaspan, B., [Jaspan95]; 468
Java, RMI, Xerox PARC RPC work influence on; 27
Jett, S., [Israel+89]; 468
Jones, L., [RFC 1928]; 452, 470
Juszczak, C.,
    [Juszczak89]; 236
    [Juszczak94]; 243

Karels, M. J., [McKusick+96]; 469
Kazar, M. L.,
    [Chutani+92]; 371
    [Howard+88]; 349
    [Kazar93]; 364
keepalives, server, with Amd; 340
Keith, B., [Wittle+93]; 473

Kent, S., [RFC 2401]; 79
Kerberos,
    See also authentication
    AFS use; 364
    authentication,
        error status values; 62–63
        errors; 62–63
        nicknames; 61–63
        protocol; 59
        version 4; 58–63
        weaknesses; 63
    credentials,
        full network name; 59–60
        nickname; 61–63
    errors, authentication (table); 63
    server verifier; 62
    verifiers, nickname credential; 61–63
    Version 5, registered entries (table); 261
key,
    common, DH; 52
    substitution, map variables and; 337–339
Kindberg, T., [Coulouris+96]; 1, 467
Kistler, J., [Satyanarayanan+90]; 251, 368
Kleiman, S., [Sandberg+85]; 91
Kline, C., [Popek+83]; 4
Koblas, D., [RFC 1928]; 452
Kohl, J., [Kohl+93]; 58
Kumar, P., [Satyanarayanan+90]; 251, 368
Kuris, R., [RFC 1928]; 452

LADDIS, *See* SFS (System File Server) benchmark
LaMacchia, B. A., [LaMacchia+91]; 58
language(s),
    C and C++ language, data structures, Rpcgen
        translation of XDR into; 17
    Cedar, RPC use; 27
    XDR; 17–23
        lexical and notation conventions; 18
last reference,
    files, implementation issues; 191, 227
latency,
    See also performance
    DNLC impact on; 86–87
    low, as NASD NFS goal; 356
    as NFS Version 4 design consideration; 453–455
    pathname evaluation and; 434–435
    performance impact; 415
    read-ahead and write-behind performance
        enhancements; 241
    term description; 415, 453
lazy replication,
    DFS, Episode support of; 371

leases,
    cache management mechanism, NQNFS; 350–351
    as model for NFS Version 4; 456
    NQNFS use; 349
    servery recovery use, NQNFS; 351–352
    term description; 350
Lee, Y., [RFC 1928]; 452
Leech, M., [RFC 1928]; 452
Leverett, B. W., [Chutani+92]; 371
lexical,
    conventions, XDR language; 18
limitations,
    export, in MOUNT protocol; 273–275
Ling, L., [RFC 2203]; 64
LINK procedure,
    NFS Version 2 (reference description); 119–120
    NFS Version 3 (reference description); 199–201
links,
    hard,
        creating, LINK procedure, NFS V.2; 119–120
        creating, LINK procedure, NFS V.3; 199–201
        symbolic links compared with; 82
        term description; 82
    linked lists, as structured XDR data type; 17
    support for, determining with FSINFO, NFS V.3;
        226
    symbolic,
        automounter daemon use; 324
        automounter problems with; 324–327
        caching of; 246
        creating, SYMLINK procedure, NFS V.2;
            120–122
        creating, SYMLINK procedure, NFS V.3;
            182–185
        fetching, in WebNFS; 442
        hard links compared with; 82
        nfspath3 data type, NFS V.3 (reference
            description); 137
        not supported, LOOKUP procedure, NFS V.3; 156
        in PC NFS; 382–383
        reading from, READLINK procedure, NFS V.2;
            106–107
        reading from, READLINK procedure, NFS V.3;
            162–164
        term description; 82, 382
        WebNFS evalution (figure); 437
        WebNFS handling; 436–438
Linn, J.,
    [Linn96]; 469
    [Linn97]; 64, 469
    [RFC 1508]; 64, 470
Linux, mountpoint cross solutions; 230

LIST procedure,
    PCNFSD Version 2 (reference description);
        395–396
listing,
    printers, PR_LIST procedure, PCNFSD Version 2
        (reference description); 395–396
    queued printer jobs, PR_QUEUE procedure,
        PCNFSD Version 2 (reference description);
        396–398
lists,
    See also data, types
    linked, as structured XDR data type; 17
    list keyword, linked list use; 17
load,
    balancing, in AFS; 364
    generation, in SFS benchmark (figure); 423
locating,
    See also access
    data, in NASD NFS; 358
lock(ing),
    advisory; 281
        (figure); 282
        LOCK procedure, Lock Manager protocol; 300
        term description; 281
    blocked, canceling, CANCEL procedure, Lock
        Manager protocol; 302–304
    creating, LOCK procedure, Lock Manager protocol
        (reference description); 299–302
    dependency graph,
        deadlock detection use; 289
        (figure); 290
    distributed, deadlock detection issues; 289
    exclusive; 281–282
        term description; 281
    file,
        cached, Lock Manager protocol; 290–291
        with CIFS; 374
        as file access protocol advantage; 3
        Lock Manager protocol (chapter); 277–319
        mapped, Lock Manager protocol; 290–291
        as NFS Version 4 design consideration;
            462–463
        reasons for omission in NFS; 277
        stateful nature of; 88
        Status Monitor protocol implementation;
            287
    freeing all, FREE_ALL procedure, Lock Manager
        protocol (reference description); 311–312
    granting, GRANTED procedure, Lock Manager
        protocol (reference description); 305–308
    Lock Manager, asynchronous procedures and
        callback (table); 283

lock(ing) *continued*
  Lock Manager protocol,
      (chapter); 277–319
      data types; 292–294
      errors; 294
      implementation, lockd daemon; 287–288
      Lock Manager protocol interaction with (figure);
          280
      procedures (reference descriptions); 294–312
      as stateful protocol; 87
  lockd daemon,
      as Lock Manager protocol implementation;
          287–288
      server crash recovery restart of; 284
  mandatory; 281
  model, Lock Manager protocol; 278
  monitored; 278–281
  netobj data type, Lock Manager protocol (reference
      description); 292–293
  nlm_lock data type, Lock Manager protocol
      (reference description); 293–294
  nlm_stats data type, Lock Manager protocol
      (reference description); 293
  non-exclusive; 281–282
  nonmonitored, limitations of; 280
  opportunistic, with CIFS; 374–376
  PC-style, HCLNFSD protocol support of; 409
  POSIX semantics, Lock Manager use; 305
  removing, UNLOCK procedure, Lock Manager
      protocol (reference description); 304–305
  shared; 281–282
  testing for, TEST procedure, Lock Manager protocol
      (reference description); 296–298
  unmonitored,
      creating, NM_LOCK procedure, Lock Manager
          protocol (reference description); 311
      DOS procedures, Lock Manager protocol (table);
          296
  write sharing need of; 172
LOCK procedure, Lock Manager protocol (reference
      description); 299–302
LockFile procedure, LOCK procedure, Lock Manager
      protocol; 300
LockFileEx procedure, LOCK procedure, Lock
      Manager protocol; 300
LOCUS distributed operating system, remote file
      access support; 4
lookup,
  of filenames,
      LOOKUP procedure, NFS V.2; 104–106
      LOOKUP procedure, NFS V.3; 155–158
  multicomponent, WebNFS use; 434
LOOKUP procedure,

NFS Version 2 (reference description); 104–106
NFS Version 2, Version 3 changes; 132–133
NFS Version 3 (reference description); 155–158
pathname evaluation, advantages; 86
Lyon, B., [Sandberg+85]; 91
Lyon, R., [Moran+93]; 323

MAC (mandatory access control), as military access
      control mechanism; 353
Macklem, R.,
  [Macklem91]; 469
  [Macklem94]; 349
Maestro, symbolic link handling; 383
making, directories,
  MKDIR procedure, NFS V.2; 122–124
  MKDIR procedure, NFS V.3; 179–182
mandatory,
  vs. advisory locks; 281
  locking, term description; 281
map(ing),
  automounter; 329–332
      direct; 329–330
      executable; 331–332
      indirect; 330–331
      master; 329
  files, locking of, Lock Manager protocol; 290–291
  NFS to DOS names (table); 380
  superuser,
      as permission implementation issue; 232
      as source of false access indication,
          implementation issues; 233
  syntax, Amd; 340–341
  UID/GID,
      MAPID procedure (PCNFSD Version 2); 405–406
      in RFS; 363
  variables, key substitution and; 337–339
MAPID procedure, PCNFSD Version 2 (reference
      description); 405–406
marking records, RPC protocol record-marking
      standard; 36–37
Marshall, L. F., [Brownbridge+82]; 4
Mason, W. A., [Chutani+92]; 371
master automounter maps; 329
maximum data request size, NFS Version 3 changes;
      134
McKusick, M. K., [McKusick+96]; 469
MCL (multicomponent LOOKUP),
  evaluating; 442–443
  WebNFS use; 434
memory,
  NVRAM,
      duplicate request cache use; 236
      performance impact; 417

performance impact; 414
virtual, mapping files into; 290
Menees, S. G., [Howard+88]; 349
Merrit, M., [Bellovin+91]; 63
messages,
    call, RPC protocol; 31–32
    reply, RPC protocol; 33–36
metadata, file, term description (footnote); 238
Miller, S., [Miller+87]; 58
Mills, D. L., [Mills92]; 50
Minnich, R. G., [Minnich93]; 323
MKDIR procedure,
    NFS Version 2 (reference description); 122–124
    NFS Version 3 (reference description); 179–182
MKNOD procedure,
    NFS Version 3,
        description; 133
        (reference description); 186–190
MLS (multi-level secure) security,
    See also security
    (figure); 353
    TNFS use; 353
MNT procedure, MOUNT protocol (reference
            description); 260–262
mode file attribute,
    comparison of support by different systems (table);
            226
    in fattr data type,
        POSIX stat comparison (table); 97
        (table); 95
    in fattr3 data type (table); 143
model,
    filesystem,
        CIFS; 373
        NFS (chapter); 81–90
    locking, Lock Manager protocol; 278
    remote procedure call; 25–27
    "trusted host", AUTH_SYS flavor; 47
Mogul, J. C.,
    [Mogul94]; 344,
    [Srinivasan+89]; 344
MON procedure, Status Monitor protocol (reference
            description); 314–316
monitoring,
    See also lock(ing)
    of a host,
        starting the, MON procedure, Status Monitor
            protocol (reference description); 314–316
        stopping all, UNMON_ALL procedure, Status
            Monitor protocol (reference description); 317
        stopping the, UNMON procedure, Status Monitor
            protocol (reference description); 316–317
    locking; 278–281

status,
    checking the, STAT procedure, Status Monitor
            protocol (reference description); 313–314
    Lock Manager protocol interaction with (figure);
            280
    Status Manager protocol; 312–318
    term description; 279
Moran, J., [Moran+93]; 323
Morgan, S. P., [Bhide+91]; 90
Morris, J., [Morris+86]; 321
mount(ing),
    automounter (chapter); 321
    dynamic addition of, autofs use; 327
    entry,
        adding, MNT procedure, MOUNT protocol
            (reference description); 260–262
        list, retrieving, DUMP procedure, MOUNT
            protocol (reference description); 263–264
    filesystems,
        MNT procedure, MOUNT protocol (reference
            description); 260–262
        without blocking, Amd operations; 339–340
    hierarchical, implementation issues; 230
    multiple; 333–334
    offset; 332
    options; 339
        scope (figure); 340
    storm, term description (footnote); 331
    table, MOUNT protocol use; 270–271
    unmounting filesystems,
        all entries, UMNTALL procedure, MOUNT
            protocol (reference description); 265
        UMNT procedure, MOUNT protocol (reference
            description); 264
MOUNT protocol, (chapter); 255–275
    filehandle access by; 85
    MOUNTPROC_XXX procedures, *See* procedures,
            MOUNT protocol
    NFS relationship to; 255
    procedures (table); 259
    revisions; 256–257
    server procedures (reference descriptions); 259–270
    transports used by; 257
    WebNFS public filehandle elimination of need for;
            433
mountpoints,
    See also authentication
    AFS use; 367
    crossing,
        (figure); 87
        pathname, issues (footnote); 261
        prohibited, LOOKUP procedure, NFS V.3; 156
        in WebNFS; 441

mountpoints   *continued*
  detection,
      as LOOKUP pathname evaluation advantage;
          86
      LOOKUP procedure, NFS V.3; 156
  filesystem, crossing, implementation issues;
          228–230
  ordering, in multiple mount requirements; 333
  replication, as mountpoint crossing solution; 229
  temporary, automounter problems with; 324–327
movement of volumes, in AFS; 367
mtime file attribute,
  comparison of support by different systems
          (table); 226
  in fattr data type,
      POSIX stat comparison (table); 97
      (table); 95
  in fattr3 data type (table); 143
multicasting, server crash recovery use; 285
multicomponent LOOKUP (MCL),
  evaluating; 442–443
  as latency reduction model, NFS Version 4
          considerations; 454
  WebNFS use; 434
multiparent, directories, not supported by NFS
          filesystem model; 156
multiple mounts; 333–334
multiprocessing, symmetric, concurrent RPC call
          handling; 234
multithreading,
  concurrent, I/O thread handling; 242
  concurrent RPC call handling; 234
  locking protocol issues; 281
  read-ahead and write-behind performance
          enhancements; 241
  in status monitor, server crash recovery use; 285

Nagle, D. F., [Gibson+98]; 356
name(ing),
  See also nicknames
  conventions, Newcastle Connection; 5
  in DH authentication; 49
  file, TNFS attribute extensions; 355
  files,
      DOS vs. UNIX; 379–381
      NFS to DOS mapping (table); 380
  full network name credential,
      DH authentication; 51–53
      Kerberos authentication; 59–60
  Kerberos; 59
  NIS name service protocol, UID/GID consistent
          mapping as driving force for; 231

named pipes,
  creating, MKNOD procedure; 186–190
  ftype3 data type, NFS V.3 (reference description);
          141
names file attribute, comparison of support by different
          systems (table); 226
namespace(s),
  See also pathnames
  CIFS; 372
      (figure); 373
  cycles, remote filesystem mounting, implementation
          issues; 228
  DFS; 370
  gaps, as hierarchical mount issue; 230
  global,
      automounter creation of (chapter); 321
      layout, automounter maps use; 329
      remote-as-local paradigm problems; 322
  in RFS; 362
  sharing, in AFS; 366–367
NASD (Network-Attached Secure Disks),
  (figure); 357
  NFS; 356–359
National Bureau of Standards, [NBS77]; 470
native paths,
  See also namespace(s); pathnames; paths
  vs. canonical paths, in WebNFS; 444
  term description; 444
Needham, R., [Needham+78]; 58
negative cache,
  benefits of; 245
  implementation issues; 156–157
negotiation,
  [RFC 2478]; 66
  security,
      as NFS Version 4 design consideration;
          459–460
      in WebNFS; 445–446
      WebNFS, NFS Version 4 model; 460
Nelson, B. J.,
  [Birrell84]; 467
  [Watson+92]; 473
Nelson, M., [Nelson+88]; 343
netgroup,
  name, ACL use, in MOUNT protocol; 258
  term description (footnote); 255
netname,
  AUTH_DES and AUTH_KERB use, for user
          identification; 231
  in DH authentication; 49
netobj data type, Lock Manager protocol (reference
          description); 292–293

network,
   address, server, portmapper determination of; 38
   independence, RPCSEC_GSS security flavor; 64
   interfaces, performance impact; 416–417
   name, ACL use, in MOUNT protocol; 258
   Network Lock Manager protocol, *See* Lock Manager
         protocol
   Network Status Monitor protocol, *See* status, Status
         Manager protocol
   Network Time protocol, Version 3, DH authenti-
         cation use; 50
   performance impact; 415–416
   processors, performance impact; 416
   protocols, bibliographic reference; 1
Netowrk-Attached Secure Devices, *See* NASD
Neuman, C.,
   [Kohl+93]; 58
   [Miller+87]; 58
   [RFC 1510]; 470
   [Steiner+88]; 58, 368
Neumann, C., [Neumann+94]; 469
Newcastle Connection, remote file access support; 4–6
nfs_fh3 data type, NFS Version 3 (reference
         description); 141–142
NFS (Network File System) protocol,
   benchmarks (chapter); 413
   data types; 92
   file attribute support, comparison with other
         systems (table); 226
   filesystem model (chapter); 81–90
   implementation issues (chapter); 225–253
   introduction (chapter); 1–8
   layering (figure); 7
   Lock Manager protocol (chapter); 277–319
   Maestro, symbolic link handling; 383
   MOUNT protocol relationship to (chapter); 255–275
   NASD NFS; 356–359
   NFS3ERR_XXX errors,
      filename construction; 85, 86
      (table); 139–140
   NFSERR_XXX errors,
      filename construction; 85, 86
      stat data type; 92
      (table); 93
   NFSPROC_XXX procedures, *See* procedures, NFS
         Version 2
   NFSPROC3_XXX procedures, *See* procedures, NFS
         Version 3
   NQNFS; 349–352
   operation mix, benchmark comparison (table,
         figure); 418

PC (chapter); 379–411
procedures,
   in NFS Version 2 (reference descriptions); 98–130
   in NFS Version 3 (reference descriptions); 147–224
server, automounter as; 322–324
Spritely NFS; 343–349
   client caching (figure); 345
TCP/IP advantages; 431–432
TNFS; 352–356
URL; 438
variants; 343–359
Version 2,
   (chapter); 91–130
   errors (table); 93
   filehandle support; 83
   server procedures (reference description); 98–130
   server procedures (table); 99
   Version 3 changes; 132
Version 3,
   changes from Version 2; 132
   (chapter); 131–224
   filehandle support; 83
   Internet and; 432
   server procedures (reference descriptions);
         147–224
   server procedures (table); 148
Version 4,
   (chapter); 449
   IETF working group charter; 451
   MOUNT protocol avoidance; 256
   stateful nature of; 88
WebNFS (chapter); 431–447
nfsd daemon,
   concurrent, I/O thread handling; 242
   concurrent RPC call handling; 234
   (figure); 235
   server crash recovery restart of; 284
nfspath3 data type, NFS Version 3 (reference
         description); 137
nfsstat3 data type, NFS Version 3 (reference
         description); 138
nfsstone benchmark; 419–421
   SFS compared with; 422
nfstime3 data type, NFS Version 3 (reference
         description); 142
NFXXX file types, in ftype data type structure; 94
nhfsstone benchmark; 421–422
   SFS compared with; 422
Nichols, D. A., [Howard+88]; 349
nicknames,
   See also naming

nicknames *continued*
  credential,
    DH authentication; 53–54
    Kerberos authentication; 61–63
  DH authentication; 50–51
  Kerberos authentication; 61–63
  verifier, DH authentication; 54
nlm_lock data type, Lock Manager protocol (reference
    description); 293
nlm_stats data type, Lock Manager protocol (reference
    description); 293
NIS name service protocol,
  map, automount map use; 329
  security issues; 58
  UID/GID consistent mapping as driving force for;
    231
nlink file attribute,
  comparison of support by different systems (table);
    226
  in fattr data type,
    POSIX stat comparison (table); 97
    (table); 95
  in fattr3 data type (table); 143
nlinks file attribute, hard links indicated by; 82
NLM (Network Lock Manager), *See* Lock Manager
    protocol
NLM_XXX procedures, *See* procedures, Lock Manager
    protocol
NM_LOCK procedure, Lock Manager protocol
    (reference description); 311
nohide option, as mountpoint crossing solution,
    advantages and disadvantages; 230
nonmonitored locks,
  creating, NM_LOCK procedure, Lock Manager
    protocol (reference description); 311
  limitations of; 280
Non-Volatile Random Access Memory, *See* NVRAM
Not Quite NFS, *See* NQNFS
notation, XDR language conventions; 18
NOTIFY procedure, Status Monitor protocol (reference
    description); 318
notifying hosts, of a state change, NOTIFY procedure,
    Status Monitor protocol (reference
    description); 318
Nowicki, W.,
  [Nowicki89]; 470
  [RFC 1094]; 470
NQNFS (Not Quite NFS); 349–352
  AFS cache consistency semantics compared with;
    365
NSM (Network Status Monitor) protocol, *See* status,
    Status Monitor protocol

null, authentication; 44–45
NULL procedure,
  Lock Manager protocol (reference description);
    295–296
  MOUNT protocol (reference description); 259–260
  NFS Version 2 (reference description); 99–100
  NFS Version 3 (reference description); 147
  Portmap protocol (reference description); 39
  RPCSEC_GSS use; 65, 67
  Status Monitor protocol (reference description); 313
numbers, program, in RPC protocol; 29–30
NVRAM (Non-Volatile Random Access Memory),
  duplicate request cache use; 236
  performance impact; 417

objects,
  caching, implementation issues; 245–246
  filesystem, in NFS protocol; 81–83
Odlyzko, A. M., [LaMacchia+91]; 58
offset(s),
  file, NQNFS extension; 352
  mounts; 332
  paths, term description; 332
Okasaki, M., [Satyanarayanan+90]; 251, 368
ONC (Open Network Computing),
  RPC protocol; 6
    (chapter); 25–42
opaque data,
  fixed-length, as primitive XDR data type; 15
  variable-length, as primitive XDR data type; 15
Open Group, *See* The Open Group
open(ing),
  files,
    ACCESS procedure impact; 160
    accessing, as permission implementation issue;
      231–232
    removal implementation issues; 227
  source,
    Amd; 341
    PCNFSD server; 385
    Samba server; 376
  systems,
    as MOUNT protocol separation from NFS
      protocol rationale; 255
    ONC RPC protocol (chapter); 25–42
    RPCSEC_GSS flavor; 64
    See also extensibility; transparency
OPEN request,
  lack of, as stateless indiccation; 87
  in Spritely NFS; 344
operation(s),
  See also procedures

idempotent,
  in NFS protocol; 88–89
  nonidempotent operations (figure); 89
mix,
  in benchmark workload; 418
  in benchmark workload, comparison (table); 428
synchronous, stable storage and, implementation
    issues; 236–239
oplock (opportunistic locks),
  See also lock(ing)
  CIFS; 374–376
    (figure); 375
  with CIFS; 374–376
option(s),
  mount, scope (figure); 340
  for mounting; 339
  nohide, as mountpoint crossing solution; 230
order(ing),
  of mountpoints, in multiple mount requirements;
    333
  replica server, automounter processing; 335–336
  XDR integer byte, big-endian; 11, 12
Ousterhout, J., [Nelson+88]; 343
overhead, of initialization, WebNFS handling; 435
owner file attribute, comparison of support by different
    systems (table); 226

packing, term description; 251
paging, executable files, permission implementation
    issues; 233
PARC (Palo Alto Research Center), RPC developed at;
    27
PATHCONF procedure,
  MOUNT protocol (reference description); 267–270
  NFS Version 3,
    description; 134
    (reference description); 218–221
pathnames,
  See also namespace(s)
  evaluation,
    latency and; 434–435
    by server; 436
    WebNFS handling; 435
  evaluation of, NFS protocol; 86–87
  filename components, handling of, in NFS protocol;
    85–86
  independence, as filehandle criterion; 84
  in NFS protocol; 85–87
  nfspath3 data type, NFS V.3 (reference description);
    137
  path data type, NFS V.2 (reference description); 98
  relative, automounter problems; 326

server mountpoint crossing, issues (footnote); 261
  term description; 85
paths,
  See also namespace(s); pathnames
  absolute vs. relative, in NFS URL; 438–439
  canonical,
    vs. native paths, in WebNFS; 444
    term description; 444
  configuration, retrieving, PATHCONF procedure;
    218–221
  native,
    vs. canonical paths, in WebNFS; 444
    term description; 444
  offset, term description; 332
Pawlowski, B.,
  [Pawlowski+89]; 469
  [RFC 1813]; 471
PC,
  clients,
    creating unmonitored locks, NM_LOCK
      procedure, Lock Manager protocol (reference
      description); 311
    file sharing, removing, UNSHARE procedure,
      Lock Manager protocol (reference
      description); 310–311
    file sharing, SHARE procedure, Lock Manager
      protocol (reference description); 308–310
  file semantics, CIFS; 373
  NFS (chapter); 379–411
PCNFSD protocol; 384–387
  HCLNFSD protocol as alternative to; 409
  PCNFSD_PR_XXX procedures, *See* procedures,
    PCNFSD Version 1
  PCNFSD2_PR_XXX procedures, *See* procedures,
    PCNFSD Version 2
  unique features, integration of, as NFS Version 4
    design goal; 453
  Version 1; 387–391
  Version 2; 391–409
Pendry, J., [Pendry94]; 339
performance,
  See also benchmarks; cache(ing)
  assessment, NFS benchmarks (chapter); 413
  as autofs automounter advantage; 327
  cache,
    efficiency, as NFS Version 4 design consideration;
      456
    locked file cache disabling impact on; 291
    policies as tool for improving; 244–251
  as design criterion for NFS protocol; 6
  factors affecting; 414–418
  as file access protocol disadvantage; 3

performance *continued*
  file, locking issues; 287
  initialization overhead, WebNFS advantages; 435
  Internet, as NFS Version 4 design consideration;
    452
  local procedure call compared with RPC; 26
  LOOKUP pathname evaluation; 86
  as MOUNT protocol separation from NFS protocol
    rationale; 255
  nickname credential advantage, in DH authenti-
    cation; 51
  NQNFS; 349
  read-ahead and write-behind enhancement of; 241
  READDIRPLUS issues; 208
  RFS problems; 363
  RPCSEC_GSS; 76
  Spritely NFS; 344, 348–349
  synchronous operations impact on; 238
  XDR; 12
permissions,
  See also authentication; security
  checking,
    ACCESS procedure, NFS V.3; 158–162
    as permission implementation issue; 232–233
    on exported filesystems, MOUNT protocol
      advantages; 255
  implementation issues; 230–233
persistence,
  as filehandle criterion; 84
  locks, issues; 288
ping tiebreaker, in replica server accessing; 335–336
Pinkas, D., [RFC 2478]; 66, 460, 471
pipes,
  creating named, MKNOD procedure; 186–190
  ftype3 data type, NFS V.3 (reference description);
    141
PMAPPROC_XXX procedures, *See* procedures,
    Portmap protocol; 39–40
policies, caching, implementation issues; 244–251
Popek, G., [Popek+83]; 4
port,
  assignment, portmapper service use to determine;
    38
  client and server; 444
  monitoring, MOUNT request validation use; 257
  NFS assignment; 433
  number,
    network address determined by; 38
    retrieving, GETPORT procedure, Portmap
      protocol; 39
  privileged, term description; 38
  registering, SET procedure, Portmap protocol; 39

  unregistering, UNSET procedure, Portmap protocol;
    39
Portmap protocol; 39–40
  as RPC protocol service, rpcbind relationship; 38–41
portmon, MOUNT request validation use; 257
POSIX,
  1003.1 specification,
    impact on MOUNT protocol; 256
    NFS filesystem model relationship to; 225
    pathconf information retrieval, PATHCONF
      procedure, MOUNT protocol (reference
      description); 267–270
  fcntl procedure, LOCK procedure, Lock Manager
    protocol; 300
  file attribute support, comparison with other
    systems (table); 226
  file locking semantics, Lock Manager use; 305
  fsync(2) system call, COMMIT semantics compared
    with; 222
  lockf procedure, LOCK procedure, Lock Manager
    protocol; 300
  path configuration, retrieving, PATHCONF
    procedure; 218–221
  stat structure,
    fattr data type, NFS V.2 relationship to; 96
    fattr data type, NFS V.2 relationship to (table); 97
post_op_attr data type, NFS Version 3 (reference
    description); 143–144
post_op_fh3 data type, NFS Version 3 (reference
    description); 146
power failure, stable storage protection against; 237
Pownell, J., [Israel+89]; 468
PR_XXX procedures, *See* procedures, print
pre_op_attr data type, NFS Version 3 (reference
    description); 145
primitive, *See* basic
principal, term description; 43
printing,
  administration of, PR_ADMIN procedure,
    PCNFSD Version 2 (reference description);
    400–401
  canceling, PR_CANCEL procedure, PCNFSD
    Version 2 (reference description); 399–400
  job queue, changing position in, PR_REQUEUE
    procedure, PCNFSD Version 2 (reference
    description); 401–402
  listing,
    printers, PR_LIST procedure, PCNFSD Version 2
      (reference description); 395–396
    queued printer jobs, PR_QUEUE procedure,
      PCNFSD Version 2 (reference description);
      396–398

in PCNFSD; 385–387
  option types (table); 386
remote,
    preparing for, PR_INIT procedure, PCNFSD
        Version 1 (reference description); 389–390
    preparing for, PR_INIT procedure, PCNFSD
        Version 2 (reference description); 393
    starting, PR_START procedure, PCNFSD Version
        2 (reference description); 394–395
    starting, PR_START (reference description);
        390–391
  services, CIFS protocol use; 372–377
  spooling, PCNFSD protocol provision for; 384
  status, determining, PR_STATUS procedure,
        PCNFSD Version 2 (reference description);
        398–399
privacy, *See also* encryption
  data, RPCSEC_GSS; 73
procedure(s),
  See also operations
  asynchronous, Lock Manager protocol use; 282–283
  HCLNFSD protocol (table); 410
  local procedure call compared with RPC; 25–27
  Lock Manager protocol,
      CANCEL procedure, Lock Manager protocol
          (reference description); 302–304
      FREE_ALL (reference description); 311–312
      GRANTED (reference description); 305–308
      LOCK (reference description); 299–302
      NM_LOCK (reference description); 311
      NULL (reference description); 295–296
      (reference descriptions); 294–312
      SHARE (reference description); 308–310
      TEST (reference description); 296–298
      UNLOCK (reference description); 304–305
      UNSHARE (reference description); 310–311
  MOUNT protocol,
      DUMP (reference description); 263–264
      EXPORT (reference description); 265–267
      EXPORTALL (reference description); 267
      MNT (reference description); 260–262
      NULL (reference description); 259–260
      PATHCONF (reference description); 267–270
      (table); 259
      UMNT (reference description); 264
      UMNTALL (reference description); 265
  NFS Version 2,
      CREATE (reference description); 112–114
      CREATE, Version 3 changes; 133
      GETATTR (reference description); 100–101
      LINK (reference description); 119–120
      LOOKUP (reference description); 104–106

      LOOKUP, Version 3 changes; 132–133
      MKDIR (reference description); 122–124
      NULL (reference description); 99–100
      READ (reference description); 107–109
      READ, Version 3 changes; 132–133
      READDIR (reference description); 126–128
      READDIR, Version 3 changes; 133
      READLINK (reference description); 106–107
      REMOVE (reference description); 115–116
      RENAME (reference description); 116–118
      RMDIR (reference description); 124–126
      ROOT and WRITECACHE deleted in Version 3;
          132
      SETATTR (reference description); 102–103
      STATFS (reference description); 128–130
      SYMLINK (reference description); 120–122
      Version 3 changes; 132–133
      WRITE (reference description); 109–112
      WRITE, Version 3 changes; 132–133
  NFS Version 3,
      ACCESS, description; 133
      ACCESS (reference description); 158–162
      COMMIT, description; 134
      CREATE (reference description); 174
      FSINFO, description; 133
      FSINFO (reference description); 214–218
      FSSTAT, description; 134
      FSSTAT (reference description); 212–214
      GETATTR (reference description); 149–151
      LINK (reference description); 199–201
      LOOKUP (reference description); 155–158
      MKDIR (reference description); 179–182
      MKNOD, description; 133
      MKNOD (reference description); 186–190
      new procedures; 133–134
      NULL (reference description); 147
      PATHCONF, description; 134
      PATHCONF (reference description); 218–221,
          221–224
      READ (reference description); 164–167
      READDIR (reference description); 202–205
      READDIRPLUS, description; 133
      READDIRPLUS (reference description); 205–211
      READLINK (reference description); 162–164
      REMOVE (reference description); 190–192
      RENAME (reference description); 195–198
      RMDIR (reference description); 192–195
      SETATTR (reference description); 151–155
      SYMLINK (reference description); 182–185
      WRITE (reference description); 168–174
  PCNFSD Version 1,
      AUTH (reference description); 388–389

procedure(s), PCNFSD Version 1   *continued*
   PR_INIT (reference description); 389–390
   PR_START (reference description); 390–391
   (table); 388
  PCNFSD Version 2,
   ALERT (reference description); 408–409
   AUTH (reference description); 407–408
   INFO (reference description); 391–392
   MAPID (reference description); 405–406
   PR_ADMIN (reference description); 400–401
   PR_CANCEL (reference description); 399–400
   PR_HOLD (reference description); 403–404
   PR_INIT (reference description); 393
   PR_LIST (reference description); 395–396
   PR_QUEUE (reference description); 396–398
   PR_RELEASE (reference description); 404–404
   PR_REQUEUE (reference description); 401–402
   PR_START (reference description); 394–395
   PR_STATUS (reference description); 398–399
   (table); 392
  Portmap protocol,
   CALLIT (reference description); 40
   DUMP (reference description); 40
   GETPORT (reference description); 39
   NULL (reference description); 39
   SET (reference description); 39
   UNSET (reference description); 39
  server,
   in MOUNT protocol (reference descriptions);
    259–270
   in NFS Version 2 (reference descriptions); 98–130
   in NFS Version 2 (table); 99
   in NFS Version 3 (reference descriptions); 147–224
   in NFS Version 3 (table); 148
  Status Monitor protocol,
   MON (reference description); 314–316
   NOTIFY (reference description); 318
   NULL (reference description); 313
   SIMU_CRASH (reference description); 317–318
   STAT (reference description); 313–314
   UNMON_ALL (reference description); 317
   UNMON (reference description); 316–317
  synchronous, Lock Manager protocol (table); 296
  unsupported, implementation issues; 225–226
processes, user-level, filehandle criteria issues for; 84
program numbers, in RPC protocol; 29–30
protection of data integrity, RPCSEC_GSS; 71–72
protocol(s),
  authentication, Kerberos; 59
  BWNFSD; 409–410
  CIFS; 372–377
  DH authentication; 51

extensibility, as NFS Version 4 design consideration;
   465–466
file access,
  vs. file transfer; 2–4
  history of; 4–6
file transfer, vs. file access; 2–4
HCLNFSD; 409–410
HTTP, connection-based security protocols that use;
  79
integration, as NFS Version 4 design consideration;
  452
IP, connection-based security [RFC 2401]; 79
Lock Manager (chapter); 277–319
MOUNT (chapter); 255–275
network, bibliographic reference; 1
NFS,
  distinguished from other remote filesystems; 4
  introduction (chapter); 1–8
  Version 2 (chapter); 91–130
  Version 3 (chapter); 131–224
NIS name service, UID/GID consistent mapping as
   driving force for; 231
ONC RPC; 6
  (chapter); 25–42
PCNFSD; 384–387
  Version 1; 387–391
  Version 2; 391–409
Portmap; 39–40
  rpcbind relationship; 38–41
RPC,
  (chapter); 25–42
  NFS based on; 4
rpcbind; 40–41
  Portmap relationship; 38–41
RPCSEC_GSS; 65–66
SSL, https URL use; 79
TCP/IP; 1
  as connection-based security; 78
  session setup with CIFS; 373
  UDP compared with; 27
transportable data and; 9–11
proxy,
  caching, as NFS Version 4 design consideration;
   456–457
  SOCKS application,
   NFS issues; 433
   [RFC 1928]; 452
public, filehandles, handling, LOOKUP procedure,
   NFS V.3; 156
  key schemes,
   DH authentication weakness related to; 57
   DH flavor use; 49

QOP (quality of protection), specification, in
RPCSEC_GSS context creation; 66
Quarterman, J., [McKusick+96]; 469
QUEUE procedure, PCNFSD Version 2 (reference
description); 396–398

Randell, B., [Brownbridge+82]; 4
rdev file attribute,
comparison of support by different systems (table);
226
in fattr data type,
POSIX stat comparison (table); 97
(table); 95
in fattr3 data type (table); 143
read(ing),
See also write(ing)
caching, implementation issues; 248–249
directories,
READDIR procedure, NFS V.2; 126–128
READDIR procedure, NFS V.3; 202–205
READDIRPLUS procedure; 205–211
from a file,
READ procedure, NFS V.2; 107–109
READ procedure, NFS V.3; 164–167
read-ahead, implementation issues; 241–243
read-only data,
disk cache use; 249
volume replication, in AFS; 368
from a symbolic link,
READLINK procedure, NFS V.2; 106–107
READLINK procedure, NFS V.3; 162–164
READ procedure,
NFS Version 2 (reference description); 107–109
NFS Version 2, Version 3 changes; 132–133
NFS Version 3 (reference description); 164–167
READDIR procedure,
NFS Version 2 (reference description); 126–128
NFS Version 2, Version 3 changes; 133
NFS Version 3 (reference description); 202–205
READDIRPLUS procedure,
NFS Version 3, description; 133
NFS Version 3 (reference description); 205–211
READLINK procedure,
NFS Version 2 (reference description); 106–107
NFS Version 3 (reference description); 162–164
readonly file attribute, comparison of support by
different systems (table); 226
"receiver makes it right", data encoding; 11
reconnecting caches, implementation issues;
250–251
record(s), record-marking standard, RPC protocol;
36–37

recovery,
crash,
client (figure); 289
client, Lock Manager protocol; 288–289
DFS grace period use; 370
server, Lock Manager protocol; 284–286
filehandle construction failure, support for,
post_op_fh3 data type, NFS V.3 (reference
description); 146
in NQNFS; 351–352
server,
client crash, leases use for; 349
(figure); 348
in NFS protocol; 88
stateful [Mogul94]; 344
in Spritely NFS; 347–348
write-behind issues; 347
redundancy, *See also* highly available NFS (HA-NFS)
servers; storage
asynchronous locking procedure; 283
as availability tool; 458
replica server use; 334
reexport, restrictions on; 273
region, locked (figure); 278
registering, with portmapper service, SET procedure,
Portmap protocol; 39
relative,
pathnames,
automounter problems; 326
symbolic link interpretation; 382
paths, absolute paths vs., in NFS URL; 438–439
URLs, evaluation; 437
RELEASE procedure, PCNFSD Version 2 (reference
description); 404–405
reliability,
as NFS Version 4 design consideration; 458–459
UDP vs. TCP; 27
performance impact; 415
workload unreliability, as Nfsstone benchmark
weakness; 421
remote, *See also* distributed; networks; NFS protocol;
RPC protocol
file sharing, *See* RFS filesystem
files, file access protocol advantages; 2
procedure call,
local procedure call compared with; 25–27
term description; 25
remote system call paradigm,
RFS (figure); 362
as RFS requirement; 361
remote-as-local paradigm, as NFS requirement; 321
system calls, in RFS; 361

REMOVE procedure,
   See also deleting
   NFS Version 2 (reference description); 115–116
   NFS Version 3 (reference description); 190–192
RENAME procedure,
   hiding files with; 191
   NFS Version 2 (reference description); 116–118
   NFS Version 3 (reference description); 195–198
renaming files, RENAME (reference description);
      116–118, 195–198
replication,
   See also redundancy
   lazy, Episode support of; 371
   mountpoint, as mountpoint crossing solution; 229
   read-only, of volumes, in AFS; 368
   replica servers,
      automounter use; 334–336
      as availability tool; 458
      (figure); 335
reply,
   RPC; 33–36
      header (figure); 33
   server, RPCSEC_GSS; 75
reporting rules, SPS 2.0 benchmark requirements;
      429
representation,
   data, XDR protocol (chapter); 9–24
   of user and group IDs, as NFS Version 4 design
      consideration; 461
reproducibility,
   nhfsstone issues; 422
   as SFS goal; 422
requests,
   batched, with CIFS; 374
   data, server processing of, RPCSEC_GSS; 74–75
   duplicate request caches, implementation issues;
      234–236
REQUEUE procedure, PCNFSD Version 2 (reference
      description); 401–402
requirements, RPC protocol; 30–31
restrictions, export, in MOUNT protocol; 273–275
retransmission,
   adaptive, for UDP, implementation issues;
      239–240
   of RPC messages, XID role in avoiding problems
      with; 31–32
retrieving,
   See also access; authentication
   attributes,
      file, GETATTR procedure, NFS V.2; 100–101
      file, GETATTR procedure, NFS V.3; 149–151
      filesystem, STATFS procedure, NFS V.2; 128–130

directories, in WebNFS; 442
exported filesystem list, EXPORT procedure,
      MOUNT protocol (reference description);
      265–267
filehandle, MNT procedure, MOUNT protocol
      (reference description); 260–262
files, in WebNFS; 441
filesystem,
   static state, FSINFO procedure; 214–218
   volatile state, FSSTAT procedure; 212–214
information, about supported services, INFO
      procedure (PCNFSD Version 2); 391–392
list of RPC service registrations, DUMP procedure,
      Portmap protocol; 40
MOUNT entry list, DUMP procedure, MOUNT
      protocol (reference description); 263–264
path configuration, PATHCONF procedure;
      218–221
port number, GETPORT procedure, Portmap
      protocol; 39
POSIX pathconf information, retrieving,
      PATHCONF procedure, MOUNT protocol
      (reference description); 267–270
printer list, PR_LIST procedure, PCNFSD Version 2
      (reference description); 395–396
queued printer job list, PR_QUEUE procedure,
      PCNFSD Version 2 (reference description);
      396–398
symbolic links, in WebNFS; 442
revisions, of MOUNT protocol; 256–257
RFC (Request for Comment); 450
   See also IANA; IETF
2339; 451
[RFC 1094]; 91, 470
[RFC 1508]; 64, 470
[RFC 1509]; 64, 470
[RFC 1510]; 470
[RFC 1808]; 471
[RFC 1813]; 132, 471
[RFC 1831]; 25, 471
[RFC 1832]; 6, 9, 18, 25, 463, 471
[RFC 1833]; 471
[RFC 1928]; 452, 471
[RFC 2054]; 439, 471
[RFC 2055]; 471
[RFC 2078]; 65, 471
[RFC 2203]; 64, 471
[RFC 2246]; 79, 459, 471
[RFC 2401]; 79, 471
[RFC 2478]; 66, 460, 472
[RFC 2623]; 80, 472
[RFC 2624]; 452, 472

RFS (Remote File Sharing) filesystem; 361–363
   device type support, NFS compared with;
      83
   as early file access system; 4
Riedel, E., [Gibson+98]; 356
RMDIR procedure,
   NFS Version 2 (reference description); 124–126
   NFS Version 3 (reference description); 192–195
RMI, Xerox PARC RPC work influence on; 27
Rochberg, D., [Gibson+98]; 356
ROOT procedure, NFS Version 2, deleted in Version 3;
      132
Rosenthal, D. S., [Morris+86]; 321
RPC (Remote Procedure Call) protocol,
   authentication; 43–65
   call,
      header; 32
      parameters; 32
   concurrent calls, implementation issues; 234
   credential, as authentication field; 43–44
   data exchange, with RPCSEC_GSS; 70–71
   errors,
      accepted status (table); 35
      authentication (table); 34
   messages, call; 31–32
   NFS based on; 4
   ONC RPC protocol; 6
      (chapter); 25–42
   program numbers; 29–30
   reducing the number of RPCs, as NFS Version 4
      design goal; 455
   RPC model; 25–27
   reply; 33–36
      header (figure); 33
   requirements; 30–31
   security based on, as NFS Version 4 design
      consideration; 459
   semantics; 27–29
   transport independence; 27–29
   verifier, as authentication field; 43–44
   versioning; 29–30
Rpcbind protocol; 40–41
   as RPC protocol service, Portmap relationship;
      38–41
rpcgen, XDR language use by; 17
RPCSEC_GSS security flavor, *See also* security
   API for C, RFC 2078; 65
   authentication; 64–78
   context creation; 66–68
      (figure); 68, 69
      successful; 68–70
      unsuccessful; 70

   credential; 66
   data,
      integrity protection; 71–72
      privacy; 73
   errors; 75–76
   as extensible authentication framework; 44
   NFS Version 4 consideration of; 459
   performance; 76
   protocol; 65–66
   pseudoflavor use; 261
   RPC data exchange; 70–71
   RPCSEC_GSS_XXX authentication failure errors, *See*
      errors, RPC, authentication (table)
   server,
      processing of data requests; 74–75
      reply; 75
   snoop session trace; 76–78

Sacco, G., [Denning+81]; 58
Saltzer, J., [Miller+87]; 58
Samba server; 376
Sandberg, R., [Sandberg+85]; 91
sattr data type, NFS Version 2 (reference description);
      97–98
sattr3 data type, NFS Version 3 (reference
      description); 146–147
Satyanarayanan, M.,
   [Howard+88]; 349
   [Morris+86]; 321
   [Satyanarayanan+90]; 251, 368
scalability,
   See also extensibility; interoperability
   AFS; 364
   as direct automount map problem; 330
   global namespace issues; 322
   as indirect automount map advantage; 331
   as NFS Version 4 design consideration; 457–458
   public filehandle advantages over MOUNT; 434
   RFS naming scheme; 363
Schemers, R. J., [Eisler+96]; 68, 76
Schiller, J.,
   [Miller+87]; 58
   [Steiner+88]; 471
Schroeder, M., [Needham+78]; 58
Secure Shell (ssh), as connection-based security; 78–79
Secure Sockets Layer, *See* SSL
secure storage, as NASD NFS goal; 356
security,
   See also authentication; credentials; flavors; verifiers
   ACL use, MOUNT protocol; 258
   in AFS; 368
   B1-level, as TNFS goal; 353

security *continued*
  connection-based,
      as NFS Version 4 design consideration; 459
      as RPC-based security alternative; 78–80
  data, in NASD NFS; 358–359
  filename protection in TNFS; 355
  flavors, *See* flavors
      AUTH_MLS; 353–354
      RPCSEC_GSS; 64–78
  government requirements, TCSEC, TNFS support
      of; 352–356
  issues with DH authentication; 58
  issues with Portmap protocol CALLIT procedure; 40
  issues with Portmap protocol DUMP procedure; 40
  labels, term description; 353
  MLS; 353
  NASD NFS; 356–359
  negotiation,
      as NFS Version 4 design consideration; 459–460
      in WebNFS; 445–446
      WebNFS, NFS Version 4 model; 460
  overloading filehandles with security flavors, in
      WebNFS; 445–446
  privileged port use, intentions and limitations; 39
  in RFS; 363
  RPC-based, as NFS Version 4 design consideration;
      459
  RPCSEC_GSS data privacy weaknesses; 73
  submount problems; 272
      (figure); 273
  transport layer, TLS [RFC 2246]; 79
  weaknesses, of AUTH_SYS flavor; 47
semantics,
  See also syntax
  "at-most-once",
      cache use; 87
      duplicate request cache use; 88
      RPC approximation of; 29
      XID use in implementing; 32
  cache consistency, AFS compared with Spritely NFS
      and NQNFS; 365
  COMMIT, fsync(2) POSIX system call compared
      with; 222
  exactly-once, not guaranteed by SETATTR
      procedure, NFS V.3; 152
  exclusive create,
      createverf3, NFS V.3 (reference description); 137
      support for, CREATE procedure, NFS V.3;
          176–177
  failure, kernel-based file locking; 287
  file, CIFS; 373
  POSIX file locking, Lock Manager use; 305

RPC protocol; 27–29
single-copy,
  DFS use; 365
  term description; 343
UNIX filesystem,
  Episode support of; 371
  preservation of, as RFS goal; 361
weak cache consistency,
  support for, pre_op_attr data type, NFS V.3
      (reference description); 145
  support for, wcc_data data type, NFS V.3
      (reference description); 145–146
sequence number, RPCSEC_GSS XID handling; 74–75
server(s),
  See also clients
  32-bit clients/servers vs. 64-bit clients/servers,
      compatibility issues in NFS Version 3;
      135–136
  administration, sending a message to, ALERT
      procedure (PCNFSD Version 2); 408–409
  client port and; 444
  cluster server, term description; 426
  configuration, SFS, Versions 1.0 and 1.1; 426
  crash recovery, Lock Manager protocol; 284–286
  data bus, performance impact; 417
  data request processing, RPCSEC_GSS; 74–75
  dead, as hierarchical mount issue; 230
  failover, in highly available NFS servers; 90
  keepalives, with Amd; 340
  mountpoints, crossing, implementation issues;
      228–230
  NFS, automounter as; 322–324
  procedures,
      in MOUNT protocol (reference descriptions);
          259–270
      in NFS Version 2 (reference descriptions); 98–130
      in NFS Version 2 (table); 99
      in NFS Version 3 (table); 148
      in (reference descriptions); 147–224
  recovery,
      of client state, NQNFS; 351
      in NFS protocol; 88
  replica,
      automounter use; 334–336
      as availability tool; 458
      (figure); 335
  reply, RPCSEC_GSS; 75
  Samba; 376
  state, loss of, lock manager handling; 278
  stateful, Spritely NFS use; 344
  stateless,
      high availability characteristics; 89–90

in NFS protocol; 87–90
open file access, implementation issues; 232
user-level NFS, automounters implemented as; 323
verifier,
DH authentication; 54–56
Kerberos authentication; 62
WebNFS,
pathname evaluation; 436
requirements; 442–444
term description; 442
services, determining which are supported, INFO procedure (PCNFSD Version 2); 391–392
session, TCP, setting up, with CIFS; 373
SET procedure, Portmap protocol (reference description); 39
SETATTR procedure,
NFS Version 2 (reference description); 102–103
NFS Version 3 (reference description); 151–155
setting,
attributes, file, NFS Version 3 changes; 135
file attributes,
SETATTR procedure, NFS V.2; 102–103
SETATTR procedure, NFS V.3; 151–155
SFS (System File Server) benchmark,
UDP checksum calculation requirement; 416
Version 2.0; 428–429
Versions 1.0 and 1.1; 422–427
running; 423–424
server configuration; 426
workload; 424–426
SHARE procedure,
Lock Manager protocol (reference description); 308–310
shared/sharing,
files,
DOS procedures, Lock Manager protocol (table); 296
DOS/Windows, Lock Manager procedures overview; 283–284
HCLNFSD protocol support of; 409
removing, UNSHARE procedure, Lock Manager protocol (reference description); 310–311
SHARE procedure, Lock Manager protocol (reference description); 308–310
locks; 281–282
term description; 278, 281
memory system, WRITE procedure impact; 172
namespace,
in AFS; 366–367
in DFS; 370

write, issues with; 172
Shein, B., [Shein+89]; 419
Shepler, S.,
[Bhide+92]; 90
[RFC 2624]; 452
side-effects, local procedure call compared with RPC; 26
Sidebotham, R. N.,
[Chutani+92]; 371
[Howard+88]; 349
Siegel, E., [Satyanarayanan+90]; 251, 368
signed integer, as primitive XDR data type; 13–14
SIMU_CRASH procedure, Status Monitor protocol (reference description); 317–318
simulating a crash, SIMU_CRASH procedure, Status Monitor protocol (reference description); 317–318
single-copy semantics, 343
See also semantics
DFS use; 365
size,
See also cache(ing); performance
data requests, NFS Version 3 changes; 134
directory, in benchmark workload; 419
file,
in benchmark workload; 419
extending, SETATTR procedure, NFS V.3; 152
filehandle, NFS Version 3 changes; 134
maximum, READ and WRITE operations; 170
UDP datagram limitations; 36
XDR structures, in NFS Version 3 data types; 136–137
size file attribute,
comparison of support by different systems (table); 226
in fattr data type,
POSIX stat comparison (table); 97
(table); 95
in fattr3 data type (table); 143
SM_XXX procedures, *See* procedures, Status Monitor protocol
SMB (server message block) file access,
See CIFS (Common Internet File System) protocol
Smith, F. D., [Morris+86]; 321
snoop,
characteristics; 7
session trace, RPCSEC_GSS; 76–78
sockets,
creating, MKNOD procedure; 186–190
ONC RPC influenced by Sockets project; 27

sockets *continued*
  UNIX, ftype3 data type, NFS V.3 (reference
      description); 141
SOCKS application proxy,
  NFS issues; 433
  [RFC 1928]; 452
SPEC (Standard Performance Evaluation Corporation),
      SPS benchmark developed by; 422
specdata3 data type, NFS Version 3 (reference
      description); 141
special,
  data, specdata3, NFS V.3 (reference description);
      141
  device, ftype3 data type, NFS V.3 (reference
      description); 140–141
  files,
    creating, MKNOD procedure; 186–190
    term description; 83
speed,
  See also cache(ing); performance
  lack of, as file access protocol disadvantage; 3
spindles, disk, performance impact; 417
spooling,
  PCNFSD protocol provision for; 384
  print jobs, PR_INIT procedure, PCNFSD Version 1
      (reference description); 389–390
Spritely NFS; 343–349
  See also filesystem(s); NFS protocol
  cache consistency,
    AFS compared with; 365
    DFS compared with; 369
  client caching (figure); 345
  NQNFS compared with; 349
Srinivasan, R.,
  [Eisler+96]; 68, 76
  [RFC 1831]; 25, 471
  [RFC 1832]; 6, 9, 18, 25, 463, 471
  [RFC 1833]; 471
Srinivasan, V., [Srinivasan+89]; 344
ssh (Secure Shell), as connection-based security; 78–79
SSL (secure sockets layer) protocol,
  HTTPS URL use; 79
  problems with; 459
stable,
  storage,
    synchronous operations and, implementation
        issues; 236–239
    term description; 171, 236
  writes, vs. unstable writes; 171
stale data,
  avoidance, as file access protocol advantage; 3

MOUNT table entries, as MOUNT table problem;
      271
standards,
  See also protocols
  canonical, XDR as; 11
  IEEE POSIX standard 1003.1, *See* POSIX
  record-marking, RPC protocol; 36–37
START procedure,
  PCNFSD Version 1 (reference description); 390–391
  PCNFSD Version 2 (reference description); 394–395
starting,
  host monitoring, MON procedure, Status Monitor
        protocol (reference description); 314–316
  remote printing,
    PR_START procedure, PCNFSD Version 2
        (reference description); 394–395
    PR_START (reference description); 390–391
stat data type, NFS Version 2 (reference description);
      92
STAT procedure, Status Monitor protocol (reference
        description); 313–314
statd daemon,
  crash, impact on clients; 285
  server crash recovery restart of; 284
  as Status Monitor protocol implementation; 287
state,
  buffers, in WRITE procedure, NFS V.3; 172
  change, notifying hosts of, NOTIFY procedure,
        Status Monitor protocol (reference
        description); 318
  client, server recovery of, NQNFS; 351
  context, required by some RPC authentication
        flavors; 88
  filesystem,
    static, retrieving, FSINFO procedure; 214–218
    volatile, retrieving, FSSTAT procedure;
        212–214
  server, loss of, lock manager handling; 278
  stateful,
    protocol, MOUNT as; 270
    server, locking requirement of; 277
    server, recovery [Mogul94]; 344
    server, Spritely NFS use; 344
  stateless,
    daemon, autofs; 327
    scalability issues; 457
    server, NFS protocol; 87–90
    server, open file access, implementation issues;
        232
STATFS procedure, NFS Version 2 (reference
        description); 128–130

static state,
  See also state
  filesystem, retrieving, FSINFO procedure; 214–218
status,
  See also errors; Lock Manager protocol
  monitoring,
    checking the, STAT procedure, Status Monitor
        protocol (reference description); 313–314
    lock manager need of; 278–281
    term description; 279
  nfsstat3 data type, NFS V.3 (reference description);
        138
  printer, determining, PR_STATUS procedure,
        PCNFSD Version 2 (reference description);
        398–399
  RPC,
    accepted errors (table); 35
    reply; 33
  stat data type, NFS V.2 (reference description); 92
  Status Monitor protocol; 312–318
    implementation, statd daemon; 287
    Lock Manager protocol dependence on; 277
    Lock Manager protocol interaction with (figure);
        280
    lock manager use (figure); 279
    procedures (reference descriptions); 313–318
    SHARE reservations not monitored by; 309
  values, Kerberos authentication; 62–63
STATUS procedure, PCNFSD Version 2 (reference
        description); 398–399
Staubach, P., [RFC 1813]; 132
Steere, D., [Satyanarayanan+90]; 251, 368
Stein, M. [Pawlowski+89]; 470
Steiner, J., [Steiner+88]; 58, 368
Stern, H., [Stern91]; 472
Stevens, W. R., [Stevens94]; 1
stopping,
  host monitoring,
    for all, UNMON_ALL procedure, Status Monitor
        protocol (reference description); 317
    UNMON procedure, Status Monitor protocol
        (reference description); 316–317
storage,
  See also disks
  flushing cached data to, COMMIT (reference
        description); 221–224
  NASD; 357
  NASD NFS; 356–359
  stable,
    synchronous operations and, implementation
        issues; 236–239
    term description; 171, 236

storm, mount storm, term description (footnote); 331
streams, TCP as stream-based protocol, record-
        marking standard; 36
strings, *See also* data, types
  as primitive XDR data type; 15
structured data types, XDR; 16–17
subdirectories, MOUNT protocol handling; 271–273
submounts,
  (figure); 272
  MOUNT protocol handling; 271–273
substitution, of keys, map variables and; 337–339
SunRPC, *See* ONC (Open Network Computing)
superuser mapping,
  as permission implementation issue; 232
  as source of false access indication, implementation
        issues; 233
symbolic links,
  See also links
  automounter,
    daemon use; 324
    problems with; 324–327
  caching of; 246
  creating,
    SYMLINK procedure, NFS V.2; 120–122
    SYMLINK procedure, NFS V.3; 182–185
  hard links compared with; 82
  nfspath3 data type, NFS V.3 (reference description);
        137
  in PC NFS; 382–383
  reading from,
    READLINK procedure, NFS V.2; 106–107
    READLINK procedure, NFS V.3; 162–164
  term description; 82, 382
  unsupported, in LOOKUP procedure, NFS V.3;
        156
  in WebNFS,
    fetching; 442
    handling; 436–438
  WebNFS evalution (figure); 437
SYMLINK procedure,
  NFS Version 2 (reference description); 120–122
  NFS Version 3 (reference description); 182–185
symmetric multiprocessing, concurrent RPC call
        handling; 234
synchronization,
  clock, DH authentication; 50–51
  file, COMMIT use; 222
  of multiple processes, byte-range locking use, DOS
        clients; 294
  operations, stable storage and, implementation
        issues; 236–239
  procedures, Lock Manager protocol (table); 296

syntax,
  See also semantics
  map, Amd; 340–341
  XDR language; 19–20
    notes; 20
system,
  remote system calls, in RFS; 361
  System authentication; 45–48
System File Server, *See* SFS

tables, MOUNT, MOUNT protocol use; 270–271
Taylor, B., [Taylor+88]; 471
TCP/IP protocol,
  See also UDP
  advantages for NFS; 431–432
  bibliographic reference; 1
  connection-based security, as RPC-based security
    alternative; 78
  data stream, compared with UDP datagram; 36
  MOUNT protocol use; 257
  NFS relationship to; 1
  session setup, with CIFS; 373
  UDP compared with; 27
  WebNFS (chapter); 431–447
tcpdump, characteristics; 7
TCSEC (Trusted Computer System Evaluation
    Criteria), TNFS support of; 352–356
temporary mountpoints, automounter problems with;
    324–327
term descriptions,
  address, universal; 40
  advisory, locking; 281
  AFS cell; 366
  authentication, flavor; 44
  automounter; 322
    maps; 329
  big-endian; 11
  broadcast, RPC (footnote); 265
  buffers, track; 237
  cache(ing),
    CacheFS; 249–250
    hierarchy; 249
    write-around; 250
    write-back; 250
    write-through; 250
  canonical,
    paths; 444
    standard; 11
  capability, data; 358
  cell, AFS; 366
  cluster, server; 426
  components, pathname; 85

  context, RPCSEC_GSS-based RPC session; 65
  data, capability; 358
  deadlock; 289
  device types; 83
  directories; 82
  exclusive, locks; 278, 281
  fid; 367
  file(s); 81–82
    metadata (footnote); 238
    special; 83
  filehandles; 83
  fileid; 81
  filesets; 370, 371
  filespace; 370
  filesystem(s); 81
  flavors, authentication; 44
  fsid (filesystem ID); 81
  hierarchy, cache; 249
  hoarding; 251
  idempotent; 28, 88, 235
  latency; 415, 453
  leases; 350
  links,
    hard; 82
    symbolic; 82, 382
  lock(ing),
    advisory; 281
    exclusive; 281
    mandatory; 281
    shared; 281
  mandatory, locking; 281
  metadata, file (footnote); 238
  monitoring status; 279
  mount(ing), storm (footnote); 331
  native paths; 444
  netgroup (footnote); 255
  offset(s), paths; 332
  packing; 251
  pathnames; 85
  paths,
    canonical; 444
    native; 444
    offset; 332
  port, privileged; 38
  principal; 43
  Remote Procedure Call; 25
  security, labels; 353
  semantics, single-copy; 343
  server(s),
    cluster server; 426
    WebNFS; 442
  shared/sharing, locks; 278, 281

single-copy semantics; 343
special files; 83
stable storage; 171, 236
status, monitoring; 279
storage, stable; 171, 236
storm, mount storm (footnote); 331
symbolic links; 82, 382
time, time-to-live (TTL); 50
track buffer; 237
TTL (time-to-live); 50
types, device; 83
universal address; 40
volumes, AFS; 366
TEST procedure, Lock Manager protocol (reference description); 296–298
testing for locks, TEST procedure, Lock Manager protocol (reference description); 296–298
text,
   See also character(s)
   case sensitivity and preservation, DOS vs. UNIX; 379
   delimiters, operating system differences; 81
   files, in PC NFS; 382
   protocol element representation as, advantages and disadvantages; 10
The Open Group,
   [TOG-NFS96]; 471
   [TOG-PCNFS96]; 471
Thiel, G., [Popek+83]; 4
threads,
   multithreading, concurrent RPC call handling; 234
   single, asynchronous locking procedure use for; 283
   timestamp validation,
      (figure); 51
      problems with; 50
throughput,
   read-ahead and write-behind performance enhancements; 242–243
   write gathering impact on; 243–244
TI-RPC (Transport Independent RPC),
   rpcbind relationship to; 40
   as transport-independent API; 27
tickets,
   Kerberos authentication use; 58
   RPCSEC_GSS error, recovery from; 76
time,
   See also clock
   asynchronous callback issues; 283
   cache,
      close-to-open consistency advantages over; 248
      consistency maintenance use; 246

client/server synchronization requirements, in DH authentication; 50
cookie validation use; 204
disconnectable cache issues; 251
lease mechanism; 350
nfstime3 data type, NFS V.3 (reference description); 142
overloading of sattr data type, NFS V.2 (reference description); 98
retransmission impact; 234
SETATTR procedure impact on, NFS V.3 (reference description); 153
symbolic link caching impact, READLINK (reference description); 163
time-outs,
   NFS request categorization based on (table); 240
   retransmission strategies; 239–240
time-to-live, See TTL
timestamps,
   validation, in Network Time protocol; 50
   verifier, DH authentication; 54
timeval data type,
   NFS Version 2 (reference description); 94
   (reference description); 94
token lifetime, as cache consistency mechanism; 370
TTL,
   DH authentication use; 53
   Kerberos authentication use; 59
   term description; 50
TLS (Transport Layer Security) protocol,
   See also security
   [RFC 2246]; 79
   (footnote); 459
/tmp_mnt/ directory, automounter symbolic link problems; 326
TNFS (Trusted NFS); 352–356
tokens,
   See also leases
   as cache consistency mechanism, in DFS; 369–370
   classes (table); 370
   DFS use for client caching control; 369–370
track, buffer, term description; 237
transaction identifier, See XID
transfer, file transfer protocol, file access protocol vs.; 2–4
translucent, filesystem [Hendricks88]; 323
transparency, as NFS advantage, over Newcastle Connection; 6
transport,
   See also TCP/IP protocol; UDP
   data, protocols and; 9–11
   endpoint, server, portmapper determination of; 38

transport *continued*
  independence,
      impact on remote procedure semantics; 28
      as RPC protocol characteristic; 27–29
      TI-RPC support of; 40
  Lock Manager protocol issues; 291
  MOUNT protocol access; 257
  in PCNFS; 387
  reliability, performance impact; 415
  security, TLS [RFC 2246]; 79
  TCP/IP advantages for NSF; 431–432
Transport Independent RPC, *See* TI-RPC
Transport Layer Security, *See* TLS
Trusted Computer System Evaluation Criteria, *See*
      TCSEC
"trusted host" model, AUTH_SYS flavor; 47
Trusted NFS, *See* TNFS
Ts'o, T., [Neumann+94]; 470
TSIG (Trusted Systems Interoperability Group), TNFS
      development; 353
TTL (time-to-live),
  See also authentication; time
  DH authentication use; 53
  Kerberos authentication use; 59, 60
  term description; 50
Tumminaro, J., [Pawlowski+89]; 470
type file attribute,
  comparison of support by different systems (table);
      226
  in fattr data type,
      POSIX stat comparison (table); 97
      (table); 95
  in fattr3 data type (table); 143
types,
  data,
      cookieverf3, NFS V.3 (reference description); 137
      createverf3, NFS V.3 (reference description); 137
      fattr, NFS V.2 (reference description); 95–97
      fattr3, NFS V.3 (reference description); 142–143
      fattr3, NFS V.3 (table); 143
      fhandle, NFS V.2 (reference description); 94
      filename, NFS V.2 (reference description); 98
      filename3, NFS V.3 (reference description); 137
      ftype, NFS V.2 (reference description); 94
      ftype3, NFS V.3 (reference description); 140–141
      implicit, XDR use of; 10
      in Lock Manager protocol; 292–294
      netobj, Lock Manager protocol (reference
          description); 292–293
      nfs_fh3, NFS V.3 (reference description); 141–142

      in NFS Version 2; 92
      in NFS Version 3; 136–147
      in NFS Version 3, descriptions; 137–147
      nfspath3, NFS V.3 (reference description); 137
      nfsstat3, NFS V.3 (reference description); 138
      nfstime3, NFS V.3 (reference description); 142
      nlm_lock, Lock Manager protocol (reference
          description); 293–294
      nlm_stats, Lock Manager protocol (reference
          description); 293
      path, NFS V.2 (reference description); 98
      post_op_attr, NFS V.3 (reference description);
          143–144
      post_op_fh3, NFS V.3 (reference description); 146
      pre_op_attr, NFS V.3 (reference description); 145
      sattr, NFS V.2 (reference description); 97–98
      sattr3, NFS V.3 (reference description); 146–147
      specdata3, NFS V.3 (reference description); 141
      stat, NFS V.2 (reference description); 92
      timeval, NFS V.2 (reference description); 94
      wcc_data, NFS V.3 (reference description);
          145–146
      writeverf3, NFS V.3 (reference description); 137
      XDR, primitive; 13–16
      XDR, structured; 16–17
  device, term description; 83
  document, in WebNFS; 442
  file,
      ftype data type, NFS V.2 (reference description);
          94
      ftype3 data type, NFS V.3 (reference description);
          140–141
      NFS Version 3 changes; 135

UDP,
  adaptive retransmission for, implementation issues;
      239–240
  connection-based security that uses; 80
  datagram size limitations; 36
  MOUNT protocol use; 257
  TCP,
      compared with; 27
      performance comparison; 415
uid file attribute,
  comparison of support by different systems (table);
      226
  in fattr data type,
      POSIX stat comparison (table); 97
      (table); 95
  in fattr3 data type (table); 143

UID (User ID),
GID mapping,
MAPID procedure (PCNFSD Version 2); 405–406
as permission implementation issue; 232
in RFS; 363
representation, as NFS Version 4 design
consideration; 461
UMNT procedure, MOUNT protocol (reference
description); 264
UMNTALL procedure, MOUNT protocol (reference
description); 265
UNICODE, CIFS support; 373
union,
See also data, types
discriminated, as structured XDR data type; 17
universal address,
See also namespace(s); URL
term description; 40
UNIX,
remote file access support, Newcastle Connection;
4–6
System V, RFS; 361–363
UNLOCK procedure, Lock Manager protocol
(reference description); 304–305
UNMON_ALL procedure, Status Monitor protocol
(reference description); 317
UNMON procedure, Status Monitor protocol
(reference description); 316–317
unmonitored locks, *See* nonmonitored locks
unmounting,
See also mounting
filesystems,
all entries, UMNTALL procedure, MOUNT
protocol (reference description); 265
UMNT procedure, MOUNT protocol (reference
description); 264
unregistering, with portmapper service, UNSET
procedure, Portmap protocol; 39
UNSET procedure, Portmap protocol (reference
description); 39
UNSHARE procedure, Lock Manager protocol
(reference description); 310–311
unsigned, integer, as primitive XDR data type; 14
UPS (uninterruptible power supply), stable storage
use; 237
URL (Uniform Resource Locator),
HTTPS, SSL protocol; 79
NFS; 438
absolute vs. relative paths; 438–439
structure; 438
U.S. Department of Defense, [TCSEC85]; 473

used file attribute, in fattr3 data type (table); 143
users,
See also UID (User ID)
identifying, as permission implementation issue;
231
UID/GID mapping, as permission implementation
issue; 232
user-level,
NFS server, automounters implemented as; 323
NFS server (figure); 324
processes, filehandle criteria issues for; 84

validation,
See also authentication; verifiers
of cookies; 203–204
of timestamps, in Network Time protocol; 50
variable-length,
arrays, as structured XDR data type; 16
opaque data, as primitive XDR data type; 15
variables, map, key substitution and; 337–339
verifiers,
See also authentication; security; validation
AUTH_NONE, AUTH_SYS credential use; 46
authentication, in RPC reply; 34
DH; 49–50
DH authentication,
full network name credential; 51–53, 59–60
nickname credential; 53–54
Kerberos, XDR description (code); 62
nickname, DH authentication; 54
RPC, as authentication field; 43–44
RPCSEC_GSS (figure); 71
server,
DH authentication; 54–56
Kerberos authentication; 62
timestamp, DH authentication; 54
versioning,
mismatch, as RPC rejection cause; 33
multiple, support issues; 226
in RPC protocol; 29–30
VFS+ (virtual filesystem interface), DFS use; 369
virtual,
filesystem interface, DFS use; 369
memory, mapping files into; 290
VLDB (volume location database),
AFS use; 367
volume replication support; 368
volatile state, filesystem, retrieving, FSSTAT
procedure; 212–214
volumes,
AFS, term description; 366

volumes *continued*
  movement, in AFS; 367
  read-only replication, in AFS; 368
  VLDB, AFS use; 367

wait, avoidance, as file access protocol advantage; 3
Walsh, D., [Sandberg+85]; 91
Watson, A., [Watson+92]; 422
wcc_data data type, NFS Version 3 (reference
      description); 145–146
weaknesses,
  See also authentication; performance
  of DH authentication; 57–58
  of Kerberos authentication; 63
WebNFS,
  (chapter); 431–447
  clients, port used by; 38
  filehandle support; 84
  MOUNT protocol optional with; 256
  NFS Version 4 relationship; 452
  public filehandles, advantages; 85
  security negotiation, as NFS Version 4 model;
      460
  symbolic link handling; 82
Welch, B., [Nelson+88]; 343
West, M. J., [Howard+88]; 349
wildcard,
  in automounter key substitution; 338
  NFS to DOS issues; 381
Windows,
  file attribute support, comparison with other
      systems (table); 226
  file sharing procedures, Lock Manager protocol,
      overview; 283–284
  LockFile procedure, LOCK procedure, Lock
      Manager protocol; 300
  LockFileEx procedure, LOCK procedure, Lock
      Manager protocol; 300
Wittle, M., [Wittle+93]; 422
Woodbury, P., [Shein+89]; 419
Woodward, J.P.L., [Woodward87]; 353
working set,
  in benchmark workload; 419
    SFS Version 1; 425
  cache efficiency benefits; 456
workload,
  benchmark performance impact; 413
  as benchmark tool; 418–419
  generation, in SFS benchmark (figure); 423
  SFS, Versions 1.0 and 1.1; 424–426
  unreliability, as nfsstone benchmark weakness; 421

Wray, J.,
  [RFC 1509]; 64, 470
  [Wray93]; 472
write(ing),
  append flag, NQNFS extension; 352
  asynchronous,
    safe, COMMIT request use for; 239
    SFS benchmark prohibition of; 426
    verifying loss of, writeverf3, NFS V.3 (reference
      description); 137
    WRITE procedure, NFS V.3; 171–172
  cache to storage, COMMIT (reference description);
    221–224
  caching,
    (figure); 249
    implementation issues; 248–249
    write-around; 250
    write-back; 250
    write-through; 250
  errors, write-behind impact on; 243
  to files,
    WRITE procedure, NFS V.2; 109–112
    WRITE procedure, NFS V.3; 168–174
  gathering; 243–244
  sharing, issues with; 172
  stable vs. unstable writes; 171
  write-behind,
    implementation issues; 241–243
    in Spritely NFS; 345–347
  writeverf3 data type, NFS Version 3 (reference
    description); 137
WRITE procedure,
  NFS Version 2 (reference description); 109–112
  NFS Version 2, Version 3 changes; 132–133
  NFS Version 3 (reference description); 168–174
WRITECACHE procedure,
  NFS Version 2, deleted in Version 3; 132

X/Open, [X/OpenNFS96]; 9
XDR (External Data Representation) standard,
  See also data, types
  as canonical standard; 11–12
  (chapter); 9–24
  data,
    types, in NFS Version 2; 92
    types, primitive; 13–16
    types, structured; 16–17
    unit; 12–13
  DH credentials stored in,
    full name credential; 52
    nickname credential; 53

Kerberos credentials stored in; 59
language; 17–23
   example; 20
   lexical conventions; 18
   notation conventions; 18
   syntax; 19–20
   variant description; 21–23
RFS use for data representation; 362
RPC call and reply header definitions (code);
   35–36
RPC call and reply message parameters encoded
   in; 31
structure sizes, in NFS Version 3 data types; 136–137

Xerox Courier RPC standard, as early RPC system,
   remote procedure call use; 27
XID (transaction identifier),
   RPC reply use; 33
   RPC requests distinguished by; 29
   RPCSEC_GSS, sequence number handling;
     74–75
   uniqueness role in RPC messages; 31–32

Zelenka, J., [Gibson+98]; 356

Quick Reference Guide to Protocol Descriptions

NFS Protocol Procedures, Versions 2 and 3

Procedure Name	Description	Version 2 Page	Version 3 Page
NULL	Null procedure	99	149
GETATTR	Get file attributes	100	149
SETATTR	Set file attributes	102	151
LOOKUP	Lookup file name	104	155
ACCESS	Check access permission		158
READLINK	Read from symbolic link	106	162
READ	Read from file	107	164
WRITE	Write to file	109	168
CREATE	Create file	112	174
MKDIR	Create directory	122	179
SYMLINK	Create symbolic link	120	182
MKNOD	Create a special device		186
REMOVE	Remove file	115	190
RMDIR	Remove directory	124	192
RENAME	Rename file or directory	116	195
LINK	Create link to file	119	199
READDIR	Read directory	126	202
READDIRPLUS	Extended read from directory		205
STATFS/FSSTAT	Get filesystem attributes	128	212
FSINFO	Get static filesystem information		214
PATHCONF	Retrieve POSIX information		218
COMMIT	Commit cached data on a server to stable storage		221

MOUNT Protocol Procedures, Versions 1, 2, and 3

Name	Description	Page
NULL	Null procedure	259
MNT	Add mount entry	260
DUMP	Return mount entries	263
UMNT	Remove mount entry	264
UMNTALL	Remove all mount entries	265
EXPORT	Return export list	265
EXPORTALL	Return export list	267
PATHCONF	POSIX pathconf information	267